Florence in the Forgotten Centuries 1527–1800

FLORENCE
IN THE FORGOTTEN
CENTURIES
1527–1800

A History of Florence and the Florentines
in the Age of the Grand Dukes

ERIC COCHRANE

THE UNIVERSITY OF CHICAGO PRESS
Chicago and London

Al popolo fiorentino
e in modo particolare agli abitanti
del quartiere di Santa Croce e del rione di Ricorboli,
i miei concittadini in affetto.

To the people of Chicago
and particularly to the residents of the South Side,
my fellow citizens by law and by affection.

The University of Chicago Press, Chicago 60637
The University of Chicago Press, Ltd., London
© 1973 by The University of Chicago
All rights reserved. Published 1973
Second Impression 1974
Printed in the United States of America
International Standard Book Number: 0-226-11150-4
Library of Congress Catalog Card Number: 72-90628

Contents

Contents

Illustrations

NOTE: Nos. 20 (AL 29380), 28 (AL 58027), and 30 (AL 4368) are reproduced by permission of Fratelli Alinari, S.p.A. Nos. 2 (44658), 3 (17360), 4 (12781), 6 (74178), 7 (7170), 13 (106782), 15 (6970), 17 (107654), 18 (107204), 19 (67190), 27 (5298), and 29 (2209) are reproduced by permission of the Assessore alle Belle Arti, Comune di Firenze. No. 5 is reproduced by permission of Alberto Cotogni. Nos. 8, 9, 12, 22, 23, and 25 are reproduced by permission of the Museo di Firenze Com'Era. Nos. 21 and 24 are reproduced by permission of the director of the Biblioteca Riccardiana. Nos. 10, 14, 16, and 26 are from photographs by Lydia Cochrane.

PREFACE

To the benevolent reader

I have written this volume more for your pleasure than for your instruction. If you are a professional historian, you will probably not have time to do more than consult it, since it does not pertain directly to any currently accepted field of historical research. If, on the other hand, you belong to that class of readers known as "educated laymen"—to the class, that is, for which Guicciardini wrote in the sixteenth century, Galileo in the seventeenth, and the editors of the *Saturday Review* in the twentieth—then you will probably not read this or any other book of history unless the author succeeds in making you want to read it.

I do assume, however, that you are generally curious about how other people have lived, thought, and suffered in other times and places, for that much of the legacy of Renaissance humanism is still alive today. I also assume that you already have some interest in Florence today and some general knowledge of Florence in the past. But I do not assume that you have any more special preparation than what you might have picked up in a college course on European history. Accordingly, I have organized each book not around a historical problem (for example, "political conditions," "religious reform"), but around a representative member of the corresponding generation; and I have thus sought (with, I hope, some scientific as well as rhetorical justification) to treat ideas, events, and impersonal forces as functions, rather than as determinants, of the aspirations, characters, and limitations of individual men. Similarly, I have explained most of the references that might not be clear to you (and you can safely skip over those you do not understand without losing the thread of my argument). I have translated all the prose quotations, taking greater care to reproduce the mood and tone of the original than to find exact, word-for-word equivalents. And I have altered the rhyme and meter patterns of the verse quotations only when forced to do so by the peculiar structure and cadence of the English language. Above all, I have left out what is usually considered to be the sine qua non of historical scholarship: footnotes.

Many of my sources are indicated in the text (for example, "as Redi wrote to Magalotti in June of 1689"). All of them are described in the bibliographical notes to each book. Most readers will not care to know exactly where I got each specific bit of information—or at least they will not care enough to warrant my adding still further to the bulk and price of this volume. Anyone who wants to have a particular page or document number need only write to me at the University of Chicago, and I will be happy to oblige him by return mail.

Yet pleasure would be artificial were it not derived from the truth. Hence I have taken care not only to check on the veracity of everything I have written, but also to submit the penultimate draft of my text to experts in the various subjects it deals with. Delio Cantimori, the pioneer of modern studies in the religious history of sixteenth-century Italy, and Bonner Mitchell, a student of Medici court music, read Book I. Hans Baron, the discoverer of Florentine "Civic Humanism," and Danilo Aguzzi Barbagli, an authority on Renaissance Platonism and on Italian literature, read Books I, II, and III. Denys Hay, an authority on all the centuries between the thirteenth and the sixteenth, and John Hale, an authority on the Renaissance as a whole and on military history, read Book II. Edward E. Lowinsky, a historian as well as a musicologist, read those parts of Book II regarding Vincenzo Galilei and the Camerata. Edward A. Maser, the founder of the *Pietra Dura* museum and one of the few art historians who has studied post-Renaissance Florence, read all the passages of all the books that touch upon his particular discipline. Paul Oskar Kristeller, whose many studies of Renaissance philosophy I have followed with care, read Book III. Giuseppe Panzini, who has managed to disentangle the structure of the Medicean bureaucracy from an enormous mass of state papers, read Book V. Ettore Passerin d'Entrèves, who has written extensively on Italian Jansenism; Furio Diaz, whose books on the *Philosophes* deserve to be better known in the English-speaking world; Keith Baker, who has written about Condorcet and the late Enlightenment; Mario Rosa, who has guided me through the controversies of the age of Muratori, Benedict XIV, and Scipione de' Ricci; and R. Burr Litchfield, my most exacting critic, who has battered down many hallowed historical commonplaces with the help of IBM cards—all read Books V and VI. I read parts of Book I to the Renaissance Seminar of the University of Chicago and parts of Book II to a faculty seminar of my own department. My wife, Lydia Goodwin Cochrane, read all the Books for style, clarity, and grammar. My students at the University of Chicago provided me with a critical and exacting audience. John Renaldo helped me to locate some of the illustrations. I am deeply grateful to them all, particularly to those of them who have expressed strong reservations about what I said and how I said it. They have saved me from numerous errors of fact and from even more numerous blemishes of expression.

Similarly, pleasure would be short-lived if it were not joined to utility. And this volume comes as close to accounting for all the significant persons, places, and events in the history of Florence between 1530 and 1800 as I could manage within the limits of space and organization. I have been gathering information off and on for the past fifteen years, and thanks to financial assistance from the John Simon Guggenheim Memorial Foundation, the American Council of Learned Societies, and the Fulbright Commission, I have spent three years doing more intensive research in Italy. I have taxed the kindness of the directors and assistants of the Newberry and the University of Chicago libraries in Chicago, of the Biblioteca Nazionale, the Archivio di Stato, the Museo di Storia della Scienza, the Accademia della Crusca, the Archivio del Comune, the Museo di Firenze Com'Era, and the Laurenziana, Riccardiana, and Marucelliana libraries in Florence. I have profited from the generous hospitality of Count Roberto Ginori Venturi Lisci, who permitted me to wander in and out of his invaluable library at will. I have made use of the diplomatic dispatches in the Vatican Archives and in the archives of the Ministère des Affaires Etrangères on the Quai d'Orsay. And I have found several important documents regarding Books II and IV in the Biblioteca Casanatense of Rome and in the Bibliothèque Nationale of Paris.

To be sure, my research has been far from exhaustive; for the quantity of surviving documents, in paint and in stone as well as in writing, is such that even a team of scholars would not be able to study more than a small part of them. But I have at least managed to read all the private papers, letters, memoranda, and diaries, both published and in manuscript, of the heroes of each book, and many of those of their friends and associates. I have looked at what most of their contemporaries left in the form of printed books, journals, and pamphlets. And I have taken note of everything I could possibly find that has since been written about the period by more recent scholars, biographers, historians, and antiquarians. Hence, students of history can find all the relevant titles they may need in the Bibliographical Note. And visitors to Florence can discover who built what, when, and why, by following the name in the index to the corresponding page. Of course, I would prefer that everyone read the entire text, beginning with the Prologue and ending with the Postscript. But I cannot object to anyone's using it, instead, as a reference book, particularly if I know that I am thereby saving him from the romantic nonsense of my best-known predecessor, Colonel George Frederick Young.

Finally, what is pleasant, true, and useful, ought also to be provocative. And I hope that those of my professional colleagues who may happen to look at this volume will find some of its theses worth testing in their own investigations. After all, I began planning for it with a legitimate historical problem in mind: that of the domestic origins of the cultural and political revival described in my *Tradition and Enlightenment in the Tuscan Academies*. I have sought to solve this problem, first, by looking into those centuries that have previously been ignored by almost all the historians of Florence since the early nineteenth century. I have sought to solve it, secondly, by putting aside the customary barriers between specialized fields of historical study and taking account of all aspects of thought and activity—artistic, economic, social, intellectual—in each succeeding generation. I have sought to solve it also by considering not just the rulers or the ruling classes, but as many other members of the community, rich and poor, educated and illiterate, as I could find traces of in the documents I have consulted.

These methodological and substantive premises have led me in turn to question the validity of several generally accepted historical concepts. The first is one which would seem as strange to a citizen of Chicago in 1971 as it has seemed obvious to Tacitus, to Leonardo Bruni, and to many modern historians of Florence: that monarchical regimes are incompatible with intellectual or cultural creativity. The second is one which has been tacitly promoted in many recent textbooks of European history: that when the radiating center of civilization moves from one place to another—from Athens to Rome, or from Florence to Paris and London—it leaves a vacuum behind. The third is one which has been contested only by some historians of art: that the Baroque is merely a degenerate form of the Renaissance. The fourth is one which has been doubted only by some recent Italian historians: that the Enlightenment was an exclusively French, or Anglo-French, phenomenon. The fifth is one which has been present in both the Italian lay tradition and the English "Whig" view of history: that the line of progress from Scholasticism to the French Revolution passes solely through Luther, and that Catholicism, particularly Tridentine Catholicism, is inimicable to free expression in all the arts and sciences as well as in theology. The sixth is one which has been questioned chiefly by historians of science: that what seems in retrospect to have been mis-calculated, ineffective, retrogressive, or derivative, is not worth studying—as if no one counted in this world except the very few geniuses who happen to have been appreciated by their posterity.

Thus, benevolent reader, you may find that this volume is informative, useful, and provocative in addition to being pleasant. But my chief concern is that you find it pleasant.

& vivi felice.

Chicago, May 1971

FLORENCE
IN THE FORGOTTEN
CENTURIES
1527–1800

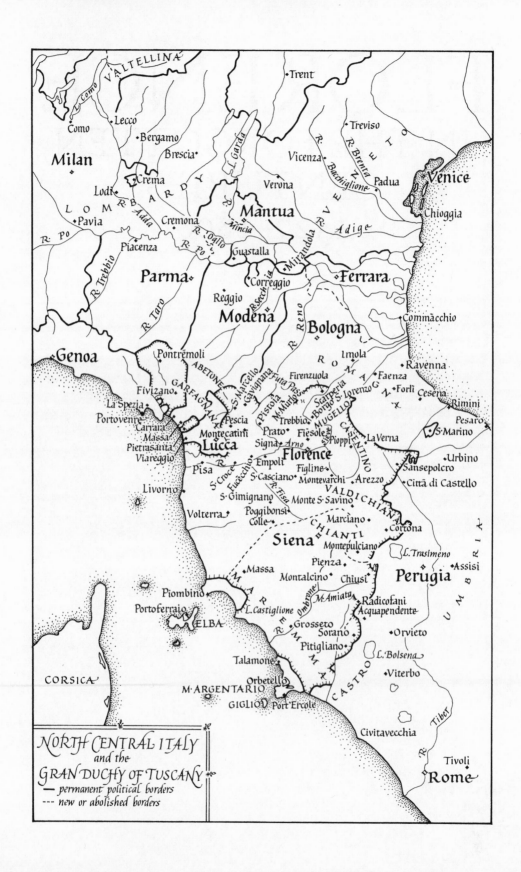

VALTELLINA

Como
Lecco
Como
Bergamo
Trent
L. Garda
Treviso
Brescia
Milan
Crema
Verona
Vicenza
R. Brenta
Padua
Venice
Lodi
Mantua
R. Bacchiglione
Chioggia
Pavia
Cremona
Mincia
R. Adige
R. Po
Adda
Piacenza
R. Oglio
R. Po
R. Trebbio
Guastalla
Mirandola
Parma
Correggio
Ferrara
R. Taro
R. Secchia
Reggio
Commacchio
Modena
Bologna
R. Reno
Pontrémoli
Imola
Ravenna
Genoa
Firenzuola
Faenza
Fivizano
ABETONE
Futa Pass
Forlì
Cesena
La Spezia
GARFAGNANA
S. Marcello
Gavignana
Scarperia
Borgo S. Lorenzo
Rimini
Portovenere
Pistoia
M. Murlo
S. Marino
Carrara
Pescia
Trebbio
MUGELLO
Pesaro
Massa
Montecatini
Prato
Fiesole
Pietrasanta
Lucca
Signa
Pioppi
La Verna
Urbino
Viareggio
Arno
Florence
Sansepolcro
Pisa
Empoli
Figline
Città di Castello
S. Croce
Fucecchio
Montevarchi
Arezzo
Livorno
S. Casciano
VALDICHIANA
S. Gimignano
R. Tisa
Monte S. Savino
Volterra
Poggibonsi
Marciano
Colle
CHIANTI
Cortona
Siena
Montepulciano
L. Trasimeno
Pienza
Perugia
Massa
Montalcino
Chiusi
Assisi
Piombino
M. Amiata
Radicofani
UMBRIA
Portoferraio
L. Castiglione
Ombrone
Acquapendente
ELBA
Grosseto
Orvieto
Sorano
Talamone
Pitigliano
L. Bolsena
CORSICA
Orbetello
Viterbo
M. ARGENTARIO
CASTRO
GIGLIO
Port Ercole
Tiber
Civitavecchia
Tivoli
Rome

NORTH CENTRAL ITALY
and the
GRAN DUCHY OF TUSCANY
— permanent political borders
--- new or abolished borders

PROLOGUE

The siege

August 10, 1530. Palazzo Vecchio, Florence.

It was almost midnight by the time the four delegates finally returned from the headquarters of the Imperial army outside Porta San Miniato. They had been there since midmorning, desperately bargaining with Baccio Valori, the personal representative of Pope Clement VII, and with Ferrante Gonzaga, the commander-in-chief of the forces of Emperor Charles V. They had succeeded in obtaining only a few face-saving concessions: the restoration of all territories formerly under Florentine rule, a general amnesty for all citizens of all parties, the right of any citizen to emigrate if he so desired, and a promise to respect the "liberty" of the city in any eventual reorganization of the government. But the delegates had had little to bargain with. After ten months of simply camping outside the walls, the Imperial army may have been tired, bored, and, as always, underpaid. But it was still intact; and the slightest intransigence could easily have provoked it into doing to Florence what it had done to Rome three years before—tear it to pieces. The usual band of young hotheads in the city may still have been ready to follow the example of the ancient Saguntines, who destroyed themselves rather than submit to the Romans. But the bulk of the citizen militia had already been disbanded. The commander of the Florentine mercenaries had submitted his resignation. All the political prisoners had been released. And mobs of half-starved plebeians were wandering through the streets shouting *Palle! Palle!*—the Medici slogan that no one had dared pronounce publicly for over three years. The city was demoralized, hungry, and exhausted. In the words of Benedetto Varchi, the chief chronicler of the events of these years:

> Everyone, men as well as women, adults as well as children, was beside himself with fright and bewilderment. No one any longer knew what to say, what to do, or where to go. Some tried to flee, some to hide, some to take refuge in the Palazzo or in the churches. Most of them simply entrusted

themselves to God and patiently awaited, from one hour to the next, not just simply death, but death amidst the most horrible cruelties imaginable.

There was no choice, then, but to accept the other articles of the agreement as well: that fifty citizens be given over as hostages pending the payment of an enormous reparations bill, that all the fortresses still held by the Republic be turned over to the Imperial general, and that all the friends, relatives, and supporters of the Medici family be released or readmitted. Nor was there any choice but to ignore the obvious holes in the agreement: the omission of any guarantee that the Medici would return merely as citizens, that the pope would relent in the pursuit of his dynastic ambitions, or that the emperor would alter his established policy of treating Florence as a prize in return for papal support elsewhere in Europe. Accordingly, the agreement was accepted the very next day, almost without debate. And two days later, on August 12, it was signed, notarized, and sent to Rome for ratification.

Until just a few weeks before, almost none of the men who governed Florence ever dreamed that they would be brought to such an extremity. The Republic had been born, or rather restored, in May 1527—at a moment, that is, when the Sack of Rome seemed to have wrecked once and for all the fortunes of the family that had dominated Florence from 1434 to 1494 and again from 1512 on. Pope Clement VII, the current head of the Medici family, was a prisoner in Castel Sant'Angelo, powerless to do anything but watch from the ramparts the wholesale plunder and murder of his subjects. And the direct male descendants of Cosimo the Elder had been reduced to two spoiled, sensual, irresponsible—and illegitimate—teen-agers, Alessandro and Ippolito. The restoration of the Republic had been greeted by an unprecedented wave of enthusiasm—even among the pro-Mediceans, who were tired of being taxed for the sole benefit of the bottomless papal treasury and who were sick of being humiliated by the arrogant, undiplomatic, and—worse yet—non-Florentine guardian of the two papal nephews. It had been accompanied by a minimum of disorder, thanks in part to the guards that were promptly stationed in front of the Palazzo Medici to prevent a repetition of the plundering spree of 1494. And it had been confirmed by the establishment of the very institution that Girolamo Savonarola, the prophet-ruler of the city in the 1490s had prescribed as the remedy for all of Florence's internal ills: the Great Council, in which almost three thousand citizens had the right to participate.

Thus, after two lengthy experiments in one-man, or one-family, rule, Florence seemed finally to have settled upon a republican constitution. Indeed, the framers of the new constitution were so convinced that their work was destined to last forever that they refused to be daunted by the eventual reversals of their initial good fortune. When the pope's escape and the gradual reassertion of his authority throughout the Papal State provoked the first signs of dissent within the city, they created a citizen militia. When a growing number of prominent and obscure citizens decided to wash their hands of "these angry madmen," as the erratic goldsmith, Benvenuto Cellini, called the leaders of the Republic, they opened the militia to all male residents, citizen and noncitizen alike—just as Niccolò Machiavelli had advised their fathers to do many years before. When the pope put aside his just resentment over the way he had been treated during the Sack of Rome and accepted the very favorable terms accorded him by the Treaty of Barcelona, they confidently showed the emperor that his best interests would be served by sending his army against the Lutherans or the Turks rather than against them. When the destruction of the last French expeditionary force outside of Naples all but sealed the Imperial hegemony over all of Italy, and when the Treaty of Cambrai finally put an end to the thirty-year-old policy of the Italian states of playing one foreign power against another, they even more confidently accepted a "promise" from King Francis I that subsidies and soldiers would arrive as soon as his children were released from captivity in Madrid.

Indeed, the hopes of the Florentine republicans grew as their situation became more perilous. When the Imperial army began slowly marching up through the Valdichiana in September 1529, they put their trust in one of the best professional generals in Italy, Malatesta Baglioni, whose loyalty seemed to be assured by his hopes of returning to power in his native Perugia. When, on October 5, the invaders began pitching their tents along the hills between San Miniato and Porta Romana, the republicans put their trust in their walls—which did indeed withstand the first major assault on October 29. And they also put their trust in the well-known tendency of the emperor's polyglot armies to dissolve after a succession of penniless paydays—a tendency that kept the commander-in-chief in a state of continual anxiety. When the Spanish and German troops failed to mutiny, and when the siege was reinforced by the arrival of unemployed mercenaries from all over Italy, they put their trust in the host of angels promised them by the current interpreters of Savonarola's prophesies in the Dominican monasteries of San Marco and Santa Maria Novella.

Unfortunately, no angels appeared, and the king of France delivered nothing but more promises. Meanwhile, the mortality rate rose rapidly, from plague as well as from undernourishment: 60 a day in February, 189 a day in April. Food supplies fell to the point where mice began to sell for high prices. Taxes and special levies drained off so much private wealth that no one could bid on the confiscated estates put up for sale to raise money. And the export industry, from which much of the city's wealth ultimately derived, languished in isolation from its foreign customers. But just as they were beginning to despair of heavenly help, the Florentine republicans discovered a human savior: the talented, ruthless, lowborn commander of the army in the field, Francesco Ferrucci, whom the Savonarolans hailed as a new Gideon when he unexpectedly recaptured Volterra in June. Late

in July, Ferrucci began to advance eastward from Pisa for the purpose of distracting the Imperial army from the siege. Meanwhile, the militia, stirred to a high
pitch of excitement by the rhetoric of its younger members, prepared to surge out
of the gates and attack the enemy from the rear. But by then Baglioni had given
up his current employers for lost and had begun secretly sounding out their
opponents for a new job. He therefore buried the urgent requests for action in a
pile of bureaucratic memoranda, and the militia was left to parade harmlessly
around the Piazza della Signoria. That left Ferrucci to face all alone the attack he
had deliberately provoked. On August 3, surrounded by the corpses of his men,
he was hacked to pieces by a band of Spanish soldiers in the piazza of the mountain
village of Gavinana—where today crowds of vacationing school children play
around the base of a huge equestrian statue bearing his name. And that eliminated
the last possible justification for further resistance.

Meanwhile, their enthusiasm for the defense of the Republic blinded the
defenders to some of its more serious internal problems. The first of these problems
was that of constitutional instability. In the 134 years between 1378 and 1512, the
Florentine constitution had been subjected to ten major revisions; and far from
overcoming the weaknesses of its predecessors, each revision simply increased the
number of citizens who longed to return to the good old days "before 1434" or
"before 1494." Hence republican regimes came to be distinguished from Medicean
regimes by their association with endless debates over fundamental institutions—
debates that the Medici learned to obviate by emptying all constitutional bodies of
any but nominal power. Even the supposedly definitive constitution of 1527
lasted less than two years. And it was then revised in such a way as to make still
another revision necessary if the government were to be provided with effective
leadership during a war: the tenure and the authority of the *gonfaloniere* (president)
were sharply reduced, the *Signoria* (chief executive council) was kept to a two-
month term and elected by lot, and the all but complete autonomy of the Justice
and War Departments (*Otto di Guardia* and *Dieci di Libertà e Guerra*) was
reinforced.

The second major problem was that of class conflict and family rivalry. In
the past, a small group of the older and wealthier citizens known as the *Ottimati*
("The Best") had occasionally succeeded in maintaining enough harmony among
themselves and enough efficiency in the management of public affairs to justify
their holding a practical monopoly of all major offices. It was they who had ruled
the city for some fifty years after the lower artisans and workers known as the
Ciompi were driven out of the government in 1381. It was they who had once
demonstrated a high sense of civic responsibility by subjecting themselves to the
first graduated income tax in history, the tax established by the *Catasto* of 1427.
And it was they who returned to power in 1527 under the leadership of the wise,
tactful, politically popular, and impeccably honest gonfaloniere, Niccolò Capponi,
whom all the historians of his own and the following generation hailed as a modern

Pericles—as one, that is, whose policies would have saved the Republic if only his less worthy successors had abided by them.

But the government of the Ottimati was soon threatened, as it often had been before, by the private ambitions of its single members—most notably by the Albizi, who had almost ruined the Ottimati government in the 1420s, by the Strozzi, whose international banking empire far exceeded the modest territorial limits of the Republic, and by the Soderini, who still remembered the prestige they had enjoyed during the presidency of Piero Soderini, between 1502 and 1512. It was even more seriously threatened by the collective ambitions of a much larger, though less wealthy, group of citizens known as the *Popolani*, who finally succeeded in gaining control of the government by the constitutional reform of April, 1529. Both privileged classes were threatened in turn by the some four-fifths of the resident population that was barred from the Great Council, and therefore from all active part in political affairs. It was this threat that led even Francesco Carducci, the less wellborn and far less experienced Popolano leader who succeeded Capponi as gonfaloniere, to lecture the plebeian militiamen continuously about the virtues of obedience. For although he had been forced to arm them, Carducci had no intention of granting them any of the privileges of citizenship. Once the charm of rubbing elbows with noblemen wore off, after all, they might well have been tempted to do what their ancestors had done at the time of the Ciompi revolt.

The third major problem was the lack of a clear ideology—one capable, that is, of uniting Florentines of all classes behind a common cause. Liberty, justice, military virtue, patriotism, and the will of God were all noble phrases. But no one, in the more than a hundred years after Coluccio Salutati made it into a slogan, had ever bothered to define liberty in relation to institutions; and as one citizen after another was thrown into exile or into prison for supposedly seditious opinions, the word lost any association it might once have had with freedom of speech. No one suggested that justice should guide the relations of Florentines with non-Florentines; and no one objected when Ferrucci threw scores of rich Volterrans into a dungeon, hanged a messenger sent to him with a white flag, confiscated all the money of the Pisan nobility, and burned most of San Marcello to the ground.

Similarly, none of the rhetorical rhapsodies about the fighting spirit of the Romans and the Spartans ever explained what Florentines should be fighting for; and even Donato Giannotti, Machiavelli's successor as secretary to the War Department, admitted that some of the fighting spirit of the younger noblemen was merely a sublimated form of their more usual rowdiness. None of the attempts to make political sense out of prophesy could come up with any more practical advice than to put on sackcloth and wait for divine intervention; even Carducci, good Savonarolan that he was, soon lost interest in the constant round of processions and public penances sponsored by the *Piagnoni*, as the Savonarolans were called. None of the tirades against the "wild beasts from farthest Spain and coldest

Germany" could explain what so many civilized Florentines were doing on the wrong side of the walls. The tirades became ever less capable of persuading the members of Florentine colonies in Venice and France to contribute to one side rather than another in what was, at least to some extent, a civil as well as a foreign war. It is not surprising, then, that, as the siege dragged on, a completely different, although equally vague ideology began to gain adherents—one that viewed the state not as a means of gaining wealth, honor, or dominion for some of the citizens, but as a means of assuring peace and tranquillity for all of them.

> If the State's in peace and ever quiet,
> Then never can its splendor wane
> But ours, like one that's fared too well,
> Whose wealth and beauty none could tell,
> Has plunged us into dearth and pain.
> (*Lamento di Fiorenza*, 2, ii)

Now that Clement VII had learned his lesson about not quarreling with Charles V, a state run by the Medici appeared to be more capable, or at least no less incapable, of achieving this peaceful end than a state run by the Ottimati or the Popolani. And the expression of *Pallesco*, or pro-Medicean sentiment, which had been terrorized into silence after the withdrawal of Niccolò Capponi's protective arm, once again became audible—even within the silent walls of the enclosed convents.

Still, the most important problem that the Florentine republic had to face was that of adjusting to the incorporation of Italy into a political system dominated by non-Italian giants. City-state republics were not necessarily anachronistic in the early sixteenth century. But, in an age of great monarchies, they could survive only under certain conditions. They could, like Lucca, Bremen, or Nürnberg, stay so small and so quiet that no one would think them worth disturbing. They could also transform themselves into financial corporations, like Genoa or Augsburg, which would be wealthy enough to dominate with credit whoever might be tempted to dominate them by force. They could become spiritual fortresses, like Geneva, which coreligionists near and far would be bound to defend in an emergency. They could draw money out of a domestic industry and a maritime empire, like Venice, and thus permit themselves a policy of relative neutrality on the continent. Or, like Holland later in the century, they could make up for what they lacked in land power with a strong navy.

But neither the Ottimati nor the Popolani, neither the Piagnoni nor the anti-Savonarolan *Arrabbiati*, were willing or able to meet any of these conditions. After centuries of rhetorical comparisons between Fiesole and Vejo and between Pisa and Carthage, they could not voluntarily give up their possessions in Tuscany. In spite of the lasting fascination of Savonarola's dream, they could not hope to erect a New Jerusalem in the face of the violent opposition of the pope, whom they still recognized as the legitimate head of Catholic Christendom, much as they condemned his politics. Having failed to build a navy a century earlier, when their commercial vessels regularly went back and forth from England, they had little chance of building one now, when Andrea Doria, in the name of Emperor Charles V, dominated the western half of the Mediterranean and the Ottoman Turks dominated the eastern half. And without a navy, they could not think of establishing an overseas empire, much as they may have been inspired, a generation earlier, by the glowing reports of Amerigo Vespucci.

Moreover, it never occurred to the Florentine republicans to adopt one measure that might have kept their enemies at the frontier rather than at the city walls—namely, transforming their city-state into a territorial state. Most of them knew, from Machiavelli if not from Polybius and Livy, that Rome had undergone just such a transformation on the morrow of the Social War and that it had thus been able to enlist all Italy, and then all the civilized world, in its support. And they ought to have realized that a unified, compact commonwealth resting on the loyalty of over a half-million industrious, prosperous members and extending from the Apennines and Lake Trasimeno to the Tyrrhenian Sea could at least have resisted external aggression—just what the sack of Firenzuola in the fall of 1529 proved that Florentines could not do by themselves. But neither they, nor any other citizen or subject of an Italian republic before the eighteenth century, ever thought of applying that particular bit of ancient wisdom in their own political decisions. For them, Florence existed for the sole benefit of some three thousand privileged Florentines; and the Florentine dominion existed solely to be governed and exploited by the *Dominante*, the "Dominant City." Having refused to enfranchise the vast majority of their compatriots, the rulers of Florence were hardly prepared to welcome mere Aretines and Pisans as collaborators. And they were not surprised when every one of the subject cities surrendered to the Imperial army in 1529–30 the moment it was abandoned by its Florentine garrison.

Thus the Republic died—as much the victim of the immoderate dreams, the mutual antagonisms, and the diplomatic errors of its ruling classes as of the vindictiveness of one of the last of the Renaissance pope-princes and of the pacification policy of the most powerful monarch Europe had known since Charlemagne. It died amidst a holocaust which, glorious as it may have appeared to the recorders of *memorabilia* in the mid-sixteenth century and to the bards of Italian nationalism in the mid-nineteenth, had turned one of the richest and most creative cities in Christendom into one of the poorest and most helpless. As Guicciardini wrote to a friend soon after his return home in September:

> I need not talk about the misery of the city and the countryside, except to say that it is far greater than anything we imagined. The wealth of men has vanished. All the houses for miles around Florence have been destroyed. The peasants have diminished infinitely in numbers. . . . In effect, the wreckage is such that no one could believe that the province was able to bear it.

Then, just to make sure that the Republic stayed dead, the new masters of the city lost no time in snuffing out whatever hopes anyone might still have of ever being able to revive it. Instead of waiting for the emperor to reorganize the government along the lines of the pre-1527 regime, they authorized an extraordinary *Balìa*, or constitutional committee, to conduct a thorough purge of all the magistracies. Instead of observing the amnesty prescribed by the agreement of August 12, they banished, imprisoned, or executed some 150 of the leading citizens and confiscated the estates of their families. By February 5, 1531, they were ready to grant full power over all the branches of government to Alessandro de' Medici, whose rank as a ruling prince had just been confirmed by his engagement to the illegitimate daughter of the emperor. The following year they had him proclaimed, not the first citizen, not the gonfaloniere, but the "Duke of the Florentine Republic," with the right of male succession.

Florence had now become a monarchy in all but name.

2. Vasari, *Siege of Florence*, detail
Palazzo Vecchio

BOOK I

FLORENCE
IN THE 1540s

*How Cosimo de' Medici turned a worn-out
republic into a well-run monarchy*

I

Election

Monday, January 8, 1537. Trebbio in the Mugello.
The Mugello has a beauty all its own in midwinter. The broad, carefully plowed fields that extend directly eastward amid rows of leafless poplars seem to wait in motionless silence for the first rays of the warm spring sun. Masses of damp, chilly fog rise slowly from the meandering River Sieve, hiding and then revealing the three main clusters of walls and tiled roofs—San Piero, Borgo San Lorenzo, and Vicchio—strung along its banks. Vine-covered hills roll upwards, first gradually and then abruptly, in the shape of a large bowl, toward blue-green chestnut forests and high bare hills on one side, and, on the other side and at either end, toward still higher mountains, which often, at this time of the year, are capped with snow. Occasionally the silent mists and the quiet, diffused light vanish before immense black clouds, which batter the valley with moving walls of rain and then envelop it in an opaque drizzle. The results can be disastrous, as they had been just a few years earlier, when

> Since Noah's time there'd never been
> a flood like this one ever seen. . . .
>
> The river did its duty well,
> sweeping all inside the dell;
> before it not a mill could stand,
> no stack of grain in all the land.
> The foe of wine soon won the day,
> and left who watched him in dismay.
> (Francesco Berni, *Capitolo del diluvio*)

At other times, however, a dry, cutting *tramontana* wind blows down out of the north, clearing the air of the last traces of humidity and redrawing all the blurred lines of the landscape with icy sharpness.

Like the other pockets carved out of the slopes of the Apennines—like the Garfagnana and the Casentino—the Mugello is set off geographically, meteorologically, and even psychologically from the rest of Tuscany. But unlike the others, it was only apparently isolated in the early sixteenth century. The main roads connecting Florence with northern Italy, and with most of northern Europe as well, came in from the southwest and then went out over the high passes toward Bologna, Faenza, and Forlì. The castle of Trebbio, remodeled as a residence a half-century earlier and now the property of the widow Maria Salviati and of her only son, Cosimo de' Medici, was particularly well located. The Via Bolognese was just minutes down the hill by horseback. And the provincial capital, Scarperia, lay strung out along a narrow hogback just five miles to the north.

Thus it was possible to gaze undisturbed at the peaceful natural spectacle spread out beneath the crenelated tower. It was possible to hunt birds and hares in the thick woods around the Quattrocento castle. And it was possible at the same time to keep fairly close track of what was going on in the world of merchants, diplomats, and assassins that seemed so far away. Indeed, Trebbio was an ideal place for a robust young man of seventeen to pass the winter—especially for one like Cosimo de' Medici, whose education had as yet elicited no noticeable vocation other than a passion for hunting, a young man whose placid, boyish face still showed no more sign of a definite character than what Rodolfo del Ghirlandaio had managed to paint into a portrait of him several years earlier, and whose life in town consisted of not much else than hanging around in the company of his licentious distant cousin, Duke Alessandro. And it was particularly convenient for Cosimo, who still had settled on no definite career, and for whom it was therefore especially important to be on call should a good prospect suddenly turn up.

Cosimo did not know it yet, but a good prospect had turned up just that morning. Sometime around noon on Sunday—the day before—he had received a rather surprising bit of news: Lorenzo di Pierfrancesco de' Medici, his short, agile, swarthy first cousin, usually called Lorenzaccio because of his morose disposition, had been seen galloping furiously into Scarperia early that morning with one hand jammed into a bloodstained glove, and galloping out again after a long session with a doctor.

Yet Cosimo was probably disposed to dismiss this latest report as just one more manifestation of his cousin's "restless, insatiable spirit . . . scornful of all things human and divine," particularly since he had no further clarification during the course of the afternoon. Cosimo was well acquainted with Lorenzaccio. They were both descendants of Giovanni "Il Popolano" ("The Man of the People"), and hence members of a lateral branch of the Medici family, although Cosimo also descended, through his mother, directly from Lorenzo the Magnificent. They were thus only distantly related to the famous main line that went from Cosimo the Elder to the current master of the city, Duke Alessandro. They had both spent their childhood in the Mugello, Cosimo at Trebbio, Lorenzaccio just over the hill at Cafaggiolo. And they had both been brought up by widowed mothers whose ambitions for their sons were inversely proportional to the reduced circumstances their husbands had left them in. Recently, it is true, they had drifted apart. To some extent the fault was Cosimo's, for he could never understand why Lorenzaccio, though five years his elder, should prefer books to the out-of-doors and solitude to conversation. To some extent the fault was his mother's. Maria Salviati had finally given up trying to get her share of the common family property by negotiation and had begun pressing claims against her sister-in-law in court. Moreover, she had come to consider her nephew as the chief obstacle to her son's advancement; and she had taken to whispering remarks about Lorenzaccio's unstable character in confidential asides to Duke Alessandro.

Nevertheless, the two families still lived, when in Florence, on the first and second floors of the same house on the Via Larga. And the two cousins inevitably ran into each other next door at the Palazzo Medici, where Cosimo—Signor Cosimino, as Benvenuto Cellini called him—served as a page and Lorenzaccio was the habitual guide of Alessandro's nocturnal escapades. To be sure, Cosimo had no way of knowing that Lorenzaccio had recently come to despise the very person he appeared to be most attached to. Nor could he have known that for three years Lorenzaccio had been hatching a plot to get rid of Alessandro and claim the ducal title for himself. But Cosimo did know that his cousin had been thrown out of Rome in 1532 for no less a crime than having knocked the heads off the statues in the Arch of Constantine. And he knew that Lorenzaccio frequently roamed around Florence at night in the sole company of a pugnacious barbarian named Scoroncolo. It was not wholly incredible, then, that Lorenzaccio should suddenly find it advisable to leave the city, wounded and at night. And it was even probable that the explanation given on the exit permit for his departure was correct. After all, his mother was indeed spending the holidays at Cafaggiolo, and his brother really had been ill.

Then, early Monday morning, another report came up from Scarperia that suddenly undermined the plausibility of this explanation. The local militia was hastily being mustered in preparation for a march on Florence. If the two events were somehow related, then Cosimo had no time to lose, hunting or no hunting. Within moments he was off. Halfway down the Via Bolognese a courier from his mother reached him with an urgent message: The duke is dead; and Messers Francesco Guicciardini and Girolamo degli Albizi request that you return to Florence at once. By the time he reached the city that afternoon, he had learned most of the astonishing details.

On Saturday evening, the night (not the *eve*) of Epiphany 1537, Alessandro, Lorenzaccio, and the two faithful bodyguards, Giomo and "The Hungarian," had disappeared in the direction of Piazza San Marco. They had then sneaked back down Via Larga to the door of Lorenzaccio's house. There Lorenzaccio had persuaded Alessandro that the delicacy of the operation required that the guards remain, for once, outside. After all, the victim of this, the most skillfully arranged of all Lorenzaccio's amorous plots, was none other than his own first cousin, Caterina Sòderini Ginori, whose dull, elderly husband Lorenzaccio knew to be momentarily out of town. He persuaded Alessandro to wait, for once without his usual breastplate, in his own bedroom, while he ostensibly went to fetch Caterina from the house that was joined to his own by a common garden. Instead, he quietly summoned Scoroncolo, slipped back into the bedroom, and then, after a struggle during which his finger was almost bitten off, sank his dagger six times into Alessandro's body. He was sure that neither the servants upstairs nor Maria Salviati in bed downstairs would think anything amiss. For he had carefully accustomed them to being kept awake half the night by brawling and scuffling in his apartment. He locked the door of the bedroom, put the key in his pocket, and shoved his mutilated hand into a glove. After a moment's hestitation about what to do next, a problem he had not thought about until then, he ran next door to the Palazzo Medici for an exit permit, mounted the first post-horse available, and headed out toward the Mugello. He did not stop, except for a bit of surgery in Scarperia, until he reached Bologna that evening.

No one gets up early on a Sunday following a holiday, not even Cardinal Innocenzo Cibo, the semiofficial representative of Emperor Charles V in Florence and actual ruler of the state in the name of the incompetent, irresponsible young duke. But Cibo was the first to become suspicious when word got around, shortly after dawn, about Lorenzaccio's precipitous departure during the night. Then, when Giomo and The Hungarian came in to ask how long they should keep up their weary vigil out on the Via Larga, he became seriously alarmed. With the emperor off in Castile, with the governor of Milan too far away to be of any help in an emergency, and, worse yet, with the commander of the armed forces, Alessandro Vitelli, off tending to family affairs in Città di Castello, Cibo's de facto power in Florence had become entirely dependent on the survival of the one who held power de jure. But Alessandro had not come home that night. He had last been seen, unprotected and unarmed, almost twelve hours before. And the person he had gone out with had since left town under very unusual circumstances.

Cibo immediately jumped to the correct conclusion—without, however, daring to verify it by actually looking for his missing ward. He went straight to the one man he trusted most, the loyal and able administrative secretary, Francesco Campana. Following Campana's advice, he swore the guards to secrecy, sealed up Lorenzaccio's house and Alessandro's own apartment, and issued a bulletin that said the duke had had an especially rough night. He then alerted the captains of the militia and sent an urgent letter asking Vitelli to return at once with all the troops he could round up. And finally, toward evening, he worked up the courage to force the bedroom door and to have the bloodstained body, which by now he was not at all surprised to find, carried secretly over to San Lorenzo for burial.

That was as much as the cardinal could do by himself. The next step would have to be an appeal to the only people who could save him from an uprising, the Florentine patriciate. And an appeal to the patriciate, as he realized after an abortive conference with a few of them that afternoon, meant restoring momentarily the de facto sovereignty of the constitutional body that held it de jure—namely, the Senate of the Forty-Eight. The initiative began slipping through his fingers. When, at the meeting the next morning, the Senate immediately rejected a motion he had planted on the floor, a motion that would have left him his power by recognizing Alessandro's infant bastard Giulio as successor, the initiative definitely escaped him; and, in a moment of weakness, he recoiled before an offer of interim authority in his own, rather than in someone else's, name. When the senators then failed to agree on any alternate solution, the initiative passed to the only group among them with some semblance of cohesion—namely, to the *Palleschi*, as the pro-Medici faction was called, headed by Francesco Guicciardini and Francesco Vettori.

It was now, about midmorning on Monday, that the name of Cosimo was first talked of seriously. Any change in regime, the Palleschi realized, could occur only at their own expense, and at the risk of provoking a direct intervention by the emperor. Some sort of prince, therefore, was indispensable—better yet, a prince with some hereditary claim to the place left vacant by Alessandro, rather than an elected president-for-life like the ones Florence had tried out before with dubious success; and rather than an extralegal strong man, or *signore*, like those most other Italian states had known off and on for over three centuries. But the only surviving legitimate descendant of Cosimo the Elder was a woman, Catherine, future queen of France. And the only surviving illegitimate descendants were two infants, Giulio and Giulia, the children of Alessandro. To find a legitimate, adult male, it was necessary to climb back up the Medici family tree to the younger brother of Cosimo the Elder, a century earlier. But that branch ended up in Lorenzaccio; and everyone agreed that he had already eliminated both himself and his brother as possible successors. The only alternative was to return to Lorenzaccio's grandfather; and his only surviving and eligible grandson happened to be Cosimo, the carefree hunter in the Mugello.

The genealogical argument was convincing. But the practical arguments were even more so. No one had ever thought of Cosimo as a possible candidate, not even Cosimo himself. Hence he was uncontaminated by the more objectionable aspects of Alessandro's government. He was hardly more than a boy; and, as far as anyone knew, he was completely devoid of political experience. Hence, he could be expected to be all that more amenable to the wise counsels of Guicciardini and Vettori. Accordingly, the Palleschi set about assuring his succession as quickly as possible. They first made contact with his mother and got a pledge of her full cooperation. They then got in touch with the die-hard republicans at the house of Cosimo's maternal uncle, Alamanno Salviati, and frightened them into submission with the spectre of a dictatorship of Cibo and Vitelli backed by Spanish troops.

Finally, they started a whispering campaign in favor of their candidate in the shops and marketplaces, where all the residents of the city were sure to show up some time during the day.

These efforts quickly had the desired effect. When Cosimo arrived that afternoon to present his "condolences," according to instructions, at the palace, and when he was then greeted enthusiastically by the crowd in the street, Cibo realized that there was no other way out of what he feared most: one of Florence's traditional popular uprisings. When Vitelli was confronted, as he led his soldiers in through Porta San Niccolò a few minutes later, not with the turmoil he had expected, but with the almost breathless calm that had reigned over the city all day, it was obvious that, for the moment at least, the only possible justification for a military coup d'etat had been removed. By ten o'clock that evening, Guicciardini had secured a promise from Cibo to nominate Cosimo the next morning in the Senate; and he had secured a promise from Vitelli to back up the election, if need be, by force.

Just how Cosimo reacted to this sudden change in his fortunes, no one knows. Somehow, probably with the help of his mother and Guicciardini, he prepared a little acceptance speech during the night and arranged a banquet for the following evening. As soon as a false alarm about an impending riot outside had silenced the last dissenting voice in the Senate, he was escorted into the hall and presented with a unanimous proclamation. Taking note of the demise of Alessandro, the absence of a pregnancy in his wife, and the disqualification of Lorenzaccio's branch of the family, the senators recognized Cosimo as the legitimate heir to the powers invested in Alessandro by the emperor and sanctioned by the constitution of 1532. They then "elected and designated" him "head [*capo*] of the Florentine Republic." And finally, they appointed an eight-man committee—composed largely of the same Palleschi responsible for the whole maneuver—to put the decree into effect.

The carefree adolescent who just thirty-six hours before had been tramping over the hills of the Mugello had suddenly, on Tuesday morning, January 9, 1537, become a prince.

Or had he? The Senate had recognized him as Alessandro's heir, it is true. But it had done nothing to clarify the rather vague stipulations of the constitution of 1532—the fundamental law of the current regime—concerning his relation as "head" to the other offices of government. Indeed, just before his election, Cibo made him promise to defend the emperor's interests in Florence and in this way to recognize the independence of his—Cibo's—authority as the emperor's representative. Right after the election, the new executive committee made him sign a decree, promulgated the next day, which recognized the independence of their authority as well. The decree accorded him the very modest title of "Signor Cosimo de'

3. Francesco and Iacopo Ligozzi, *Election of Cosimo I*
Palazzo Vecchio

Medici" and associated the title with that of "his magnificent counsellors,"
making it clear that Alessandro's title of "duke" had been purely personal and
that Florence was a republic, not a duchy. It limited the appointment of magistrates, both in the city and in the dominion, to "true original Florentine citizens,"
thus suggesting that they would hold their positions by right rather than at the
prince's pleasure. Finally, it cut the salary of their "head" to 12,000 *scudi*, 6,000
less than Alessandro's had been. Perhaps, then, Cosimo was not a prince at all, but
merely the president of an oligarchy.

Similarly, the Senate had acted entirely in its own name, not in that of either
of the two powers which in fact had imposed the constitution of 1532: the Empire

and the Papacy. Yet just how free it was to act in its own name became clear within a few hours after the election, when Vitelli's soldiers, at the instigation of their commander and with the complicity of the mob, ransacked Cosimo's as well as Lorenzaccio's house and carried off everything of value they could lay their hands on—including, apparently, most of Cosimo's boyhood letters. Then, early the next morning, Vitelli seized the fortress—the Fortezza da Basso—and moved himself, Cibo, and Alessandro's widow, Margherita of Austria, inside it, together with every scrap of jewelry, silver plate, and money they could haul out of the Palazzo Medici. Still worse, Vitelli saw fit to justify his act not to Cosimo and his magnificent counsellors, but to the governor of Milan and, through him, to the emperor, whom he now recognized as his sole superior. The fortress, which had been built to defend a prince from his subjects, was now turned, on behalf of objectives shared by none of them, against both prince and subjects alike. Suddenly Cosimo had lost much of the wealth that was supposedly his by inheritance. Suddenly the state of which he was supposedly the head had lost all but the shadow of independence. And Florence was threatened with the application of a clause in the imperial decree of October 1530—a clause by which the authority conferred upon Alessandro was to devolve upon the emperor himself in the event of a default in Alessandro's male succession. That, after all, is just what had happened to Milan less than two years before.

Thus Cosimo found himself all but powerless before what soon appeared to be a still graver challenge to his new position: an armed invasion from abroad. The exiles at Bologna, Venice, and Rome—all those many citizens, that is, who had found the established regime incompatible with their ideals or interests or whom the regime had found incompatible with its ideals or interests—were rapidly recovering from their initial shock over what Lorenzaccio had done. And they soon decided that this was, in the words of one of their leaders, "the last act of the comedy, which must be played out well, and fast." Within less than a week they had started hiring troops in and around Bologna and Mirandola, and within a fortnight they had moved an army up from the south as far as Montepulciano. At the same time, two thousand Spanish troops had disembarked in the Lunigiana —no one knows just why—and were heading down the coast. And Pierluigi Farnese, who was as eager as his father, Pope Paul III, to redraw all the borderlines of northern Italy, had almost succeeded in grabbing the fortress at Pisa, the only one still fully loyal to the Florentine government.

Meanwhile, the morale of the population inside the city was degenerating into near panic. It took no more than a report of a brawl among some of Vitelli's soldiers, one morning, to bring the shutters of every shop crashing down in unison. Most of the former protégés of the deceased duke soon decided that their security had expired with the last breath of their patron. Many of the citizens who had fled after the siege of 1530 and who subsequently had returned under pressure decided that any change in government could benefit none but their enemies.

They scattered, some to the countryside, some across the borders, and at least one, the future art historian Giorgio Vasari, to the hermitage at Camaldoli. Many nonpartisan citizens started leaving too, persuaded that they were now faced either with a sack or with an equally ruinous forced loan. These voluntary exiles were not necessarily hostile to Cosimo. "I have never even thought of doing anything that might displease you," wrote the wealthy businessman Francesco Valori as soon as he reached Bologna on June 1. But they were terrified of those elements in the government, most particularly Cibo and Vitelli, whom Cosimo, they realized, was unable to control. "I had learned from a person of good faith," Francesco continued, "about certain things said [in my regard] by someone of authority in the government, which frightened me and forced me to get out of town." Just enough debtors had sudden "doubts," in the corridors of Palazzo Medici, about the loyalty of their creditors, and just enough respectable citizens vanished without explanation in the direction of the Bargello, to justify his fears.

Outside the city, similarly, disorder was turning into chaos. A captain from Pisa, following Vitelli's example, had taken possession of the fortress at Livorno; and there was no reason to suppose that he would not encourage his fellow citizens to call in the Spanish, as they had once called in the Venetians, in order to get rid of the hated Florentines. In fact, for a day or so in April, everyone in the capital was sure he had done just that. The inhabitants of Borgo San Sepolcro were already lining up on either side of a family feud that was soon to invite armed intervention from the outside. And the Pistoians had used the first report of Alessandro's death as an excuse for immediately reverting to their age-old pastime of butchering each other, all the way from the Valdinievole to San Marcello.

The prophesy of one well-informed observer at the end of January was not wholly incredible: that Tuscany would soon be another Piedmont, torn apart in a struggle among foreign powers, or else another Lombardy, ruled by a foreign governor and a foreign army. In such circumstances merely becoming a prince provided very little guarantee of remaining one for long.

2

Survival

Fortunately, Cosimo was not completely devoid of resources. First of all, he could draw upon the lasting fame of his father, Giovanni. One of the most popular and romantic heroes of the early sixteenth century, he was usually called Giovanni delle Bande Nere ("of the Black Bands") after the professional army he had commanded. Cosimo had never really known his father; Giovanni had been killed prematurely in 1526 while trying to block the advance of the Imperial army that was to sack Rome the following spring. Indeed, the stilted little note he wrote at the age of seven, asking "Your Illustrious Lordship to permit me to pay a visit before you depart," suggests anything but familiarity and affection for a father who, as a matter of fact, preferred the wild women of Rome to his straitlaced wife, and who deprived his son of what might have been a decent inheritance by refusing to demand what was due him from his patrons. At one point, he even sent the insignia of the Order of St. Michael back to the king of France and tore up the bank draft that accompanied it, simply because he was too proud to accept advance payment for services he had not yet rendered.

What Cosimo remembered, then, was not his real father, but the somewhat exalted image of him that had been subsequently created by his widowed mother, whose devotion to her husband increased with her distance from him, and by Pietro Aretino, the man of letters whom Giovanni had patronized and in whose arms he had expired. "Let our hearts repose in the joy of his many honors! Let us recall his victories and become like lamps lit by the rays of his glory!": Cosimo heard phrases of this sort repeated over and over, along with constant exhortation to "resemble, if not surpass" the model that was held before him. And he apparently heeded the exhortation, for in January 1537 those who knew nothing of the son could still recognize in his bearing traces of his famous father.

Cosimo could also depend upon the support and encouragement of his mother. Maria Salviati was in many respects the exact opposite of her husband—a solid,

down-to-earth, old-fashioned aristocratic matron, one who wore no other ornament than a plain white veil over her black gown, who managed her small estate
with scrupulous care, and who probably never got around to reading even the
little book that Jacopo Pontormo made her hold when he painted her portrait
several years later. "The instant the blessed soul of my lord consort left me," she
noted proudly, "I decided to live solely for my son." Indeed, everything she did
thereafter was carefully aimed toward a single purpose: that of getting for Cosimo
what she thought had been unjustly denied to Giovanni. On him she poured out
all the affection that had been pent up during her years of none-too-happy marriage.
For his sake she turned aside all the suitors her brother persisted in finding for her.
For him she willingly made any sacrifice, even that of incurring a rather large
monetary debt with Cosimo's future archenemy, Filippo Strozzi. In him she
inculcated the three principal virtues that had been notoriously lacking in her
husband: ambition, financial punctiliousness, and marital fidelity. After his election, Maria was always at hand, ready to give advice, particularly on how to handle
the principal Florentine families, about whom she was well informed. But at the
same time she carefully avoided interfering in matters that, as she soon realized
after a few indiscretions, were not within her competence. Now that her ambitions
had been fulfilled—far, indeed, beyond her fondest hopes—she changed roles.
Instead of a solicitous mother, she was an affectionate baby-sitter, one who spent
most of her time in the nursery with Alessandro's orphan daughter Giulia,
with the baby Bia, whom the impeccable Cosimo somewhere and by someone—
nothing more specific is known about the incident—managed to beget before his
marriage in 1539, and with Cosimo's many legitimate children thereafter. She
also became a "lady of mercy," a *donna pietosa*, whose charity toward the poor and
generous contributions to religious foundations did much to reconcile Florentines
with their new ruler.

Cosimo owed something still more important to his mother: his self-reliance
and his experience in the ways of the world. Maria adored her son; but—and this
is really to her credit—she never tried to dominate or protect him. Quite the
contrary: no sooner had Giovanni died than she sent Cosimo off to be presented,
alone and not from behind her skirts, in the high society of Venice. In December
1532 she sent him to Bologna, where she hoped some nice scraps might fall his
way from the appetizing table that the pope and the emperor, at their second
meeting in three years, were displaying before the big and small of all Italy. To
be sure, she put him officially in the care of his tutor, the stuffy, pompous Pierfrancesco Ricci, whom Benvenuto Cellini later called, somewhat unjustly, the
"dirty little pedant [*pedantuccio*] of Prato." She also saw to it that he lacked nothing
in the way of proper attire and equipment, from his own personal bed to horses
and game bags. She covered all his expenses, in spite of the astronomical prices in
a city that had now become an established center for international political conventions. And she wrote anxious petitions on his behalf to Pope Clement, to her

rich and influential but hardly paternal father, Jacopo, who "had enough cloth to dress whom he pleased," and to her decidedly unfraternal brother, Cardinal Giovanni, whom Cosimo was to find even less helpful in 1537 than he had been in 1532. But she insisted that Cosimo do the rest himself. She knew that the whining, homesick Ricci could teach him no more than how to write horribly misspelled Italian speeches sprinkled with correctly spelled Latinisms, and how to recite them with due dignity. But in a century when extreme youth was respected as much as old age, and when cardinals in their teens kept princely households in their own names, there was no reason why a fourteen-year-old boy could not be his own advocate. She therefore instructed him "not to wait for my father or anyone else to do your job for you, but to do it all by yourself." And she admonished him to "take courage and himself ask a favor from the pope," rather than relying, as his father had foolishly done, on the empty promises of the pope's nephews.

None of Maria's elaborate schemes came to anything in the end. Cosimo got neither a post in the government of the Romagna nor a sinecure in Florence. And he was denied the hand of Maddalena Cibo Cajazzo, the heiress to a minuscule feudal domain in Lombardy, whose tight-fisted and financially distressed mother was determined to find her a more promising husband. Cosimo had nothing better to look forward to, on his return from Bologna later that spring, than a modest, though respectable, career either as a decorative hanger-on at Alessandro's court or as the head of one of the several Florentine families—and one far from the most prominent—whose members happened to bear the same surname as the duke.

But the experience turned out eventually to have been extremely profitable. Cosimo had learned to move easily in the company of princes, ambassadors, and cardinals. He had learned to kiss the foot of the pope and to hunt with the emperor, whose passion for the chase, he found, was as undampened as his own by the chilly, drizzly Emilian winter. He had learned the art of using balls, banquets, and masks, which at Bologna had gone on almost steadily for three solid months, as a way of preparing negotiations. And, after the conference, he had been exposed to the desolating consequences of war and the stimulating prospect of sea power during a trip through the principal cities of northern Italy, from Bologna to Genoa. Meanwhile, his formal education had furnished him with a good supply of anecdotes from Ariosto, Livy, and Cicero, without infringing upon the unadorned, colloquial, irregular, but crystal-clear language in which he was to express himself thereafter. Thanks, then, to his mother's pushing and to his tutor's affectionate neglect, Cosimo turned out, on January 9, 1537, to be somewhat less inexperienced and immature than most of the senators thought him to be; and he could rely first and foremost, in moments of crisis, on himself.

Cosimo could rely on himself. But he also could rely, insofar as their interests happened to coincide with his own, on those who at the moment shared or limited his authority. Cardinal Innocenzo Cibo, first of all, the somewhat sensual, long-bearded éminence grise he had inherited from Alessandro, fortunately had no other ambition than that of holding on to what power he already enjoyed. His family was not much of a problem. For most of them were still desperately trying to stay where they had landed after the election of Pope Innocent VIII had catapulted them out of a remote corner of eastern Liguria a half-century earlier. And none of them was yet settled enough to think of using his cardinal-uncle as a means of moving elsewhere. Money was not a problem for Cibo either. Beside what he could milk from the Florentines, he could count on his regular salary as archbishop of Turin, archbishop of Genoa, archbishop of Messina, abbot of San Siro and of San Paolo a Ripa d'Arno near Pisa, and rector of a score of churches in various parts of Christendom—all positions, in those blissful days before the Council of Trent, for which he did not have to perform the least service in return. Moreover, he was far more interested in the technical details of power than in its actual exercise. Instead of trying to dictate policy, he was usually content to collect stories from his numerous spies and to figure out little plots and intrigues, few of which had any other concrete effect than to annoy his patrons and charges, Alessandro included. Cibo had to be put up with as long as the emperor declined to remove him. But at times he could be useful, particularly since he had committed himself, in yielding to Guicciardini's maneuver on January 8, to getting the emperor's approval for Cosimo's election. At times he could be sidestepped or ignored. When necessary, he could be reminded of his moral obligations to the family of Leo X and Clement VII, to whom he owed most of what he now possessed.

Alessandro Vitelli, the professional soldier who had seized the Fortress on the morrow of Cosimo's election, was somewhat more difficult to deal with. Indeed, it was "that valorous and sincere honor of the Vitellian race," as Pietro Aretino had the bad taste to call him, who terrorized the citizens with his ill-behaved Spanish soldiers, who interfered with the business of the magistrates, and who disrupted negotiations with the exiles. Moreover, he was determined to take full advantage of the emperor's willingness to forget about legal scruples when faced with an advantageous fait accompli. Yet even Vitelli could be useful at times. He was a fairly good general. His interest in Florentine politics was limited to the fairly simple objective of preventing the return of anything resembling the republican government that had executed his father during the war with Pisa. His own personal ambitions were limited to the fairly modest goal of becoming lord, or *signore*, of some small autonomous domain, preferably in his home town of Città di Castello, just over the border in the Papal State. And above all, he was completely dependent on the emperor, whose word alone would have been sufficient to break him. Fortunately for Cosimo, the emperor at the moment was eager to get the pope's cooperation in a war against the Turks, and he had no intention, therefore, whatever many Florentines may have thought, of occupying directly a state, like Florence, that his potential ally also had designs on. One way to control Vitelli, then, was to persuade the emperor that Cosimo was more dependable than any of the semiofficial Imperial representatives in his government. And that is just what Cosimo managed to do between January 19, when his first special emissary left for Spain, and May 21, when the Marchese Del Vasto, the Imperial governor of Milan, came out definitely in his favor.

Far more reliable, and considerably more competent, were the leaders of the Palleschi in the Senate, particularly the most eminent of them, Francesco Vettori, best known today for his correspondence with Machiavelli, and Francesco Guicciardini, whose massive *History of Italy* is still recognized as a classic of historical writing. Vettori and Guicciardini both descended from families in the inner circle of the republican oligarchy. Both, accordingly, had been launched into political life at an early age, and both had become, in the course of time, men of letters as well as men of action. Their subsequent experiences had been somewhat different. Vettori, after a period in Rome as Florentine ambassador and adviser to Clement VII, had returned home to take his place as a member of a corporate political body, whereas Guicciardini had remained abroad as governor of the Romagna and had become accustomed to governing alone as the absolute master of a subject population. But both had begun as dedicated advocates of an aristocratic republic; and both, after careful reflection, had become resigned to some sort of authoritarian regime, one which they then hoped to temper by an informal council of a few wise men like themselves. Vettori, indeed, had drawn up, in a private letter to Pope Clement in 1530, what turned out to be almost a blueprint for the constitution of 1532, and he had participated in all the various ad hoc commissions that finally had set up the government of Alessandro.

Guicciardini, similarly, though he largely had given up belief in the efficacy of political action, hastened to respond favorably to Alessandro's appeal to him as the man "I have always held in the place of a father." "The duty of good citizens when their country is in the hands of a tyrant," he reflected, is not to waste their energies in futile attempts to remove him, but "to get into his confidence in order to persuade him to do good and desist from evil." He therefore became a sort of guardian, or "vice-duke" to Alessandro, drafting a defense brief for him at Naples in 1535, putting up with the diplomatic blunders he occasionally committed on his own, and chiding him for riding around Florence, ill-dressed and unprotected, with Lorenzaccio slouched behind him on the same horse.

Indeed, it was these elder statesmen, along with their immediate colleagues in the Senate, who were chiefly responsible for saving the state in the crucial moments of January 1537. It was they who willingly "endured labors beyond all belief," even though they had "the rank and the resources to live [quietly] elsewhere." It was they who strove desperately to realize "some small benefit for the city" at a time when "for hundreds of years [it] had never been in such need." It was they who went on working, when all their plans came to naught, "at least for the satisfaction of not having shrugged [their] duty." It was they, with their unsurpassed knowledge of politics in general and of the current political situation in particular, who most clearly realized the absurdity, at a time like this, of "talking about Brutus and Cassius and about turning the city back into a republic." It was they who first recognized as the single immediate goal of the new government, the goal for which everything else had to be sacrificed, that of keeping the city from being gobbled up by the Empire. And it was they who pointed out what Cosimo soon adopted as his own long-range goal—namely, reasserting the city's full independence.

Yet the services of these elder statesmen, indispensable as they were, were not without a price. And all Cosimo had to do to find out how much they cost was to reread the electoral agreement they had made him sign on the morning of January 9. It would have been naïve to suppose that those who had guided republics, advised popes, and ruled provinces would suddenly turn into submissive subjects. It would have been unrealistic to ignore the secondary motive of their eloquent pleas to the exiles on Cosimo's behalf—their desire to reinforce their own position in the government by getting their rich, influential friends back home. And young though he was, Cosimo was anything but naïve or unrealistic. If, then, he were ever to free himself from the interests of the big Palleschi, if he were ever to become something more than just "Signor Cosimo and his magnificent counsellors," he would have to look for more support than this. And that is just what he did during the first months of 1537.

The first element to respond favorably, at least by refraining from the violence everyone expected of them, were the lower classes of the city's population. The manual laborers and industrial workers, the "extreme part of the multitude who are abject and vile and are not members of the city except . . . as servants who minister to the needs of our bodies"—these "plebeians," as they were disdainfully called— had nothing to gain from the restoration of a republic which had never admitted them to citizenship even in its most democratic phases. They wanted bread, which they believed Alessandro had assured them by putting a ceiling on the price of grain. They wanted work, especially after the terrible economic depression brought on by the siege. And they did not care why the Fortress was being built as long as the bricklayers were kept employed. They expressed their gratitude to Alessandro by turning him, in a string of rather monotonous popular tales, into a sort of Robin Hood, one who made Roberto Acciaiuoli restore the bribes he had extracted from a peasant and who forced Baldo de' Medici to pay back a poor linen worker he had cheated. They expressed their confidence in Cosimo by lining the streets and shouting *Palle! Palle!* at anyone who dared challenge his authority.

The *Popolo*, on the other hand—the bigger artisans and the smaller merchants who had dominated the city during the last year of the last republic and who were scorned as "our enemy and yours" by the Palleschi oligarchs—had gradually come to realize that the word "liberty," at least in the mouths of those who now seemed most eager for it, had changed its meaning since 1529. It now meant, apparently, nothing more than the privilege of high-born ruffians like Piero Strozzi to beat them up and raid their shops with complete impunity. And when Alessandro let the *Otto di Guardia*, or central police office, throw Piero into the Bargello, they began to wonder whether the tyranny of one was really much worse than what amounted to the tyranny of many, and whether "liberty" was really preferable to what had apparently become its direct opposite, equality. They were undisturbed by the much-lamented, but rather vaguely documented irregularities of Alessandro's love life, which after all involved not their wives but those of patricians. And they were as flattered as Guicciardini was shocked by Alessandro's habit of "wandering around the city with a flute in his hand . . . , not considering his greatness at all," and occasionally stopping in at a shop, just like any other Florentine, "to pick up a bit of conversation." The *popolo* had one small weakness, to be sure: religious fanaticism. Just to be sure, therefore, that no one was tempted to make Savonarola's prophesies come true, Cosimo strictly forbade the carrying or possession of arms; and he made the least criticism of his or his predecessor's government a capital crime.

Cosimo also found support in the subject cities of the *Dominio*. One of the first things he did, after writing to the pope and the emperor, was to write, and to have his mother write as well, appealing to "the affection you [the chief magistrates of the subject cities] have always borne," not toward any particular Florentine government nor toward the House of the Medici in general, but "toward our [own immediate] family and our illustrious father [Giovanni] of happy memory." It was an audacious move. For the first time in history a Florentine ruler had deigned to consider as collaborators those who had always been looked down upon as mere subjects; and he did so at a time when most citizens still remembered the resentment they had felt, in the years before 1527, at being governed by a regent from Cortona. It was a clever move, too. For it undercut the plans of Cibo and Vitelli to use the *Dominio* for their own purposes by having it declare for the emperor. Above all, it worked. The citizens of the subject cities were by and large indifferent to the constitutional experiments that so excited Florentines while always leaving their own constitutions as authoritarian as ever. But the latest experiment seemed at last to offer certain advantages. If their ruler were a prince rather than a board of magistrates, he might be less tied to the particular interests of the dominant city and more responsive to their own special needs. If he could stop the Florentines from fighting among themselves, he might spare them what had always been the bloody and expensive consequences of Florentine civil disturbances. And if he could replace vacillation and mutability with firmness and consistency in the supervision of their own internal affairs, he might free them once and for all from the internecine strife that they had never been able to resolve on their own.

Hence their favorable response: "The emperor in Italy . . . and Signor Cosimo in Florence. May God maintain them both in greatest happiness!" And hence their steadfast loyalty, even in the presence of hostile armies that might well have tempted them to follow the example of Pisa in 1494 and of Arezzo in 1503. The city councils sent in spontaneous pledges of loyalty directly to Cosimo, and they addressed him perfectly openly as "Your Excellency . . . the Duke of Florence," without bothering about any of the subtle formulas prescribed by the Senate. Better yet, they gave their support to what was soon to be Cosimo's chief counter-weight to Vitelli's Spanish soldiers—the militia, which Alessandro had already started recruiting in the provinces, not in Florence, under the command of provincial, not Florentine, captains. It was these captains, from Pietrasanta in the northwest to Cortona and Montepulciano in the southeast, who were among the first to assure Cosimo, and Cosimo alone, of their "sincere loyalty and inviolable fidelity."

Plebeians, *popolo*, subject cities, and the rudiments of a militia: all these were very important. But they would not have been enough without at least the tacit consent of a good part of the Florentine patriciate—of that part, namely, which had no other political ambitions than the honor of an occasional magistracy, which wanted above all to get back to business, books, and comforts, and which had the private financial resources that all Florentine governments had relied upon in emergencies. A Roberto Acciaiuoli, for example, might indeed have been "avid, avaricious, unscrupulous," as his modern biographer says he was. But by 1537 he was left alone, in his villa at Montegulfi and his home and office in Borgo Santi Apostoli, to make himself "as rich as his father had been poor." An Ottaviano de' Medici, similarly, the warm, genial, generous friend of just about everyone and the affectionate brother-in-law of Maria Salviati, was willing to forego the authori-tative position in government he had occupied for the preceding eight years. He was adamant, in fact, in refusing all suggestions that he claim the succession to Alessandro, which he had almost as much right to as his distant cousin Cosimo. All he asked for was honor and respect—and the right to spend his ample spare time and his still more ample spare cash patronizing artists and poets.

To some outside observers—to Pietro Aretino, for example—this attitude looked like a surrender of principles, like that of "a young maid who bit by bit lets her breasts be touched and her clothes undone and ends up doing what is asked of her." But to people like Alessandro Antinori, who came through with a large and apparently unsolicited contribution to Cosimo's treasury in the crucial moments of late July, it was merely an intelligent adjustment to the realities of the situation. They needed Cosimo as the only defense against revolution or invasion. Cosimo needed them for their prestige and their pocketbooks. He therefore obliged them by doing away with some of the more annoying aspects of the former government. He abolished a few harmful taxes. He made it clear that he would never commit such outrages as commandeering Ottaviano's house without his permission, and at a moment when his wife was in the last stages of pregnancy, as Alessandro had done. Best of all, he sacrificed the most hated of Alessandro's lowborn foreign henchmen: the cruel, arrogant police secretary, Ser Maurizio, whom two young Florentines had the privilege of murdering, right under the walls of Siena, after his escape from prison in late April. Just to make sure, then, that no one mistook favors for weakness, Cosimo ruthlessly bore down on all suspected dissidents—on the "very honored citizen" Paolo Tolomei, for instance, who had removed the arms of Alessandro from his house, and on Giuliano Salviati, who had "spoken ill" (*sparlamenti*) of Cosimo in a private conversation.

Still more important were those members of the patrician and citizen families who had already given up politics for administration and who could be counted on for their loyalty to any government that showed signs of stability. The process of transforming a patriciate into a bureaucracy had still not gone nearly as far in Florence as it had, say, in Milan. Especially in the earlier years, Cosimo had to depend to a considerable extent on professional jurists and administrators—upon Bernardo di Colle, upon Francesco Campana, who had been secretary to Lorenzo, duke of Urbino, and then to Alessandro, and upon Ugolino Griffoni of San Miniato, who was nicknamed "The Broom" by those who did not like him and "The Olive" by those, like Maria Salviati, who did. These "secretaries," as they were called, had the particular advantage of being non-Florentines and of humble origin—and therefore of being completely dependent upon the prince who hired them.

But the transformation of the patriciate at least had begun, and Cosimo could already count on a number of wellborn assistants of considerable experience and technical ability. He could count on Francesco Guicciardini's brother Luigi, the "wise, severe man, quick and lively in the dispatch of affairs" who had been commissioner in Arezzo and was soon to be entrusted with the almost hopeless task of imposing law and order in Pistoia. He could count on the wealthy banker and skilled diplomat Lorenzo Cambi, who was soon to be charged with soothing the equally ruffled tempers of Paul III and of the citizens of Borgo San Sepolcro. He could count on Averardo Serristori, the son of an ardent partisan of Lorenzo the Magnificent, who now, at the age of forty, was about to be charged with two of the most delicate positions in the foreign service. He could count on his future military expert, Girolamo degli Albizi, to control Pisa, on Antonio Ricasoli to hold the Valdichiana, on Vincenzo de' Nobili to check the exiles at Montepulciano, on his cousin Chiarissimo to get money and men out of Pisa without causing a stir, and on "my distinguished relative and friend," Bernardo de' Medici, bishop of Forlì, whom he sent to the emperor in January.

Unlike the secretaries, these citizen-servants did not simply execute orders. They took the responsibility time and again for telling Cosimo politely but firmly what he ought to do; and with all the confidence of men of means and good background, they did not hesitate to point out what he ought not to have done. "Your Excellency . . . will give me orders as to how I am to answer the Cardinal [of Paris]," Serristori wrote sometime later. "But good servant that I am, I wish

not to omit reminding you to consider if you don't think it well to respond . . ."—
and then follows exactly what Serristori wanted Cosimo to order him to say.
After all, "I am now [in Rome]," he pointed out, and "I know the humors of
these persons better than those who cannot see and hear what is heard here."
Cosimo appreciated their cooperation. Never—and this is perhaps one of the
secrets of his success as a politician—did he resent their guarded reprimands, not
even Serristori's discomforting story of how he and the pope secretly decided to
burn up one of Cosimo's over-frank letters and ask for another one (which
Serristori then drafted) instead. Indeed, he often as not left them completely to
their own resources and in face of the most difficult circumstances. It is not surprising, therefore, that Serristori and Luigi Guicciardini were the authors of many
of the measures he adopted with regard to Pistoia, Spain, France, and the Papacy.

Obviously, none of these various groups and individuals would have done
Cosimo much good had the emperor decided to get rid of him. Foreign policy,
not domestic policy, was to make or break the new government. But, in turn,
the question of internal stability was to determine the government's worthiness
to survive. If Cosimo managed to keep quiet what turned out to be the most
turbulent city in European history between Ghent in the fourteenth century and
Paris in the nineteenth, then the emperor might be brought to accept another
fait accompli, as he had in the case of Vitelli and the Fortress.

It was thanks to all these resources, and thanks also to the amazingly pre-
cocious talent for politics apparent in the very first of his dispatches, that Cosimo
overcame, one after another, the crises of the following months. The first crisis,
an imminent invasion from the south, he thwarted in the third week of January,
when he persuaded the three Florentine cardinals to leave at Monte San Savino the
army they had brought up from Rome, and to come privately to Florence for a
conference. By letting one of them, his maternal uncle Giovanni Salviati, believe
that he really might be able to run Florence himself through "the authority he
[would certainly have] exercised over his nephew," Cosimo and his ministers even
succeeded in accomplishing the incredible: getting the cardinals to disband their
own army. That at least ended the threat from the south. And while Vitelli saw
to it that the cardinals were carefully isolated from any possible sympathizers in the
city, Cosimo turned his attention to the exiles in the north. They were first deprived
of the support of the local Papal governor, a small triumph of the Florentine
ambassador at Rome. They were then forced to move up into the Apennines,
where they were soon as discouraged by bad logistics as they had been encouraged
by an unexpected and very unusual wave of spring-like weather. And they were
finally subjected, individually and collectively, to a demoralization campaign,
culminating in the decree of January 30, which offered complete pardon and
restitution of all confiscated property to whoever would give up and come home.

The reconciliation that Cosimo, and the Palleschi as well, earnestly hoped for
did not come about at the time. It failed because Vitelli, backed up by the governor

of Milan, deliberately sabotaged it. And it failed because neither a powerful international banker like Filippo Strozzi nor a wealthy ecclesiastical prince like Cardinal Niccolò Ridolfi had any intention of suddenly submitting to the law of an upstart boy—they, who had never submitted to any law, moral, natural, or civil. Some Florentines, in other words, had simply become too big for Florence to contain them. But the offer had the positive effect of breaking the united front the exiles had managed at last to patch together under the impact of the events of early January. It permanently eliminated one of the protagonists, Cardinal Niccolò Gaddi, who decided that he preferred living in quiet luxury in Rome to tramping around the camps of northern Italy. And it set the rest of them back to the same old arguments about political principles that had so often impeded their effective action in the past.

The next crisis, therefore, did not occur until April—not, that is, until the initiative had passed into the hands of the French ambassador in Venice and the French representative in the College of Cardinals, and into the hands of Filippo Strozzi's brash, violent, unprincipled young son, Piero. Piero had only two objectives: glory—his own glory—and revenge—revenge for having been put in jail by his sometime playmate, Duke Alessandro. But he caught the imagination of the many young Florentine students at the universities of Padua and Bologna, who looked upon him as a providential agent for the realization of the wonderful ideals they had copied out of Demosthenes and Plutarch. Best of all, he came up with a new plan: a surprise attack aimed not at seizing Florence but at establishing a permanent foothold on Florentine territory.

The plan might have worked, in spite of its audacity. Everyone in Florence remained breathless as Piero's enthusiastic band swept across the frontier and headed toward their goal at Borgo San Sepolcro. It might have worked, that is, had Cosimo's efficient spy network not kept him informed of every word spoken in Bologna, had Piero not forgotten completely about the small, not very romantic question of supplies, had the peasants and villagers he encountered not to a man slammed their doors in his face, and had Vitelli not sent a regiment of soldiers with lightning speed to block his access to Borgo. When Piero's exhausted, drenched, and half-starved followers finally straggled out into the Duchy of Urbino a week later, the new government had passed its second test. The city had held firm in January. The countryside had stayed loyal in April. And at least one of the young enthusiasts, the poet and philosopher Benedetto Varchi, whom Cosimo later commissioned to write a history of Florence, decided that military expeditions were definitely not to his taste, and quietly retired to his books and literary conversations.

The next crisis was far more nerve-racking than the first two, partially because it lasted longer, partially because it involved not an open war with a near-equal enemy, but a diplomatic struggle with the most powerful monarch in all Europe—Charles V, Holy Roman Emperor, King of Castile, Naples, Bohemia, Sardinia, and Aragon, Count of Holland, Flanders, and Catalonia, Archduke of Austria, Lord of the Indies, etc., etc. At the beginning of May, the long-awaited personal representative of the emperor finally arrived, in the person of Juan de Silva, Count of Cifuentes, one of those polished but tough minor Spanish noblemen who were more and more being entrusted with the administration of Charles's empire. The first thing Cifuentes did was to let it be known that he considered as merely provisional everything done since January 7. He then got up a committee of senators—only one of whom he let Cosimo appoint—to advise him on the constitutional question. He next summoned representatives of the exiles, one of whom happened to be their outstanding expert on the theory and practice of government, the budding political philosopher Donato Giannotti. He drew·out the patricians by letting them think they might indeed persuade him to modify the regime in their favor. He kept Cosimo in suspense by holding out the prospect of a marriage with Alessandro's widow, Charles V's illegitimate daughter Margherita, whom he even had moved out of the Fortress and into the house of Cosimo's favorite counsellor of the moment, Ottaviano de' Medici. Only after weeks of lording it over the Florentines, whom he disdained as much as his master did, and only after interminable formal speeches before the Senate and an endless round of receptions, balls, and dinners, for which, of course, the Florentines were expected to pay—only then, on June 12, did he finally announce his decision. The decision contained less than Cosimo had hoped for. The question of Margherita was left hanging, the question of the fortresses was resolved in favor of Vitelli, and the question of the relation of Florence to the Empire was made more equivocal than ever before. But at least it granted the indispensable. It recognized Cosimo as the legitimate successor to Alessandro, even though as "head" and not as "duke", and it sanctioned the status quo as the only legitimate form of the Florentine Republic. All, of course, subject to eventual confirmation by the emperor himself.

The decree of June 12 at last freed Florence from the nightmare of outright annexation. But at the same time it made the next crisis almost inevitable. For by putting an end to the emperor's old game of playing off the regime against its enemies, and thus sucking the greatest advantage out of each, it threw the exiles once and for all into the arms of the French. The only alternative to submission, they now realized, was force backed up by subsidies from King Francis I and by the immense financial resources of the Florentine banks in Rome, Venice, and Lyon. For the moment they hesitated. The cardinals had qualms about contributing any more money. Filippo Strozzi was afraid of being stuck with the bill once again—and anyway he hated camping, he was scared to death of soldiers, and he really wanted to get back to his Greek texts, to his account books, and to Tullia d'Aragona, the lovely, witty mistress he shared with some of the best people in Rome.

But action could not be put off forever. The pressure from the great mass of minor exiles, those who had no resources abroad and whose estates at home were being confiscated, was becoming increasingly unbearable. At the same time, the leaders were letting themselves be consistently misinformed about conditions in Tuscany—to the point, indeed, of believing that all the foreign troops had left, that Prato and Pistoia were on the point of rebellion, and that Guicciardini and Vettori were ready to desert. A rumor—truer than anyone imagined—that France and the Empire were negotiating an armistice, the discovery that Cosimo's spies had got hold of all the exiles' secrets, and a furious family fight in which Piero Strozzi hurled every imaginable swearword at his humiliated father, were enough to overcome the weakest wills. In the last week of July two hundred wildly enthusiastic citizens and several thousand less enthusiastic hired soldiers started pouring over the Apennines and down along the route that today is marked by the Bologna-Florence railroad line.

The result was the Battle of Montemurlo, one of the most spectacular disasters of all Florentine history. While Maria Salviati arranged for prayer vigils in all the hospitals and monasteries, Cosimo imposed a tight curfew on the city, collected the huge sum of 100,000 *scudi* from the Senate, and moved the near relatives of the chief exiles into protective custody. He then ordered the Spanish troops in Fiesole and his own troops in the Pian di Ripoli to move as quietly as possible toward the castle, a little over half-way to Pistoia, where the exiles were assembling. All his resources, financial and military, had been committed; and there was nothing to do but wait. At twelve o'clock the next day, August 1, 1537, the news arrived: the exile army had been totally crushed and almost all its leaders had been captured. Two hours later the lugubrious procession started down the Via Larga, amid the tolling of bells and a din of *Palle! Palle! Vittoria!* There was Baccio Valori, the high commissioner of the Papal army of 1530 and master of Florence in the months after the siege, now "dressed in a ragged army jacket, without even a cap on his head." There was Antonfrancesco degli Albizi "of noble birth and proud disposition," who had deposed the president of the Republic in 1512, now being "led miserably on foot." There was Filippo Strozzi, "the first man of Italy, praised in the name of every great virtue." There was Baccio's son Pagolantonio, Lodovico Rucellai, Bacciotto Tagi, and a score of others, bearing some of the most famous names of the sixteenth century. There they were, exposed to the insults of a furious mob and then pushed to the ground before the placid, motion-less eighteen-year-old youth who had become the symbol of all they hated.

The danger of external agression had suddenly, and unexpectedly, vanished. All that remained to do was to set off a fireworks display, proclaim August 1 as an annual civic holiday, start chopping off heads in the Piazza della Signoria, and send out official announcements of the victory to the emperor, to Andrea Doria, and to the governor of Milan. The victory had not been complete, to be sure. Piero Strozzi, for one, had escaped. Several others had bribed their way to freedom. Still others had to be bought from the Spanish troops who had captured them. Worse yet, the biggest of them all, Filippo Strozzi, had been "stolen" by Vitelli and was now reposing, for whatever advantage Vitelli might hope to get out of him, in the Fortress—right under Cosimo's nose but just beyond his reach. Moreover, some of the most pressing of Cosimo's problems were still outstanding: the problem of Margherita's marriage, the problem of the Spanish troops in Tuscany, the problem of the fortresses. And their resolution was still to require many months of pulling strings, distributing favors, and waiting patiently as the emperor either greeted the hard-working Florentine ambassadors in his perfectly fluent Italian or else rebuffed them in the Spanish only one of them could understand.

But in the meantime, the opposition in Florence had crumbled. "Since this victory," the Sienese ambassador reported, "Signor Cosimo has been much more courted by the citizens than ever before . . . and almost every afternoon he goes hunting"—hunting, at last, after so many months of hard work! By the end of September, Cosimo had obtained the emperor's confirmation of the decree of June 12. By mid-autumn many of the citizens, like the young scholar Pier Vettori, who had retired to the country, were beginning to return to the city. And by the end of the year Cosimo could report to Andrea Doria that "even though it has been reduced to poverty by the late troubles," his state "was beginning to breathe again."

Cosimo was still far from being the master of his own destiny. But what had looked, in January, like little more than a makeshift arrangement had begun, eight months later, to show definite signs of lasting.

3

Affirmation

Eight years later, in 1545, the promise had become a reality. Cosimo spent most of August that year out in the villa of Poggio a Caiano, which Giuliano da Sangallo had ennobled with a gracious Attic portico for Lorenzo the Magnificent in the 1480s, and which Jacopo Pontormo had just recently decorated with startling frescoes under the direction of Ottaviano de' Medici. Cosimo was still as busy as ever, between hunting on the thickly wooded slopes of Monte Albano, dictating to his secretaries, entertaining visitors, and keeping an eye on the dome of the cathedral, which he could see from the terrace, ten miles straight eastward across the flat Arno valley. But now he also had time occasionally to stand still while Pontormo's affectionate, affable assistant, Agnolo Bronzino, who was usually off playing with those "adorable angels," Cosimo's children, got back to work at the easel. The suit of armor Cosimo had ordered for the occasion was just as uncomfortable and far less appropriate than the one in which Bronzino had painted the duke of Urbino a few years before. But Cosimo was sure that this would be the best of the many canvasses, "absolutely true to nature and done with incredible diligence," which had recently made Bronzino one of the most sought-after portrait artists in Italy.

Cosimo looked a bit more than his twenty-six years, with his large eyes, high forehead, and slight beard, with a placid, determined, and at the same time complacent expression, and with little trace of the "Machiavellian duplicity" or the "impenetrable gaze" that certain romantic tyrannophobes read into Bronzino's portrait three centuries later. He had a right to be contented with himself, after all. For almost all the grave problems he still had had to face after August 1537 had been solved, some very successfully, the rest at least not too unsatisfactorily. They had been solved in part because of the hard work of the Florentine diplomatic representatives abroad—of able, experienced citizens like Cosimo's distant cousin Bernardo de' Medici, who had just returned, honored and respected, from the court of France, and like Giovambattista Ricasoli, bishop of Cortona, who had impressed even the hostile authorities in Milan some years before by "speaking like a great Guicciardini." The problems had been solved also by carefully adhering to Serristori's advice of January 1538: "Don't ever run out of money," he had told Cosimo. "Save every cent you can," and "always have a good reserve on hand for unforeseen circumstances."

Above all, the problems had been solved by following Guicciardini's advice to remain firmly in the Imperial camp. The policy seemed contradictory, for it proposed regaining independence by openly siding with the very power that had done the most to reduce Florence to dependence. And it was risky, for, as Cosimo's ambassador repeatedly reminded him, "they all [at the Spanish court] look upon this present affair just as they have upon all past ones: as a way of eating Your Excellency." But at least it was realistic, for it recognized that the days of the French in Italy were numbered. And it was certainly more effective than the kind of debilitating vacillation that Machiavelli had denounced in the government of Piero Soderini before 1512.

Cosimo started, it is true, with a few partial checks. First of all, he lost Margherita. In spite of the constant pleas of the Florentine ambassadors, and in spite of the constant reminders of Margherita's own agent in Spain that "she was happy to remain in Florence . . . and [should be] left to enjoy this noble state destined for her by heaven," Charles V finally decided to exchange his daughter for a bit of papal goodwill. Cosimo lost much more than a bride, for once Margherita had been reconciled to being torn away from the only home she had ever known and to being sold to the highest bidder on the market of international politics, she put in a claim for a good part of the property of her first husband. And because this case, like all the others she had ever been involved in, was settled by a political and not a judicial decision, Cosimo ended up having to pay rent even on the Palazzo Medici. Indeed, he was left finally with little more than the pleasure of watching the furious teen-age girl make her captors' lives miserable for months before she would consent to cohabit with the pope's fuzzy-faced grandson, later Ottavio Farnese, duke of Parma.

At the same time, Cosimo paid dearly—far too dearly, it turned out—for the one thing he wanted more than Margherita: Filippo Strozzi. With Filippo alive in the Fortress—and particularly with Filippo freely walking about the ramparts, dining in state, and running his business by correspondence—Cosimo was constantly faced with a visible reminder of the strict limitations on his effective authority. He was also faced with the possibility that Vitelli, who was very flattered by the company of so honorable a guest, might suddenly accept the huge bribe that had been offered for Filippo's freedom. And if the emperor went through with the plan to sell Milan to the king of France, then Cosimo could count on facing a coalition of French power and Strozzi money right on his doorstep. But several examinations, with torture, failed to extract from Filippo a confession of complicity with Lorenzaccio—a confession which would have been completely false, but which alone would have forced the emperor to let Cosimo have him.

Filippo himself finally relieved Cosimo of his embarrassment. Having been abandoned by his son Piero, shunned by his brother Lorenzo, bored with his translation of Polybius, and exasperated by an increasingly hopeless situation, he suddenly, in a fit of despondency, committed suicide. Thus vanished one of the great men of the Italian Renaissance—one so great, indeed, that he could dispense with all the moral principles and political ideals that governed the actions of lesser men, one incapable of imagining a social order directed to anything but satisfying his appetites and magnifying his family, and one who, in the end, fell victim more to his own indecision than to the malice of his enemies. He left behind him a testament that has since been read out of context by generations of noble spirits as a great monument of republican patriotism. And he left a fortune which, even after the confiscation of his property in Florentine territory and the plundering of much of his property abroad, still amounted to the huge sum of 500,000 *scudi* in liquid assets alone.

These were temporary setbacks, true. But they were amply offset by several notable gains.

First of all, Cosimo acquired a title—a clear, unequivocal title, as duke of Florence, and not merely as duke of Nemours or of Penna, like two of his Medici predecessors, and certainly not merely as "head" of a republic. That ended all question about the nature of the regime, even if it left open, to be settled in practice rather than in theory, the question of whether his title came to him by inheritance, by election, or by investiture.

Cosimo next acquired a wife—not the illegitimate daughter of the emperor, to be sure, but someone just as good: the perfectly legitimate daughter of one of the most powerful noblemen in Spain, Pedro de Toledo, who was then, and who was to remain for thirteen years thereafter, viceroy of the kingdom of Naples. Eleonora was duly welcomed into Florence on June 29, 1539, with fireworks, choruses, orchestras, plays, and a triumphal procession through the streets. Cosimo's marriage made him at least potentially the equal of Marguerite of Hungary in Flanders, of Andrea Doria in Genoa, of the Marchese del Vasto in Milan, of the Duke of Alva in Castile—of all the actual rulers, that is, of the various autonomous parts of Charles V's heterogeneous empire. In other words, it raised him from the position of a temporary protégé to that of a permanent member in what amounted to an Imperial federation. His new position was duly symbolized by the headdress designed for "Flora" (Florence) at the wedding banquet: six red eggs (the Medici balls) in a nest being set on by an (Imperial) eagle. And the position was finally solemnized in Charles's instructions to his son Philip on January 18, 1548. "The duke of Florence," the emperor wrote, "has always shown himself most devoted to me. . . . Given his relationship with the House of Toledo . . . and the situation of his said state . . . you will do well to keep him in his sentiments of good will and to favor him in all his doings."

In Eleonora de Toledo Cosimo acquired his closest and most constant companion, one who equaled him in physical energy and almost equaled him in spiritual energy; who went hunting with him and traveling with him even in advanced stages of pregnancy; whose passion for gambling and whose disconcerting changes of mind he gladly put up with. Eleonora turned out to be well worth the huge dowry his father-in-law had forced Cosimo to put up for her. She provided him with domestic happiness almost unheard-of in an age of exclusively arranged marriages. "The duke and the duchess are deeply in love," reported one well-informed observer in 1541, "and one is never apart from the other." Better yet, she provided him with children—the first just nine months and thirteen days after her arrival in Florence, the second just ten months later, the third in the fall of 1543, and so on and on until it became almost routine to congratulate "the most happy and most fecund duchess . . . who from single has been made double of body. And God will that it come out a male!"

The predicament of January 1537 would not, apparently, recur. What had been a family threatened with extinction had now become a dynasty capable of surviving the sudden eclipse of whoever happened at the moment to be its head, and, apparently, capable also of magniloquent comparisons to the greatest houses of Greece and Troy:

> Mediceam laudare domum si tentet Homerus,
> haud fuerint numeri, haud Attica verba satis.
> illa suis adeo pro avis at avisque refulget
> ut vincat Graecas, Iliacasque domos.*
> (Francesco Vinta in *Carmina*, p. 34)

The test came in October 1543, when Cosimo lay for weeks at the point of death; Eleonora, with the help of Campana, showed herself fully able to hold on to what her husband had acquired until one of her infant sons should come of age.

At the same time, Cosimo managed to get rid, one by one, of all his "protectors," both foreign and domestic. The turn of the big Palleschi came in June 1537, when the emperor's plenipotentiary, Cifuentes, put them into the same category as all other Florentine citizens and chose to negotiate directly with Cosimo alone. They still retained their positions as "magnificent counsellors." They still maintained their prestige as elder statesmen. But when Guicciardini found Cosimo in

---

* "If Homer tried to praise the House of Medici, Attic speech would hardly suffice. So brightly does it shine, in itself and in its ancestors, that it overcomes the [great] houses of Greece and Troy."

late August "already informed of everything" concerning the matter he thought he alone knew about—worse yet, when he discovered that Cosimo was perfectly willing to let him accept a position that was about to be offered him in Rome—it was evident that their advice had now become purely consultative. Guicciardini quietly retired to his villa, to revise and expand his great *History of Italy*. Francesco Vettori gradually resigned himself to being no more than a technical consultant. Both were disappointed, particularly Vettori, who was obsessed by what he thought, erroneously, to be a "soft" policy toward Spain. But they had to admit that there was no alternative, and that in fact Cosimo was doing very skillfully exactly what they would have done in his place. "It seems that our age is at last beginning to be happy," admitted Guicciardini after watching Cosimo maneuver his way through a particularly delicate affair. "For it is now free of having [constantly] to extend its thoughts and calculations beyond the next day." That was at least some consolation for two great men who, by the time they died a few months apart, in 1539 and 1540, had already become historical personages, admired for what they had done in the past rather than looked to for what they might still do in the future.

The retirement of the two greatest citizens was followed, soon afterwards, by the reconciliation, or at least the submission, of most of the rest. Some opposition there still was, to be sure, even inside the city. But it was voiceless, and it is recorded only in a few private memoirs that came to light many decades later. It was also wholly disorganized. Just to make sure it stayed disorganized, Cosimo issued a series of draconian decrees prohibiting "any kind of assembly, congregation, or conventicle" and punishing even the intention of subversion with death for the guilty and banishment and confiscation for all the male heirs. The one serious attempt against the regime proved the efficacy of these measures. No one, not even his closest friends and relatives, seems to have been the least bit aware of the elaborate plot of the husband of one of Eleonora's ladies-in-waiting, a certain Giuliano Buonaccorsi, to shoot Cosimo from a window in August 1543. In fact, the only motive the grueling examination could get out of him was a mere fascination with audacity for its own sake. And Giuliano's fate served to frighten off any other lone plotters. He was hauled through the streets of Florence, tormented with pincers and hot pokers, torn down from the scaffold half-alive, dragged by one foot around the Fortress, and disemboweled in public. What remained of him was then dumped first on his sister's doorstep and then into the Arno—whence Cosimo, in a moment of compassion, had him fished out for a decent burial.

The only alternative to silence, then, or to private grumbling, was exile, and exile often led in turn to banishment and confiscation of all property left behind in Florence. To be sure, life abroad was not without its attractions, at least for those Florentines who managed to find a good position as a secretary in some court or as an employee in one of the many Florentine firms in Rome, Venice, and Lyon, which always hired compatriots in preference to natives. Life was very pleasant indeed for Bartolomeo Cavalcanti, who became the right-hand man of the chief representative of French interests in Italy; for Luigi Alamanni, who earned the complete confidence of the future queen of France; for Donato Giannotti, who enjoyed the sparkling company gathered in Cardinal Ridolfi's magnificent villa at Bagnaia; and for Luigi Del Riccio, the friend of Michelangelo and an interlocutor in one of Giannotti's dialogues, who became one of the directors of the Strozzi bank. "I am healthier and more full of life than I've ever been before," wrote Giovan Battista Busini in 1550. "I have enough books to keep me busy and enough friends to console me." And he, like so many others, had no desire to go home.

But exile had serious drawbacks, too. It was not easy for an old-fashioned republican "to live here [in Rome] among all these priests . . . bowing and scraping and holding your hat in your hand." It was even less easy for a self-conscious citizen suddenly to find himself a courtier, forced to dress up in outlandish clothes, wait idly in drafty antechambers, and "conform to the will of the patron." It was a positive hardship, indeed, for almost any Florentine to live outside Florence, and not one of them was free from frequent pangs of homesickness. Thus, when Cardinal Ridolfi found himself reduced to drying his feet with rags, he had to send back to Florence for new towels ("and please make sure they're made out of domestic cloth")—and for wine, shirts, cheese, fruit, and just about everything else. Obviously nothing of proper quality could be had within the borders of the Venetian Republic, even if it was, probably, the richest state in Europe.

Only the hope of eventually getting back home—on terms, of course, other than those Cosimo insisted upon—could provide any comfort amid such inconveniences. But the exiles had been deprived of all their leaders in 1537. They had lost confidence in the cardinals. And they still mistrusted the hotheaded children of Filippo Strozzi. So there was very little they themselves could do to make the hope come true. "I thought that *cacaruola* of Montemurlo could have made you a bit wiser," wrote Pietro Aretino to one enthusiastic Ciceronian in the fall of 1537. "And I am surprised that you have not made a vow before all the Annunciations in the world never again to talk about liberty and soldiers." But the longer the exiles waited for someone else to rescue them, the more improbable it became that fortune or the emperor or the king of France would do so. Cosimo did not drop dead, or resign, or move to Naples, or get chased out by a providential army, in spite of the false rumors that circulated in Venice during the early 1540s. Hence some of the exiles began to doubt the wisdom of their decision. Cavalcanti admitted that he really did not have any grudge against Cosimo himself. Vincenzo Martelli, after loudly proclaiming the "affection he had always felt for Filippo [Strozzi], his country," etc., etc., was soon asking his friends in Florence "to kiss humbly the hands of His Excellency the Duke and of Signora Maria."

Switching sides was not considered treasonable or even inconsistent in the sixteenth century. Even Martelli's own employer, the famous Ferrante Sansovino, Prince of Salerno, turned overnight, after a spat with Cosimo's father-in-law,

Pedro de Toledo, from an ardent imperialist into an equally ardent francophile. There was no reason why the exiles had to carry their principles to the bitter end, either. Few of them actually had returned as yet. But when Cosimo proved to be as flexible in such matters as anyone else, when he opened his arms even to Silvestro Aldobrandini, who had been the first to open his arms to Lorenzaccio, and when he greeted Martelli "with the greatest demonstrations" of goodwill in spite of Martelli's passionate sonnets about "the bitter yoke" of the imperialists, the exiles were sorely tempted.

More important still, Cosimo's opponents found it harder as time went on to figure out just what they were opposed to. They railed against the basic immorality of all princes in general and of Duke Alessandro—and Peisistratus of Athens and Dionysius of Syracuse—in particular. But Cosimo, who neither starved his mother nor poisoned his relatives nor raped the wives of his subjects, turned out to have very little in common with any of the standard textbook tyrants. They blamed him for banishing and persecuting respectable citizens. But Savonarola and Francesco Carducci had done the same thing. They charged him with acts of violence. But the behavior of their own roughnecks in Naples in 1535 and in Rome in the late 1540s was far from exemplary. They accused him of selling out to the emperor. But they themselves had offered Pisa to Charles as an outright gift and Florence as a virtual protectorate. Still worse, they could think of only one way to get rid of the emperor, namely, to replace him with the king of France. And only the most naïve could really believe that "in the spirit [of Francis I], full of sincerity and prudence, there is no place . . . for sinister opinions and evil counsels," indeed no place for any lesser cause than "giving back Florence her liberty." Substituting one foreign domination for another was not much help. And when Piero Strozzi's soldiers rushed into Serravalle in June 1544 shouting, not *libertà!* and *popolo!* but *Francia! Francia!* who could throw the first stone?

In fact, even the grumpiest of anti-Mediceans had to admit that some elements of Cosimo's government were not very bad. Eleonora might be, whatever everyone else said to the contrary, haughty, domineering, cruel, and, worse yet, a Spaniard. But Maria Salviati was the incarnation of all womanly virtues. Cosimo might throw away money on frivolities. But he also issued what all virtuous republicans considered the noblest laws in Florentine history—those, namely, which prescribed perforation and then amputation of the tongue on the first and second convictions for blasphemy and the stake on the third conviction for sodomy. Some, indeed, even began to wonder whether the old regime had been worth saving after all. Perhaps it was true, as Giannotti himself pointed out, that it had not been a republic but just a multiplicity of conflicting tyrannies. And perhaps it was true, as even Jacopo Nardi admitted, that "the diversity of opinion" in such governments "always makes consultation lengthy and execution weak and tardy."

Opposition gradually gave way to acquiescence, and acquiescence ended up in a tacit agreement about which of the electoral conditions of January 9, 1537, to keep and which to let drop. Cosimo granted the Florentine patricians a virtual monopoly of all ordinary government offices, which is what they really had wanted all the time. The patricians in turn forgot all about the strings they had so anxiously attached to Cosimo's personal authority. At times, indeed, acquiescence even gave way to applause. Vice, noted Francesco Vettori's studious young cousin, Piero, in 1546, had been replaced by modesty, uniforms by the simple dress of his ancestors, unruly soldiers by a well-disciplined militia, the threat of invasion and disorder by peace and prosperity.

The eulogy was a bit premature, and it was not strictly accurate in all details. But it expressed what had become a fairly widespread sentiment in Florence, one now shared not only by those who had worked for the establishment of the new regime from the start, but also by those who had come, regretfully, to accept it as the least of possible evils. Certain precautions were still advisable, to be sure— such as a bodyguard made up of German, rather than Florentine, soldiers. But Cosimo was at last free of what had been the most fearful nightmare of all Florentine governments until then: sedition and insurrection. He alone was master. Everyone else, including the four "magnificent councellors," was a subject. And no one any longer complained, not even the counsellor Bernardo Carnesecchi, whom Cosimo hardly had to remind, during a minor difference of opinion some years later, "that our advice is our will and that we consider as adversaries all those who oppose it." All the artillery that had been piled up in the Fortress was therefore unnecessary. And in 1544 most of it was moved out into the *Dominio* for the defense of Florence against external enemies rather than for the defense of the Prince against Florentines.

Thus Cosimo rapidly disposed of his domestic "protectors." The turn of his foreign protectors—of those, that is, whose authority in Florence descended from the emperor rather than from the government that supposedly employed them—came next.

The moment the excitement of Montemurlo died down, Cosimo instructed his ambassadors to keep up a steady wail about "the disorders of these Spanish infantrymen . . . whose presence here brings daily more ruin to this afflicted country." At last one of the ambassadors managed to get his hands on some very compromising documents. And after a bit of very skillful negotiating during the international conference of Nice and Aigues-Mortes in June and July 1538, they managed to obtain the dismissal of Vitelli, who went off in a huff to Rome. At the same time they procured the reduction of the Spanish garrison to a maximum of 200 troops. That turned over control of military power in Florence from an army of occupation to the native militia. But it also made increasingly uncomfortable the presence of the militia commander who had been forced upon Cosimo by the governor of Milan. Luckily, the general was as irascible as he was head-

strong and bad-mannered. And his behavior one evening out at Poggio, where he
let Eleonora's favorite dwarf goad him into a violent, undignified temper tantrum,
was all Cosimo needed to make the emperor swallow the whole list of valid charges
and less valid insinuations forthwith prepared for him. Within a month or so
Cosimo had a new commander, Stefano Colonna, who was sure to be responsible solely and exclusively to the prince who had hired him and who paid
him.

As the military protectors moved out, so did the civilian one. The bill Cosimo
received for the traveling expenses to Nice of one who, after all, enjoyed some of
the fattest benefices in Christendom, put Cardinal Cibo into the category of a
rather expensive luxury. He had also become an intolerable nuisance, since he
never missed a chance to show off Alessandro's son Giulio, whom he had in effect
kidnapped from Maria Salviati in 1538, and whom he kept in state, under a heavy
guard, in his own house. Cosimo's opportunity soon arose. A few months later
he found out "that no one opens his mouth or even pisses in my house without
its first being known down there [in Rome]." Where was the leak? Not among his
secretaries, nor among the "magnificent counsellors," whose faces Cosimo
scrutinized closely as he announced his discovery to see if any of them changed
expression. No, it was rather just where he least expected it, but where he was
more than happy to find it. Cibo, it seems, had been passing on tidbits regularly
to his sister-in-law, Ricciarda Malaspina, who then passed them on to her current
bedmate, the Imperial ambassador in Rome. That was enough for Cosimo to
start a campaign of careful denigration. "I will never fail to pay him the honor and
reverence due his station," Cosimo wrote his father-in-law. "But to speak frankly
to Your Lordship, considering his light-headedness and the way he lets himself be
governed by persons who wish well neither to His Reverend Lordship [i.e., Cibo]
nor to me . . . I am forced no longer to confide in him."

The next move was Cibo's, and it turned out to be fatal. He started spreading
rumors around Spain that Cosimo had hired a certain poison-maker named
Biaggio to assassinate little Giulio. This was pure, unwarranted slander, which no
one really could have taken seriously. Cosimo immediately had Biaggio examined
before no less authoritative judges than Guicciardini and Matteo Strozzi. Then,
"one morning while the cardinal was eating," Cosimo "made Biaggio appear
before him saying, 'the duke sends me to Your Lordship with the request that
you do what you want with me.'" The cardinal, faced squarely with his own
unjustifiable misdeed, "remained half-dead, looking . . . as if someone had thrown
soup in his face." By the time a blow-by-blow description of the entire affair, all
written out in Cosimo's earthy style, had reached the emperor, Cibo was already
packing. He spent the rest of his life in rather noisy retirement at Massa Carrara,
trying, amid the bloody quarrels of his relatives, to hide the ignominy of having
been completely outwitted—he, the nephew of one pope, the favorite of two others,
and three times an archbishop—by a mere boy of twenty.

With his "protectors" now out of the way, and with his place in the Imperial system relatively secure, Cosimo could start eliminating some of the more expensive and less agreeable aspects of his dependence on the emperor. He no longer had to put up with the annoying little bribes to Charles's ministers, for instance—with the 1,000 *scudi* paid to Antoine Perrenot de Granvelle and with the 10,000 *ducati* promised to Francisco de los Cobos in 1537. He could send presents instead, like Bronzino's *Deposition*, now in the gallery of Besançon, knowing that he would receive similar tokens of esteem—like a couple of Moorish slaves for Eleonora—in return. He no longer had to put up with the insolence and calumny of certain Spanish generals; and it took no more than a little chat with Campana in 1540 to reduce the tough, haughty, and tactless Juan de Luna practically to tears. Above all, he no longer had to put up with the practice of "wintering" Spanish armies in his dominions—at his own expense, needless to say, the emperor's military treasury being chronically in arrears. When the usual "request" from the Marchese del Vasto arrived in 1541, Cosimo pointed out dryly that "this is not the stall and stables of all this wandering riff-raff, nor is it the sewer of His Majesty's states in Italy." And just in case it occurred to Vasto to dump his troops into the Lunigiana anyway, as he had always done before, Cosimo added that he now had the means "to defend this state and thus serve His Majesty in other occurrences." He no longer had to grovel or beg. He could now talk from a position of strength.

At the same time, Cosimo had become an expert in using the Imperial alliance to his own advantage, particularly when it came to relations with his immediate neighbors. Italy in the sixteenth century was not yet a system of states. It was rather a system of big families, all engaged in a desperate game of musical chairs, and all intent upon using any means, from bulls of excommunication to trumped-up court cases, from bribery to assassination, from solemn alliances to sudden treachery, to seize one of the few available states of the peninsula whenever the music stopped—as it did periodically when a pope was elected, a prince died, or the emperor and the king momentarily stopped fighting. Some families had done fairly well up till then—the Gonzaga at Mantua, the Este at Ferrara and Modena, the Della Rovere at Urbino, and of course, more recently, the Medici at Florence. Some had lost the last round, like the Strozzi, the Baglioni, and the Colonna, but were ready to bounce back at the first opportunity. Others, like the Sforza in Milan, the Borgia in the Romagna, the Bentivoglio in Bologna, and the Varano in Camerino, had been eliminated altogether. One family, the Farnese, had just entered the competition; and they knew they had no longer than the lifetime of their current head, Pope Paul III, to score their indispensable first point in the game.

It was as a move in this game, then, and as an instance of the general rule that the advantage of one contestant was automatically the disadvantage of the others, that Cosimo viewed the interference of the Este in the Garfagnana. It was a similar move when Serristori publicly embarrassed the ambassador of Ferrara at a big reception in Rome, "as his silly presumption warranted," thus setting off a quarrel over who would sit where in papal audiences and in the imperial chapel that was to last for many decades. It was in these terms, finally, that Cosimo and his counsellors judged every move on the part of their greatest antagonist, Pope Paul III. The defense of Christendom against the Turks, they decided, the defense of Catholicism against the Lutherans, the Peace of Nice, and, eventually, the Council of Trent, were merely tactical maneuvers aimed at setting up the pope's son Pierluigi—or his grandson Ottavio—in Milan, or in Piombino, or in Siena, or even, so the ambassador in Rome wrote in 1539, in Florence itself. Luckily the ambitions of the Farnese usually ran head-on into the interests of the emperor. Or at least their ambitions countered the interests of Charles's chief representatives in Italy, who let out a furious howl when Milan was rumored to be up for sale in 1543. Cosimo could be sure, then, of Imperial support—except, of course, in those rare moments when the emperor and the pope managed to agree on something. And he stood firm before an onslaught that started within a few months of his election and ended only with a very advantageous compromise five years later, an onslaught that included two interdicts on the city and an attempt to transfer one of the richest ecclesiastical benefices in Tuscany to another of Paul's grandsons, Cardinal Alessandro.

Cosimo had nothing to lose. The Florentine bankers in Rome, the usual hostages in such circumstances, were all on the side of his enemies anyway. Among his subjects, "there [was] not a person left," he discovered to his delight, "who would not prefer to live two years under interdict than to pay a single *scudo*" of the heavy ecclesiastical tax demanded of him. Ecclesiastical sanctions had lost their force because, clearly, they were being used not to block the Turks but to ruin a perfectly Christian government. And because Paul was, as Campana pointed out, "malevolent, iniquitous, unprincipled, and the most double-faced of all men," one who "would be a thousand times worse than Pope Alexander [VI] if only he had a man instead of a sheep for a son," Cosimo's conscience was at rest. He regretted only that the emperor kept him from actively supporting the city of Perugia when it rose in revolt against the Papal government in 1540. For "considering . . . the actions of the priests of the Roman Church in these times," and given "the cruelty and obstinacy with which the pope is burning and desolating the countryside," the right was, Cosimo assured himself, on his side. The most he could get away with, though, was letting his general, Rudolfo Baglioni, a descendant of the former lords of Perugia, slip back across the border and keep the rebellion going for a month or so longer.

Relations with the four minor states of Tuscany were somewhat simpler. For one thing, all of them put together were far weaker than Florence alone, even in 1537. For another, they were all in one way or another within the Imperial sphere of influence. All Cosimo had to worry about was keeping the peace and breaking down somewhat the wall of ill-will that had been built up by the expansionist policies of almost every Florentine government during the preceding two centuries. The Republic of Siena was the largest of the states, with a *dominio*, or subject territory, that covered most of the southern third of Tuscany. But it was also the least stable, for its four mutually hostile parties, or family-interest groups, called *monti*, always stood ready to throw each other out of office, and the Farnese and the French stood ready to help out whichever of them might extend an invitation to intervene. Cosimo was not yet prepared to pay the price of intervention. He was still unwilling, that is, to get himself tangled up in the inextricable web of Sienese party politics, which was apparently the only alternative to destroying the city altogether. Nor was he willing to let the more aggressive imperialists annex Siena outright to the Empire, which is just what would have happened had he yielded to their pleas for an armed invasion. But when a confession tortured out of a captured Sienese rebel in 1541 made it clear that the next revolution would certainly establish a French regiment in Port'Ercole, Cosimo hastened to assemble the militia along the frontier and to sign a mutual defense pact with the latest coalition government. And he renewed the treaty after another coup d'etat four years later, even though it swept away what Granvelle, in the name of the emperor, had established with so much effort.

The state of Piombino, a historical accident of the early fifteenth century perched on the rocky island of Elba and the adjacent continental promontory, was somewhat closer to Cosimo, personally, geographically, and, because of its ancient iron mines, economically. The fourth wife of the incompetent reigning prince, Jacopo Appiani, the wife who finally managed to bear him a son, was a Florentine, after all, and even a near relative of Cosimo's mother. Piombino was *too* close, as a matter of fact. "Would to God," Cosimo scrawled at the bottom of a dispatch to Giovambattista Ricasoli in 1543, "that [it] were as far off as Mirandola. I'd gladly have washed my hands of it six times. But, damn it, there it is . . . and I'd be very poorly repaid [for all my efforts] if one of my enemies got a chance to sit his ass down there." The worst of his enemies were the Turks, for whom Piombino would have been a convenient stop-off point on their periodic visits to their French allies in Toulon. And a stop-off by Barbarossa, or by his equally bloody successor Dragut, inevitably meant the destruction of everything they could not steal and the slaughter of every inhabitant they could not carry off into slavery. That is what happened twice to Elba in a matter of a few years. Unfortunately neither the emperor, nor Jacopo, nor, after the latter's death in 1545, his widow, was able or willing to construct proper defenses; and Cosimo quickly realized he would have to do it himself. Starting in 1543, with the emperor's permission, he rebuilt the old fort on the mainland and built a huge new one at Portoferraio, both of them so solid and impregnable that they are intact today. And so eager was he to have both forts under his immediate jurisdiction that he twice bought the whole principality from the emperor, though the emperor ended up taking all of it back (without a cent of refund, needless to say) except for a few square miles around Portoferraio.

Of the two tiny states in northwestern Tuscany, the Republic of Lucca gave Cosimo the least trouble—merely a few incidents along the ill-defined borders, a certain amount of indignant protesting when one of Vitelli's protégés robbed a silk train in 1538, and a rather useless campaign to re-route the Rome-Genoa mail line for the benefit of Lucca's merchants. The only real trouble occurred in 1546, when a certain Francesco Burlamachi, a prominent citizen who spent a bit too much time poring over Plutarch, turned up with a plot worthy of Rabelais' Picrochole during the War of the Cake Merchants. He dreamed up a scheme to sneak out of town one night with a band of Lucchese militia (who were not to be told what was up), catch the Medicean guards asleep at Pisa, then, with the help of the Pisans, march to Pistoia, topple the walls of Florence with shouts of *Libertà! Popolo!*, and conquer Siena and Perugia, while Lucca voluntarily acceded to the successful initiative and agreed to head a league of free Tuscan communes.

There was just enough plausibility in the plot to make Cosimo nervous—but not enough to justify the truculent attitude he assumed toward the innocent Lucchesi. The incident finally persuaded the oligarchs at Lucca of the futility of annoying their bigger neighbor. When they then realized that a sort of Florentine protectorate was the best guarantee against a repetition of the silkworkers' uprising of 1531, they relieved Cosimo of any further incentive to intervene. The magnificent reception they gave his son Francesco during the carnival of 1559 was in substance the consecration of the independence they had fought so many centuries to maintain. Lucca relaxed thereafter into a dignified tranquillity that was to last until the advent of Napoleon.

The tiny principality of Massa Carrara, on the other hand, gave Cosimo far more trouble than it was worth. It had involved him in a bitter and bloody feud among the various members of the Cibo and Malespina families—including Cardinal Innocenzo himself, who, even in the evening of his life, could not resist the temptation of pitting one furious cousin against the other. The contestants there were also constantly travelling across his dominions and in and out of his capital because he was constantly besought to act as arbitrator. But as long as the marble quarries beyond Carrara were safe, and as long as the threats to call in the Este, the Spanish, the Genoese, or—worst of all—Piero Strozzi came to naught, Cosimo was content to bide his time. Eventually the principality fell to the last remaining heir, Alberigo Cibo, who turned what was left of it into a miniature Eden, with tree-lined streets, elaborate public works, and a literary academy. And so it remained until it was annexed to Modena in the eighteenth century.

Unlike almost all his republican predecessors, Cosimo was not for the moment interested in pushing the frontiers of the Florentine dominion into the three corners of Tuscany. The only bit of rounding out he proposed before 1555 was in the direction of Pontremoli, where a family of Genoese rebels threatened the security of the several small towns in the Lunigiana that had voluntarily put themselves under Florentine rule. For the rest, he wanted peace, quiet, and no influence greater than his own. He was perfectly willing to turn a border town over to the Sienese and then let it become a small autonomous principality for the family of Pope Pius IV. Not annexation, then, which might well have had unfortunate international complications, but dependent states—and the more of them the better. "It's too bad " as Serristori put it in 1550, "that Siena and Lucca are not split up into many [separate] pieces. For then you could easily be the boss of them all, or at least be sure of having them always on your side."

By the early 1540s, the policy of parsimony, audacity, and a guarded, vigilant fidelity to the emperor had turned Cosimo into a peer among Italian princes and a peacemaker among Tuscan citizens. It had also won him a good bit of *riputazione*, or reputation, which in the sixteenth century was an essential ingredient of power, not just its reflection. As early as 1540, Pedro de Toledo expressed admiration for his son-in-law, who "behaved with such prudence and such dexterity." A few years later the Imperial minister Granvelle declared that Cosimo was one of the few persons he knew who did not have to go to school: "he already knows too much, and, if anything, is too wise and too acute." And by 1547 "the fame of his honored achievements" was recognized even in the Campo dei Fiori of Rome, "the true book of the predestined" as well as the gossip center of all Europe, in spite of the incessant efforts of the Genoese and the Florentine exiles to discredit him there.

Best of all, Cosimo's policy eventually won him his biggest single prize since the Battle of Montemurlo: the Fortress. By May 1543, the emperor had been persuaded of what Cosimo had been telling him ever since the summer of 1538— that his fears about the Florentine government "again falling into the hands of the plebeians" were completely unfounded. Moreover, with the French once again pressing him in Piedmont and Flanders, and with their allies the Turks heading toward the western Mediterranean, the emperor desperately needed all the men and all the money he could scrape together. Just then Cosimo and Eleonora turned up to meet him in Genoa bearing, among other little gifts, a draft for 100,000 *scudi*. That was more than even Charles could resist, in spite of his penchant for holding on as long as possible to whatever he had once got hold of. The Florentines were overjoyed, or at least immensely relieved. Almost overnight they raised the cash to cover the check. And on July 3, 1543, they all, practically to a man, followed the magistrates out to the Fortress in solemn procession. As the Medici banner rose on the flagpole, Juan de Luna, who had been draining them of their earnings ever since he had replaced Vitelli in 1538, marched out of the gate. And with him marched the Spanish soldiers who for six years had insulted them, provoked them, robbed them, and made their streets unsafe at night. Florence was at last independent, or at least as independent as any other state in

Italy after Venice and the Papal State, and more independent than it had been since Giovanni de' Medici had become Pope Leo X in 1513.

Cosimo was elated. He was a completely free prince, he informed the king of France with an understandable splash of exaggeration. He had no obligation to anyone beside God, and his bonds to the emperor were based solely on sentiments of gratitude, not on force. To be sure, there was still much to do. Membership in the Imperial system, he soon found out, meant membership in one of the two major parties at the Imperial court—for him, the one led by his in-laws, Toledo and Alva. It also meant a more or less open conflict with those of his colleagues, headed by the ambitious new governor of Milan, Ferrante Gonzaga, who had come to consider the Empire not as the embodiment of Christendom, but as an appanage of Spain, and who were determined to turn as much of Italy as possible into a Spanish province. Just how determined they were became clear two years later, on September 10, 1547, when Ferrante murdered Pierluigi Farnese and seized the city of Piacenza without even bothering to get the prior consent of the emperor. At the same time, the Venetians were not completely persuaded of Cosimo's independence, and they declined to reciprocate when he appointed a resident ambassador. Nor was the new king of France, Henry II, persuaded, even though his wife, Catherine de' Medici, was impressed enough by the success of the cousin she had snubbed so long to send him four magnificent carpets, "all covered with gold brocade," as well as eight beautiful boar-hunting dogs and four puppies of the same breed for Eleonora.

Cosimo was at least strong enough by then to get rid of a few more past or potential enemies. Fazio da Pisa, who had so often snarled at him from the fortress at Livorno, soon fell under the knife of an assassin. Giovanni Bandini, the ambassador to Spain he had inherited from Alessandro and to whom he had written hundreds of frank, confidential letters, suddenly vanished into the dungeon of Volterra, ostensibly on a charge of homosexuality, but actually because he had received one too many presents from the Strozzi and one too many honors from the emperor. Even Lorenzaccio, after ten years of sneaking around Europe, was finally caught off guard, right on the streets of Venice, and the thug who put a poisoned knife in him lived thereafter on his 7,000-*scudi* prize and his 300-*scudi*-a-year pension while boring the citizens of Volterra with his account of the great deed.

Then came the boldest move of all. On August 31, 1545, Ottaviano de' Medici and Pierfrancesco Ricci walked over to the Dominican monastery of San Marco and posted a notice on the door—a notice which gave the fifty-odd monks inside exactly one month to clear out. That struck a blow simultaneously at the most active religious center in Florence, one of the most influential religious orders in Catholic Europe, the pope, and half the College of Cardinals. The grounds for the expulsion were political, not religious. "The *frati*," Cosimo insisted, "have long made a public profession of being contrary to me," and he now no longer had

4. Bronzino, *Portrait of Cosimo I*
Uffizi

to put up with them. "With their intrigues, their dirty-dealing, their infernal and heretical confabulations, they are a bunch of devils, from which may almighty God liberate me and this city for *infinita saecula saeculorum. Amen.*" To the delegation of monks who rushed in immediately for an explanation, Cosimo was caustically brief:

Cosimo: Tell me, my fathers, who built this monastery? Was it you?
Monks: No.
Cosimo: Who put you in this monastery, then?
Monks: Our ancient Florentines and Cosimo the Elder of good memory.
Cosimo: Right. And it's the modern Florentines and Cosimo the Duke who are throwing you out.

To the powerful of the world, he was shrilly intransigent. "I don't need to justify what I have done to anyone except God," he shouted, "and as an independent prince I may do as I see fit." Luckily Cosimo's opinion of the monks was shared, rightly or wrongly, by all his supporters in the city and by many of his opponents— Donato Giannotti for one. Private donations, which in fact were at the bottom of much of the controversy, dried up immediately; and they resumed as a mere trickle when Cosimo finally agreed to the one tiny face-saving compromise of letting the non-Florentine Dominicans come back.

Cosimo could at last indulge in a bit of self-satisfaction. As soon as he saw Bronzino's finished portrait, he ordered it sent off immediately to the emperor. And when Bronzino offered to paint another, still better, he replied, with complete disregard of the creative process, "I don't want one more beautiful. I want it done exactly the way it is already." And that, by the way, is why only slight variations of the same portrait are now on exhibit in Berlin and New York as well as in the Pitti and the Uffizi.

4

Consolidation

In the sixteenth century the word "state," or *Stato,* was usually used in the passive sense, as something that was possessed, acquired, or dominated, rather than in the modern, or active sense, as something that levies taxes, declares war, rewards, and punishes. That Cosimo "had a state" in the first sense by the mid-1540s, no one could deny. That he would keep it and pass it on to his heirs, almost everyone admitted to be highly probable, if not certain. But having a state still left open the question of just what kind of a state it would be. Florence could not be treated merely as the inert object of whatever action Cosimo, following the precepts of the utopian philosophers, might choose to exert on it. It could not be considered simply a state in the abstract, one which, following the example of the Borgias and the Sforzas, he might exchange for any other. Unlike Alessandro's father, Lorenzo de' Medici, who had settled for Urbino, and unlike Pierluigi Farnese, who would have settled for Piombino or Siena had he not been able to have Parma, Cosimo was not interested simply in being a prince. He was interested only in being prince of the city he was tied to by birth and affection, for its benefit as much as for his own. Florence, in other words, had a particular physiognomy, a distinctive character, and a special historical tradition all of its own. And Cosimo, as a patriotic Florentine, was determined to develop and elaborate what was peculiar to Florence, even at the cost of limiting his own freedom of choice rather than to replace it with something entirely new.

Florence was first of all an economic organization. To trade, indeed, it owed its origins in the eleventh and twelfth centuries. To banking, which grew out of and accompanied trade, it owed its rank, in the thirteenth and early fourteenth centuries, as one of the richest cities in Christendom. And to manufacturing, which developed particularly after the bank crash of the 1340s, it owed its position as the chief furnisher of high-quality finished wool cloth to most of Europe and the Levant. But the succession of political crises, economic failures, plagues, and invasions between 1494 and 1537 had reduced the city to a shadow of its former self. By 1540 it had barely more than 50,000 inhabitants, and many of them indigent at that, as compared with some 90,000 in the 1480s and 120,000 in the 1340s.

Cosimo knew nothing about running a business or about running a state for the benefit of business: unlike most well-born Florentines, he had had no experience in a family firm. But he knew a good bit about spending wisely what he had, not spending what he did not have, and keeping well-balanced credit-and-debit columns constantly before him. He also knew that his own wealth as a prince depended largely on that of his subjects, for, unlike most of his Medici predecessors, he started off with hardly a cent to his name. And he knew also that money was the essential ingredient of a foreign policy deprived of the only alternative to money, military force. While he was unwilling to follow the good Florentine tradition of tying politics to economic interests, he was willing to do all he could for the economic recovery of his dominions—even to the point of reaching into his own slim tax revenues for an occasional subsidy.

Neither Cosimo nor any of his better-informed and more experienced advisors had any new ideas about how to realize their good intentions. None of the businessmen in the city had any new ideas about how to improve the traditional methods of organizing, producing, distributing, or marketing. None of them wrote anything corresponding to the technical manuals of the fourteenth century, and none of them had even heard of the now-famous guide book for the virtuous merchant-citizen, Leon Battista Alberti's *On the Family,* which was not rediscovered until some two hundred years later. Those of them who were quietly investing their liquid capital in land, often to the detriment of the subject cities, seem to have ignored completely the experiments with new crops then being conducted in other parts of Italy—most notably with a "grain called maïz" (corn), which, according to one enterprising farmer from the Veneto, multiplied twice as fast as wheat. True, they were now discovering the delights of digging, planting, and grafting with their own hands. But they all continued, like their forefathers, to regard agriculture as a means of conserving rather than of expanding their wealth. Florentine writers produced several masterpieces in the genre of agrarian literature during the lifetime of Cosimo, masterpieces that rank with that of the ancient Roman agronome, Columella. But even Pier Vettori, who carefully checked in his own garden all the information he culled from ancient writers and frequently came up with innovations of his own, was interested more in praising than in profiting from what he raised. And indeed he said nothing about what to do with the olives once the trees he so admired started to bear fruit. Even Giovan Battista Tealdi, who had gone all over Europe in search of new plants for his villa and who figured out how to raise grapes without seeds and artichokes out of season—even Tealdi was mostly interested in presenting his friends with such curiosities as dwarf apple trees and grapes growing in wine bottles.

For those who vacationed in the country, and almost everyone of means did so, it was a wonderful place for getting back to the good, simple life prescribed by Virgil, Sannazzaro, and all the other ancient and modern Arcadian poets. But for those who worked there (and many did), life went on much as usual. "Do you think I have much joy and amusement," wrote the wise rustic moralist Isabella Guicciardini to her husband Luigi, then governor of the Florentine Romagna, "living here in the sole company of two servant girls, spending most of my time ordering and paying for repairs, buying [and selling], and keeping accounts?... In this world, whoever wants to be happy had better learn to take pleasure in those things which displease him, for otherwise he'll always be in torment." And she went on producing everything from wine to wheat, eggs to kindling wood, in the same way they had been produced for centuries, without ever looking for happiness, or at least for greater results from the same hard labor through new methods, new crops, or new markets.

The best the new regime could think of doing was simply to do more efficiently and thoroughly what had been done by its predecessors. It reissued the regulations of 1476 and 1487 aimed at maintaining the "ancient reputation" of manufactured goods. It still further isolated supply from demand by rigidly fixing prices. It enforced the jurisdiction of the ancient guilds and left them, as integral parts of the bureaucracy, with much of the political and economic authority they had always enjoyed. It increased restrictions on the movement of foodstuffs, even within the *Dominio,* and then put the blame, as usual, on supposed hoarders and speculators when the prices jumped wildly back and forth from *lire* 1.14 to 3.15, from 1.10 to 7.10. It guaranteed the metallic content of Florentine coins and forbade the circulation of foreign ones on the vain assumption that money could have a fixed value. And it did all this with the full support and advice "of the wisest and most experienced [tradesmen] of the city," in whose name, indeed, many of the edicts were issued.

All these measures were probably no more harmful than similar measures had been in the past, though in the long run they discouraged innovation, blocked individual initiative, and prevented adaptation to changing conditions. But what business lost by economic legislation, it largely made up through the beneficial by-products of policies adopted for other than economic reasons. The establishment of internal peace withdrew one of the greatest deterrents to economic activity and let the businessmen at last get back to work. The Imperial alliance opened up the Spanish dominions to Florentine bankers and manufacturers, particularly after Cosimo pointed out to the emperor that clothing his troops in Florentine wool was a very good way of consolidating a friendly regime in Florence. The gradual reconciliation of the exile communities abroad eventually revived the "white imports," or profits from foreign investments, that had always represented a considerable portion of Florentine revenue. And the reform of the direct tax rolls removed much of the uncertainty that previously had discouraged investment and risk. By plugging up the remaining loopholes and eliminating all but a few special privileges, Cosimo made the tax rate as nearly proportional to ability to pay as was then possible. Except for extraordinary indirect taxes, and except for the *accatti,* or forced loans, to which Cosimo, like all his predecessors, had recourse in emergencies, businessmen could calculate in advance just how much they would be held to.

Still, it was probably more to the lasting vitality of its traditional business enterprise than to innovation or legislation that the Florentine economy owed its rapid recovery between 1540 and the last decades of the century. Just how extensive the recovery actually was cannot yet be determined, since no one has yet had the time, patience, and technical training to go through the immense quantity of surviving financial records. But enough is known to wipe out the nineteenth-century myth about the economic collapse of the sixteenth. Florence was still, in 1551, an industrial and commercial city, one in which 34 percent of the heads of households were employed in the cloth industry alone, in which wool production had apparently returned almost to the levels of the mid-fifteenth century, in which a prominent patrician like Luca degli Albizi still spent most of his time manufacturing silk, and in which a busy bureaucrat like Averardo Serristori still took time off to help run a family banking firm—a firm big enough to furnish the government with a sudden short-term loan of no less than 120,000 *scudi* in 1558. Florence was still the center of many international commercial companies, like that of Piero di Niccolò Cambi, who specifically forbade his heirs to transfer the money he had invested all over southern France and northern Italy from business to real estate; like that of Lorenzo Guicciardini in Bologna, and Giovanni Boti in Seville, Fabio Baldi in "Sarmartia" (Poland); and like scores of others spread all the way from Lisbon and Bruges to Transylvania.

There were still signs of weakness, to be sure. Several of the best families (that of Chiarissimo de' Medici, for instance) happened to have some of their money invested in the business of prostitution, which few modern economists would qualify as generative of further wealth. Almost a quarter of the adult population was tied up in what modern demographers would call an inactive status—as monks, nuns, and domestic servants. And the increasing number of abandoned children and unemployed adults in charitable institutions suggest that the new wealth was being anything but widely distributed. Still, Florence was soon rich enough again to leave Cosimo, even after the disastrously expensive war of the 1550s, completely free of debts outside his own dominions, and able "to pay back the money" he owed to banks in Florence "with perfume on it."

Florence was an economic organization, then. It was also, or at least it had been, a political community, one whose experiments with different kinds of government had given rise, in the hundred-odd years between Coluccio Salutati and Niccolò Machiavelli, to the most original school of political thought since the times of Thucydides, Aristotle, and Cicero. But Florence as a political community had failed spectacularly in 1530. When even the most nostalgic republicans admitted the inefficiency of government by semiautonomous committees, and when even the Senate had to complain, in 1534, that elected officials were shirking their responsibilities, the political community was in grave danger of disappearing altogether.

Cosimo himself had very little idea of how to reanimate the body politic in the first years of his reign. Neither, for that matter, did even a thoughtful anti-republican like Luigi Guicciardini, who could suggest nothing better than having an absolute prince do everything all by himself. Political philosophy in the tradition of Leonardo Bruni went almost entirely into exile after 1530 and 1537— all of it, that is, except the tiny remnant that ended up in the ridiculous pretend-republic of a private club called the "Academy of the Plain," in which a popularly elected "dictator" read magniloquent decrees to the "citizens" after the in-dispensable "solemn repast with excellent food and choice wines." "Seeing that these Florentine brains cannot stand idle," commented Cosimo, who detested constitution-making as a serious occupation, "it's just as well that they busy themselves with such pastimes."

But even the best of the Florentine political philosophers abroad were as vague about how to put their ideas into practice as they were often perspicacious in analyzing the defects of former regimes. Bartolomeo Cavalcanti, for instance, became so fascinated with what Plato, Aristotle, and Polybius had said about politics that all he could think of doing, when he was at last called upon to advise the Republic of Siena, was to juggle around the same old communal offices in still another manner. Donato Giannotti, similarly, became so absorbed in the virtues of Venice that he was surprised to find, in 1540, that they had become irrelevant to conditions in Florence. And his second major work, the *Florentine Republic,* accurate though it was in its diagnosis of past constitutional ills, bogged down in a purely imaginary sociology ("Florence is a community of inhabitants divided into poor and rich, noble and ignoble . . .") as soon as it came to remedies. Hence his ingenious proposal for a regime that would satisfy the ambitions of all classes turned out to be pure theory, for its application depended wholly on the assumption that the "tyranny" in Florence would soon collapse by itself.

Because the old school of political philosophy was getting more and more involved with the planning of utopias, Cosimo and his collaborators were forced to work out a new philosophy of their own, or at least to devise something that might serve as working principles for the new regime. They were not altogether successful, to be sure—partially because they disdained their opponents, and partially because they expressed themselves not in comprehensive treatises, but in a number of scattered reflections, recommendations, dedications, and panegyrics. They thus ignored the basic problem of political vitality that had been raised by the writers of the republican era. They brushed aside the whole burning question of the relation between religious and political morality. And they forgot completely the question of institutional, rather than merely moral limitations, on the power they accorded to the prince. But often, under the disguise of statements about what Cyrus, Alexander the Great, or even Cosimo had already done, they put forth some rather precise suggestions as to what ought to be done in the future, along with reasons for doing it. And at least one of them, the experienced state official Gianfranco Lottini, ended up with what amounted to the first step towards a theory of an administrative, or bureaucratic, state.

One of the first principles that the apologists for the new regime attributed to it was efficiency. After all, inefficiency, overlapping jurisdictions, and lack of coordination had been among the most noticeable defects of the Republic. And they were also among the qualities that the fastidious, orderly young prince could least abide. Efficiency, for Cosimo, meant first of all the absence of jurisdictional squabbles. Therefore, he scrupulously eliminated, consolidated, or divided administrative offices the minute he found that they were getting in each other's way. Efficiency also meant keeping records in such a way that they could be easily looked up. He deposited all administrative papers in a single state archive (rather than let his administrators keep them in their private family archives, as was the rule in most states of Europe until well into the following century), and he had them provided with a rather rudimentary, but at least workable index. Efficiency meant "having the resources of the empire constantly before him," like Lottini's idealized Emperor Augustus. He tabulated in his own hand the results of the two censuses he ordered in 1551 and 1561—censuses as accurate and comprehensive as any done before the time of Carlo Borromeo in Counter-Reformation Milan, or, for that matter, before the eighteenth century. Efficiency meant coordinating administrative procedures in such a way that an incumbent could easily be understood by a successor from another office. Cosimo prescribed every detail of the work-sheet for each office; in at least one case, he determined even the exact number of pages and the quality of binding to be used for the receipt books.

Finally, efficiency meant changing the requirements for office-holding from wealth and influence to technical competence. Cosimo did not much care where his qualified assistants came from. In some cases, particularly when he needed someone absolutely dependent on himself, a provincial or even a foreigner was preferable to a citizen. That, after all, he knew from the example of the Republic, which had always brought in certain judges and secretaries from the outside as a guarantee of impartiality. In some cases, though, particularly in diplomatic missions in which rank was of considerable importance, citizens, the more prominent the better, were preferable to those of lesser status. But in all cases, competence was essential. If Cosimo tended to hire noncitizens, especially in the early years of his reign, it was not so much because he wanted to crush the remnants of the republican governing class as because few citizens yet had the requisite training. But the distinction between citizen and noncitizen broke down in theory as well as in practice, for those of humble origins were usually rewarded with wealth, Florentine citizenship, and at times even a seat in the Senate, the ultimate goal of all social climbers. To be sure, some old-time anti-Mediceans grumbled quietly about the haughty "new Solons" like Jacopo Polverini of Prato, the man chiefly responsible for the reform of the court system. But the patrician administrators, who needed neither money nor honors but were well rewarded with both anyway, had no trouble getting along with the newcomers. The sincere affection that passed between the provincial Bartolomeo Concini and the distinguished aristocrat Agnolo Niccolini is ample evidence of the cohesion of the new bureaucracy. "I salute, embrace, and kiss you," wrote Niccolini, then archbishop of Pisa and governor of Siena, early in 1564; "since I have no lady to pass the carnival with, you'll have to do instead."

The same principle of efficiency was also applied in what Cosimo regarded as two other branches of the administration: the army and the church. The army, it is true, was not completely his to direct. The foreign soldiers brought in for special services usually had to be left with the kind of organization they were used to. The professional generals hired to lead them usually had to be left with the tactics and rules established by the international market of military talent they were drawn from. And the military or knightly Order of Santo Stefano, which Cosimo founded largely for the purpose of enhancing his prestige abroad, had to follow the pattern of the old crusading orders, particularly since its principal occupation consisted in little more than outright piracy. But the militia was dependent upon Cosimo alone. And after ten years of perfecting the project he had inherited from Machiavelli and Alessandro, he ended up with an efficient and effective corps of volunteers. The captains were drawn from the ranks. The soldiers had a stake in preserving the regime. And the supreme commissioner, Antonio degli Albizi, although a patrician by birth and a civilian by profession, had made himself a specialist in the science of military organization.

The church was not completely Cosimo's to direct either. After all, its basic structure and its various geographical subdivisions, inconvenient though they were at times, had been determined long before and by an authority external to Florence. Some current practices that he might have changed, moreover, were far too convenient for political reasons to be given up, even though they did not correspond to what some reformers, and eventually the Council of Trent, held to be proper and salutary for religious reasons. For instance, plural benefices could provide deserving civil servants with handsome incomes at no cost to the state. And "reversions," or the yielding of a benefice to a cousin or nephew before resignation, could assure a well-disposed patrician family, most notoriously the Tornabuoni, of a steady source of revenue. As a consequence, what Cosimo did in ecclesiastical affairs did not always correspond to what he did in civil affairs. Because appointments to the hierarchy, which he had almost complete control of after the death of Paul III, were usually made for political rather than religious reasons, promotions from the lower to the higher ranks of the clergy remained as rare as they had been since the high Middle Ages, when such promotions had become a monopoly of the patriciate. Hence the church did not regain its ancient function as a means of social mobility; and the zeal and talent from below that might have reanimated it were directed instead toward the regular orders and the civil bureaucracy.

Nevertheless, Cosimo was no more capable than anyone else at the time of considering religion and politics as separate spheres; and he accepted full responsibility for all those ecclesiastical affairs which fell, or which he thought ought to fall, within his jurisdiction. He was well aware, even before the episcopal visitations of the late 1560s, of a number of grave defects in the Florentine church. He knew that many convents were not observing their rules, that many pious institutions were being despoiled by their lay administrators, that parishes were being neglected by their pastors, and that most of the dioceses were being run by incompetent vicars in the name of irresponsible, nonresident ordinaries. He was persuaded, moreover, that no one else would lift a finger to correct these defects— not the pope, not the superiors of the regular orders, and certainly not the "small-minded, despicable" archbishop of Florence, Andrea Buondelmonti, who had bought his mitre from Cardinal Ridolfi right after the siege of 1530, who had reimbursed himself by selling absolutions for breaches of the Lenten fast, and who had made himself the laughingstock of the city by fulminating from the pulpit about a pair of stockings he thought had been stolen from him.

Cosimo had no interest in theology. His own religious experience was limited to fearing a distant Power that punished careless princes in this world and wicked ones in the next. He seems never to have heard of any of the great religious reformers of his time, with the possible exception of Girolamo Seripando. And he regarded with suspicion the one indigenous religious force dedicated to reform, Savonarolism. It is not surprising, then, that he fell back, in his conscientious effort to make the church run smoothly, on the same principle of efficiency that guided him in civil matters. The bishops or their vicars had to be men of administrative ability, whatever their other qualifications. All of them were expected to send in regular reports of "all [their] ideas and actions," as his bishop of Fiesole and sometime representative at Trent put it, "so that Your Excellency can correct whatever is not in conformity with Your will." "Lutheran" books were confiscated and suspect preachers were suspended; while the right of determining who might be prosecuted for heresy was reserved for the duke. Ecclesiastical tribunals were prohibited from interfering in what Cosimo decided were civil cases, although their jurisdiction over what he deemed to be purely spiritual ones was respected. Anyone who stepped over jurisdictional boundaries was mercilessly pursued, as one of Paul III's collectors found out the moment his master died. An ad hoc citizens committee threw the collector into jail, invited claims of extortion from all those he had supposedly "taxed," and then turned him over to the hangman. Finally Cosimo ordered a general housecleaning. The decree of April 17, 1545, empowered a four-man commission to eradicate abuses in institutions under lay or episcopal control, and it charged a three-man commission with reporting to the proper religious superiors the abuses found in exempt institutions.

In all these measures, Cosimo could count on the enthusiastic support of almost all his subjects, whose anticlericalism was matched only by their religiosity, and who were by then thoroughly disgusted with what Boccaccio had once been willing to pass off as funny. The typical monk had become for them something like Anton Francesco Doni's Fra Bonaventura, who lived "in an apartment . . . with more rooms, desks, loggias, halls, and more little bays than the cupola of Santa Maria dei Fiori," and who earned his "sausages, cakes, and those nice little wines that sparkle in the glass" by rolling his hypocritical eyes, uttering unfelt sighs, and rattling off meaningless Masses for gullible bigots. The typical priest had become one of the dirty canons of San Lorenzo, whom the art connoisseur Vincenzo Borghini accused of letting Michelangelo's statues be stained with smoke from the church's charcoal burners. The chief cause of this deplorable situation, they all agreed, lay in the Court of Rome, whose ministers, as Cosimo put it, "want to set up shop with the things of Christ . . . and bind the hands of the bishops so they can't take care of disorders in their own dioceses." And the usual remedies, they added, were worthless—most particularly the one that had been used in the days of St. Francis, St. Bernardino, and even Savonarola: inviting in outside preachers. They thus made one eminent Franciscan furious by yawning through what was probably an admirable apotheosis of the Franciscan theologian Duns Scotus. And they simply ignored a curious, rag-clad Spaniard named Jacopo Lainez, soon to become the second general of the Society of Jesus, whom Eleonora brought to court in 1545. Cosimo's own unenthusiastic response to the first Jesuit missionaries earned him the wrath of almost all the historians of the Society thereafter; but it faithfully reflected the attitude of Florentines, who were not disposed to have mere Spaniards tell them, the heirs to Savonarola's New Jerusalem, anything new about piety.

Popular support, however, was not enough. Some of Cosimo's measures succeeded because they fell within the realm of jurisdictional disputes, which he was an expert at resolving. Others succeeded only later—and Cosimo's own analysis showed that there was still much to do even in the 1560's—because they

ran into the same red tape that had strangled most other attempts at reform from
below before the Council of Trent. And some of them failed completely because
the church was something more than just the well-run, efficient administrative
organization Cosimo thought it to be.

The first principle of Cosimo's government, then, was efficiency. The
second was continuity.

Much as it satisfied his ego, Cosimo dared not emphasize his role as a "new
prince" in the delicate area of foreign policy; for the Este and the Savoia were
trying to prove he was just that in their efforts to get their ambassadors admitted
before his in foreign courts. But even in domestic policy he found it convenient
to qualify his regime as the fulfillment rather than the negation of the Republic,
and to picture himself as the heir to a family of first citizens rather than as the
founder of a dynasty of monarchs. Keeping on the citizen magistrates cost far less
than hiring new ones, after all, for they expected no more recompense than honor
and an occasional gratuity or, at the most, a token salary. Moreover, this lent a
certain sense of dignity and legitimacy to those decrees and appointments "that
seem to be of greater importance and universality," and that Cosimo was always
careful to submit to the formalities of Senate approval. Above all, it preserved for
the Principate what almost everyone, particularly Lottini, considered the most
valuable practice of the Republic: deliberation. While execution was left completely
in the hands of the prince, policy was often determined only after a full discussion
among the "magnificent counsellors" or, from the late 1540s on, among the
members of a sort of informal cabinet called the *Pratica Segreta*.

Thus Vasari correctly represented in the mural sequences of the Palazzo
Vecchio "the just undertakings . . . of the Florentine people of old and . . . of our
most illustrious princes," as if one were merely the continuation of the other. Thus
Saints Cosmus and Damianus, the patrons of the Medici family, were portrayed as
Cosimo the Elder and Cosimo the Duke. And thus Pier Vettori pointed out that
"you acceded to the government of the city not by evil artifices or by force, but
by the will of the citizens." For Cosimo left intact the constitution of the Republic,
just as formerly the Republic had left intact the constitutions of the Tuscan
communes over which it extended its *dominio*. The Eight of Pratica still went on
being elected for the usual six-month terms, though Cosimo often "suggested"
whom to elect. The Six of Mercanzia and the Eight of Balìa still sat for the usual
four-month terms. And the Council of the Two Hundred still met to formalize
decisions regarding elections, citizenship, and dowries. Indeed, Cosimo even
insisted that the magistrates take seriously the administrative responsibilities he
left to them. When he found that some of them were "getting lazy . . . in the
discharge of affairs," he had a bell rung every morning and a fine of seven *lire*
put on anyone not at his desk a half-hour later. He adopted another well-tried

republican institution: permanent secretaries, or "auditors," the heirs of the great chancellors of the Quattrocento, who maintained continuity between one set of elected officials and the next, furnished the officials with professional advice, and made sure they acted in harmony with the other parts of the administration. And when, on one occasion, he found the magistrates still unworthy of their position, he told the Senate to replace them at once, even before the end of their terms. It looked, then, as if government by deliberation might at last be made to work, although, as Cosimo put it, "no two Florentines ever manage to agree on anything." For the government now was coordinated by a single, stable, unifying force, which none of the long- or short-term gonfalonieri had ever been able to provide for the Republic.

After efficiency and continuity, the next principle of Cosimo's government was justice. Justice, to be sure, had long been a commonplace of Florentine political thought. But in the 1540s it received additional force from a new school of jurisprudence: that of the humanist jurists, or *Culti*, as they were called. The school was actually Italian in origin, though it had developed largely in France and Germany during the first decades of the century. It was then brought back to Italy by the famous Milanese jurist Andrea Alciati, and it was brought to Florence by Alciati's close friend, and Cosimo's chief legal advisor, Lelio Torelli of Fano. The new school differed from the old largely in its insistence on a historical or philological rather than a logical interpretation of Roman law. It started by scrapping the voluminous commentaries that had accumulated since the eleventh century and went to the texts themselves, particularly to the text of Justinian's *Pandects*, which had been kept under lock and key in Florence since 1405 and which Torelli published, for the benefit of law students, in 1553. It then sought to explain the various parts of the text by reference not to the present, but to the specific historical moments in which they had been written. As a result, Roman law, and hence the common law of Florence as well as of most other states of Italy, became much less amenable to twisting and turning in the hands of a clever lawyer—which is probably one of the reasons why the new school flourished more among professors of literature than among professors of law. But at the same time it became a much more rigid standard by which particular political acts could be judged. And in the face of the careful definitions inscribed in the *Pandects*, the concept of justice, or *giustizia*, could no longer be so easily used as a cover-up for purely personal interests.

Hence the term "absolutism," often applied to the new regime, must be used with caution. Neither Cosimo nor any of his apologists ever suggested that his will, like the will of Francesco Sforza, Cesare Borgia, or the other traditional lords of Italy, was superior even to statutory law. The law might emanate from him, or through him from a body politic—these were philosophical subtleties that no one bothered to argue about. But he was as subject as any other man to the moral principle from which all law derived. The task of a prince, then, was to see that individual acts of the government did not conflict with the principle, as they usually had done in the past. What gave Cosimo the special right to be prince was that he, the impeccable, uncorruptible son of Giovanni delle Bande Nere, happened to know the principle better than any of the Florentine citizens, individually or collectively.

Hence Cosimo took care, or at least so he said, not "to contradict ourselves [even] on those occasions in which we would very much like to." He held himself bound by "the laws, the order, and the magistrates of this our city," and he held everyone else to be so too, regardless of birth, wealth, or political influence. What seemed like occasional infractions of the principle were merely, as Serristori explained, the means prescribed by the times—by times, that is, in which "seditious, evil citizens" were doing all they could to prevent the principle's realization. What seemed to later generations like undue harshness was really the only way anyone then thought that crime could be eradicated; and the English traveller William Thomas, as well as all of Cosimo's subjects, found the extraordinary punishments prescribed by the criminal laws not only irreproachable, but positively commendable. What seemed to many of his contemporaries like a lack of liberality was simply a refusal to yield before the increasing tendency in other parts of Italy and Europe to seek exceptions from the law (*grazie*) instead of applications of the law (*giustizia*). And to the numerous petitions that poured in for special favors—from Benvenuto Cellini, from Pietro Aretino, and from any number of still more authoritative personages accustomed to the different mores of France, Ferrara, and Rome—Cosimo was proudly crisp. "In answer to your letter," he replied,

> it behooves us to inform you that under no circumstantes will we grant an exemption [*grazia*] ... for we have no intention of mixing private with public affairs.

With his own conscience at rest, and with Torelli's Ulpian and Tribonianus to back him up, Cosimo saw no reason to sacrifice his principle, even in the name of practices condoned elsewhere. Just to make sure that *grazia* made no headway in his dominions, he energetically completed the reform of the tribunals begun in 1532. He separated criminal from civil jurisdictions and courts of first instance from courts of appeal, and he intervened personally whenever he thought anything had gone wrong. He then beheld his work and found it far superior to any other court system of the age, most particularly to that of the Roman Inquisition, which he always suspected of letting justice succumb to "individual passions and ambitions."

From the third principle of Cosimo's government, followed the fourth—equality. If everyone was made to obey the law, then everyone was entitled to its protection. The concept *equality* thus came to comprehend the new version of the old concept of *liberty*, which now meant the right to be left in peace for the pursuit of private affairs rather than the right to participate in the management of public affairs. Cosimo accordingly did all he could to mitigate the distinctions between citizens and noncitizens and between the rich and well-off and the poor, even though he left the former with their constitutional monopoly of elective offices and their control of the production and distribution of wealth. For the first time in Florentine history, a government became particularly solicitous for the lowest classes of the population, whom the Republicans had always disdained, but whom Cosimo would no longer allow to be mistreated.

Still more important, he did much to break down the legal distinctions, common to all medieval communes, between the dominant and the subject cities and between city and country dwellers. He did not abolish the distinction. But he soon became aware of some of its more unfortunate consequences. Subjection to Florence had drained the several parts of the *Dominio* of their energy and talent, without, at the same time, giving them any sense of unity among themselves or of identification with the city that ruled them. Going from Florence to Pisa, Empoli, or Cortona, was like moving back two centuries—or rather like moving into the petrified, dilapidated, deserted remnants of what had existed two centuries earlier. Arezzo was no longer capable of anything but Romeo-and-Juliet family fights. Pistoia still had, even after the substantial recovery of the 1560s, only two-thirds of the inhabitants and two-thirds of the houses it had had in 1310. And at least one formerly flourishing suburb of Prato had become, according to one observer, nothing but "a cluster of trees and vines, a nest of foxes, a den of wolves."

Cosimo started with the same remedy he had used in other administrative questions: applying more thoroughly the methods he had inherited from the Republic. He left all the local ordinances, privileges, and offices standing as he had found them. He increased still further the authority of the governors appointed from Florence. And he tightened the chain of command between local and central authorities. But he also made some innovations. He eased the economic restrictions once imposed for the benefit of Florentine industry, and in Pisa he sponsored a revival of silk manufacturing. He founded two new settlements: "Cosmopoli" (from "Cosimo"), or Portoferraio, on Elba; and "The Place of the Sun," in the Florentine Romagna—though he did this for military purposes rather than for the utopian ideals that have sometimes been attributed to him. He began the construction of a port at Livorno and the drainage of the swamplands in the Maremma, projects that were to be among the most important concerns of his successors. Most important of all, he did what no Republican but Machiavelli had ever thought even to advocate. He went to live among his subjects, spending at least three months of every year in Pisa and another three months tramping about the rest of the *Dominio*. And he had Florentine citizenship conferred upon the leading residents of the subject cities without obliging them to live in the capital.

The unity of Cosimo's dominions was still far from complete, to be sure, even by the end of his reign. Economic recovery—of which the production figures for Pistoia in 1569 were at least a hopeful sign—was still thwarted by internal trade barriers. Political recovery was stifled even more by the elimination of almost all remnants of local autonomy, even in financial matters. Thus when Empoli was forced to surrender its last remaining source of revenue, a market tax, it had also to give up any hope of liquidating the tiny debt of 400 *scudi* it had contracted more than thirty years before. For that matter, the administrative structure as a whole was still far from perfect, even according to Cosimo's own standards. As long as the ever-present, never-resting Cosimo kept poking his nose into every obscure corner, the bureaucracy could not acquire the consistency and the esprit de corps that it soon had in the larger, less personal states of Europe. Moreover, attention to too many details could eventually rob officials of their ability to think for themselves—as it did, apparently, in the case of the architect Bartolomeo Ammannati, who felt obliged, in spite of specific instructions to the contrary, to refer to Cosimo even the request of a young art student to copy a picture in the gallery. Similarly, too-frequent interventions in the courts could lead judges to confuse justice with the will of the one who all too often reversed their decisions. "Should Your Excellency," wrote one of them, "for whom every penalty is arbitrary, wish us to alter the provisions of the statute and fix the penalty in this case in a different manner . . . we will not fail to execute what You see fit to communicate to us." And the judge wrote this in spite of the oft-repeated admonition, inscribed once again at the bottom of this particular note, "Let the sentence stand as it is, for otherwise justice will be defrauded."

But for a man who hated nothing more than sitting at a desk, for one who complained "I am standing here like a falcon on his perch" when a rainstorm kept him inside for a day, for one who usually gave orders while rushing around the palace or climbing onto a horse, the accomplishment was considerable. The political community had been reconstituted, if in a very different form. The first major step had been taken in transforming Florence from a medieval commune dominating other medieval communes into the capital of a modern, bureaucratic territorial state.

5

Elaboration

Still more than an economic organization and a political community, Florence was a city of creative minds—of "wise and valorous men," as one observer noted, "from whom it derives all its splendor." But of valorous men, it now had very few. They had started leaving as early as 1513, when the wealthiest of their patrons moved to Rome as Pope Leo X. And they had continued to leave in the wake of the crises of 1527, 1529, 1530, and 1537, until finally "the poor, afflicted city [was] completely abandoned . . . by those men of quality in which it once abounded." All that were left, indeed, were the occasional lecturers at the Badìa Fiorentina, the small circle of artists that Ottaviano de' Medici had inherited from Duke Alessandro, and the informal group that gathered in the store of the witty paper merchant Antonio "Il Marzano" in Via del Proconsolo. The disciples of Marsilio Ficino's successor, Francesco Cattani, were almost all in exile. The school of the philosopher Francesco Verino, the most recent incarnation of the Platonic Academy, had broken up. The bookstores were empty. The libraries were in disorder. And the attractions of Padua and Bologna, Venice and Rome, were on the verge of turning Florence into a provincial outpost of what was rapidly becoming a national culture, one freed of its former local and municipal roots and rapidly gravitating toward the capitals of the two major independent states of the peninsula.

In the beginning, at least, Cosimo knew next to nothing about arts and letters. In fact, he thought he could deal with them just as he dealt with questions of civil administration; this was to the amazement of Cellini, for one, who had never heard of submitting written reports, setting prices, and going through channels. But Cosimo knew, nonetheless, that he could not do without the arts. After all, his carefully publicized image as the successor to the family of Cosimo the Elder and Lorenzo the Magnificent required that he too help "bring to light every lost work of genius." The high social status of writers and artists all over

Italy at the time made it essential that he have the good will of at least some of them, even if he could not, like the emperor, the king of France, and the duke of Ferrara, try to pay off all of them with expensive gifts. The number and complexity of the problems he was faced with made it advisable to keep a sort of reserve of talent handy for eventual emergencies, particularly given the general belief of the age that talent, whatever its specific field of competence, could be put to work effectively on just about anything.

The task was not easy. Culture did not cost too much in the mid-sixteenth century, it is true; or, at least, 20 *scudi,* plus materials, for Bronzino's portrait and 300 for Vettori's salary as a lecturer was not much in comparison to the 1,200 a year paid to the captain of the fortress at Pisa. But for the moment, Cosimo had not a cent to spare. Getting rid of the conditions that had brought about the emigration, of course, could be of some help; and already by 1542 internal peace and stability were such that

> the Tuscan nymphs,
> fearless of the wolves,
> guarded by their shepherds,
> go happily through the woods,
> singing of their loves.
>   (Varchi, *Sonetti,* p. 174)

Encouraging the efforts of others to create conditions that might stop the emigration altogether turned out to be even more beneficial. As soon as Cosimo heard, early in 1541, that a group of young patricians had been meeting regularly since November "to learn about . . . and enrich the Florentine language," he was quick to act. "Remembering that Cosimo the Elder . . . had organized such an academy," he raised them to the status of a public institution, with the title of *Accademia Fiorentina,* the Florentine Academy. He then provided them with permanent headquarters, first in the Palazzo Medici and then at Santa Maria Novella. And soon after, he made their *consul*—as the president they elected every six months was called—a salaried magistrate, with the job of supervising public instruction and the book trade and with the right to sit in the Council of the Two Hundred. Cosimo's encouragement added just what was needed to make the venture an immediate success. The old philosopher Verino "went wild with joy," especially when some two thousand people turned up to hear him speak before the academy. By the following year "the fame of this academy of yours" had reached Rome, according to Giannotti, "because of the many great men that are working in it." And instead of dying out after an initial spurt of enthusiasm, as did most of the other such institutions that mushroomed all over Italy at the time, the Accademia Fiorentina was to last, with its ups and downs, until 1783.

Yet the academy took care only of the current generation, not of the next one. Accordingly, in 1542 Cosimo sent his secretary Campana down to Pisa in order to see about reviving the ancient but moribund university and rescuing whatever of the former endowments could still be located. Universities had played only a minor role in the elaboration of earlier Renaissance culture; but now they were regaining their position of influence and prestige, and Florence could not afford to remain behind. When Cosimo himself went down with Eleonora for the formal inauguration the following November, he was pleased to find that 250 students had already enrolled and that Campana was expecting still more before Christmas.

After the university came the press. Four years later Cosimo sent 200 *scudi* to Venice in order to encourage the volunteer exile Anton Francesco Doni to move the printing press he had just established to Florence. That, he hoped, would enable the academy to publish its proceedings and at the same time free him from the only printers then operating in the city, the Giunti, whose political opinions he was unsure of. When Doni's mismanagement and the intrigues of the Giunti then put the enterprise into bankruptcy, Cosimo negotiated another contract—not with Doni, whom he had no intention of bailing out of debt, but with a Brabanter named Laurens Lenaerts, soon to be famous by the name of Torrentino, one of the great printers of that great age of printing. This time Cosimo was successful—at no greater cost than a 500-*scudi* down payment, a 100-*scudi* annual subsidy, and a monopoly to Torrentino on the trade in foreign books. Within eight months of April 1547, the "two presses fully supplied with nine sets of letters, six Latin and three Greek," were ready to start on their assigned task of "keeping the cities of Florence and Pisa . . . abundantly supplied with every and whatever sort of book regarding every discipline." And there, in the house next to Sant'Apollinare, they were to remain, under the care of the successive "printers to the grand duke," until the end of the eighteenth century.

Florence was thus provided, by the end of the decade, with a self-supporting and easily controllable center of learning, with a rapidly growing university nearby, and with a high-quality and trustworthy press. The first, it was hoped, might soon recapture the glory of the old Platonic Academy, while avoiding, as long as the members stuck to the literary and linguistic questions in their program, the political complications that had arisen from the Rucellai Garden, where Machiavelli had read his *Discourses*. The second might, with enough attention, come to rival the two great universities of the north and keep ahead of the one that the governor of Milan was soon to revive at Pavia. At least it was assured of attendance by Cosimo's own subjects, who, like their contemporaries in Venice and Milan, were forthwith forbidden to take degrees abroad. The third would probably keep Florentine writers from being lured abroad by the great foreign printing houses—by the Gioliti of Venice, Cardinal Marcello Cervino and Francesco Priscianesi of Rome, and the Grypho of Lyon. Thanks to all three of these institutions, Florence soon became a much more attractive residence for men of talent.

The next step was to get them to come live there. Cosimo scored his first success as early as 1538, largely because Pier Vettori was too much of a Florentine, and too independent financially, to prefer the attractive position offered him in Rome to the modest lectureship he was given at home. The second success came in 1540, when Cosimo's counsellor Giovambattista Ricasoli persuaded him to accept a promise of good behaviour from Baccio Bandinelli, the ill-tempered, money-mad sculptor Clement VII had imposed on Alessandro: Cosimo kept Baccio in Florence by putting him in charge of art work in the cathedral. The third, and somewhat bigger, success came in 1542, when Cosimo's unofficial cultural advisor, Luca Martini, handed him some sonnets by a young poet named Benedetto Varchi—the same poet who had publicized Lorenzaccio as a new Brutus, who had followed Piero Strozzi on the ill-fated expedition to Borgo San Sepolcro, and who had since been serving as tutor to several prominent exile families. Cosimo "carried [the sonnets] around for several days, and read and showed them to many persons." He then sent a rather peremptory invitation to Varchi through one of the academicians. In the meantime, Varchi had been beaten up by Strozzi toughs on the streets of Padua. He had quarreled with his most recent patron. He had been bypassed as a candidate for a rich benefice near Naples. And he had lost his favorite nephew when an ill-constructed balcony collapsed underneath the nephew in Bologna. He accepted, therefore, without a moment's hesitation. By summer he was back in Florence, with the decrees of banishment and confiscation against him abrogated and with a small fee for a series of lectures he had promised to give in the academy.

With the return of Varchi, Cosimo suddenly acquired, at very little cost, the reputation he had been seeking as a "liberal prince"; and Florence became, once again, a distinct possibility for men of letters looking for a place to settle down. "The villa in Fiesole [you mentioned] has given me pleasure and sorrow at the same time," wrote no less distinguished a writer than Annibal Caro, "for I don't see how I can get up there to enjoy it with you." As news of what was going on in Florence gradually spread abroad, the Florentines at home started putting pressure on their friends. "If you had the least bit of sense in your head," wrote one of them, "you'd leave Rome and the pope and everything else and come back immediately." Their appeals were so effective that the offers soon were coming in faster than Cosimo could handle them. "I am a musician, a writer, an expert in the vernacular, and decently proficient in Greek," wrote one, "and I devotedly offer you part of my virtue to perpetuate [your name] in future centuries." "It is my desire," wrote another, "to serve you not only for one or two statues, but for all my life, as a most faithful servant."

Meanwhile Cosimo had begun a systematic search for talent on his own. As early as 1542 he sent the future president of the university, Filippo Del Migliore, off to Bologna, Ferrara, and Padua, with full powers to bid as he saw fit against all the other high-bidding governments in Italy in the highly competitive market of university professors. In 1544 he sent Bartolomeo Panciatichi off with a similar commission, and with the added instruction: "Don't let money stand in your way."

Cosimo's efforts were not always rewarded with success, to be sure. The famous jurist Andrea Alciati got caught in a tug of war between the duke of Ferrara, the governor of Milan, and the emperor, and had to send a young disciple instead. Varchi's former philosophy professor, Lodovico Boccadiferro, could not bring himself to leave Bologna. The great Titian would do no more than stop briefly in Florence in 1546 on his way home from Rome. Luigi Alamanni, the only Florentine poet of distinction at the time, showed no inclination to leave France. And Michelangelo, who would have been the biggest prize of all, and on whom Cosimo and Vasari and just about everyone else in Florence exerted every possible art of persuasion, simply could not extricate himself from one more great project after another. And that, by the way, is the only reason he himself ever gave for not leaving Rome and "coming back to Florence," of which he always declared himself a proud citizen, "to rest and to die," even though some modern art historians are convinced that he could not possibly have preferred the drab tyranny of Cosimo de' Medici to the enlightened commonweal of Pope Paul IV.

But several notable victories soon compensated for all the failures. The first one occurred by chance, when Benvenuto Cellini dropped into Florence to check up on his poor relatives, without "any intention of remaining." But when Cosimo then suggested that he do a Perseus for the Loggia dei Lanzi, he remained —for the rest of his life, in fact, in spite of the irregularity of his paychecks, the regularity of his quarrels, and his constant threats to go back to France. The second victory occurred after some negotiation, when Cosimo persuaded two Flemings, whose names were immediately Italianized as Giovanni Rosso and Niccolò Fiamingo, to teach Florentines how to make tapestries and to set up the tapestry factory whose products were to be famous for two centuries thereafter. The third had been carefully prepared ever since May 1537, when Cosimo seems to have offered the "slightly lascivious and avaricious, but most rare" historian, Paolo Giovio, some notes for his current book, and when he then promised to replace the white horse one of Alessandro's captains had stolen from Giovio in Genoa. The correspondence went on for another twelve years, accompanied by little favors and occasional reminders of the standing invitation. Finally, in September 1550, Giovio arrived, old and ailing, to supervise Torrentino's printing of the first part of his monumental *History*. So happy was he at last to be in the company of his old acquaintances, Varchi, Bronzino, Pontormo, and Torelli, and so engrossed was he with the information he was gathering for the final chapters, that he kept putting off his resolution to return to his delightful Plinian villa on Lake Como. He was still in Tuscany when he died early in 1553. And he is still there today, eternalized in Francesco da Sangallo's marble statue, imparting an episcopal blessing on his twentieth-century colleagues as they start up the staircase towards the Laurenziana Library.

The last victory was perhaps the most important, and it was accomplished, even more than the third, with the help of Torrentino's press. Since Giorgio Vasari had fled Florence early in 1537, he had been building a reputation as one of the most versatile and prolific painters in Italy. He had frequently been in and out of Florence, where Ottaviano always had been happy to put him up; and indeed, it was his *Deposition* for the monks at Camaldoli and his *Allegory of the Conception* for the exile Bindo Altoviti in Santi Apostoli, that started the succession of bigger and bigger commissions he received from 1540 on. But he probably would have settled down eventually somewhere between Arezzo and Rome had it not been for a second vocation, one first suggested to him by Paolo Giovio: "Write, my brother, write, for . . . you will be happier, richer, and more glorious for having written this work than if you had painted the [Sistine] Chapel of Michelangelo himself." No one, certainly, had seen and studied so many art works in so many different places, and no one so well combined a thorough training as a painter, a well-developed faculty for critical judgment, a familiarity with what were then the latest methods of historical research, and a command of Tuscan prose. By about 1547 the manuscript of the first great masterpiece of art history—and, in spite of its occasional errors of date and fact, one of the great masterpieces of history in general—was ready; and Vasari turned it over to the printer he thought would do the best job on it, the Torrentini. On March 8, 1550, he sent the first volume of *The Lives of the Most Excellent Painters, Sculptors, and Architects* to Cosimo, "not having any other purpose nor other hope than in your goodness and good will." The formal invitation from Cosimo soon reached him. And after several trips to finish up important contracts elsewhere, "the man who revives the dead and prolongs the life of the living," as his hero Michelangelo affectionately called him, was established once and for all in Florence, with an official position as superintendent of all Cosimo's art projects.

With the return of those who had left, then, with the coming of others from the outside, and with the maturity of those who had remained, the Florentine cultural and intellectual community, which had been on the verge of disintegration in 1537, was largely reconstituted by the early 1550s. Florence had become, at least in the eyes of Pier Vettori, who had done so much to make it so, a center from which the fruits of productive thought radiated once again through the whole world.

Meanwhile Cosimo had finally managed to become, after considerable effort, a fairly discerning patron. By carefully studying Vettori's orations, he had picked up a taste for good Latinity. By conversing at length with Giovio, and by reading the *History* as it came page by page off the press, he learned something about historiography—enough, at least, to read critically the manuscript of chapter VII of Filippo de' Nerli's *History of Florence* "with even more pleasure than I have the others," and to add "a number of little marginal notes in my own hand" where Nerli's account seemed to differ from what he remembered from his own experience. By hovering over the woodcutters and jewel-setters he had working in his *guardaroba,* and by demanding of Cellini not only his aesthetic judgments but a rational explanation for them as well ("Tell me distinctly, Benvenuto, what the 'great force' you're so amazed at in this master consists of"), he learned to ask intelligent questions of the artists and not to accept uncritically their answers. By 1548 he was already on the verge of outshining his chief rivals, the Farnese. "These turbulent times," Giovio wrote, with his usual taste for exaggeration, "have castrated the Maecenases"; the arts and letters would disappear altogether, he asserted, if it were not for "Your Excellency, on whom all good men have pinned their hopes."

The new community of talent that had finally been put back together was not always a happy one. All Florentines tended, noted the Aretine Vasari, to "spend most of their time and energy hanging around the shops . . . busy with nothing other than speaking ill of the work of others." Some of them went farther than just words. Varchi's enemies got him thrown into the Bargello in 1545, not, as they had hoped, because he had yielded once again to his unfortunate appetite for young men, but because he did not have the heart to betray his gardener, who had seduced a twelve-year-old girl next door. The enemies of Anton Francesco Grazzini, or "Il Lasca," as he was usually called, got him thrown out of the academy a year or so later, even though he was one of the charter members; and, during the quarrel about whether or not the Florentine language descended from ancient Aramaic, they went so far as to stop the printing of his anthology of carnival songs by presenting false testimony against the authenticity of one of the texts. Even Cellini's *Perseus* became a subject of factional fighting—not so much because anyone really dissented from the unanimous praise accorded to even the first sketches, but because Cellini was friendly with Varchi, and therefore with Bronzino, Adriani, and Lasca, and because they in turn were not friendly with Giovan Battista Strozzi, Carlo Lenzoni, and the chief of the "Aramaists," Pierfrancesco Giambullari. The most violent altercation of all took place right in the Palazzo Vecchio, with Cellini on one side, Bandinelli on the other, and Cosimo trying to keep a semblance of order in the middle. And it ended only when Bandinelli, whom Cellini called "the filthiest ruffian ever born in this world," screamed "Oh shut up, you dirty fairy!"—knowing full well that that was the one accusation the author of the antisodomy laws could not pass over lightly.

To some extent this internecine bickering was a reflection not so much of petty jealousies as of a characteristic of the Florentine intellectual community at the time—namely, its individualism. In spite of the tendency of some recent historians

5. Bandinelli, *Ercole*, and Cellini, *Perseo*
Piazza della Signoria

to pass it off as "courtly," and therefore as uniform and monotonous, the community was actually composed of a number of very striking individuals—of
persons, that is, whose idiosyncrasies and peculiarities of character were far more
evident than what they had in common. Who, for instance, could have been more
different from the "jolly and extravagant" merchant, traveler, and sometime

soldier, Giovanni Mazzuoli, called *Lo Stradano,* than his grave, somewhat plodding, spaniel-eyed friend Giambullari, who had helped him put together the nucleus of the Accademia Fiorentina in 1540? Who could be more different from the "sweet, courteous" Bronzino, who "has never done the slightest injury to anyone," than his strange, solitary, tormented master, Pontormo, who pulled the ladder up behind him whenever he retired to paint in his attic, and who would probably have starved on the tiny rations of almonds, plain lettuce, and omelettes (*pesce d'uovo*) he fixed for himself at home, had not Bronzino filled him up with chicken and veal every Sunday? It is not surprising that Varchi, who took beatings like a timid dog, and then went right on pompously talking down to everyone, did not get on too well with Vettori, whose modesty and benevolence kept him aloof from polemics even in the face of an attempt to discredit him professionally. But it is remarkable that he should have been so close to Vasari, whom an unbroken series of personal triumphs made oblivious to the least defect in his own work or character.

The differences among Florentine writers and artists were not limited to matters of temperament and personality. They extended to what was written and painted as well. While Vettori, for instance, spent much of his time trying to explain what Aristotle actually had said in Greek, Varchi went right on explaining in the vernacular what a philosophy professor in Bologna, on the basis of a Latin translation, said that Aristotle had said. Bandinelli thought that beauty was a function of anatomy and that therefore what started out as an Adam could very easily be turned into a Bacchus. And he went right on multiplying his muscled statues, indifferent to the nasty sonnets that were inevitably pasted onto them. He might, indeed, have been still more intransigent had he foreseen that the decaying skulls and more-than-lifeless body of his *Pietà* would, four centuries later, merit votive candles from the pious *habituées* of the Basilica of the Annunziata. Vasari thought that beauty was achieved by a proper "manner" or style. And he went on incorporating into his own paintings perfect imitations of the various "manners" he observed in every other painter of his time, to the point of distracting subsequent students of his work into a chase after sources. Pontormo, on the other hand, said that beauty was essentially "grace"—*grazia.* He therefore went on "improving on nature," with "splendid, surprising things . . . such that nature has never made," and "arranging and composing them where they seem best"— where they seemed best on the surface of the canvas, that is, and not where they ought to have been according to reason, experience, or Alberti's rules of one-point perspective.

These differences may help to explain why the artistic school decried as "Mannerist" in the seventeenth century and praised by the same name in the twentieth is so hard to define. In Florence, at least, it was not so much a school as an assortment of distinct individuals who may have eaten, talked, and even worked together, but who in paint, on stone, and in writing, followed thoughts and methods that were largely their own, even when they picked up suggestions from their colleagues. Their purpose was not primarily to communicate or to teach, but to work out wholly individual impressions and preoccupations; and they hit upon a number of fascinating technical innovations. Whoever looks first at the horrifying distortions of Rosso Fiorentino's monocolored nudes, then at the 45° parallel lines that shoot out of the frame of Bronzino's *Dead Christ,* and then at the brash perpendiculars and terrifyingly unanatomical dwarfs of Francesco Verdi's *Deposition*—whoever looks at all this variety, appropriately located today in one room of the Uffizi Gallery, will wonder why some recent critics say these works are vitiated by "a preoccupation with content" (*preoccupazioni contenutistiche*), as well as by "provinciality" and lack of originality.

Differences in point of view and in method were recognized in theory as well as in practice. Florence in the fifteenth century discovered the value of the individual *man*. But Florence in the sixteenth century pushed the discovery to its logical conclusion by admitting the value of individual *men*—of men, that is, who were respected, or at least tolerated, for qualities that were peculiarly their own, rather than for the qualities of, say, Alberti's *uomo universale* or Castiglione's *Courtier,* to which everyone might aspire. Hence Vasari, the very critic who first explained the aesthetic merit of the Sistine Chapel when everyone else judged it on moral grounds, was willing to reserve judgment when he finally encountered something that simply did not fit any of his critical categories—namely, Pontormo's frescoes in San Lorenzo. "Since even I, who am a painter, can't understand them," he concluded, "I have resolved to leave the judgment to whoever will come look at them." And when later he took charge of decorating the *Studiolo* of Prince Francesco, he let one of his assistants (Domenico Buti) shrivel up the feet of the

6. Pontormo, drawing

7. Domenico Buti, *La Fondaria*
Studiolo di Francesco I

nude Achilles being instructed by Chiron how to make steel, and he let another
(Sebastiano Marsilli) stretch Atalanta into the shape of an eerie boomerang—all
this in spite of the "rule, order, and perspective" he followed in his own work.

This recognition of the value of differences, this tendency to leave systems
open-ended rather than to exclude what could not easily be comprehended, was
encouraged in part by the considerable freedom of expression enjoyed by
Florentine artists and writers at the time. To be sure, freedom stopped short of
political dissent, heresy, misrepresentation, and even pornography: Agnolo
Firenzuola decided to leave the other "altars covered" when his dialogue about a
perfect woman got down as far as "those two hills of snow and roses, with two
little crowns at the top." Freedom of expression was regulated by a rather
rudimentary prior censorship and by the threat of sudden clamp-downs, as
Domenichi discovered when one of his books was found to be a paraphrase of
Calvin. But it was otherwise not seriously abridged, even in the delicate fields of
religion and ethics, until the early 1560s—that is, until the Tridentine Index
of Forbidden Books, which Cosimo had no choice but to accept, replaced the
Index of Paul IV, which he had done all he could to disregard. Freedom was even
supported by Cosimo's acceptance of the current theory concerning the relation
between patron and the patronized, a theory that made each indispensable to the
other but left the latter completely in charge of planning and executing what the
former had hired him to do.

Independence of thought and judgment thus came to be respected, not just
tolerated—so much so that the literary quarrels eventually gave way to polite
discussion. After listening to Cosimo's firm suggestion that they be as "courteous"
in writing as he made them be on the streets, and after reading the classic of all
books on manners, the *Galateo,* which Giovanni Della Casa published in 1559,
Florentines came to recognize that independence was not incompatible with
"modesty," which Varchi said "ought to be observed by all men, and especially
by those who make a profession of letters." They realized that being "pious, just,
affable, and friendly toward one another" was the best way of maintaining
"civility and conversation"—which, by the way, were among the greatest
achievements of the age.

Still, these differences of opinion and temperament might well have dissipated
the energies of Florentines in a number of purely individual undertakings had it
not been for the basic unity that underlay them all. The unity of the Florentine
cultural and intellectual community was such that it managed to cut right across
class and professional barriers. It brought together artisans like Gelli and
patricians like Vettori, men of humble birth like Bronzino and men of ancient
families like Bernardo Segni. It put bureaucrats next to professors: Campana, for
instance, collaborated with Vettori on his edition of Cicero, and Francesco Vinta
helped Vasari avoid errors in his historical murals by reading him passages from
Guicciardini as he worked in the Sala dei Cinquecento of the Palazzo Vecchio.

In a certain sense, this unity reached all the way from the duke, who made regular rounds of the workshops of the painters and the studies of the writers, to the whole population of the city, which turned out en masse, to applaud or condemn, every time a new painting or statue was unveiled.

The unity of Florentine culture cut right across fields of specialization, too. Indeed, the attempt to separate the amateurs from the serious philologists of the Accademia Fiorentina in the late 1540s soon had to be given up, for it was impossible to distinguish one from the other. Artists, in conversations of the time, were expected to talk intelligently about poetry: Bronzino, for one, wrote plays and sonnets and claimed to know the whole *Divine Comedy* by heart. Poets, in turn, were expected to talk authoritatively about art, as did Varchi in arbitrating between painters and sculptors in their argument about whose form of expression was the best. Similarly, physicians were expected to pass from a lecture on digestion to one on Dante. And men of letters were expected to pass just as easily from a line of Petrarch to a detail of anatomy. Some people were expected to talk about everything—which may be the reason that many of them never got around to talking about the subjects they announced on their title pages. At times, it is true, this disregard for distinctions among disciplines broke down into superficiality. To say that poetry was talking painting and that painting was mute poetry, for instance, did not really add much to the understanding of either. But just as often the disregard led to valuable insights. It permitted that most rambling of all the sixteenth-century polygraphs, Cosimo Bartoli, to transfer to music the critical concepts usually reserved for the plastic arts, and thus to get rid of the limited functions assigned to music by the Neoplatonists.

At times, indeed, the entire community got together on a single project—like the annual San Giovanni parade, the pageants to welcome visiting dignitaries, and the decoration of the Palazzo Vecchio. Cosimo Bartoli and Vincenzo Borghini, on such occasions, would prescribe the themes. Pier Vettori would compose the inscriptions. Vasari would design the costumes. Tribolo and Cellini would make the statues. Bronzino and a dozen or so assistants would paint scenery. Lasca would provide the lyrics. Antonio da Lucca and Cosimo's band of musicians would play the scores—all while the general public commented and criticized, and while various pieces gradually and spontaneously grew into one harmonious whole. Spectacle was no invention of the mid-sixteenth century. But it was now carried out more fully and more elaborately than ever before. Nor was it the invention of a prince intent upon distracting his troublesome subjects Its greatest promoter, in fact, was not Cosimo at all, but Il Lasca, who, far from being bread-and-circused into passivity, kept presenting projects for still "gayer," still "more delightful" shows.

What distinguished one Florentine from another, then, was offset by, and to some extent even made possible by, what bound them all together. And what bound them together was above all a common heritage. The writers and artists

of mid-Cinquecento Florence were still the heirs of the humanists of the Quattrocento, and through them of the ancient Greeks and Romans, whose works the
humanists had done so much to recover. They still accepted many of their
predecessors' basic theses: the superiority of the active to the contemplative life,
the justification of study as a stimulus to creativity, the refusal to accept the word
of an authority in preference to what was observable, the prescription of philology
as the foundation of learning, and the assurance that the moderns already had
surpassed, or would soon surpass, the ancients. They also accepted the principal
literary forms, like the personal letter and the dialogue, in which these theses had
been presented. Indeed, epistolary treatises became still more spontaneous in
appearance and still more carefully cultivated in fact; Varchi, for one, managed to
perfect the dialogue to the point at which he could write one inside another
inside another without losing track of where he had started. They accepted the
humanists' models of the good life as well. In fact, the latest incarnation of the
ideals of Bruni and Alberti happened to be the favorite schoolmaster of many of
them, Francesco Cattini. "Although a philosopher," Cattini "did not shirk from
civic duties" or from marriage. He switched into the vernacular whenever any of
his listeners appeared not to understand Latin. He explained himself as clearly to
children as to adults. And he encouraged one of his many sons to gain "the same
credit and reputation among the most honorable merchants" as he himself
enjoyed "among the most brilliant men of letters."

Thus Florentines of the 1540s shared a common cultural tradition; and what
a few recent historians have taken as a revolt against that tradition, or an "Anti-
Renaissance," was actually an attack on the aberrations of humanism, like
pedantry and sophistry, an attack which often sounds very much like Petrarch's
attack on the aberrations of scholasticism two centuries earlier. But they also
shared a certain sense of detachment from their tradition, a detachment that
became more marked as a new generation grew away from the generation that
had educated it. Varchi, for instance, dutifully edited Francesco Cattani's *Three
Books on Love*; but he avoided any mention of Cattani's philosophical doctrines in
the biographical preface. Giannotti respectfully acclaimed the *De Amore* of "that
saintly, learned old man" Francesco Verino when it appeared in 1542; but he
barely managed to read beyond the first few pages. Beginning art students still
copied the paintings of Andrea del Sarto for practice; but they looked for
inspiration to the Pontormos and the Vasaris, for whom Andrea had become only
a precursor.

As it forgot its teachers, the new generation also lost interest in much of what
they had transmitted to it from their own past. True, old favorites were still
"rediscovered" from time to time. Gelli popularized Giovanni Pico's *Oration*,
Doni recommended Matteo Palmieri's *City of Life* for publication, Domenichi and
Bartoli translated the aesthetic treatises of Leon Battista Alberti, and the
Torrentini put out Giovanni Villani's *Chronicle,* complete with the long-lost

Books XI and XII. The ancients were still read—to a greater extent, in fact, since Pier Vettori and Bernardo Segni, among others, had made many more texts available in more correct and better-annotated versions. But in general all the Latin literature of the fourteenth and fifteenth centuries went out of circulation, partly because it no longer came up to the Ciceronian standards of Pietro Bembo. And most of the vernacular literature went out of circulation too, partly because it was written in a language that was fast becoming antiquated, and partly because it seemed less actual and less important than what was being written at the moment. In other words, while the ideas of earlier Renaissance humanism lived on, the writings in which the ideas had first been expressed were increasingly forgotten. And interest in the writings had all but vanished by the time the printers of Basel finally started putting them out, for the benefit of northern European rather than Italian readers. All that remained, in the end, were the great classics: Dante's *Divine Comedy,* Boccaccio's *Decameron,* and Petrarch's *Canzoniere,* which forthwith became the subjects of intense, line-by-line commentaries in the academy, and required reading, if not required memorizing, for any Florentine who considered himself half-way literate.

Detachment therefore had some disadvantages. But it also had one notable advantage: that of encouraging an independent and often creative elaboration of certain elements of the heritage. First of all, the philological methods of Poggio and Poliziano, that is, the methods of determining from faulty or discordant manuscripts what an author really said, were further developed—to the point where such stumbling blocks as the "Lake of Arezzo" in Strabo, which corresponded to nothing in ancient or modern geography, could at last be overcome. By altering four letters in the Greek and by putting two words together, the text was made to read "Trasoumena," or Lake Trasimeno, which really did exist. The methods were then applied to the one or two new texts still left after the great discoveries of the previous century, most notably to Aeschylus and Euripides. And they were also applied to a great variety of major and minor Greek authors, from Aristotle to Porphyry, from Dionysius of Hallicarnasus to Clement of Alexandria, which the Quattrocento philologists, with their greater interest in Latin than Greek literature, had not had time for.

Secondly, historiography became far more voluminous than it had been in the days of those who were still considered the models of good historical writing— Bruni to some extent, Guicciardini later on, and, above all, Machiavelli. It also became more universal in scope. Thus Adriani expanded his history of Florence into what turned out to be really a history of Europe, and Giovio expanded a history of Europe into a history of the Turks, Persians, and Egyptians as well. It became less concerned with current politics. Thus Borghini and Giambullari, neither of whom had ever held a political office, could study, respectively, the fourth century and the eight and ninth centuries A.D. with as much scholarly aloofness as anyone before the time of Leopold von Ranke. Above all, history became more accurate. For historians became much more aware of the importance of archival documents, which Cosimo gave some of them free access to and which they then quoted at length in their books, often to the point of boring their readers. Cosimo himself made it clear that he did not appreciate such collections of unfounded flattery as Domenichi's *Sienese War*. He was sufficiently sure that the plain truth would bear him out in the long run that he saw no need for imposing an "official" version of the past on the historians he supported.

Similarly, theology—humanist, and hence nonacademic theology, that is, conceived as a guide to piety rather than as a science—was enriched in the 1540s by the addition of two new sources: many more of the writings of the Greek Fathers and the works of contemporary Italian religious reformers. Consequently, the criticism, as well as the remedies that Florentines proposed, were often very similar to those of the leading humanist theologian of the previous generation, Erasmus of Rotterdam, even though few of them seem to have known directly any of his works but the *Adagia*. As Borghini's monks at the Badìa began studying St. Gregory Nazianzen, as Giovio began reciting Marcantonio Flaminio's Italian Psalms, as the confraternities began singing Filippo Neri's popular *lauds* and reading Antonio Brucioli's translation of the Bible, they became increasingly intolerant of the "endless quarrels of the black and gray friars" over obscure, and, as far as they were concerned, irrelevant points of dogma. They became even more intolerant of the continued use of Latin in the liturgy, which went against all current theories about the function of language, and which Gelli, for one, denounced as a trick of "the priests and the friars . . . to keep [the faith] hidden . . . then sell it back to us," and thus "live sumptuously." Had they succeeded in joining humanist theology to traditional forms of popular piety, had they managed to join the practical biblical and spiritual manuals of, say, an Ambrogio Catarino, a Paolino Bernardini, or a Simone Porzio, to the intense spirituality of the Savonarolan mystic Caterina de' Ricci, they might have produced a genuine religious revival in their day. They failed in the long run, to be sure. For an authority far above them determined that Florentines should go on praying "like jays and parrots," as Gelli put it. And even Gelli's most recent editor, four centuries later, felt obliged to replace Gelli's perfectly accurate passages from the New Testament with the Latin of the Vulgate, a language that St. Paul never heard of and that Gelli's contemporaries found inexpressive and inelegant.

This sense of detachment from their heritage thus encouraged Florentines to add to it. It also permitted them to introduce one subject that had long seemed incompatible with, or at least extraneous to, the heritage, namely, the Aristotelian philosophy, or more precisely, the physics and metaphysics in the Averroistic and Alexandrian interpretations of Aristotle that had long been cultivated in the great universities of the north. When Varchi brought back in 1542 what he had learned during his exile in Padua and Bologna, and, better yet, when he divested it of the academic jargon so annoying to their ears, Florentines responded enthusiastically.

To a generation tiring of what seemed like the inevitable vaguenesses of Platonism, the philosophy of Aristotle had one great advantage: it gave them quick, clear answers to almost any question, and it planted the solutions firmly on such undeniable axioms as "The whole universe is divided into things eternal and things not eternal." The reading of Aristotle then drew their attention to the works of other philosophers, ancient and modern, who had dealt with similar matters. Soon, what they could not find in Aristotle they were looking up in Galen, whose second century A.D. textbook was still authoritative in the medical schools; in Andrea Vesalius, who had become the most celebrated anatomist of the sixteenth century; and, better yet, in Realdo Colombo, professor of medicine at Pisa, who promised to overthrow both Galen and Vesalius on the basis of his own researches.

Thus philosophy in general soon led to natural philosophy in particular. Needless to say, what Varchi and the Accademia Fiorentina thought to be natural philosophy was often far from scientific, even according to the standards of the times. His description of the male sperm, for example, as "what is left over of nourishment after the final and perfect digestion," and of the testicles as nothing but weights that permit the sperm to pass, was as ridiculous as his conclusion—that castration is no impediment to virility. Unfortunately, such theories occasionally had deleterious effects outside the realm of science. For instance, they cut short of its logical conclusion the argument from humanist ethics and anthropology which might well have ended up in the emancipation of women. Thus after letting the feminine interlocutor in the *Circe* assert her right to be a companion and collaborator of her husband, and not just his servant, Gelli ran head-on into the "scientific" verity that the male alone, at the moment of conception, provides the *anima sensitiva*. That left the female contemporaries of such outstanding women as Vittoria Colonna and Giulia Gonzaga still shut up at home, incapable of generating anything better than purely passive *anima vegetale*.

Yet the mere presentation of these theories made up, to some extent, for the damage they may have done. Varchi, for one, never pretended to do anything but report on what he had heard from the specialists. He insisted that what he reported were merely working hypotheses, no matter how authoritative their source, and that they were therefore subject to eventual rectification in the light of new evidence. He was receptive to any novelty, and he made a point of interrogating the inventors, as he did his old Sienese friend Vannoccio Biringucci about his "pyrotechnics," even when he found what they proposed contrary to all that seemed rational. He suggested, moreover, at least by implication, that natural science was an independent and respectable discipline in its own right, even when it arrived with conclusions that seemed incompatible with his own religious convictions. He thus contributed to the establishment of a science wholly different from the one he thought would last forever. He did so not by foreseeing the scientific revolution of the following century, but by taking the first steps toward the formation of an informed, open-minded lay audience which would eventually be capable of supporting the leaders of the revolution against the attacks of their professional colleagues.

Philosophy and science were looked upon as bodies of knowledge that had already been fairly well worked out; and philosophers and scientists were called upon not so much to add to what they had accumulated as to make it available to others. The same was true for most other disciplines. Florentines in the age of Cosimo the Duke came to consider as their principal task that of giving back to the world what their predecessors had so carefully gathered from it since the age of Cosimo the Elder. The main purpose of critical editions of the classics, they held, was to help students, not to enlighten scholars; and what Vettori did in his study was considered merely a continuation of what he did in the classroom. The main purpose of the Accademia Fiorentina was to provide public lectures for the citizenry, not to hold private seminars for its members; and its public sessions were conducted more like modern adult education courses than like meetings of a learned society. The main purpose of the university was to train the young, not to subsidize research; and the worst thing the rector could say in his reports to his superiors in Florence was that a given professor was failing to show up for the number of private and formal lessons imposed by the statutes. For Cosimo was even more unaware than his educated subjects of the value of what Galileo was later to think possible only in monarchy—the independent pursuit of knowledge for its own sake. And Cosimo's own investments in knowledge tended to be strictly proportionate to the number of people he thought might be given access to it.

No one thought of reconsidering, it is true, the methods of education handed down by the humanist educators of the fifteenth century, and the University of Pisa took over without question the traditional program of instruction still observed by the prehumanist universities of Padua and Bologna. Knowledge, nevertheless, became even more identified with pedagogy than it had been in the days of Guarino da Verona, and what was taught became ever less important than the mere fact that someone was learning something. Even the much-debated question of what was the proper medium for the elaboration and communication of ideas, which the Accademia Fiorentina inherited from the discussions in the Rucellai Gardens of Machiavelli's generation and which it then passed on to its successors for the next three centuries—even the *questione della lingua,* as it was called—was usually resolved in terms of the "Florentine" language that the audience most easily understood. Unlike their colleagues of the *Pléiade* in France, whose work they heard of indirectly through correspondents in Lyon rather than directly through the texts, the Florentine linguists did not have to create a national literature. They already had one. They did not have to prove the equality of their own with ancient languages. Pietro Bembo and Sperone Speroni, the chief language authorities of the day and Varchi's old friends in Padua, had already settled that point to their complete satisfaction. What they had to do, rather, was to break down the growing barrier between the learned and the educable and between writing and speech. Their audience now consisted not only of Bruni's cultivated bankers and merchants, or only of Ficino's elite of part-time philosophers. It consisted also of Gelli's cobblers, storekeepers, and pharmacists, who had neither the time nor the inclination, after a day of hard work, to realize the humanists' dream of a perfectly bilingual culture. It was essential, therefore, that authors write not in Latin, nor even in the somewhat artificial "Italian" of the courts of Rome and Urbino, but in a cross between the language of Boccaccio's merchants and the language of Doni's storekeepers. And after a number of ingenious experiments with new letters and new accent marks, which fore-shadowed the phonetic alphabets of modern dictionaries, they succeeded in blocking the tendency in contemporary Italian to let spelling follow etymol-ogy, as it has ever since in English, and in making it follow pronunciation instead.

This emphasis on the dissemination and popularization of learning encouraged a considerable increase at least in the volume of literary and artistic production. Lodovico Domenichi, for instance, managed to compose or translate fifty-nine tomes in less than twenty-five years. Vasari and his atelier managed to produce up to a dozen major art works every twelve months. And Varchi supposedly could compose a score of sonnets in a single day. In spite of occasional complaints about "paper dirtiers" (*imbrattacarte*), moreover, quantity turned out to be not incompatible with quality. Indeed, the criterion of quantity was somewhat ennobled by Vasari's ambition to cover the world with objects of beauty. So anxious was Varchi to bring his audience up to his level rather than to lower himself to theirs, that he carefully supplied lists for further reading every time he judged it opportune, for rhetorical purposes, to skip over the more technical aspects of an argument. The result, then, was not a decline in quality, but a change in kind—a change that was encouraged by the appearance, for the first time, of a group of professional writers who lived largely, if not completely, from the sale of their works, and who, unlike even the "professional" writers of Elizabethan England, were no longer wholly dependent on the good graces of a wealthy patron. What these writers introduced was a new kind of prose literature—one intended to be skimmed through rapidly rather than read carefully out loud, and to be enjoyed rather than, or as well as, profited from. Anyone who takes the trouble to read what they wrote from the point of view of the audience they wrote for rather than from that of the modern literary scholars they never dreamed could exist will appreciate how well they succeeded. And he will probably refrain from looking for logical coherence or philosophical profundity in Gelli's rambling dialogues about everything and nothing and in Doni's fantastic anticipa-tions of modern science fiction—in books, that is, which were never intended to be either profound or coherent.

To be sure, not all was perfectly healthy in the Florentine intellectual community. Too much energy was being expended on eulogistic and festive orations. Too much artistic talent was being invested in papier-mâché. Too many comedies were being sacrificed to the interludes. Too many writers were being tempted to let flattery take the place of work, in spite of Cosimo's efforts to resist the flattery. Too many differences of opinion were ending up in appeals for a decision on the part of political authority, in spite of Cosimo's insistence that he was not competent in literary and artistic matters. Moreover, at least one field of activity—and one of the most promising, at that—was beginning to show signs of exhaustion. When Varchi let what was supposed to have been his major work be marred by page-long sentences, when he, and the whole Florentine colony in Lyon, got involved in a sterile and largely unjustified campaign of denigration against Giovio, when Adriani failed to understand the potentialities for political history of Vasari's experiment with cultural history, and, finally, when Jacopo Nardi started railing against "those impudent, shameless historians who . . . turn bad into good and black into white," it should have been obvious that something was wrong with historiography. And when most of the historians abandoned their manuscripts on their desks, or locked them up in cabinets, it was apparent that they were beginning to lose confidence in the value of what they were doing.

But for the moment, at least, these blemishes were hidden beneath a widespread optimism about what had been and what still might be accomplished. Depending upon their points of view, Florentines in the 1540s and 1550s had several different ways of judging the present in relation to the past. To some, notably Vasari and Borghini, the return to ancient art in the fourteenth century and the recovery of ancient letters in the early fifteenth had initiated a process of continual improvement that had recently culminated in the art of Michelangelo and the critical texts of Vettori. To others, like Nerli, some four centuries of political development in the "New Rome" (Florence), had at last ended in the perfect government of the "New Augustus" (Cosimo), who happened, as everyone knew, to have been born under the same constellation as his more famous, but, according to Adriani, less fortunate predecessor. To still others, like Varchi, the advent of Cosimo had providentially saved Florence from the "suffering and calamities" that had been the lot of the rest of Italy ever since the catastrophic French invasion of 1494.

In spite of occasional reminiscences about the Republic of Soderini, then, and in spite of an unbounded admiration for "the most stupendous event ever recounted by any author," the siege of 1530, most Florentines were convinced of the superiority of their own over all previous ages. So convinced were they, that they saw nothing wrong with Vasari's pulling down the antiquated rood screen in Santa Maria Novella and painting over Masaccio's old-fashioned frescoes—all on behalf of the "order and proportion" that Vasari knew more about than any of his precursors. When, in the second edition of his *Lives,* Vasari decided to put Michelangelo at the beginning of a new epoch as well as at the end of the last one, and when Cosimo Bartoli noted that "those who study . . . can now accomplish much more in a few days than they could until just recently in many years," Florentines became convinced that the future would be even brighter than the present. "The singular industry of men and the rare felicity of this century," they concluded, "have scattered the clouds . . . of times past." They had "good reason," they believed, "to hope now for surer, more certain things" to come.

6

Triumph

The year 1559 was an important one for Cosimo. The cordial reception of the presents he had recently sent to Constantinople held forth the double prospect of freeing the Tuscan coast from Turkish raids and of opening up a vast new market for Florentine manufactures. The accidental death of King Henry II suddenly removed one of the greatest troublemakers on the Italian political scene and put the government of France in the hands of Cosimo's distant cousin, Catherine de' Medici. The long-awaited death of Pope Paul IV, "the man of steel who turns the stones he touches into fire," as Serristori called him, removed the second greatest troublemaker, one whose disastrous pontificate had brought to the steps of St. Peter's the very Spanish armies he had sworn to drive into the sea. Finally the Peace of Cateau Cambrésis at last put an end to the Hapsburg-Valois rivalry that had kept Europe in an almost constant state of war for more than forty years. Cosimo's gamble to remain firmly on the side of Spain and the Empire had paid off. His own personal prestige was now backed by the power that enjoyed an undisputed hegemony over most of Italy, and his effective authority was reinforced by his success in procuring the election of Pope Pius IV, who never lost a chance thereafter of expressing his gratitude.

Most important of all, Cosimo had just emerged from the severest test of his whole career: the Sienese War. He had abandoned his policy of benevolent neutrality late in 1553, when the appointment of none other than his chief enemy, Piero Strozzi, as commander-in-chief of the French forces in Tuscany threatened to make Siena a bastion not only of the French or the Spanish but also of the Florentine exiles. On the night of January 24, 1554, under the cover of absolute secrecy and a frigid downpour, he had sent his troops in a three-pronged march across the frontier. Unfortunately, the war, which turned out to be a civil war rather than a war of pacification or conquest, had lasted not four weeks, as he had hoped, but five years. It had begun with the failure of the Florentine incursions into the Maremma and the Valdichiana, with a frightening raid by Piero right across the Arno to Montecatini and Pescia, with a costly victory at Marciano, and with an exhausting nine-month vigil under the walls of Siena, which finally surrendered, on conditions, only after the defenders had been reduced to the last gram of bread. The war had then settled down to endless skirmishes, barely kept within the limits of the French-Imperial truce of March 1556, against the various outposts to which the diehard Sienese and their French and Florentine protectors had retired after the fall of their capital.

The Sienese War had brought out at least one disagreeable strain in Cosimo's character: cruelty. He manifested this in his treatment not only of captured exiles but also, occasionally, of Sienese peasants and citizens. Worse yet, it had cost the gigantic sum of 2,000,000 *scudi,* which had to be raised in part by suspending the salaries of state employees and letting the poor starve on the streets of Florence. In the end the war left Siena desolated, depopulated, and deprived of its natural seaports, Orbetello and Talamone, which King Philip of Spain insisted upon keeping for himself after reluctantly agreeing to exchange the rest of Sienese territory for the cancellation of his debts. But the war had also revealed two new talents in Cosimo: that of a military organizer—he turned out to be a much better tactician than the expensive general he had hired for the occasion—and that of a governor of a conquered people, whom he, with the help of his gracious, tactful representative, Agnolo Niccolini, managed to win over in a remarkably short time. Best of all, the war had increased the size of his state by one-third.

Cosimo had reason to be satisfied, then. He duly assumed the new title of Duke of Florence *and Siena*. His trip to Rome the following spring turned into a triumphal march, as he and Eleonora were received at the gates of the city by four thousand horses, one hundred coaches, and six cardinals—and by the entire Florentine colony, which finally put aside its once implacable hostility and welcomed him as its protector and benefactor.

Triumph, it is true, had not been without moments of disappointment. Cosimo was shocked, for instance, to find that one of his favorite young companions was plotting to blow him up with gunpowder in the cathedral, and he was surprised to learn that his son Francesco was being drawn away from him by certain unscrupulous associates. Indeed, triumph was accompanied by one major personal tragedy: in December 1562, his sons Giovanni and Garzia and then his wife, Eleonora, all died within a few days of each other. While venting his wrath against his would-be assassin, however, Cosimo managed to confront the other crises with a truly remarkable spirit of paternal affection and Christian resignation. "God disposes of us and our life and death as pleases His immense goodness," he reflected, and "our loss is [nothing compared to] the infinite number of people all over Italy who have already died of [the plague]." His attitude was at least more justifiable than that of Lorenzo Torrentino, who, with all the best intentions, put the blame on the absence of rain during the autumn solstice and on the "superabundant heat" in all fruit picked thereafter.

But there were moments of intense satisfaction as well. The Piazza della Signoria and the Ponte alla Carraia had been repaved as early as 1543. Bernardo Tasso's Mercato Nuovo, now known familiarly as the "Straw Market," had been opened in 1549, thanks to contributions from the Florentine colonies abroad. The suburbs destroyed during the siege had already been replaced, in 1550, by villas, gardens, and fountains, "which give great pleasure to the viewer, hearing the murmuring, whispering waters flowing from all sides."* The remodeling of the Palazzo Vecchio had been largely completed by 1560—not, fortunately, with the huge facade of classical columns proposed by Bandinelli in the 1540s, but at least with a propriety worthy of the *nunc dimittis* of the aged artist Ridolfo Ghirlandaio. "I can now die happy," he supposedly said, "for I can report to our artists in the next world that I have seen what was dead come to life, what was ugly become beautiful, what was old turn young again." Vasari was already busy turning the Palazzo Vecchio into a showpiece; and the enlargement on the palace Eleonora had bought from the Pitti family many years earlier soon reached the point at which Cosimo could move into his new, far more sumptuous residence across the Arno, leaving what was thereafter called the "Old Palace" (*Vecchio*) to Francesco. By 1561 enough money had been collected to launch a huge urban renewal project in the "low, dirty" quarters, inhabited by "persons of sordid occupations," between the Piazza della Signoria and the river. As the old buildings came down, at no little loss to the owners, the greatest architectural achievement of the age started going up—the Palace of the Uffizi, which was paid for, and then occupied by, the various government offices (*uffizi*) whose titles or mottoes still appear above the huge doors under the colonnade.

Meanwhile, Cosimo's example, as well as the law of January 28, 1551, giving the right of eminent domain to whoever would "put up . . . palaces . . . or expand those already built," encouraged a wave of private building. The heirs of Lorenzo Strozzi began work again on their half of the family palace in Via Tornabuoni. The heirs of Filippo began work on the other half as soon as Cosimo restored it to them in 1568. The Ugoccini put an immense cornice on their house. The Ricasoli cleared space for a new palace at Ponte alla Carraia and built a villa and a garden, on the advice of Cosimo Bartoli, at the Porta San Gallo. Many families followed Cosimo across the river, and the Via Maggio soon became the most elegant street in town. Many others renovated old facades with the chiaroscuro arabesques that Bernardo Buontalenti was soon to perfect on the house of Bianca Cappello. The entire city, in other words, was becoming a work of art, one in which individual initiative was coordinated through Vasari as superintendent of the Uffizi, and through the new Accademia del Disegno (Academy of Fine Arts) founded in January 1563.

With some seventy artists already at work, with over two dozen students enrolled in the first courses of the academy, and with the sudden influx of ancient

---

* That charmingly confused image is Leandro Alberti's, not mine.

art objects that followed Cosimo's trip to Rome in 1561, Vasari's dream of surpassing the age of Augustus seemed closer to realization than ever before. Florence was already "full of aqueducts, fountains, . . . statues, and temples, and adorned with palaces and an infinity of other ornaments." It was still further embellished in 1565 by the huge column that had been hauled from Rome to Civitavecchia on rollers, from Pisa to Florence on barges, and finally erected, at great expenditure in money and labor, in the Piazza Santa Trinita. And Cosimo was willing to believe Vasari's report, after a tour of northern Italy in 1567, that Florence was already more elegant than Venice and more magnificent than Rome.

Cosimo's work was finished. He now had "no other obligations of dependency" abroad except those he chose to assume on his own initiative. He was "without debts . . . and with enough ordinary revenue" to satisfy all his needs. He had 200 pieces of artillery and he could gather together 24,000 infantrymen and 20 galleys in less than eight days. His subjects were protected from the designs of evildoers by an efficient system of justice. His neighbors were all obligated to him without his being in the least obligated to any of them. And he was content to manage his own affairs without "molesting, disturbing, or disquieting" those of others. Or at least so he boasted in a letter to Emperor Ferdinand in 1563. He therefore turned over the direction of all but foreign affairs to his son Francesco, who had just returned from a very expensive, if honorable, sojourn in Spain. He then provided him with a royal bride, the daughter of the emperor himself, and thus elevated the Medici family once and for all to the rank of a European ruling house. Finally, in December 1565, in honor of the arrival of the new princess, Giovanna d'Austria, he put on the biggest show of his life. The celebration began with five months of feverish preparation— erecting three huge triumphal arches, repainting the facades along the Borgo Ognissanti, covering a whole piazza with gigantic allegorical figures, constructing a fountain that poured forth, for the benefit of "the German nation," real wine, and building a street along the bank of the Arno east of the Ponte alla Carraia. A procession of four thousand soldiers, eighty knights, all the city magistrates, and fifty young patricians with a baldacchino accompanied Giovanna from Poggio a Caiano to the courtyard of the Palazzo Vecchio, which Vasari had just finished redoing with the stuccoes and the murals that still provide such a contrast to the stern medieval exterior. And balls, banquets, comedies, a mock hunt with a real lion in the Piazza Santa Croce, and a real attack on two mock castles in Piazza Santa Maria Novella then followed, day after day, week after week, until Lent mercifully put an end to everything but the bills, which in the end amounted to well over 50,000 *scudi*.

There was nothing left for Cosimo to do, then, but to travel endlessly around Tuscany, to overeat (especially garlic and onions) and overhunt, to amuse himself with two girlish, and, alas! worthless mistresses from good Florentine families, and to lapse slowly into a premature old age. Cosimo was still capable at times of noble actions—as when, for instance, he persistently protected, without any advantage to himself, the one condemned heretic who really did deserve his fate: the lily-fingered, light-minded prelate, Pietro Carnesecchi. He was still capable of putting conscience before politics, as when he went right ahead and married his second mistress in spite of loud complaints from his son Francesco and his son-in-law, the emperor. And he was still capable of skillful diplomatic maneuvering, which at last earned him the title of Grand Duke of Tuscany, promulgated by Pope Pius V in 1569 and officially bestowed during another triumphant trip to Rome the following February. But he soon began to show signs of physical as well as spiritual exhaustion. For most of 1571 he was confined to bed. In July 1573 he suffered a stroke that left him paralyzed on one side. And on April 21, 1574, he died, at just fifty-five years of age.

BOOK II
FLORENCE
IN THE 1590s

*How Scipione Ammirato solved just about
all the problems of his age*

I

The Countryside

June 27, 1591. Villa La Petraia, just above the road to Prato, where the broken slopes of Monte Morello finally tumble down onto the plain.

Scipione Ammirato, a well-preserved gentleman of average height and of not quite sixty years of age, with slightly staring eyes, a sharp straight nose, a long narrow face, and a pointed beard, meticulously dressed in a black ecclesiastical biretta and a starched white collar, stepped out of the heavy door in the exact center of the villa's broad rear facade. A vast rectangular terrace stretched out on either side toward two carefully drawn beds of flowers and then, at right angles, turned back toward a long row of tall cypresses guarding the upper entrance to the villa. Two straight staircases descended directly down from the delicately wrought balustrade to the far corners of a reflecting pool, from which an ample gravel walk reached outward toward identical circles of clipped fruit trees. And a straight path, like the axis of a series of augmenting isosceles triangles, led slowly downward from the pool between a double series of absolutely symmetrical patterns of hedges and pergolas to the back wall, where the line of equidistant espaliered trees was divided exactly in two by a small gate leading out to the road below.

The garden could have been more elegant, it is true. It had not yet been adorned with Giambologna's delicate fountain of Venus, which was moved over from the nearby Villa del Castello only in the eighteenth century. It had none of the woods, fountains, and long promenades, and none of the stone population that had recently been installed around the late grand duke's retreat at Pratolino. And it bore little resemblance to what Ammirato himself had once thought nature should look like: the natural settings he had designed back in the 1570s for his tree-shaped genealogical charts included crenelated villages on top of irregular hills, ruined arches along craggy seacoasts, fishermen dragging nets along windswept beaches, and ships racing towards swirling clouds beneath flocks of migrating geese. But he had since come to realize that nature could be enhanced

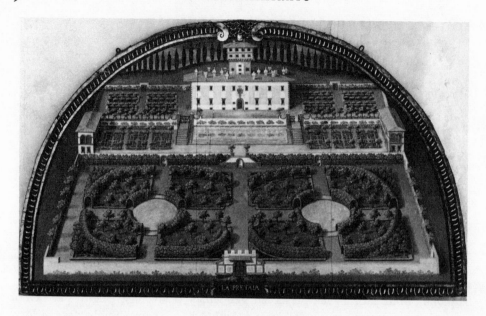

8. Villa La Petraia in the late sixteenth century
Museo di Firenze Com'Era

more effectively by "certain little things," such as a fragment of an ancient inscription, than by all the fountains and loggias of Naples. He had also become accustomed to the way Florentines insisted upon projecting geometry onto their surroundings—and to the way they were just then, thanks in part to the grand duke's late cousin, Queen Catherine de' Medici, projecting it onto the landscapes of France as well.

As Ammirato strolled back up from the lower garden, he turned to admire the villa, which still looked much more like the painting in the Museo di Firenze Com'Era (Florence's "Historical Topographical" museum) than like what it has become today, thanks to the plushier tastes of its most recent resident, King Vittorio Emanuele II. The stately solidity of the old Tuscan castle that Cardinal (now Grand Duke) Ferdinando de' Medici had bought for himself years before had not been obliterated. The plain whitewashed walls sparsely broken by equidistant window casings and topped by a straight tiled roof still betrayed the rather unimaginative fortified farmhouse it once had been. By simply altering a few details in the basic design, the celebrated architect Bernardo Buontalenti had created an overall impression of lightness and gaiety—by rearranging the four center windows in the north facade into two pairs, by tapering off the door with two smaller apertures on either side, and by carrying up to the overhanging tower the uneven dark gray stones that outlined the four corners of the main building.

Ammirato felt very much at home at La Petraia. Here he had come, as a guest of Cardinal Ferdinando, shortly after his arrival in Florence in 1569. Here he had remained, as a permanent guest of the proprietor; for Ferdinando soon tired of personality conflicts with his older brother, Grand Duke Francesco, and retired thereafter to the much more lavish Villa Medici that he had built on top of the Pincio in Rome. Here Ammirato's patron, who gave up his cardinal's hat to become the third grand duke of Tuscany in 1587, would visit him during his long last illness several years later. And here he would die, attended by a few close friends and by his faithful secretary and adopted son, Scipione Ammirato, Jr., in 1601.

Ammirato climbed back up to the terrace and turned about to behold what was probably the most spectacular of all the attractions of La Petraia: the view. The abrupt, bare, still unforested mountainside on the far left hid Fiesole from him, but it graciously moved aside just in time to reveal most of the tall gate towers of the city's walls toward which the house-lined streets stretched, like the fingers of an open hand, over the deep green of enclosed orchards. In the far foreground, he could see Duke Alessandro's cannon-proof Fortezza dal Basso trying to camouflage itself beneath a coating of grass and trees. And just above it, though in reality at the other extremity of the city, he could see Grand Duke Francesco's equally impregnable, but far more decorative, Fortezza del Belvedere, which served also to remind the citizens of the approach of the dinner hour by a blank shot fired every day at noon. Far in the distance he could see the Prato Magno, emerging like a giant whale out of the early morning mists. And down to the right he could watch the Arno, now withered beneath its artificial banks to half of what it had been after the last spring rains, a month earlier, as it flowed out of the city, skirted along the already browning hills on the south edge of the valley, and then plummeted into the pine-ridged gorge at Signa toward Montelupo, Pisa, and the sea.

A splendid sight! As he looked down on the crisscross of carefully cultivated fields of ripening wheat, on the rows of neatly tied vines, on the polka-dot patterns of dusty green olive trees, and on the occasional patches of mulberries that Grand Duke Francesco had cajoled proprietors into planting for the benefit of the Florentine silk industry—as he looked down on the patiently cared-for valley below him, Ammirato would have been somewhat surprised at the adjective "sterile" that the Venetian ambassador had applied to the land around Florence in 1588. True, the crenelated towers and high tiled roofs that peeked out from behind clusters of cypresses all over the hills and plains around him were intended mostly for pleasure and show, and not, like the agricultural enterprises into which the Venetian patriciate was pouring its money, as a capital investment. But then nature had not granted the bushy slopes and swampy flatlands of northern Tuscany any of the lush fertility of the Veneto; it was man, by centuries of hard work, who had turned it into a garden. It was thanks to man, moreover, that all Tuscany had become, as the ambassador's successor two years later had to admit, "most abundant in every kind of crop—so much so that it produces enough not only to supply all the needs of the inhabitants, but also to permit selling considerable amounts abroad"—at no small profit to Tuscan growers.

And yet Ammirato could have pointed out that both the ambassadors had exaggerated somewhat. For in spite of all the money the grand dukes had spent building drainage canals around Pisa and in the Valdinievole, and in spite of all the new plants they had imported from as far away as America, food production could still at times fail disastrously. Most of the land in Tuscany was still, as it had been for the past two centuries, in the hands of city-dwellers. And most Tuscan landowners still looked upon their estates as safe, rather than as potentially productive, investments. True, some of them had recently begun to admit agriculture as a subject worthy of discussion in the literary academies they belonged to. But none of them ever supposed that their discussions had anything to do with the practical problems of planting, harvesting, and marketing. Indeed, the "agronomes" of the late sixteenth century would have been surprised to find themselves credited, by their successors of the late eighteenth century, with the authorship of scientific technical manuals. Bernardo Davanzati wrote his treatise *On the Cultivation of Vines and Trees* for the same reason that he wrote all his other works: to show how well he could imitate the telegraphic prose of the Roman historian Tacitus. Giovanni Antonio Popoleschi wrote his treatise *On the Method of Constructing and Maintaining Bird Traps* to amuse his friends with clever anecdotes about the ornithological predilections of Alexander the Great. And Giovan Vittorio Soderini, the "bizarre and restless" nephew of the gonfaloniere of 1502-12 and a former law student at Bologna, wrote his treatise *On the Preservation of Vines* "in order that our language not be wanting in georgic compositions" and in order to pass away idle hours during a vacation at Luigi Alamanni's villa near Volterra.

Thus, in September 1589, when a flash flood destroyed most of the expected harvest all over Italy, and, two months later, another downpour turned much of Florence and the Arno plain into a vast, chilly lake, neither Ammirato nor anyone else could think of a solution. Periodic famines and floods, he decided, were simply part of the nature of things. Even Rome, after all, which had conquered the world, had never been able to conquer the Tiber. He could only be thankful that Florence was not wholly dependent on the land around it for sustenance. And he could be sure that it would be rescued from the next disaster as quickly as it had been from the last by the apparently limitless wealth and the proverbial business sagacity of Grand Duke Ferdinando, who had just discovered in the distant parts of Poland a new source of profit for himself and a new source of grain for the whole western Mediterranean.

Natural disasters were bad enough. But the Tuscan countryside was troubled by still another ailment that Ammirato found to be just as incurable and even more frightening: brigandage. He himself had had one terrifying run-in with brigands many years before in the mountains east of Naples, where he had barely escaped with his life after losing all of his belongings. To be sure, Tuscany was not the Kingdom of Naples or the Papal State, where legal and semilegal violence made extralegal violence almost inevitable. Yet the danger was never far away, particularly in the mountains beyond Pistoia, where chronic poverty and an ill-guarded frontier made law enforcement particularly difficult. For over a decade a wellborn cutthroat named Alfonso Piccolomini, who could boast of a family tree with two popes in it, had successfully played off Pope Sixtus V against the grand duke and the French against the Savoyards. Just the previous August, while Ammirato was still applauding Grand Duke Francesco for having had Piccolomini shipped off to get wounded in distant Flanders, the brigand had suddenly sneaked back across the Apennines with the secret connivance of the Spanish governor of Milan: Piccolomini's five hundred henchmen had quickly swelled into a horde among the poverty-stricken mountaineers. It had taken most of an army to clear the horde out of Tuscany; and it had taken constant diplomatic pressure and a good bit of bribery among the Papal officials in the Romagna to have Piccolomini himself hauled back to be hanged in front of the Palazzo Vecchio.

There was little chance, to be sure, that the well-tempered states of the late Cinquecento would quake before another John Hawkwood or a Marco di Sciarra, the famous *condottieri* of the fourteenth century. Bandits these days were thieves and assassins, not heroes. But Ammirato was highly sceptical about the effectiveness both of the Duke of Alcalá's project for a well-guarded highway to Puglia and of Pope Gregory XIII's policy of forbidding the storage of any robbable commodity outside city walls. He knew that the threat of terrifying punishments had so far done nothing but create more bandits. And he doubted that the much grander remedies he himself had proposed would have been much more effective. Brigandage, he reluctantly concluded, was an "incurable disease," one which even the best Roman consuls and emperors had been unable fully to cope with. It was a disease engendered as inevitably by all civil societies as boils were by human bodies, rats by houses, and vermin by garbage.

At least, Ammirato reflected, the countryside he now beheld would probably never again be ruined by rebellion or civil war. Fifty years had passed since the Battle of Montemurlo, and by now all the would-be successors to Filippo Strozzi and his sons had disappeared. Thirty years had passed since the last of the stiff-necked republicans had returned home from Montalcino, and nothing but an occasional campaign of wall-scribbling against the Jesuits had since ruffled the benevolent firmness of Medici rule in Siena. Moreover, fifteen years had passed since the last of the Florentine Brutuses, Orazio Pucci, had swung from the gallows as a sign of the futility of all further plots against the regime. Pucci had possessed none of the unscrupulous daring of Lorenzaccio, and he showed none of the generous idealism of Zanobi Buondelmonti and Jacopo da Diacceto, the would-be tyrannicides of the anti-Medici plot of 1522. He seems to have been animated by nothing more noble than a personal grudge, which twelve years of friendly gestures from the prince who had executed his father as a rebel had not managed to remove. Everyone in Florence would probably have laughed at the melodramatic scheme dreamed up by some of the overgrown teen-agers in his tiny blueblood gang in 1574—to butcher every single member of the Medici family at a banquet. But laughing had turned to pity when the assassins hired by the grand duke mercilessly—and unnecessarily—tracked down all over Europe the accomplices whose names Pucci had unheroically written down after an abortive attempt at suicide. Even Francesco must have realized that his dignity would have been better served by releasing Pucci after a paternal scolding. For once the incident was all over, he took regular evening strolls through the city in the company of only two or three unarmed gentlemen whenever he was in town. And it took a hysterical letter from none other than Caterina de' Ricci, the Dominican mystic whose suspicions were universally held to be warnings from God himself, to induce him to have the basement of the Uffizi searched before attending a performance of Giovanni de' Bardi's latest comedy on February 16, 1585. "Having now become completely accustomed to life under the dominion of an absolute prince," concluded the Venetian ambassador in 1589, "the country now enjoys a continuous peace and a most happy tranquillity."

There was even less chance that the fields of Tuscany would again be devastated by armies from abroad. The natural barriers along two sides of the grand duchy were amply supplemented by a string of heavy fortresses on the third; and a trained, equipped army of 35,000 native soldiers, ably commanded by loyal and well-paid generals, stood ready to man them in any emergency. The seacoasts were adequately guarded, especially now that the menace of Turkish raids had dwindled to only an occasional scare, by the military installations at Livorno and Portoferraio, by four big warships, and, when necessary, by the fleet of the Order of Santo Stefano. What force could not definitely prevent, moreover, diplomacy could avoid. The marriage of Cammilla Martelli's daughter Virginia to Cesare d'Este in 1585 put an end to the grand duke's ridiculous snobbery contest with the court of Ferrara, which at times had sharpened into raids back and forth across the ill-marked borders of the Garfagnana. The influential position of Cardinal Ferdinando in Rome, the scrupulous cordiality of Francesco toward Pope Sixtus V, and the filial protection accorded at Pratolino to the infant heir to the duchy of Bracciano notably diminished the endemic chaos along the sparsely populated frontier areas of the far south.

After his accession in 1587, Ferdinando rapidly perfected what his less courageous brother had begun. Francesco's actions had been guided by two fairly simple lines of policy: preventing any interference with his absolute authority in internal affairs, particularly on the part of emissaries from the Roman Curia, and avoiding any temptation to involve himself in the affairs of others. He was haunted by suspicions, it is true, and he kept a small army of spies roving about Italy just to make sure that nothing went wrong. But he remained to the last "perfectly happy with the state I already possess," as he told the Polish ambassadors who had tried to entice him with the crown of their distant kingdom; and he never entertained any "thought of undertaking greater things."

Ferdinando's actions were guided by the much more ambitious policy of preserving the peace, and what was left of the independence, of all Italy. He successfully arbitrated a border dispute in the north before the governor of Milan could take advantage of it. He quickly patched up the long quarrel with Venice over the indiscretions of his pious pirates of the Order of Santo Stefano. And he effectively checked the only Italian prince who failed to respond to his soothing assurances, the duke of Savoy, by threatening to attack Provence and to "buy" the French rights to the March of Saluzzo, which the Savoyards had recently seized.

Furthermore, Ferdinando had learned, as its cardinal-protector in Rome, that the Spanish lion was growling these days more than it cared to bite. And now that the Armada had been wrecked in the English Channel, he had no scruples about twisting the lion's tail in a way Francesco would never have dared to do. He started by declaring null and void his father's promise to clear all Medici family alliances with the king. He then went right ahead and arranged for a marriage with a French princess, Cristina of Lorraine—which was just what the Spanish ambassadors were bribing officials in Nancy to prevent. Finally, he cut off the flow of credit that his brother had felt obliged to sanction from his own well-stocked treasury to the perennially empty treasury of the king of Spain, fully aware that not a cent of it would ever be returned. To everyone's surprise, these audacious acts paid off. The Spanish envoy did show up at the wedding celebrations in 1589 in a rather bad humor. But at least he showed up; and he carried with him not only an official letter of congratulations but also an unconditional investiture for the State of Siena, which King Philip II still claimed as a feudal dependency.

Spain had passed the crest of its power, although Ferdinando was about the only Italian prince to suspect this. France was only beginning to recover from the ravages of civil war. The emperor no longer objected to the grand ducal title bestowed by Pope Pius V. And Ferdinando carefully protected himself against an eventual resurgence of France by marrying his niece Maria to King Henry IV whose reconciliation with the Papacy he had done so much to arrange.

The dream of Cosimo I had at last been realized. Tuscany was now wholly free from the danger of foreign occupation. Ferdinando could start thinking about a few adventures of his own abroad—in Marseilles, in the Aegean, and even in South America.

Ammirato suddenly broke off his meditations. By now the sun had risen halfway up the eastern sky, and its sharp rays had smothered the remnants of the refreshing morning breeze. His carriage was ready. He hurried away, fearful of being exposed to the torrential radiation of a Florentine summer noon before arriving in the city.

2

The city

An hour or so later, Ammirato had passed the customs officials at the gate and
was riding down between the severe, windowless walls of the convents and
monasteries that lined Via San Gallo: San Clemente and Sant'Agata on one side,
and, on the other, Santa Maria Regina Coeli, or the "Chiarito," where one of the
nuns kept the impeccably neat account books which, three hundred years later,
would permit a modern economic historian to chart price fluctuations on the
Florentine market for most of the sixteenth century. Just beyond the hospital of
Bonifazio, which shielded its orchards and well cared-for paupers from the world
outside, severity suddenly gave way to gaiety—first in the gracious palace of the
Pandolfini, built by Sangallo and Raffaello some fifty years earlier, and then, just
beyond a spacious garden, in the cloister of the wealthy confraternity of the
Scalzi, long famous for its frescoes by Andrea del Sarto. Turning first to the left,
and then, between two long walls, to the right, he came upon the broad white
facade of the Casino, once the site of Lorenzo the Magnificent's permanent art
fairs, which Buontalenti had recently converted into one of "the most glorious
buildings in all Italy": he had added considerably to its elegance with delicately
carved window casings and a wavy stone ribbon beneath a miniature balcony,
and he had carefully preserved the geometrical simplicity of the original form.

Simplicity—the subservience of external decoration to the basic lines of
architectural structure—was the essence of beauty in Florence, Ammirato realized.
It was echoed in the still-bare entrance to the basilica of San Marco, just across
the street. It was reflected, along the first block of Via Larga (now Via Cavour), in
the tiny garlands and miniature balustrade that Giovan Antonio Dosi had set off
against the neutral face of the new house of the Pestellini. It was recorded even
in the immense Palazzo Medici, in which, according to the contemporary guidebook by Francesco Bocchi, "the simplicity of all the various parts" made the
whole "wondrously resplendent in all that is beautiful." Even Bartolomeo

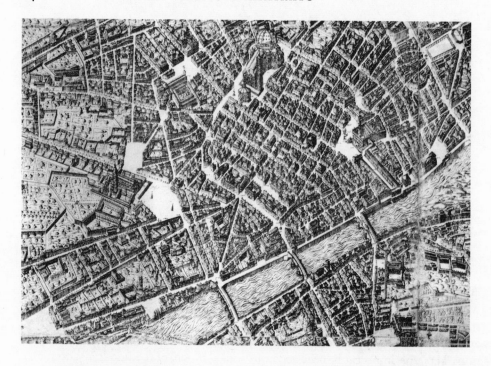

9. Stefano Bonsignori and Bonaventura Billocardi, Map of Florence, 1584, detail

Ammannati, who seldom passed up a chance to experiment with new forms, had dared add nothing to the stark exterior of the little church and college opposite the palace, which he designed, built, and endowed for the Jesuits. At the other end of Via de' Martelli, just behind the row of houses that still shielded it from the baptistry, Dosio had so carefully avoided breaking up the straight lines of the facade and the regular succession of immense arches in the courtyard of the new episcopal palace that the archbishop once complained about having to live in a "hospital."

To be sure, Florentine architects were not averse to novelty. They willingly covered flat facades with elaborate colored arabesques. And they put aside all the restraint they might feel before stone whenever they were faced with papier-mâché instead. Even the well-disciplined Buontalenti let his imagination run wild on the stage sets for the baptism of Prince Filippo and on the dripping grotto in the courtyard of Palazzo Pitti: the scrambled confusion of his designs for the facade of the cathedral, as well as his financially profitable experiments with fireworks displays, soon earned him the nickname of "Bernardo delle Girandole." But the architects never let decoration obscure structure. Santi di Tito, a painter as well as an architect, used just enough decoration on the house he built for the Zanchini to draw the eye of the viewer from the square windows on the ground floor to the arcades on the *piano nobile*; and he avoided it almost entirely on the house he built for himself on Via delle Ruote. Indeed, in Santi di Tito's sober, balanced, and at times almost nude buildings, the Quattrocento seemed suddenly

10. Buontalenti, Portal of the Casino

11. Ammannati, *Fountain of Neptune*, detail
Piazza della Signoria

to descend from the past to warn the late Cinquecento against the exaggerations of its more popular architects. Just at the moment when Romans were boldly experimenting with the first stages of what later would be called baroque styles, Florentines were cautiously reinforcing what had been bequeathed to them from the past. And no one could appreciate as well as Ammirato the way in which new and old blended together in his adopted city in one harmonious tribute to the genius of its citizens. "Cast your eyes about you," he proclaimed, texts and documents in hand, "You will see nothing but marvels and wonders—loggias, granaries, two public palaces, four bridges, and so many towers . . . that no one can count them." Ephesus waned before the splendor of Florence's temples; and Corinth yielded before the magnificence of its private dwellings.

Ammirato was not a Florentine by birth. He had been raised in Lecce, a quiet but relatively prosperous agricultural center down in the heel of Italy. He had been educated in Naples, and he long afterward remembered with nostalgia the long walks along the bay, "that marvelous cup wrought by the hand of nature." He had lived briefly in Venice, where he had met many of the current leaders of Italian culture. And he had once thought of settling down in Rome, where one high-ranking curial official assured him he was expected more eagerly than the Messiah among the Jews. But he had established connections with Florence from his earliest days. In Lecce he had come to know and admire Braccio Martelli, the former bishop of Fiesole and one of the "model bishops" of the Catholic Reform, who had been transferred as far away from Florence as possible in punishment for his anticurial position at the Council of Trent. In Naples he had met several wealthy Florentine business agents, and from them he had learned to make favorable contrasts between the Florentines, who were "still faithful to the ancient customs of Italy," and Neapolitans, who spent most of their time "chasing after whores and boys, wallowing in the pleasures of the table, and tossing away a whole fortune in a single night of gambling." He had not hesitated for a moment when Grand Duke Cosimo suddenly offered him a position as state historiographer at the respectable salary of 300 *scudi* a year. As soon as he arrived, he resolved never to leave again:

> Up, then, with new arguments!
> Speak to me of piety
> toward the agéd father,
> toward the sweet virgin sisters I leave behind.
> Remind me of my homeland, of the sea;
> stir me, beseech me,
> put forth your every effort;
> string me round with the cleverest of plots:
> You'll never get me back!
>
> (*Contro la speranza, 1569*)

Indeed, as Ammirato started down the second most fashionable street in Florence, Via de' Tornabuoni, he wondered why anyone ever left so pleasant a city. The recent transformation of vigor into civility and the quest for power into a quest for comfort was aptly illustrated by the palaces on either side of the street. To the left stood the gigantic cornices and the repelling stone blocks (*bugné*) of the fortress-palace of the Strozzi, a monument of times gone by when residences were meant first of all to be defended. On the right stood the smiling facade, with windows, not bars, and with a door, not a gate, on the ground floor, which Dosio had just built for Ammirato's frequent host, Lorenzo Giacomini—a monument of an age when residences were meant solely to be lived in and enjoyed.

Some Florentines, it is true, still lived up to their old reputation as the world's "fifth element." A whole colony of them was resident in Rome and was soon to flourish once again under another Tuscan pope, Clement VIII. An even larger colony was resident in Venice, where it supplied most of the skilled labor for the growing wool industry and where it eventually took over much of the banking business. The Guicciardini were still settled in Antwerp, the Capponi and the Rinuccini in Lyon, the Vecchietti and the Bardi in Lisbon, the Cavalcanti and the Giraldi in Madrid, the Cecchi in Cracow, and the Alberti in Lwow. Some Florentines wandered still farther afield. Giambattista Vecchietti, son of a Florentine silk merchant in Calabria and advisor to the grand duke's oriental press in Rome, had gone to Egypt, Syria, Persia, and beyond. And Filippo Sassetti, who had worked his way through the University of Pisa and spent long hours over genealogical tables with Ammirato, went all the way to Goa in India, where he died in 1589. Similarly, Florentines who stayed at home were as curious as anyone else in Europe at the time about their expatriate countrymen's adventures. They eagerly read all the more or less open letters that Sassetti sent back on every ship from India; and they plied him with commissions—for notes on fauna and flora, for traces of Alexander's armies, for snakebite remedies, mahogany knickknacks, and scented wood. They were enchanted by the four Japanese ambassadors who debarked at Livorno in 1584. Indeed, they permitted their puzzled guests to go on to Rome, laden with presents, only after they had established the "fact" that Japanese lived for 150 years, never got sick, and extracted wax from trees. Finally, they were still interested enough in recent Spanish discoveries in the New World to applaud such poetic panegyrics of them as Giulio Cesare Stella's *Colombiade* and Giovan Battista Strozzi's *America,* which were read out loud in the Accademia degli Alterati.

But Ammirato knew that this curiosity seldom went much farther than what could be read or heard—that returning travelers were expected to amuse, rather than instruct, the Florentine academies with the reports requested of them, and that except for those who chose to change their names from Lorenzo to Laurens and to look for wives in France rather than, as was customary, in Florence, very few of them passed up a chance to return home or to make their children return. For instance, when the banker Cosimo Martelli died at Lyon in 1580, he left 2,500 *scudi* to each of his two brothers on the condition that one marry a Florentine and the other take his family back to live like a gentleman in Florence—even though a third brother now called himself *Hugolin,* not *Ugolino,* and had advanced from the family bank to a respectable position in the Gallican episcopacy. Perhaps he too, like Duti in Leonardo Salviati's comedy *Il granchio,* felt himself

> drawn by an occult virtue, the love of my country, to pass my remaining days where all my forefathers have lived in respectable condition for lo, these many hundreds of years.

Moreover, those Florentines who might once have sent their sons abroad for an education now hesitated to expose them to "the grossness and drunkenness" of the Germans, the "venomous heresies" of the Flemish and English, the "ferocity and cruelty" of the French, and, above all, the "vanity and false pride" of the Spanish, which had had a very unfortunate effect on that dissolute swaggerer Don Pietro de' Medici. Similarly, those whom business or adventure enticed out of the city usually ended up disenchanted. They rebaptized the Spanish capital, somewhat inelegantly, as *Merdid*; they proclaimed the position of *podestà* of the Tuscan village of Montespertoli to be far preferable to that of viceroy of Aragon; and they wrote back nostalgically that, in comparison, even colorful Malabar was a great bore—at least for young Giovanni Buondelmonti. "Here [in Spain] among such a throng of people," the ambassador Bongianni Gianfigliazzi confessed to Ammirato in 1583, "I cannot but recall at every hour of the day the good friends left behind in Florence. May it please God to bring me back safely and quickly!" Some, of course, were forced to leave because of their inability to consent to the religious establishment. But even Fausto Sozzini, or Socinius, the apostle of Anti-Trinitarianism, had found what he later denounced as "the seat of sloth and vanity" attractive enough for almost a decade to warrant his keeping his convictions to himself. And Francesco Pucci, after wandering for some time about Germany, declared himself willing to retract whatever "God's Vicar" asked of him, provided only that the grand duke "open the gates of Tuscany" to him once again.

By now Ammirato's carriage had turned left at the approach to Ammannati's gracious new bridge, the Ponte Santa Trinita, guarded at each end by two of the four seasons. And as he rode up the recently opened bank (*lungarno*) along the north side of the river toward the Ponte Vecchio, it may have occurred to him that this self-satisfaction—this tendency to think that everything of importance took place in Florence and to consider the rest of the world as merely a grab bag of curiosities—could be a bit stultifying. Certainly his own exercises in political philosophy might have benefited from some of Giovanni Botero's notes on the governments of Turkey, China, and Mexico, as well as from some reflection on the theory of sovereignty of his famous French colleague, Jean Bodin. But none of the Florentine critics and poets he knew read anything but Italian poetry— none of them, that is, except the somewhat erratic Antonio degli Albizi, who once interrupted a lecture series on Petrarch with some comments about a certain French Petrarchian named *Ronsardo*. None of the Florentine moralists had ever heard of Montaigne. None of the playwrights had ever heard of Shakespeare or Marlowe. And they would have not understood what they might have heard, since only businessmen and the intimates of the grand duchess spoke French, only

Albizi spoke German, and absolutely no one at all spoke English. Florentines
had so long taught others that they had forgotten how to learn. They never
stopped to think that the vitality and autonomy of their own cultural tradition
might be strengthened, rather than diluted, by exposure to stimuli from the
outside. And Ammirato was no exception.

It may also have occurred to him, as the driver followed the traffic into the
busy Via Por Santa Maria, that some of the exiles were coming home for other than
purely sentimental reasons. The civil wars in France had all but ruined Lyon, and
the high ransoms levied on the foreign colonies every time the city passed from
the hands of one party into the hands of another had already driven one Florentine
banker to drown himself in the Sâone and had forced all but one of the rest of them
to close up shop. Similarly, the Sack of Antwerp had wiped out most of what was
still left of Florentine commercial operations in Flanders after the English fleet
had blocked the maritime route to Spain. The systematic draining of the Papal
State for the sake of beautifying Rome and defending the borders of Catholic
Christendom had made Florentine tax-farmers ever less able to meet their pledges.
And the lack of productive investment opportunities had forced the Florentine
bankers in Rome to throw their money into the private bond issues of spendthrift
cardinals and, worse yet, into the immensely popular, but disastrously unproductive, game of speculating on future papal nominations. Four of them went
bankrupt when Sixtus V created the wrong cardinals in 1587. Several others were
caught short by Gregory XIV's prohibition of bets on the election of his successor.
All of them were constantly harassed by Pius V's anachronistic and antieconomic
usury laws. And none of them could successfully compete with the new semipublic
Banco di Santo Spirito, which hid its interest rates behind the facade of charity.
Hence, the many handsome new palaces that were embellishing the face of
Florence were not all signs or instruments of growing wealth. More often they
were simply *pietra serena* mausoleums of once-lucrative and now liquidated
international corporations. They served not to reinforce public confidence in the
business ventures of the proprietors, but to drain capital out of production and
into consumption.

To be sure, the failure of some of its foreign investments had not yet robbed
Florence of its vitality as a commercial and manufacturing capital—as Ammirato
could have noticed by looking into the well-stocked shops as he approached the
business center of the city around the palace of the Wool Guild, or *Arte della Lana*.
Fine wool cloth, Florence's principal export commodity, had been hard hit by
the recession of 1581–85, when a drop in demand, particularly in Sicily and Spain,
coincided with an influx of money—partly from Rome, where Pope Sixtus V put
5 million new *scudi* into circulation, and partly from Medina del Campo, where the
greatest of the Spanish merchant bankers, Simón Ruiz, suddenly found himself
overwhelmed with liquid assets. In 1584 wool prices dropped to 20 percent of
their former levels, and by 1589 wool production had dropped to one-half of

what it had been in 1572. Several prominent bankers followed the declining curve into bankruptcy: first Strozzo Strozzi, then Bernardo Soldani, then Piero Canigiani in Pisa. But a softening in one sector of the economy was compensated for by growth in the others. Silk manufacturing continued to prosper, to the point at which it absorbed not only most of the raw silk of Calabria and Sicily, but also all that now produced, thanks to the grand duke's encouragement, in the Lunigiana and the Pistoiese. When demand fell in one place, Florentine silk merchants were quick to find new markets: in the West Indies, for example, where they were favored by privileges from the Spanish crown, and in Poland, where one Bernardo Soderini, "un gentilhombre muy noble y honrrado y rico,"* made enough money to maintain an estate estimated at 80,000 *scudi*. Raw wool continued to be an important article of commerce, thanks in part to the well-known wisdom of Florentine wool buyers, to whom the Spanish herdsmen still sold much of each year's clippings. And what could no longer be disposed of to domestic manufacturers was shipped off to clients in Venice.

Similarly, the losses of its competitors often turned out to be Florence's gain. The closing of Antwerp led the Portuguese to redirect their pepper shipments to Germany through Livorno; and although Grand Duke Francesco wisely backed away from purchasing a monopoly from them, most of the business fell into the hands of the Manelli when the two Portuguese agents moved on to Venice in 1581. The plundering of the Kingdom of Naples lined Florentine as well as Genoese and Spanish pockets—not only those of the grand duke, who was one of the largest nonresident landowners, but also those of his subjects like Ludovico Serristori, who, to the horror of the Apostolic visitor, invested the revenues from his ecclesiastical benefices in his family's commercial company in Florence. And the renewal of civil war in the Netherlands and the preparations for the Armada against England provided the iron mines in Elba with a constant stream of orders for cannon balls. Most important of all, the attempt of King Philip II of Spain to free himself from the stranglehold of the Genoese bankers led momentarily to a shift in the market for *asientos* (the commissions to supply gold to the troops in Flanders in anticipation of the arrival of the next silver fleet in Seville) from Genoa to Florence. The grand duke led the way by overlooking Philip's haughty language and humbly accepting the very attractive trade concessions he won for his merchants in Spain. His lead was soon followed by two big private consortia: the Strozzi-Carnesecchi Company in 1580 and the Avena-Caccia Company in 1582. Florentine banks eventually proved incapable of meeting the demands made on them, and the Genoese succeeded in keeping control of the Wall Street of late-sixteenth-century Europe: the so-called "Besançon Fair" at Piacenza, where all major financial transactions were cleared. In the meantime, Florentines had won at least a modest place in the risky but

* "A very noble, honored, and rich gentleman": in Spanish in the original letter of Baltasar Suárez to Simón Ruiz.

highly profitable business of international credit. What they had won was further
secured by Grand Duke Ferdinando's creation of a subsidiary money market at
Pisa in 1596. Their place was still secure enough in the third and fourth decades
of the following century to permit them to challenge the Genoese once again,
right in their own domain at Piacenza.

Thus Florentines had some grounds for being relatively optimistic about
the state of the economy. Prosperity seemed to be reflected in the recovery of the
city's population, which rose from 59,557 in 1551 to something approaching
the archbishop's estimate of 80,000 in 1589. It seemed also to be reflected in the
rise of wages. To be sure, real wages—that is, wages calculated in food prices
rather than in money—declined in Florence, as they did all over Europe at the
time. But at least they declined much less rapidly: only from 108.88 to 94.34
index points for master masons between 1540 and 1600. And monetary wages
rose accordingly: from 50 to 90 points for weavers, notwithstanding the recession
in the wool industry, between 1550 and 1590. Prosperity seemed to be guaranteed
by the 7 million *scudi* that Grand Duke Francesco was said to have amassed in
his treasury. And it seemed to be directed toward further expansion in the future,
both by Grand Duke Ferdinando's ambitious overseas schemes, and by his
success in turning Livorno into one of the principal emporiums of the western
Mediterranean. As one observer wrote in 1598, "our countrymen get lots of
money out of other countries* and send forth lots of merchandise. Many of them
have grown rich in the cities of Italy or in Flanders, France, Germany, and
England. And when they return home with what they have earned, it naturally
comes into the possession of their relatives in Tuscany."

Yet the unpleasant sight of beggars on all the street corners and in front of
all the churches may have suggested to Ammirato that this optimism was not
always completely justified. He himself thought of mendicancy as a self-contained
phenomenon, one attributable to no other cause than the "idleness" (*ozio*) of
the mendicants; and he could think of no better solution for it than the kind of
public works projects he could see now across the Piazza della Signoria (or the
Piazza del Granduca, as it was then called), where the grand duke had just begun
construction on a large, but unnecessary extension for the rear of the Palazzo
Vecchio. Other observers were less superficial. The Venetian ambassador put the
blame on Grand Duke Francesco for having raised indirect taxes. The former
bank clerk Bernardo Davanzati, in one of his very few violent outbursts, put the
blame on "princes" in general, without specifying which ones, for having
reduced the florin to one-fifth its original value. Shopkeepers put the blame on
gambling, which they complained had "grown to such a point that [their]

---

* The expression "get money out of [*cavano denari*]" better corresponds to contemporary
notions of the nature of wealth than the modern equivalent: "make money in." The inelegant
repetition of the word "country" is in the original: *paesani* and *paesi*.

business had fallen off gravely." Apparently the magistrates agreed with the shopkeepers, for they wore themselves out trying to prohibit bets on anything, then excluding only those on the sex of expected children of members of the ruling house, then placing them all under the supervision of a Bureau on Bets for Papal Elections and Promotions, and then prohibiting them all, quite as futilely, once again.

Actually, the causes of what appear now to have been the signs of impending economic stagnation were much deeper than anyone at the time could have imagined. First of all, the rise in wheat prices—from an index number of 51 in 1560 to 123 in 1590—may have benefited the landed proprietors. But it certainly did not benefit the tenant farmers (*mezzadri*), who usually had barely enough for their own consumption after giving half of each year's harvest to their landlords. And their real income is estimated to have fallen from 138.90 in 1520–29 to 81.17 in 1600. No wonder, then, that so many of them gave up, preferring the free, if inadequate, soup lines in the city to hard and profitless work in the country. Second, the "economic miracle" of the decades after 1559 had been accomplished with only one minor technological innovation: the *ricorsa* and the *accomandite* contracts, which gave somewhat greater flexibility to the temporary partnerships upon which all Florentine commercial and industrial enterprises had previously been based. In general, Florentine businessmen continued to follow the methods of their forefathers and to ignore even the inventions of their close neighbors— like the experiments conducted in Bologna in the 1580s with a grain-sowing machine and the new credit instruments devised by the Banco dello Spirito Santo in Naples. Third, political expediency often took precedence over economic interest. Thus, when the grand duke decided not to put an end to the profitable and pious piracy of his knights of Santo Stefano, who kept Livorno well stocked with plunder from Turkish merchantmen, Florence lost what careful diplomacy at Constantinople had almost won for it: a part in the current revival of the Levant trade. When he decided to purchase the good will of the king of Spain at the enormous price of 1,414,667 *scudi* worth of *asientos,* he tied the Florentine economy to a royal treasury on the verge of its third bankruptcy in a half century and to a national economy on the verge of collapse.

More important still, the institutions of Florentine manufacturing and commerce proved incapable of changing with the times. Instead of encouraging diversification, the guilds merely tightened their old restrictions. Instead of looking for new products and new markets, they merely repeated with tiring monotony the words "conserve," "restore," "maintain." Instead of reducing their overhead, they freed their formerly volunteer officials from the obligation of engaging actively in business; and they thus burdened themselves with a professional bureaucracy that followed the tendency of all other bureaucracies to multiply: to forty-three employees in the Linen Guild by 1578, and from six to fifty-one in the Por Santa Maria Guild by 1589.

Most important of all, business went out of fashion among the very citizens who might have been able to stimulate or redirect it: the intellectuals. In the twenty-two years that he had been in Florence, Ammirato had often heard echoes of the solid business mores of the good old days, which everyone still professed to admire. He may have heard the young Filippo Valori rant against "those wiseacres who deny"—in spite of the well-known examples of Venice and Athens and in spite of the statues of famous merchant-philosophers that adorned his father's house near San Pier Maggiore—"that liberal studies can flourish . . . in a city where most [citizens] are engaged in mercantile traffic." And he had certainly heard the remarkable discourse of Marcello Adriani to the Accademia degli Alterati in 1589 about the social utility of private wealth, the nobility of manufacturing, and the beneficial effects of commerce upon world peace—a discourse that sounds today like a cross between the views of the Quattrocento humanist Matteo Palmieri and those of the eighteenth-century political economist Adam Smith.

But these were isolated voices. Filippo Sassetti was the only example that Adriani could cite for his ideal in his own generation. And actually Sassetti never said any of the things that Adriani attributed to him. In fact, skilled businessman though he was, he openly affected an ignorance of and a disdain for business; and he lamented having to return to it in 1578 as a tragic sacrifice of an infinitely more worthy vocation for letters. Similarly, Bernardo Davanzati, the only Florentine writer of the period who treated such subjects in print, was careful to remind his readers of what they could have gathered after the first sentence: that his treatise *On Money* was meant for their "entertainment, not instruction." Tommaso Buoninsegni, the only other writer who pretended to treat of such subjects, intended his *Treatise on Just and Ordinary Commerce* merely as an index to recent papal bulls; and he accordingly took his information about commerce not from current practices, which he pretended to know something about, but from Thomas Aquinas, Aristotle, and the Old Testament.

Even those wealthy businessmen who claimed also be be intellectuals did all they could to cover up their principal occupations. No one could guess from all his much-applauded and much-padded orations that Sassetti's cousin, Lorenzo Giacomini, actually soiled his hands by running boats between Pisa and Genoa. No one could guess that that model of all Florentine gentlemen and later patron of Galileo, Filippo Salviati, who "never appeared at a dance, a tourney, a joust, or any public spectacle without his entrance first being admired for its magnificence," who could outdo everyone in singing, dancing, throwing the javelin, and playing musical instruments, who taught himself Latin in one year at the age of forty-four and quickly romped through Sallust, Tacitus, and the whole of Pier Vettori's editions of Aristotle—no one could guess that this reincarnation of Castiglione's courtier actually made enough money from heaven-knows-what sordid affairs (his biographer did not think them worth mentioning) to offer to equip a third of the army the grand duke was thinking of sending off to the War of Monferrato.

Leon Battista Alberti's attempt to work out an ethical justification of economic activity was no longer even a memory. Buyers and sellers were ejected from the temple of the muses. Begging money from a prince was considered more noble than earning it. The omnipotent Aristotle had disenfranchised everyone who supported society instead of just living off it. And no one was left to rescue Florence from the next economic crisis. When the Ricci bank suddenly collapsed on September 17, 1595, the Florentine intellectuals simply turned their backs and thought of something more pleasant—or more noble.

By now the carriage had emerged from the narrow Via de' Calzaiuoli and exposed its passenger to the sight of the bare front of the cathedral, which the grand duke had just shorn of its classical facade and left in the form of raw bricks. It turned right at the foot of Giotto's tower, rolled past the Confraternity of the Misericordia, and stopped in front of the cathedral workshop-warehouse, the Opera del Duomo. Ammirato stepped cautiously onto the pavement, hobbled through the gate, and walked slowly up to the halls of the Accademia degli Alterati, where his companions were already awaiting him.

3

How Ammirato solved Machiavelli's dilemma by putting politics and religion together again

Ammirato felt a particular affection for the Accademia degli Alterati. He was a rather isolated scholar—one who occasionally showed up at court on a special invitation from the grand duchess, but who usually wandered alone from one library to another or closeted himself with his books and papers at La Petraia. The learned games and serious discussions put on by his wellborn associates had become, especially in recent years, his favorite form of recreation.

Indeed, recreation was one of the academy's chief functions, as Ammirato had learned on those memorable evenings back in 1587. On March 17, the academy proposed a debate about the propriety of the word *urn,* previously used to designate the box into which the members were obliged to deposit their original compositions. The first speaker, Giovan Battista Strozzi, opened the session with a well-pondered, quotation-filled "opinion." But no sooner had he got beyond the first few sentences than Ammirato rushed in to challenge him on a question of precedence—just as if Ammirato were the ambassador of one Italian prince trying to push his way into the imperial chapel ahead of the ambassador of another. When he succeeded at last in winning a favorable decision from the chair, the meeting degenerated into pandemonium, "everything being filled with confusion, tumults, and noise." That was just the opportunity Giuliano Gianfigliazzi had been waiting for. He accused the regent of "cowardliness, timidity, and do-nothingness" and called upon Ammirato to deliver an oration against him.

The ensuing chaos made a suspension of the debate unavoidable. When it was resumed three days later, Ammirato was ready with a new tactic. He rose to proclaim himself "dictator" and to demand as his own the most prominent seat in the hall. The regent, who happened to be the same Marcello Adriani whose discourse on the nobility of commerce the secretary did not think worth recording, tried to counter by ordering the seat removed. When the maneuver failed, "he took the seat in his hand, and with great strength and force broke it to pieces on the ground." At that point the fighting passed from questions of procedure to questions of political theory: whether the assembly was superior to the regent, or vice versa, with perhaps a chilling reminder of the version of the same question which had been carefully sidetracked by the Florentine Senate back in 1537. Adriani tried to stall a decision by calling on Strozzi to condemn Ammirato for his unconstitutional intervention. And when Ammirato tried to defend himself by evoking the precedent of a half-dozen Roman consuls, Strozzi "openly declared war on him"; and chaos ensued once again. The next meeting, on April 16, opened in a tense calm, with a number of deliberately dragged-out administrative details. Then silence, in trembling expectation. Finally the apprehensive regent could stand it no longer; and when he asked Strozzi if perhaps he hadn't something to say, the news was out! He and Ammirato had secretly made peace. That brought the fury of the assembly on them both, and one passionate orator after another rose to remind his panicky listeners that the ruin of the Roman Republic had begun with the reconciliation of Caesar and Pompey. . . .

It was an amusing game, and Ammirato was an expert player.

At the same time, he felt a particular obligation toward the Alterati. It may have been relatively easy for outsiders like the Piedmontese Carlo da Pozzo and "provincials" like Piero Usimbardi of Colle to climb up through the Medicean bureaucracy to distinguished positions, even in such recognized Florentine monopolies as the Tuscan episcopacy and the Senate. But to an outsider whose only claim to distinction was literary, and especially to one who, as a Neapolitan, might be suspected of the taint of Spanish manners, the doors were barred tight. The Florentine patriciate jealously guarded one of the last domains it was still permitted to control, that of culture; and it was little disposed to yield even to a special recommendation from the prince. Fortunately, Ammirato had arrived in Florence just a few months after the first "seven gentlemen began to hold exercises together for composing lectures and poems . . . and to order themselves under a small number of laws." Few of the original members were more than twenty years old at the time, and most of them had a rather rebellious attitude toward their stuffy elders and conformist contemporaries in the Accademia Fiorentina. Hence, they probably found it convenient to have as a mentor one whose experiences with other academies elsewhere might be of some practical help and whose lack of acquaintance with the city had kept him free of compromises with the establishment.

It may, indeed, have been in part the guiding hand of Ammirato—or *Il Trasformato,* to give him the academic name he chose in memory of the Accademia dei Trasformati ("The Transformed") in Lecce—that saved the Alterati ("The Altered") from the fate of the many similar groups that mushroomed during the 1560s "in every village, in every hamlet" of the peninsula, only to die when their requests for subsidies were ignored. The original members had stayed on after they began to make a name for themselves. New members with already established reputations had then joined them. And recently even a prince had accepted an offer of election—the talented general, architect, and musician, Don Giovanni de' Medici, Cosimo's illegitimate son by Eleonora degli Albizi, whose adventures in romance were to shock the matrons of the court during the following decades. Old and new members shared the enthusiasm that rescued the academy from occasional moments of lethargy—like that time in April 1580 when the regent was left "to pace up and down all alone for an hour" while his negligent colleagues "strolled about the streets" outside. Some of them established a branch in Pisa. Others would reconvene after dinner to carry on the discussion begun in the regular meeting. Almost everyone turned up at the biannual "general assemblies" in February and July. And no one ever missed the frequent banquet meetings, at which Ammirato himself sometimes acted as host.

This combination of serious discussion and conviviality, this alternation between lectures on poetics and lectures on "whether philosophy has a place among the cups," had made the academy so popular by the late 1580s that it was running serious competition with what, after all, was supposed to be the center of cultural life in Florence. Or at least the difficulties encountered by the Accademia Fiorentina in getting someone to accept the presidency for 1584 and in persuading its large membership to show up for the dull round of formal eulogies and the routine bestowal of honors on distinguished Italian writers eventually led the consul, in 1588, to complain that the "private" academy was robbing the "public" academy of its best talent. The Alterati took the complaint as a compliment. They were so pleased with their institution that they had haughtily turned down, just four months before, a perfectly reasonable proposal by two newer academies, the Desiosi and the Crusca, to join forces—and, still worse, they had censured those of their associates who had dared attend meetings of other academies or who had spoken in favor of the merger.

Yet today, June 27, 1591, Ammirato had a special reason for being present. It was his turn to speak from the rostrum, and he had promised his colleagues at the preceding meeting finally to read them a chapter or two from the book he had been working at, off and on, for the past six or seven years, the *Discourses on Cornelius Tacitus*. Most of them had probably already seen some of the chapters, either in manuscript or, as one recent historian has suggested, in an earlier, incomplete edition. And all of them were interested in Tacitus, who had become, particularly since the appearance of the editions and commentaries of Beatus Rhenanus and Andrea Alciati, one of the most widely read ancient authors in all Europe. Ammirato had read enough of Tacitus as a student to be able to decorate his earliest dialogues with the usual tales about Tiberius and Caligula. He was probably aware of the critical editions just then in the process of emendation and correction by the greatest of all the sixteenth-century textual critics, the

Belgian scholar Justus Lipsius. He may even have run across some of the able Italian Tacitists—Paolo Manuzio, Latino Latini, Francesco Benci—who had welcomed Lipsius to Rome, just as Ammirato was passing through on his way to Florence, in 1569. He may have seen the heavily annotated volumes of Lipsius's friend and critic Marc-Antoine Muret, who had been teaching in Rome since 1560. He may have seen some of the preparatory work by the Florentine scholar Curzio Pichena, based on the most ancient of all the manuscript sources, the Mediceus I and II, which were kept just three blocks away in the Laurenziana Library.

But it was the Alterati who first had drawn Ammirato's attention to Tacitus as a subject for serious study. In July 1583, Bernardo Davanzati had submitted to the academy the first book of his translation of the *Annals*; and from then on the academicians, Ammirato included, regularly discussed each succeeding book as it came out, right down through three complete drafts to the final version of the entire *Works,* dedicated to them in 1599. To be sure, the shy, retiring Davanzati, who had been forced against his will into accepting even so ordinary a position as the consulate of the Accademia Fiorentina and who finally produced his treatise *On Money* only after considerable pressure from the academy in 1587, seldom could summon up enough courage even to attend the meetings of his most loyal supporters. But he had very personal reasons for studying Tacitus. He found in the author of the *Annals* and the *Histories* of imperial Rome a person much like himself—namely, an incorrigible idolizer of the good old days. He was delighted to learn how to let Tacitus speak for him from the way Tacitus had put his own opinions into the mouth of the British general Galgacus. And he carried out what he had learned by burying away in his unpublished critical notes the occasional blasts, as passionate as they were vague and unjust, against the Medicean regime, which had exiled his father, confiscated his patrimony, and barred his access to public office. He may also have found that translating the works of another provided his uncreative mind with an intellectually respectable relief from the distasteful task of making money, which his poverty forced on him after his return from an apprenticeship with the Capponi bank at Lyon in 1547, and which he managed to shield from both friends and posterity with as much blushing meticulousness as any of Henry James's expatriate Bostonians.

More important, Davanzati discovered in "the briefest writer of all times" an excellent weapon against the excessive exaltation of the humanist principle of "copiousness"—the "sea of eloquence," that is, which one victim of too many academic orations warned was rapidly drowning out Tuscan prose. Davanzati shunned polemics and never mentioned names. But his friend Francesco Bonciani made it perfectly clear that his Tacitus was directed, or could have been directed, against one of Davanzati's sometime companions, the nervous and nearsighted, but also brilliant and unscrupulous dictator of linguistic propriety, Leonardo Salviati. Salviati had established a literary reputation back in 1562 by dragging

out a funeral eulogy for Don Garzia de' Medici for more than three hours—all
without ever inserting a single concrete fact about the deceased fourteen-year-old
prince. He had rapidly become a master at avoiding almost any issue, from ancient
gymnastics to the war in Flanders, by piling words on words—by adding
meaningless epithets, like "a most flourishing city in Greece" to already obvious
references like "Athens," by throwing in two adjectives when one would do, and
by strangling his heroes in garlands of meaningless metaphors:

> Amid so many flashes, amid so many rays, amid so many lamps, amid so
> many lights, amid so many stars, there stood firm the flash, the ray, the lamp,
> the light, the star of Don Luigi [d'Este].

And to think that Salviati thought of doing this sort of thing to Tacitus himself!

Davanzati must have shuddered at the prospect, for his standard of style was
exactly the opposite of Salviati's. Both would have agreed that "we speak in order
to be understood and to move others," since the statement had been a commonplace for a century and a half. But Davanzati insisted further that "the shorter
and simpler our speech, the better and more quickly it is understood and moves."
That was the standard which Tacitus had held up against the Ciceronians of the
first century A.D. That was the standard that Justus Lipsius, Marc-Antoine
Muret, and even Montaigne borrowed from Tacitus on behalf of the anti-
Ciceronians of the late sixteenth century. It was the standard that quickly turned
the Tuscan Tacitus into a minor classic of Italian literature, that made the
translator the stylistic mentor of the Alterati, and that provided even Ammirato
with the inspiration for the terse ablative absolutes (*Teodosio trovatili prodi*) and
squashed-down neologisms (*inconfidenza*) of his own Tacitan prose. And it may
have been Davanzati's stylistic innovations that were ultimately responsible for
the development of the clear, crisp, and down-to-earth periods of the Galilean
scientists of the following generation.

Most important of all, Tacitus enabled Davanzati to come to the rescue of
his countrymen at a particularly grave moment in the history of Florentine
culture. In 1578 they had suddenly run across a new book ("that French book"
as Davanzati still called it many years later) by a certain Henri Estienne, whom,
apparently, no one recognized as one of the most eminent Hellenists of the age.
Estienne had long insisted on the superiority of French to all other modern
languages, and he had led a violent campaign to rid it of what he held to be
unnatural and unnecessary Italianisms. He now added still another argument:
not only was French closer to the best of all possible languages, Greek, but it was
closer to Latin as well. As proof he cited the experiment of that tireless translator
of the classics, Blaise de Vigenère, who had managed to use nine fewer words
than Giorgio Dati in rendering a chapter of Tacitus's *Histories*. The blow was a
severe one, particularly now that the stature of Florentine culture was depending
more and more on the recognition of the superiority of the Florentine language.

Florentine, or Florentine Italian, had already won the battle against Latin, at least in all the nonprofessional fields. It had also triumphed over the other Italian dialects; and Leonardo Salviati himself had become the chief expert in all Italy on proper vocabulary and orthography, the one to whom such famous non-Tuscans as Battista Guarino and Francesco Panigarola turned for help in rooting out their Lombardisms. Its triumph was about to be crowned with the monumental *Vocabolario,* the first great dictionary of a modern European language, which Salviati's Accademia della Crusca was just then beginning to work on.

Now, however, a challenge had come not from Italy, but from a foreign country; and Davanzati, with the support of Salviati, with the help of Salviati's new (1582) edition of Dati's standard Italian translation, and with the encouragement of the Alterati, set out to meet it. He buried himself in the scholarly tomes of Guillaume Budé, Carlo Sigonio, Lipsius, and Pichena. He carefully compared Tacitus's locutions with those of all the other Latin writers of the first and second centuries. And he peeled away from Italian all but the most essential of the articles and prepositional phrases that inevitably padded out the translations of the more telegraphic dative and ablative forms in Latin. His search for brevity, it is true, occasionally led him into errors of grammar, as when he refused to accommodate a participle to a change in gender after a second subject. It also led him into errors of logic, as when he let one fortunate lady be *sverginata* (deprived of her virginity) two times, just to avoid putting in another verb. Similarly, his search for clarity and intelligibility led him to reverse subjects and predicates and to call what Mithridates did to the Romans a "Sicilian Vespers."

But after twenty years of hard work, Davanzati finally proved his point. The Florentine language could express with the utmost precision every single concept in all of Tacitus, and it could do it with 37,000 fewer letters than French. Even better, it could do it with 5,000 fewer letters than Tacitus's own Latin. The Alterati breathed a sigh of relief. The superiority of the Florentine language, and with it the preeminence of Florentine letters as a whole, now rested on an irrefutable mathematical proportion: Florentine 9, Latin 10, French 15.

The Alterati had still other reasons for encouraging the study of Tacitus. One of their favorite literary exercises consisted in the presentation of a thesis by one member and a counter-thesis by another, followed by a general debate and a decision by the regent. Very often the more usual literary or philosophic questions —whether comedy was more useful than tragedy, whether Ariosto was more praiseworthy than Tasso—gave way to such questions as whether the Romans rose to greatness through virtue rather than fortune and whether a militia was more effective than a professional army, questions behind which lurked, needless to say, the ghost of Machiavelli.

Florentines had been shocked when their own Machiavelli had suddenly appeared on Paul IV's Index of Forbidden Books. They had been dismayed when he turned up again on the Index of the Council of Trent, especially since his heirs had long since given up the futile task of preparing a "corrected" version. To be sure, none of them was yet so silly as to stop reading him just to please the strange tastes of the Holy Office, even though they usually followed Ammirato's discretion in hiding his name behind such expressions as "a certain author" or "someone has said." Indeed, they continued to read all his works, and not, like some of their Transalpine contemporaries, just *The Prince*, or what Innocent Gentillet or even Henri Estienne said about *The Prince*. But more and more their august ancestor had become a source of annoyance that they gladly would have had removed. Machiavelli had insisted that the only durable political order was not the comfortable and comforting monarchy they all had come to enjoy, but a turbulent mixed republic, one in which all the citizens were expected to sacrifice dinner parties to public service, private duels to field campaigns, and tranquillity to occasional street brawls with plebeians. Worse yet, he had demonstrated that the ethics of politics was essentially different from, if not at times openly opposed to, the ethics of Christianity. And those were just the points that the carefree subjects of Pius V and Francesco de' Medici no longer wanted to concede.

Hence the hopes the Alterati placed in Tacitus. If a study of the historian of the Roman republic had produced the disturbing doctrines in Machiavelli's *Discourses on Livy,* perhaps a study of the historian of the Roman principate would come up with something more appropriate to the changed circumstances of the late sixteenth century. The parallel was already too obvious to be missed. In a day when horoscopes were taken with dead seriousness, everyone knew that Duke Cosimo had been born under the same stars as Augustus. Now that Francesco was dead, everyone realized that a second Tiberius had at last been succeeded by a second Trajan, Ferdinando. For Ferdinando turned out to be as little disturbed by busts of Filippo Strozzi as his ancient counterpart had been by statues of Brutus and Cassius, and he was equally effective in reconciling the most obdurate of modern Tacituses to the new Principate.

Moreover, even though Ammirato had warned them that the science of politics could be apprehended only through an empirical investigation of the concrete data of history, most of his compatriots sincerely looked to Tacitus as a means of avoiding the uncertainty that empirical investigation inevitably brought with it. Uncertainty was just what Ammirato's contemporaries feared the most, after disorder. They sought to banish uncertainty regarding the principles of literary criticism by raising Aristotle's *Poetics,* or some modern or ancient version of the *Poetics,* to the position of an authoritative text. They sought to overcome uncertainty regarding proper vocabulary and syntax by substituting Boccaccio, whose language would not change, for current usage, which Salviati warned would produce chaos if used as the basis for correct language. If Tacitus, then, could be elevated to the same rank as Aristotle and Boccaccio, all those annoying problems Machiavelli had brought up would be swept away once and for all. If it were true, as Ammirato himself later suggested, that "princes have their authoritative masters (just like all the other noble arts)—namely, the historians, in whom they must place no less confidence than do physicians in Hippocrates and jurists in Ulpian," then the Alterati could forget about Machiavelli's "long experience with modern affairs" and all but some five hundred pages of his "continual reading of those past." Just to make sure, then, that Ammirato would fulfill their expectations, they assigned one after another of their associates to "contradict" everything he said "by putting forth the opposite opinion of Machiavelli."

Ammirato knew that his task was not an easy one. For one thing, Tacitus left much to be desired as an authoritative text for a Christian political scientist in late-sixteenth-century Italy, especially for one like Ammirato who was committed to using his texts in a somewhat less high-handed manner than Machiavelli had. The portraits of the early Roman emperors were really not edifying enough to be held up as models for imitation. And, needless to say, neither Tacitus nor any of the political personages he wrote about were Christians. Moreover, the Alterati were so accustomed to thinking in Machiavellian terms that their minds were not easily changed. That morning Ammirato spent some forty minutes showing that Tacitus' off-hand comment (XVIII, 159) about money being "the nerve of war" was borne out both by the theoretical statements of Pericles and Cicero and by the practical experience of Alexander, Hannibal, and the Venetians. He then pointed out (and modern critics agree with him) that the arguments of "the above-mentioned author" to the contrary were based on a misreading of Herodotus III and of Justin XXV, 201, which he identified as the sources. He pointed out that these arguments completely overlooked what Thucydides said in Book I about the strength of the Athenians in the Peloponnesian War and that they deliberately left out the sequel to the Battle of Agnadello in 1509, when the Venetians, ignorant of Machiavelli's depreciation of the role of money in war, bought back all they had lost by arms to the pope, the emperor, and the king of France. He concluded, then, that the thesis of *Discourses,* II, 10, was wrong, and that, properly qualified, the thesis in Tacitus was "as firm a proposition in the government of states as is [the axiom] among the mathematicians about the whole being greater than any of the parts" (XVIII, 9).

All this, apparently, to little avail: for the Alterati still hesitated to abandon the long-accepted positions put forth once more in the rebuttal of Francesco Bonciani.

Yet with time Ammirato managed to overcome both the difficulties of his text and the habits of his audience. The first he took care of by showing that modern as well as ancient princes were not bound by human law, that some Roman emperors had in fact behaved in a perfectly Christian manner, and that conscience had been as effective a deterrent for the pagan emperors Nero and

Tiberius as it had been a millenium later for the Christian king Alfonso II of
Naples. Tacitus, therefore, could be used as a source of political maxims as
safely as the Bible, which unfortunately contained very few of them. Overcoming
the second difficulty took much more effort. Ammirato first admitted a number of
Machiavelli's specific theses, even some of the more disquieting ones. He completely accepted Machiavelli's position on the method, the approach, the form,
and even the language of political philosophy, even though he was later to have
some doubts about the validity of a basically inductive method. Indeed, after several years of study, he had come to respect, even to admire, the author his Florentine friends expected him to remove from their shelves, and even in his most
critical passages there is not a trace of the violent indignation and misinformed
fury of a Reginald Pole, an Ambrogio Caterino Politi, a Pedro Ribadeneyra, an
Antonio Possevino, or any of the other creators of *Machiavellianism*.

Thus Ammirato was in a position to combat Machiavelli on his own grounds.
He first resolved the question of the best constitution by eliminating the chief
competitors of monarchy. Fortunately, aristocracy had already eliminated itself.
For by the end of the sixteenth century, the Florentine patriciate had disassociated
itself from all remnants of the "natural" nobility of the Quattrocento philosophers.
It had been detached from its former responsibilities for the welfare of the
commonwealth. And it had become, in treatise after treatise, merely an illustrious
parasite, defined not by valor or virtue but only by blood, and expected not to
work, not to lead, not even to administer (the grand duke's lowborn technocrats
did that very well), but to "shine." The plebeians took a bit more space. Ammirato
showed them to have been wrong in every quarrel with every prince from Tiberius
to Pius V. He found them incapable either of the well-pondered decisions that
Pericles credited them with or of the spiritual fortitude that Machiavelli attributed
to them. He concluded that they were, in short, "light-minded, lazy, timorous,
precipitous, desirous of new things, ungrateful—a mixture of all the vices without
the benefit of a single virtue." And the elimination of two of its three essential
elements left Machiavelli's mixed constitution nothing but an empty dream.

Ammirato then resolved the question of the relationship between political
and Christian morality by turning to history. The Romans really believed in their
augurs, he said. The laws of Numa were strikingly similar to those of Moses.
And Roman religion resembled Christianity in most of its fundamental teachings,
for both rested on a "natural" religion inherent in every rational creature. He
then showed that Christian morality was effective in the realm of politics—that
Syracuse owed its stability not to cruel Dionysius but to his just and merciful
successor, that Ferdinand of Aragon maintained himself in Naples by sparing,
rather than killing, the son of his deposed predecessor, that princes best gained
their ends by keeping their promises, and that the Christian religion kept subjects
in line better than any other. He next found a way of justifying acts apparently
incompatible with Christian teaching by advising princes to flip through the Old

Testament for precedents that might be lacking in the New. Just in case they were so impious as to suppose that God had changed his mind about slaughtering the wives, children, and cattle of an enemy, let them remember that "the oracles of God are [by definition] good laws, and whoever follows them follows the laws of God himself." Finally, he rescued the church from Machiavelli's attack by alternatively moving it in and then out of the realm of human institutions. He relieved the Papacy of all responsibility for the division of Italy and then insisted that it had served Italy's interests best by keeping it divided. He attributed papal elections solely to the inspiration of the Holy Spirit and then advised princes that a military alliance with the pope was the best way of realizing their purely temporal ambitions.

To be sure, a modern reader with a taste for consistency will probably find Ammirato's theses somewhat less than convincing. He may find it difficult to understand what the pursuit of fame has to do with Christian humility, why the Turks should be excepted from the general rule against admitting a new religion (even a "true one"), and why Christ's injunction about admonishing wayward brothers should prove the political value of public accusations. He may also be somewhat confused by the constant jumping around from one subject to another, by problems that are skirted without being solved, and by questions that are buried in interminable digressions or piles of mere *exempla*. But then Machiavelli himself presents almost as many difficulties, or at least he did before his works finally came to be studied in chronological order. In any case, Ammirato's contemporaries were enthusiastic. The *Discourses* went through four Italian editions before 1599 and two more at the beginning of the next century. They were translated into Latin for the benefit of German readers in 1609 and 1618 and appeared in French translations twice in 1618 and in 1628, 1633, and 1642. Better yet, the work completely realized its main objective. Florentines at last could lock up Machiavelli's works in their "prohibited books" cabinets; and for a century and a half thereafter they were to make barely a reference to any of them. They could ignore Paolo Paruta, Hugo Grotius, and all the other vigorous political writers beyond the Apennines and Alps. Indeed, they could even stop talking about politics, either theoretical or practical, altogether. So successfully, apparently, had Ammirato solved the problem posed by Coluccio Salutati, Leonardo Bruni, Matteo Palmieri, Donato Giannotti, and scores of others of the best minds of the city, that one of the most flourishing fields of Florentine intellectual activity during two centuries suddenly died out. There is scarcely a word about the structure and the purpose of political organization in all Florentine literature between the publication of Ammirato's *Discourses* in 1594 and the appearance of Lodovico Antonio Muratori's *Defects of Jurisprudence* in 1742.

To some extent, the rapid success of the *Discourses* can be explained by their style—by the brevity, concision, and perfect balance of the sentences, by the well-placed echoes of Sallust, Tacitus, Guicciardini, and Ammirato's other stylistic mentors, and by the augmenting series of witty anecdotes—all of which make the book as delightful to read today as it must have been to hear back in 1591. Its success may also have been owing in part to its very lack of organization. Ammirato intended it, after all, to be read either bit by bit as it came from his pen ("secondo mi abbatteva a cosa che mi piacesse"), or in the topsy-turvy order he presented it to the Alterati (XVIII, 9; XVIII, 5; XII, 3; XIX, 3, etc.), or, perhaps, like a manual, from the subject index backward. Thus the browser could concentrate wholly on what was being said at the moment, without being too much worried about what had been said three pages, or three months, earlier.

But the book had still greater attractions. Ammirato inspired the confidence of his audiences by including a number of subjects, such as public finances, demography, and commerce, which Machiavelli had overlooked, and by drawing upon a much wider variety of written sources, which, everyone admitted, amply compensated for his lack of practical experience. He also comforted them by converting into blessings those defects in the established order over which they no longer had any control. The Spanish, for example, could not be chased out of Italy, but, then, the "gentle rule" of a foreign Philip was certainly preferable to the "tyrannical domination" of a Neapolitan Alfonso. The basic structure of society could not be altered, but, then, it was less bad than any of the known alternatives. Finally, he suggested to his listeners that there were still ways in which intellect might affect political action. It was useless, he realized, to charge them with the responsibility of creating a better, more just world, for no Italian prince would ever be induced to adopt the extreme measures that any right-minded counsellor would recognize as desirable. It was even more useless to entertain them with another of the imaginary republics of contemporary Italian utopia-builders or to abandon them to the passive role of observing an inexorable "reason of state." Princes might move on a plane infinitely removed from that of ordinary mortals. But they could still on occasions be influenced—not, it is true, by a rational demonstration or a well-thought-out memorandum, but by a timely appeal to their vanity, to their consciences, or to easily manipulated tales about whatever hero they could be brought to identify themselves with: Caesar, Trajan, Theodosius I, or Cosimo de' Medici. Political philosophy had become, then, far more a matter for contemplation than a guide to action. But within certain very narrow limits, an intelligent man could still hope to do something, however small.

On one or two occasions Ammirato, strangely, forgot all his careful calculations. He had often felt obliged to insist that, in principle at least, moderns were not one bit inferior to ancients. He had been forced to conclude, therefore, that *virtù,* in Machiavelli's sense of the term, might still break through the status quo to accomplish great things. It had done so, after all, in the notable cases of Columbus, Giovanni delle Bande Nere, and . . . yes, even Martin Luther. Indeed, just three years before, such a breakthrough had seemed imminent. The beginning of the Persian War had momentarily taken the eyes of the Turks off the West. And it had coincided with the accession of Grand Duke Ferdinando, who gave promise of being more adventurous than his equivocating predecessor. The war also coincided with the pontificate of Sixtus V, who was anxious not to die before accomplishing at least one deed as memorable as those of Pius V, the mastermind of the Battle of Lepanto. Suddenly the rhetorical commonplaces that Ammirato and everyone else had been repeating for years about the Eastern menace took on an air of actuality. Ammirato shoved aside his scholarly dissertations, opened his copy of *The Prince* to the last chapter, and dashed off a fervent appeal to the pope. This is the moment, he cried, the unforeseen "occasion," to draft the unemployed into a national militia, to turn the orphanages into military academies, to convert the bickering nobility into crusaders, to rekindle "the still not-completely-spent *virtù* in the Italian blood,"* and to destroy once and for all the age-old enemy, the Turk.

The occasion of 1588 had rapidly slipped by. The pope forgot even to answer, and Philip II sent his fleet into the English Channel rather than into the Bosporus. But five years later a similar occasion was to present itself—when, in 1593, the Turkish drive toward Vienna coincided with the recent election of Ammirato's old friend Cardinal Aldobrandini as Pope Clement VIII. Now all Europe was alarmed. The pope sent secret messages to potential rebels among the Christian population of the Balkans. He sent an apostolic vicar to persuade the Poles and Russians to stop fighting each other and the Swedes and to turn south instead. He sent an ambassador to Persia to talk the shah into reopening the eastern front. And Ammirato hauled the 1588 oration out of a drawer, appended a translation of a similar one written a century earlier by Cardinal Bessarion, and sent them both off to the grand duchess.

There was not a minute to lose. While Ferdinando, at his consort's intercession, was puzzling out how to put his nonexistent surplus of farm labor into uniform, Ammirato summoned up his last ounce of high-pitched rhetoric and hurled it at his old compatriots in Naples, whose weaknesses and ambitions he knew so well. "Already I can see aged fathers coming to embrace their departing sons with affectionate tears and a thousand kisses. . . ." This time he got a response, or at least enough of a response to imagine that all Naples was practically in arms. In a burst of enthusiasm, he wrote out another set of orations for Clement VIII and Philip II, which he entitled the *Clementines* and the *Philippines* and sent around to the princes of Italy with the suggestion that a small subsidy might enable him to write a *Gonzaghine* or a *Roverine* as well. But alas! the papal secretaries promised only to "present it at the first possible moment." By the end of September 1594, the Neapolitans had gone back to their games. The exhausted king of Spain decided to save his remaining strength as a deterrent to the ambitions of the king of France. The German electors voted against any eventual involvement in Polish

---

* A paraphrase of Petrarch's famous sonnet, quoted by Machiavelli at the end of *The Prince*.

or Muscovite affairs. And the pope decided that Ferrara was more enticing than Greece or the Holy Land. The crusade was over. The poor balding priest who had dreamed up the whole fabulous adaptation of Tasso's *Jerusalem Delivered* staggered back to the prosaic but tolerably pleasant realm of the little that was possible, resolved never again to tax the patience of his indulgent listeners.

Such diversions did not in the long run detract from Ammirato's accomplishment, for his listeners appreciated his charm and good sense too much to reproach him with inconsistencies in his own actions. Nor were they disturbed by his failure to investigate thoroughly the whole question of the relationship of government and its subjects, which had been so prominent in Machiavelli, for they had already dismissed it as irrelevant. Ammirato himself may have entertained doubts about the omnipotence of, say, the duke of Mantua, and Sassetti may have thought Francesco de' Medici incapable of altering the laws of supply and demand. But most Florentines agreed with Ammirato's sometime sparring partner and faithful disciple, Giovan Battista Strozzi, who had pointed out that the authority of princes derived not from legitimate succession, not from innate or acquired virtues, not from wisdom, but from God. Most of them agreed with Lorenzo Giacomini in regarding loyalty to a commonwealth rather than to a single man or family as somehow subversive. Or at least no one objected to his cutting out the words *to your country* from the phrase "the piety you owe to your country and to your noble blood," and *unhappy* from "the unhappy war of 1530" in his edition of Jacopo Nardi's biography of his uncle Antonio in 1597. Most Florentines also agreed that princes, and therefore politics, were not subject to law. They were convinced that the practice of law amounted simply to matching specific cases with specific commands. They were sure that the theory of law had no more useful function than that of helping "elevated spirits" to contemplate an Unchanging that never changed anything beneath it, and that jurists did little more than twist technical jargon around until even their clients were penniless. And that, outside of an occasional course at the university, was the end of jurisprudence in Florence for another hundred years.

Some men of letters were willing to go still further. Ammirato's own excursions into servile language (and he was an expert at it) probably reflected little more than his practical advice on how to get princes to pay attention or come through with what today would be called a grant-in-aid. But Lorenzo Giacomini seems really to have thought of Francesco de' Medici as the "most abundant fountain of . . . all that we have," as he wrote as early as August 29, 1566; and Leonardo Salviati seems really to have considered himself nothing but "parched earth" at the disposal of the quickening spirits of one of his Apollos—so much so, indeed, that he expected the grand duke not only to pay him, but also to decide whether he should write a history of Florence, a sonnet, or an oration. Apparently, Cosimo's policy of subsidizing men of letters had succeeded beyond all expectations. By the end of the century almost all of them had followed Alessandro Canigiani's advice to "put aside [their] private concerns and direct [their] thoughts totally to the commands of this prudent prince."

It helped, of course, to be governed by a prince who merited at least some of the praise heaped upon him. Francesco, it is true, had never attracted much sympathy. He was a man of "quiet thoughts . . . and much care and circumspection in speech." His parsimony bordered on an obsession. His intolerance of corruption matched his forgive-and-forget attitude toward the brother of Orazio Pucci, his would-be assassin. And his taste for iced wine probably had no more to do with his death, as the Venetian ambassador thought, than did the "immoderate embraces of his consort" which everyone gossiped about. Probably he served the cause of learning more by retiring to the sumptuous isolation of Pratolino than by the lectures he enjoyed delivering to his intellectually inclined subjects on painting, pharmaceutics, mathematics, cosmography, the "secrets of nature," and all the other arts and sciences he considered himself proficient in. He spent most of each day locked up in the *casino* of his garden. It was here that he dictated letters to a secretary so as to "transform pleasure into business and business into pleasure . . . without wasting any time." It was here that he arranged to feed the reindeer that a Lucchese merchant had sent him from Sweden and to pot the plants that Sassetti had sent him from India. And it was here that he invented, with some success, new ways of manufacturing crystal glassware, fireworks, fake jewels, porcelain dishes, and poison.

Ferdinando, on the other hand, was greeted by wild enthusiasm the moment he arrived to see his morose brother off to the next world. He was a strikingly handsome man, unlike most of his family, slightly on the heavy side, with wide eyes, a full, rounded nose, bushy eyebrows, and ruddy cheeks; and his closely cropped beard and slightly receding hairline combined the last traces of youth with the first signs of the square-chinned majesty that twelve years later Giambologna was to put into bronze on the giant horse guarding the entrance to the Via de' Servi. While fully conscious of the magnificence of his station, he was also a remarkably affable man, who had learned the value of tact during many years of negotiating at the Roman court, and who had mastered the art of manipulating others during many more years of patching up Medici family quarrels: He could quickly win the affection of the humblest as well as the proudest without ever descending to the level of either. He liked money and knew how to earn it. But he also knew how to spend money in huge public displays—like the *mascherata* that the papal nuncio found so *graziosa* in 1589, with Pietro de' Medici acting as the Seine, Virgilio Orsini impersonating the Arno, and himself and his consort mounted on a huge float amid angels and musicians. His actions matched his character. He personally distributed dowries each year to poor girls in a colorful ceremony at San Lorenzo. He built hospitals in Florence and a college for scholarship students at Pisa. He created hundreds of new jobs through his massive building projects. And he did all this with the flair of a well-trained public relations expert. Thus, in November 1589, when he risked his life crossing the flooded valley in a small boat and then walked about the stricken sections of the city personally distributing the emergency rations he had efficiently collected, his subjects cheered enthusiastically.

But to Ammirato's readers, the popularity or the merits of an individual man were secondary to the fact of his being a prince. What they said about Ferdinando may have been more sincere. But as a matter of fact it was exactly what they had already said about Francesco, and in both cases the flat metaphors were equally remote from the flesh-and-blood realities they supposedly referred to. "Oh mirror of prudence," sang a young medical instructor from Fivizzano in 1587,

> Oh mirror of prudence, high splendor of Italy,
> eye of princes, whom thou dost teach
> how to govern themselves and men;
> Oh great soul, who dost show
> the value and honor of every virtue . . .

No one would have known he was talking about the herb-presser at Pratolino if the title had not pointed it out. Stranger still, exactly the same things were said about Francesco's sometime mistress and later consort, Bianca Cappello. Leonardo Salviati's hymn

> Ah, Lady ever more beautiful,
> ever honest and lovely,
> above the flowers, above the waves,
> yea, above the sun itself . . .

could have been addressed to Laura, Beatrice, or the Virgin Mary. For there was not a single specific detail to identify it with the ambitious young woman whom a dashing Florentine merchant stole from one of the first families of Venice; whom the grand duke "borrowed" from her husband until the husband and the grand duchess conveniently died; whom the best poets and musicians of all Italy compared to Venus and Diana as she ascended the Tuscan throne in one of the most lavish fetes of that lavish age; and whom even the Venetian Senate, swallowing its pride, proclaimed "Daughter of the Republic" after she had completely subjugated the ruler of the second richest state in Italy. Florentines may have been shocked by some aspects of her behavior. But they willingly exchanged silence, or inflated eulogies, in public for the privilege of passing around the most salacious rumors by word of mouth. The nearest thing to a criticism in all the literature of the time is an offhand observation by Ammirato about a ninth-century warrior who let himself be dominated by his wife.

To some extent, of course, the apotheosis of the Medici had a practical purpose. Raising the holders of political power above the vicissitudes of time and of human caprice was one way, at least, of blocking any possible return to what Ammirato chillingly recalled as the "horrors and calamities" of the former regime. But to some extent this way was not the result of a free choice. It was, as Ammirato sourly noted, the inevitable consequence of the loss, or surrender, of financial independence by the intellectuals. The ideal man of letters was no longer a Leonardo Bruni, who earned a salary, or a Donato Acciaiuoli, who enjoyed an independent income. He was, rather, a Leonardo Salviati, who fed himself and all his whining cousins on the wholly unmerited grace of his patrons. He was no longer an Anton Francesco Doni, who lived from his pen, but a Giambologna, who never accepted fees, only gifts. "Those who live by the bread of others," noted Ammirato, "are no longer masters of themselves. . . . They are bound to place themselves, their energies, and all their works at the service of those by whose good will they are nourished."

In the same way that he could avoid the constitutional issue, Ammirato found that he could glide over even the more obvious discrepancies among politics, morality, and religion—for the reason, that is, that such questions had already lost much of their former actuality. No one really cared that Salviati could find no higher purpose for massacring the Flemings and scorching the earth of Flanders than that of permitting Philip II to keep his thumb on Italy. No one cared whether "arms" were superior to "letters," because Lorenzo Giacomini, who juggled these concepts around, was not even conscious of Bruni's and Alberti's efforts to link Christianity with a workable ethic for this world. And none of the assiduous readers of Giovanni Della Casa's *Galateo* seems ever to have sensed the author's tragic realization that men in his time had lost control over good and evil. Salviati's violent tirades against "pride" and "ambition" were really a way of escaping from an unpleasant reality into comforting but empty abstractions. And Davanzati's harangues against "our women today," so many "Agrippinas . . . borne in triumph over the trampled remains of modesty and care of family," could be politely and safely applauded, because the real problems of the real daughters and housewives, who never set foot out-of-doors, could then be ignored.

Thus moral philosophy became a watertight compartment of its own, with no relation either to the purely "contemplative" science of theology or to the daily experience of ordinary Florentines. It was rather a method of extracting precepts from authoritative texts—from "the books of Aristotle [which contain] all there is to know about morality," from Seneca and Epictetus, "the true masters of human life," and from Plutarch, whom Marcello Adriani translated for the Alterati and whom "all the wise men of our age admit to have written down more rules . . . than any other philosopher." Precepts, arranged in logical order under such wholly innocuous abstractions as "magnanimity" and "modesty," became an end in themselves. Ammirato's readers could be counted on not to ask what the

Stoics had to do with St. Paul, not to wonder what Ammirato's tempered version of the traditional "universal man" had to do with Christ, not to worry about what Salviati's syllogisms about "justice" had to do with his scrambling all over Italy in search of strange new poisons. Morality could not possibly contradict religion or be contradicted by political practice: it had been completely isolated from both.

Florentines could rest assured that nothing their rulers could do would ever really trespass on the domain of the sacred. They had no doubts about the thoroughly Christian character of their city, especially now that a certain patriotic expatriate named Paolo Mini had exploded all the baseless rumors he had heard in France and that the Venetian ambassador later circulated around the Senate about the city's supposed atheism. Externally, indeed, Florence looked like a city of saints. Some 5,000 nuns filled its many convents. Twelve endowed hospitals provided 300 beds for the homeless and free medical care for 800 invalids. Well-furnished orphanages housed some 2,000 children, and over 10,000 laymen supported at least 113 confraternities. The tolling of the Angelus brought the city to a standstill each evening. The passing of the Sacrament through the streets brought crowds to their knees. Thousands of citizens flocked out to Impruneta for the magnificent procession of 1581. And thousands of country-dwellers flocked to the capital for the indulgences of 1575.

Moreover, religious life was well cared-for by zealous pastors. When at last the quiet, studious Antonio Altoviti, archbishop since 1543, found it safe to return to his see after almost twenty years of nonresidency, he had been transformed by the enthusiasm of the last days of the Council of Trent into a vigorous, though gentle, reformer. By August 1569 he had visited every parish within his jurisdiction, and by the time of his death in 1573 he had turned the diocesan and provincial synods prescribed by the Council into regular institutions. His work was carried on by the nervous but good-humored son of Cosimo's second cousin, Alessandro de' Medici, who may or may not have pouted when, as a child, Duchess Eleonora had given him a toy sword instead of a saint-doll, but who certainly succeeded in combining the intense piety he had learned at San Marco as a young man with the skill as a diplomat he had acquired as Cosimo's ambassador to Pope Pius V and as Gregory XIV's legate to King Henry III. At the same time, he never forgot how to exchange wisecracks with his old friends back in Arezzo, even when he found himself overwhelmed by the awesome responsibilities his high office had cast upon him. "Remind everyone to pray for me," he wrote Pietro Vasari on the day after his nomination, "and I really mean remind them, for I feel the burden I carry and I need as much help as possible."

Alessandro's political duties kept him, much to his regret, out of his diocese as often as in it. He was one of the chief agents in procuring the absolution of King Henry IV in 1595, and as papal legate once again he was responsible for reestablishing diplomatic relations between France and the Papacy. But he never neglected what he regarded as his first obligation. He raised the salaries of the cathedral clergy and then forbade them to hire substitutes. He ordered all the hundred-odd nonresident curates he found back to their parishes on pain of losing their benefices. He broke, or rather tactfully overcame, the resistance of the stiff-necked patricians in the cathedral chapter. He quietly made the rounds of the convents without ever embarrassing the inmates by writing down what he had discovered. Like his fellow model bishop, Gabriele Paleotti of Bologna, he hired a historian—no less a historian than Vincenzo Borghini—to help him adapt his reform measures to the traditions of his episcopal predecessors. He systematized old rites, with fixed hours for Masses and the daily Angelus. He introduced new rites, particularly the Milanese Forty Hours Devotion, which he inaugurated on the Feast of the Immaculate Conception in 1589 "with an immense quantity of lamps and a huge number of silver candelabra . . . truly a sight to behold!" And he was rewarded for his efforts, a few weeks before his death in 1605, by being elevated to the papacy as Leo XI.

Alessandro's work was seconded by his colleague, Francesco Cattani da Diacceto, grandson of Marsilio Ficino's successor as head of the Platonic Academy and a close companion of Ammirato. Francesco, who succeeded his saintly uncle Agnolo in the see of Fiesole in 1570, supplemented his pastoral vigilance with a constant stream of homilies, treatises, saints' lives, and translations from the Fathers and the Scriptures. Alessandro's example may also have inspired the reforms later carried out in Arezzo by a former bureaucrat, Piero Usimbardi, and in Pisa by an assiduous member of the Accademia degli Alterati, Francesco Bonciani. And it may even have been carried across the Alps—at least by the Florentine academician Alessandro Canigiani, who became archbishop of Aix-en-Provence and one of the earliest exponents of the Tridentine reform in France. This work was not always easy, to be sure. Alessandro often found his position in Rome undercut by the intrigues of Bianco Cappello and her ambitious protégé, Fra Geremia of Udine. He found his authority at home undermined by the nosy papal inspectors of 1575. And the influential parents of the girls he had thrown out of convents forced him to pay back the girls' dowries from his own pocket. His efforts succeeded, nonetheless, in turning Florence into a small-scale version of St. Carlo Borromeo's Milan, one which conformed as closely as could be expected to the standards set forth by the Council of Trent.

Strangely enough, neither Alessandro nor any of his colleagues, except perhaps the bishop of Fiesole, ever chose to look for support from the one element in Florentine religious life that might have responded favorably: the spiritual heirs of the prophet Savonarola. True, the fervor of the first decades of the century had suffered a heavy blow when Savonarola's religious brothers in the monastery of San Marco were expelled. It had since dwindled all too often into a fascination for extravagant prophesies that even the vigilant papal nuncio found too ridiculous to bother about. It had occasionally succumbed to a naïve credulity about pious legends that Cesare Baronio, the official historian of the Roman Church and the acknowledged expert on legends, dismissed as unworthy of consideration. And it had frequently degenerated into an almost hysterical veneration of Savonarola, one which threatened to turn the civic leader and religious reformer of the 1490s into nothing but a miracle-worker interested solely in making Latin scholars out of illiterates overnight and in helping Clement VIII take Ferrara away from the Este.

Yet religion in Florence still showed signs of considerable vitality—in the lasting influence of the mystic Caterina de' Ricci, for instance, and of her Savonarolan sisters at San Vincenzo in Prato, and in the efforts of a certain P. Remigio to make the scriptural portions of the Mass more intelligible to the unlearned. Its vitality was manifested in works of charity—in the efforts of Vittorio dell'Ancisa to follow the example of St. Filippo Neri in the hospital he founded in 1584. Its vitality was manifested in works of learning—in the efforts of the university professor Flaminio Nobili to make available the texts of the Greek Church Fathers. Its vitality was also manifested in the vernacular hymns written in simple language to simple, if rather monotonous, tunes—the last outburst of congregational singing before the professionals drove it out of the church:

Lo-da-te fan-ciul-letti in suon'e can-to . . .

Praise him, o children, in sound,
praise the good Jesus in song,
praise his thrice-holy name,
which all the world adores.

(Razzi, *Laudi,* No. 1)

Above all, the vitality of the Florentine religious tradition was manifested in the saints' lives, the inspiring biographies, and the translations from the Scriptures and the Rhineland mystics of that tireless and deeply pious Savonarolan Dominican, Serafino Razzi. And Razzi's intense spirituality may even be reflected in Ammirato's own versions of the Psalms and Canticles, which are touchingly sincere even if they fall short of great poetry. Some Florentine Christians, in other words, were still "subjects," to use modern theological terms, rather than just "objects" of ecclesiastical reform.

Instead of trying to encourage or direct this living tradition, Archbishop Alessandro decided to stamp it out. Just why he should have conceived such a morbid fear of everything connected with Savonarola is not quite clear. Nor is it clear why he should have gone out of his way to persuade Grand Duke Francesco that the Savonarolans had been behind Pucci's assassination plot and that they were still busy organizing a vast conspiracy against the monarchy. It is outright astonishing that he should have wasted so much of his overtaxed time in confiscating medals, tearing down icons, and sending suspects to the inquisitor or into exile. But it is clear why he succeeded—why the Dominican general at last agreed to make even the good Razzi speak only of "a certain Friar" without naming him, and why Clement VIII, whose own mother had venerated Savonarola, answered the stirring request for canonization which Razzi brought all the way to Rome on foot with a decree banning Masses in the reformer's honor. For one thing, traditional Florentine religion had very little in common with the Society of Jesus, the papacy of Pius V, and, in general, the spirit of post-Tridentine Catholicism. It was rather a curious amalgam of thirteenth-century millenarianism, fifteenth-century humanism, the doctrines and prophesies of Savonarola, and the good-humored, down-to-earth wisdom of Filippo Neri, the Florentine Savonarolan mystic who founded the Roman Oratorio. It was nourished by the ever brighter memory of Savonarola's "New Jerusalem" of 1495–98, by a rather hazy Old Testament and Pauline concept of the church as a mystical body of lay as well as ecclesiastical members, and by a more sentimental than scholarly association with the age of the Apostles. And it expected spiritual regeneration to proceed upward from the ordinary laymen of Florence, not downward through the hierarchy from Rome, which indeed it often regarded, rather blindly, as the center of all corruption.

For another thing, Savonarolanism encouraged an attitude that seemed to the archbishop "not completely respectful of the clergy and the Holy See." The observation of disparities between the ideal and the reality of ecclesiastical administration was exactly what the bishops and the Curia now claimed as their exclusive prerogative. Such observations were exactly what the itinerant preacher Lorenzo da Brindisi denounced all over Italy and Germany as the first step toward heresy. Worse yet, Savonarolanism stimulated a sense of personal dignity and pride among mere artisans and other "middling sorts of persons." And that was exactly what sent the Medici and all right-minded noblemen into nightmares about the republican regime of 1529. Traditional religious piety in Florence, then, particularly in its Savonarolan form, was an annoying impediment to the orderly, well-disciplined, centralized administration that the post-Tridentine papacy was trying so hard to set up; and it was a discordant note in the hush-hush campaign then being directed against the very ebullience and zeal that had made possible the convocation of the council.

Alessandro concluded that it would be better to promote a very different kind of religious life. Accordingly, genuine religious experience was confined to the cloisters. It was closed up in the lightless cell and ornate chapel where Antonio Maria Montusi kept his flesh subdued with a whip and a hair shirt and where he talked to no one but Christ, the devil, his confessor, and a score of angels for some nine years before his election as general of the Servites in 1597. It was walled off in the impenetrable convent of the Carmelites, then located across the Ponte alla Carraia in the building occupied today by the archdiocesan seminary. There, in the company of the daughters of the best families of Florence, lived Maria Maddalena de' Pazzi, who, since the age of fourteen, had been deprived of all contact with the outside world except for what was revealed to her in raptures; who frightened her aristocratic sisters and amazed the sober lawyers from the chancery by being suspended in midair for a quarter of an hour at a time; and who perfected the Christian virtue of raising enemies to the level of friends by according indiscriminately to both only the signs, not the substance, of affection.

To be sure, cloistered piety was not completely lacking in social utility. For one thing, it provided a living example of the efficacy of human initiative in the process of salvation—an efficacy far greater, indeed, than the Tridentine doctrinal decrees were willing to admit. "We direct all our efforts," Maria Maddalena wrote, "so to sanctify ourselves with holy virtues and other practices pleasing to the Lord that we will *merit* becoming a temple *worthy* of the Celestial Spirit" (italics mine). For another thing, it provided divine sanctions for the Tridentine reform decrees—as, for instance, when Maria Maddalena was ordered to order Archbishop Alessandro to give up his nonepiscopal duties in Rome and France and return instantly to his diocese. It also stimulated a certain sense of responsibility for "those creatures, members of God, [whose faith is imperiled] by their lacking the necessities of life"—a responsibility that could easily be assumed, needless to say, without in any way touching the established social and political order. Finally, the prayers of the mystics could sometimes procure valuable advice and substantial rewards for those in power. When Maria de' Medici went off as bride to King Henry IV, for instance, the Virgin Mary told Maria Maddalena to advise her that her first duty would be to have the Jesuits readmitted to France and have the Huguenots exterminated; and she added that if the queen fulfilled her duty she would be assured of numerous offspring.

But in general, all the good souls outside the cloister were excused from having to engage in any other kind of prayer than the constant repetition of Paters, Aves, and the Rosary (in Latin, of course), which Maria Maddalena assured them was sufficient for persons in their station. They no longer needed to assume any other obligation than that of mortifying their human sentiments and of paying for the firewood, the nut-oil, the furniture, and the table delicacies that the nuns always found time, between one rapture and the next, to request of them. They no longer had to aspire to sanctity, because sanctity was now the special preserve of the celibate, and because the seventh sacrament, holy matrimony, which the Renaissance humanists and the Council of Trent had tried so hard to defend, was reduced to the level of "pleasures of the flesh," or, in Ammirato's words, to "slavery." That, at any rate, is what one latter-day

Savonarolan mystic by the name of Ippolito Gallanti found out when he tried to organize religious discussion groups for married couples and to get his students involved in assistance to immigrant peasants. Gallanti's final humiliation was provided by his Jesuit biographer, who carefully reworked his life on the model of St. Luigi Gonzaga, whom Gallanti had never heard of, rather than on that of St. Antonino, the fifteenth-century bishop of Florence, from whom he drew much of his inspiration.

Indeed, ordinary laymen no longer had to bother even with the official liturgy of the church, in spite of all the hard work of the council and the papal liturgical commissions. For their pastors and preachers now drew their attention to much more immediate subjects of meditation. Cattani da Diacceto offered them the bones of his earliest predecessors in the diocese of Fiesole. Alessandro presented them with well-lit processions and once, when a poor boy accidentally stained the floor of the cathedral with a bloody nose, with a well-publicized three-day exorcism. Carlo Borromeo of Milan commended to them the great quantity of relics in their treasuries, which he took several hours of his one-day stopover in 1582 to inspect. Maria Maddalena furnished them with scraps of the hair shirt of a recently deceased Dominican preacher—or at least what was left of it after the systematic plundering of his possessions. And all held up for their admiration the miracles, or *prodigi,* that now occurred with ever increasing frequency. Similarly, laymen no longer had to search for the historical word in the Scriptures, for one of their fellow citizens was in constant contact with the eternal Word; and the Bible could not be left to Turks and Arabs, on whose behalf alone Ferdinando's skilled Orientalists and his skilled typographers were working tirelessly, and fruitlessly, in Rome. Indeed, they really did not have to bother about anything except the "atrocious pains of Purgatory, where [the dead] cry out in direst affliction." And they were accordingly kept busy—and out of the hair of the hierarchy—with the various external acts prescribed as a way of avoiding those pains: attending fifteen-minute Masses at the altar where Cosimo I's funeral had been celebrated and choosing from among the 164 pages of indulgences granted by Sixtus V to the new confraternity at Santa Croce. Religion for the chosen few was an excruciating burden. For everyone else it was just a matter of following a few easy rules.

Needless to say, the practical consequences of this sort of piety were not very gratifying. Alessandro himself had to admit, after fifteen years of hard work, that "superstition" was still the lot of most of his charges. His closest friends still looked on the church as a grab-bag of sinecures. The Florentine nobility still looked on the Tuscan hierarchy as a way of taking care of extra sons. Fathers still looked on convents as a comfortable alternative to ruinous dowries. Academic eulogists still looked on the elevation of Cardinal Luigi d'Este at the ripe age of fourteen as a sign of his virtue. And even Ammirato, the sometime employee of the vigorous reformer Girolamo Seripando and the admirer of his own model bishop, Braccio Martelli—even Ammirato, "not being able to recall [at the moment] the precise rulings of the Holy Council of Trent," decided that "it would be proper not to refuse a benefice of 25 *scudi*," even though, at a distance of some 600 miles, he had not the slightest intention of ever visiting it.

And yet the new piety had certain undeniable advantages. First of all, it kept mysticism from upsetting the administration of the affairs of this world. The mystics of the early Catholic Reform had often prolonged their lives by founding, or by inspiring others to found, new religious institutions—like the Oratory of Divine Love and the Society of Jesus. The mystics of the later Counter-Reformation remained isolated individuals. The only way in which Maria Maddalena could serve as a model to others was by pouring boiling wax over her arms. And the most her imitators could do was to rip up each others' backs with iron chains in the lugubrious, but socially innocuous, "companies of the night." Second, the new piety thwarted any attempt to apply Christian concepts of justice to the established social order. Maria Maddalena's wellborn companions, like Suor Margherita *Medici* and Suor Carità *Rucellai,* shielded her from all contact with the lower classes (forcing her therefore to "play" beggar in the kitchen), and that sixteenth-century combination of St. Bernardino, Bossuet, and Billy Graham, Francesco Panigarola, demonstrated in one stirring and studied sermon after another that nobility of birth was practically a prerequisite for sainthood. But above all, the new piety proved to be of inestimable value in overcoming any contradiction between religion and politics. It reduced private worship to the role of getting individual Christians into heaven and public worship to that of entertaining crowds of passive spectators. It made the sacraments a way of escaping from, rather than of sanctifying, the world, and it turned theology over to the exclusive care of the experts. It limited Christian moral teaching to screeching denunciations of the one last solace still left the poor wool-workers— the taverns—while quietly ignoring all the real ailments of individuals and society. It left the Church Militant with no other arms than Lorenzo Giacomini's blasts against purely imaginary monsters and Francesco Bocchi's meaningless tirades against "the dirty, filthy tongue" of someone he had once heard of called "Martino Lutero of Saxony." Finally, it reconstructed the Church Triumphant into a glorified replica of Pratolino and the Palazzo Pitti, in which the Medici, the Cappello, the Aldobrandini, and all their lavishly dressed courtiers and bureaucrats took the place of the cherubim, seraphim, apostles, and martyrs. The only relevance religion might still have to the state was the one that Ammirato had tried hard to avoid. But Leonardo Salviati in the 1560s, Giovan Battista Strozzi at the turn of the century, and just about all the theorists of "reason of state" made it perfectly clear. Religion was politically "useful." It made soldiers fight harder. It kept rebellious subjects in check. And it alone, not civic spirit or the constitution, accounted for the remarkable longevity of the Venetian Republic.

And that, as far as Ammirato was concerned, resolved once and for all Machiavelli's dilemma about the relation between Christian morality and politics. In fact, the dilemma was now so thoroughly resolved that Florentines ceased worrying about it. And thereafter Ammirato's *Discourses* were more often read not in the original but in the two French translations, which were to become, in the age of Richelieu, the foundation of the Tacitan school of French political thought.

4

How Ammirato made historiography obsolete by writing a definitive history

Thus, after reading from the *Discourses* all through the following month, Ammirato decided to put it aside and try out his other major work on the Alterati. It was the one which he had originally been commissioned to write for Cosimo I, but which, after numerous delays and many distractions, he was only now getting around to finishing. Accordingly, on August 8, he brought in the first chapter of his *History of Florence*.

"Tuscany," he began, "is located almost in the middle of Italy; and two rivers, the Tiber (once called the Albula) on the east and the Magra on the west separate it respectively from the Campagna [Romana] and from Liguria." He went on to chuckle at the heroic genealogies and the "extravagant and unusual feats" attributed to "the powerful Etruscan kings" by that master of historical fictions, Annio di Viterbo, by that "curious hunter of antiquities," Curzio Inghirami, and, more recently, by that defender of Florence's "nobility," Paolo Mini. Scientific Etruscology was still more than a century away. Etruscology based solely on a few passages in ancient Roman authors sounded, in the critical sixteenth century, like patriotic myth-building, and Ammirato would have none of it. He therefore jumped to the first major, properly documented event: the founding of Florence, which he, like Angelo Poliziano before him, attributed to the last Triumvirate on the basis of a passage in Dionysius of Halicarnassus and on a general knowledge of Roman colonial policy. He then posed the criterion of relevance to modern times in justification of his decision to concentrate on the most recent, rather than on the most ancient, of the Etruscan cities. It was Florence, he pointed out, and not Cortona or Fiesole, which eventually extended its dominion over all the others. Hence, what the Alterati were hearing about the distant past was not merely a collection of curiosities, but the first step in a long process that had been completed in their own day.

The Alterati had no reason not to be pleased with the *History*. For one thing, it included "a much greater quantity of facts" than any of its predecessors: with thirty-five books, it was some four times longer, and just as dense, as the *History* of Machiavelli, and it extended not just to 1492, but all the way to 1574. For another thing, it was more comprehensive. Ammirato had made use of all the relevant literary and archaeological remains then available for the earliest centuries. He had read an immense number of Genoese, Venetian, and Neapolitan, as well as Florentine, chronicles for the later centuries. And he had carefully checked all the literary histories of Florence since Bruni's—all of them, that is, except for such works as Guicciardini's *Cose fiorentine* and Bernardo Segni's *Storie* which were not discovered until much later. Moreover, the work reflected all that Ammirato had learned about the use of sources from Flavio Biondo, Carlo Sigonio, and the other representatives of the erudite tradition of Renaissance historiography; and it preserved all the stylistic elegance he had worked out in the *Discourses* on the basis of the best of the Greek, Latin, and Florentine monuments of literary historiography. It studiously avoided, or tagged with an "it is said," whatever could not be backed up by a specific document; and only once or twice did it get caught up in a Guicciardinian gerund—as in the sentence:

> . . . and that the king came to Tivoli ostensibly to visit the pope, but actually because, *dying,* he could be present to create a pope favorable to himself . . . ,

where *dying* could, grammatically at least, refer either to the pope or to the king (V, 229). It included a good smattering of the philosophizing, moralizing, and purely personal asides that everyone expected in a work of history, without letting any of them ever take the place of historical explanation. It scrupulously inserted, like an almanac, complete lists of all officeholders and complete texts of important documents. It gave apparently definitive solutions to all the historical questions that had been debated for the preceding half-century—particularly to the one about the destruction and rebuilding of the city by Totila and Charlemagne. It had the advantage of being written by one who, being a non-Florentine by birth, had almost no personal connections or sympathies with any of the people or events he described. And above all, it presented a plausible, well-supported, and often original scheme of periodization. Machiavelli's Golden Age of Theodoric the Goth declined precipitously through the ninth century. The capture of Fiesole heralded the rise and eventual triumph of the medieval commune. And the ascent of the Medici family prepared for the stability and tranquility that were finally achieved in the late sixteenth century.

The *History of Florence* offered nothing really new to the method or the scope of history. It stuck wholly to political and military affairs and made no attempt to integrate the recent specialities of art, literary, and ecclesiastical history. But it did succeed admirably in bringing to perfection one of the most productive schools of historiography of all times. Ammirato did no more than what Bruni, Poggio, Machiavelli, Varchi, and Borghini had already done: but he did it with a thoroughness and a consistency that all of them would have admired.

This time the reaction of the Alterati was anything but encouraging. They applauded politely and asked a number of intelligent questions. They even, a few months later, elected the author to a second term as regent. But even though the negligent secretary lost the records for most of the meetings during the next year or so, it is doubtful that they asked Ammirato to go on with his readings from the *History*; and the obvious dwindling of the last chapters into a string of disconnected events suggests that even Ammirato lost interest in what was supposedly his magnum opus. He managed to get only about one-third of it to the printers before he died. His diligent, loyal heir put off publishing the rest until almost a half century later. And the labor of some thirty years ended up in little more than a couple of thousand uncut pages.

Why had he bothered at all? Certainly Ammirato must have realized that all those questions he had induced the Alterati to argue about back in 1575 and 1576—whether a work of history should be confined to a single action or a single nation, whether events should be presented in strictly chronological order, whether the historian should pass judgment upon the persons he writes about— certainly he must have realized that such questions concerned not history, but "the art of history" (*ars historica*), which all over Italy had become a speciality completely detached from the actual writing of history itself. Certainly he must have realized that, with one or two exceptions, his friends were referring even their methodological and philosophical questions—whether history was harmful or useful, whether a narrative of events should include also an analysis of their causes—not to the experience of real historians, but to the rules laid down by the authorities. In other words, they were referring their historiographical questions not to Livy or Guicciardini, but to Aristotle, Cicero, and Quintillian. Now that Vasari's cycle of murals in the Palazzo Vecchio had been completed for more than twenty years, Ammirato must have known also that the friendly fight between Girolamo Mei and Vincenzo Borghini about whether Roman Florence had been a colony, a *municipium*, or merely a military camp, had lost much of its actuality. And now that Ferdinando had successfully asserted the complete external in- dependence of the grand duchy, he knew as well that it made little difference whether Charlemagne had refounded the city—and thus placed it legally under imperial sovereignty forever thereafter—or whether he had merely reassembled its scattered citizens.

Apparently, then, the past no longer had much to do with what went on in the present. It could sometimes serve to glorify a prestigious institution. For instance, the author of a *History of the Servites* scrupulously eliminated from the record of his order everything that could not be substantiated after "all due diligence in research." Everything that then remained had therefore to be "true." But when he tried to apply this method in establishing the scantily recorded visions of the order's founder, he was forced to rely largely on his own fertile imagination. And when he attempted to establish as "true" that an angel, not a man, had painted the portrait of the Virgin at the Annunziata, he did so by comparing it not with other portraits of the thirteenth century, but with a portrait of the Virgin's Son recently fished out of Lake Bolsena—a portrait that seemed to reveal a family resemblance and that certain "experts" dated in the reign of Nero. Similarly, the past could sometimes be illuminated by contrasting it with the present. Francesco Bocchi drew up two lists of categories of political and military conditions, one for modern and one for ancient Italy. He then canceled out all the categories in each list that were basically the same: virtue, domestic concord, military organization, and so on. That left only the system of colonies and alliances peculiar to ancient Italy; and he thus discovered the real cause of Rome's spectacular rise to greatness. Yet neither Bocchi nor the Servites ever thought of following the example of Baronio and rewriting ecclesiastical history according to the standards of its founder, Eusebius. Nor, since they studied the past largely as a way of escaping momentarily from the present, did they ever think of following the example of their distinguished ancestor, Leonardo Bruni, whose classic of early Renaissance history writing was based on the assumption that the past was implicit in the present.

Yet the study of history was not therefore completely useless. It might assist an intellectual elite in isolating itself from the corrupting influences of the vulgar herd:

> Ere this troubled, sinful world
> further entices and deceives me, . . .
> I shall withdraw to solitary, pious haunts,
> where with my sweet, elect companions,
> to whom I'm tied by bonds of endless love,
> I'll live my days amid the holy, taintless bands.
>
> (Leonardo Salviati)

That, after all, was the purpose of the literary exercises that the Alterati conducted behind closed doors. That was the purpose Ammirato himself had assigned to poetry when he commended Plato for not letting it be cast to the swine. And that was the increasingly prevalent concept of the function of learning as a whole which eventually divested the intellectuals of all responsibility toward the rest of society. History might also serve to perpetuate the names of the patrons who paid to have it written. Young Luigi Carafa would only have himself to blame, Ammirato warned him in 1584, if he ended up as a Homer-less Achilles. He need only follow the example of the Medici to have his deeds "written and sung about . . . by us poor nobles of the long robe." Finally, history might aid in stimulating the moral virtues of the reader, as Ammirato and just about everyone else from Bruni on had claimed. It sought

> to impress on our memories . . . the actions of men of the past, and to show
> us the consequences of the actions . . . either in praise, grace, and honor, or

in ill-will, blame, and vituperation, depending on the goodness or the badness
of the action.

But, then, inquired Leonardo Salviati with unflinching logic, why history?
Davanzati had answered: because the reader will associate himself more readily
with what actually happened than with a poetic fiction. Not so, said Salviati.
What impresses an audience is not what actually happened, but what it is disposed
to believe actually happened. If, therefore, the purpose of history is to wrap up
moral principles in a veil of examples, then the better the historian the less he
need bother with the truth, and the more readily will he be able to get away with
deliberate falsehoods, *bugie,* which are at times more "useful" to his ends anyway.
What affects the present is not the past, but the appearance of the past. And with
that, Salviati knocked away the last prop that kept history from collapsing into
poetry.

What Ammirato probably did not realize was that the very notion of the
single, the concrete, and the irreducibly unique, upon which history as a discipline
ultimately depended, had been swallowed up, in most of the other fields his
friends were busy with, by its exact opposite: the general and the abstract. Pier
Vettori had been the last great defender of historical "facts" in Florence, right up
until his death in 1585. And Ammirato still remembered affectionately the "Florentine Isocrates," who even in his eighties kept his young disciples busy analyzing
difficult passages and whose almost legendary physical fitness seemed to belie the
wrinkles forming about his large, sparkling eyes. Vettori had taught two generations of Florentines to respect the singular—to restore the texts they were editing
as nearly as possible to what Aristotle or Cicero or Porphyry had written many
centuries before, rather than fixing them up in accordance with modern notions of
logical coherence and orthography. One of them, the cranky expatriate Girolamo
Mei, was so impressed by Vettori's success in perfecting the science of critical
philology that he endowed it with a still higher end. Philology, Mei insisted, was
the key to certainty; and certainty—certainty about anything, however insignificant—was the one thing that could save Italian culture from the wave of moral
and religious as well as historical relativism that he feared would soon engulf it.
Yet even Mei had given up by the 1570s and refused to come home. By the 1580s
it was apparent that, in spite of a constant stream of flattering eulogies, Vettori
was being sought after not so much for scholarly advice as for letters of recommendation. And the direct descendants of Niccolò Niccoli, Angelo Poliziano, and
the other founders of modern philology gradually stopped editing ancient texts—
just at the moment when the Scaligers, the Lipsiuses and the Casaubons beyond
the Alps were taking on the job with such spectacular success.

Philology still had its uses in Florence. It could help the Alterati find out
exactly what Aristotle had said about a disputed point, particularly now that the
question "What actually is?" had been replaced by the question "What is

written about it?" Philology could also keep Leonardo Salviati from letting his incurable predilection for logical rigor disfigure the Trecento expressions he was cataloguing in that monument of linguistic scholarship, the *Avvertimenti,* or "Observations on the Decameron." But in most of the other fields to which it traditionally had been applied, philology was fast succumbing to Mei's "partisans and flatterers" and to a concept of certainty that was taken not from Vettori, but from Aristotle. In the art of the funeral oration, for example, which was one of the most highly cultivated art forms of the age, facts were completely deprived of their objective validity and reduced to the role of merely illustrative ornaments —ornaments which, according to one authority (and to Ammirato as well), could be switched around at will from one "virtue" to another. Similarly, biography became less a way of reconstructing a whole, unique personality in a particular historical context and more a way of chopping up real people into the neat categories—memory, intelligence, manners, and the like—which Salviati had deduced from the axiom: "What men have is either given them or acquired by them," and which he applied with equal success to Cosimo de' Medici, Benedetto Varchi, and a dozen others. Literary criticism became more involved with fitting everyone from Homer and Euripides to Dante and Tasso into the unchanging categories extracted from Aristotle's *Poetics* (or from Castelvetro's Aristotle); and it became less concerned with discovering the peculiar quality of each text or the intentions of each author. So also the famous "language question" turned into a search for a completely a-temporal and unchanging "genius of the language" through Petrarch, Bembo, and the other "authors" soon to be canonized by the new Accademia della Crusca. The last-minute intervention of the "silent" Bernardo Davanzati and his Sienese friend Belissario Bulgarini on behalf of local dialects and unrestricted coinages faded away into a quiet exchange of personal letters.

Whatever was left over by the critics and the linguists, finally, was finished off by the one professional philosopher whom Florentines would occasionally let out of the Pisan ivory tower, Francesco de' Vieri, better known as Verino II to distinguish him from his philosopher father, Verino I. Verino was willing to speak in Italian, and the members of the Florentine academies who invited him up as a guest lecturer had had, during their prescribed four years at the university, quite enough of Latin discourses and of the "barbarous, rough" jargon which Ammirato found so disagreeable among philosophers. Even though he actually spent less time reading Plato than reconciling Plato with Aristotle, Verino passed as a Platonist—as an heir of Marsilio Ficino, from whom Florentines still borrowed most of their poetic conceits and metaphysical commonplaces. Indeed, he even had hopes of getting out of Pisa, where a vigilant Aristotelian orthodoxy had for twenty years kept his "extra" course off the required list, and of setting himself up, at Ferdinando's expense and at double his current salary, as director of a revived version of Ficino's Platonic Academy. Verino may have impressed his audiences somewhat less than he thought he did, and he apparently did not impress Ammirato at all. But at least he could lend an expert's sanction to what they already had come to assume: that the general was deduced from the universal, not induced from the particular; that theory served not to guide practice, but to escape from it; that contemplation aimed not at stimulating action, but at rising above it; and that philosophy sought to understand "things human and divine" not as a way of exploring the range of man's intellect but as a way of "making man like God." Hence there was no real reason to search for patterns of change among the particular moments in the past for the purpose of directing the course of change in the future.

Because no one else could tell him why he should write history, Ammirato had to figure out a reason for himself—some other reason, that is, than simply having been hired to do it. He had started his literary career not as a historian at all, but as a poet—a much more prolific poet than anyone realized before his manuscripts were discovered in the National Library of Rome, and not a bad one either, at least within the conventions established by the Neapolitan Neo-Petrarchists of the mid-sixteenth century. He had been something of a critic as well, one who added to the usual critical standards of his time a refined sense of the sonorous qualities of the language, who could overlook, in some perceptive notes on the *Divine Comedy,* what appeared to all his contemporaries as the "coarseness" of many of Dante's expressions, and who managed, in his *Dedaglione* of 1560, to save poets from Plato's *Republic* even at the risk of returning to a pre-Renaissance "veil" theory of poetry.

But soon after his arrival in Florence, Ammirato gave up his earlier occupations. To be sure, he changed the dedication on some of his verses to fit new situations. He dutifully got out, in 1584, an edition of the works of some of his old friends in Naples and Lecce. And he occasionally, like everyone else, put his applications for subsidies in rhyme and meter. As late as 1585, moreover, he let himself be dragged into the war between the partisans of Tasso and the partisans of Ariosto—a war that enlivened several decades of debate in the Alterati and that gave the new Accademia della Crusca a baptism by fire. But his heart no longer followed his pen. When in 1582 the regent of the Alterati called on him to take part in the current discussions of poetics, he "excused himself as being too far away from the thoughts of the academy."

Perhaps Ammirato realized that his one attempt at comedy (*I Trasformati*) and his several attempts at *novelle* failed to rise above the level of the endless contemporary reworkings of Terence, Plautus, and Machiavelli. Perhaps, like the sculptor-architect Ammannati during his fits of depression, he suffered from occasional attacks of Counter-Reformation prudery. "When I was a youth," he told the grand duchess in 1597, "I wrote, spoke, and acted like a youth." He now shrank back from the "lascivious loves"—and, he might have added, from the dirty puns and the obsession with sexual intercourse—that filled the novels and comedies of most contemporary Florentine writers. More probably he suffered from having exchanged a stimulating environment for one in which poetry was criticized to shreds (he had only to remember Battista Guarini cowering before the omniscient Leonardo Salviati), but in which nothing much was actually produced except the streams of unpoetic verse "ordered" by the academies. He may also have been discouraged by a school of criticism that, after an outburst of brilliance, had let itself be trapped within the limits of its authoritative texts. And he may have been silenced by a poetics which, in spite of its express profession to the contrary, ended by discouraging the writing of poetry.

What had first aroused Ammirato's interest in history was not history itself. Indeed, he had been more than willing, in the late 1560s, to drop his projected history of Naples as soon as he realized it would not bring him a single *scudo* of profit. Nor was it the "lives" he read to the Alterati in the 1570s, which he himself admitted amounted to nothing more than wittily told moral tales. Rather, it was genealogy. Ammirato had arrived in Florence with a pocketful of notes taken from the records of his former patrons and with an established reputation as a designer of the *imprese,* or symbolic devices and mottoes, that were one of the passions of all Italy at the time. He knew how to play on the fashion, introduced by the Spanish, for ever more superlative forms of address, even though he realized that it would soon leave God with no titles of honor of his own. He knew how to take advantage of the ambitions of Neapolitan commoners to establish ancient rights to the fiefs they were buying up. He knew how to muffle his laughter over claims to "nobility" based on nothing better than birth and over the desperate pushing and shoving that even an eminent scholar like Scipione Bargagli was willing to indulge in just for the sake of altering a coat of arms. He had also mastered the art, or the science, of making family trees, perhaps with some help from his new fellow citizen Vincenzo Borghini, the expert on the subject; and the success of the first of his well-documented genealogies, later collected in his *Noble Families of Naples* (1577), had been such, notwithstanding a bit of jealous snickering, that he opened shop for Florentines as well. So pleased were his new clients, in turn, in spite of the violent objections of some of the Ricasoli, that he aimed still higher: the Aldobrandini, the Sforza, the Gonzaga, the pope, and even the king of Spain, with whom the Tuscan ambassador, Bongianni Gianfigliazzi, acted as his agent.

But Ammirato soon realized that genealogy was more than just a way of making money. It was a way of winning a place in the already crowded republic of letters:

> Since every man should do his utmost to help others, since I recognize that
> my slender forces permit me to arrive at this goal only through the study of

letters, since even in this [field] . . . almost all the positions through which I might win glory for myself . . . are occupied by a great quantity of writers . . .

It was a way of amusing such latter-day Atticuses and Varros as the wealthy, humane, and urbane Maecenas, Baccio Valori, who, while serving as grand ducal high commissioner of Pisa, discovered the *Cenotaphium Pisanum*—an inscription that was to challenge the leaders of the revival of antiquarian scholarship a century later. Finally, genealogy was a way of adding still more items to the already crowded galleries of miscellaneous rarities, like the one described by Raffaello Borghini:

> Where are displayed little statues of marble and bronze . . . precious stones of all sorts, porcelain and crystal vases, sea shells of many kinds, medals, masks, fruits and animals frozen in stone, and so many new and rare things brought from India and Turkey that it is marvelous to behold.

Ammirato soon came to realize that genealogy might also be considered a branch of a much broader discipline, namely, history. He then discovered that the major discipline had one great advantage over its branch: it permitted him to behold "the beautiful and simple face of Truth" without letting his vision be clouded by the demands of his clients. He therefore turned with enthusiasm to the researches he was supposed to have been conducting all along. And he found them to be very much to his taste. "So wound up am I," he admitted,

> in my curiosity about ancient objects . . . that I pass days on end, from morn till night, covered with the dust and mouse-dung of the monasteries of Tuscany, reading the records of the last seven hundred years, which have furnished me already with so many fascinating bits of knowledge that I have become a veritable storehouse of antiquities!

Ammirato did not like the past particularly; in fact, his work on the *History* confirmed his conviction that the "tranquil conditions of the present times" were incomparably preferable to all previous centuries put together. But he was fascinated by it. If the study of the past did nothing else—and he was not sure it did—it served admirably to give "incomprehensible delight" to the student. That, as far as he was concerned, was a perfectly sufficient reason for its being.

Thus the last and most complete of the Florentine histories of the Renaissance was written for the author, not for the reader. No one in Florence was to write another history of the city—or any other kind of history for that matter—until the middle of the eighteenth century.

5

The twilight of a perfect day

The sun was already hanging heavily over Pistoia when Ammirato started back toward La Petraia that evening. Some of the friends he had seen an hour or so earlier in the academy were now standing casually on the steps of the cathedral. Instead of arguing about war and finances, they were exchanging news and wisecracks. And instead of proclaiming their immeasurable superiority to the *plebe,* whom they repeatedly scorned in academic orations, they were now mixing freely with the artisans and errand boys who shared, after all, the same language, the same traditional Florentine wit, and the same willingness to risk fractured legs and cracked skulls in that sweaty and classless forerunner of modern soccer known as the *gioco di calcio.* Others of his friends—and, *Dio buono,* didn't they look better since the grand duke made them stop putting their hair up in curlers!— were now strolling over to enjoy the first evening breeze from the Ponte Santa Trinita, perhaps remembering the debate of some years before in the Alterati on the question of whether (on scorching days like this one!) it was better to show up at the academy or to take a plunge into the Arno. Still others were heading toward the Porco on the Corso degli Adimari, or toward the Bertucce, the Chiassolino, and the other night-spots where "enormous blasphemies, robberies, cheating, falsehood, . . . and other crimes" were regularly committed over the gaming tables, "to the ruin of many, especially of young noblemen," and to the distress of the stern but helpless magistrates of the Police Office, the *Otto di Guardia.*

Not all the attractions of the city, Ammirato admitted, were exactly uplifting. As the metal shutters came rattling down along Via de' Calzaiuoli, he could see the first of the "women clad in bright garments" emerging from the crowded quarter behind the Palazzo Vecchio, where Cosimo's remodeling of the ghetto had forced them to move. The number of prostitutes had grown noticeably in recent years. But it never occurred to Ammirato that this growth might have something to do with the instability of the economic curve. Nor did he realize

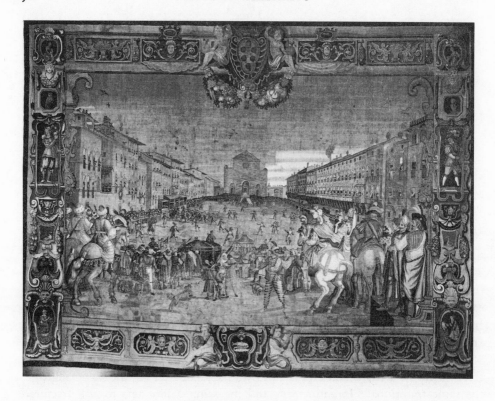

12. Gioco di Calcio, Tapestry
Museo di Firenze Com'Era

that prostitution might be a consequence of the latest method of keeping up an estate without working for it—namely, the condemnation of most potential wives to convents and of most potential male heirs to permanent bachelorhood. But at least he did not hold the prostitutes themselves responsible, as did the archbishop, who barred them from the churches and then rounded them up from time to time for an obligatory harangue about their sins. Ammirato put them in the same category with beggars and bandits—as one of the few incurable blemishes on an otherwise fortunate age, whom even the pope had to tolerate "in order to avoid the worst." All he could do was to complain about the way they rode around triumphantly in carriages. Even Cleopatra herself, he pointed out, did not get away with that.

In general, Ammirato had good reason to be pleased with his life in Florence. Vasari, Varchi, Lasca, Vettori, and all the other leaders of the old generation had now vanished; and the premature death of Salviati in 1588 had left him as the most prominent man of letters in the city. He had good reason to be content with his work, too. One by one, he had succeeded in solving, at least to the satisfaction of his new compatriots, most of the problems that had bothered them for the past two hundred years. Indeed, he had succeeded in convincing them that the hopes and aspirations of the great age inaugurated by Dante had at last been realized. True, some Florentines still had doubts. Marcello Adriani, for instance, warned that "ignorance" and the quest for pleasure were on the verge of driving the last remnants of good literature to France and England. Bernardo Davanzati suggested that the age of Lorenzo the Magnificent and Poliziano was now as remote and done-for as the age of Pericles and Demosthenes. And Francesco Bocchi still maintained that the happiness of Italy had been permanently compromised by the catastrophic French invasion of 1494. But these were only a few isolated voices in a chorus of contentment and satisfaction.

Actually, neither Ammirato nor Salviati nor Giacomini really had much to worry about. They had no fear that anyone would look up the original formulations of the problems they claimed to have solved: the linguistic purists had banned all but the vernacular literature of the Trecento from current reading shelves, and the Accademia Fiorentina had removed all but a few passages of Ficino and Pico from the literary heritage of the Quattrocento. For another thing, they could rest assured that self-conscious Florentines would not willingly expose themselves to any of the new books from abroad in which the old problems were presented in new forms. And just in case anyone should be tempted by attractive titles, they could now rely on the pious vigilance of the ecclesiastical censors. For although the Index of Forbidden Books could not be enforced to the letter, it had at least made suspect in the eyes of nervous readers any work written by any author or put out by any publisher who had ever been accused, however unjustly, of a slip from orthodoxy. And that kept them away not only from most of the writings of the Italian humanists, which were available only in transalpine editions, but even from the expurgated versions of Erasmus's *Colloquies* and *Adages,* which were published with official approbation in 1575 and 1585.

At times, the literati found censorship a bit annoying. The booksellers and physicians complained bitterly to Cosimo I in 1559 when they were threatened with losing their stocks and their textbooks. Vettori and Borghini grumbled audibly about having to alter the words of Boccaccio's *Decameron* in 1573. And Ammirato was frequently annoyed at having to hold up his most urgent projects for months on end just because of bickering between the ecclesiastical and the civil censors. But none of the grumblers had any real objection to censorship itself, particularly after the much more flexible and more easily enforceable Tridentine Index, with its provision for prohibitions "until corrected" (*donec corrigatur*), replaced the ridiculously rigorous Index of Paul IV, which Cosimo managed to get around by waiting patiently until its author died. They could find little comfort abroad, for censorship was at times even more arbitrary and extensive in England, France, Geneva, Spain, and almost every other part of Europe aside from Venice. They admitted that what once might have been innocent jokes or frank reporting of fact might, in an age beset with heresy, "lead the minds of simpler folk away from the straight path." They agreed that no mere author could claim to be the final judge in matters of religion, morals, or the reputation of princes. They conceded that "it is better that one book be lost than that our souls be endangered by bad opinions." And they did not even bother to inquire to what extent Francesco Bocchi's *History of the Rebellion in Flanders* or the *Commentaries* of Enio Silvio Piccolomini (Pope Pius II), which were first published in 1584, had been touched up by the time they got into print.

Neither state nor church had to exert much pressure on the authors. Grand Duke Francesco let Fabio Benvoglienti put out two editions of his plea for religious toleration, the *Discourse on Why the Ancients Did Not Make War over Religion,* even though the thesis was rather remarkable at a time when the St. Bartholomew Day's Massacre in Paris was celebrated with parades and fireworks all over Catholic Europe. And Grand Duke Ferdinando entrusted wholly to Ammirato's well-known discretion the choice of what to include in or exclude from the *History of Florence.* Florentine writers were sometimes more than cooperative. Salviati put out a still more expurgated version of the *Decameron* completely on his own initiative in 1582; and his eulogist, Pierfrancesco Campi, got away with proclaiming this unnecessarily emasculated version to be a restoration of the original text, although it seems to have been prompted solely by the editor's hope of making money. While it might be rather ample in practice, then, freedom of thought and expression rested on no firmer a foundation than that of convenience. When, in the last decade of the century, the Holy Office decided that it would henceforth assume the same responsibilities for philosophy and science that it had previously assumed for religion and morality, Florentines acquiesced without a murmer. Ammirato and his friends had forgotten about Girolamo Mei's warning of 1566: that censorship, either voluntary or involuntary, could lead to stagnation. For in the meantime they had discovered in it a hitherto unhoped-for instrument of self-defense—one that rendered practically impregnable the whole admirable edifice of ideas and attitudes that they had built up during thirty years of hard work.

Little did they suspect, then, that this edifice was not quite ample enough to cover all the areas in which their fellow citizens were still active. They thought that they had fully accounted for one of them back in 1564: the fine arts. It was then, during the funeral ceremonies for Michelangelo, that Salviati did away with all further problems of aesthetics by transposing the arts into perfectly understandable Aristotelian categories. It was then that Vasari proclaimed the arts never before to have been "so great and so abundant." It was then that the new art academy, the Accademia del Disegno, in what amounted to its first public exhibition, promised to guarantee forever the maintenance of painting and sculpture at the unsurpassable level that the "divine" Michelangelo had raised them to. How was Ammirato to know, as he echoed Vasari's complacent observations about the flourishing state of Florentine art twenty-five years later—how was he to know that the optimism of 1564 had rested on no better evidence than a census of available craftsmen? How was he to remember that Salviati's "solution" depended completely on the assumption that color automatically instilled an "insatiable avidity" and an "ardent longing" in the viewer's soul? After all, Vasari and Vincenzo Borghini had kept quietly to themselves their snide observation about what the Accademia del Disegno was really up to a decade after its foundation, and not even Salviati had felt obliged actually to look at real paintings when he talked about their final causes.

Fortunately, the artists themselves paid very little attention to what the philosophers said they should do. Some of them simply went on reproducing what they had learned from their masters—particularly since one master, Vasari, had the bad taste to outlive his prime and to cover the ceiling of the cathedral with a fresco that they politely honored by not mentioning. Some of them went on catering to the aesthetic preferences that their masters had instilled in the mind of Grand Duke Francesco, who, unlike his father, pretended to be an expert on art as well as on politics. It is not surprising that much of the work of Battista Naldini, Bernardino Pocetti, Battista di Lorenzo, and the other favorite painters of the moment looks like a shallow imitation of Bronzino and Pontormo. Nor is it surprising that it often seems to make an end of what once had been the technical means of Mannerist art: anatomical distortion, unnatural color, and two-dimensional abstract design.

This apparent waning of creativity, this "Cinquecento on the verge of death," has so puzzled a few recent art historians that they have gone outside the field of art history in search of a cause—namely, to something they call the "Counter-Reformation." This Counter-Reformation has nothing whatever to do with the religious, ecclesiastical, and theological movement usually denoted by the same name. It was, say these art historians, the product of "the discovery of new trade routes" and the consequent "collapse of the great mercantile bourgeoisie," which no social or economic historian of the age has yet been able to discern. It consisted, they point out, in "a Catholic counter-offensive that tried by every means, from persuasion to coercion, to regain lost terrain"—even though nothing of the sort occurred in the one diocese, Bologna, where the actual relations of a reforming bishop and his artists are well known. This reformation is documented not by the decrees of the Council of Trent, which made only general stipulations about liturgical decorations, but by a rather senile crisis of conscience on the part of one Florentine artist, which none of his colleagues seem to have shared, and by a dialogue on *The Errors of the Painters,* which no one in Florence seems to have heard of. Finally, its effects are supposedly visible in all those elements of the pictorial, but not the written, record of the age which seem to viewers in the twentieth (but not necessarily in the sixteenth) century to be sad, morose, morbid, irregular, or otherworldly.

This explanation may well be correct. But anyone whose professional commitments restrict him to purely human or natural, rather than meta-historical, explanations for historical events will have to look elsewhere. He may notice that Florentine artists were not wholly dependent either upon the court or upon the church hierarchy for their commissions and that at least one of them painted as often for shopkeepers, carpenters, and lay confraternities as he did for wealthy state officials. He may also notice that Florence suffered from an overproduction of art at the time—an overproduction deliberately fostered by the Accademia del Disegno in spite of the increasing difficulty it encountered in selling off its stocks after every public competition. He may further notice that art prices declined just at a time when most other prices were rising—that 3.7 *scudi* for one of Andrea Boscoli's portraits and 23 *scudi* for one of his vast murals was rather little compared to the 14 *scudi* paid for a set of six silver knives and forks and the 25 *scudi*-a-month pension that one artist found completely inadequate for the support of his family.* Finally, he may notice that the once exalted social position of the artists had begun to slip—to the point, indeed, at which the new Bureau of Public Works established in 1588 lumped them together indiscriminately with "jewelers, gardeners, porcelain workers, and distillers."

At the same time, anyone looking for "causes" may have to admit that the decline of late Mannerism was relative rather than absolute. First of all, Mannerism did not rule out the possibility of occasional innovation within the established styles. At least such innovation is apparent today in Alessandro Allori's "Annunciation" in the Accademia, where attention is drawn away from the more traditional apparition of the angel toward the event that the angel is announcing; and in the cold, eerie, off-white light that surrounds the playful Baby Jesus and his carefree playmates in Allori's "Virgin and Child." It was also apparent to Allori's contemporaries who were then working on Philip II's Escurial: they found Florentine mannerists as worthy of imitation as the greatest of the Spanish mannerists, El Greco. Second, decline did not preclude the extension of forms previously worked out on canvas to a new medium, namely, architecture. And Mannerist architects achieved such lasting triumphs as the Ponte Santa Trinita by Ammannati and the facade of the church of Santa Trinita by Buontalenti. Third, decline did not impede Florentine artists from breaking through the isolation characteristic of most other aspects of Florentine culture at the time to learn from the example of foreigners. They were charmed by the Audubon-like drawings of plants and animals that Jacopo Ligozzi specialized in after his arrival

---

* The figures extracted by Detlef Heikamp from Boscoli's account book are given in *lire*, the money of account. I translate into the more common money of exchange, *scudi*, according to the rates set by the edict of July 15, 1556: 1 *scudo* = 7 *lire*, 12 *soldi*.

from Verona in 1578. And they were overawed by the Fleming who soon became
the most celebrated sculptor in Florence, Giambologna, in spite of his inability to
distinguish critical judgments from platitudes and to distinguish the speech of his
homeland from that of his adopted country:

> ... La casson che ce molto che veder, et teniama gran obliga al Sig.
> Cavalier. . . . Di pieu ce mena per la cita a veder le cose bella che veramente
> lo trava affectionatissimo a li servizio di S.A.S. . . .*

Similarly, decline did not prevent the organization of a number of vast collaborat-
ive projects in which the overall conceptual unity made up, to some extent, for
deficiencies in the individual parts. That, at any rate, is what happened in the
decorations for the funeral of Cosimo I, in the *Studiolo* of Francesco, in the chapel
of San Luca at the Annunziata, in the chapel of the Salviati at San Marco, in the
sacristy of the Spanish chapel, and, above all, in the great cloister of Santa Maria
Novella, where Cristoforo Allori turned manna into roast pheasant and had
water poured by a voluptuous female from a weightless jar.

The very nature of the decline was to some extent conditioned by the artists'
awareness of it—an awareness expressed by Bocchi's and Davanzati's study of
stylistic differences between the generation of Brunelleschi and the generation
of "our fathers," Michelangelo and Bronzino. It was also conditioned by the
artists' willingness to look for a remedy. Some of them proposed returning to
the direct study of anatomy—to such an extent that Alessandro Allori kept his
students nauseated with the jars of pickled arms, legs, and hands in his studio.
Some of them, most notably Santi di Tito, tried to return in their own work to
the pre-Mannerist Florentine tradition. One of them, Lodovico Cigoli, sought to
combine what he had admired in the works of the High Renaissance with what
he learned from his contemporaries in Bologna, Rome, and Venice. And all
of them were inspired by the one really relevant theoretical treatise of the age:
the "conversation" among the artist friends of the knowledgeable patron
Bernardo Vecchietti, which a little-known ex-bank clerk named Raffaello
Borghini wrote down in a dialogue called *Il riposo,* after the name of Vecchietti's
villa outside of Porta San Niccolò. They were thus exposed once again to the
long-forgotten principles of Leon Battista Alberti. They became critical of
exaggerated departures from exact representation (*verosimile*), particularly those of
Francesco Salviati. They learned to test Pliny's reports about the rhetorical effect
of ancient painting by reference not to theory but to their own impressions of
modern painting. And they prepared themselves to discard Mannerism altogether
for what one recent historian has called the "Second Renaissance"—which is

---

* In English the passage sounds something like this: "The raison is that moch is to sea;
et oui are verry obligés to the gentleman ... who laid us autour the cité to sea the beautiful
choses whome trouly oui found most devoted to the services of H.R. Highness."

what Santi di Tito began to do in the 1580s and what Cigoli was to do much more successfully in the next two decades.

At the same time, a similar juncture of practice, theory, and scholarship was producing a still larger crack in Ammirato's admirable edifice. Ammirato himself seldom listened to music. But he was at least aware that the musical *intermedi* between the acts of contemporary comedies were becoming more important than the dull rehashings of the same old plots—so much so, indeed, that one playwright, Lasca, wrote directions for the *intermedi* right along with his texts. He also knew that the ingenious and expensive parades that regularly wound through the streets to the accompaniment of popular "carnival songs"—*canti carnascialeschi*—could, when moved into the courtyard of the Palazzo Pitti, turn into the huge displays of artistic talent that he himself acclaimed as "the greatest, the proudest, and the most stupendous . . . that the world has seen since the days of the ancient Romans." He had met the rich, talented, and somewhat grouchy patron of music in Florence, Giovanni de' Bardi. He had heard the philosophic explanations of soccer games and the casual travelogs about Hadrian's villa at Tivoli which Bardi occasionally recited in the academies. And he had been as annoyed as the consul of the Alterati when Bardi rudely disrupted one meeting by scheduling one of his private concerts at the same hour.

Yet neither Ammirato nor most of his academic friends seem to have realized that the group of amateurs and performers whom Bardi had gathered together in an informal association called the *Camerata* were preparing one of the most important revolutions in the history of music. Nor were they aware that the principles of the revolution were already being applied—bit by bit so as not to shock audiences or disrupt the traditional programs of court festivities—in such spectacles as the one put on for the marriage of the grand duke two years before. Or rather, they knew about all this, but they took no account of it when dealing with the subjects that interested them intellectually. And when they referred to music in academic discourses, they simply fell back, like Verino and Bocchi, on the same old watered-down Platonic arguments about its soothing effect on troubled nerves and the dangers of too much of it in vigorous republics. They were thus deaf to the Camerata's condemnation of those modern musicians "who aim at nothing but delighting the ear." And they failed to appreciate the new ends that it proposed for music: "to express the passions with greater effectiveness and to communicate these [passions] with equal force to the minds of mortals for their benefit and advantage."

But perhaps the academicians did well to leave music alone. The Camerata looked to antiquity not, as they did, for definitive answers, but for provocative suggestions. Vincenzo Galilei, the father of the great Galileo and music mentor of the Camerata, set forth his theses in the form of dialogues, like his humanist forebears, rather than in the form of treatises and orations, which the academicians had become accustomed to. Indeed, Galilei insisted upon arguing from the phenomena rather than from the authorities. He judged the quality of music not by its conformity to mathematical ratios but by its emotional impact upon the listener. Music was thus divorced from metaphysics and allied to rhetoric, just as art, political philosophy, and historiography had been in the days of Bruni and Alberti. Accordingly, Galilei included Alessandro Striggio's "Lament of Psyche" in his anthology of exemplary pieces because, according to Lasca, it had made Grand Duke Francesco's wedding guests cry when they heard it sung in 1565. He readmitted certain elements of the counterpoint he had once condemned in his still-unpublished *Seconda pratica* of 1588. He refused to present his own experiments with dissonance until they could be "set forth in an orderly manner." And he abstained from publishing his more startling innovations until they could be tried out in practice.

To be sure, the Camerata did not start the revolution, whatever the mud-slinging of Galilei's *Dialogue on Ancient and Modern Music* of 1581 might imply. The revolution had begun over a century before, at almost the same time that a similar revolution had occurred in the visual arts. It had been furthered by Josquin des Prés, among others, who freed music from its remaining medieval patterns and endowed it with thematic unity and the function of expressing emotions and states of mind. And it had been brought to Florence by some of Josquin's contemporaries, who, as early as 1520, had managed to write scores that took account of "the sense and the value of words"—which may be why Galilei looked so favorably upon Florentine folk and popular songs. Nor did the Camerata work wholly alone. Nicola Vicentino and Gioseffo Zarlino in Italy, Heinrich Loriti (Glareanus) in Switzerland, and Pontus de Tyard in France had all been searching for a kind of music that would better realize the new ideal. And they had all been prodded by what they read in certain ancient writers about the extraordinary emotional effects of Greek music. But Galilei went beyond his predecessors and contemporaries in objecting to the increasingly cerebral quality of recent polyphony, even Palestrina's. He exceeded them in his optimism about the possibility of reproducing in his own time the effects attributed to the Greeks in antiquity.

It was just at this moment that Pier Vettori's school of philology came to his rescue, in the person of the same Girolamo Mei who had fought with Vincenzo Borghini over the Lombards and who, after wandering about from Venice to Lyon, finally settled, amid frequent attacks of the gout, in Rome. Tracking down references for Vettori's projected edition of Dionysius of Halicarnassus had led Mei, in the early 1570s, to undertake a purely historical study of Greek music. And just as he finished drawing out all the relevant information contained in literary sources, lo! there at the bottom of the Vatican Library he discovered two pieces of real Greek music: the "Tables" of Alypius and the "Hymns" of Mesomedes of Crete. To be sure, Mei could not really read the scores he found. Even modern scholars dare offer no more than good guesses as to how they should be played. But they did offer him what he considered to be clear proof that Greek music was more expressive than sixteenth-century music, and that it was so for two reasons: because it was monophonic rather than polyphonic and because it emphasized the sound and the meaning of the words it was set to.

Galilei was enthusiastic. He immediately set forth to make choruses sing only in unison, to permit instruments only in accompaniments, to sacrifice abstract beauty for emotional impact, and to impose universally the kind of unmelodic recitative that even his admirers found a bit "coarse and antiquated." But he was still left with only modern music, not ancient music, as the basis for his principles. Hence, what he did—and what Giovanni's son Piero Bardi, Jacopo Corsi, Jacopo Peri, and Giulio Caccini did—was not so much to create a wholly new music as to bring the many isolated and purely empirical experiments of the recent past within the framework of a well thought-out and carefully tested theory. They then put the theory into practice—first in the *intermedi* for Ferdinando's wedding, then in the musical settings for Ottavio Rinuccini's pastoral play, *Dafne,* and finally in Peri's *Euridice,* which was written and performed for the wedding of Maria de' Medici and Henry IV in 1600. Peri's off-beat accents, his sudden shifts of harmony, his skillful use of dissonance, and his arrangement of melodic cadences according to the changes in moods and ideas succeeded so well in accentuating the meaning of each line of the text that the *Euridice* has proven capable of moving an audience even at the distance of almost four centuries —as Howard Brown made clear by putting it on at the University of Chicago in January 1967. Just as Cigoli abandoned what had become a purely ornamental and decorative art in the name of Alberti and Andrea del Sarto, so Peri, following Galilei, abandoned the music of delight for the music of rhetoric in accordance with the methods and purposes of Quattrocento humanism. And when he combined his music with Rinuccini's poetry and Buontalenti's stage sets, he gave birth to a completely new form of art: the opera.

Yet the most serious threat to Ammirato's edifice did not come from music and the arts, which he managed fairly well to isolate from his principal concerns. It came rather from the sciences. Science, or "natural philosophy," as it was then called, was the discipline that Ammirato thought to be the safest—the one, that is, in which the greatest number of problems had already been solved. True, even he, like Benedetto Varchi before him, occasionally let slip a vague doubt about the validity of certain hallowed theses—as, for example, when he admitted that an illiterate Venetian fisherman might know more about ichthyology than the most learned professor. But then any of his friends who had yawned through the regular philosophy courses at the university could easily have reassured him. A few doubts, they knew, were not enough to compromise the system as a whole; and anything that Aristotle himself had not been able to figure out could easily be provided by reference to Aristotelianism, the metaphysical system of which his writings were merely the most authoritative manifestation. Hence the study of natural philosophy still consisted in commenting upon a few universally accepted texts. It had nothing to do with the acquisition of knowledge about single objects, which was within the scope even of the unlearned. And it set forth a rational, intelligible, comprehensive, and rather comfortable cosmos, which even the doubters were very happy to live in.

Unfortunately, occasional discrepancies among the authorities and—worse yet in an age that was rapidly accumulating an immense quantity of unassorted information—occasional discrepancies between the authorities and the specific data they supposedly had "explained" were beginning to create serious difficulties. In fact, the most proficient scholars of the day were spending much of their time trying desperately to overcome these difficulties. Giovan Battista Benedetti worked for years on an up-to-date version of Aristotle's *De Coelo,* as the musicologist Girolamo Mei acknowledged after hearing his lectures in Rome. Francesco Buonamici, the one university professor whom Filippo Sassetti omitted from his list of laughable academic cranks, struggled constantly with the most upsetting point in Aristotelian physics: the theory of motion. Jacopo Mazzoni, who had been warmly welcomed in the Florentine academies in 1588, had already resolved 5,197 discordant *quaestiones* in Aristotle, Plato, and "many other Greek, Arab, and Latin authors" by the time he arrived at Pisa; and he immediately set to work resolving as many more.

None of the university philosophers was more dedicated to the task of saving the authorities than a shy, mild instructor in medicine named Andrea Cesalpino. Indeed, Cesalpino went to such efforts to back up what Aristotle had said about the nature of sleep that he accidentally came up with what several historians have noted as an anticipation of Harvey's discovery of the circulation of the blood. There was no reason, he pointed out in his major work, the *Peripateticarum Quaestiones* of 1571 and 1593, to bother with new books. The foundations of science had already been laid down far more thoroughly and comprehensively in the old ones, which by then were available in easily accessible modern editions. But when he then noticed that Galen said one thing and Hippocrates said another and that certain flowers sent to him from Pistoia and Goa failed to fit the species and genera of either Theophrastus or Dioscorides, he had to admit that his admonition was not completely reliable. After all, Cesalpino was not just a teacher of academic medicine. He was also the supervisor of the herb-loving grand duke's botanical garden. He was responsible for sick soldiers in Livorno and sick knights in the Order of Santo Stefano. He was expected to render competent judgments

about the authenticity of the bones of St. Donatus in Arezzo, about the physical
effects of ecstasy on the corpse of St. Filippo Neri, about the way to expel a demon
from a suspected murderess, and about the quality of the balsam and poisons that
Grand Duke Francesco was thinking of buying. Sometimes he just had to figure
out an explanation of his own. Because he had once been a pupil of the philologist
Pier Vettori, he knew how to drop the principles when they failed him and look
solely at the individual and the concrete. When he began applying the standards
of philology to the rocks and plants in his collection, he hit upon a "working"
method of classifying them which was to remain unexcelled for almost a
century.

Cesalpino had merely suspended for a moment the system he was trying to
defend. But he occasionally went farther—as when he suggested that science might
consist of a constantly growing number of only relatively true hypotheses—*velut
aquae fluentes in continua renovatione* "continually being renewed like flowing
waters"—rather than a fixed body of doctrine. Others went still farther. An
obscure teacher of perspective named Ostilio Ricci told his pupils at the Accademia del Disegno that the new equations worked out by the mathematicians at
Padua and Bologna were not merely intellectual exercises: they might rather serve
as a substitute for Aristotelian logic in reorganizing the whole structure of the
cosmos. Worse yet, one of the most diehard Aristotelians—one for whom
"conformity with the doctrine of Aristotle" constituted "the sole rule of all
truth"—had the audacity to announce, right at the height of the Counter-
Reformation, what his predecessors had suspected for over a century: that
Aristotle was no longer capable of providing a metaphysical foundation for
Christianity. "Above the Eighth Sphere [of the fixed stars]," he decided, there is
neither God nor angels nor saints. And if the Lords Inquisitor persist in their
contrary opinion, he added, carefully shielding himself behind the grand duke's
determination to preserve freedom of speech at the university, they will find
nothing up there but "a plate of macaroni." Ammirato had made religion
compatible with politics. But what had he achieved if it then turned out to be
incompatible with physics?

Ammirato did not know—and did not care. He was getting old. And so, for
that matter, were most of his associates. He chuckled quietly as he recalled how
that now respected ecclesiastic, Francesco Bonciani, had once dressed up in an
outlandish costume and helped half the young thugs of Pisa throw the other half
over the Ponte di Mezzo. He smiled as he remembered how that now middle-aged
patrician, Cosimo Rucellai, once rushed "into the piazza . . . in a gold *faresettin*
and a huge feathered cap, jumped at the ball, kicked it off, dashed in all directions,
gave some punches and received many more, and often fell down and rolled
around on the ground." Those days were gone forever. The upstart Accademia
degli Alterati had become an established institution, and the brash teen-agers of
the 1570s had become the first citizens of the 1590s. Indeed, they themselves

were conscious of the change in generation, and within a few years they were to renovate the academy by voting in their sons and nephews en bloc.

But Ammirato did not really understand what these young people were up to. He had never met Ricci or Buonamici. He was not upset when Cesalpino accepted a higher salary from the pope and went off to Rome. And he was not at all interested in Vincenzo Galilei's bright young son, the one who occasionally cropped up in Ammirato's conversations with Giovan Battista Strozzi and Baccio Valori. This was the son who, three years before, had given a rather dull lecture on Dante's *Inferno* in the Accademia Fiorentina, who talked endlessly about things called conic sections and centers of gravity, and who just then was packing up to go to Padua, after half starving for a year at Pisa on one-twentieth the salary paid to the big-name professors.

It was late that evening when Ammirato's carriage finally clattered back through the heavy iron gate at La Petraia. He was relatively content. After all, his speech had been applauded. His wit had been commended. And his position as the leader of the Florentine intellectual community had once again been recognized. But he was also tired. And, he had to admit, he was a bit lonely.

BOOK III

FLORENCE
IN THE 1630s

*How Galileo Galilei turned the
universe inside out*

PROLOGUE

How Galileo came home after eighteen years abroad

January 7, 1610, in Padua.
Galileo Galilei, the distinguished and respected, if somewhat iconoclastic professor
of mathematics at the University of Padua, climbed once again to the roof of his
house as soon as it got dark, apparently heedless of the damp, penetrating chill
of the Venetian winter. For the past two weeks he had been up there every
evening, at least whenever the usual fog cleared enough for him to see the sky.
He had been looking at the moon, not with his naked eye, which is the only way
anyone had ever looked at it until then, but through what he called an "eye-reed"
(*cannocchiale*) and what soon came to be called a "telescope." He had gradually
come to the startling conclusion that the moon was not the perfectly smooth
sphere that almost everyone had always thought it to be. Rather, it was "sharp
and unequal . . . and full of eminences and cavities," much like the mountains
and valleys of the earth. This evening, however, he turned the telescope toward
Jupiter. There, to his even greater surprise, he discerned not just the familiar
planet, but three tiny discs, two on one side and one on the other. They were
discs, he noticed—round, luminous areas. Hence, they were not stars, which even
through the telescope appeared merely as points of light surrounded by rays.
Moreover, they changed position relative to each other during the course of the
evening. Hence, they must be moons. And Jupiter, far from being an eternal lamp
embedded in an impenetrable crystalline sphere, must be a freestanding body
much like the earth.

Galileo was so excited by his discovery that he forthwith descended from the
roof and spent the remaining hours of the night describing what he had seen
in a terse, compact, and polished letter to his most influential friend at the court
of Florence.

Galileo returned to his roof the next evening and almost every other evening for the rest of the month. He was soon able to add still another moon to Jupiter and to baptize all four of them, in a stroke of well-planned diplomacy, the "Medicean Planets," in honor of Grand Duke Cosimo II and his three brothers. He then succeeded in attributing the glow on the dark portion of the new moon not, as had been customary, to Venus or to some sort of inherent lunar luminosity, but to the reflection of the sun's light off the earth. He discovered that the Milky Way was not simply the irregular blobs that had "vexed philosophers through so many ages," that the nebula of Praesepe was not a strange concentration of an imaginary space-filler called "aether," and that the sword and belt of Orion contained not just nine but at least eighty stars. "As these observations are infinitely marvelous," he exclaimed, "so infinitely I give thanks to God that he has been pleased to make me the first one to see things so marvelous, hidden throughout all ages."

The discoveries were more than just "marvelous." They seemed to confirm what several leading philosophers had recently come to suspect: the explanation of the structures of the universe first proposed by Aristotle and almost universally accepted for over a millennium could no longer be maintained. At the same time, they offered a large amount of spectacular, if not yet conclusive, empirical evidence in favor of another explanation, one that had been known in antiquity and that had been re-proposed, some sixty-five years before, by the Polish astronomer Nicholas Copernicus. For Jupiter could have moons and the moon could have mountains only if the following propositions were true: celestial bodies were subject to laws of motion identical to those observable on earth; the planets revolved around the sun while the "fixed stars" really remained "fixed" in relation to it; and the earth was, in Galileo's words, "a wandering body surpassing the moon in splendor" rather than an immobile "sink of all the dull refuse of the universe," as the Aristotelians supposed. Galileo therefore put aside his telescope and set to work on what was soon to be one of the most enthusiastically acclaimed pamphlets of all time, the *Siderius Nuncius,* or "Starry Messenger," which he dedicated to Cosimo II and published in Venice on March 4.

Certainly no one of his generation was as well prepared as Galileo to make the discoveries, to understand their importance, and to explain them to others. First of all, he was a mathematician. He had been introduced to the subject by a pupil of the leading mathematician of the mid-sixteenth century, Niccolò Tartaglia. He had also learned, partly from the ancient mathematician Archimedes of Syracuse, and partly from his fellow students at the Accademia del Disegno in Florence, that what hitherto had been regarded as solely a speculative science might have important practical applications. He had then gone on to work out several practical consequences of Archimedes' theories in his first two published treatises. His skill as a mathematician had won him both his teaching positions—first as an underpaid instructor at Pisa, in 1587, and then as an increasingly well-paid professor at Padua, in 1591. It was his ability to express in mathematical terms what he saw through the telescope in January 1610 that finally assured him of not being deceived by an optical illusion.

Galileo was also a technician and an inventor. On commissions from the Venetian government, he had devised one new instrument for increasing the efficiency of oars on naval galleys and another for "raising water and irrigating fields, very easy and very inexpensive to operate." He had then constructed a rudimentary slide rule for calculating mechanically the interest due on varying amounts of capital and a still more rudimentary thermo-barometer which, in spite of its defects, at least permitted temperature to be expressed in numbers for the first time. Galileo had even gone into the business of inventing: he installed a workshop in his house that soon grossed several thousand *lire* a year, and he vigorously protected his patents in at least one noisy lawsuit and one vituperative pamphlet. He was thus quick to guess at the potential utility of an ingenious combination of concave and convex lenses that some Dutch artisans had recently put on the market in Paris. No one else thought of it as anything but a toy, an outrageously expensive toy at that, according to the Tuscan ambassador, who refused to buy one for the grand duke. Whoever was familiar with current theories of optics dismissed it as "a huge deception, [one which] makes objects seem to be where they are not and which changes their sizes, colors, and movements." But being a mathematician rather than just a theorist or an artisan, Galileo realized that its magnifying power could be calculated mathematically. After sparing "neither time nor expense" for over a month, he managed to construct one that enlarged distant objects not twenty or thirty but a thousand times their apparent size. And when the senators who followed him up the Campanile in San Marco realized that their captains might spot pirate ships on the Adriatic as clearly as the senators now beheld the otherwise invisible facade of Santa Giustina in Padua, they placed a standing order for as many of the new instruments as he could make and doubled his salary at the university.

More important still, Galileo was a teacher. Indeed, he dressed almost ostentatiously in academic garb: a long, straight beard and closely cropped hair over a flat white collar and a plain brown gown which, in the age of waxed Van Dycks, multicolored bloomers, starched lace, and other such "Spanish subtleties," looked fifty years out-of-date. His inaugural lectures in 1591 had drawn an overflow crowd and a stream of congratulatory letters. In the next few years he managed to attract many of the most talented, serious, and wellborn students at the university. Some of them shared his roof and his table, in accordance with a long-standing Paduan tradition of receiving paying boarders into professors' houses. Many of them eventually became his chief collaborators and patrons:

the eccentric Venetian patrician Giovanfrancesco Sagredo and the wealthy Florentine nobleman Filippo Salviati, for instance, both of whom appear as interlocutors in his two principal dialogues; the brilliant Benedictine monk Benedetto Castelli, who worked out many of his unsolved mathematical problems; and the mechanic and architect Paolo Aproino, who applied his principles to the science of acoustics. Indeed, Galileo's students took the place of a family in his affections. For them he shunned the company of his doting mother, his whining sister, his shiftless brother, and his demanding brother-in-law. For them he was to abandon his mistress, later in 1610, almost without a tear. For them he put the two daughters she bore him in a convent as soon as they were of age and put off recognizing for almost a decade the son she also bore him. For them, finally, he developed a new kind of expository prose—a kind capable of persuading them, or of getting them to persuade themselves, of the absolute validity of his scientific theses.

Galileo's prose owed very little to his favorite authors—to Petrarch, whom he ransacked for forceful adjectives, to Dante, whose *Inferno* he plotted out in conic sections, to Francesco Berni, whom he used as a model for his satirical poem "Against Wearing Togas," and to Il Lasca, whom he may have read as inspiration for his own abortive attempt at a comedy. It owed nothing at all either to the forty-odd volumes of philosophy and ethics in his meager private library or to the prolix orations he had listened to as a member of the Accademia Fiorentina in the 1580s. Galileo followed three simple principles. The first was clarity: he wrote "obscure" over every line of his favorite poet, Ariosto, that could not be instantly understood. The second was relevance: he constantly upbraided his least favorite poet, Tasso, for "filling up the page" when there was really "nothing more to say." The third was effectiveness: a period that was "cold and forceless," he insisted, might just as well be left unsaid. Galileo thus learned to bridge the gap between a literary and a spoken language, to express the loftiest matters in the form of casual conversation, and to alternate rapidly between the deadly serious and the gently ironic, between humor and gravity. Better yet, he learned to communicate his theses not just to the academic elite to which he belonged by vocation, but to the society of nonspecialized educated laymen to which he, and most of his students, belonged by birth and by choice. His works were acclaimed as models of literary excellence in his own generation. They have been held up ever since as evidence that good science and good letters are not necessarily incompatible.

But what Galileo really aspired to be was a philosopher—a philosopher, that is, according to the then current definition of the term as one who seeks to understand the nature and function of the universe. He had studied at Pisa under two of the more prominent academic philosophers of the age, Francesco Buonamici and Giovan Battista Benedetti; and he had been impressed enough by their attempts to solve the most pressing problem of contemporary philosophy—

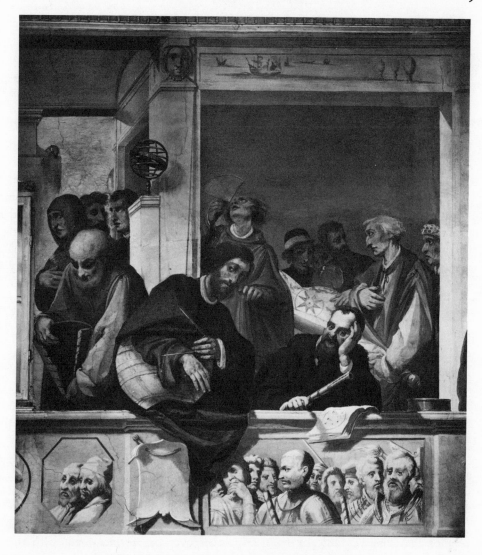

13. Cecco Bravo, *Galileo among the Philosophers*
Casa Buonarroti

how to patch up the widening cracks of the Aristotelian cosmos—to offer a
solution of his own. In the meantime he had also come into contact with one of
the most promising professional philosophers of the age, Johannes Kepler, the
court astronomer at Prague, with whom he soon began corresponding, as well as
one of the most ebullient nonacademic philosophers of the age, the Neapolitan
monk Tommaso Campanella, whom he met in Venice in 1592. With their help
he soon became convinced that the Aristotelian cosmos could no longer be
saved either by the *impetus* theory of the fourteenth-century Parisian doctors or

by the Neoplatonic props discovered by the most vocal successor to Buonamici and Benedetti at Pisa, Jacopo Mazzoni, with whom he occasionally collaborated. When he succeeded in explaining the motion of falling bodies and the pendulum in a manner as compatible with observation as it was incompatible with the Aristotelian theory of substance, he quietly let that cosmos drop. And when, on the night of October 10, 1604, a new star suddenly appeared in the constellation Sagittarius—a star that observation showed could be located nowhere but in the Aristotelians' impenetrable, unalterable supralunary spheres—he openly rejected that cosmos.

Yet being a philosopher, Galileo could not do without any cosmos at all. And being a mathematician as well as a philosopher, he could not admit the traditional relegation of astronomy to the role of a mere calculating device. That, indeed, had been the chief weakness of the so-called Ptolemaic system. In order to account for the irregular course of the planets, it had to imagine that they revolved around moving points on their orbits while their orbits wobbled around a variety of moving centers near to, but not coincident with, the earth. But it never supposed that in reality the planets revolved in any other way than in the perfect concentric circles prescribed by philosophy, since philosophy alone had the right to determine what existed. Thus when, as early as 1597, Galileo decided to try out the Copernican astronomical system as an alternative to the one he was giving up, he realized that he was adopting far more than just a purely hypothetical means for predicting celestial motions—which is all that Pope Gregory XIII's commission on calendar reform was willing to give Copernicus credit for. Indeed, the Copernican system had not yet proved noticeably superior in fulfilling that function than the Ptolemaic system; and Galileo did not share Kepler's optimistic prognosis that it ever would be, as long as observation was limited to what the naked eye could see.

Rather, Galileo was adopting a completely new cosmos. It was one that still suffered from puzzling lacunae, such as its failure to account for the apparent immobility of the earth and the evident motion of the planets. It was also a cosmos that differed radically from any other ever before imagined, with the possible exception of the one recently proposed by the Danish astronomer Tycho Brahe, which made the planets revolve around the sun and the whole solar system around the earth. It was quantitative rather than qualitative, in that it contained no more color, soul, beauty, or goodness than what human fantasy chose to project into it. It was democratic rather than aristocratic, in that it was comprehensible through numbers, which any man could read, rather than through signs and symbols, which were accessible only to the initiate. It was infinite rather than finite, and it assumed the existence of what Aristotelian nature abhorred: empty space, or a void. It operated according to inexorable laws, laws which might be understood for the general benefit of all men, but which could not be manipulated for the particular benefit of a clever genius. It had to be studied with the support of such disciplines as mathematics, astronomy, and technology, which cosmographers had always thought were irrelevant. And it had to be studied in complete isolation from such disciplines as theology, ethics, and aesthetics, which cosmographers had always looked upon as related fields.

Galileo soon realized that he would never succeed in establishing so radically different, and, at least from a purely human point of view, so unattractive and lifeless a cosmos simply by writing to philosophers in the language of philosophy, which is what Kepler advised him to do. He would have to write to the general public of cultivated laymen in the only language they were willing to read, the language of Doni, Gelli, and the Accademia Fiorentina. He would have to gain the support not so much of the universities, which most Italians still looked upon largely as training schools for civil servants and prelates, but of the literary academies, the courts, and the religious orders—those institutions that had the money, the prestige, and the power to impose their views on others. Finally, he would have to enlarge his already unprecedented combination of professions. No longer could he be only a mathematician, a technician, a teacher, a literary stylist, and a philosopher. He would have to become a publicist, or a missionary, as well.

Becoming a missionary soon forced Galileo to reconsider a problem he had long thought settled: the problem of residence, or, more specifically, the problem of whether to remain in Padua or return to Florence. For he now had to think not only of where he might most conveniently pursue his philosophic speculations but also of where he might most effectively launch his campaign.

Padua had notable advantages. It assured him of a lifetime appointment at one of the most prestigious universities of Europe. It provided him with the company of stimulating and friendly colleagues: even the diehard Aristotelian Cesare Cremonini gladly helped out in moments of financial difficulty. And a teaching load of only sixty half-hour lectures a year (less than a third of the normal load in modern American universities) left most of his time "perfectly free and absolutely *mei juris,*" as he gratefully admitted. Moreover, Padua was close to Venice. The latter, which was now an industrial as well as a commercial metropolis, could offer both the assistance of highly skilled artisans, to whom Galileo later paid tribute in the opening lines of his *Dialogues Concerning Two New Sciences,* and the conversation of many wealthy and cultivated gentlemen, at whose houses Galileo was often a welcomed guest. More important still, Padua lay within the jurisdiction of the Venetian Republic. The government of the Republic, which had just emerged victorious from a bitter contest with the Papacy, was pledged to regaining its former position of power in international affairs; and it was also pledged to maintaining the intellectual freedom of its professors, as Galileo knew from his frequent conversations with the ideological mentor of the Republic and future historian of the Council of Trent, Fra Paolo Sarpi.

However, most of these advantages could be found in Florence as well. Florence also had skilled artisans, like the jeweler Bastiano Guidi on the Ponte Vecchio and the glassmaker Antonio Neri, who manufactured multicolored lampstands as well as eyeglasses and pharmacists' beakers. It had so many of them that some Florentines boasted of finally being able to produce "everything that the human mind has devised to procure the good life" right there in their own city. Florence also was a monumental city:

> Has perhaps the proud machine
> come tumbling down, which Brunelleschi matched
> 'gainst all Antiquity? Has the Pitti waned,
> and have the noble bridges broken
> which guide us o'er the Arno at all hours?

It was surrounded by a countryside that was even more beautiful, if perhaps somewhat less productive, than the Paduan plain:

> There are the hills,
> waiting for the harvest time to come,
> and lovely to behold in ev'ry month;
> there's the valley,
> where gracious Triptolemus strides;
> there the gardens
> which guard the riches of Pamona.
> And there's the cypress,
> where sprightly naiads play.
>   (Chiabrera, 1805 ed., Pt. II, p. 265)

Florence also was well populated with educated gentlemen. Indeed, its gentlemen were so well educated and, after over a half-century of one-man rule, so thoroughly depoliticized, that there was little chance of any of them ever insisting upon the superiority of a political to a scientific vocation—as did even the most devoted of Galileo's patrician disciples in Venice whenever they were called to an office.

Moreover, Florence had by now achieved a level of social and political stability that once had been thought possible only within the framework of the exemplary Venetian constitution. It had done so at the cost of relegating all important affairs of state to the category of *arcana,* which the prince alone was capable of penetrating; and it had left even the chatty court diarist, Cesare Tinghi, with nothing to write about but gossip and parades. But it also had done so by removing all causes of potential discontent. The urban patricians were happy because Ferdinando I, who had no taste for routine, had turned over all purely administrative responsibilities to the old republican magistracies, thus saving them from the status of empty honors. The urban plebeians were happy because their princes protected them from injustice and from famine while providing them with a constant round of entertainment. The citizens of the subject cities were happy because, unlike their counterparts in the Venetian Republic, the more ambitious and talented of them could aspire to the highest positions in the state bureaucracy. Sarpi may have condemned Cosimo II as "a new prince and the usurper of a republic." But Cosimo's subjects praised him as the guarantor of "the amenities of concord . . . in this garden of the world":

> Beneath your wise and placid yoke,
> beneath the Balls you raise on high,
> gaily, and without a sigh,
> proud Arno bows her willing head.
> (Giambattista Marino,
> *Rime,* 1601 ed., I, 113)

Their praise was not wholly unwarranted. For Tuscany was spared the peasant uprisings, civil wars, class conflicts, and regional revolts that afflicted almost every other country in Europe during the following decades.

Better yet, Florence continued to enjoy, quite as much as Venice, the benefits of the economic "Indian summer" of the late sixteenth century. Prosperity was reflected in the high level of ordinary tax receipts, which remained at some 1,300,000 *ducati* a year, and in the low level of interest rates paid by the *Monte Comune,* or state bank, which still attracted sizeable foreign deposits at only $5\frac{1}{2}$ to 6 percent. Prosperity was encouraged by the grand duke's efforts to open new markets for Florentine manufactures in Morocco, Syria, and even Persia, where a commercial mission was set up in 1610. It was further stimulated by extensive capital investments in docks and warehouses at the port of Livorno, which by 1609 had doubled its polyglot population and attracted five permanent foreign consulates. It was well served by Ferdinando's private business transactions: exporting wine, capers, and "other foodstuffs particularly to the taste of the queen" to England, importing grain from Poland and the Ukraine, and selling off the contents of the "infidel" ships captured by the Knights of Santo Stefano on the high seas. It might even have been served by his more adventurous schemes, like raising sugar cane in Brazil and discovering gold in the Orinoco river, had their chief architect, the vagabond English explorer Robert Dudley, been a bit more realistic about the nature of the Spanish monopoly in the New World. As it was, the most expensive of the grand duke's transatlantic fleets returned with nothing but eight Indians, seven of whom promptly died of smallpox. And the most adventurous project he had a hand in, Francesco Carletti's trip around the world, ended in a fruitless attempt to get the Dutch to restore Carletti's captured cargoes—along with a fascinating account of his travels.

Best of all, the government of Florence succeeded almost as well as the government of Venice in realizing what both of them professed to be the chief aim of their foreign policies: the "liberty" or, more correctly, the independence,

at least of their own states if not, as they claimed, of all Italy. Florence did so
partly through an efficient, well-staffed diplomatic corps. And Galileo could not
afford, in an age of notoriously unreliable postal communications, to overlook
the potential services of the competent Tuscan ambassadors at London, Madrid,
Rome, Paris,* and Prague—particularly after May 22, 1610, when they were
formally instructed to comply with all his requests for the collection and
dissemination of scientific information. The government of Florence also
succeeded in its foreign policy by adopting tactics just the opposite of those of
Venice, that is, by maintaining cordial relations with all the great powers instead
of trying to play one off against the other. For example, Ferdinando managed to
discuss a marriage alliance with King James I without offending James's ideological archenemy, Pope Paul V. He managed to encourage the expansionist
ambitions of King Henry IV of France without weakening his ties with King
Philip III of Spain. And he managed to help negotiate a settlement favorable to
the Venetians in 1607 while permitting his subjects to publish pamphlets in
defense of the Papacy.

To be sure, Florentines preferred spectacular to routine achievements as
much as any of their contemporaries; and the grand dukes obliged them—not,
alas, by liberating Sion and subduing the Ganges, as one poet expected, but at
least by sacking the city of Bône in Tunisia in 1607 and by capturing a Turkish
fortress in Syria in 1613:

> In the water of his fountains joyfully he plays,
> Cosimo [II], beloved of the heavens.
> And in the hearts of courteous strangers he awakes
> sentiments of sweet amazement.
>
> But in the water of the seas, there's nothing there of play;
> Up go his sails, and out his lightening bolts,
> which fill barbarian breasts with fright and horror.
>
> (Chiabrera, pt. III, p. 71)

They then obliged them more concretely by "rounding out" the borders of the
grand duchy with Pitigliano and Sorano in the south and with three more
"castles" in the Lunigiana in the north. They obliged Galileo in particular by
ingratiating themselves with the two institutions from which he expected the
greatest help in his forthcoming campaign: the court of Rome, which still
resented the humiliation it had recently suffered at the hands of the Venetians, and
the Society of Jesus, which the Venetians adamantly refused to readmit to their
territories. Hence, Traiano Boccalini, the current gadfly of Italy, was not
completely incorrect when, after weighing one by one all the states of Europe in

---

* The ambassador at Paris in these years was none other than Scipione Ammirato's adopted son, Scipione Jr.

his political scales, he awarded the prize to "the most flourishing state of the grand dukes of Tuscany." Nor was he too far wrong in commending the political sagacity of those who, in such troubled times, preferred "good government, abundance, peace, and lasting quiet" to quarreling among themselves and with their neighbors.

At the same time, Florence no longer suffered, in the 1610s, from what Galileo might have judged to be a grave disadvantage twenty years earlier: artistic and literary sterility. In the visual arts, first of all, the rebellion against the remnants of late Mannerism had finally led to the creation of a wholly new style of painting, the undisputed leader of which was one of Galileo's most faithful correspondents, Lodovico Cigoli. In 1603, after the triumph of his revolutionary "Last Supper," Cigoli set down in theory what he had worked out in practice. Beauty, he said, is the product of a rigorous unity among all the parts of a work, of a strict adherence to "the truth" of observation, of a perfect geometric arrangement of shapes and spaces, and of the elimination of everything distorted, unnatural, "dishonest, or lascivious." This theory particularly impressed the leading Roman art critic of the age, Giovan Battista Agucchi, who passed it on to the theorists of Roman baroque in the following generation. It also impressed Galileo, who objected as much as Cigoli to "strange chimeras" and "confused and inordinate mixtures of lines and colors," even in the art of Michelangelo. And he formally accepted the theory in a long letter-treatise that drew out still farther the obvious parallel between the new art and the new philosophy.

Cigoli's was only one of several experiments with new forms of expression. For instance, the *maniera vaga* of Matteo Rosselli, who inherited the workshop and all the unfinished commissions of the antimannerist painter Gregorio Pagani in 1605, came much closer to purely realistic representation. Rosselli's style was uninhibited by Cigoli's puritanical religiosity—or, for that matter, by any other nonartistic criteria than the rules for "civil, Christian living" that he imposed on his numerous students. By 1620, when he started to work on his masterpieces in the Casino, it had been perfected to the point where he could execute both delicately subdued chiaroscuros and vast fresco cycles "without the slightest error in drawing." Similarly, the realism of Cigoli's pupil Giovanni Billivert ended up in a fascination with just those parts of nature that Cigoli avoided—like the frightening, macabre, and shockingly realistic Marsyas under Apollo's knife and the morbid and sensuous details of his many versions of such popular contemporary subjects as "Judith and Holofernes" and "The Chastity of Joseph." Realism in sculpture was often combined with a delight in technical virtuosity. Or at least it was in the work of the boy wonder from Massa, Pietro Tacca, who succeeded Giambologna as director of the school and foundry in Borgo Pinti in 1608. Tacca began by correcting what he detected as defects in his master's huge equestrian statue of Ferdinando I before it was set up, later the same year, in Piazza Santissima Annunziata. And he then cast the 12,400-pound "Henry IV"

14. Pietro Tacca, Fountain, detail
Piazza Santissima Annunziata

that now stands, complete with bas-reliefs designed by Cigoli, on the Pont-Neuf in Paris. At times technical virtuosity could realize a handsome profit—as it did most notably for another of Giambologna's pupils, Antonio Susini, who sold the half-dozen bronze statuettes he managed to produce each week for over 200 *scudi* apiece. It could be used to transfer one form of art into another: that, at any rate, is what Orazio Mocchi and the *intarsia* artisans of the Galleria did when they reproduced Billivert's painting of Cosimo II before the altar of St. Carlo Borromeo in jasper, lapis lazuli, gold, and no less than 263 diamonds. It could also make possible the blending of several forms of art into one. Giulio Parigi, the son of Vasari's successor as architectural director of the Uffizi, had learned about architecture from Buontalenti and about painting from Cigoli. And he put all his lessons together in bigger, more elaborate, and more beautiful stage sets than any yet constructed, with torches hidden for indirect and spot lighting, with waves that seemed to bear real dolphins across a sea, and with revolving floors that could turn Livorno into hell or into Vulcan's workshop in a matter of minutes.

In literature, poetry finally managed to free itself from the stifling regulations that Leonardo Salviati and the academic critics had once imposed upon it. And that is just what Galileo said it should have done. As organ playing must be learned from organ players, he insisted, rather than from organ manufacturers, so poetry must be learned "from continually reading the poets" rather than from the theorists of poetry. If precepts make the poet, then Aristotle should have been the greatest poet of antiquity, which he most obviously was not. The Accademia della Crusca evidently agreed with him. For it abandoned its interminable debates over Tasso and Ariosto and got to work on its first dictionary of the Italian language, the *Vocabolario,* which was finally published at Venice in 1612.

Florentines were still not ready to produce significant poetry of their own. For instance, one potential poet, Curzio da Marignolle, wore himself out devising elaborate practical jokes, like stealing the hoods of the monks of Vallombrosa off their clothesline and then parading them on the heads of donkeys right underneath the windows of the monastery. But at least they were ready to listen to poets from other parts of Italy. They applauded the audacious young iconoclast from Naples Giambattista Marino; and they were shocked neither by his occasional dips into pornography nor by his irreverent attitude toward all past poets—which, after all, was not much different from Galileo's attitude toward all past cosmographers. They also applauded the chestnut-skinned, nearsighted wine connoisseur from Savona, Gabbriello Chiabrera, who actually lived in Florence for much of the first two decades of the century. They particularly appreciated his efforts to enrich Italian verse with forms borrowed from Ronsard and Henri Estienne in France as well as from Pindar, Sappho, and Anacreon. And they fully sympathized with his declaration of poetic freedom: "a poet may do what he pleases," Chiabrera declared, "providing he does it well." A poet might invent the most horrible nightmares or the most fantastic paradises and describe them in the most outlandish language imaginable. But he need not thereby infringe upon the laws of "order, coherence and verisimilitude" that bound the philosophers and scientists. For poetry was now as completely isolated from prose as were qualities from the Copernican cosmos. No one should any longer be led astray by a poetic aside in a scientific work; everyone could safely read Galileo's joke about the comet of 1618 lighting up an intimate tête-à-tête between Mercury and the sun without thereby concluding that the comet would disappear when Mercury emerged from its conjunction. For the purpose of prose was to expound the truth. The purpose of poetry was to shock, surprise, delight, or, as Chiabrera put it, "raise eyebrows." And the witticisms, jokes, and other amenities with which Galileo, following good Renaissance precedent, decorated his dialogues had no more bearing on the scientific quality of his argument than did the mountainous moon beneath Cigoli's Virgin on the aesthetic qualities of his "Assumption."

But if Florentines produced no great poets, they did produce one fairly good dramatist: the polished, wealthy great-nephew of Michelangelo and one of Galileo's closest friends, Michelangelo Buonarroti, Jr. By stringing together the *intermedi* of Cinquecento plays and by getting rid of the dull comedies that previously had kept them apart, Buonarroti created a new form of theatrical entertainment, one in which dramatic unity was the least important element. What counted was not the connection between beginning, climax, and conclusion, but the single scene or situation. He therefore created what essentially amounted to a series of individual, and only barely related, *tableaux*. He populated his stage with a charming collection of contemporary Tuscan shopkeepers, peddlers, soldiers, magistrates, peasants, and streetsweepers. He made his characters talk alternatively in the roughest Florentine vernacular, in legal and medical jargon, and in the cultivated diction of the academies. He had them play upon the peculiarities of Italian consonant clusters:

> Spacciatevi, studiatevi,
> sforzatevi, sferzatevi,
> co' salti avvanteggiatevi,
> faccende, e camminiam!*
> (*La Fiera,* II,
> Introduction)

in which nothing really mattered but the sound of the words. And when their conversations began to wane, he made them sing:

> Chi desia di saper che cosa è amore,
> io dirò ch'e' non sia se non ardore,
> ch'e' non sia se non dolore,
> ch'e' non sia se non timore
> ch'e' non sia se non furore†
> (*Il passatempo,* in Solerti, app. VI)

—lines, in other words, as empty of content as they were easy to learn by heart. The result was first *La Tancia* in 1611, then *Il passatempo* ("Pastime") in 1614, and, best of all, *La fiera* ("The Fair"), five separate "days" of five acts each, in 1618. Although these plays have been forgotten by literary historians ever since, they were wildly applauded at the time—at a time, that is, when dramatists were expected not to elevate or inspire, but only to amuse:

> May all deep thoughts from your breasts take flight,
> and your spirits be soothed by this rustic delight!
> (*La Tancia,* Introduction)

So Galileo decided to go home. He was sure of being well received. The new grand duke, Cosimo II, had studied mathematics with him during his long paid summer vacations at Villa Artimino; and the dowager grand duchess, Cristina di Lorena, who called him "the greatest mathematician in the world,"

---

* "Spread yourselves, urge yourselves, force yourselves, whip yourselves, seize the opportunity with leaps, you affairs, and let's get going!"

† "Who wants to know what love is, I'll tell him that it's nothing but ardor . . . sorrow, fear, furor."

had repaid him for the "devices" (*impresse*) he had invented for her by finding a job for his incompetent brother-in-law Benedetto.

All he needed was an invitation. And that is just what the discoveries of January 1610 finally procured for him. On June 26 he was officially appointed not just "mathematician" but "philosopher" to the grand duke, with a considerable increase in salary and with no teaching obligations whatsoever—a provision that the pragmatic Venetians refused to consider. On September 4, after two months of feverish preparation and a visit to the University of Bologna, he entered Florence, riding in a litter that had been sent across the Apennines by the grand duke himself.

Meanwhile, the publication of the *Starry Messenger* had created a sensation all over Europe. Buonarroti broke into verse:

> So Ferdinando, whose eyes too soon were closed
> that once the borders of Etruria guarded,
> opens them again, seated in the lap of Jove,
> and the fateful virtue of his noble offspring sees:
> four god-like, radiant chairs await them,
> with promise of immortality.
>
> (*Opere,* vol. X, p. 412)

So did Piero de' Bardi, on behalf of the Accademia della Crusca:

> You Galileo have opened the treasuries of heaven,
> Tuscany's kings you have made into stars of the sky.
> Fame to the glasses illustrious that four add to seven!
> Fame to the hero whom horrors of darkness now fly!
>
> (*Ibid.,* p. 399)

So also did Chiabrera, Girolamo Magagnati, and even Thomas Seggett, a British friend of Kepler's then visiting the imperial court. Galileo was now the talk of all Florence, so much so that a riot broke out in the Mercato Nuovo one day when a messenger walked in with a package marked "Padua" that looked big enough to contain a telescope. He was also the talk of Brescia, Venice, Bologna, Rome, Ingolstadt, Augsburg, Prague, Munich, and Paris. It was all he could do for the next two months just to keep up with an endless stream of letters.

The first authoritative declarations of adherence began to arrive as well. Kepler was reserved at first, but within a few months he was ready to apply to Galileo the famous motto of Julian the Apostate: *Vicisti, Galilaee*! ("You have won, oh Galileian")—which is a perfect pun in Latin. Father Christopher Clavius of the Society of Jesus spent three months gazing through the telescope that Galileo's friends were careful to supply him; and then he too succumbed, along with—after a long evening of eating, drinking, and debating—the whole Collegio Romano, the society's chief educational and scientific institution. Early the next

15. Matteo Rosselli, *Cosimo II Being Shown the Telescope*
Casino

year, the partly religious, partly scientific confraternity in Rome known as the
Accademia dei Lincei elected Galileo to membership. That at once gave him the
support not only of the pious, pensive, and insatiably curious "prince" of the
academy, Federico Cesi, but also of such distinguished corresponding members as
Mark Welser in Augsburg and Giovan Battista Della Porta in Naples.

Complete success, Galileo thought, was just a matter of time. So he put
away his telescope. He retired to Filippo Salviati's villa of Le Selve overlooking
the Arno above Ponte a Signa. And he set to work, patiently but firmly, responding
to objections, explaining obscurities, and smashing down the reluctant with wit,
sarcasm, forebearance, or vituperation, as the occasion demanded.

PREFACE

Condemnation and abjuration

The hardest task for believing men who are dedicated to their world is not the task of justifying themselves before the world. It is the task of justifying themselves before the Church.
(Daniel Berrigan, S. J., *Consequences*: *Truth and*..., p. 37 [Macmillan, 1965])

Tuesday, July 12, 1633. Florence. The Refectory of Santa Croce.
Only Taddeo Gaddi's fresco of the Last Supper still recalled the original purpose of the long, rectangular hall. It was now furnished not with the customary table but with rows of benches, a raised platform, and a podium. Only Taddeo's portraits of St. Francis and St. Bonaventure showed that it still belonged to a Franciscan monastery. For it was now used almost exclusively by the Dominicans, the Servites, and the Jesuits who were on the staff of the Office of the Inquisition for Florence. It had not yet become a museum. Cimabue's "Crucifixion," which was to disintegrate beneath eight meters of oil and mud three centuries later, was still in the basilica. So were the works of Cigoli, Alessandro Allori, Santi di Tito, and other post-Renaissance painters, which none of the published reports of the tragedy deemed worthy of mention, but which were to be just as badly damaged on the morning of November 4, 1966.

By the time the inquisitor arrived, over fifty persons were waiting in the refectory. It was a distinguished audience. Besides the official "consultants," it included "as many mathematicians and philosophers as can be found"; and that meant, in Florence, just about everyone of any social and economic as well as intellectual importance. It was also a somewhat apprehensive audience. For no one had any clear idea of why he had been called in so suddenly. No one knew, that is, except the inquisitor himself. And he, the good-natured, timid, and not very efficient Clemente Egidi of Montefalco, was too upset to tell anyone. It was his name, after all, that appeared right there behind the title page of Galileo's *Dialogue Concerning the Two Chief World Systems,* a book he now wished he had never heard of. It was his career, not anyone else's, that was at stake. For he was not a gentleman of Florence, not a philosopher, and not a professor. Indeed, he was not anything but an ecclesiastical bureaucrat. It was he whom the pope was to make, a few weeks later, the scapegoat of the whole disagreeable affair. Egidi was so upset, in fact, that he forgot to send in a report about the meeting he had called that morning. He was thus forced, in September, to implore the forgiveness of his superiors in Rome for an error he knew them, not himself, to be guilty of. For it was they who had let him grant the imprimatur in the first place. And they might easily have revoked their permission at any moment between 1630, when he granted it, and February 1632, when the book finally came out.

The inquisitor, therefore, said nothing. He just ordered that the two documents he had received from Rome be read aloud.

"We the cardinals," the first document began,

> specially commissioned by the Holy Apostolic See as general inquisitors against heretical depravity ... say, pronounce, and declare ... that you, Galileo ... have made yourself vehemently suspect of heresy by having held and believed a doctrine false and contrary to the Holy Scriptures, namely, that the sun is the center of the world ... and that the earth moves [about it]. You have consequently incurred all the censures and penalties of the holy canons ... against similar delinquents. From which we are happy to absolve you, providing that you first abjure ... the said errors and heresies; ... [and] we condemn you to formal prison in this Holy Office at our discretion.

"I, Galileo Galilei of Florence," the second one read,

> seventy years of age ... kneeling before Your Eminences ... wishing to remove from the minds of ... every other faithful Christian this vehement suspicion justly conceived about me, with a sincere heart and in perfect faith, abjure, curse, and detest the said errors and heresies. I swear never in the future to say or to assert, in voice or in writing, anything that might again bring such suspicion upon me. ... I further swear to fulfill and observe entirely all the penances imposed upon me. ... I, Galileo Galilei, have abjured as above in my own hand.

There were no questions, no comments, no discussion. The inquisitor did not wish to humiliate himself or his audience any further by asking them to subscribe to the abjuration. He certainly did not wish to revive the old Tridentine "loyalty oath," since it had not been imposed on anyone for some seventeen years. So he let the matter drop. The meeting was adjourned.

I

The campaign progresses

The reaction of most of those present was one of shock and surprise. To be sure, the campaign to convert the world to the new cosmology had run into difficulties almost as soon as it was launched. It had first aroused the ire of two university professors, although neither was particularly qualified to deal with matters of science and philosophy. It had then provoked the fury of two Dominican friars: the old-fashioned, wellborn Niccolò Lorini, and the lowborn, reckless, ambitious Tommaso Caccini. Neither of the friars, as the inquisitors soon found out, had any more than the vaguest notion of what Galileo was talking about. But together they managed to drag the argument out of the realm of philosophy and into the realm of theology, where they thought they had a better chance of winning. The first attack boomeranged. It simply provoked Galileo's masterly *Letter to the Grand Duchess,* which was theologically far sounder, by Renaissance as well as by twentieth-century standards, than anything they could have produced against it, and they were laughed out of the Tuscan court. The second attack was more successful. They gave up theology and turned to calumny. And they shifted their field of operation from Florence to Rome. There, with encouragement from the frustrated, irascible, anti-intellectual Pope Paul V, and with shoulder-shrugging from everyone who might have known what they were up to, they managed to obtain the momentary cooperation of the Holy Office. Copernicus's *On the Revolutions* was "suspended until corrected." The book of a Carmelite Copernican was prohibited. Certain statements reported as Galilean by Lorini and Caccini were declared to be "foolish philosophically" and "contrary to the Holy Scriptures." And Galileo himself was privately admonished to stop talking about what went around what in the heavens.

Nevertheless, the Galileans had good reason to interpret the incident as no more than a temporary setback. The university, first of all, did not seem to pose a serious threat. Even the commissioner (*provveditore*) himself joked about it:

"Bologna, lovers; Padua, students; Pisa, monks," he wrote in his diary. "The first trimester both teachers and students study. The second, teachers only. The third, neither teachers nor students." And the Galilean instructor Benedetto Castelli simply ignored the stern injunction of the arch-conservative rector and went on teaching what he pleased in private lessons. The Magisterium of the church, moreover, seemed to pose no more than a few minor difficulties. Its chief theologian, Cardinal Roberto Bellarmino, was too weary of pointless battles to rush into still another one. He was reluctant to tear up the little treatise he had written about the mind ascending through the planetary spheres to the *primum mobile*. But he was just as reluctant to damage his own reputation, as well as the reputation of the church and of the Society of Jesus, to which he belonged, by breaking openly with the most applauded philosopher of the day. So after a little lecture about "hypotheses," he sent Galileo an open letter full of expressions of esteem. The Accademia dei Lincei, which was in close contact with top ecclesiastical and intellectual circles in Rome, then gave Galileo positive encouragement. It ignored the decree about Copernicus. And it severly reprimanded one of its members who started to take the decree seriously. All that seemed necessary, then, was a temporary change in tactics—a brief digression into other, less inflammatory aspects of the same campaign, until Bellarmino and Paul V would finally have passed away.

In August 1623 the seven "years of silence" were at last rewarded by the election of the handsome, cultivated Maffeo Barberini as Pope Urban VIII. Urban was a Florentine by descent, a poet by avocation, a friend and admirer of Galileo, and an active member of the Lincei. His own compatriots exulted, with days of parades and fireworks and with reams of sonnets. They then rushed off to Rome to grab up the manna that rained from the pope's patriotic generosity. One of them, the antiquarian Carlo di Tommaso Strozzi, was commissioned to brush up the Barberini family tree—since obscure bankers from an inconspicuous village half-way to Siena could not by themselves account for the superhuman virtues of their most recent descendant. His cousin, Giovan Battista Strozzi, was honored with a reception "usually accorded only to great princes . . . lodgings in the Vatican at the pope's expense, long audiences, frequent presents," and a pension of 100 *ducati* a year. One of Urban's ambitions was to outdo his predecessor, Leo X, as a patron. He subsidized so many men of letters that the refugee German scholar Gaspar Schopp ran into thirty-nine of them merely by accident during a brief trip to Rome in 1636. His other ambition was to outdo Leo as a Florentine. He lodged two of his nieces in the ultrafashionable Carmelite convent once inhabited by the famous mystic Maria Maddalena de' Pazzi. And in 1628 he rewarded the nuns for their hospitality by building new quarters for them in Borgo Pinti, which were forthwith turned into a gallery of contemporary painting and adorned with an enormous Barberini coat of arms.

Galileo, therefore, delayed only long enough to be assured of a proper

16. Convent of Maria Maddalena de' Pazzi, portal with coat of arms of Pope Urban VIII
Borgo Pinti

reception. Then he too followed the procession to Rome. He did not, it is true, obtain all he had hoped for. Instead of a formal retraction of the decree of 1616, he received only the assurances of the pope's regrets and a warning about limiting God's omnipotence to any definitive cosmological system. But he was feted all over the city. He was six times honored in formal receptions at the Vatican. He was instructed not to deprive the world any longer of the products of his genius. His most recent work, the *Saggiatore* ("Assayer"), one of the greatest masterpieces of satire in the history of literature, was read aloud, amid applause and laughter, at the papal dinner table. A "feeler" he circulated in manuscript shortly after—a rebuttal to an anti-Copernican—provoked none but favorable comments in authoritative circles. He concluded, therefore, that the time had come for another change in tactics. Though he could no longer expect the church to endorse Copernicanism openly, he could at least be sure of its impartiality. All he had to do, apparently, was admit that other kinds of cosmos were "possible." He would then be free to bring forth all the evidence he could find in support of the one he thought most "probable." And that is precisely what he set out to do the moment he returned to Florence.

Meanwhile, the Galileans were steadily growing in strength and influence. In Florence, the "universality of men who want to know" was soon completely converted. Galileo's most effective supporters were those well-to-do citizens who had studied mathematics—citizens like the brothers Arrighetti, who wrote scientific letters to one another, like the son of the musician Jacopo, Dino Peri, who made his money as a lawyer and spent his time as a philosopher, and like Michelangelo Buonarroti, Jr., the patrician dramatist and art connoisseur. They in turn were actively supported by professional men—by Francesco Rondinelli, who took care of Galileo's property during his absence in Rome, and Bernardino Nardi, an accomplished surgeon, who was to die, at the age of sixty, while reading a commentary on Lucretius. Both rich citizens and professional men were supported by painters like Gismondo Coccopani, by architects like Giulio Parigi, and by such a jack-of-all-trades as Cosimo Lotti, "a very bright man," as Galileo put it, "an engineer and inventor of machines, and my especially dear friend," who sat with him from time to time on state advisory commissions.

The Galileans were a knowledgeable circle. They were fully able to understand Galileo's arguments and to offer helpful suggestions as they listened to the *Dialogue* read aloud to them, night after night, in the house of Canon Niccolò Cini. They were a gay circle, too. They summoned each other to their frequent dinner parties with jokingly peremptory invitations:

> Your Lordship [in this case Galileo himself] is cited to appear in the said place at 17 o'clock, under penalty of going without dinner and of being deprived of the olive oil you requested.

But, above all, they were an influential circle. They had the sympathy of Cosimo de' Bardi, archbishop of Florence in 1630 and the son of Galileo's father's patron in the *Camerata*. They had the sympathy of Ascanio Piccolomini, archbishop of Siena since 1628 and future host to Galileo after his release from Rome. They had the sympathy of the many diocesan priests who in 1633 said daily Masses for the happy issue of his trial. They dominated the Accademia Fiorentina, of which Galileo's collaborator, Mario Guiducci, and then Galileo himself had been elected consuls. Better still, they had the wholehearted backing of the grand duke. As soon as Ferdinando II came of age, he honored Galileo with a seat on the Council of the Two Hundred. He granted full citizenship to Galileo's illegitimate son. He paid his travelling expenses, together with free lodging at the embassy, whenever he went to Rome. And he vigorously squelched the underhanded attempt by some of Galileo's opponents to challenge the legality of paying his salary out of ecclesiastical tithes, which Cosimo I had obtained for the support, not of scholars, but of teachers at Pisa.

Still, Florence alone was too small to support so great a cause, and the Galileans lost no time moving in on the very center of power: Rome. Almost the whole Florentine colony, which the election of Urban VIII had greatly increased in size, was soon theirs. The colony included the grand duke's uncle, and his official representative in the Curia, Cardinal Carlo de' Medici. It included most of the names on the guest lists of the wife of the Florentine ambassador, Caterina Riccardi Niccolini, soon to be godmother to Galileo's grandson and already one of the most accomplished hostesses of the city. It included Caterina's distant cousin Niccolò Riccardi, better known as *Padre Mostro* ("Father Monster") because of his enormous bulk and massive erudition, who had been driven from Spain in the wake of one more fight over the Immaculate Conception, and who then, as Master of the Sacred Palace, had charge of licensing books for publication. It included Giovanni Ciàmpoli, a close friend of Galileo's since their first meeting at Artimino in 1608, whose talents for improvisation had once made him the highlight of Giovan Battista Strozzi's dinner parties, and who now held the important position of secretary for papal briefs. It included the whole Magalotti family, of whom one, Lorenzo, had just become archbishop of Ferrara, and another, Costanza, was married to the pope's brother, Carlo. It included the Rinuccini family—particularly Giovan Battista, then archbishop of Fermo and later nuncio to Ireland, whose eloquence could "enrapture the spirits of the most eminent personages in the world," and Giovan Battista's brother, Tommaso, who had worked for six years for the pope's nephew before returning home, as consul of the Accademia Fiorentina, in 1631. It included the main line of the Orsini family, whose head, Paolo Giordano, the son of the ill-fated Lucrezia de' Medici, had been raised at the court of Florence. To some extent, the Florentine colony included even the pope's own family, the Barberini. For it enjoyed close ties with young Taddeo, whom Castelli had been tutoring since 1627. And it was often joined by the "cardinal nephew," Francesco, whom Chiabrera called the "sun of the Tiber, from whom blazes the light that ne'er the mists of adversity will fear, the noble hope of the famous Hills. . . ."

Moreover, the colony was not alone. Galileo was admired by no less eminent a personage than Sforza Pallavicino, then under consideration as successor to Cesi for the presidency of the Lincei, and soon to become famous as the author of the official rebuttal to Sarpi's *History of the Council of Trent*. Galileo had at least the tacit approval of the heads of three great religious orders—of the Capuchin Giovan Antonio Montecuccoli, of the Dominican Niccolò Ridolfi, another Florentine, and of the Theatine Giovanni di Guevara, who sent him the manuscript of a treatise on mechanics for correction. He also gained the unequivocal support of the most recent institutional expression of Counter-Reformation piety, the *Scuole Pie*. The Scolopians, as the Fathers of the "Pious Schools" were called, were attempting to bring to a logical conclusion what the humanist pedagogues of the fifteenth century had started. They offered free instruction to the children of the poor. And they offered it to all the children, not just to those whose natural brilliance might commend them to a wealthy patron. Realizing that mathematics was fast displacing metaphysics as the foundation of all the sciences, the founder and general of the order, José de Calasanz, sent his associates to Florence, where the most famous mathematician of the age lived. The school they opened at Orsanmichele in 1629 soon became the most exciting—and the most thoroughly Galilean—religious community in the city, as well as in the whole church. Best of all, Galileo had every reason to think he had won over the pope himself. On his next trip to Rome, in 1630, Urban received him "with many signs of affection" (*moltissime carezze*). He sent him home "completely satisfied about the prospects . . . of that aromatic business of his," the publication of the *Dialogue*. And he at last came through, that fall, with the two ecclesiastical pensions he had promised back in 1624, one of them increased by 40 *scudi* a year as a sign of special favor.

2

The campaign falters

It is not surprising that the Galileans felt confident of imminent victory. True, some of them had occasional moments of doubt and urged Galileo to get back to pure science, which the troublesome friars would not be capable of understanding. But most of them shared their leader's determined optimism. He was not a Kepler, they knew, who would bury his discoveries in unreadable Latin tomes. He was not a Descartes either, who would retire to a neutral haven to avoid having to argue with anyone. He was too loyal a Catholic to stand idly by while the church was chained up to an outworn metaphysics. He had no intention of running away, either to Venice, where he was offered complete freedom and a high salary, or to Holland, where the States General was interested in his device for calculating longitude. Running away would simply have given his enemies the chance they were waiting for—to add apostasy to their charges of "heresy sympathizing"; and Rome might have been lost forever. The Galileans therefore backed him in his resolution to fight to the finish. They put up with his fits of petty jealousy, even when directed against themselves. They joined him in hurling vituperation at the least indication of dissent. They were sure that the *Dialogue* would rapidly win over all those of good faith who were still uncommitted. And they were fully confident "in the integrity . . . of the Lords of the Congregation [of the Holy Office] . . . who are sure to recognize your [Galileo's] manifest sincerity and to approve of your actions and your writings." So, at any rate, thought Mario Guiducci as late as May 21, 1633, when an adverse decision had already been taken.

Unfortunately, the Galileans failed to recognize that the church had undergone considerable change in structure and administration during the preceding fifty years. They still looked for support from the bishops; for observing the intense pastoral zeal of some of the Florentine bishops misled them into supposing that the episcopacy still enjoyed the authority conferred upon it at Trent. After all,

Cosimo de' Bardi gave his life for his flock when he died of the plague, rather than escape to the country, within months of his appointment. Similarly, Giovan Battista Rinuccini refused to abandon his flock when offered a more lucrative see; he left it temporarily only to accomplish an urgent mission for the pope, during which he carried a message in a rowboat to the beleaguered Catholics in Ireland right under the nose of the English fleet. But the Galileans were wrong. The bishops no longer had any effective power except as delegates of the Roman Curia, which kept an eye on them through the papal nuncio in Florence.

The Galileans still looked for support from the cardinals, too. They thus forgot that Clement VIII had broken up the College into separate congregations and that Urban VIII had caustically forbidden the individual members to speak, even in consistories, unless specifically invited to do so. Indeed, when the crucial moment came, only three of the several members of the Congregation of the Holy Office sympathetic to Galileo avoided affixing their signatures to the condemnation; and none of those three dared whisper his dissent. All initiative had become concentrated solely in the hands of the pope. And since the pope could not tend to everything all by himself, it passed, by default, into the hands of the papal bureaucrats. It was they who collected the evidence and prepared the briefs. And it was they who delivered the decisions, which the pope could not possibly reject without compromising in practice the infallibility he constantly, though not too successfully, claimed to possess.

To be sure, the bureaucrats followed procedures that were anything but arbitrary, at least according to the Florentine specialist on the subject. But the role of absolute secrecy on one hand, and the desire to expedite cases with the least possible fuss on the other hand, led them to adopt certain measures which, as Ferdinando II was shocked to find, would never have been permitted in Tuscan courts. They went right ahead and built their case against Galileo on an obviously forged memo that had been planted in his file back in 1616. They called in only those witnesses who had the approval of the plaintiffs and permitted all prospective defense witnesses to be terrorized by a malicious whispering campaign. Worse yet, they based their judgments not on fully articulated theses but upon single statements ripped from context. They based them, for example on statements like "The sun is the center of the world," which, without a supporting argument, was neither true nor false but simply meaningless. Moreover, they extended this method well beyond the domain once considered strictly theological. When Galileo tried to show, in the famous *Letter to the Grand Duchess,* that a Copernican universe would have enabled Joshua to stop the sun more easily than a Ptolemaic one, he backed himself into the same corner with Francesco Patrizi and the Platonists, who never tired of repeating St. Augustine's theological judgment in their favor. Hence both of the last-ditch tactics of the Galileans were doomed in advance. The bureaucrats in the Holy Office had neither the time nor the inclination to try to understand Galileo's statements in their contexts. They had no intention of getting embroiled in a major doctrinal issue, which would have resulted in what they all feared the most, another general council. And they were fully persuaded that theologians, not philosophers, were the best judges of what was true and false in philosophy.

As the Galileans misjudged the structure and function of the church, so also they misjudged the personality of its head. For Urban VIII, the arts and sciences served one ultimate end: that of exalting the Papacy. The international chaos later known as the Thirty Years War was just then offering him an unprecedented opportunity for recapturing the Papacy's long-lost role as political arbiter of Europe. The Papacy in turn served the end of exalting the Barberini family. Urban was determined to set up his relatives with an Italian principality, even at the cost of reintroducing the open nepotism that his predecessors had worked so hard to eliminate. He understood the artists, since they were visibly turning Rome into an architectural wonder commensurate with his image of himself. But he never took the trouble to understand the scientists. He thought that technology had nothing to do with philosophy. He therefore kept Castelli employed as a flood-control expert for years after he had sacrificed Castelli's master, Galileo. He thought that philosophy was merely a matter of intellectual fantasy. He therefore refused to see Galileo's cosmos as anything but one more of the stupendous but purely hypothetical constructions of the late Renaissance. He thought that astronomy was a branch of astrology. He therefore actually believed that Galileo was maliciously tampering with his horoscope. Moreover, whenever the policies that really interested him ran into trouble, he was willing to throw aside all the works of genius he supported. That is just what happened in 1632, when he was caught negotiating indirectly with the Protestant king of Sweden against the Catholic emperor. Urban, the impartial arbiter, turned out to be a pawn in Cardinal Richelieu's anti-Hapsburg games. He thus suffered the first of the series of humiliations that was to culminate, finally, in the failure of his nephews to hang onto the duchy of Castro, and then, posthumously, in the exclusion of papal delegates from the Congress of Westphalia. The more apparent it became that his ambitions would be thwarted, the less efficient he became in pursuing them. "Since the present pontificate is so weak," noted Grand Duke Ferdinando a few years later, "it makes much of things of little moment and pays no attention to those of real importance." And nothing seemed less important to Urban VIII in 1633 than idle but troublemaking disputes over the sun and the planets.

While the pope, then, was unwilling to give the Galileans the backing they needed, the grand duke, who represented the second of the great powers they were counting on, was unable to do so. Ferdinando II was just as intelligent and even more convinced of the value and the validity of Galileo's campaign than his

two immediate predecessors had been. He was just as affable, though less flam-
boyant, than his grandfather. And he was just as sensitive, though far more
modest, than his father:

> Behold how he reclines secure
> upon inherent majesty.
> Nor ever will his heart endure
> that pride which is but vanity.
> Behold, how artfully he reigns,
> and e'en the humblest ne'er disdains.
> He hides the light that round him bounds;
> and thus th' invidious he confounds.
>
> (Chiabrera, I, 12)

Moreover, he was just as committed to their overall policy of peace at home and
blood-and-thunder on the Mediterranean. But where Ferdinando I and Cosimo II
had succeeded, Ferdinando II faltered. The imminent intervention of France into
what until then had been an exclusively German war threatened to wreck the very
foundation of the policy he had inherited; and Ferdinando had no choice but to
greet the troops Cardinal Richelieu sent across the Alps in 1630 as the manifestation
of "generous and holy intentions." The marriage alliances, which had been the
principal means of implementing the policy, had all broken down. Ferdinando's
great-aunt Maria had been driven out of France. His mother had just died on a
fruitless mission back home to Austria. His grandmother's Guise relatives had
managed to escape from Nancy only by fleeing in disguise at night. And they were
thereafter able to provide him with nothing but the doubtfully useful pleasure of
being entertained, at his expense, in Florence. All hope of reconstituting the
alliances was then shattered by the demotion of the Medici to a lower rung on the
ladder of European dynasties. Ferdinando's brother Carlo, who wanted to marry
a Neapolitan princess of modest means, had to give way to an undistinguished
Spanish nobleman. And Ferdinando himself, the grandson of an emperor and the
great-nephew of a king, had to be content with nothing more than the dispossessed
heiress to the defunct duchy of Urbino.

In circumstances such as these, there was little point in talking about crusades
or colonies. Ferdinando balanced the cost of maintaining a fleet against the
decreasing revenues of piracy and then sold most of his great galleys to the French.
He put aside Robert Dudley's magnificent projects in the New World. All that
was left of them was a magnificent portolan atlas, with detailed charts of every
known coastline in the world, which he had printed in 1646 for no other apparent
purpose than that of making handsome presents in foreign courts. It was all he
could do to maintain his position in Italy. He could not afford to intervene in the
War of Monferrato, that Italian backwash of the Thirty Years War; and he had to
stand idly by as Spanish troops tore the city of Mantua to shreds. He could not

prevent the viceroy of Naples from seizing that long-coveted plum, Piombino, just as the will of the last of the local princes seemed to put it finally within his grasp. He could not turn down the huge subsidy of 500,000 *scudi* demanded by the Spanish for their campaigns in Lombardy. He could not even keep his own subjects from using foreign connections to circumvent the laws of Tuscany. And most of his interventions on their behalf abroad produced little more than expressions of regrets on the part of the authorities at "not being able in this case to do all that Your Highness might desire." If Tuscany was, in the end, spared "the rapine, the burnings, and the sacrileges" perpetrated in northern Italy "by the vile refuse of mankind," this was due more to fortune than to calculation. Fidelity to the policy of his predecessors brought Ferdinando only two concrete results. He placed a few of his more glory-hungry subjects—as well as his brother, Gian Carlo—in respectable foreign military commands. And he rounded out his borders with two more of those tiny relics of the Middle Ages—the fief of Santa Fiore in the extreme south (1629–33), and Pontremoli, in the vacuum between the Este and the Genoese, in the far northwest (1650).

The decline of Tuscan power abroad was to some extent a reflection of the waning of political leadership at home. For the first eight years of his reign, Ferdinando was a minor; and his mother and grandmother, as joint regents, could think of no higher goal for political action than living up to Urban VIII's commendation of them as examples of "devotion . . . to the Apostolic See." For the next six years, until the death of the lovable, jovial, but not very practical dowager Cristina in 1636, Ferdinando continued to defer to Cristina's favorite minister, Andrea Cioli. And Cioli had good reasons for doing nothing that might estrange the most active of the still independent states of Italy, the Papacy.

Ferdinando readily followed Cristina's and Cioli's advice, largely because those of his subjects who might have suggested an alternative to him—the cultured gentlemen who had backed Galileo—had by now become completely apolitical. So apolitical had they become, indeed, that they equated responsible citizenship with subversion. They accused a critic like Cicero of trying to destroy society just because he criticized it. And they reduced even the "reason of state" doctrines which that angry Venetian, Traiano Boccalini, was extracting from Tacitus, to nothing more than "a little collection of political sonnets," utterly devoid of references to any real political situation since the death of Nero. Political philosophy, then, remained at the point where Scipione Ammirato had left it forty years earlier. So also did jurisprudence. The nearest that the eminent jurist Piero Girolami came to making jurisprudence relevant to the government of Ferdinando II was to draw up a list of the "virtues" of St. Louis, King of France; Girolami preferred, during his consulship of the Accademia Fiorentina in 1637, to arrange for lectures about card games. According to Galileo's devoted friend, Giovan Battista Doni, the "theory of the laws" consisted solely of "the study of texts and of the information about antiquity contained in them." It had nothing to do with "the practice of the courts . . . particularly of those in Florence." Doni soon gave up ancient law, which he found to be useless, for ancient music, which still seemed to be of some practical value.

Bereft of the vigilance of an informed public and of the leadership of an exigent prince, the bureaucracy began to lose some of its much-vaunted efficiency. The magistrates occasionally tried to "provide a remedy for the disorders" by reissuing the edicts of Cosimo I—particularly those prohibiting "any official in any town, locality, or castle . . . or their assistants from . . . taking any kind of present, gift, or favor." Nonetheless, exceptions from the law tended to undermine the authority of the enforcers of the law. For example, the eccentric painter Giovanni da San Giovanni got the grand duke to "except" him from the law against hunting in the Cascine. He then displayed his privilege by letting the policemen who arrested him drag him all the way to the Mercato Nuovo before exhibiting his permit—just to make sure a big crowd would join him in ridiculing the naïveté of the policemen who still thought the law to be universally binding. The ladder of advancement at court from "gentleman" to "cup-bearer" began to take precedence over the more customary *cursus honorum* through the republican magistracies, even though successful aspirants like Luigi Antinori never did much except act as decoration at the grand duchess's villa of Poggio Imperiale. Commented one observer,

> Mad is he who seeks
>   a good career through merit;
> for sadly will he learn, poor man,
>   that there's no court can bear it.
>   (Soldani, *Satira I*)

Similarly, malicious gossip occasionally took the place of accurate information—as it did most notably in the case of the sensitive sculptor Pietro Tacca, whose death was hastened by worrying about what was said behind his back. More and more big fish managed to break through the judicial net. When the wife of Jacopo Salviati had his mistress hacked to pieces by hired assassins, and when she wrapped up what was left of the body in a bundle of clean linen for him to find, it was they, not she, who paid the price for the crime that she alone had so diligently arranged. Some Florentines, like Galileo's disciple Niccolò Aggiunti, let these scandals be buried under the same old commonplaces about the court as a "school of lies." Others hid them under the mantle of "custom," which could be questioned only at the risk of appearing "uncivilized, intractable, and bestial." Most simply ignored them, as did Galileo himself, confident that "under [Ferdinando's] happy dominion there is no one who is troubled by any of the hardships that afflict the [rest of the world] these days."

3

Plague and depression

Political debility in itself, of course, was not irremediable. Indeed, it was partially overcome in the next few years. The ministers left over from the regency soon died off. The particular weaknesses of the grand duke himself were soon made up for by the special talents of his younger brothers, who brought the Tuscan government as close as it was ever to come to collegial direction. Hence, by the early 1640s Ferdinando was able at least to say "no" once in awhile. He rejected a highly recommended promotion as incompatible with his "rule of seniority and talent." He obliged French troops crossing his territory to pass in groups of not more than 150. He made the Spanish spend their own money, not his, when recruiting soldiers in Tuscany. And he countered the high-handed measures of the Barberini with an armed force.

Yet Ferdinando's efforts to regain fully his grandfather's international position were constantly frustrated by the loss of the one resource that for centuries had offset Florence's poverty in land and men: money. To some extent, Florence was a victim of the same widespread depression that economic historians have recently shown to have occurred all over Europe at the time, from Seville to Lyon, from Normandy to Danzig. But Florence also suffered from special circumstances of its own, circumstances that made the "times" seem so "calamitous," even as early as 1621, that one orator felt obliged to dispense with the sugary optimism usually required for ceremonial speeches at court. Several extremely cold, wet winters led, in the crucial year 1619, to the most disastrous crop failure ever recorded "in the history and the memory of past times." The closing, bemoaned by one observer, of many of "the ancient and most active manufactures of the city" led to a steady decline in wool production, long the mainstay of the Florentine economy, from 14,000 pieces in 1602 to 10,700 in 1629, and to 5,647 in 1644. Grain prices rose by 20 percent and fluctuated so erratically thereafter that no one could plan more than a month ahead. Then, first in the winter and spring of 1630–31 and once again in the spring and summer of 1633, Florence was struck by the worst disaster of all, the plague.

The effects of the plague of 1630–33 were not completely negative. Mortality was far less than it had been during the Black Death of 1348 and substantially inferior to what it was during the same years in Milan or Venice. Just how many people actually died is difficult to determine, since one set of the house-to-house surveys that have survived gives a drop in population of 10,000 between 1622 and 1630, and another shows a rise from 63,143 to 66,056, between 1630 and 1632. The eighteenth-century historian Riguccio Galluzzi, who had more documents before him and whose conclusions have been accepted by historical demographers ever since, probably came closest to a correct figure. He calculated 7,000 victims, or slightly more than 10 percent of the total population, in the three years.

If it is true, as some authorities claim today, that overpopulation was one of the chief causes of the depression, then the plague may even have been beneficial. It was certainly beneficial to public morality. Florentines were justly proud of the civic spirit and self-discipline with which they responded to the emergency. No one broke the forty-day quarantine. No one touched the property of the helpless—no one, that is, except the clever thief who managed to get away with 1,500 *scudi* worth of the grand duchess's silver plate in March 1633. None of the some thousand gentlemen and their assistants who were appointed by the specially created Office of Public Health shunned the unpleasant tasks imposed upon them—fumigating stricken houses, scrubbing floors, burning mattresses, and carrying off the sick. None of the residents went without the necessities of life—bread every day, meat three times a week, four ounces of oil once a week, cheese on fast days, and clean sacks for the homeless beggars. The grand duke himself made a daily round of the city—on foot, at that, since his carriages and horses had been commandeered for public service just like those of his subjects. The city had never been (and it would never again be) so clean, for the streets were continually swept from one end to the other. The citizens had never been so well cared-for, since most of the physicians were drafted (at good salaries) into state service, and they treated the sick of all classes gratuitously in the two fortresses and several suburban villas that were made over into public hospitals.

Most important of all, as far as Florentines themselves were concerned, the plague was beneficial to religion. Everyone agreed in attributing the disaster to the individual and collective sins of the people, and to the consequent wrath of God. Just as much effort, therefore, went into removing the causes as into correcting the effects, which a specialist from Portugal, then lecturing at Pisa, was hastily summoned to identify in a *Compendium of Advice on Preventing and Curing the Plague.* Masses were multiplied and were celebrated out in the streets, where they could be watched from the windows. Special fasts were instituted. All relics were exposed. The Confraternity of San Francesco in Palazzuolo—better known by the name *Bacchettoni,* which soon joined the many other variants of "bigot" in the Italian vocabulary—paraded in bare feet and crowns of thorns. The faithful of San Marco knelt en masse, candles in hand, before the prior—the same Ignazio Del Nente whom Galileo rejected as a censor for the *Dialogue*—and vowed to fast thirteen extra days that year and to visit the body of St. Antonino. Only one person in the whole city seems to have succumbed to the eat-drink-and-be-merry attitude described by Boccaccio three centuries earlier. And when he, the antisocial miscreant, started up a rope one evening toward the ladies' quarters on the second floor of a villa full of wellborn, storytelling refugees, he slipped, fell backwards, and was found days later floating in a nearby well.*

The plague of 1630–33 seems to have turned Florence not into a moral chaos but into an impeccably administered "terrestrial Paradise." Consequently, it produced not another *Decameron,* but a couple of wordy eulogies, a detail-laden chronicle by Galileo's solicitous neighbor, Francesco Rondinelli, and one or two spicy "case histories" for the collections of Jesuit casuists. On May 21, 1633, while Galileo was awaiting the verdict of the Holy Office at Palazzo Madama, the miraculous Madonna was brought down from Impruneta. She was carried through the deserted streets of San Frediano, over the Ponte Santa Trinita to the cathedral, and back up the Costa San Giorgio. Just before she departed, loaded with expensive presents, she squeezed out a drop of milk to indicate her approval. The Office of Public Health was sure it had at last found a cure. And within six weeks the hospitals were once again empty.

The plague, then, may have had some beneficial effects. But it had far more harmful ones. First of all, those that it killed were more often from the active and productive than from the passive and dependent elements in society. They were Capuchins, for example, who did the dirty work during the plague, rather than the cloistered nuns, who suffered no other inconvenience than having to wash their own dishes. They were artisans, who stayed in their shops, rather than absentee landlords, who fled to their villas. Secondly, those it did not kill it terrorized—first as it moved irresistibly down from the Brenner to Milan, then to Bologna, then—in spite of extra guards to prevent anyone from crossing the frontier—to Trespiano, and finally—in spite of the severest measures to expel the vagabonds, deodorize the Jews, and lock the city gates—to a rooming house in Via del Garbo.† Terror in many ways was worse than the sudden high fever, the huge, stinking boils, the delirium, and the splitting headaches that were the prelude to violent death. For terror struck everyone, with the sole exception of those few who recovered from an attack and were then rewarded with a thanksgiving procession and presents from the grand duke. Terror gripped everyone, day and night, month after month, as they starved themselves, purged themselves, sprayed themselves with acid and snake poison, and paid clerks in the shops by dropping

* The Jesuit casuist G. D. Ottonelli claims to have gotten this story from "un sacerdote degno di fede"—a trustworthy priest.
† Now Via Condotta, just north of Piazza della Signoria.

coins into a vat of vinegar. All communication with the outside world was cut off—
except for what Galileo and a few others managed to sneak into the diplomatic
pouches. Nothing but the tinkling bells of the carts carrying off the stricken to
the hospitals broke the deathly silence of the streets.

> Look, look upon your country!
> behold the body of her who is your mother;
> see how pestilence has covered her with wounds!
> Her blood-stained breast is bereft of its inhabitants,
> and has become a trench for bones and corpses.
> Her streets are horrid, turbid torrents
> of death and lamentation.
> (Carlo Casini, *Il Monte Senario*, 1631)

The economic effects of the plague were still worse than the psychological
ones. For six months in 1631 and for four in 1633, all business was at a complete
standstill. Of the 144 able-bodied adults living in the dark, dank district between
the Ponte Vecchio and the Uffizi in February, 1631, 67 were unemployed silk- or
wool-workers. Fifty-one out of a total of 159 families were completely without
means of support. Two of the six small hotels had already been boarded up, and
only one had more than a couple of guests. Practically the only people able to
support themselves at all in this district were the nine shopkeepers and the court
servants. No one had enough left over to support the dogs; and a fence had to be
put up around the common graveyard to keep the dogs from beating the grave-
diggers to the bodies. Florence had become a city of industrial workers without
industries. The only alternative to mass starvation was the mass distribution of
public charity. Ferdinando distributed some 150,000 *scudi* of it in 1631 alone, not
counting his subsidies to monasteries bereft of their usual alms and the special
outlays voted by the city magistrates.

The price was enormous; and, at the moment, there was only one way to
pay it, namely, by drawing on the state bank, the *Monte Comune*. The draft did
not at once produce a crisis, however. Quite the contrary: it seems to have
stimulated still further the already marked tendency to take money out of business,
which had become increasingly risky and unprofitable, and put it into state bonds,
which brought in a regular 5 percent without the slightest effort. Galileo himself
bought 3,000 *denari* worth of them just before leaving for Rome. Bonds (*luoghi
di monte*), after all, were a safer investment than shares in the Capponi bank, which
collapsed in 1640 with 400,000 *scudi* in unredeemable deposits. They earned far
more than the 326,708 *ducati* that Giovan Battista Strozzi had invested in Roman
real estate, and the 162,235 he had lent out to cardinals in expectation of future
ecclesiastical benefices. And they apparently earned more than the huge inherited
fortune and the 14,000 *scudi* dowry of his cousin Carlo, who was reduced to
charging fees for his genealogies and to begging salary increases from the already

hard-hit members of the Merchants Guild, of which he, the least businesslike of all the indolent descendants of the once enterprising Strozzi family, had, ironically enough, been appointed chairman. Hence the new bond issues floated in 1634 and 1637, the latter for a million *scudi,* sold out almost immediately.

One big problem still remained: how to reinvest the deposits so as to insure the payment of interest. Merchants and manufacturers, the only borrowers who might have used the money to make more money, were apparently not interested. By the middle of the century they held only 21 percent of the loans of over 500 *scudi* in Siena, as opposed to 62.4 percent for "nobles"; and the percentages were probably not much different in Florence. Hence the money just sat there, or else was absorbed into the state fiscal system; and the interest was paid by raising taxes—that is, by draining off that much more of the rapidly shrinking supply of wealth available for productive investments.

Obviously, a debacle was inevitable. That it came so quickly was due to noneconomic circumstances beyond the control of the grand duke. He had lost enough "face" in 1631, after all, by quietly letting the pope grab Urbino and not pressing his own claims to it. He had lost still more face in 1641, when he had done nothing but protest as the pope seized the Farnese fief of Castro, right along his southern border. Now, however, the French and Spanish were tied up elsewhere and would not interfere. Venice and Modena had signed an alliance with him on behalf of the good old slogans about the "freedom of Italy." He still had to prove himself worthy of his grandfather's reputation; and the brash, brilliant victim of Barberini ambitions, Duke Odoardo Farnese of Parma, was threatening to outshine him once and for all with another lightning invasion of the Romagna. The moment of glory had arrived, and Ferdinando dared not let it pass.

Not until the eighteenth century did anyone discover the striking similarities between the War of Castro and Tassoni's famous parody of medieval intercity wars, the *Secchia rapita* ("The Stolen Bucket"). Except for a few conscious-stricken preachers, who were forthwith banished from the country, there was not a single discordant note in the chorus of applause that followed the grand duke and his two brothers off toward the Chiana frontier on June 5, 1643, at the head of an army much more colorful than the last one Florence had sent out, some eighty years before, toward Siena. There was even more applause when all of Umbria was quickly conquered—and plundered—and when Pope Urban, in one of the last acts of his long and disastrous pontificate, was forced to hand back all he had taken from the Farnese.

But then the bill was presented. The *Monte* had been completely drained. The king of Spain had refused once again to repay a cent of his enormous debt. New taxes were out of the question. There was nothing to do but cut the interest rate, first by half, then by three-quarters. Few investors withdrew their deposits, since they had no clear idea of how to reinvest them. Hence lowering the interest amounted to reducing the actual amount of their invested capital by roughly the same proportions. The city that had once been able, even during the severest crises, to buy off the most powerful rulers in Christendom, had, first gradually and then suddenly, become poor. No one had any solutions to offer. No one, indeed, and Galileo least of all, was even particularly aware that a radical change was taking place. Florence had little chance, in the foreseeable future, of becoming anything but still poorer than it was already.

4

The campaign loses its auxiliaries

Galileo was thus abandoned, at the most crucial hour, by one of the great powers of this world; and he was supported much less actively than he had hoped to be by the other. At the same time, he was let down to some extent by those who might have been, and indeed who wanted to be, his most effective propagandists, the poets. The poets' intentions were beyond reproach. They tried their best to put mathematical formulas into meter. They discovered that "triangles and circles" rhymed, more or less, with "what you search for" (*triangoli e cerchi/quel che tu cerchi*). They made shepherds tell shepherdesses about the mountains on the moon and about the "admirable instrument" that had permitted "the new Endymion" to observe them. They hailed "your just and well-earned glory" and foretold the "confusion of your opponents and persecutors." But shifting once and for all from one cosmos to a completely different one was beyond their powers of imagination. Jacopo Gaddi, for instance, put a Copernican sun in one line and an Aristotelian sun in the next; and he then wrung his hands in a marginal comment over the "ambiguous variety of opinions" that beset him. Marino let his shepherd fly off to the "sphere of Mercury" after delivering a purely extraneous lecture on Galilean astronomy. Antonio Malatesti figured out a way of saying "telescope" metaphorically in Stanza 5 (it was "a serpent that frightens no one"); and then he fell back on the epicycles of Jupiter to describe a windmill in stanza 41.

In other words, Galileanism in poetry failed to penetrate the substance of poems. Similarly, Galileanism in poetics failed to come up even to the standards Galileo himself had set in his Archimedian recasting of Dante's *Inferno*. For example, Mario Guiducci, the protagonist of the debate over the comet of 1618, got bogged down when he tried to read Galileo's projectiles, as well as Gilbert's magnets, back into the poems of Michelangelo. All he could do was to take five minutes off for a straightforward scientific explanation of the matter. Poetry and the new science parted ways after their first brief tryst. And their wedding (just to drag out the metaphor in good baroque fashion) was put off until the "scientific poets" of the following century had fitted out a bridal suite in Arcadia.

The main trouble lay in the inability of the poets to conceive of poetry as a means of persuasion, instruction, or indoctrination. What really interested them was continuing to experiment with new forms. Francesco Ruspoli, whom Don Antonio de' Medici made "tutor" to his pet bear, invented a variant of the Petrarchan sonnet with four extra stanzas of one short and two long lines each. Benedetto Fioretti worked out a kind of eleven-syllable "Fidenzian" verse composed of anagrammatic words. Jacopo Soldani spiked Juvenal with a bit of seventeenth-century pornography,

> Some find advancement through the ivory thighs
> [of their beardless brothers]; to others, the bellies
> [of their sisters] are no less effective.

which the prudish editors a century later replaced with dots.* Francesco Maria Gualterotti discovered that Tuscan was as amenable as Greek to composite words: and three centuries before *Time* magazine introduced *cinemactor* into English, he made *drunkfestive* girls *sparkledancejoke* and *singhowl* through pages and pages of his charming dithyrambs:

> Seguia il suo dir; ma intanto
> piu donne ebrifestevoli
> ivi arrivar, che liete
> brilliballischerzavano,
> corisalti facevano,
> e ripiene di vin cantiululavano.
> (*La morte d'Orfeo*, 1628)†

Giovan Carlo Coppola outdid Tasso with a long epic about a heroic "Cosmo" who drove the "Scythians" and a dragon out of Florence in the sixth century A.D.:

> Of arms I sing, and of the valor of the Tyrrhenian hero . . .

Stefano Vai undercut Tasso by returning to Berni, always one of Galileo's favorites:

> Your Lisa, ah, your Lisa,
> She is white and fresh as cottage cheese.

And finally, Lorenzo Lippi, the poet, painter, and musician who kept Ferdinando's aunt Claudia spellbound with his deadpan acts and whose passion for hiking under the midsummer sun finally killed him, turned Tasso completely upside down. He

---

* The curious reader will find the omitted passages in the manuscript Magl. VII, 10.44 in the National Library of Florence.

† It would be sacrilegious to translate this delightful passage into a sharpharshsongless language like English; yet I dare not keep it from those readers who may know some Italian.

did so in a small masterpiece, called the *Malmantile Regained,* where he described, in lowbrow Florentine vernacular, a cosmic battle fought for the possession of the villa of one of his friends, located just over the hill from where Filippo Salviati had put up Galileo in 1612:

> O Muse, who stretch out gladly in the summer sun,
> atop a fence post, whence your songs abound;
> that I may fight this contest to the end,
> scratch my belly, and give my voice some sound.
>
> (*Il Malmantile racquistato di Perlone Zipoli,* I)

Some of the experiments were eventually abandoned—the exact replicas of Pindar, for example, which "offended Tuscan ears," and the "lascivious filth in Marino's sea" (*Mare Marini*—a pun in Italian). All of them were intended to be laughed at and applauded by the witty crowds that gathered at the home of the Baldinucci in Florence, at the pharmacy just off the Ponte alla Carraia, and at Alessandro Valori's villa near Empoli. In spite of an occasional repetition of commonplaces about the moral value of poetry, and in spite of one or two dreadful attempts at putting the commonplaces into practice, none of these experiments was ever intended to chastise, stimulate, uplift, or inspire anyone on behalf of anything.

Poetry did not prove, then, to be very helpful. But neither, for that matter, did prose, which Galileo himself had specifically distinguished from poetry. The *Dialogue,* to be sure, turned out to be a masterpiece, perhaps the greatest masterpiece of Renaissance prose literature. It avoided all the flowery exuberance of the "official" style, which the leading current authority on the Tuscan language, Benedetto Buonmattei, was just then pouring forth from a new professorial chair in Florence:

> To language in general it is so difficult to give rules, that I believe the task
> impossible, since various peoples, separated by long plains, by rapid rivers,
> by high mountains, and by thick woods, seldom visit among themselves.

Such syntactical somersaults and piled up particulars could prove nothing except that Buonmattei's cat, Romeo, had mastered all the liberal arts—which everyone knew to be true anyway. The *Dialogue* also kept itself free of Buonmattei's valiant and voluminous efforts to squeeze Tuscan—which, alas! had no case endings—into the forms of Latin grammar:

IV	*Nom.*	Mondo
Declension	*Gen.*	Di Mondo
	Dat.	A Mondo
	Acc.	Mondo
	Loc.	O Mondo, etc.

At the same time, Galileo resisted the campaign of the Jesuit stylists, from Famiano

Strada to Sforza Pallavincino, to replace Plato and Cicero with Aristotle as the model of philosophical discourse; for they would have confined him strictly within the limits of unadorned syllogisms. The *Dialogue* succeeded in its intent, which was rhetorical, precisely because it was humanistic rather than Platonic, because it was discursive rather than expository, because it left questions open rather than imposed definitive answers on them, and because it made the interlocutors not abstract "figures" but real people, with all the peculiarities of personality—people whom all their old friends immediately recognized from the speeches put into their mouths. Hence the reaction of the first readers: "It is full of wonderful, new things, explained in such a way that anyone can understand it perfectly"; "it has had the same effect on me as [Ariosto's] *Furioso*: wherever I start reading, I can't put it down."

The fault, in other words, lay not with the prose, but with the audience. For the broad, educated, lay reading public to which the *Dialogue,* like its predecessors of the fifteenth and the sixteenth centuries, was directed, had by now split into two groups: the very few well-prepared specialists who could grasp the substance even without the amenities, and the many more nonspecialists who enjoyed the amenities but did not quite follow all the particulars of the substance. The first group was already persuaded. After all, they had heard Galileo talking about these things for years. But the second group was becoming ever less capable of being persuaded by anything. They were slowly learning, from the meetings of the various new "academies" everyone belonged to, that all intellectual endeavor served no other purpose than that of amusing the participants. Amusement was the declared aim of the *Svogliati* ("The Will-Less"), who met in the garden of Jacopo Gaddi, of the *Infiammati* ("The Enflamed"), who met at the Company of San Giorgio on the Costa, and of all the other such societies that took the place, in the 1620s and 1630s, of Scipione Ammirato's hard-working *Alterati.* Amusement was at least the implicit aim even of the Accademia degli *Apatisti* ("The Apathetic"), the only one of these societies destined to endure, which the earnest young cleric Agostino Coltellini organized in 1632 on the model of St. Filippo Neri's *Oratorio.* For in spite of their tributes to the "spirit of brotherly charity" and to "all the sciences and letters," most of the members spent most of their time in "long and various arguments," "many and frequent conferences," and "most learned and ingenious disputes" about what academic name each of them should adopt. Most of the "academicians" admitted that cosmology was very amusing. But Galileo was asking much more of them. He was asking that they make an exception to what had now become a general rule about all subjects and to commit themselves to one of them, body and soul. And that is what they were no longer willing, or able, to do.

At the same time, those in both groups, the specialists as well as the amateurs, consciously cut themselves off from the great mass of the uneducated beneath them. When Galileo, right in the dedication of the *Dialogue,* distinguished between those who were and those who were not philosophers by the irremediable diversity of their intellectual powers; when Giovan Battista Doni distinguished between those "who appreciate well-ordered things" and the "ignorant populace"; when Giovanni da San Giovanni waited until the crowd had finished applauding the mural he had unveiled at the Porta Romana and then hacked it to pieces just to show how little he valued their applause—then nothing remained of the ambitious program of the founders of the Accademia Fiorentina in 1540 to bridge the cultural gap between butchers and bakers and intellectuals. Ammirato had already thrown the plebeians out of the realm of politics. Galileo now threw them out of the realm of the letters and sciences. The "plebeian" language frequently adopted by the poets and playwrights was meant solely for the entertainment of gentlemen. No real plebeian ever heard a word of it.

To be sure, this transformation of a leading elite into a closed caste was more theoretical than actual. After all, even some of the most antiplebeian Galileans, like Niccolò Aggiunti, had themselves broken the barrier between the two classes by "the force of genius and industry." Nor did it reflect any real change in the structure of society. Upward mobility seems to have increased, not through economic activities, perhaps, but certainly through the arts and letters and through the bureaucracy. The musician Jacopo Peri had been raised in a foundling home near the Porta San Gallo; but he managed to change his name to "de' Peri" and manufacture a family tree almost as convincing as that of the Barberini. The sculptor Pietro Tacca from Carrara rose to membership in the Council of the Two Hundred, where he was the peer of Galileo, and married his children into good middle-class (though not patrician) families. Admissions to Florentine citizenship, if Carlo Strozzi's lists are at all correct, rose from twenty-one in the first decade of the century to thirty-four in the second and to thirty-seven in the third. Moreover, individuals—though not yet whole families—could move down the social scale as well. "The most noble and respectable men" often mixed with "plebeians and the lowborn," as one moralist complained, in at least one levelling pastime: that of "having commerce with these infamous women" and "freely, yea shamelessly, going into their houses in broad daylight."

On one occasion the purely human instincts of the bluest of blood produced an outburst of savagery. Giovan Battista Cavalcanti was one of the richest and certainly the handsomest young men in all Florence in the 1630s. So handsome was he that "he robbed husbands of their wives and wives of their husbands." One of the friends he carefully cultivated after he had been married off to a respectable but dull Capponi girl was Luigi Antinori. Luigi had just become the not-too-willing husband of the beautiful Maddalena Del Rosso. And Maddelena was the young woman whom Giovan Battista had been madly in love with ever since they used to romp together, as teenagers, over the fields between their neighboring villas at Signa. The Del Rosso were soon bribed into feigning ignorance. And Luigi was charmed into turning his back, even for the "premature" birth of a daughter seven months after his return from an embassy in France. The affair was soon going so well that Giovan Battista simply moved into Palazzo Antinori—instead of having Maddelena slip out the side door—whenever Luigi was out of town or up at Poggio Imperiale. There was only one flaw: a poor cousin named Zanobi Carnesecchi, who had become indebted to the Cavalcanti and who had been rebuffed after making a pass of his own at Maddalena. One night Luigi came home unexpectedly to find the door, naturally, locked tight. His banging roused the nearby Zanobi, who rushed up with torches; and half an hour later Zanobi's henchmen caught Giovan Battista sneaking out without his breeches. *Dai! dai!* they screamed, and tore him to pieces with daggers. Meanwhile Maddalena had escaped to the house of a widowed aunt near Santo Spirito. But in vain. One of her brothers, bloated with a sense of "honor," borrowed a ladder from a nearby barber, crawled over a coach-house roof, waited until the maid went out into the garden, and then dispatched his sister with no less than eleven stabs in the breast. Luckily the family chapels of the Antinori and the Cavalcanti were next to each other, so the two lovers could be buried side by side. Luckier still, no one was prosecuted. The grand duke was less interested in enforcing justice than in maintaining an untarnished image of the aristocracy.

The Florentine patriciate, then, occasionally had troubles. But it was usually distracted from them by its persistent efforts to become a "nobility," just like the one in France. Mere family names and senatorial rank would no longer do. For neither the transalpine nobles whom Florentines met at foreign courts, nor those on the "grand tour" whom they met at home, had the slightest idea of what it meant to descend from republican magistrates. Whoever had money and influence could sometimes acquire the title of "count of the Holy Roman Empire" from the emperor himself, as four of the Strozzi did in 1623. Whoever had the proper family tree could look back into the distant past for titles, to precommunal feudal domains, from which Cosimo II obligingly removed the disabilities of republican legislation. Thus the Della Stufa family, which for centuries had disguised its nonmercantile origins, once again became the "counts of Talcione." Those who had neither the right ancestors nor enough money could now have new feudal domains created specially for them, and they became marquises and counts of hundreds of godforsaken pieces of deserted land in the romantic wilderness of the Maremma, all after an elaborate investiture ceremony at court worthy of the most chivalrous stanzas from Tasso's *Gerusalemme liberata*.

The rush for titles created some difficulties. For one thing, it added that many more separate legal jurisdictions to those already left standing by the Republic and the Principate. For another, it brought up endless questions of protocol. If "Very Illust.rs" was banned as unworthy of anyone, and if equals had to be addressed as "M'st Illstr. my Worshp.fl Patr.n," then superiors had to become "M'st. Ecc.nt L.rd my Worshp.fl L.rd Patr.n"—a form which could be augmented somewhat by writing out one or more of the abbreviations or toned down by sticking in another "my" somewhere and adding or subtracting a curlicue after the name of the city on the envelope. Being a "nobleman" was expensive, too. It required maintaining a string of country villas. And after 1664, when Cardinal Fabio Chigi, the future Pope Alexander VII, brought one back from France, it required riding about in a *calesse* with gold plate, crystal ornaments, and a metal shock-absorber.

Nevertheless, the new customs fitted perfectly with the efforts of contemporary theologians to think up still more titles for the Virgin: one Florentine Servite listed as many as twenty-one of them, in one long run-on sentence, by dipping into a sea of dubious similes (*tanquam rupes in medio erecta mari . . .*). The customs were imposed upon the younger generation by moving well-bred soccer players off the streets, where they might rub shoulders with the vulgar, and into the Riccardi gardens at Gualfonda,* where they could be supervised by their tutors and properly refreshed with "fine wines and delicate iced waters." Finally, the new customs were reinforced by fashions in clothing and makeup. The men raised their collars still higher, put on flowing capes with bold embroidered designs and gold buttons, and stood defiantly on elevated platforms, like Arnolfo (a good chivalric name!) de' Bardi, whom Carlo Dolci painted in 1632 with a boar being captured off at the right. The women took off their collars, put on thirty pounds and twenty years, powdered their great expanse of flesh until it blurred off into the surrounding atmosphere, and let their puffy mouths hang open and their watery eyes drift upward, like a cross between Sustermans' Magdalene and Guido Reni's Cleopatra. Thus both men and women of quality were easily distinguishable from the peasants and workers (but less so from the lackeys and butlers), who still wore canapa shirts and straight hose held up with a rope.

The quest for nobility, then, demanded an immense expenditure in time, money, and energy. But in the long run it was successful. Galileo occasionally grumbled at excessive formalities, though he knew how to use them as well as anyone. A few others still regretted the days when the magistracies were open only to merchants; they put the blame, as usual, on the Spanish and the Neapolitans. The artists, finally (happy souls!), were permitted to go on being as bohemian as ever. They could even play practical jokes on their customers. When a respectable monastic order unveiled the "Charity" it had commissioned from Giovanni da San Giovanni, it discovered instead a picture of two donkeys scratching each other. But everyone else willingly, even enthusiastically, complied. When Jean Baptiste L'Hermite de Souliers made an inspection tour of Florence in 1643, he found that all was in order. "The illustrious house of the Bardi," it seems, had never owned a bank, which is what historians remember them for today. Quite the contrary: it had been in possession of two real counties, "de la Verne et de Mangona," "since time immemorial." And L'Hermite accordingly recognized Florence as worthy of inclusion in his international social register.

* Just to the northeast of the railroad station, on the site of the present Exhibition Hall.

17. Carlo Dolci, *Vittoria della Rovere*
Palazzo Pitti

5

The campaign fails

This sort of aristocratic snobbishness inevitably rubbed off onto the Galileans, some of whom were aristocrats anyway, and all of whom accepted social conventions as uncritically as the rest of their contemporaries. The effectiveness of Galileo's rhetoric was thus limited to a privileged few, while the vast majority of Florentines were left to pick up their notions of science and cosmology from the only source of information available to them, the pulpit. The pulpit, in turn, was controlled not by the secular clergy, many of whom were favorably disposed toward Galileo, but by the regular clergy. More precisely, it was controlled by only some of the regular clergy. Two orders took almost no part in public preaching: the Benedictines, who had given Galileo one of his most brilliant apostles, and the Scolopians, who were among his most faithful disciples. For the first were without a large establishment in Florence, and the second were under harsh attack for encouraging disrespectful manners among the poorer classes. The task of preaching, therefore, fell largely to five other orders. Two of them were Florentine in origin and membership: the Vallombrosans at Santa Trinita and the Servites at the Annunziata. Two of them were mendicant and mostly non-Florentine in membership: the Franciscans at Sante Croce and the Dominicans at San Marco and Santa Maria Novella. And one of them was a relative newcomer: the Jesuits at San Giovannino, who were just then beginning to break down the widespread prejudice against them because of their connections in Spain.

The attitude of these religious orders toward Galileo varied from total indifference to open hostility. The two Florentine orders were simply uninterested. The Vallombrosans had apparently forgotten about the attack one of their members had launched against the *Starry Messenger* in 1611. As just about the most exclusive club of wellborn bachelors in the city, they were now intent solely on getting their portraits and coats-of-arms painted onto the walls of their newer, more pleasant refectory, despite some grumblings about the "worldly" nature of the project. The Servites were intent upon preserving the memory of Angelo Maria Montusi, the only theologian of note that they had produced in the past hundred years. For Dionigi Bussotti and Gherardo Baldi della Gherardesca, his two main successors in the 1630s and 1640s, preserving his memory meant holding inflexibly to his sensational reduction even of the Trinity to logical categories garnered from Aristotle and Peter Lombard. It meant adhering faithfully to his line-by-line explication of the Bible and defending the faithful against that "standard-bearer of impiety, Luther, a man without moral law, wrapped up in false words . . . ," and so on. And it meant keeping all the sciences, particularly anatomy, firmly within the domain of theology.

The Servites were also intent upon improving their reputation as agents of special divine favors. That meant carefully chronicling the miracles worked by their relics and intercessors. Both relics and intercessors were kept busy in the first decades of the century: the Swaddling Clothes of the Annunziata produced several painless childbirths when exposed in delivery rooms; Pietro de Bertis cured no less than thirty-one sick persons within a year of his death in 1610; and the founder of the order, Filippo Benizi, bestowed so many favors upon those who made vows to him that he was elected patron of the city of Todi in 1620. The Servites' reputation also had to be guarded against the denigration that was then being heaped upon their brothers in Venice, all of whom had sided with the Republic against Pope Paul V. Accordingly both Sarpi, Galileo's old friend and mentor, and Fulgenzio Micanzio, his enthusiastic disciple, were carefully omitted from the official history of the order published in the following century.

The mendicants, on the other hand, were somewhat better informed. Or at least a few of them made some effort to become so, once they realized how closely their orders had missed being permanently damaged by the grossly misinformed statements about science made by some of their brethren in 1614 and 1615. Indeed, one Dominican preacher, a certain Raffaello delle Colombe, who was a friend of Giovan Battista Strozzi and possibly a relative of Galileo's noisy antagonist Lodovico, figured out a way of avoiding further collisions. Don't rip biblical passages out of their contexts, he warned. Don't pad sermons with elaborate metaphors and oratorical bombast. Stick to the words you find in the Crusca's *Vocabolario* and to a "natural and familiar way" of speaking—like that of Galileo, he might have added, rather than that of Marino. Above all, don't pretend to be authorities on anything but "what belongs in our own shop." For if "we try to sell ourselves off as astronomers, philosophers, physicians, jurists, historians, and, I might add, artisans and technicians," we'll just show "that we know nothing about anything."

Few of his fellow Dominicans heeded his words. For over four centuries they had defended one particular combination of Christianity and philosophy. They had not succumbed to sharp metaphysicians like John Duns Scotus or

William of Occam. And they had no intention now of yielding to a mere mathematician. At the same time, they were busy defending their reputation as "a seminary of saints" against lingering suspicions of Savonarolism. Therefore, the slightest rumor of being anything but more orthodox than the orthodox had to be avoided, particularly since the most formal "abjurations" were held in their own mother church in Rome, Santa Maria sopra Minerva. They were also busy defending the reputation won for them by the pious, learned Domenico Gori before his death in 1619—the reputation, that is, of being the best teachers of logic and philosophy, as well as piety, in all Florence. Hence, Gori's successor, the sincere, sympathetic, but none-too-intelligent Ignazio Del Nente, dedicated himself "to rousing the whole order . . . and to recalling . . . the fruits of the spirit" through the examples of his great predecessors, principally Henry Suso, the fourteenth-century German mystic, and Sister Domenica dal Paradiso, whose intercession had saved Florence from being sacked in 1530. As far as Del Nente was concerned, Galileo was no different from "that wise philosopher Epicurus" mentioned somewhere by Justus Lipsius: he was a pure speculator, one whose speculations served no other purpose than that of encouraging the young to strive for wisdom. As far as Del Nente's colleague in Rome, Vincenzo da Firenzuola, was concerned, Galileo was guilty of letting what Vincenzo himself admitted to be the truth interfere with the proper functioning of venerable old institutions. And it was he, the perfect monk without the slightest taint of personal dignity, who was charged with getting a "confession" out of his illustrious captive in April 1633.

Unlike the Servites and the Dominicans, the Jesuits had known all about Galileo from the very start. After all, that was their business. They were no longer primarily apostles, as they had been in the age of Ignatius of Loyola and Peter Canisius. They were not yet primarily preachers and spiritual advisors, as they were to become, in Italy at least, in the age of Paolo Segneri. Instead, they were concentrating wholly upon building a reputation as men of learning. "The Muses everywhere proclaim your wisdom," admitted one Florentine in 1620. "The world applauds your studies; and the Temple of Fame is full . . . of your virtuous trophies." It was they who, as early as 1594, first formulated the guide lines for properly distinguishing between faith and scientific inquiry that were later adopted by the Galileans.

Unfortunately, building a reputation eventually became an end in itself. Thus when Galileo questioned their competence in subjects they claimed to excel in— when he exposed one Orazio Grassi of the Collegio Romano to the biting ridicule of his *Saggiatore* and when he threatened the career of one Christopher Scheiner by denying his pretended priority in the discovery of sun spots—the Jesuits closed their ranks in a massive move of collective self-defense. They were trapped by their vow of unquestioning obedience to the pope—or to whoever could get away with speaking in the name of the pope; and after 1616 they had no choice but to fall back on the Tychonian system, which many of them knew was only second best to the "condemned" Copernican system. Apparently, then, the would-be intellectual leaders of Europe were beginning to lose their intellectual vitality. They were also losing their taste for innovation; and after failing to obtain approval for a female branch of the society, they promptly squelched the plan of a Florentine lady named Eleonora Montalvo Landi to do in Florence what the famous English "Jesuitess" Mary Ward had tried to do across the Alps. They may even have begun to lose confidence in themselves—at least some authorities have suspected none other than Galileo's groveling persecutor of 1633, Melchior Inchofer, as the author of a vitriolic satire on the society that soon began to circulate in manuscript. Then, when their own self-appointed task of bearing witness before the church to the truth of the sciences fell by default to an admittedly not very polite gadfly, they turned upon him with uncontrollable fury. It was they, more than any others, who were responsible for what happened in the spring of 1633.

The old universe did not simply dissolve when it was struck by the full force of Galileo's dialectic in 1632. To many, indeed, it seemed at last to have been cured of all its ills and rendered as immortal as Christianity itself. For a supposedly infallible authority had shifted the foundations of the universe from science, which was no longer able to hold it up, to faith, which Galileo himself admitted to be its one sure guarantor. Moreover, it still enjoyed the unequivocal adherence of the vast majority of the population, which the Galileans had not bothered, or had not been able, to reach. It still enjoyed the passive adherence of many of those they had reached. For some philosophers really were, as Baldi della Gherardesca told Grand Duke Ferdinando, too old to start their education all over from scratch, and they really could not be thrown together, as the Galileans uncharitably tried to do, with men "so stupid and so inhuman . . . that they won't even open their eyes."

At the same time, the new cosmos was still marred by serious defects. For instance, Galileo had turned the comets into optical illusions, which obviously contradicted his statements elsewhere about the value of sense perception. He had not bothered to assimilate the more important recent discoveries of those he should have considered his colleagues—most notably, the discoveries of Kepler. He had not yet formulated his later approximation of Newton's law of inertia and had thus left the planets to propel themselves by some sort of mysterious force inherent in perfect circles. He had tried to clinch his argument about the movement of the earth by connecting it to a visible phenomenon, tides; and all his best friends soon told him that the ebb and flow simply did not occur according to the schedules he assigned to them. Finally, he had completely ignored the question of substance—what was the universe made of? Until some of his successors revived the ancient theories about atoms and the void, the Aristotelians still provided the only available answer to this question.

Galileo himself, then, was in part responsible for the survival of the old universe. But by far the greatest responsibility lay with those many powerful people in the many powerful institutions who found they had too great a stake in the Aristotelian universe to let it die. By the early 1630s they had good reason to be frightened. When requests for letters of recommendation came more and more to be addressed to Galileo instead of to them, when Cavalieri became more and more entrenched at Bologna, and when Dino Peri and Niccolò Aggiunti provoked a wave of "apostasy" from "Peripateticism and Justinianism" among the students of Pisa, the control of the academic job market, and of the universities and the schools as a whole, was on the verge of slipping through their fingers. To be sure, they could have gotten to work rewriting their lecture notes from beginning to end. They chose instead to join forces with the Jesuits, the Dominicans, the curial bureaucrats, and all those many members of the "establishment" who were anxious, after the exciting but fatiguing task of reforming the church and consolidating the state, to relax into a quiet, well-run normality.

The church rejected the services offered it. The campaign to convert the world by converting its most prestigious institution thus ended, twenty-one years after its brilliant inauguration, in total failure.

6

The Galileans hold out

The "philosophers and mathematicians" of Florence were dismayed, then, as they walked back out into Piazza Santa Croce on July 12, 1633. They were also somewhat apprehensive. A moderate, polite, but nonetheless dangerous rebuttal of the *Dialogue* had just appeared a few months earlier. It was one which went beyond the same old arguments about the unreliability of the telescope. Indeed, it touched upon some of the chief weaknesses in Galileo's thesis, such as the explanation of tides and of the shape of planetary orbits. The author was a mild, broad-minded humanist and philosopher from Lorraine named Claudio Berigard, and he was soon rewarded with several promotions at Pisa and then, in 1639, with one of the best chairs at Padua. Berigard was backed up by a certain Scipione Chiaramonti, who had already taken on Tycho Brahe and Kepler and who was ready to take on Galileo as well. He was backed up by Paganino Gaudenzio, the linguist, theologian, and orientalist, who the very next year was once more to proclaim Aristotle the beginning and the end of all wisdom. The three of them organized an academic pressure group called the *Circulus Pisanus,* which prepared an explication of all branches of Aristotelian philosophy for presentation to the grand duke in 1643.

The worse was still to come. Convinced that the condemnation of the statement "The earth moves" constituted a final decision in their favor, the Aristotelians became more adamant than ever. So also did those, particularly the Jesuits, who had let themselves be forced unwillingly into an Aristotelian position and who now had to pacify their consciences. Either they studiously ignored Galileo—for instance, by picking Tasso as the modern master of the dialogue form; or else they prefaced their books with Latin translations of Galileo's abjuration and built "an impregnable fortress . . . with many compliments to themselves and much disdain of Galileo" out of fragments gleaned from the constructive criticisms offered Galileo by his friends. The Holy Office became vindictive. It specifically excluded the *Dialogue* from the coverage of the blanket permissions it sometimes gave reliable people for reading books on the Index. It ordered all the local inquisitors, from Lisbon to Lithuania, to have the condemnation announced publicly. And it doubled its vigilance over booksellers, even in Paris, and over the libraries of the deceased. The pope became implacably hostile. Constant diplomatic pressure had forced him to transfer Galileo's "prison," first to Siena and then to the villa at Arcetri. For the "prisoner" still was, after all, the "First Philosopher and Mathematician to the Most Serene"—and gravely offended— "Grand Duke of Tuscany." But Urban went out of his way to pick fights with the ambassador, Niccolini. He threatened the dungeons of Castel Sant'Angelo if anyone disturbed his sleep with another petition for a mitigation of the sentence. And he became almost hysterical when, in 1642, he heard of a proposal to erect a monument to the "penitent of the Holy Office" in Santa Croce.

He who claimed to be infallible had been caught in error. Hence, his fury knew no bounds. It paralyzed the church. And it offered ambitious underlings the chance they had been waiting for. They had already shipped Ciampoli out to the coldest corner of the Papal State in 1632, for reasons that are still unclear. Soon after they had Niccolò Ridolfi deprived of his position as general of the Dominicans, in spite of the order's rigid provisions against outside interference. One of the bureaucrats, a certain Mario Sozzi of Montepulciano, managed to wreck the entire order of the Pious Schools simply by denouncing his colleagues as a bunch of Galileans, which they most certainly were. He first had himself made head of the house in Florence and promptly purged it of its Florentine members. When the grand duke threw him out of Tuscany, he turned on the general himself, José de Calansanz, who was forced to walk through the streets of Rome in penitential garb and then acquiesce in the dissolution of the order he had dedicated his life to building.

The Galileans were apprehensive, then; but they were not disconcerted. The same sort of sporadic persecution, they knew, could just as easily be turned against some of their enemies. Aristotelianism contained the germs of something far worse than heresy: atheism. And the Holy Office proved to be as vigilant as ever when it came to the philosophic theses of Cremonini, Galileo's old colleague at Padua. Galileo eventually quarreled with one of Cremonini's disciples about the question of the moon's light. He denounced another of them as an "ignorant ox." And he may have derived some satisfaction from the troubles his old antagonist of 1616, Tommaso Caccini, got into when he presented his tedious, pointless *Ecclesiastical History* to the "correctors" in 1638. Galileo had no reason to yield on religious grounds. Although not profoundly religious himself, he was sure that the solid Catholicism he had inherited from his ancestors was better than the religion his opponents defaced with an outworn metaphysics. Though probably sympathetic with Aggiunti's reluctance to fast during Lent, he realized, as his daughter reminded him, that "these disturbances and setbacks" might well

serve him who "had penetrated the heavens with the eye of a Lynx [Linceo]," to
understand the "vanity . . . of all earthly things." He was certain that he, and not
the few unscrupulous plotters who had temporarily usurped the central organs
of the church, represented the "true" Catholic tradition of the Apostles, the
Fathers, and the Doctors, whom he cited continually. And he had no doubt at
all about his own innocence. Therefore, he did not hesitate to accept the explanation soon worked out by his friends for what had happened. The pope, they
claimed, had been misled into thinking that the Aristotelian position was
unfavorably presented in the *Dialogue* and that the spokesman for the Aristotelians,
Simplicio, was to some extent a parody of himself. The explanation was far from
accurate, for it labeled as "misconceptions" what many readers congratulated
Galileo on having set forth so clearly. But it served the Galileans well. For it freed
their consciences from the least shred of remorse. And it allowed them to maintain
their respect at least for the Papacy, if not, perhaps, for that particular pope.

Thus the Galileans had nothing to worry about just because the chief
institutional form of their religion now frowned on them. For religion in
Florence, and in much of the rest of Catholic Europe, had become largely a
matter of individual piety by the 1630s. It was still bolstered by a familiarity with
the Bible, that "school of true wisdom, which alone can make men divine,
immortal, blessed," as the literary critic Benedetto Fioretti called it after reading
it through eighteen times. Religion was still supported by the remnants of a
philological approach to the Bible—that is, by a method which preferred the
Hebrew original or the Chaldaic equivalent to the Latin translation, and which
demanded at least the same attention to the single words of the Bible that Fioretti
accorded to those he extracted from the *Vocabolario* ("Dictionary") of the Crusca.
Biblical scholarship in Florence never even approached the high standards being
set for it in France by the greatest of the Counter-Reformation scholars, Denis
Petavius. But it was at least sincere. And it occasionally produced an outburst of
enthusiasm—like that of the jovial, loquacious, vagabond cathedral chaplain,
Bastiano Masotti, who finally had to be barred from the ghetto when his interminable recitations of Old Testament passages began to bore, rather than edify,
his street-corner audiences.

Moreover, religion in Florence had recently been reinforced by the fame
of the harsh austerities practiced among the reformed Franciscans at Fiesole.
They dressed themselves in hair shirts and chains. They spent several hours each
day in mental prayer. And they left their overworked janitor almost every
morning with the job of mopping up the blood they had spilled "administering
the discipline" the night before. Religion had been still further inspired by such
latter-day Savonarolans as Bartolomeo Cambi da Saluto, who entertained huge
audiences with denunciations of the clergy, who hung his crucifix from a rope—
to the scandal of all right-thinking people—and who ended his days in a state of
continual ecstasy at a hermitage near Rieti. Finally, religion had been made a

matter of the highest concern by Pandolfo Ricasoli Baroni, whose *Angelic Doctrine* was published at almost the same moment as Galileo's *Dialogue,* and whose teachings sometimes sound like borrowings from his more famous contemporary, François de Sales. Every Christian, Ricasoli promised, "in whatever state or way of life God has placed him," can aspire to the highest forms of mystical experience. He can arrive there not by going through anything so rigorous as the "purgation" of Catherine of Genoa or the "dark night of the soul" of John of the Cross. Let him begin, as a child, playing with toy altars. Let him then "make use of created things insofar as they aid us in reaching our end." Let him continually recite the psalms and canticles and read the Bible and pious books. Such meticulous preparation will not fail to produce in him the gift of "consurrection," by which his mind, while retaining a degree of autonomy, will become inseparably united with the mind of God.

Ricasoli's promise fell on receptive ears. Florentines had already learned how to realize his promise from the popular Dominican teacher Benedetto Gori, who had revived many elements of Renaissance Christian humanism in the *Spiritual Exercises* he administered to the "businessmen"—*persone impiegate in mercatura*—of the confraternity of San Benedetto Bianco. They had learned still more from his successor, Ignazio Del Nente, who directed the Company of the Good Death at San Marco. They therefore plunged into an exhausting round of pious observances. Girolamo da Sommaia, the commissioner of the university who added compliments in his own hand every time he sent Galileo a paycheck, described an ordinary day in this manner:

> To Mass at the Carmine . . . and to lunch at the Colombaria. Then Vespers at Santa Maria Novella and thence in a coach around the walls with Ruberto Ridolfi and Alessandro Rinuccini. Evening office at San Benedetto with a sermon by the chaplain and with devotions by Father Gori . . . .

Jacopo Peri, the musician, almost killed himself in 1630 when he sneaked out of bed with a high fever in order to go to Mass; it took his son Dino three days to revive him after he collapsed on the floor of the church. Similarly, Carlo Strozzi showed up every week for the "discipline" at the Theatines. He got a bill of indulgence signed by none other than Urban VIII. He enrolled all his family, and himself twice, as Third Order Franciscans. And, just to make absolutely sure that everything would go all right after his death, he left money for no less than four hundred Masses for his soul.

Florentines had apparently overcome, in the generation of Galileo, the fear of hell and the misgivings about heaven that had beset the generation of their fathers. Confident of possessing all the necessary means, they devoted themselves tirelessly to attaining the twofold end of sanctity in this life and instant admission to paradise in the next. When the similar efforts of one of their ancestors were finally awarded with canonization—a fairly frequent occurrence in the first decades of the century—they all rallied round to celebrate. Thus in June 1629, the one hundred-ninetieth anniversary of a victory won by the Florentines through his intercession, the new saint, Andrea Corsini, was honored with a fake marble facade on the Carmine, with three days of fireworks, and with a procession of sixty singers, eighty German bowmen, the whole Senate dressed in purple, all the magistrates with torches, and the grand duke with his family and attendants— most of this paid for by Andrea's latest descendant, Filippo, who now called himself, according to the latest fashion, the "Marquis of Sismano."

Unfortunately, this purely personal quest for sanctity had certain dis- advantages. It robbed ecclesiastical institutions of the benefits of criticism, of collaboration, and, therefore, of a sense of responsibility among its members. It left to the archbishop alone the disagreeable task of bewailing, in synod after synod, the same old cases of "turpitude" in the confessional, of "curates ... who forget completely their obligations ... by remaining absent from their parishes," and of priests who, "unconscious ... of their dignity ... frequent public and private assemblies of men *and women*" (my italics). It induced the laity, and most of the clergy, to assume that all the necessary reforms had been carried out by competent authorities and to think only of themselves. It made them helpless before the excesses of relic collection, for example, the enormous expenditures needed to acquire the bath sponge of St. Carlo Borromeo and the bones of St. Benedict the Martyr. It lured them into such purely sentimental cults as that of the rosary, which Matteo Rosselli celebrated in several huge canvasses and which a special confraternity promoted with a barrage of large and small indulgences. It encouraged them to confuse morality with casuistry, a literary genre which strung together—for no other apparent purpose than the titillation of its many devotees—a great variety of piquant "cases of conscience" under such lurid chapter headings as "Men Who Die Impenitent because of Excessive Attachment to Whores."

For many Florentines religion became solely a matter of exterior acts. And exterior acts in turn bred hypocrisy—like that of the "privileged penitents" of the Annunziata, who "went about with downcast eyes and few words," but who were "so insolent and so intent on their own advantage that they would have made even Socrates lose his patience." One poet remarked:

> There they go, heads bowing,* over the street,
> muttering *Aves* and crunching out psalms;
> Scoundrels, they, all of them; but oh, how it's sweet,
> always to boast of your prayer books and alms.
>   (Francesco Ruspoli, Sonetto no. 10)

---

* *Torcicollo*: still another word for "bigot." It is surprising that English-speaking peoples, who have been as fecund as Italians in producing the phenomenon, should be so sterile in words to describe it.

Another poet, Andrea Cavalcanti, felt obliged to suggest a way for keeping "all monks and other devout persons" from "annoying other people's women": have "cats jump about on their genitals . . . every time they are beseiged by the enticements of the flesh." And while the wits laughed, the pastors wrung their hands. As that late survivor of Counter-Reformation piety, Giovan Battista Rinuccini, put it:

> We have arrived at the Antipodes of primitive Christianity. . . . We pay attention to exterior appearances. We denigrate the interior substance. We put aside the meaning and the force, and we turn splendor and pomp into idols. . . . No matter how much bishops strive these days, theirs, which is the greatest of all occupations, usually ends up being taken as little more than a frivolous pastime.

Nowhere was the demise of "primitive Christianity" more evident than in the convents. Some of them were largely refuges for the wealthy, admission being as costly as it was unconnected with a true religious vocation:

> To take the veil and to prepare
> for cloister, choir, and matins,
> the highborn virgin puts on lace,
> she feasts and sings and sets the pace
> in flirts with men in satins
> (Soldani, *Satire,* no. 5)

Others suffered severe financial hardship and had to beg the archbishop to put pressure on the relatives of the inmates for further contributions. Many of them were badly administered, though few probably had as inefficient a manager as Domenico Bonedi, pastor of San Felice a Ema, who had charge of the accounts of Galileo's daughter's convent of San Matteo. Somehow he figured out a way of ending up in the black in 1633—with *lire* 13,411:2:3 credits and 12,159:2:4 debits. But most of the endowment was invested in urban real estate—in two shops near San Lorenzo, in a house behind Santa Croce, in a shop with an extra room on the Ponte Vecchio (which brought in the highest rent). The endowment was therefore particularly sensitive to economic recession. Profit or no profit, the nuns avoided starvation only by begging food from their families, and they kept from freezing only by huddling in borrowed blankets.

Still, the greatest problem in the convents was keeping busy. Maria Celeste, Galileo's daughter, managed to run about from dawn to dark preparing medicines and jams, cutting out dresses, and giving music lessons; often she could find time only for a brief note to her beloved father. But most of her associates were no more certain of their monastic vocations, and no better able to distract themselves from the consequences of a mistaken vocation, than their famous contemporary, immortalized in the nineteenth century by the novelist Alessandro Manzoni, the

Monaca di Monza. Theirs was a holy life, they knew, a life specially protected from abuse by the thick walls, the double grates, and the doddering gardeners prescribed by the archbishop in 1601. And it was guarded by the careful regulations for admittance described by the grammarian Buonmattei in his *Method of Consecrating Virgins* of 1622. But at least one of them, the unfortunate Maria Felice Orsini, who was let out at fourteen to be married to an unknown Frenchman and then shut up again when Louis XIII had him executed, must have been grateful only for being spared the twelve childbirths that had finally killed her mother at the age of thirty-four. One other, absolutely ignorant of what ailed her, smashed her head to pieces against the wall of her cell—to the utter bewilderment of her friend, Maria Celeste Galilei. And still another of them, a certain Arcangela Tarabotti, burst out into a violent denunciation of the whole male sex, which, she said, locked up thousands of unwilling women in convents for the sake of "reason of state . . . worldly pride, and accumulating riches." Unfortunately this diatribe ran up against the usual antifeminist "authorities," Aristotle and St. Jerome; and Arcangela could think of no alternative to the supposed "imperfection" of women but the "criminality" of men. Still, she could cite all the appropriate conciliar decrees in her favor, and she could look forward, in the next world, to watching mobs of heartless fathers drown for all eternity in "the river . . . formed by the tears of these miserable captives."

Religious individualism, then, had its drawbacks, at least from the point of view of religious people. But for ordinary Florentines it had one great advantage. It mitigated, to some extent, the widening breach between the rich and the poor by forcing the former into an endless round of works of charity. For the Galileans, it had an even greater advantage. It enabled them to remain faithful, even devout, Catholics, while they continued to believe firmly what Galileo certainly did not say at the moment of his abjuration: *Eppur si muove*—"the earth really does move." The church may have condemned the proposition, they admitted. But the Christian religion, which the church itself distinguished from purely administrative matters, had not condemned it.

At the same time, the Galileans had still another good reason for not changing their minds—namely, that two of the other major fields that interested them were still as "Galilean" in the 1630s as they had been in 1610. In music the combination of theory and practice and of Hellenism and technology enabled Florence to produce one of the greatest musicologists of the age, Giovan Battista Doni. Doni had gotten to know half the scholars in Europe during his travels as a student of law and as a papal secretary. He had studied under one of the most bizarre of them, a Scottish Catholic "made for war and contention" named Thomas Dempster, who taught at Pisa until 1619 and who was to achieve posthumous fame, a

century later, as the founder of modern Etruscology. Doni had joined the scholars'
ranks by producing a huge supplement to Janus Gruterus's collection of ancient
inscriptions and a score of treatises on various antiquarian and archaeological
subjects. Antiquities soon led him back to the letters of Girolamo Mei and to the
writings of Vincenzo Galilei, "the father of the presently famous philosopher
and mathematician," which he procured through the courtesy of the son of the
founder of the Camerata, Piero de' Bardi. By the fall of 1633 he was sure he had at
last found the way of "ridding our music of the barbarism into which it has fallen
since the invasion of the Germanic nations and of restoring it to its ancient
splendor." He invented a "new instrument" that enabled him to make as many
"marvelous observations" in music as Galileo had with the telescope in astronomy
and "to succeed in a few months where whole schools had until now labored in
vain." He had gone beyond Vincenzo Galilei and Jacopo Peri—or at least so he
thought. He had at last discovered all the secrets of Greek music. And he could
actually transform what he discovered into sound on the agglomeration of
crisscrossed strings and stops which he called, after the patrons who paid for his
experimental concerts, the *Barberini lyre*.

Just how far Doni actually managed to affect the practice of music in Florence
is still unknown. Historians of music are all familiar with the work of his friend
and contemporary, Girolamo Frescobaldi, who was organist at St. Peter's until
1632. But none of them has yet discovered what it was that Francesco Rovai's
"conversation" of young noblemen who "went around singing . . . every week
in the principal churches" performed. None of them has yet found out what the
sixty-man chorus performed at the cathedral under the direction of Marco da
Gagliano and Domenico Melani. None of them has yet examined even the printed
scores of the prolific Matteo Coferati, whose *Corona* was republished several
times before the end of the century. Probably Doni's effect was negligible on
dramatic music. For costumes by now had obliterated the personages represented,
to the point where shepherds were expected to appear in white ermine jackets.
Alfonso Parigi's "machines" and Angelo Ricci's flame-throwing dragons had
overshadowed the actors. Dancing horses—the most popular "invention" of
contemporary choreographers—had outshone dancing men. Poetic unity had been
sacrificed to standardized scenes and eulogies of patrons, so that the quality of
suspense consisted solely in waiting to see how Andrea Salvatori or Giovan Carlo
Coppola would manage the indispensable sea scene and the required references
to the grand duchess. Finally, musical unity, which Jacopo Peri may still have
gotten away with in the score he wrote for Salvadori's *The Precedence of the Ladies*
in 1625, had completely vanished by 1637, when the libretto was divided between
five different composers for the sake of "variety."

Doni, then, may have failed in the long run. But the Galileans understood
perfectly what he was trying to do. After all, he had been the first of them to get
in to see Galileo immediately after the condemnation. They welcomed him with

open arms when at last he came home to stay in 1640. They agreed with him that study and experiment served "to discover new things," not "to wear out the brain in abstractions or to feed a vain curiosity." And they fully supported him in chiding the other great musicologist of the age, Marin Mersenne, for occasionally mixing astrology and symbolism with what Mersenne himself admitted to be a purely scientific, and therefore basically mathematical, discipline.

The visual arts were still Galilean too. Or at least the artists remained as fascinated with new techniques, as irreverent of "authority," and as dedicated to "nature" as they had been three decades earlier. Giovanni da San Giovanni, while shut up at home with the gout and protected from the watchful gaze of patrons, let his imagination run wild painting baskets and straw rugs—at no small monetary profit to himself. Carlo Dolci managed to squeeze a whole crowd of Tuscan peasants in between the legs of the sweaty workers pushing the Cross into place. Lorenzo Lippi, who refused to look at Correggio's cupola for fear of being influenced by it, stuck to the "truth" about flower petals in his paintings as carefully as he had reproduced Florentine colloquialisms in the *Malmantile Recaptured*; and he duly respected the "truth" about the family of Maddalena Carnesecchi, whom he had been commissioned to portray, by including the one stillborn child she had borne, along with her seventeen live ones. Pietro Tacca kept a live wild boar in a cage in order to perfect the *Cinghiale,* or "Bronze Pig," as it was then called, which he adapted from a Hellenistic statue in the Uffizi and set up in the Mercato Nuovo in 1640. He made the joints so smooth in his grotesque fountains in front of the Annunziata that the curly tails gave no sign of having been cast separately. He also learned how to make his giant horses more and more active. After innumerable sketches from real life and a careful study of an equestrian portrait by Rubens, he managed to make one of them, with King Philip IV of Spain in the saddle, stay reared up on its hind legs, even though the apparent center of gravity lay over nothing but empty space:

> Motionless to motion aspire,
> up to the stars, ever higher,
> where the praise of the maker can't fade,
> nor the fame of the marvel he's made.
>   (Rovai, Sonnet No. 46)

Florentine artists went on producing "novelties" in the name of the principle that Matteo Rosselli had adapted from Galileo's *Dialogue*: that all the rules of Leonardo were useless unless tested in practice. Unfortunately, they too, like the musicians, eventually ran into difficulties. In 1619 they had produced the greatest monument of *graffito*: the elaborate painted facade of Palazzo Antella in Piazza Santa Croce. In the 1620s, they had decorated the interior of Buontalenti's Casino with a series of frescoes that admirably integrated each of their individual styles with Matteo Rosselli's overall plan. Throughout the 1620s and again in the mid-1630s many of them were busy with the paintings, frescoes, and chiaroscuros that Michelangelo Buonarroti, Jr., was having erected as memorials to his famous uncle. And they were so successful in blending unity with diversity that only the discovery of a manuscript notebook in the National Library has at last permitted the identification of the several contributors. Then in 1635, Giovanni da San Giovanni, the ablest fresco artist in the city, started in on the vast project of painting the ground floor of the Pitti. Just as he was about to realize the full potentiality of his technique—just as he was about to cast aside the frame borrowed from canvas painting and to make the walls vanish into an infinite space—the grand duke brought in from Rome another artist who had already done just that on the ceiling of the Barberini palace. The Florentines could do nothing but watch with amazement as Pietro da Cortona—who had enough Florentine background in him to be comprehensible, but enough experience elsewhere to be completely independent of his inheritance—swept away all local traditions and swept in the new Roman baroque, which he had done so much to create. "Oh Curradi, Oh Curradi," exclaimed one of them, "how tiny we all are in comparison." Pietro then took over the art life of the city. He dominated the parties and

18. Pietro da Cortona with Ciro Ferri, ceiling, Sala di Marte
Palazzo Pitti

discussion groups. He removed the late sixteenth- and early seventeenth-century art from the cathedral. He painted an "Allegory of Quiet" for Prince, now Cardinal, Gian Carlo de' Medici, which has recently been identified in the house of the Venturi Ginori Lisci in Via della Scala. He laid out the plans for the most recent religious community in the city, the Oratorians of St. Filippo Neri. And he left his disciple, Cirro Ferri, to finish what he had begun in the Pitti.

Art in the Florentine tradition suffered a momentary eclipse. Much of what the artists of Galileo's generation did was soon forgotten in the darker corners of churches, packed away in cellars, or sold off to foreigners. Some of it was eventually destroyed, like the frescoes that were whitewashed over in what has become the jail of the Court of Appeals. And most of what was left might have vanished forever in the flood of 1966 had not one or two farsighted art historians appreciated its value. Michelangelo Buonarroti, Jr., was almost prophetic when he wrote about his 22,000 *scudi* gallery:

> The pictures and statues I hold so dear may some day serve as targets for balls and rackets . . . and my house may become a barracks to be let out to French and German soldiers.

For it certainly would have become a barracks for German and American soldiers during World War II had it not been providentially walled up. And it would still be walled up had not one of the biggest banks of the city subsequently put some 400 million *lire* into restoring it as a public museum. But in 1633 the Florentine artists were still unaware of their fate. They were also fully sympathetic with their current national hero. And one of them—in fact the least "Cortonesque" of them, whose *bravura* earned him the nickname Cecco Bravo—appropriately expressed their sympathy two years later by painting an amusing caricature of him right in the middle of the "famous philosophers and mathematicians" in Buonarroti's gallery.

7

The Galileans win

In the meantime, the Galileans were comforted by the return of Galileo himself, after a pleasant and productive sojourn—an all too-pleasant one, according to one Holy Office spy—with his old friend and disciple, the archbishop of Siena. He was not exactly in Florence when he returned, for he was forbidden to leave his villa. But then, Arcetri was not a disagreeable place to live in. The broad terrace opened onto one of the most beautiful views in all Tuscany—olive orchards that rolled down toward the Greve and back up again to the Certosa monastery. And the view had not yet been ruined by the Capuchin friars, who flouted both good taste and public building codes in the 1950s and '60s by turning their monastery into a sprawling, "modernized" eyesore.* A three-minute walk up the hill to what is now the observatory offered the even more remarkable view of the whole city, with Fiesole on one side and the plains heading out toward Pistoia on the other. His daughter, Maria Celeste, who provided him once again with the family affections he had lost in the 1590s, was practically next door at San Matteo. His son Vincenzo was nearby on the Costa—whenever he was shirking his duties and not residing in one of the provincial magistracies his father worked so hard to obtain for him. Vincenzo's in-laws, the Bocchineri, of whom Galileo was particularly fond, could easily get in from Prato.

Life in a villa, then, was not completely the life of "penance" the Holy Office intended it to be. Everyone else, after all, particularly after the plague, spent as much time as possible in the country, which had at last been rid of bandits by the latest version of Machiavelli's militia—"faithful subjects, not foreigners, honorable citizens of their towns and villages . . . able to nourish a horse from their own . . . business activities." The Arrighetti brothers lived just over the hill at San Miniato. Niccolò Cini lived just down the Ema valley at Le Rose. No one really worked in his villa—except perhaps, like Galileo himself, to tend a few

* For the particulars: *La nazione*, August 8, 1966, p. 5.

lemon trees, to prune a vine or two, or to cultivate an artichoke bed between conversations and paragraphs. The country air was found to be especially conducive to poetry. Hence the excitement when a real live "peasant poet"—and not just one of Antonio Malatesti's imaginary rustic "verse distillers"—was discovered near Arcidosso: he was straightway invited to come recite before the court. Country food turned out to be simple and healthy:

> A pinch of salt and pepper
> On a slice of good roast pork,
> some raisins, sausage,
> a bit of fennel;
> and all you need's a fork . . .
> (Malatesti, *La Tina*, stanza v)

—though occasionally the meat and eggs could be spruced up a bit by being served *en gelée,* with a branch of laurel on top "for looks"—*un piatto da farsi vedere.* So Galileo had no objection to living outside the city, though he was painfully annoyed at not being able to receive anyone without a permit from the inquisitor. Neither, for that matter, did his fellow "exile" Ciampoli mind his rustic environment, though he carefully edited out of his published correspondence his former expressions of contentment with the studious solitude "among the cliffs of the Apennines." And the cultural life of Florence followed them out into the country.

Now that the plague was over, Florentines hurried back to normality. The Accademia Fiorentina brought in thirty-six new members in 1634, and the next year it elected Galileo's pupils to all its offices. The Accademia della Crusca at last reopened in 1640 under the leadership of none other than Michelangelo Buonarroti, Mario Guiducci, and Filippo Pandolfini—all of them Galileans to the core; and the following July they put on a huge party for fifty-six members and two Medici princes, with fourteen torches in silver holders, dozens of clever speeches "in praise of thirst," and "the most exquisite dishes." Now that the "campaign" was over, Galileo got back to work, back to the purely "scientific" problems of motion, which many of his friends had been urging him to take up again for years, back to the tight demonstrations that less spectacularly, but much more thoroughly than the most impassioned appeals in its favor, reinforced the new cosmos. And in 1638 his second great masterpiece, the *Dialogues Concerning Two New Sciences* was published at Leiden.

Galileo's disciples also got back to work, not only as scientists but also as propagandists. Niccolò Aggiunti soon had several students presenting Galilean theses at Pisa. The new rector, Marcantonio Pieralli, turned a funeral oration of 1638 into a eulogy of "the great Lynx (*Linceo*)" who had made the university famous once again; and he noted that "the heavens tell of the glory of God" by making the planets—though not necessarily the one he was standing on—revolve about the sun. Another professor, the Olivetan monk Vincenzo Renieri, became a specialist on Galileo's works, which he began assembling for eventual republication, and from which he extracted astronomical tables for the use of antiquarians.

None of the Galileans yielded. Some of them indulged in a bit of revenge by denouncing the search for science in the Bible as Manichaeism and by repeating the statements of Lactantius on the difference between geometry and theology. Others worked out a still better tactic, the one Pascal had usually been credited with. They softened up their opponents rather than charging them head-on; and they proclaimed themselves, not the so-called Aristotelians, to be the true followers of Aristotle. They, after all, were following his example by looking impartially at nature and by refusing to accept any previous hypothesis as an absolute truth. They thus left the task of denigrating Aristotle, that disagreeable noisemaker "who sullied his reputation with so many vices," to people like the Minimite monk Giovan Battista Neri and the prior of San Marco, Ignazio Del Nente.

Twenty-five years of teaching and twenty years of combat now gave way to ten final years of serenity. The vigorous, lively old man whom the court portraitist, Justus Sustermans, painted in 1635 gradually withered into the emaciated old man, his sightless eyes staring into space and his bony knuckles wrapped around a telescope, whom Sustermans again painted just before Galileo's death in 1641. But his mind remained as alert and as full of new projects as ever, even while he sat by the fire at night listening to one of his young pupils read Ariosto aloud. Two of his older disciples, Castelli and Cavalieri, were busy working out some of his suggestions in pure mathematics, suggestions that he had always been too impatient to follow up himself. One of his more recent disciples, the young Florentine Evangelista Torricelli, was busy working on the famous barometer, which, in 1644, was to establish the existence of the vacuum experimentally and thus supply the new cosmos with an answer to its still open question of substance. The kindly priest Niccolò Gherardini, who had followed him back from Rome and then settled down with a benefice at a nearby church, was busy planning the first biography. The dedicated Scolopian Fabiano Michelini and the enthusiastic secretary Vincenzo Viviani, who was still barely out of his teens, had moved right into his house; and they could assure him, at the moment of his death, that still more disciples would carry on his work for at least another generation.

Meanwhile Galileo's books were spreading all over Europe. One of his telescopes was presented to the emperor of China. His major works were, within two decades, reduced to a compendium in English for the use of the schools of the Massachusetts Bay Colony. His methods were soon adopted, in a slightly Baconian disguise, by the chief scientists of England. And Florence became a Mecca for distinguished pilgrims—for John Milton, for instance, for John Evelyn, for Balthasar de Monconys, and even for the prince of Denmark, who came not only to admire "one of the most magnificent pieces of art in the world," as the Medici chapel was thought to be, but above all to meet Viviani, Torricelli, and Renieri, and to find out what their great master was doing.

Thus even though the old cosmos still survived, the new cosmos emerged stronger than ever. In the long run, it was not Galileo who lost the "campaign." It was the Society of Jesus, which became a symbol for intellectual mediocrity and duplicity. It was the church, which divorced itself from the sciences and turned into a regressive force in the development of European culture. It was all the Catholic apologists right down to the time of Agostino Gemelli and even Emmanuel Mounier, who have had to go on repeating "it's too bad, but . . ." and "if only Galileo had not . . ." without convincing or comforting anyone. It was Protestant Christianity, too, which managed to cover up its share of culpability for Galileo's misfortunes only with the help of the now discredited "Whig" myth about Luther as the founder of liberal democracy. It was organized religion as a whole, which fell into the same old errors when confronted with the Rights of Man in the eighteenth century, with geological and biological evolution in the nineteenth, and with Freudian psychology in the twentieth.

The victors, then, were the Galileans, and the many great men of science and piety from the time of Galileo to the time of Pasteur and Teilhard de Chardin. They triumphed among the scientists in 1633. And they finally triumphed among the theologians too, on December 7, 1965, when chapter 36 of the second Vatican Council's decree on "The Church in the Modern World" proclaimed their doctrine of the just autonomy of terrestrial affairs to be the official teaching of the Catholic Church.

BOOK IV

FLORENCE
IN THE 1680s

*How Lorenzo Magalotti looked in vain for a
vocation and finally settled down to
sniffing perfumes*

I

How Magalotti started out being a scientist

No one could have expected anything but the most brilliant of careers from the bright, handsome young man of twenty-two who arrived in Florence in 1659. He was "equipped with all the ornaments of chivalrous exercises, as befits a noble and well-trained patrician"—sure in the saddle, nimble in the ballroom, and charming in the antechambers of princes. He had received the best possible education: four years at the Collegio Romano and three years at the University of Pisa. He belonged to one of the oldest and still one of the most prominent families of the city. True, his spendthrift, black-sheep father, Orazio, had been no more than a clerk in the Papal post office. But his uncle Lorenzo, archbishop of Ferrara, had been one of the most influential members of the Roman Curia. His cousin Filippo was now rector of the University of Pisa. And his aunt Costanza was the mother of the nephews of Pope Urban VIII. One of his mentors was not far wrong when he concluded: "From the brilliant dawn of his adolescence our country can justly look forward to a still more resplendent noonday in his manhood."

Yet Lorenzo Magalotti suffered from one grave difficulty: he could not make up his mind which career to embark upon. He had tried out law, only to find it boring. He had tried out medicine only to find it hopelessly antiquated. He had tried out mathematics under no less authoritative a teacher than Galileo's principal disciple, Vincenzo Viviani; but although he dutifully worked out the problems Viviani handed to him, he could not bring himself to look on mathematics as anything but a pastime. Eventually indecision took on a physical form: a painful abdominal rash that neither his doctor's vile concoctions, nor his mother's daily visits to the Madonna di Santa Chiara, nor even a twenty-day retreat managed to cure. And he retired in desperation to soak for three months in the sulphur baths at San Casciano.

Fortunately an opportunity then arose to try out still another career, or at least to keep himself so busy that he could no longer worry about his indecision; and the rash promptly vanished. Three years earlier, on June 19, 1657, a group of philosophers and amateurs at court—*virtuosi,* as they called themselves—had decided to form a permanent institution for the pursuit of scientific research. They had called it, after their sponsor and protector, the Academy of the Most Serene Prince Leopoldo. Posterity, in recognizing it as the first of the many great scientific academies of late seventeenth-century Europe, has called it, after the name on its heraldic device, the *Cimento.* Such an institution would not have been feasible among Galileo's immediate friends and contemporaries, for most of them had followed their master to the grave in rapid succession: Castelli in 1643, Torricelli and Cavalieri in 1647, and Galileo's own son, Vincenzo, in 1649. The most able disciple in the years immediately following was none other than the grand duke, Ferdinando II, who regularly had in guests to watch him manipulate the instruments Galileo had left him. But Ferdinando, after all, was the grand duke, and only occasionally could he sneak away from his impossible wife and his administrative duties to the quiet of his well-equipped laboratory.

By the mid-1650s, however, the generation of younger disciples who had known Galileo in his last years had at last grown up. Viviani was now thirty-five, no longer the child prodigy who had entertained the court at Livorno by outdoing Euclid at the age of sixteen, but an accomplished and recognized mathematician. Francesco Redi, the bright young scholar-turned-physician from Arezzo, was now thirty-one, and he had just returned, after five years in the service of Cardinal Colonna, to be pharmacist to the grand duke. Carlo Roberto Dati, a lecturer at the university since 1647, was now almost thirty-eight; he had just recently applied what he had learned from Galileo and Torricelli in a stirring *Exhortation on the Study of Geometry,* directed at his future associates. Alessandro Marsigli of Siena, who still treasured the memory of his interview with Galileo back in 1633, was far the oldest of the group; by now, at fifty-six, he had at last lost faith in the Aristotelian doctrines he had been teaching for so long at Pisa, though he still hesitated about what to put in their place. This core of Tuscan Galileans had just been reinforced by an influx of Galileans from abroad. The anatomist and astronomer Carlo Renaldini had come down from Ancona and Bologna to teach at the University of Pisa eight years before. The eccentric Jesuit Antonio Uliva had resigned his position as theologian to Magalotti's cousin, Cardinal Federico Barberini, and come up from Rome just one year before. And Giovanni Alfonso Borelli, a former student of Castelli's in Rome, had just arrived from Sicily, bringing with him the manuscript of his first major work, *Euclid Restored,* which came out under the auspices of the grand duke in 1658.

Most important of all, Prince Leopoldo, the youngest (he was then just forty-nine), the ugliest, possibly the most intelligent, and certainly the most sympathetic of the four sons of Cosimo II, had at last returned definitely from a stint as governor of Siena, and, for the moment at least, was free of official obligations. Leopoldo was not really a scientist, as his brother Ferdinando was. He was interested in absolutely everything: "manuscript reports on the geography, customs, and inhabitants of countries . . . in every part of the world . . . books of criticism, gallantry, satire, and curiosities," as Magalotti told one of the prince's book-buying agents abroad. "You may forward," he instructed him, "documents of natural history, like that [description] of a fish I sent you or like that [account] of a strange pregnancy you didn't bother to acknowledge—what the devil ever became of it?—or like that skeleton so similar to a human one that Giovanni Trullo found at Castel Gandolfo; information about medals, newly-discovered statues, cameos and other ancient relics, architectural designs, tall tales with a bit of spice—anything will do," especially the latest editions of the fathers of the church and the newest biblical commentaries. Experimental science, from Leopoldo's point of view, was just one of the subjects he delighted in during the four hours he spent each day "up to his neck in books." "Like boys with a piece of bread," Magalotti reported, "he always keeps a book in his pocket to chew on whenever he has a free moment." He did not dominate the academy, as the bombastic eulogies of his admirers have led some historians to imagine. It was, and it remained, a free association of whatever qualified scientists happened to be in the city; and Leopoldo always took great care to show up at meetings "as an academician, not as a prince"—a rare concession in so rank-conscious an age—and to discourage any but the most carefully disguised adulation.

What Leopoldo did do was to provide the academy with a rudimentary form of organization. He insisted that it work as a single body and that it publish its discoveries anonymously, in the name of the academy as a whole. He tactfully intervened, with his winning personality, his good humor, and his unquestionable sincerity, every time ruffled tempers and ticklish jealousies threatened to turn one member against another. He furnished the academy with permanent quarters in the Palazzo Pitti. He initiated, supervised, and signed much of its correspondence with learned men abroad—the name of a prince, after all, a Medici at that, being the surest guarantee of a quick answer. He saw to it that the members were supported by well-paying sinecures at court or at the university. And, above all, he covered the sizeable expenses for equipment, maintenance, and supplies:

> From the chariot of virtue, invincible Prince,
> you spend for Minerva both hours and gold [*l'oro e l'ore*]
>   (A. Coltellini in *Rime varie*)

Thanks, then, to the solicitude of an unemployed young prince and to the enthusiasm of the group of budding scientists he gathered about him, the academy soon flourished. When Alessandro Segni resigned as secretary to accept a post in the diplomatic corps early in 1660—and when he quietly left buried in his own files all the records of the first three years that were to be discovered only a century later—Leopoldo searched around for a worthy, and more reliable, successor. He found him, probably at Viviani's suggestion, in the young man who had already been indoctrinated in the principles and prejudices of the academy, who regretted only having been born too late to see the great Galileo with his own eyes, who by now had gotten rid of the last traces of his Roman accent, and who had just been appointed a gentleman of the chamber by the grand duke.

Certainly Magalotti could not have wished for a more exciting moment to be admitted to the academy. During the preceding months the members had been occupied in testing some of Galileo's theories about the pendulum. The problem was not a new one in Florence, needless to say. Galileo had already worked out most of the theory, and his son Vincenzo had been working on putting it into practice at the moment of his death. But the problem had come up again rather suddenly with the arrival, earlier in the year, of designs for a new clock recently constructed in Holland by a still unknown mathematician named Christiaan Huygens. The academicians were enthusiastic. A flawless timepiece, based on natural rather than man-made motions, was exactly what they were looking for to execute properly their projected experiments with the speed of sound and light.

Just then another bit of news about the young mathematician arrived from Holland, again through Carlo Roberto Dati's old friend, Nicholas Heinsius. Huygens had at last perfected studies of the planet Saturn that he had started four years earlier, and he was now prepared to announce that the two little balls Galileo had noticed on either side of the planet back in 1610 really represented a flat ring around its equator. The epoch-making *Systema Saturnium,* dedicated to Leopoldo, unfortunately went astray in the mail, as did so much transalpine correspondence in those days. But the academicians apparently had already procured some specific information through another of Dati's and Leopoldo's regular correspondents, the future president of the Académie Française, Jean Chapelain, who had seen the preliminary reports back in 1656. They asked Heinsius for specifications regarding Huygens's telescope. And by May their highly skilled instrument-maker, Anton Maria Del Buono, a brother of two of the academicians, had begun constructing a still bigger one, suspended, for easier manipulation, like a boom from the mast of a sailboat.

The academicians had to be cautious, even though they were sympathetic from the start. They were pledged not to accept any hypothesis, their own included, or even to become enthusiastic about it (*appassionarsi* was Leopoldo's word), until it had been "tested and retested" according to the academy's motto, *provando e riprovando.* This particular hypothesis, moreover, was fraught with dangers, for it asserted the existence of a phenomenon, a ring, that had absolutely no parallel in anything that had yet been observed in the heavens. It also seemed to contradict one of Galileo's metaphysical asides concerning the natural tendency of all matter to assume the shape of a sphere. The hypothesis was already under fire from the best instrument-maker in Rome as well as from Magalotti's former teacher in the Collegio Romano, Onorato Fabri, both of whom attributed the ring to defects in Huygens's lenses. Even after the repeated observations of July and August 1660, the academicians hesitated to make a pronouncement. They had not yet been able, and Huygens had not thought, to check on the supposed solidity of the ring by looking at it against the background of the Milky Way. And they had discovered some shady spots in the upper right-hand portion of the globe, which Huygens had not yet reported.

Nevertheless, the astronomers of the Cimento succeeded in providing the first sustained confirmation of Huygens's discoveries. Every time they looked through their improved telescopes, they saw the same single, flat ring, which wobbled up and down according to the season. They then constructed a model of Huygens's Saturn: a globe encircled by a flat ring. And every time they looked at it from afar through a weak telescope, they saw not the ring, but just what Galileo had seen in 1610 and what Fabri still saw in 1660: two balls; and that threw Fabri's argument about an optical illusion right back at him. Better still, they supplied a physical and mathematical explanation of what had been seen. Whatever the ring was made out of—and Borelli showed that the question was relatively unimportant—it bore the same relation to Saturn that the Medician Planets did to Jupiter. The one could not be rejected without also rejecting the others—which, of course, before Newton, was still philosophically, though not practically, possible.

"The most marvelous mechanism in the universe" was now all but an established fact. It needed nothing more that a few final calculations by the pope's mathematician, Matteo Campani, and an extra ring or so from the Bolognese astronomer, Giovan Domenico Cassini, later known as Jean Doménique of the Académie des Sciences in Paris. No one was more elated than the young secretary. Even *he* had been asked to write an opinion on the subject, which may indeed have turned out to be little more than a schoolboy exercise in drawing out far-fetched analogies, but which Leopoldo nonetheless had included, to Dati's embarrassment, in the same package with the others. Who cared whether his Saturn was surrounded by an atmosphere three times thicker than its diameter? Who cared whether its surface temperature corresponded roughly to that on earth? What mattered was that the unknown author suddenly found himself associated as "ingegnosissimus Magalottus" along with "subtilissimus Borellius" and a lot of other famous people in all the scientific circles of Europe. Perhaps, he thought, he had found his true calling. "The great book of nature," he exclaimed enthusiastically, "is laid open before my eyes, and I am filled with a burning desire to understand the wondrously beautiful characters I see inscribed on it."

Fortunately, the book of nature had many chapters, one more fascinating than the other, and the academy was not in principle committed to any one of them. Many of its experiments were intended to do no more than carry on where Galileo and Torricelli had left off—its experiments on air pressure, for instance, which started with Torricelli's mercury tube of 1643, and those on the process of congelation, which started with one of Galileo's off-hand comments to the effect that "ice was rarefied, not condensed water." No intentions could have seemed more appropriate at the time. Dati just then was busy defending the priority of Torricelli's mathematical discoveries against the claims on behalf of Mersenne. Leopoldo was reminding Huygens that Galileo and his son had already worked out in all but tiny details the pendulum clock he had claimed for himself. Viviani was circulating a story about how such a clock had actually been sent to the States General of the Netherlands in 1636. And the older academicians were trying to outdo each other with boyhood reminiscences about Galileo, "the greatest ornament of our country," who had patted their heads and given them bonbons. Indeed, they soon turned Galileo into the object of a near-religious cult. And Magalotti soon became one of the most ardent worshippers. He filled even his after-dinner speeches at the Crusca with random quotations from the *Dialogue on the Two World Systems,* and he went so far as to imply, in one of his half-serious *Scientific Letters,* that science consisted chiefly in picking up the "many precious, beautiful gems" preserved either in the written revelation of the master or in the still fairly reliable oral tradition about him.

Sometimes this kind of hagiolatry ended in ridiculous exaggerations. To speak of Galileo's difficulties with the Roman Inquisition was taboo. To suppose that he had retired to Arcetri for any other purpose than "to enjoy a sweet and well-earned tranquility" was inadmissible. To suggest that he had ever really believed in the motion of the earth was blasphemy. To notice that he had ever written letters to a certain enemy of the church named Fra Paolo Sarpi was plain denigration, obviously the work of unredeemed Jesuits; and Viviani, who had turned his house in Via dell'Amore into a kind of museum in honor of his mentor, announced himself ready to go all the way to Amsterdam and tear up the letters he had heard some Dutch publisher had obtained, no matter how much he had to pay out in bribes. Even the law courts were affected. When, in June 1679, several customs officials were caught red-handed pocketing receipts at the city gates, one of them had his five-year prison term commuted to a short exile on Elba simply because he happened to bear the name of "the most noble family Galilei."

Still, "the excessive affection for the infinite merits of Signor Galileo," as Dati put it, did have certain good results. For one thing, it inspired Viviani to search for relevant documents in every corner of Italy and at last, after interminable delays, to publish his famous biography, which is still, notwithstanding a few errors, the sole source of much of what is known about Galileo today. For another, it acted as an important cohesive force among the various members of the academy, whose conflicts of interest often left them with little else to agree on. Finally, the apotheosis of Galileo provided a stock of ready-made hypotheses—hypotheses which members could be fairly sure of on the authority of their master, but which the master himself had insisted upon having demonstrated in practice. Indeed, their confidence in being able to substantiate Galileo's hypotheses was largely responsible for the high quality of the many scientific instruments they devised and constructed. Many of the instruments, incidentally, with their delicately carved bases and sculptured handles, turned out to be works of art as well as marvels of technical ingenuity.

On the other hand, some of the experiments arose simply in response to questions that happened to be current at the time, or that happened to interest one or another of the members separately. Since 1656, for instance, Marcello Malpighi had been carrying on at Pisa the studies of the heart that were soon to make him one of the most acclaimed anatomists of the day. By 1660 anatomy had attracted enough attention even in literary circles to warrant the publication of Agostino Coltellini's *Institutions of the Anatomy of the Human Body . . . Explained in Verse,* which Magalotti may have heard read aloud at the Accademia degli Apatisti. Thus when that stiff-necked religious bigot, Grand Duchess Vittoria della Rovere, finally succumbed to her curiosity and asked Antonio Uliva to teach her about this new thing called the circulation of the blood, he had no trouble making her a wax model based on all the latest discoveries.

The search for new medicines also attracted considerable attention; and while one of the physicians in town was getting ready to launch his new "Gelli pill" on the market, the academicians were busy, from November 1660 on, "extracting salts from all kinds of things" in the hope of finding still better recipes. Hydrostatics was also a subject of considerable interest, particularly after the grand duke became involved in one more quarrel with the Papal government about whether the waters of the Chiana Valley should flow into the Arno or the Tiber. Accordingly, Magalotti, Viviani, and Dati were commissioned, in December 1664, to test out the latest theory of water motion, a theory that turned out to contradict empirical evidence because it supposed flowing water to press only downward on the river bed, not outward against the banks.

On the other hand, one new branch of the sciences, the study of "electrical virtues," was somewhat less important. Indeed, the study was almost inexplicable in a universe from which "virtues" had been banned, and it had advanced very little beyond the point where William Gilbert had left it some seventy years before. Nevertheless, it was fascinating; and watching how charged amber behaved in a vacuum or at high temperatures could at least serve the purpose of debunking Plutarch. It could also serve the purpose of providing Magalotti with material for his next two treatises—the *Historia Electrica* and the *Philosophia Electrica,* although Ottavio Falconieri apparently had the good sense to throw away the only copies as soon as he received them.

Other experiments in the academy seem to have been motivated solely by curiosity—curiosity about such "marvelous effects of nature" as cool water boiling in a vacuum and pearls producing a mass of froth in an acidic solution. There was nothing wrong with curiosity, as the academicians were quick to point out. It had been put into the hearts of men by nature herself for the wholly commendable purpose of stimulating their minds. And it had nothing to do with the "indiscrete curiosity" that so annoyed Magalotti during his visit to Naples in April 1663, when he was dragged about by "a mad herd of philosophers" to gawk at "the wondrous pool, the Baths of Cicero, the geyser of Pozzuolo, the grotto of Agnano, and finally, the sum total of all asininity past, present, and future, the vortices of Vesuvius." Curiosity alone, of course, could end up in pure observation without any attempt to understand the reasons for what was observed. But when guided by a proper method, curiosity could turn a successful demonstration into a new problem. It could start with the examination of the strange fish, sent up in a salt-water tank from Livorno, that supposedly opened up oyster shells. It could start from a two-headed cat that Magalotti found interesting enough to have drawn for Cassini. And it could then go on to more general subjects of zoology and anatomy. It could start by focusing a microscope on the gizzards of chickens to see what had become of the cork, cypress wood, and pistol bullets that had been jammed into them—and then go on to focus it on just about any other kind of living tissue. It could lead from the discovery of how crickets managed to sing, "a great and admirable problem that so far has eluded the intelligence of the greatest men," to a more proper understanding of the nature of sound. And that, as a matter of fact, is just what happened.

Still other experiments were provoked by the latest scientific literature from abroad, which the correspondents of Dati and Leopoldo were charged with rushing to Florence as soon as it came off the presses. Thus they read in Jean Pequet's anatomical work of 1651—but not, strangely, in Blaise Pascal's *Experiences nouvelles* of 1647, which they never mentioned—about the change in barometer readings between the bottom and the top of the Puy-de-Dôme. They then made much more exact calculations themselves by constructing a still more elaborate barometer and hauling it up at dawn on a windless day from the courtyard to the tower of the Palazzo Vecchio. They read about the recent experiments of Gilles Personne de Roberval, one of the founders of the Académie des Sciences; and they too built a mercury tube inside a mercury tube and a bladder that could be filled or emptied from the outside in order to perfect his observations.

Then, in 1660, the academicians suddenly received word of still further experiments by a little-known English scientist named Robert Boyle—experiments that bore directly upon their work with Torricelli's tube. When, just a few months later, they discovered that one of the English tourists in town happened to be Boyle's good friend, Robert Southwell, they had him escorted immediately to the Pitti, where Leopoldo received him with every expression of honor and affection. Unfortunately a vacuum pump they tried to build according to Boyle's directions failed to silence a small hand-organ that had been fitted into a crystal cylinder; and since there was no feasible way of floating such an object up through quicksilver, the relationship between sound and air had to be left in the realm of hypotheses. Boyle himself was not much help in the matter. Perhaps he still remembered how shocked he had been by the carnival parties, the brothels, and the rest of what he called disgusting manifestations of popery during his grand tour of 1641—as well as by the efforts of his Florentine guides to compromise his well-guarded Protestant virginity. For he refused even to acknowledge Viviani's and Leopoldo's requests for collaboration, in spite of Southwell's appeals to the rules of courtesy.

What held all these various experiments together was not some sort of inner relationship among the particular objects of investigation. Even the words that today mark off one scientific discipline from another had not yet been coined. What kept the well-groomed experimenters from suffocating in their eminently impractical lace cuffs and brocaded knee-length jackets, what kept them sweating through long summer days as one frog after another bloated up and popped in an evacuated tube, what kept them shivering in the *tramontana* through long winter nights as ice formed in vases of a hundred different sorts—what animated all these endeavors was a commitment to a method of research. The method was purported to be strictly and exclusively Galilean; and it began, accordingly, with geometry. By "geometry" was meant not simply a means of "measuring distances and heights, [or of] describing some figure," as Seneca had thought, but rather "the general rule that conditions the human mind to imbibe all the arts and sciences" and that "gives us wings to traverse the heavens." Geometry, therefore, was indispensable for scientific inquiry—so ran the official doctrine of the Cimento in the elegant garb of Magalotti's crisp prose—"for it brings the inquirer directly to the truth and frees him immediately from further striving and uncertainty." Geometry, in a sense, was self-sufficient: it could thus establish Galileo's theory that the motion of light occurred in time, not instantaneously, even though instruments had not yet been devised to show that it actually did so in practice.

But geometry alone had limitations. It "leads us a good way along the path of philosophical speculations, but then it suddenly abandons us," Magalotti wrote on behalf of his colleagues; and we are left with the much more arduous task of observing individual phenomena and of "testing and retesting" to discover their causes. The doctrine was still officially Galilean. But the Cimento had surreptitiously expanded the area reserved for inductive reasoning far beyond the point that Galileo had permitted. It then added another important distinction. The realm of geometry is finite, it insisted. Eventually all the theorems deducible from the basic self-evident axioms will be discovered. On the other hand the realm of knowledge induced from the phenomena of sense perception is infinite; and no one will ever arrive at the end of it. Geometry yields certainty. Observation yields a series of theses that constantly approach but never attain certainty. Geometry, or deductive reasoning, can adequately be dealt with by one or two men of extraordinary genius. Observation requires the close cooperation of as many men as possible, men whose chief qualifications are not so much brilliance as patience and precision. Observation was the task of the Cimento. Accordingly, the solitary hero of Arcetri gave way to the bustling society of Palazzo Pitti, surrounded by a clutter of bottles and burners.

The Cimento did not state explicitly that what had started as a difference in degree had become a difference in kind. It simply acted as if that is what had happened. It described its observations even when it could not supply an explanation. It published its achievements even when the results were unsatisfactory. And it challenged others to succeed where it had failed. It gave clear, precise instructions on just how to make the instruments it so laboriously invented, and it referred whatever artisans who might be employed to make them to Antonio Neri's manual of 1612 on *The Art of Glass*. It welcomed doubts, questions, and criticisms, no matter how farfetched, and it did all it could to avoid getting into fights. It cordially invited the learned men of all Europe to attend its sessions in Florence, and it appealed to all "the diverse assemblies scattered . . . in all the more illustrious and conspicuous regions of Europe" to enter with it into a network of "free communication." Finally, it entitled its transactions not "discoveries," but "essays" (*saggi*), by which it meant, as Magalotti reminded one of the censors, that none of the experiments described therein could be considered finished (*finite*), since the matters they dealt with were by their very nature infinite (*infinite*).

This sort of empiricism had one great advantage: it got rid of metaphysics, and therefore of any possible bond between religion and theology on the one hand, and science on the other. One could say, for instance, that outer space contained no air and that the top of a barometer contained no mercury vapor, for experiment had established the absence of both. But one could not say therefore that a vacuum did in fact exist or that all space was not permeated with some sort of imperceptible quintessence. One could say that the Medicean Planets revolved about Jupiter and that comets went regularly in and out of the solar system. But no one had to say that the planets did not in fact revolve about the earth, because the academy somehow never got around to making observations that would have required such a statement. One could say, after "testing and retesting" hundreds of times, that "it seems possible to believe with some semblance of truth" that a given explanation was valid. But no one had the right to elevate the explanation to the level of irrefutable truth. One could measure the flow of water. But whether water flowed because of an inherent liquid quality or because of the rotundity of its component particles, was a question that the Cimento declined to consider. Any statement, in other words, concerning the structure of the universe, the nature of matter, or the certainty of scientific propositions was considered metaphysics. It was forthwith banished from the realm of experimental science— and from the realm of religion and morality as well.

Leopoldo, Borelli, and all the more pious members of the Cimento were immensely relieved. No longer, they secretly reflected, would science and theology get mixed up in the kind of "misunderstanding" that had occurred in 1633. They had saved both at the same time. And with religious zeal they set out to batter down any attempt to bring the two together again. Aristotelianism they denounced as a "philosophy reduced to words alone," and they had Magalotti admonish Falconieri "to be a good boy in the future" and forget all about the "prime matter" he was known to chat about in his Roman salon. Cartesianism, the modern equivalent of Aristotelianism, they saw as a huge inverted pyramid teetering on a very feeble base—on "a bit of nonsense about vortices," as Borelli put it. Atomism they refused to talk about. They rejected the label Epicurean or Democritan, and pretended to be nothing but "ingenuous, dispassionate philosophers." They may have taken comfort from Boyle, who, atomist though he was becoming, shrank from the blasphemous corollary that motion was inherent in the basic particles of matter. Similarly, they studiously ignored all the updated, Galilean versions of late sixteenth-century cosmologies that were then circulating about Naples; Magalotti, who occasionally went to Naples, never mentioned one of the best-known of the Neapolitan system-builders, Elia Astorini, even after Astorini came to work at Siena in the mid-1690s. Finally, they denounced all supposed sciences that admitted nonmaterial elements as just the same old hocus-pocus of Della Porta, Paracelsus, and Digby; they especially distrusted chemistry, a "sticky dough" into which they had no intention of "putting their hands." They were so determined to avoid such questions that they failed to notice what Boyle was just then doing to separate chemistry from alchemy and to wed it instead to physics. They were thus unable to explain why water distilled in lead vessels became cloudy and then, with a few drops of vinegar, became clear again.

Science without metaphysics might easily have ended up in a mass of unrelated observations about nothing in particular, in the sort of minute descriptions, for example, completely devoid of the least trace of a general concept, that Magalotti reeled out, for the amusement of Leopoldo, in such essays as "On the Marvelous Extravagances of a Flower." The academicians were not unaware of the danger. They knew that the atypical was scientifically relevant only insofar as it was potentially typical, and that describing the single was valuable only as the first step toward comprehending the general. That may be why they so willingly spent Monday evenings at the home, and long weekends at the villa, of the one philosopher they all respected, Orazio Ricasoli Rucellai, sometimes known as "The Prior" from his honorary post in the Order of Santo Stefano, sometimes as "The Florentine Socrates" from his taste for interminable conversations, and sometimes as "L'Imperfetto"—The Imperfect One—from his title as a member of the Accademia della Crusca.

Rucellai was already fifty-eight years old when Magalotti first got to know him, in November 1662. He was still a very striking man, with large eyes, a huge slightly hooked nose, and a tiny moustache above his grinning lips. He had a jovial disposition that earned him the benevolence of "all ages, all sexes, and all professions." And he had only one tiny defect: a passion for cheese, which led him, according to one of his colleagues in the Crusca, to get himself elected president only for the purpose of running off with the cheese platters at the annual banquet. As "the only man in Florence who can safely be introduced to all foreigners alike," he had come to know men of letters all over Europe, and Magalotti predicted that Rucellai would feel perfectly at home were he, at the end of the world, suddenly resurrected by mistake at Saint-Germain. He had inherited two of the best names in Tuscany. He had been presented at court at the age of ten, sent as ambassador to the king of Poland and the emperor at the age of thirty, appointed tutor to one of the grand duke's children, and finally, in 1657, made director of the Laurenziana Library. But what he spent most of his time doing was poring over the works of the ancient philosophers. In the early 1660s he came to the conclusion that what Galileo had done, and what Viviani and Dati were then doing, could best be explained by Plato—by Plato, that is, as translated and interpreted by Marsilio Ficino, and as rounded out by occasional bits from Anaximander, Heraclitus, St. Augustine, and the two "radiant lights . . . of our own city," Dante and Galileo.

Rucellai set out to expound his conclusions in a series of dialogues, all consciously modelled on Boccaccio to make them fun as well as instructive to listen to: three on the *Timaeus* were ready by November 1665, one on Anaximander by January 1666, one on the "Universal Soul" by March, one on Heraclitus by July, and so on for the next two years until they filled twelve large manuscript volumes. He was encouraged from the beginning by the discovery, through Ottavio Falconieri, that none other than the patriarch of Aquileia, Giovanni Delfini, was just then composing equally Boccaccian treatments of exactly the same subjects. The two philosphers exchanged their manuscripts to check on each other's linguistic purity and Galilean orthodoxy, and they then turned them over to be read aloud, one after another, in sessions of the Crusca. Florence was suddenly glutted with Platonism, far more than it ever had been since the days of Ficino's Platonic Academy.

Rucellai's Plato seemed to provide a welcome antidote to Aristotle, Democritus, and Descartes. For instance, it showed that space was infinite, that the heavens were corruptible, and that cold was merely the privation of heat. Better yet, it showed that everything known to philosophy concerning God, the soul, and the nature of matter was known only relatively, whereas certainty proceeded from no other source than "our infallible Catholic faith." For a moment it looked as if the Cimento had found something that had all the advantages of a metaphysics without any of the complications.

Alas, the whole beautiful vision started to fade away even before it had been fully contemplated. The Crusca applauded the "delicate pen" that had incorporated one more subject, metaphysics, into the domain of the Tuscan language; but it paid no attention to the content. The men of science and letters gathered in Rucellai's library began to nod as their well-meaning host paused for an instant to turn from the bottom of page 1105 to the top of page 1106. Within a few years they were making little jokes among themselves about the Platonic idea of cheese and about the one-track mind that "finishes everything happily . . . because it notices . . . only what crops up in the course of its studies." By 1674, when he was composing the verses for a funeral eulogy, Magalotti could not remember too well just what the dialogues had been all about. Thirty-five years later he thought they had something to do with anatomy and morality. No one thereafter ever discovered what they actually did contain until a few of them were finally printed, for the laudible purpose of saving young people from the corrupting influences of liberalism and romanticism, in 1833.

What saved science in the Cimento was not Plato but the pious priest-philosopher of Aix-en-Provence, Pierre Gassendi. During the four decades before his death in 1655, Gassendi had attacked both Descartes and Aristotle in the name of an empirical version of Galileo. He had restored the Renaissance image—and the Hellenistic image—of Epicurus as a pre-Christian saint. He had denounced the incursions of metaphysics into theology as well as into the sciences. He had turned over the search for the truths of religion to the biblical and patristic scholars, the search for substances and qualities to the angels, and the search for the causes of observable phenomena to teams of patient experimenters. Most important of all, he had worked out the corpuscular theory of matter, carefully purged of all its atheistic overtones, that Boyle officially adopted as his own in 1666.

The scientists of the Cimento did not have to make so explicit a declaration. After all, quarrels about philosophy might have interfered with the quiet pursuit of their experiments, and most of what they took from Gassendi could just as easily, and much less noisily, be attributed to Galileo. Instead, they simply assumed, as they applied a hand pump to a closed vessel, that they actually were decreasing the finite number of air particles within it; and none of their conclusions could possibly have supported the contrary thesis: that the enclosed space was still as "full" as ever of the same, though now "rarefied," substance. They then added a string of laudatory epithets to "that sublime writer, that blazing light of modern schools," Gassendi, whenever they had a chance to mention his work as an experimental scientist.

Whatever ambiguities remained in the Cimento's position were soon to be cleared up by a young philosophy instructor at the university—a sometime protégé of Leopoldo, a former classmate of Magalotti, an ardent and devoted disciple of Borelli, and later an accomplished mathematician in his own right, Alessandro Marchetti. The form Marchetti used to expound his ideas was, oddly enough, an Italian translation of Lucretius, that archenemy of the gods and

of god-fearing mortals roundly condemned by Cicero, and by a millenium and a
half of Ciceronians thereafter, for everything but his style. The translation had
considerable literary merit, or at least it was duly praised by all the leading critics
right down to the time of Giosue Carducci. At the same time, it afforded Marchetti
the possibility, every time he got into trouble over it, of defending himself with
the boast that he was simply applying the program of the Accademia Fiorentina
to the last great work of classical antiquity still to be incorporated into the Tuscan
literary heritage.

But none of Marchetti's sympathetic readers was fooled at the time, as
successive versions of the manuscript did the rounds of Florence, Rome, and
Paris during the last three decades of the century. None of the arch-Aristotelians
was fooled either. And that most reliable guardian of their academic interests,
the Congregation of the Index, condemned the first edition the moment it was
published, at London in 1717. When Marchetti deliberately toned down the
elevated quality of the original with all the mollifying devices permitted by
current poetic tastes, it was obvious that he was tearing Lucretius out of the
niche reserved for all the Latin classics by the Council of Trent. When he
substituted the word "Tuscan" for "Latin" and the name "Gassendi" for
"Epicurus," and when he added a passage about Messina and Borelli right
after the one about Syracuse and Archimedes, it was perfectly obvious that he
wanted the contents to be considered as well as the style. When, finally, in 1670,
just as he was finishing the first draft, he launched a counterattack against the
Peripatetics at the university, it was perfectly obvious that he had found in
Gassendi's revision of ancient atomism the most adequate philosophical explanation for the work of his fellow scientists in the Galilean tradition. Luckily, none
of the Galileans suspected that the real Lucretius was soon to become a weapon
in the hands of such determined anti-Christians as the Baron d'Holbach, who
kept twelve copies in his library. Marchetti's Lucretius provided them with just
what they needed to support their working hypotheses about the atoms and the
void, the purely subjective nature of secondary qualities, the infinity of space, and
the heliocentric solar system.

Thanks to its network of correspondents, however, the Cimento did not have
to wait for Marchetti to have its principles accepted and its discoveries recognized.
As soon as he received his appointment, Magalotti was charged, as secretary,
with sending regular reports to the Florentine prelate-mathematician Michelangelo
Ricci, whose high position in the Curia assured their rapid diffusion and favorable
reception in Rome. Ricci in turn passed them on to his correspondent Melchisedech
Thévenot, the Orientalist and voyager, who had spent some time in the French
embassy in Rome, and who shortly after his return to Paris in 1654 had organized
an informal scientific salon in his own house. Similar reports from Dati were
sent to Nicholas Heinsius, the Dutch scientist and scholar, who passed them
around among his friends in Holland. Still others from Leopoldo reached the

astronomer Ismael Boulliau, who had been offered a chair at Pisa back in 1647, and whom Magalotti described, after their meeting in June of 1668, as "the most refined, the most loveable, the most bizarre, the most agile ... and the most witty old man that can be found to turn the Ideas of the Platonic universe upside down." And Boulliau passed them on to his associates, first to those in the Montmor circle at Paris, and then, after 1663, to Colbert's new Académie des Sciences. Still others went directly to the Académie Française, and others, through the Tuscan ambassador in London, to the Royal Society, after its incorporation in 1662.

The initial reactions to the academy's work were very encouraging. Ottavio Falconieri, in a very elegant sonnet, immediately complied with Magalotti's injunction to bid farewell to Aristotle. Ricci hesitated, and then became embarrassingly enthusiastic: "Those things we consider relatively unimportant," Magalotti noted in 1663, "he thinks excellent; and those we call excellent, he calls marvelous and stupendous." The University of Pisa gave in, for the moment at least, when one of the academicians, the moderate and hence somewhat more tactful Alessandro Marsigli, assumed the rectorship in 1662. Rome began to yield soon afterwards when none other than Pope Alexander VII, whose mind "was completely alien to scholastic subtleties," became so fascinated with the experiments that he asked Magalotti to instruct him in the use of the instruments. It yielded completely with the founding of a new periodical in 1668, the *Giornale de' letterati,* which gave long reviews to all that reached it from Florence, as well as from Paris and London. Even the Society of Jesus appeared to concur. By 1664 the Cimento's own Antonio Uliva had "pissed on [too] much snow in Stagira," as Magalotti put it, to revert to the half-way position between Aristotle and Galileo maintained by most of his fellow Jesuits. The general, Gian Paolo Oliva, was so pleased with Leopoldo's nice comments about his sermons in the Vatican that he extended his sugary compliments to Leopoldo's scientific interests. Better yet, the society's foremost prose writer and literary critic, Sforza Pallavicino, was so anxious to get his monumental *History of the Council of Trent* cited in the next edition of the Crusca's *Vocabolario* that he decided not to quibble with Florentines about other matters. Once reassured that he need never pronounce the forbidden phrase "the earth moves," he gladly accepted an unofficial position as the Cimento's reader for theological and stylistic questions.

None of the academicians was more gratified than Magalotti. His commission obliged him to compile the transactions. By the end of 1660 he was busy every night on the *Saggi,* or *Essays on Natural Experiments,* that were soon to win him acclaim, perhaps not as a scientist, but certainly as one of the best scientific writers of his age.

2

How he then gave it up

Then, gradually, Magalotti lost interest in science, First of all, the *Essays* turned out to be a much more burdensome task than he had anticipated. The ecclesiastical censors gave him little trouble, it is true. For the academy enjoyed the unqualified backing of Pope Alexander VII, who had long been an admirer of Galileo and was still a close friend of Galileo's sometime host, and now Magalotti's frequent correspondent, Ascanio Piccolomini, archbishop of Siena. But the academicians, conscious of Galileo's example as a prose writer, insisted upon literary impeccability as well as scientific accuracy; and they made Magalotti revise draft after draft of the *Essays* as they argued for hours on end about whether to write *146th* or *one hundred forty-sixth,* whether to write *o* or *ho* for "I have," and whether to use the verb *asolare* ("to frequent") even though it did not appear in the Crusca's *Vocabolario.* Pallavicino and Ricci made the task still more difficult. The academy depended upon them to iron out any possible theological knots in the text. But it had no intention of accepting technical advice from a mere mathematician or linguistic advice from a mere Lombard; and both of them constantly exceeded their commissions by offering what they thought were helpful suggestions in all aspects of the composition. Hence, Magalotti soon acquired "an invincible distaste" for the whole project. By July 1677, when Ricci ("damn it, but that man makes life difficult," Magalotti scrawled) came up with one more tiny annotation, he threatened to send the proofs off to Geneva, the traditional source of subversive literature in Italy. He finally handed them over, still incomplete, to Orazio Rucellai's son, Luigi.

What had once seemed like a great opportunity to make a name for himself had become, after "seven years in the secretariat of philosophy," merely a source of annoyance and frustration. When the *Essays* were finally published, late in 1667, and when they finally reached him in London the following March, Magalotti was unmoved. Only about half the experiments had been included, after all;

and even those friends of his in Brussels who had been pestering him for a copy since January had known about all of them for some time. So had his friends in the Royal Society, whose sessions he was just then attending as a guest. Henry Oldenburg, the secretary, graciously made a stab at translating the chapter headings out loud; and he then handed the book over for an eventual report to "someone more conversant with the Tuscan tongue." The very limited edition that Leopoldo had distributed gratis to the wise and mighty of Europe did serve the purpose of glorifying the donor and of erecting a lasting monument to what Boyle called "the justly famous Florentine academy." But it did nothing for practicing scientists, who had not felt obliged to wait for the published accounts before making use of the academy's discoveries. Thus what was supposed to have been a manual turned out to be merely an historical document. Another twenty-three years went by before anyone thought of reprinting it.

Second, Magalotti was increasingly distressed by the personal rivalries among the individual members, which constantly undermined the academy's dedication to collective research. "Whenever two or three Florentines are gathered together in the name of the Lord," he reflected, "there in their midst are contradiction and animosity." The greatest culprit, certainly, was not a Florentine, but a Sicilian: the brilliant, irascible, "troublesome—I almost said unbearable" Borelli. Borelli had begun his tenure at Pisa by quarreling with the students and with the rector; his fits of jealousy and bad humor had made life miserable for everyone else ever since. But the very Florentine Viviani was almost as disagreeable. Small-minded, procrastinating, backbiting, he considered himself the sole guardian of the heritage of Galileo; and woe to anyone who, like Marchetti, dared to challenge his monopoly. When, in 1659, he pulled strings at court to stop the publication of Borelli's edition of Apollonius until he could get out his own clever anticipation of the contents, he set off a violent feud that eventually infected not only his colleagues, but a whole generation of their disciples as well.

At the same time, one after another of the members became distracted by other concerns. They tended to look upon the academy as if it were a sort of graduate school in the sciences—which to some extent it was. Once they had acquired some degree of maturity and self-confidence, they preferred to invest their time in projects that might contribute more concretely to the advancement of their own careers. Redi became absorbed in his snakes, his insects, and his duties at court. Dati and Viviani were lured by subsidies from Louis XIV into producing something more worthy of a dedication to the Sun King. Magalotti himself got involved in his usual family complications, which took him to Rome for the winter of 1661–62 and to Rome and Naples for the winter and spring of 1662–63. Three others left once and for all in the first months of 1667—Borelli for Messina, Uliva for Rome, and Renaldini for Padua; and the academy suddenly found itself all but memberless.

Leopoldo's tireless efforts to fill the gaps were at least successful in bringing one outstanding and one good scientist to Florence. The young Danish anatomist Nils Stensen, better known as Nicholas Steno, arrived from Copenhagen by way of Leiden and Paris early in 1666. The Norman astronomer Adrien Auzout, inventor of a device for measuring planetary diameters, arrived in 1668, fresh from a quarrel with Colbert and armed with a letter from Magalotti, who by then had become Leopoldo's main talent scout abroad. But individual scientists could not make an academy, particularly since Leopoldo no longer had the time to impose a sense of unity upon them. During the last long illness of his brother he was burdened with all the responsibilities of state; and when he became a cardinal the following December, he had to assume the additional duties of chief represent-ative of the Medici family in Rome. In an authoritarian society that discouraged collective activity in all other walks of life, the attempt to introduce it exceptionally into one of them could succeed only by the fiat of someone in authority. Once he disappeared, the exception quickly yielded before the rule.

Yet Magalotti was perfectly aware that the end of the Cimento did not mean the end of science in Florence. Some of the most significant work of the academicians, after all, had been accomplished independently of the academy. For instance, Borelli's treatise on the Comet of 1664 and his *Theory of the Medicean Planets* pushed the explanation of planetary motion right up to the very doorstep, as Newton himself acknowleged, of universal gravitation. Borelli's study of kidneys laid the foundation for his later *On the Motion of Animals,* which applied the principles of Galilean physics to organic matter. And his ponderous *On the Force of Percussion,* published the year of his departure, brought about a greater advance in mechanics than anything done since the death of Galileo.

Similarly, Steno's *Fish of the Dog Family* led to outstanding discoveries in two important new fields of scientific research. The boy wonder from Denmark had already established his reputation as an expert anatomist several years before with his study of a sheep's brain. He had learned the elements of geology in 1665 from the English physician John Ray, whom he had met during an excursion through southern France. Still more important, he had found in the Cimento a systematic confirmation of the methodological principles he had sketched out somewhat provisionally during his debates with the Cartesians in Thévenot's salon in Paris. "No one can clearly indicate the parts of muscles or effectively observe their movements," he then concluded, echoing Borelli, "unless the science of muscles becomes a part of mathematics," Thus when, in July 1666, he set to work cutting up the huge pregnant shark that Ferdinando had sent him from Livorno, he was able for the first time to give an accurate description of the process of ovulation in females—a description he was to expand and generalize several years later in what has since been recognized as a landmark in the history of genetics, the *Anatomical Observations Regarding the Eggs of Viviparous Animals.* At the same time, he noticed that the teeth of the shark corresponded exactly to those in some of the fossils he had picked up during his wanderings about Tuscany on a commission from the grand duke to explore the mineral resources of the country. He first put his rock collection in order—in an order, by the way, far more rational than anything tried out since Andrea Cesalpino, the mineralogist-biologist-physician of late sixteenth-century Pisa. He then went on to notice, for the first time, the peculiar structure of crystals. And finally, in his famous treatise *On Solid Bodies Naturally Contained Inside Solid Bodies,* he arrived at the first fumbling statement ever to be made (and one that was almost stillborn because of its radical novelty) of a theory of geological evolution.

What Borelli and Steno did in anatomy and geology, Francesco Redi did in what later came to be called microbiology. One morning in June 1663, a crate of snakes was delivered to the pharmacy of Palazzo Pitti. While the grand duke and his sons stood around wondering what to do if anyone was bitten, Redi, the pharmacist, began working out plans for the slaughter of thousands of reptiles of every sort, kind, and condition, in order to find out just where the venom came from. He slaughtered thousands of chickens, too, which he injected with venom or had bitten by snakes, and which he then happily discovered to be still as good to eat as ever. And he might also have slaughtered his brave, iron-stomached assistant, as well as some of his overconfident friends, had he given them a draught big enough to correct his erroneous thesis: that venom was harmless when swallowed.

By the time his letter-treatise to Magalotti *On Vipers* was published in 1664, Redi was already at work on his even more remarkable letter to Dati *On the Generation of Insects,* which had grown out of a conversation with Ferdinando about some cocoons in a nearby elm tree. After a whole summer of stinking up the grand ducal residence with the decaying flesh of horses, steers, bulls, lions, capons, tigers, sparrows, frogs, river snakes, tuna fish, fresh and salt water shrimp, and a score of other wiggling and walking creatures—enough, that is, to eliminate at least one of the variables—he arrived, "testing and retesting" in good Cimento fashion, at his epoch-making conclusion. Whenever flesh, either raw or cooked, is exposed to the fly-filled air of Tuscany, it produces worms, which consume the flesh, form cocoons, and metamorphose into the same common flies which, in that less hygienic century, buzzed around everyone's dinner table. It never, however, produces bees, as Pliny, Virgil, Varro, Origen, and Philo erroneously asserted. And when it is covered securely—Aristotle, Albertus Magnus, J. B. Van Helmont, Onorato Fabri, and just about everyone else notwithstanding—it does not produce anything at all. What William Harvey had suspected, experiment had proved. Living things are born from the eggs of other living things of the same species, and from nothing else—not from wood, not from excrement, not from putrefying flesh, no, not even from the body of Pope Pius V, which supposedly had engendered a mouse several decades after the pope's burial. And that got rid of one of the most tenacious errors of all times: the theory of spontaneous generation—or at least it did so until Needham and Buffon tried to revive the theory in the middle of the following century.

A great intellectual revolution took place in Europe during the decade that opened with the foundation of the Cimento and closed with Newton's appointment at Trinity College. And Florence, whatever some historians may have said about decadence, lethargy, inquisitorial severity, and court frivolity, was one of the three or four major centers from which the revolution proceeded.

After 1670, Florentine science changed somewhat in character. For one thing, the direct heritage of the Cimento lost its immediate connection with Florence, since the departing members carried it all over Europe—to Bologna, to Padua, to Naples, to Leiden, to Copenhagen. For another, the new grand duke, Cosimo III, did not really understand what science was all about, in spite of his careful education; or rather he understood only that part of it which was directly relevant to his greatest fear, death, and to his greatest preoccupation, the salvation of his soul. He made an honest effort to imitate the benevolent and open-minded patronage of his father, and perhaps also that of his uncle-in-law, King Louis XIV. He kept on even the more troublesome Galileans at the university. And he offered chairs to eminent scholars from as far off as Spain and Holland. But his attention usually focused on his two favorites. The first was Steno, who, as a convert to Catholicism, could do no wrong and who was back in Florence in 1674 working on geology and mineralogy. The other was Redi, who, as his personal physician for some forty years, could control almost all the state appointments in the medical and scientific fields and who, after the death of Leopoldo and the retirement of Steno, enjoyed unchallenged preeminence as the last active member of the disbanded academy. Florentine science, in other words, tended to become concentrated in the hands of fewer and fewer scientists until, by the mid-1680s, only one of them was left.

Redi himself did not have any special predilection for one kind of science over another, except perhaps that he preferred the infinitely small, which was just as full of undiscovered marvels as the infinitely great. Most of his spectacular discoveries arose merely from chance. When the court was at Pisa for the winter, he dissected fish. When it moved to Cerreto for the hunting season, he collected fossils—of the same fish. When Cosimo presented him with a cage full of squirrels and chipmunks, he noticed that everything previously written about their internal structure was wrong. When he himself caught a pregnant boar, he verified what Steno had previously found about the formation of the fetus. When he ran into references to two-headed snakes as he was browsing through some obscure Greek poets, and when he noticed that Ulisse Aldrovando in the sixteenth century and Thomas Willis in the seventeenth had reported similar phenomena, he launched into an incredible massacre of Arno slugs, Tunisian scorpions, and half the grand duke's hunting catches—a massacre that ended up in his fascinating, and delightfully nauseating, *Observations on Living Animals Found in Living Animals,* first published in 1684. The book revealed among other things, that even the simplest forms of animal life had sexual organs, that the supposedly medicinal bones of sea-bunnies reacted to acids in the same way as all others, that Molière was perfectly right when he said, in one of his plays, that turtles could walk around for hours with their heads cut off. Most important, and most blood-curdling of all, the book revealed that almost every living creature supported a menagerie of little worms—worms that continued to live after the host-creature was dead, that were absolutely immune to all the cures ever tried on them, and that were, particularly in Redi's artfully engraved illustrations, as horrifying to the sight as they were damaging to health.

Most of Redi's time, however—and most of that of his disciples and associates, too—was devoted to medicine. Medicine, after all, was their principal means of support, since all the natural sciences still had to be squeezed into the medical faculty at the university. Medicine also enjoyed every conceivable form of research assistance—a blank check from Cosimo III for all the animals and equipment Redi needed, a new library at Santa Maria Nuova, a botanical garden at Pisa, and the right to have criminals strangled instead of hanged whenever the anatomists put in an order for a special kind of corpse. But above all, medicine was without doubt the most talked-about subject of the day. Seldom have so many people spent so much time complaining of, or meditating upon, their ailments. Those whose ailments were not serious enough to warrant serious attention could always console themselves by reading the "medical letters" of prominent physicians, which became one of the most popular literary genres of the age. Those who were not actually ill could at least claim to suffer from the fear of being ill in the future; and their psychological state was obligingly raised to a level of a bona-fide illness in its own right, complete with a Hellenic name, *hypocondria,* and with a respectable physical cause: the concentration of nervous fluid in the cerebral cavity. It is not surprising that Redi aroused considerable curiosity when he began applying the same experimental methods that had been so successful in microbiology to the time-honored texts of the Galenists, which he himself had once accepted as authoritative. Even such traditional remedies as bleeding and violent purgatives were soon proven to be positively pernicious. Most medicines, ancient as well as modern, were proven to be more often harmful than beneficial. And the role of the physician was reduced to that of removing artificial obstacles to natural recovery. "Mother Nature," said Redi, "knows how to work much better [all by herself] than anything we could possibly desire."

Redi's Galilean criticism thus swept away two thousand years of accumulated wisdom at one stroke. But at the same time it laid the foundations for a completely new kind of medicine. It encouraged such bold new experiments as blood transfusion, which had just recently been proposed theoretically by Louis XIV's physician, Jean-Baptiste Denys, and which Magalotti learned about from a Latin poem dedicated to him by an obscure Jesuit named Ridolfo Aquaviva. It joined internal medicine firmly to anatomy—so much so, indeed, that Lorenzo Bellini, the most prominent physician at the university during the last decade of the century, turned all medicine into a branch of anatomy, at least in his popularizing lectures before the Accademia della Crusca. It sought to explain diseases, as far as possible, as the result of purely physical maladjustments—to the point of reintroducing a form of the banished four-humor theory and prescribing liquids for the cure of "dry" parts of the body. It admitted its ignorance of the causes of most ailments, and it insisted upon observation as the only way of ever finding out what they were. True, it was willing to condescend at times to the inveterate habits of patients with a sprinkling of unintelligible jargon. "Take," wrote Redi with a grin,

> senna in the leaf, vj drams; cream of tartar pulverized, dr. iij. . . . Infuse for 12 hrs. in sufficient quantity of common water over hot coals. Add choice manna of the whitest kind, ounces iij, and juice of squeezed lemon, on. j with white of one egg. R̉: Of the resulting paste: on. vj to take each morning, 5 or 6 hrs before dinner.

But none of its high-sounding and foul-tasting prescriptions ever did anything but produce a mildly laxative effect. And none of them was ever meant as a substitute for what Redi called "the good rule of life"—namely, to eat less, drink less, avoid rich foods, take plenty of water, get enough sleep, and stay away from pharmacies. Thus medicine ended up as dietetics; and had everyone followed the daily regimes that Redi dictated by the dozen—had they tried out his vegetable broths, endive salads, cooked fruit, boiled beef, and chicken breasts instead of consuming immense quantities of roast partridge and Montepulciano wine with a pinch of ground poppies to relieve acid indigestion—the sickest generation in Florentine history might have turned into the healthiest.

After the dissolution of the Cimento, then, Florentine science became less concerned with physics and astronomy and more concerned with microbiology, genetics, geology, and medicine. But that was not what bothered Magalotti, who still kept up with every detail of every experiment and with every word of each new treatise. What bothered him was his gradual realization that the Cimento had been a bit too encouraged by the initial response to its work. He had only to look at the subsequent record. All those astronomical observations, he noted, and still some people went right on trying to fit the new discoveries into a Ptolemaic or a Tycho Brahe cosmos. All those experiments on the vacuum, and still a certain Giovanni Maffei at Pisa had the nerve, in 1673, to denigrate Gassendi publicly in the name of Aristotle and, still more, to play on the timorous piety of the grand duke in order to procure an edict banning Galileo from philosophy courses at the university. All those careful dissections, and still someone in France had the audacity to maintain, in a rather acrimonious refutation of Redi's findings, that snakes were dangerous only when they got angry. Redi's reply to his critic was just as ineffective; for a certain Nicholas Lémery simply used it as an authority for a sweating potion he had invented—a potion made by dropping live, angry snakes into boiling water and then distilling the broth. All that work, in other words, and the same old errors persisted as before.

Magalotti was probably even more discouraged by the discovery that the supposed converts of the 1660s really had not been converted at all, and most particularly those in the Society of Jesus. Father Athanasius Kircher, whom the society had committed itself to defending as the most learned man of the century, kept on sending a stream of books and pamphlets to Florence, where they were always politely acknowledged and then quietly put aside for reading "at the first possible moment." But Kircher went right on proving, by what he thought were impeccable Galilean rules, that meteors were effluxes of subterranean fire, that fossilization worked backwards by transforming mineral into animal substances, that ocean currents always moved from east to west, and that the crosses observed "by perfectly trustworthy persons" after the recent eruption of Vesuvius, and carefully illustrated in his costly copper plates, were produced, perfectly naturally, by a conjunction of snow flakes and rising saline vapors. Father Daniello Bartoli, similarly, after dedicating years of effort to his monumental history of the society, became an enthusiast of Galilean science. He went even so far as to rewrite Seneca's ethics and Bellarmino's manual of piety in Galilean, though of course not in Copernican, terms, and to propose that the physics of the Cimento was far more conducive to morality and religion than any other. But when, in 1681, one of the Cimento's disciples brought some of its experiments to their logical conclusion and reduced heat and cold to pure motion, Bartoli missed the point completely. And out came so much more empirical evidence to show that Boyle was wrong about his corpuscles and that Aristotle was still right. The one thing the society would not put up with was Redi's constant ridiculing of the new drugs it was importing from Asia and America at no small profit. When it then blocked all of Leopoldo's efforts to prevent the astronomer Onorato Fabri from dying in the prison of the Inquisition, when it "buried" the single Jesuit pupil of Borelli in Tuscany under a round-the-clock schedule of teaching moral philosophy, and when it encouraged one of its fiery preachers to go on with his violent pulpit invectives against the atomists in Naples, the illusion was broken. "A Jesuit mathematician," Magalotti told Francesco Maria de' Medici in 1686, "is a rarity worthy of being put into a museum." And that was all he had to say for the institution that had so long pretended to be at the forefront of learning.

What was even more distressing was that the scientists themselves gradually lost confidence in their ability to convince anyone. "Redi has stopped dead in their tracks all the pharmacists in Florence, Pisa, and Livorno," wrote his former student, Giacinto Cestoni, in 1699. "But I can assure you that within very little time they'll be right back manufacturing all those medicines they have had to toss out in the last fifteen years." Why? Because, he answered, "men want to be deceived," and there is not much the scientists can do about that.

The criticism was perceptive, and it was one that Cestoni alone could have offered, thanks to his humble origins and nonacademic occupations in the commercial city of Livorno. But his teachers were completely unaware of the problem. Many years before, on a morning in April 1665, they had let word get out of their comfortable laboratory in the Pitti that Venus was visible in broad daylight. Within minutes the Mercato Nuovo was filled with hysterical men, and the windows and doorsteps of the whole city were bulging with screaming women and children. The scientists might, at that moment, have felt moved to send out another message explaining that the event was a perfectly natural phenomenon, and not, as everyone else thought, a portent of imminent doom. After all, no one would have noticed it had they not pointed it out. Instead, they laughed—and then went off to dinner. In other words, neither the possibility nor the utility of communicating with the uneducated ever occurred to any of the scientists. "Sir," wrote Magalotti to a friend, "we have a great advantage over ordinary men, even over the so-called great among them. We know how to learn and to keep what we learn for our own enjoyment. . . . Just think how few there are in this world today who are capable of searching out and finding the mysteries [of science]. In Florence . . . there remain but you, me, and one or two of our disciples." When the scientists found that they had trouble in communicating with the educated as well, and when Magalotti discovered that "no one ever closed the mouth of a companion bent on contradicting him," the last glimmer of the Renaissance faith in the power of words disappeared. Science in late seventeenth-century Florence, in spite of its many remarkable achievements, lost the sympathetic audience it had enjoyed at the time of Galileo. And the scientists were reduced to a small elite isolated in a desert of incomprehension and ignorance.

Why, then, bother with science at all? What good did it do, for example, to chart the stars, when even a mediocre telescope would reveal hundreds of new ones—unless, perhaps, it was to immortalize a friendship in the heavens by naming some of them the *Ottavie* or the *Falconiere*? Well, science could at least prove once and for all that deer brain was good to eat—all the long-accepted opinions to the contrary notwithstanding. It could prove that the worms in ship hulls at Livorno (which, by the way, no one figured out how to get rid of) had "a more delicate, more odorous taste" than any shell fish—no matter how much Magalotti might tease Redi about his dreadful little animals. It could show that boiling water, fire, and acid all changed the color of lobsters to the same tone of red—and thus baffle the peripatetics with the problem of attributing one effect to three different causes. It could delight the reading public with microscopic monstrosities and sordid anatomical details—so much so that Marcello Malpighi of Bologna, one of the foremost scientists of the age, felt called upon to reproach his colleagues, and especially those in Florence, for attending solely to *penem, anum, vulvam, et testes* and forgetting all about man as a whole.

But except in medicine, science seemed to have no real possibility of being applied in practical uses. It could not alleviate poverty, increase wheat production, stop floods, avoid famines, or improve the techniques of wool manufacturing. Given the Cimento's careful distinction between knowledge derived from the senses and knowledge derived from divine revelation, it could not even serve to elevate the minds of the scientists to the Author of what they were studying. Hence the successors of the Cimento exaggerated still further the empirical elements in the Cimento's methodological principles; eventually nothing was left but an unsorted collection of bits and pieces that were as useless as they were occasionally delightful. The result was Magalotti's own inch-by-inch description of coconuts. And coconuts, two centuries before the invention of the coconut carts that are today an indispensable ornament of every park and piazza in the city, had not the slightest relevance to anything that could be seen or used in Tuscany.

Even Redi eventually gave up. By 1684 he had come to regard his great work on insects as nothing but a bunch of "silly little observations," *osservazioncellucce*; and he laughed away his latest book, *Concerning the Things of Natural History,* as just "a few trifles of mine," a disconnected assortment of miscellaneous curiosities no more valuable than his "poor and miserable sonnets." His only response to a violent attack on his work in 1691 was simply: "I couldn't care less.... Let everyone think as he pleases." Science in the Galilean-Cimento tradition had failed to find a purpose beyond itself. And it went temporarily into hibernation.

Magalotti had already arrived at Redi's conclusion some twenty-five years earlier. He knew as well as anyone that a scientifically valid explanation of the comet of 1664 could have made an important contribution to an explanation of the whole solar system. But instead of attempting one, he amused himself with the obviously ridiculous thesis that the tail of the comet was an optical illusion. As soon as he saw Cassini's much more penetrating and much better-informed explanation, he admitted that he "cared no more for comets than for rainbows." He studiously ignored all the other comets that appeared during the following decades, including the one that took the name of its best-known observer, Edmund Halley.

No, Magalotti was not meant to be a scientist. He was only a "simple gazeteer of the sciences." It was just as well: for soiling his hands in a laboratory hardly befitted a *cavalliere,* a gentleman, like himself. Then, when Cardinal Flavio Chigi decided that he really did not need the services of a "courtier and philosopher"—someone, that is, who would just sit around in elegant attire and occasionally bring his patron up-to-date on the latest scientific smalltalk, Magalotti had to give up all thought of entering even that rather subsidiary career. Still ambitious, and still "marvelously desirous of praise," as he admitted, he had to look around for something else.

3

How Magalotti went traveling
and then came home

For the moment, however, postponing a decision was easier than making one. But it was also becoming increasingly embarrassing to face friends and patrons who expected such a decision from him. When, therefore, early in the summer of 1667, his boyhood friend Paolo Falconieri came up with a suggestion of how to avoid both embarrassment and a decision at the same time, Magalotti listened attentively.

The idea of traveling, either as a way of satisfying his curiosity about foreign lands or as a way of escaping his responsibilities at home, had occurred to Magalotti before. Indeed, it may have occurred to him as early as 1660, when one of Leopoldo's former protégés, a certain Cosimo Brunetti of Siena, passed through Florence after completing a secret mission to find a colony-site in the West Indies for the persecuted friends of the Parisian monastery of Port-Royal. And he had certainly heard Brunetti regale his former patron with glowing descriptions of "the softness of the air, the fertility of the land, the infinity of springs and streams, the goodness of the beaches, [and] the incredible abundance of all kinds of fish and game" in that earthly paradise, Martinique. Five years later he had met Sir John Finch, a graduate of the University of Padua and a former lecturer at the University of Pisa, who arrived as English minister to the Tuscan court in 1665. From Finch he may have learned the first elements of the English language, which he was later to speak with considerable fluency. He had also met Henry Neville, the unredeemed Cromwellian who spent three years in Florence and Rome after being released from the Tower of London in 1663. Neville had let him look at the first drafts of *The Isle of Pines, or A Late Discovery of a Fourth Island in Terra Incognita*, which was soon to become one of the most popular travelogs of the century. He had spent some fascinating evenings learning about Macao, Peking, Lhasa, Nepal, and a hundred other exotic places from the German Jesuit Johann Grueber, who had stopped off in Florence on his way back from the Far East in

1665. He had undoubtedly browsed through the intriguing descriptions of Algiers, Morocco, and Mexico that he was responsible for keeping on file in the Cimento's reference library. He had read the letters that Dati received from his many transalpine correspondents. He had heard the glowing panegyrics of Amsterdam that Leopoldo received from his roving agents, Francesco Riccardi and Alessandro Segni. And he began to get restless. Hence, when Paolo asked him to come along on another information-gathering expedition to northern Europe for Leopoldo and Viviani, Magalotti accepted, little realizing that he was beginning a twelve-year term as "the postilion of Europe."

The two companions left Florence in mid-July, crossed the Alps into Switzerland, and arrived at Augsburg in the first week of August. By early September, after a boat trip down the Danube and a stopover at Regensburg, they were in Vienna. By mid-October they were "wandering around—*a zonzo*" in The Hague. By early December, after a tour of Leiden, Haarlem, and Texel, they were in Amsterdam, where a visit from none other than Prince Cosimo, the future grand duke, detained them for over a month. Most of January they spent in Antwerp and Brussels. Most of February and March they spent in London, with a seven-day side trip to Windsor, Hampton Court, and Oxford. And they ended up, toward the end of April, in Paris.

For Magalotti, the trip was a great success. It had started out merely as a way of avoiding reality and of satisfying a vague curiosity about the strange and unusual. But it turned out instead to be a course of instruction. "I would not trade what I've picked up around inn-tables in the countries I've visited," remarked Magalotti many years later, "for all the learning of the scholars. For it has taught me how to get along with other men rather than just nude, crude science." To be sure, he had been terrified by "the everlasting horror of the Alps," just like almost every other traveler before the age of Romanticism.

> Ice-covered heights and the fog-bounded cliffs,
> snow blown about by the wind's violent breath;
> signs are all these of a frightening death,

he commented, regretful of not being able to cut a shorter trail with some of Hannibal's vinegar. But after a day or two in Switzerland, he discovered that Protestants were hospitable and unusually moral people, in spite of all that his teachers had told him about the "impious license" of "the ungrateful rebels against the Holy See." He was overwhelmed by Amsterdam, a city that talked more about commerce than courts and that seemed to have fully regained its prosperity since the recent war against England. He picked up all kinds of information about distant places quite as fascinating as any he had heard of from Grueber—about the new port just opened on the Arctic Ocean by the Prince of Muscovy, about an elective monarchy of Black Catholics near Gambia, about the incredibly delicious oysters in Sierra Leone, and about a bird brought back from the Barbados too extraordinary even to describe. In London he was shocked to see how much money the English spent on cock fights and how much mess was still left over from the Great Fire. But he was favorably impressed by the "public garden" and by the "shops full of every sort of merchandise." In Paris he discovered the delights of female society, delights quite unknown to the exclusively male world of scholars in Italy; and he quickly gave up the "wonderful libraries" for "the drawing rooms of certain ma'm'selles, who have sliced up my heart like a Sienese cake."*

The books of Redi and Borelli and the letters of Dati and Leopoldo opened the doors of the great and famous almost everywhere. Nicholas Heinsius received the travelers at The Hague and was delighted to discover that the author of that little treatise on Saturn was "an extraordinarily urbane man, a compendium of Tuscan elegance." The greatest classical scholar of the age, Isaac Vossius, also received them and expressed "an unbearable impatience" to hear about Redi's insects. In Leiden they met Jacob Gronovius, the accomplished antiquarian who was later to accept a chair at Pisa. At one of Prince Cosimo's receptions, they met the exiled French publicist and man of letters, Charles de Saint-Evremond, whose essays and poems Magalotti was to study so attentively in later years. In Paris they met the erudite lawyer Habert de Montmor, founder of the famous scientific salon, who invited them to a "solemn symposium" at his house and drank innumerable toasts, "in the most appropriate and respectful manner" to Leopoldo. They met the septuagenarian poet Jean Chapelain, whose editions of Marino, Chiabrera, and Tassoni had made him one of the most authoritative specialists on Italian literature outside Italy; and they found "nothing wrong with him that could not be remedied by taking thirty years off his age and improving his complexion." They met the accomplished epistolographer and venerable secretary of the Académie Française, Valentin Conrart, whose many subsequent letters to Magalotti none of the editors of Conrart's works has ever bothered to publish; and they found him to possess "one of those eye-compasses our Galileo used to talk about that enable one immediately to distinguish correct proportions and make proper measurements." They met the orientalist Melchisedech Thévenot, the astronomer Ismael Bouillau, and the quarrelsome mathematician from Normandy Adrien Auzout, whom Magalotti was now willing to absolve of plagiarizing the Cimento's instruments in the hope of recruiting him as a member. Finally, they met that garrulous Italianist Gilles Ménages, who soon bored them to tears by reciting his farfetched Italian etymologies.

In England, the two young Florentines were still more fortunate in their introductions, thanks in part to a resident compatriot, Bernardo Guasconi, who had fought bravely for King Charles I and who had just returned, after a three-year vacation in Italy, to enter the service of Charles II. Guasconi provided them with

* Magalotti does not say *pan forte,* although he is probably referring to its forerunner.

what they had most desired of their trip to England: an invitation to the weekly meetings of the Royal Society. A lecture-demonstration by Robert Hooke, as well as a warm reception by the secretary, Henry Oldenburg, quickly overcame their initial disappointment in finding the society somewhat less formally organized than they had expected. The arrival, finally, of the published version of the Cimento's *Essays* gave them the opportunity of taking an autographed copy to King Charles himself, whom they were delighted to find well acquainted with Italian poetry. At Oxford they spent two long evenings talking about air pressure, vacuums, and the merits of Leopoldo with none other than the great Robert Boyle, whose generous hospitality more than compensated, they found, for his reluctance to answer letters. And one or two confidential acquaintances at court gave them enough information to draw up a fairly complete list of the peers, prelates, officers, and scandals of the realm.

Magalotti did not meet everyone, to be sure. Many of the most acclaimed dramatists, poets, theologians, and statesmen of the age are not mentioned in his letters, and their names are often incomplete, or misspelled, when they appear in the lists of his official memoranda. He seems to have gone to the theater only once—a strange omission for a contemporary of Molière and Dryden. Moreover, by not reading up beforehand on the countries he was to visit and by relying almost wholly on personal interviews once he got there, he sometimes mistook the surface for the substance. Thus he scrutinized individuals but ignored institutions. He described current practice but said nothing about historical precedent. He judged thirteen pages on intrigues at court to be worth one on the House of Commons. And he cultivated an air of curious detachment that sealed him off personally from much of what he was exposed to—like the misery of the Irish peasants under the heels of the English landlords who wined and dined him so elegantly the next year.

Still, one of the main purposes of the trip had been fully realized. "Receiving courtesies from wise and learned men," he wrote Dati, "is ample recompense for all the trouble and money spent on traveling." And a score of prominent scholars and one real king was not a bad record for a thirty-year-old tourist of as yet no particular accomplishment.

Magalotti was all too happy to seize the next opportunity to resume his travels. And such an opportunity arose almost as soon as he got back to Florence that summer, as the result of complications in the personal relations among the members of the ruling family that went back some seven years. In 1661, Grand Duke Ferdinando had scored a minor diplomatic triumph by getting his heir-apparent, Prince Cosimo, betrothed to the favorite cousin of King Louis XIV of France, the beautiful, vivacious, headstrong, and thoroughly spoiled Marguérite

Louise d'Orléans. The marriage by proxy at the Louvre had been solemn, the sea escort from Marseilles had been magnificent, and the official reception in Florence had been stupendous—at least according to Magalotti's predecessor as secretary of the Cimento, Alessandro Segni, who published a description of it, and according to the traveling scholar, Jacob Spon, who compared it to the triumph of a Roman emperor.

The exorbitant cost of these festivities seemed to have been fully justified, for it enabled Ferdinando to act as mediator between the king and the pope and to place himself on what he correctly estimated to be the right side in the forthcoming struggle for power in Europe. But as soon as the festivities were over, the troubles began. Marguérite Louise, it seems, had been brought up with the expectation of becoming a queen; she was furious at finding her way suddenly blocked, by an article in the recent Peace of the Pyrenees, at the level of a mere grand duchess. Still worse, she had left behind a lover, a dashing young sportsman at the French court with whom the well-meaning but pious and taciturn Cosimo simply could not compare; only her royal cousin's ultimatum of Florence-or-convent had managed to tear her away from him. Finally, she was an incorrigible Gallic snob, and she poured ridicule on everything, from dress to manners, that did not exactly correspond to current fashions in France.

Ferdinando was understanding at first. After all, he had as much experience with unhappy marriages as anyone, and all his children had been born of brief moments of reconciliation with his incorrigible wife, Vittoria della Rovere, whose last act of conjugal vengeance was to outlive him by more than three decades. He then tried to be patient and long-suffering. Finally, he sent all her French servants home and cut off her correspondence with her mother: these people, obviously, were to blame, not the nice little princess. At the same time, he got the pope to send theologians, bishops, and monks, and the king to send letters, ambassadors, and even her old nurse. All this pressure forced her to yield just long enough to conceive one child, Ferdinando Maria, who was born in 1663. But it also had the effect of intensifying the steady stream of invective she let loose day and night at the grand duke, at the whole house of the Medici, at the Florentine landscape, at the Tuscan people, and above all at the plaster-faced, unathletic husband upon whom the future of the dynasty, and the preservation of the state, depended. A bit of solitary confinement at Poggio a Caiano at last brought repentence—and, to everyone's joy, another pregnancy. But four months later the princess tried to run off with a French soldier at Pisa. After that, she tried to bring on a miscarriage, first by violent horseback-riding, then, when the horses were confiscated, by equally violent hiking, and finally by starvation. She had to be confined again until August 1667, when she gave birth to a girl, Anna Maria Luisa, the last direct descendant of Cosimo I.

Just two children, of course, were not yet enough for a dynasty reduced to a single available male; and Ferdinando turned in desperation to extreme measures.

He sent Cosimo off on a long and, he hoped, instructive vacation through northern Italy and over the Alps to Augsburg, Brussels, Amsterdam, Hamburg, and Bremen. After six months of separation and an exorbitant bill of some 25,000 *scudi*—not counting the tips and the cartloads of expensive bric-a-brac Cosimo had picked up in the shops of Holland—the princess was as intractable as ever; and Ferdinando had no choice but to send his son packing again—this time in another direction. Cosimo, of course, would need a proper retinue, even though he was to travel incognito. He had much enjoyed the company of the two young Florentines who had paid him a visit in Amsterdam. He knew that they had mastered the art of getting comfortably from one place to another, and he knew that one of them could be counted on to describe a voyage as elegantly and precisely as he had described the experiments of the Cimento. He therefore appointed them *cavalieri* for the next expedition. And Magalotti, along with Filippo Corsini, who had acted as recording secretary for Cosimo's last trip, was given the job of keeping a diary for future reference. Thus traveling acquired still another purpose. What had once been a pastime, an escape, a course of instruction, and a tour through the gallery of great men, had become, at least for the time being, a paying profession.

The party of five gentlemen, four aides, a director, a treasurer, a confessor, a physician, and fourteen secretaries, servants, and interpreters sailed from Livorno on September 18 and arrived at Barcelona by way of Portofino and Monaco on September 29. They proceeded by land to Montserrat, Zaragoza, and Madrid, where they spent almost a month. They crossed Castile to Córdoba, Granada, and Seville, passed through Portugal from Lisbon to Oporto and along the north coast of Spain. At La Coruña, they boarded another ship which took them through a very uncomfortable storm off Brittany to Kinsale in Ireland and then to Plymouth. After a leisurely coach trip through Devonshire and Dorsetshire, they spent some three months at London, Cambridge, and various country houses. They then went on to Rotterdam, where they were received by Cosimo's former host, the wealthy Florentine merchant Francesco Feroni. They continued through Holland to Aachen for the obligatory homage at Charlemagne's tomb, through the Ardennes for a six-week visit in Paris, and finally, by way of Lyon and Marseilles, back to Florence, which they reached at the end of February.

From Cosimo's point of view, the second European tour was much more profitable than the first. In half the countries he visited there were many more churches and monasteries to hear Mass in, and he could occasionally forego his regular evening religious exercises to practice the art of writing dispatches to his father. In every major city he was officially greeted by the entire diplomatic corps, as well as by the leading dignitaries of the government: and after long private conversations with each of them separately, he managed to learn a good bit about the conduct of international politics. In England he made a number of good friends from among the over one hundred distinguished persons who came to call on him. Some of them (including Charles Calvert, Lord Baltimore) later became his correspondents, and many of them thereafter received an annual case of Chianti wine. Indeed, Cosimo became a dedicated Anglophile: "In this world," he confessed cautiously upon his return to Tuscany, "I hope for nothing so vehemently as to see once again that kingdom . . . the paradise called England. . . and to embrace all my old friends there." In Paris he carefully practiced what he had learned about proper behavior in courts and made a surprisingly favorable impression on his uncle-in-law, the Sun King. Once back home, he managed to make a somewhat less unfavorable impression on his wife—partly because travel had sanded down some of his more peculiarly Tuscan traits. And in 1671, a year after he had followed his father, Ferdinando, to the throne, a third child was born, his successor and the last Medici grand duke of Tuscany, Gian Gastone.

From Magalotti's point of view the trip was at least partly successful. Lisbon filled him with almost as much enthusiasm as it had Filippo Sassetti some eighty years before, with its spectacular situation, its handsome modern buildings, the "numerous large vessels" in the Tagus, and an air of buoyant optimism still left over from the War of Independence against Spain. Visiting England gave him a chance to renew his old contacts, not only with Boyle, but also with Sir Samuel Morland, who soon fulfilled his promise to send copies of his calculating machine and his loudspeaker—the *tuba stentorofonica*—to Florence. He learned to appreciate even more the striking similarities between the empirical bent of English science and that of the Galilean-Cimento tradition he had been brought up in. He perceived the metaphysical implications of English empiricism and prophesied that the fame of Isaac Newton would far outlast that of Thomas Hobbes. He resumed his study of English politics, this time with additional help from Harrington's *Oceania*. He perfected his command of the English language, and he was soon able to write polished English letters, to act as official host for distinguished English visitors in Florence, to sight-translate English scientific treatises for Redi, and to begin the first Italian version of the latest masterpiece of English literature, Milton's *Paradise Lost*. He also learned to speak one more foreign language, Spanish, and to acquire the rudiments of still another, Portuguese.

Other aspects of the trip, however, fell decidedly short of Magalotti's expectations. Moving about in the train of a rank-conscious prince, wasting hours on end doing silly little errands, and just hanging around in the ante-chambers for instructions, made traveling somewhat less than exciting. Moreover, not all the countries he visited were equally admirable. Spain in particular he found to be bankrupt and demoralized, proud and lavish—exactly the opposite of the great, invincible power that he, and most other Italians, still thought it to be. Its poetry was still somewhat alive, thanks, he surmised, to the importation of new themes from America. But its learning was hopelessly out of touch with that of the rest of Europe. And its religion consisted largely of elaborate processions, gaudy reliquaries, and fables. The librarian of Philip II's priceless collection at the Escurial had classified Copernicus under "astrology." None of the professors at the University of Alcalá could speak more than three words of Latin. Many houses were collapsing from want of inhabitants. And most of the streets reeked of several months' accumulation of defenestrated chamber pots. Worse yet, all Magalotti's dreams of returning to Italy "loaded with virginal scarfs and with the spoils of the most famous beauties of all Spain" were soon shattered. After twenty-four days in Madrid, the group of very eligible young Florentines had managed to attract only one cripple and one gypsy!

England and France might have made up for Spain. After all, English physicians possessed "what little is known in this world" about medicine, and French scientists possessed a profundity of thought that contrasted favorably with the Italian habit of "knowing a bit of everything without ever going deeply into anything." But Magalotti soon came to the conclusion that all Frenchmen suffered from one major defect: *leggerezza,* or superficiality. Even the proud Italianist Ménages carefully avoided talking anything but French in their presence. The scientist Denis de Sallo did not seem to know that Galileo had studied the motion of the pendulum. And the *Journal des sçavans,* one of the first learned periodicals in all Europe, turned out to be little more than a collection of "baroque arguments"—*argomenti in barocco.*

Thus one possible reason for traveling had to be ruled out, namely, the hope of discovering something abroad that might profitably be adopted at home. Magalotti was perfectly aware of his compatriots' shortcomings: their passion for eating, their lack of patriotism, their willingness to serve for low pay in foreign armies, and their penchant for aping foreign manners and speech. But he was doubtful that foreigners could offer much in the way of a remedy. England, he thought, was on the verge of another and much more destructive civil war. The literary products of the incipient age of Louis XIV in France—the age, that is, of Racine, Molière, La Fontaine, et al.—were destined to wither away in a vain effort at popularization. Italy still had much more to teach than to learn. Magalotti observed that Italy's prospective students admitted as much by "erecting altars and a cult" to Redi's works "in the farthest lands of the north" and by regularly reviewing them in the *Journal des sçavans* and the *Philosophical Transactions.* But teaching was no more fruitful an occupation than learning. When the French turned Redi's conclusions upside down, when the Royal Society put away the Cimento's *Essays* until it could find a translator, and when that literary chauvinist Doménique Bouhours launched a virulent campaign to rid French literature of all Italian influence, Magalotti chose to respond not with a documented defense, as his successors were to do in the next generation, but with a compassionate shrug of the shoulders. When Ménages came out with the outrageous observation that no Italian knew Greek, he merely walked over to a bookshelf, pulled out the first

Greek text he could find, and told Paolo to start reading out loud. He had already failed, as secretary of the Cimento, to convert Pisan pharmacists to Galileo. And he had little hope now, as an ambassador of Italian letters, of converting an entire nation to Petrarch and Chiabrera.

Traveling, then, did little good for those who traveled and even less good for those who came into contact with travelers. Still, it might be made to serve another, if somewhat less serious, purpose. It might be used, that is, to provide the necessary factual basis for the more or less fanciful "descriptions" of distant and exotic lands that were now in great demand all over Europe. Magalotti had learned the art of writing travelogs from several contemporary masters—from Henry Neville, from Jacob Spon, and even from one of his own compatriots, Francesco Negri, whose book on the wonders of Lapland was finally published, with a dedication to Cosimo III, in 1701. He therefore set to work rewriting what he had heard from Jean Chardin, who had just returned after many years in the Near East, about Persia. He set down an account of his earlier conversations with Johann Grueber on China and Central Asia, to the great delight of "all those who are curious about information pertaining to the most remote nations." He gathered together the data he had collected in Holland about the Isle of Martinique. He unearthed and edited the accounts of Francesco Carletti, the most eminent Tuscan voyager of Galileo's generation. Finally, he arranged in proper literary form the fascinating details he had culled from an English translation of a Portuguese Jesuit's account of Ethiopia—details to which he gave an aura of authenticity by denouncing the "frivolous conjectures" of all the previous authorities on the same country.

Yet this sort of literature never became anything more than an occasional pastime; and those pieces that finally were published appeared only years after they were actually composed. For Magalotti to have become a Tuscan Hakluyt, or a competent compiler of others' travels, he would have needed a technical competence that he was simply not willing to spend the time acquiring. He had once made a stab, it is true, at learning Arabic, and he still remembered enough, many years later, to carry on intelligent conversations about it with the Maronite priest Peter Ambarachius, whom Cosimo invited up from Rome in 1698 to resurrect the long-neglected Oriental press of Ferdinando I. But able linguist though he was, Magalotti never managed to do anything more than choke on Arabic gutturals and aspirates that one of the grand duke's former slaves tried to make him pronounce. And he quickly gave up any pretense of some day being able to meet the only standards he knew were acceptable—those of the great Orientalist Barthélemy d'Herbelot, who "knew more languages than [the Apostles at] Pentecost," and who had been received with highest honors during a visit to Florence in 1666. A few strange words might add a bit of learned luster to a "scientific letter" on the souls of animals. But that was not sufficient to let the author pass as an authority on the countries where the languages were spoken.

Chinese and Syriac, then, Arabic and Coptic, would have required far too much effort for anyone who hesitated to commit himself to them for life; and certainly the miserable state Magalotti heard poor old d'Herbelot was living in after 1670 did not encourage him to make such a commitment. But Greek, which Magalotti knew well enough to make a graceful translation of Theophrastus, and Latin, which he had been soaked in at the Collegio Romano, were all the preparation he needed to master another, and much more serious branch of learning, the branch that was then defined as the study of "antiquities" and that today would include archaeology, numismatics, and the organization of museums and libraries.

The study of antiquities had recently been encouraged all over Italy by Pope Alexander VII, who hoped that the records of past monuments would "raise the eyebrows of the most powerful monarchs in Europe," and particularly those of King Louis XIV, as much as the monuments themselves had once awed the barbarians. It had been given official status in Tuscany by the appointment of several outstanding scholars at the university: the Hellenist Valerio Chimentelli, who rediscovered and edited an important inscription at Pisa; the theologian and ecclesiastical historian from Verona, Enrico, later Cardinal, Noris; and, for a short time, the Dutch scholar, Jacob Gronovius, who already enjoyed a world-wide reputation by the time of his arrival in 1673. This study soon produced several works of merit. For instance, Carlo Dati's elegant and accurate biographies of the Greek painters were based on years of painstaking examination of all the extant literary sources and made a big enough impression beyond the Alps, the flattering dedication to Louis XIV aside, to win a handsome subsidy from Colbert. Ottavio Falconieri's edition of Famiano Nardini's *Roma Antica* took the place of Flavio Biondo as the best account of ancient monuments in Rome before Ridolfino Venuti's revised edition came out in the middle of the following century. Cosimo Della Rena's *Series of the Ancient Dukes and Marquises* continued to be cited as a basic guide to early medieval Florence for another seventy-five years. And Cardinal Noris's *History of the Pelagian Heresy,* his *History of the Fifth Ecumenical Council,* and his *History of Investitures,* to mention but a few of his many works, laid the foundations for much of the ecclesiastical historiography of the age of Muratori—and of Voltaire.

Magalotti was perfectly aware of the accomplishments of the antiquarians. He was kept informed of their most spectacular discovery at the time—not the *Republic* of Cicero, which someone claimed to have turned up in Naples in 1663, but the complete *Satyricon* of that forthright chronicler of Roman high-life, Petronius. He appreciated their claim to be as orthodox Galileans as the members of the Cimento. He knew that they threatened, by picking away at the established authorities, to tear down the accepted view of history as thoroughly as the scientists had destroyed the Aristotelian cosmos. And for a moment in 1665 and 1666, just when he was tiring of test tubes and barometers, he had been seriously tempted to follow in their footsteps, especially after Ottavio Falconieri pointed to himself as an example of how scholarship favored promotions in an ecclesiastical career.

But the moment never returned. Magalotti soon realized that the study of antiquities was suffering from the same excessive empiricism that had afflicted post-Cimento science. When he noticed the insouciance with which Dati jumped from a passage in Pliny to an ancient medallion and then to one of Steno's sharks, he concluded that such study was incapable of yielding even the most tenuous hypothesis about the connections among single phenomena. The study of antiquities might have been made to serve a purpose beyond itself. For instance, it might have provided an effective defense of true Catholic piety against Molinism, Jansenism, Deism, and "libertinism." But Enrico Noris's suggestions to that effect failed to evoke any other response than a blast from the Spanish Holy Office; and the similar suggestions of other scholars elsewhere in Europe went totally unnoticed in Tuscany. For such suggestions presupposed a connection between "antiquities" and history that no Florentine was able to perceive. History, as Magalotti pointed out even before he had learned about the other, more famous historical Pyrrhonists of his age, "rested on a foundation of false-hood." And historians could only "be considered as liars in good faith if they're sincere and [as liars] in bad faith if they're corrupt." The heroes that history once celebrated no longer appealed to an unheroic, nonchalant (*svogliata*) generation, he observed. "Princes want no more Rodrigones; conquerors want no more laurels; soldiers want no more stirring speeches; and even Venetian boatmen no longer speak in *recitativo*." The past ages that once invited comparison with the present had lost their charm, or at least the only past age that still seemed at all attractive was Carlo Dati's second century A.D., the least historical-minded of all centuries before the seventeenth.

Florentines were content to let history slumber in the innocuous categories prescribed for it by Agostino Mascardi's *Art of History*; and they were still willing to borrow what few schemes of periodization they needed from Baronio, Vasari, or Bellarmino. Like his compatriots, Magalotti saw nothing incongruous in writing about Philippe de Commynes and King Louis XI as if they were contemporaries of Bossuet and Louis XIV. He never bothered to look at Redi's rare copy of the *Magdeburg Centuries,* that manifesto of Lutheran historical concepts which had provoked Baronio's vast *Annales Ecclesiastici* a century earlier. He never bothered to find out why a group of Belgian Jesuits known as the Bollandists should have asked Redi to lend them his copy, or why they should have taken such pains to produce the first monument of modern Catholic erudition, the *Acta Sanctorum*. He put aside Carlo Sigonio's *Italian Kingdom,* one of the greatest achievements of late Renaissance historiography, as soon as he had looked at the title page.

The study of antiquities had to be satisfied with a more modest role. It could, for example, be used to shield antiquarians from the world about them, just as it had in the days of Livy; even Noris bitterly resented being distracted from his quiet research by his administrative duties as director of the Vatican Library. It could also furnish subjects for commemorative medals, although the best Ottavio Falconieri could come up with for Prince Cosimo's trip abroad was a picture of Nero returning from a dancing tour of Greece, which was hardly appropriate. It could assist the pope in finding a better place to put the Chair of St. Peter in the Vatican. It could amuse the king of Sweden with details about the spots on the painting of a lion recently unearthed at Rome—so many details, in fact, that Paolo Falconieri's memorandum on the subject took "until three days before Doomsday" just to read. It could force the canons of the Baptistry to change the date of their dedication feast in accordance with a letter of Pope Nicholas II discovered in the basement of Santa Felicità. For, as the antiquarians pointed out, "antiquity must be respected" (*servanda est*).

But for Magalotti, at least, none of these roles was particularly exciting. Or rather none of them was exciting enough to make up for what was the indispensable condition of all scholarly activity at the time: submission to that incarnate encyclopedia of scholarship, Antonio Magliabechi, librarian to the grand duke and founder of the world-famous collection that still forms the core of the National Library in Florence today. Magliabechi did not have to give proof of his learning by writing books: the scores of authors who applied to him for information kept his name prominently displayed in the dedications and acknowledgments of half the books published in Italy during his lifetime. He had read everything that was then in print and much that was not, and he could recall every word in almost every line he ever read without so much as looking at a note. He corresponded with all the learned men of Europe, and he soon succeeded Dati as the chief channel for information passing from one side of the Alps to the other. Thanks to the debts owed him by all the scholarly clerks in the Roman Holy Office, he could get anyone permission to read any book on the Index—which is why Magalotti had to apply to him in 1666. And thanks to the unshakable confidence accorded him by Cosimo III, he enjoyed almost as much influence over promotions and appointments at the Tuscan court as he claimed to have.

Magliabechi's cooperation was therefore both a prerequisite and a guarantee of success in the field of scholarship. But the price for his services was high. Whenever clients went to England, they were expected to send him assurances that the "name of the incomparable Sig. Ant.o Magliabechi was the most sacred and venerable of all" among the English. Whenever they went to Holland, they were expected to send him "catalogues of all those men of letters in Leiden and Amsterdam who have spoken of [him]." When they stayed at home they were expected constantly to remind their correspondents "that nothing escapes his immense erudition" and to hide their real opinions about him behind a barrage of flattery. They were even expected to pay regular calls at the unaired, unswept house he lived in opposite Santa Maria Novella—and to be spied on through a peep hole before being admitted. They had then to avoid tripping over the disorderly piles of books that filled every corner of every room, slipping on the breadcrusts and apple peels scattered about the floor, sitting on the "miserable bed" littered with papers and garbage, and looking at the deformed face, frozen between a smile and a sneer, which nature had given the proprietor in order "to make the beauty of his intellect shine forth more clearly." They had to suffer the stench of clothes never washed and never even taken off. And they had to touch those "black, dirty, filthy hands," grimier, according to Magalotti, than the pots in the kitchen of the Zoccolanti friars. Even then they ran the risk of being praised to the skies in one breath and of being secretly denigrated ("please burn this letter the moment you finish reading it!") all over Europe in the next.

The price was too high for one like Magalotti, who had a sensitive nose and an even more sensitive consciousness of his rank. He stopped even bothering to check the quotations from ancient authors that dropped copiously and haphazardly into his letters. And he forever renounced the career of those who "toured the world [just] to copy epitaphs and count the steps in bell towers."

But traveling as a career still had one other possibility. After another expedition abroad in 1673 and 1674—an expedition that took him to Brussels, Köln, Hamburg, Copenhagen, and Stockholm and that permitted him to study at close hand the negotiations then in progress for the termination of the Franco-Dutch War—Magalotti was unexpectedly appointed as Tuscan ambassador to the imperial court. His instructions were simple: stay away from the French, get the confidence of the Jesuits, avoid quarrels over precedence, and make sure that the grand duke's aunt, Archduchess Anna de' Medici, remembers her nephew in her will. Vienna turned out to be comfortable, in spite of the menace of another Turkish attack, amusing, thanks to the number of foreigners living there, and full of news, which poured in from all the countries of eastern Europe. Magalotti happily settled into a little suburban villa, well equipped with flower vases, two admirable perfume dispensers, and an Italian-style garden.

Then, just as he was about to conclude that diplomacy was the vocation he had long been searching for, Magalotti began to have doubts; back came the old annoying rash that always before had accompanied moments of indecision. For one thing, he could not get along with Germans; and his one attempt to entertain Turks had been a disastrous failure. For another thing, he discovered that his allowance was insufficient to cover the clothes and coaches that endless court ceremonies constantly required. Worst of all, he began to wonder whether diplomacy really accomplished the ends expected of it. He realized that it provided the last remaining barrier to total anarchy in the relations among the great powers, and he knew that it necessarily involved scrupulous attention to complicated rules of protocol, like those he and Carlo Strozzi wrote out in a memorandum of 1671. But since tiny Tuscany could not hope to be admitted to the councils where all the important decisions were made, Magalotti also realized that his role as a diplomat would always be more that of an observer than a participant. Most of Grand Duke Cosimo's grandiose projects came to naught: converting England, northern Germany, and India to Catholicism, battering the Ottoman Empire by land and by sea, and establishing permanent commercial relations with Persia. Although some of his more modest projects succeeded—such as maintaining the strict neutrality of Livorno and getting himself accorded "the same honors, prerogatives, and preeminence" as rulers of royal rank—Magalotti was not sure they were worth the vast amounts of money spent on them.

Magalotti's disillusionment with diplomacy was heightened by a growing disillusionment with politics in general. Insofar as it involved the making of effective decisions, he realized, politics was the sole responsibility of the prince. And princes, he admitted, were "above all limitation, above all fundamental laws." The most a minister or a courtier could do was to give his advice whenever it was asked of him. Usually his duties consisted solely in observing a series of elaborate ceremonies: in providing decorative background for audiences at the Pitti, in following the grand ducal household from Pisa to Artimino and from Livorno to Poggio Imperiale, in carrying baskets of fruit to visiting dignitaries, and in attending all-night parties in the Boboli whenever someone of importance had a birthday or an anniversary. Occasionally the duties were rather arduous: waiting on the table of a foreign diplomat, getting an enraged noblewoman to back her carriage out of Via de' Guicciardini when the equally obstinate English envoy had driven his into the other end; turning over an entire palace to a traveling German prince—which is what the Salviati were asked to do in 1690; or arranging for the reception of the Bavarian bride of Prince Ferdinando—which is what Alessandro Segni was ordered to do in 1688. Segni had just been awarded the title of senator, not for his accomplishments as a scientist, a scholar, or a diplomat, put for having organized a particularly magnificent parade two years before. Often, however, the duties consisted solely in endlessly multiplying ceremonial procedures. Before the new French ambassador was presented to the grand duke in 1689, for instance, he was picked up in two carriages driven by eight liveried men and solemnly fed in the presence of four noblemen, who cut his meat, poured his wine, and held his napkin. The next day he was taken to Mass at the Annunziata and given a black velvet prie-dieu with two torches on either side. The third day he was driven out into the country in a six-horse coach—with another four-horse coach following close behind. Only after another week of such comings and goings was he finally permitted to go up to Poggio Imperiale with what turned out to be merely a list of high-sounding compliments.

Most Florentine patricians were happy to perform these tasks, even at the risk of losing the very memory of their former pride and self-sufficiency. No one, not even the officials who continued to be elected to the old republican magistracies, was ever expected to take any initiative, to accept any responsibility, or to consider his job as anything but a way of gaining prestige and rounding out his income. But to Magalotti, the life of a courtier was no different from the life of a canary in a golden cage:

> Tell me, then, do,
> if between me and you
> you can note any difference in fate,
>
> if in the end,
> they seem just to blend,
> or if a court is the same as your grate.
>
> (*Il passero di canaria*)

He had had enough experience as a courtier to draw up for the new grand duke in 1670 a carefully selected list of prospective appointees to state offices. But when the foreign minister assured him that his place on the bench was waiting for him if he ever wanted to come home, he could only answer: "What kind of fantasies are you dreaming up ? You certainly have followed my sailings about during these last twelve years, [and thus you should] know how unwilling I am to pilot my way into a port for fear of having to grease the palm of its governor. If [at the moment] I can't go on, I prefer to stay on board ship and wait for the wind to change."

Still, if Magalotti did not want to engage in politics, he could always write about it. He had acquired some knowledge of the contemporary political theory which was soon to produce the masterpieces of John Locke in England and of Bossuet in France. And he was well acquainted with the most famous political theorist of his own national literature, Machiavelli. Indeed, he had spent a whole evening in 1665—after obtaining the necessary ecclesiastical dispensations—going over all the available manuscripts of Machiavelli's works with Magliabechi and Panciatichi. He had helped one of his friends to conduct a fruitless search for an autograph copy of *The Prince*. And he knew the text well enough to commend the Tartars on having anticipated the rule about conquerors living in the countries they conquered.

But the moment Magalotti actually started to write about politics, he ran into difficulties. For one thing, he himself was too much a victim of Cimento empiricism to imagine that any of the specific information he had collected could possibly yield a general guide to action. The only maxim (*massima*) he dared to hazard after dozens of tightly packed pages on England was that the behavior of English noblewomen contradicted the Tuscan proverb: "Who won't pay the whore pays the doctor." And the only recommendation he could make after scores of pages on Sweden was that the next king go to Poland for his education, then conquer Denmark, and then come home to subdue the nobility. For another thing, he never seems to have understood what Machiavelli—or what Henry Neville, for that matter—was talking about. Like Carlo Dati, he read the fifteenth chapter of *The Prince* not for its methodology of political science, but for proof that the eagle is not the king of birds; and he read the *Florentine Histories* not for reflections on the weakness of republican institutions, but for new words for the forthcoming edition of the Crusca's *Vocabolario*. He therefore left to Neville the task of making Machiavelli applicable to the political problems of his own times—and of publishing the principal works in English translation in 1675. And he left to the *Acta Eruditorum* of Leipzig, and to the French translators of the *Discourses,* the task of blasting the myths of the sixteenth-century anti-Machiavellians.

More important still, it never occurred to Magalotti that anything he had seen abroad had the slightest relevance to the political institutions of his own country. He could conceive of only one kind of government: one in which all power was concentrated in the hands of a single monarch and in which physical force was rendered unnecessary by the moral force of the Catholic religion. That was exactly the kind of government that existed in Tuscany; and all that anyone might add to the standard eulogies of Cosimo III would be "a firm but polite reproach to those who rule their states in a different manner."

Tuscany was a model to be imitated, not a patient to be treated. It too had its defects, to be sure. The mobs of hungry peasants shouting "bread and work!" outside the Pitti in 1698 were only the evident sign of a severe economic depression —and of the futility of the still more draconian restrictions that had recently been placed on agriculture and industry. Justice was occasionally sacrificed to intrigue. One night in 1681, two gentlemen were sealed up in the dungeon at Volterra without a hearing or a trial and simply left there to die. In 1690 a wealthy widow named Elisabetta Mormorai was locked up in a convent simply because a disappointed suitor was influential enough to make the law into an instrument of personal vengeance. And when a certain Roberto Acciaiuoli tried to get her out, he was forced to flee to Switzerland, and she was transferred to the Fortezza da Basso, leaving her children doubly orphaned at home. But then the grand duke's decrees were universally identified with a form of justice far superior to the logic of mere mortals. Famine and depression were invariably attributed not to the mismanagement of men, but to the wrath of God. The stringent regulation of courtship was held to be beneficial to public morality rather than an invitation to hypocrisy. And, strangely enough in the age of Colbert, no Tuscan ever dreamed that politics had anything to do with economics or that the state might be judged according to the material prosperity of its subjects.

Actually, this complacency was not completely unjustified. For the government of Cosimo III was certainly no worse, and probably somewhat better, than that of most other states at the time. The occasional exactions of troops, mules, money, and ships for the defense of Hapsburg outposts in Hungary and Venetian outposts in the Aegean was nothing compared to the wholesale conscription, the ruinous taxes, and the actual military devastation imposed upon much of France, Germany, and northern Italy during the wars of Louis XIV. Graft and corruption were kept to a minimum, as most foreign visitors remarked with amazement: indeed, one tiny indiscretion in the Salt Office led the grand duke's secret agents to track down the culprit right into the heart of the Veneto. Offices were filled by election or appointment, not by purchase or inheritance, as was customary elsewhere. Prostitutes were confined to the red-light district between the church of the Oratorian Fathers and Santa Croce, and small arms were prohibited on the streets, with no little benefit to the cause of public safety. And even though elections were controlled and appointments were made according to influence rather than merit, fees for administrative services were posted publicly to prevent the incumbents from fleecing those whom they were meant to serve. Princes, cardinals, and ministers had to pay the same customs duties as "the least of the inhabitants of the city," as the French ambassador was shocked to learn; and judges in the criminal courts were strictly enjoined to recognize no class distinctions among defendants or witnesses. The law may have been tangled, confused, and full of loopholes, in spite of the efforts of one industrious lawyer to make some sense out of them. Sometimes they were as ridiculous as they were unenforceable, as when they tried to prevent Jews in Livorno from frequenting Christian prostitutes. But at least no one was exempt from them. And at least they bore some relation to the lofty, if by then rather commonplace principles set forth in such documents as the *Instruction for the Captains . . . of the State of Siena,* published in 1671, and Ruberto Pandolfini's discourse to the Senate of 1682. The joke picked up by the German tourist Heinrich von Huyssen about the statue of Justice in Piazza Santa Trinita—that it had been put on top of the column to prevent the poor from climbing up to it—was obviously intended merely as a joke.

Thus Magalotti's treatise on *The Concord of Religion and Principality* was doomed to failure from the start. The sentences were often so complex that they failed to make sense even after several rewritings. The subjects were so scrambled about that any logical connection among them became imperceptible. The argument frequently got caught in blind alleys, most notably when a reference to the Holy Trinity almost made oligarchy, not monarchy, the best form of government. The only thesis that had any possible relevance to the problems of the day—the warning about excessive piety in princes—was quickly suffocated in a blanket of vague generalities. The concrete examples used to illustrate the theses were drawn from situations no less remote than King David's Israel, Emperor Arcadius's Rome, and that unattainable paradise of the Jesuit missionaries, China. The only authorities thought worthy of quotation were Aristotle, Jerome, Erasmus, François de Sales, and the Jansenist moralist Pierre Nicole, none of whom had much to say about the appointment of judges, the pardoning of criminals, or any of the other matters listed in the various drafts of the Table of Contents. Magalotti continued to work on the treatise for at least a year after his return to Florence. But he never managed to produce more than three rough chapters and a mass of scattered notes. Finally, he added a postscript—one which consigned all political philosophy to the realm of idle utopia-making. And he put the manuscript away—so carefully that it was not found again until the end of the nineteenth century.

By January 1678 Magalotti had given up all hope of finding a vocation abroad and was seriously thinking about going home. Florence, he knew, was now much less isolated than it once had been. By now other Florentines had picked up his taste for travel; and they could be counted on to follow his example in keeping their compatriots informed of their adventures. More foreigners were coming to Florence, which was now equipped with a new tourist guidebook, one properly stuffy pension, and two hotels—the Albergo di Monsù Massè and the Aquila Nera—respectable enough to accommodate the bastard sons of the kings of England and Denmark.

Florence was also a fairly comfortable city to settle down in. Its climate was sometimes rigorous. But its houses were built so that the inhabitants could move (like migratory geese, said Magalotti) from the first to the top floor and back to the mezzanine, according to the season. And since no one had yet heard of stoves, not to mention central heating, no one complained about the cold and damp. Similarly, hygienic conditions fell rather short of modern standards. Even a gentleman "of every good quality and refinement" like Niccolò degli Albizi felt no qualms about urinating right at the foot of Ponte Santa Trinita. And Magalotti let a pet goat wander freely about his house until it died from drinking the contents of a chamber pot, although he was sure the pot was not his, since "anything that comes out of my body, which contains such a beautiful soul, could not possibly be poisonous." But foreigners were amazed at the relative cleanliness of the streets, which were paved in such a way that the rain carried off the refuse instead of letting it stagnate. Above all, Florence was quiet, and hence particularly conducive to "the philosophic life" that Cardinal Leopoldo despaired of finding in noisy Rome. Even Regnier Desmarais admitted that he preferred Florence to Paris, where errands and courtesy calls took up more than half of each day.

Magalotti had no idea what he would try next. For this time what had begun as another crisis of vocation turned out to be a crisis of character as well. He was ambitious—without having enough energy to realize any of his ambitions. He was hard working—up to the moment when his work began to be troublesome as well as enjoyable. He was realistic—yet he soon let the defects obscure the merits in everything he took up. He was cordial and open-minded—as long as he did not have to accept as social equals many men he met who were of different social classes and backgrounds. Being an ambassador had the enormous disadvantage of making him subject to a mere bureaucrat in the Foreign Ministry, "a man," he insisted, "so insensitive to the touch of humanity . . . that he wouldn't get near his wife, if he had one, except from a purely rational decision to beget children." Worst of all, he suffered from two contrary weaknesses at the same time: egotism and indecision. In spite of pretending to be objective, he judged almost everything he saw solely by how it pleased or flattered him, never by how it served or satisfied others. And in spite of his efforts to avoid looking critically at himself, he had to admit that he was like "one of those reckless pilots in the Baltic, who sail about without map, compass, or any other guide than an eye for the north wind."

Thus suddenly, in May 1678, without asking the grand duke, without informing his friends, without even closing his house in Vienna, he came home. It was unreasonable, he explained to Redi, that "we Florentines be asked to stay for more than six months beyond the reach of the shadow of the Cupola."

4

How Magalotti became an art connoisseur, a lexicographer, a poet, and a literary critic

The weary traveler was glad to be back at Lonchio, his favorite villa outside Florence. The unpretentious house revealed the "not too much money of its founder" and "the very little money of its present owner"; but it occupied "the most marvelous piece of land that can be found within some hundred miles around." From the window of the main floor he could catch in one glance the mountains of Pistoia, the towers of Prato, and the whole "immense and formidable array of villas and habitations that encircle Florence . . . in a friendly, yea, obsequious siege." One row of cypresses followed a winding road to the main door. Another led upward past a series of small meadows interspersed with grape vines and clusters of pear and peach trees to a small secluded chapel. Two brooks gushed out of natural springs and broke into a "serenade for five voices" as they splashed down past the walls into an artificial pond. The house was high enough to catch the least westerly breeze, the *Ponentello,* during the summer, and to attract, in the early hours of the morning, the soft dew that descended, apparently, from the Milky Way. It was low enough to be hidden from the sun by the high hills on the other side until almost midday; and the contented proprietor could have his lunch served comfortably out-of-doors, instead of groping around, like his friends in the city, behind the tightly closed shutters of first-floor apartments.

It was indeed a pleasant life. There was solitude when he wanted it—long walks through the chestnuts and oaks and across the great stretches of bare rock with his favorite companion, Becar:

> Becar, my dog,
> my gentle tiger,
> my barking Iberian;
> Becar the true, the wise, the proud—
> of all the Spanish races,
> there is none like him.
> (*Canzonette anacreontiche,* p. 25)

There was company, too, when he wanted that—company in the city, just eight miles away through the Porta San Niccolò, where he could drop in at court or at an evening gathering without ever having really to become involved, and company in the country, where all of Florentine society that counted spent at least four months of the year. Rucellai was only a few hours away at San Casciano, and Giovan Battista Strozzi was only a few hours away at La Colombaia; and while going from one to the other, he could stop off and join Panciatichi in "reading, walking, killing thrushes, and eating enormous cabbages." There also was variety, for he could always move, when he felt like a change, to his other house at nearby Belmonte; and he could ride back to Mass at the Badìa a Ripoli along the banks of the river Ema.

It was an easy life. The ever-indulgent Cosimo soon forgave his truancy with a tidy little pension. His servants dressed and fed him. His secretary, Materno Collez, kept his correspondence in order. And his brother Lodovico took complete charge of all the administrative burdens of his estate: overseeing the tenants, repairing the water mains, planting the olive trees. It was a life, moreover, that fulfilled all the aspirations of the unsocial age he lived in for quiet, detachment, and timelessness:

> Mosquito, I pray you,
> your buzzing awakes
> the anguish, the torments
> that sleep from me takes.
> Begone with your noisome,
> importunate sounds,
> while dream's arms embrace me
> and stillness abounds
> (Carlo Dati, in Andreini, p. 55)

It was, finally, a life that Arcadia, the new literary movement just then being formed in Rome, was soon to decorate with shepherds and nymphs and raise to the level of a national ideal. Neither Pliny's Como nor St. Basil's Pontic vales had anything to compare with Lonchio—and neither, as the Florentine poet Benedetto Menzini could have assured Magalotti, did Tivoli and Tusculum. The traveler was tempted just to settle down and enjoy it.

Yet complete retirement soon turned out to have certain drawbacks. After a long, painful illness, and after giving away much of his salary in poor relief as commissioner at Volterra, Lodovico died, early in 1680; and Magalotti found himself not only with what proved to be a poorly kept account book, but also with the administration of an abbey belonging to his older brother, Alessandro, then a resident priest in Naples. Moreover, Lonchio and Belmonte were dangerously close to Florence. And as one gay party after another showed up unannounced just in time for dinner, Magalotti realized that he would have to exchange his suburban villas for the wilds of the Maremma if he wanted to be left alone. When, then, one of his friends told him frankly that "this retreat of yours does not please me a single bit" (*nè punto nè poco*), he recalled what Vincenzo da Filicaia had told the Crusca about its vacations:

> Blessed be your idleness; for it prepares
> works still more beautiful;
> and blest be rest: 'tis she who bears
> an offspring still more bountiful.
>
> (*Canzone* no. XIII)

He became conscious of what Regnier Desmarais was to warn him about several years later: "Sometimes living in solitude does nothing but give you more time to gnaw on yourself from within." And he at last conceded what he had vaguely suspected as soon as he returned from Vienna—that a bright, cultivated, charming man of slightly over forty simply could not do nothing at all. "It's a sin," proclaimed Regnier, paraphrasing the New Testament, "to hide under a bushel a lamp that should be placed in a candelabra."

The big question that had to be answered was just what to do. Getting married, or rather "assuring the perpetuation of the ancient and most noble stock of the Magalotti in Tuscany," as Redi put it, was one possibility. As his family's last available male heir, Magalotti had given some thought to matrimony as early as 1677, when Redi warned him of the possible negative effects of the cold Austrian climate on his virility. He even went so far as to contract a somewhat shady liaison with a certain Marchesa di Grana, who left him with a long list of errands to do every time she went out of town. The liaison soon became serious enough, in spite of his efforts to write it off as the invention of German scandal-mongers, to provoke a polite rebuke from the foreign minister. He thought of marriage once again after his return to Florence. His brother Alessandro found him a wealthy widow in Naples. By 1680 the negotiations he had opened with her guardians had proceeded far enough to involve the grand duke, the viceroy, the viceroy's wife, and the Tuscan ambassador in Madrid.

But Magalotti hesitated. Marriage in late seventeenth-century Florence had very few amenities. It had nothing to do with love: that sentiment had been reduced to such a purely poetic convention that not even the poets were permitted to experience what they wrote about—as Magalotti pointed out when Redi wondered whether his love poems were autobiographical. It had nothing to do with companionship, either. For women, according to Ricasoli Rucellai's interpretation of Plato, were endowed with beauty, not intelligence; the only woman at the time to receive a respectable education was kept carefully shut up in her house at Pisa. Above all, marriage had nothing to do with sex, except insofar as husbands were expected occasionally to perform their "duties." For sex as pleasure had been banished from the marriage bed and confined exclusively

to such places as the house of La Pisanella or the apartment of La Maiorchina—
the latter of which was located, appropriately enough, on the Via delle Pinzochere
("Bigots' Street") behind Santa Croce. This arrangement had the notable
disadvantage of letting gaiety degenerate into brawls. On August 7, 1688, Count
Giovan Francesco Dal Benino murdered Giulio Rucellai at La Pisannella's. On
May 20, 1670, a hotel keeper and a lumberjack murdered their rival, the son of
Senator Giorgio Tornaquinci, right in front of his house. On July 29, 1670,
Giovan Carlo Ricasoli Rucellai, a son of the philosopher Orazio, fatally wounded
his cousin Giovanni Alamanni, after a noisy chase around Piazza Santa Croce.
And neither he, nor La Maiorchina, nor any of the witnesses was indiscrete
enough to reveal any of the highly embarrassing details, even under torture.

Marriage was thus reduced to the role of a "prison," one from which,
according to Carlo Dati, probably the least unhappily married man of his time,
death alone gave freedom. It might bring in a dowry, but Dati still found that he
had to give up "more polite studies" and waste his talents in an "abhorrent"
silk business just to support his numerous dependents. Magalotti calculated that
the usual female extravagance would quickly wipe out the added revenue he
might expect even from his Neapolitan heiress. Marriage might also provide
offspring. But neither the Squarcialupi, nor the Sassetti, nor the Panciatichi, nor
the Viviani Franchi were particularly upset about the imminent extinction of
their families at the time—partly, perhaps, because the family as an institution
had lost much of its former political and economic importance, and partly because
it now frequently consisted of little more than a group of quarrelsome bachelors.
Indeed, most well-to-do Florentines were as bent upon limiting, if not eliminating,
their heirs as were their contemporaries in Venice. They put 44 percent of their
daughters into convents; the average age of those of their sons they permitted
(or ordered) to marry advanced from 29.38 years in the first half of the century
to 36.37 in the second. Hence Magalotti saw no real reason to jeopardize the
comforts and conveniences of a single life for purposes that almost no one regarded as worth while. He was not afraid of celibacy. He knew St. Luigi Gonzaga
and St. Filippo Neri had both won their crowns largely by observing vows of
"perpetual virginity"; and much of his behavior in the following years supports
his claim to have followed their example from 1678 on. At the same time, he
was shocked at the prospect of having to throw Becar off one side of the bed
just to make room for a jealous wife on the other. He therefore looked on
passively as one set of negotiations crumbled and a new set was begun. And finally
he broke them all off by telling the negotiators that he had become impotent.

Magalotti decided that he was better suited for some sort of intellectual
activity. He might have become interested in music. After all, music was still

one of the liveliest of the arts in Florence. Both Alessandro Scarlatti and Georg Friedrich Handel visited the city during the following decades. Francesco Nigetti was remembered long afterwards as one of the best organists and choirmasters ever to be appointed at the cathedral. Prince Ferdinando, "the Orpheus of princes," kept enough musicians on his payroll to supply an orchestra of a hundred pieces in 1687. And one of the instrument-makers he brought to Florence, a certain Bartolomeo Cristofori of Padua, eventually succeeded in transforming the harpsichord, not into one of Nigetti's multiple keyboards, but into a completely new instrument—one that later came to be called a *pianoforte,* or piano.

Magalotti might also have become a connoisseur of the visual arts. As early as 1664 he had been appointed to the commission charged with supervising the decoration of Palazzo Pitti; and from then on, right up until the year of his death, he made a point of getting to know all the practicing artists of the city. He put together a small private gallery of his own, and at least once—on his way to Vienna in 1675—he turned up at one of the big public auctions regularly held in Venice. Through Paolo Falconieri, that "great and cavalier master of all the arts," he learned the principles of architecture. Through Panciatichi he kept track of the current project to transform the ceiling of the Uffizi into "a

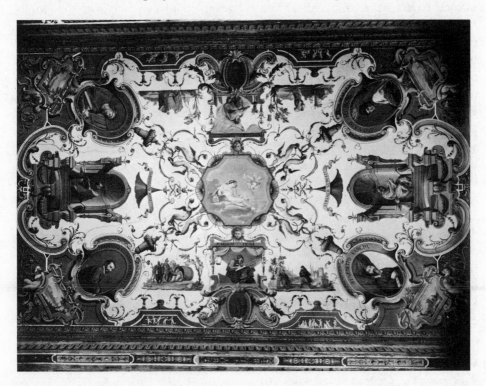

19. *The Philosophers,* ceiling in the Uffizi Gallery

universal history . . . of all rare talent that the city of Florence has produced in
the last four centuries." It may have been his advice that accounts for occasional
departures from traditional iconography in some of the thirty-one panels: for
instance, the inclusion of Varchi as well as Ficino among the "philosophers"
and the inclusion of Machiavelli among the "politicians" as well as among the
"historians" and the "secretaries." Indeed, Magalotti worked out two principles
that he consistently applied in all his critical judgments. Quality, he supposed,
was a function of clarity and rhetorical effect. Salvator Rosa's "Conspiracy of
Catiline" was a good painting because it represented the scene much more
forcefully than Sallust's narrative. And Cirro Ferri's "Miracle of San Zanobi"
was "marvelous" because the concept (*invenzione*), the background (*architettura*),
and the arrangement of the figures all enhanced the single impact on the viewer.

Yet Magalotti dared not commit himself to music. For one thing, he admitted
to being tone deaf. For another, all the interesting music of the time was performed
not by Florentines but by the foreign musicians whom Prince Ferdinando
recruited through the Tuscan diplomatic service. And it served the purpose not
of stimulating domestic creativity, but of magnifying the prince's Olympian
festivals at Pratolino—to which Magalotti was never invited. He dared not commit
himself to art collecting, either. For he never could compete with Leopoldo,
Louis XIV, all the cardinals in Rome, and all the princes in Italy whose standing
orders on the inflated international art market had pushed up prices far beyond
his means: 2,000 *scudi* for a single Domenichino, for instance, and 4,300 *scudi*
plus a rent-free house and a year's supply of grain, wood, and wine for a single
major project by Cirro Ferri.* He hesitated even to commit himself to art criticism.
For the current critical vocabulary was still limited to the same old Vasarian
adjectives, like "stupendous" and "marvelous," and to the same old platitudes
about *disegno,* color, and disposition that had been drained of meaning by generations of overuse. The one attempt to repeat Benedetto Varchi's experiment in
inducing a new vocabulary through a poll of the practitioners yielded only
technical information, not potential value judgments. The few attempts to arrive
at philosophical definitions of beauty succeeded no better than Rucellai's
definitions of substance in escaping the closed world of Platonic ideas. And no
one dreamed of deriving workable guidelines from such philosophical definitions—not even from those that bore the prestigious name of Antonio Bellori—
until the advent of Neoclassicism in the middle of the following century.

Art criticism had retreated into art scholarship, into the science of establishing
correct dates and attributions and of fixing the limits between one style and
another. And art scholarship, together with such amenities as the right to explore
the Duke of Mantua's treasuries and to attend weekend parties at Alessandro

* Supposing Galileo's annual salary of 1,200 *scudi* to be roughly equivalent to the $25,000
usually paid to holders of big-name chairs in modern American universities, Ferri's fee comes
to $89,500.

Valori's villa, might have tempted Magalotti had the field not already been completely taken over by one of the most meticulous scholars of the age, Filippo Baldinucci. Baldinucci was first of all an expert draftsman—so expert, in fact, that Emperor Leopold of Austria asked him to copy the Virgin of the Annunziata solely on the basis of what was said about the portraits he had made of the Valori family. He was also a tireless traveler; and his photographic mind enabled him to remember every line and every shape he had seen during the art-hunting trips he took up and down the peninsula as an agent for Cosimo III. He was a voracious reader as well; and his verbal memory enabled him to recall almost every word every artist had ever written in the many volumes of unpublished "artistic correspondence" that had recently begun to arouse the curiosity of aristocratic collectors. More important still, he was the curator of the grand duke's art archives. And the laborious process of cataloguing their chaotic contents finally convinced him that sketches and preliminary drawings were as important as the finished product in understanding a work of art. He forthwith set out to correct all the errors in Vasari, to identify scores of hitherto anonymous canvasses, and to rearrange the history of Italian art not according to individual biographies but to stylistic similarities among the artists. Thanks to the efforts of his equally diligent son, Francesco Saverio, his *Studies of the Professors of Drawing Since Cimabue* turned out to be so exact and so thorough that it is still used as an authoritative reference book by art historians.

Baldinucci's triumph as a scholar left the artists with little choice but to follow in the footsteps of their masters' masters. Bernini was still acclaimed as the last word in architecture; and Baldinucci joined the acclamation by accepting a commission from Queen Cristina of Sweden for the first full biography. Pietro da Cortona was still revered as an absolute authority in painting—partly, as Baldinucci admitted, because of the absence of any trace of "obscenity and ugliness" in his works. And even Magalotti prescribed meditation under his ceilings as the best way to train aspiring artists. Hence, Alessandro Gherardini dared depart from Cortona's concept of space only to the extent of making the clouds on his ceilings in Palazzo Giugni and Palazzo Corsini seem a bit more solid. Cirro Ferri dared depart from his cartoons for the unfinished rooms of Palazzo Pitti only to the extent of toning down his colors. And Anton Domenico Gabbiani, who succeeded in passing off what he copied as originals, dared vary what he had learned from Ferri in Rome only to the extent of admitting an occasional element from another of Magalotti's favorites, Carlo Maratta.

It never occurred either to the artists or to the patrons of the late seventeenth century that they would one day be charged with the responsibility of saving Florence from Roman baroque. No one objected when Giovan Battista Foggini, the most versatile sculptor and architect of the time, transformed the Feroni chapel at the Annunziata into a minor masterpiece of baroque decoration, with scores of stucco bodies wiggling up past twisted columns and windblown

20. Foggini, Capella Feroni, *Santissima Annunziata*

branches into a spiraled infinity. Certainly Cosimo did not object; for it was he who had sent Foggini to study under Ferri in Rome. Certainly Prince Ferdinando did not object, for he had especially admired the bust that Foggini had done of his uncle Leopoldo. Certainly none of the men of letters who regularly took part in the vivacious conversations at Foggini's Villa Mezzo Monte ever objected; for they knew he had read all the books prominently displayed on his shelves. Far from ostracizing him for his departures from Florentine tradition, they rewarded him with an unending list of orders and offices: two more statues in the Annunziata, a monument to Francis Xavier that Cosimo III shipped to Goa, a new altar for the Knights of Santo Stefano at Pisa, the direction of reconstruction at Poggio a Caiano, Pratolino, and the Laurenziana, and, in 1694, the position of first architect to the grand duke. Neither did anyone object when a whole team of painters and architects created an entirely baroque interior for the new convent of Santa Maria Maddelena de' Pazzi in Borgo Pinti. And everyone applauded when the Corsini family brought in the least Florentine of all contemporary baroque artists to do their chapel at the Carmine—Luca Giordano of Naples. Giordano was immediately commissioned to decorate the great hall in the Palazzo Medici, which the Riccardi had recently bought from the grand duke. When he there succeeded beyond all expectations in making the current members of the ruling family float upward from the clutters of allegorical landscape around the four sides, he was forthwith elevated to the rank of Cortona himself, not as an example for Florentines to shun, but as a model for them to imitate. And imitation became almost automatic when the skilled but unreflective Alessandro Gherardini set out to decorate the ceiling of San Marco without having made so much as a preliminary sketch: the originality of his work consisted simply in adding a few elements from Cortona and Salvator Rosa to the forms that had been indelibly engraved on his mind by Giordano.

Even those artists who seemed to resist contemporary fashions avoided making any commitment in principle. After all, ancient art, the source of inspiration for three centuries of their predecessors, had now been handed over to the antiquarians; and even Ottavio Falconieri failed to notice the aesthetic potentialities of the very unbaroque bas-reliefs he copied from a pyramid in Rome. Similarly, all Italian art between Cimabue and Cigoli was relegated to the category of mere anticipation of the "perfection" of art in the seventeenth century—even by Baldinucci, who admired Giotto largely for having done so much with so little. Finally, all non-Italian art was considered valuable only to the extent that foreign artists remembered what they had learned as students at Rome. And a translation of Roland Fréart's attempt to derive an aesthetic theory from the Romanized French painter Poussin was thought so uninteresting by the translator himself that it was not discovered until 1810. Hence, those architects who followed the original designs when they added a wing to the Pitti and when they extended the Palazzo Medici-Riccardi along Via Larga did so only to prevent one palace from looking like two. Those architects who toned down their Roman models in the facades of San Gaetano and Ognissanti did so only out of respect for the Cinquecento simplicity of the surrounding buildings. And the one painter who consciously returned to pre-Cortonesque Florentine traditions, Baldassare Franceschini ("Il Volterrano"), did so with such subtlety that his borrowings from Giovanni da San Giovanni in the Annunziata ceiling went unnoticed for another two centuries. Not until the 1690s did anyone think of complaining about twisted lines and broken arches; and the one who complained —Lorenzo Bellini—was a poet and an anatomist, not an artist. Not until the twentieth century did anyone become so infatuated with Quattrocento purism as to destroy the aesthetic unity of Foggini's masterpiece for the sake of a fresco that he, with equal indifference to unfashionable relics of the past, had once covered over. Florence, then, may have escaped the architectural diversity that was imposed upon most other cities between Turin and Palermo in the age of Filippo Juvara. But the credit belongs to its artists' innate sense of harmony and congruity rather than their aesthetic principles.

Thus the visual arts turned out to be either too imitative, or too expensive, or too demanding; and Magalotti decided to look for a vocation in the verbal arts instead. The *Saggi* had already established him as something of a prose stylist, one capable, that is, of making the most technical details attractive to a lay audience. The travelogs had then rid his writing of its earlier traces of grammar-book artificialities. And his extensive private correspondence had perfected his command of a literary genre—the "familiar letter"—which was both suited to his character and sanctioned by the lingering remnants of Renaissance humanism. The verbal arts, along with the natural sciences, constituted the one remaining field, besides natural science, in which Florence could still claim a certain supremacy over its neighbors. And when this supremacy was suddenly challenged, in the mid-1650s, by some of the foremost writers of Italy, Magalotti had not hesitated to come to the aid of Carlo Dati, the hard-working chairman of the Crusca's dictionary committee.

The challenge had been a particularly grave one. Daniello Bartoli, the brightest star among contemporary Jesuit authors, had complained bitterly about the "you-can't-say-that" attitude of Florentine linguists. Sforza Pallavicino, the acclaimed master of Italian literary elegance, had complained just as loudly about their refusal to accept Tasso as anything but an unrepentant prodigal son. And Ottavio Falconieri, the Crusca's unofficial representative in Rome, had warned that the rest of Italy was on the verge of secession from the Tuscan linguistic empire. If the Cruscans failed to respond to the increasingly urgent requests for a revision of the *Vocabolario* that were flooding Prince Leopoldo's mailbox, and if they acquiesced to the offer of a Dutch publisher simply to reprint the second edition, they would soon find their authority as arbiters of correct speech cut short at the borders of the grand duchy.

Unfortunately, the academy's plan of attack was so ambitious that it soon outran the patience even of its most dedicated members. The commission to refute the thesis that "in our language we have no writers on scientific and philosophical matters" ended up with no more than a long list of words which Magalotti and Vincenzo Capponi had extracted from the works of Galileo. The commission to bolster new definitions with a barrage of texts from more recent Florentine authors bogged down after the publication of the first volume of Carlo Dati's *Prose fiorentine* in 1661; and the remaining four volumes did not begin to appear for another seventy years. The commission to trace the derivation of all accepted words back to their Lombard, Gothic, French, Greek, and Arabic as well as their Latin origins was cut short by a communication from Ménages—a communication that contained not the offer of collaboration requested of him but the printed sheets of his own forthcoming *Origins of the Italian Language*. Hence, the academicians simply lapsed back into their usual round of gay dinner parties, mock orations, *débauches,* and *jeux*—occupations which *Il Sollevato* ("The Raised up"), as Magalotti called himself, found very enjoyable, but which the official historian of the Académie Française found unworthy of the *exercises d'esprit* of their colleagues on his side of the Alps.

But the Crusca was not permitted to shirk its responsibilities for long. Late in 1676 it was shocked to learn of the foundation of a rival "Academy of the Tuscan Language" in Turin by an ex-professor of the University of Pisa. Early in 1677 it adopted the more limited, and therefore more feasible, project presented by its new arch-consul, Francesco Redi, who by now was thoroughly bored with snakes and willing to try his hand at words instead. It accordingly abandoned to others the compilation of special dictionaries—like Giovan Battista Strozzi's *Observations on Writing and Speaking* of 1674, and like Filippo Baldinucci's still valuable glossary of artistic terms. And it agreed to concentrate solely on preparing a new edition of its standard *Vocabolario* of the Tuscan language.

Magalotti, who was just then beginning to have doubts about his career as a diplomat, was delighted when the news reached him in Vienna. He immediately sent in a couple of complimentary sonnets to be read at the forthcoming annual banquet. During the following summer he put together a lengthy memorandum on how to make the third edition far more useful and authoritative than the second. The vitality of the Tuscan language, he warned, was now being threatened not by Latin but by French; and no amount of joking about *Boelo* (Boileau) being barred from a Petrarchian Parnassus could save Tuscan from decline unless those who spoke it stopped fighting among themselves. In other words, what had been the private preserve of an elite in a single city would have to be elevated, like its rival, to the rank of an international language. He insisted, therefore, that the new dictionary be written for Indians, Lapps, Japanese, and Germans as well as for Florentines and Romans. He insisted that it codify modern Italian, which was the only language acceptable abroad, rather than Trecento Florentine, which not even modern Florentines spoke. He insisted that it admit all major Italian authors of the last century as normative, no matter where they came from and no matter how often they departed from previous standards of orthodoxy. And he insisted that it sanction the use of foreign expressions whenever native authors failed to supply one of equivalent force. Why, he asked, should Italians be obliged to "put a matter on the table" when the French could teach them to put it "on the carpet"?

Unfortunately, Magalotti soon discovered that his fellow Cruscans had neither the will nor the energy to adopt his recommendations. They completely missed the potentialities of Redi's own research into Provençal and Aretine dialect—partly, to be sure, because the study of dialects was still a hundred years ahead of the times, but also because Redi himself qualified it as "a joke." They failed to recognize Gabriele Fasano's attempt to transform Neapolitan into a literary language, even though Redi and Magalotti read his translation of Tasso with great interest. And they received comfort, not reproaches, from their correspondent in France, Regnier Desmarais, who was just then trying to block the normal development of French orthography and to impose his conservative grammar on the Académie Française. Magalotti was therefore happy to be excused from the endless committee meetings and the months of painful proofreading that he knew getting out a dictionary would require. And he was just as happy to be dissociated from what the third edition turned out to be after eleven more years of backbreaking labor: just an enlarged and better-documented version of the second. Its main purpose, he realized, was to amuse the grand duke with such trifles as the "unspeakable quantity of meanings [it distinguishes] in the verb *fare* ['to do, to make']." If it also managed to prolong the linguistic supremacy of Florence for another few decades, it did so only because some of the younger generation of non-Tuscan writers voluntarily abandoned the rebellious attitudes of their fathers. So Magalotti decided to let the critics rage and purists rant, to let the Crusca bar Gallicisms and the Académie Française banish Italianisms, and to let Tassoni take the place of Tasso as the prophet of the anti-Cruscans. He henceforth would follow his "marvellous penchant for the morbid qualities of this age" and throw in French, Spanish, English, and Portuguese expressions whenever he felt like it, without the slightest regard for "the severe honesty of our forefathers." While the lexicographers betrayed the language by freezing it, he would serve the language by using it.

As a would-be poet, Magalotti had the good fortune to be born into one of the least inhibited ages in the history of Florentine literature. Not since the death of Poliziano had poets been so free to write what and as they pleased. Not since the advent of Leonardo Salviati had they been so free to ignore the dictates of the philosopher-critics. Poetry had divorced itself as completely from poetics as art had from aesthetics. But unlike the artists, the poets were not bound by the models of the preceding generation; if they disliked the products of what one of them called "this depraved century," they could move back in time as far as Dante or Theocritus and abroad in space as far as London or Lisbon. They were not bound by Baldinucci's moral precepts either; if they chose not to elevate or edify, they could simply ridicule, delight, or entertain, without making the least apology. As long as they did their homework for the Crusca's committee-meetings, they were not even bound by the definitions they themselves wrote into the *Vocabolario*. For they knew as well as Redi that laziness, not conviction, accounted for their admittedly inadequate word lists. Indeed, they were bound by nothing but a single taboo: the one on sex. And since no one in that celibate, misogynist generation dared approach even the Song of Solomon without the protection of the heavy blinders of allegory, they willingly observed the taboo.

Thus the poets themselves set out to establish their own critical principles. They did so not in order to impose their authority on others and even less in order to revive their ancestors' quarrels about the relative merits of Ariosto, Tasso, and Marino. Rather, they did so in order to guide their own pens. They wrote no formal treatises: even Menzini's adaptation of Horace was considered more of a poem than an *ars poetica*. They addressed their compositions to none but the same small, select audience that read their scientific treatises—the same audience that showed up at Carlo Dati's soirées and Giovan Battista Strozzi's house parties at the *Colombaia*. Instead, they wrote hundreds of specific commentaries on each others' first, second, and third drafts; and they worked out their principles not in the order in which each one followed logically from its predecessor, but in the order in which each one emerged from a specific problem in a specific text. As a member of what Redi called "The Tribunal of My House," Magalotti gladly joined in this joint endeavor. The lengthy correspondence he carried on with Redi and Regnier Desmarais during the decade after his return from Vienna is ample evidence of the seriousness with which he accepted his charge.

Criticism, Magalotti decided, was an empirical discipline, just as much as physics and biology had been in the Cimento. Critical principles were to be found not in the works of Aristotle, Castelvetro, or Salviati, but in the works of the great poets of all ages and of all nations. Aspiring poets should begin by studying those who had succeeded in their art—not only Tasso, Della Casa, Luigi Alamanni, and the other poets generally read and appreciated in the seventeenth century but also Boccaccio, who was usually condemned as a "shameful author . . . of the ugliest kind of immorality," and even Dante, whom almost no one any longer understood. To encourage the poets in their studies, Magalotti had made a pilgrimage to "the blessed bones of the divine poet" at Ravenna in 1667. And to help them in their studies, he began a commentary on the *Divine Comedy,* a commentary which sought to overcome textual obscurities not by repeating Carlo Dati's patriotic exclamations, nor by reworking Francesco Ridolfi's geometrical gyrations, but by looking up Dante's own explanations in the *Convivio* and the *De Vulgari Eloquentia*.

Poets, then, should try to imitate the authors they had studied. They should not copy them, for even Petrarch wrote a few unfortunate lines, even Dante succumbed to "rancid scholasticism," and even Anacreon was capable of writing "bow, wings, and arrow" instead of "bow, arrow, and wings." But they should carefully adapt the forms the great poets had invented to new arguments and adopt their more felicitous expressions in new contexts. They should then seek to surpass their models. For "as long as we try [just] to imitate Petrarch, [Della] Casa, and Tasso, we will ... never manage to equal what we imitate; and as long as we limit outselves to imitation ... we will end up repeating the words of Michelangelo before Brunelleschi's Cupola: 'Like you, I want not; more than you, I cannot.'"* Obviously, originality was generally the result not of effort but of an infused "poetic spirit" (*fato*); and probably few poets could ever rise to the level of Redi, who, as "a citizen ... not a guest ... in Parnassus, [had] crossed the confines of the old world and no longer needed either a compass or the north wind" to guide him. But originality could at least be prepared for by following the general rules implicit in the works of those who had achieved it.

The first rule was clarity. Giovan Michele Milani's *On Light* was good because "it expounds all modern and ancient philosophy with miraculous clarity." Menzini's verse portraits were good because they were more true to life than Sustermans' oil portraits. And some of Magalotti's sonnets were bad because Redi's cook, the only judge with appellate jurisdiction over the "Tribunal," failed to understand them when they were read to her the first time. The second rule was propriety. Pagan deities were obligatory in dithyrambs, but they were forbidden in religious verses, Sannazzaro notwithstanding. For poetry, like Cimento science, had to be kept strictly isolated from religion, as even the theologians admitted in submitting their poems to the judgment of the poets. And it may have been Milton's error in mixing Virgil with Moses that led Magalotti to abandon his translation of *Paradise Lost* after the first canto. The third rule was veracity: Redi was warned not to put "poisoned arrows" into the hands of undisciplined cupids until he had checked on how they were actually used by the natives of Java. The fourth rule was naturalness: Filicaia's *The Sacrifice* earned Redi's praise as "the best thing written ... between Guittone and the present day" because of the unforced manner in which it expressed "the most robust concepts." The fifth rule was rigorous balance in rhyme and meter: Magalotti was forced to give up his harsh alliterations (*acciocché in cuor*) and his confusion of pure vowels and dipthongs (*fuore* and *esteriore*), even though the

* That is, "I do not wish to do one exactly the same as yours, but I am unable to do one that is any better."

words fitted perfectly the sense of his poem. The sixth, and final standard was significance: "I cannot approve," said Magalotti," the maxim of those . . . who hold quality . . . to consist more in the way a thing is said than in the thing itself. Nor am I pleased by . . . a sentiment that floats on elocution like a rowboat on the sea."

Magalotti was sure of the validity of his rules. Whenever he put them into practice in the one form of literature in which he could count on the aid of his *fato*—namely, discursive essays and descriptive letters—he succeeded very well. He learned how to lighten heavy arguments by interspersing in the exposition successive episodes of an amusing anecdote. He learned how to hammer in an important thesis by recapitulating it in patterns familiar to his readers—as in this adaptation of St. Paul:

Are you witty? They were witty too. Are you learned? So were they.

He learned how to put complex matters in the form of a simple dialogue:

Spiritus Domini ferebatur super aquas. What's this Spirit you ask? If it's God himself, then we're attributing local motion to God. And that won't do. . . . Well, well, you say: it's not true. As for me, I reply, I don't understand. But then we have to understand.

He learned to reinforce a thesis with long sentences—sentences which jumped back and forth from the elevated to the familiar, which made use of all the potentialities of Italian subjunctives, accrescitives, diminutives, *vezzeggiativi,* and *spreggiativi,* and yet which held together, line after line, in accordance with an impeccable but carefully disguised logic. He learned to be elegant and flowery, to the point of frustrating the efforts of modern language historians to classify him as a Galilean purist. And he also learned to write, when the occasion demanded, just as he spoke, "in pieces and mouthfuls, without observing any order whatever." Finally, he learned to dissolve the last barrier between author and audience and to associate with those who heard him on a level of complete equality. If they would not waste their time pedantically checking the Vulgate text of Genesis 1:2, neither would he; after all, the incorrect word, *Domini,* got his meaning across as well as the correct word, *Dei.* As a prose writer, Magalotti admitted to only one fault: his execrable handwriting, which, he insisted, could be read, rather than deciphered, only with the help of necromancy. He therefore took care to have his secretaries copy out everything destined for more than two eyes—a category which, unfortunately, constitutes only a small part of his extant writings today.

When he tried to apply his rules to imaginative prose ficiton, his *fato* deserted him, and he got stuck at what he himself had called the pre-creative state: that of mere imitation. Trying to imitate Boccaccio in an age when no one any longer seemed to have possessed the equipment necessary for falling in love—Magalotti's

---

* "The spirit of God was stirring above the waters" (Gen. 1:2, Confraternity version).

seppur tutti . . . innamorati sono ("Although all are in love") notwithstanding—produced a ridiculously emasculated *Decameron,* one in which the handsome lover realizes his folly before gaining his shameful objective and lives ever after in perfect Platonic harmony with the old husband and the young wife. When, on the other hand, Magalotti tried to apply his rules in verse, he was somewhat less unsuccessful. He had had plenty of practice as an adolescent under the exacting guidance of Agostino Coltellini, the mentor of the Accademia degli Apatisti. He had had even more practice as a young man, when he presented the Sapphic verses of Ascanio Piccolomini, the archbishop of Siena, at Dati's Sunday soirées. He had composed a farfetched comparison of Saturn engendering rings and the grand duchess getting pregnant that was as pleasing to the tastes of the 1650s as it was to be incompatible with the standards of his more mature years. From then on he managed to turn out as many as two sonnets and one *canzone* a week whenever, as he put it, his muse had an attack of diarrhea.

Most of his compositions were free adaptations of ancient or foreign poems —of the Psalms and Lamentations, of John Philip's *On Cider,* of Saint-Evremond's *Idea of a Woman Who Has Not Yet Been Found and Never Will Be,* and, last but not least, of Anacreon, the latest fruit of the quest for adaptable Greek models, who was Tuscanized by no less than four Florentines as well as by one Italophile Parisian, "The glorious swan on the Seine," Regnier Desmarais. But some of Magalotti's compositions were largely original: for instance, the delicate stanzas of his *Butterfly,* the charmingly alliterated verses of his *On a Pearl*:

> la battuta
> combattuta
> candidetta pellegrina.

and the heavy periods of his own contribution to that favorite of all themes, the liberation of Vienna from the Turkish siege.

Unfortunately, very few of these lines came up to the author's own standards. The love poems amounted to nothing but watered-down paraphrases of Petrarch, without the slightest reference to Magalotti's own experiences or his own frustrations. They turned a suggestive "short life" into a meaningless "certain death":

> Poiché la morte è certa,
> e lo spirto vien meno all'alta impresa.*

They turned Laura's eyes, which had sent Petrarch into a cloud of introspection, into Emilia's hands, toward which Magalotti remained coolly indifferent:

> Oh man leggiadra, ove 'l mio ben alberga.

---

* "Since death is certain, and the spirit falters before the high undertaking."

And they turned love into a surgical operation performed by a bandit cupid with an alliterated knife:

> E tratto il cor tra palpitante e morto,
> il pongo in mano al masnardier malnato.*

Similarly, his religious poetry did nothing but water down the Vulgate with a shower of unnecessary verbiage. Four words in the Magnificat:

> Et exultavit spiritus meus†

became six lines, with nothing but padding in between:

> Quindi il sopito, e morto
> *mio spirito,* ebro, ed assorto
> nell'essenza infinita,
> ch'è mar di luce, e vita,
> e che in se stessa si riposa, e stagna,
> d'alto *piacer si bagna,*

and with the forceful "exults" diluted into "bathing in pleasure." Although Redi consoled him with a flattering comparison to Chiabrera, his *Magnificat* was far inferior to the scriptural paraphrases by the two best religious poets of the age, Ludovico Adimari and Vincenzo Capponi. Finally, his attempt at an *Italia mia* merely repeated the long-forgotten context of Petrarch's original. It contained not a word of genuine remorse for what a half-century earlier was still occasionally mourned as the loss of Italian independence. It contained not the slightest echo of Magalotti's own observations on the homeland of the current lords of half of Italy, the Spanish. And it failed to approach even the vapid treatment of the same theme which Vincenzo da Filicaia unwittingly bequeathed to the grade-school anthologies of the late nineteenth century.

Magalotti did not even try to write satires, since they would have required a pen as mordant, and a character as ungovernable, as that of poor Benedetto Menzini, whom Redi's occasional handouts kept from starving between one precarious job and the next. He did not try to write comedies, either—partly because Adimari already kept the Florentine stage well supplied with superficial intrigues, and partly because the more successful comedies, like those of Giuseppe Giacomini and Andrea Moniglia, required the support of music, which lay beyond his competence. He was even less tempted to write tragedies. For he knew that Florentine audiences would not stand for the elevated tone that was

---

* "And drawing forth my heart, still beating but almost dead, I place it in the hand of the ill-born bandit."

† "And my spirit rejoices [in God my Savior]."

The other passages are really not worth translating. The italicized words in Magalotti's version are the only ones that correspond to those in the Latin original.

an essential element of the great tragedies then being produced in France; and he gladly left the task of adulterating ancient tragedy to Redi's Venetian friends, Carlo de' Dottori and Cardinal Giovanni Delfini. Magalotti showed no more interest in the theater after his return to Florence than he had while living in London and Paris. He never attended any of the dramatic spectacles put on by the Corsini in their garden at Porta al Prato. He never set foot in the new theater that Ferdinando Tacca built in Via della Pergola in 1656 and that Prince Ferdinando remodeled in 1688. He never dreamed that its construction was to mark the first step in the transition of an aristocratic and courtly into a popular and commercial form of art.

In spite of his misgivings, Magalotti was called upon to participate—along with all the other men of letters in Florence—in the creation of the greatest minor masterpiece of the age, Francesco Redi's witty, polished, delightful *Bacco in Toscana* ("Bacchus in Tuscany"). But as successive drafts of the manuscript circulated among the studios of the city, and as Redi kept adjusting the text to introduce a reference to one more fame-starved member of the Italian Republic of Letters, it soon became apparent that poetry, for Magalotti, could never be anything but a pastime. Bacchus mounted his throne at Poggio Imperiale and began his enchanted monologue—so musical in words alone that it needed no musical accompaniment. He tasted one wine and then another, carefully following a map of Tuscany in order to miss none of them. He became excited in a string of short lines:

> Accusato
> tormentato
> condannato
> sia colui che . . .*

and then more rational in a series of long lines. He tasted the sweet *Mammolo*:

> che colà imbottasi
> dove salvatico
> il MAGALOTTI in mezzo al Solleone
> trova l'autunno . . .†

He mixed up his words and jumped from Brindisi, the sea port in Puglia, to *brindisi,* "a toast!" He lapsed into ecstatic inebriated nonsense:

> Arianuccia, leggiadribelluccia,
> cantami un po',

---

* "Accused / tormented / condemned / be he who . . ."

† "that there is put into a barrel, where, like a man of the wilds, / Magalotti in the heat of the summer sun / finds autumn"—which is exactly the same way in which Magalotti himself described life in his villa.

> cantami un po',
> cantami un poco, e ricantami tu
> sulla viò
> sulla viola la cuccurucù,
> la cuccurucù
> sulla viola la cuccurucù.*

Finally, staggering forward with a raised cup, he promulgated his verdict: "Montepulciano of all wines is king!" And as the collaborators and petitioners searched for concrete evidence of their election to immortality in the thirty-odd pages of footnotes that accompanied the text, the festive Baccanti broke into a frolicking dance and the satiated satyrs stretched out on the warm grass for a deep snooze.

Magalotti could only conclude, as he watched the *Bacco* go to press, that "I am no poet, as you well know." But he had already begun to wonder why he or anyone else wrote poetry at all. I compose, he told Paolo, "for the same reason you do . . . : at times to amuse myself, and at times to cure my brain of an itch." None of his friends could give him a much better answer. Adimari wrote, apparently, only to cultivate his own religious spirit; for almost no one could have afforded to pay for the huge margins and expensive plates that adorned his published books. Francesco de Lemene and Carlo Maria Maggi, the only two non-Tuscan poets whom Redi and the critics of the next generation were willing to admit to the Tuscan school, wrote, more often than not, simply to remind the other of a hat left behind at his house. And Redi himself wrote "not as a professional poet, but [only] to kill time while I'm on a vacation or at court or when I don't feel like working." Even glorifying a great monarch, which was the only real reason Regnier Desmarais could think of for writing poetry, was completely inapplicable to Tuscany. The closest approximation of this reason Magalotti could come up with was the same one proposed for all the other disciplines he had looked into: the amusement of the grand duke.

Poetry, and creative literature in general, got caught in the same dilemma that had afflicted the sciences: a lack of purpose. It had not occurred to the scientists that their methods and discoveries might eventually be used to improve the material well-being of their fellow citizens. And it never occurred to any of the poets that their sonnets and odes might be prescribed as an antidote to Marinism, as they were within a few years by the theorists of the Arcadian movement, and as they have been by literary historians ever since. But Magalotti went right on writing anyway. In fact he, as well as Redi, Menzini, and Filicaia,

---

* "Ariana," of course, is Bacco's female companion; *leggiadribelluccia* is another one of those run-on words that had been popular among the poets of Galileo's generation. The rest of the stanza is onomatopoeic nonsense involving the sound of Ariana's voice, of violas, and of bird chirping, and cannot be translated.

were among the first Italians outside of Rome to join the Roman Arcadia and to encourage the foundation of Arcadian "colonies" all over the peninsula. For Magalotti now had a purely personal reason for writing, one that he dared not confess to anyone. He had discovered that poetry served very well as a cover-up for what he was sure, after 1682, was to be the vocation he had so long been searching for: theology.

5

How Magalotti became a theologian

Theology could have been an important subject in late seventeenth-century Florence, for it might have served as a guide to the numerous expressions of popular piety. Religion took up much of the spare time of most of the citizens. Many of them belonged to confraternities, like the Company of the Good Death at San Giovannino. And that meant daily Masses and examinations of conscience, weekly offices before a privileged altar, monthly general communions "to be applied toward a good death," and, on several occasions, a pilgrimage on foot to as far as Rome or Loreto. Many of the citizens' wives belonged to female congregations, like the Company of San Pio at San Marco. That meant raising money for the decoration of poor country churches, making peace among friends, reciting a Pater every time a viaticum bell sounded, and then recording another seventy-day indulgence for each one of these good works. Many of the citizens' sisters belonged to religious orders. That meant following a constant round of exercises in imitation of the current model of feminine religiosity, the late sixteenth-century mystic, Maria Maddalena de' Pazzi, who was canonized in 1670. At least once, these exercises succeeded in their aim. Camilla Strozzi (Suor Maria Minima) had reacted to her stepmother's mistreatment by getting a religious vocation while still a child. She had then responded to her father's announcement of an imminent engagement by getting seriously ill. And once safely inside the Carmelite convent in which Maria Maddalena had once lived, she was rewarded for her sufferings with visions of the devil, who climbed into bed with her in the form of "a horrible bear"; with an incurable wound in her breast; and with the privilege of receiving communion from the hand of an angel.

Religion provided the chief source of public instruction. So highly was this function regarded that the opening of a new series of sermons was usually announced by a festive reception for the preacher at the city gates and by a magnificent procession of all the civil and ecclesiastical dignitaries through the streets. Religion also provided the chief source of public charity. It was the gentlemen of the Congregation of San Giovanni Battista who kept the unemployed from starving, by personally distributing rice and bread in the sections of the city assigned to each of them, during the frequent years of economic crisis and high food prices. Finally, religion provided the chief source of public entertainment. Aside from the regularly celebrated holy days, hardly a year passed without several days of processions, Te Deums, and mass communions in honor of a newly discovered or newly donated relic: the bodies of St. Mauro, St. Cosimo, and St. Victor the Martyr in 1663, the bones of St. Crespinus in 1669, the crucifix that had bowed to St. Giovanni Gualberto in 1672, and the miraculous Madonna outside Porta Pinti, which attracted a crowd of some two thousand on May 17, 1682.

Theology might also have served to correct some of the more obvious abuses of contemporary religious life. It might have warned the casuistic monks of the Annunziata against trying to make a single votive Mass count for the hundred they had been paid to say. It might have cautioned the bishops of Fiesole and Florence against letting their jurisdictional feuds degenerate into open battles, as they did in 1685, when the two bishops had each others' proclamations ripped off the walls of disputed parish churches. It might have checked the tendency of some sermons to follow the pattern of a Prato fair, "where horses, mules, dried chestnuts, wool cloth, and herbs are all displayed for sale, [and] where the Holy Girdle is exposed on one side of the piazza while Pasquariello sings the tarantella on the other." It might have saved some preachers from the kind of practical jokes played on one of them during a party at the Corsini gardens: after he had pronounced another of his usual "trivial conceits for old women," a hidden trapdoor on the lecture platform suddenly opened up, and he found himself upside down in a pond. If properly applied to the real moral problems of the day, theology might have spared some well-intentioned laymen from the barbs of the Sienese playwright Girolamo Gigli, who adapted Molière's *Tartuffe* to a Tuscan setting for their correction. It might have moderated the misdirected zeal of a certain Anton Maria Vannini, who spent five hours on his knees in church each morning, who spent most of each afternoon berating whores, gamblers, beggars, and merchants, and who was rewarded for reciting the rosary in a loud voice on street corners with insults and pellets from disrespectful urchins. And it might have prevented piety from withering, as it all too often did, into uncharitable bigotry:

> When once my conscience still was free
> of scruples and calculation;
> then sharp-tongued malice did I flee,
> by natural inclination.

But now that bigotry's taken hold,
and long-faced piety I show,
I can't but bite and carp and scold
at those whose impious acts I know.
    (Magalotti to Redi, August 26, 1673)

But contemporary theologians declined to accept any of these tasks. And it never occurred even to Magalotti that theology had anything to do with the church, just as it had never occurred to him that political philosophy had anything to do with the state. Magalotti knew as well as Rucellai that the court of Rome was truly "the theater of the world"—one where "everyone disguises himself as something other than what he really is." But he had no intention of criticizing a system that served him, and all other prominent Florentines, so well; and he was only "sorry" about the cardinals who scandalized two visiting French Benedictines in 1685 by playing cards during a conclave. He knew as well as Pope Alexander VII that the charitable activities of the confraternities really did little but encourage poverty among the beneficiaries, and that only jobs, not doles, could give the poor a sense of dignity and thus enable them to solve a problem that no one else had yet been able to solve for them. But he never lifted a finger to implement the plan he translated from a French text on commission for the grand duke—a plan proposed by the city of Montaubon for replacing private with public charity and turning the poor into productive citizens. He knew that "indulgences by the caseful" and "pardons shot about like bullets" served only to devaluate the church's spiritual treasury. But he could not condemn the Jesuits for prescribing such exterior practices as a corrective for the excessively interior piety of the preceding half century. And he could not deny that one of Magliabechi's indulgence charts had at least the advantage of freeing Florentines from the attempts of a few old-fashioned preachers to evoke piety through fear. "The horrible torments of the martyrs" may still have been "a mere shadow compared to the sufferings of just souls in purgatory." But with indulgences so plentiful, almost no one had to worry any longer about purgatory at all; and Magalotti's theological adviser prudently advised him to leave the whole subject out of his polemical pamphlets.

Magalotti had still a better reason for avoiding a critical examination of the institutions and practices of religion in his day: his conviction that nothing was basically wrong with them. Lacking even the rudiments of a historical perspective, he could not imagine either going back to something better in the past or going forward to something better in the future; what he heard about current proposals for ecclesiastical reform in France simply confirmed his belief in the superiority of the least bad of all possible worlds that he was used to at home. Moreover, the piety of his learned friends was not sufficiently different from the piety of the unlearned to permit it to be used as a standard of judgment. The interminable "religious lectures" in the Crusca were no less padded with meaningless exclamations that the average sermon at San Lorenzo. And Magalotti's own lectures were no exception to the rule:

> Oh fleeting goods of this world! Oh truly frail happiness, subject to the vicissitudes of the human heart! Oh voluble aspirations! Oh mere shadow of pleasure—the source of bitterness, not joy, of trouble, not repose, of worry, not contentment!

Similarly, Redi's veneration for the Madonna of Montenero was no less sincere—for all his jokes about it—than the ordinary Florentine's belief in the power of the crucifix at San Jacopo in Via Ghibellina to stop rain. And even the best theologians had trouble finding real problems toward which they might direct their critical zeal. One of them was left with nothing better to do than devise a prayer for people who found themselves without a confessor at the moment of death. Another devoted pages simply to proving that priests could smoke in a sacristy without danger of mortal sin—providing that they kept the smoke out of the church, and providing that they did not "expel excrement from their bodies or heads." Like them, Magalotti concluded that the few blemishes of the Florentine church could safely be overlooked—or rather, as Steno put it, that the weeds in God's garden should be left alone lest some of the grain be pulled up with them. He agreed with Steno that Florence was, its blemishes notwithstanding, the holiest city in all Europe.

Indeed, almost all of Magalotti's compatriots were fully persuaded that Florence had come as close to being a New Jerusalem as was possible in this imperfect world. The Florentine Jerusalem was strictly Catholic in doctrine; not even the cosmopolitan Magalotti was willing to support his resident Anglican friends, a few years later, in their request for permission to hold private religious services. But within the bounds of Catholicism, it was much less monolithic than either its predecessor in the age of Savonarola or its successor in the age of Scipione de' Ricci, in the 1780s. It carefully avoided a commitment to any contemporary school of ecclesiology, whether Gallican or Papist. Even though the grand duke prided himself on having been made a canon of St. Peter's during a Holy Year pilgrimage in 1700, he did not hesitate to defend the autonomy of his civil courts from interference by the Inquisition and the validity of his relics from the doubts of a Roman congregation. The Florentine Jerusalem also carefully avoided a commitment to any current school of theology. While Cosimo showered money on the Jesuits' College of San Giovannino, he appointed as state theologian none other than Enrico Noris, whose Augustinian sympathies were anathema to the society. And he permitted his more learned subjects to go on discussing all the authors—from Paolo Sarpi to Cornelius Jansenius—who had been included in his uncle Leopoldo's heterogeneous reading list.

What really convinced Florentines that they had achieved this lofty goal was the great number of their fellow citizens who succeeded in qualifying as religious heroes, or as what were then considered to be religious heroes. The most conspicuous of them was the grand duke himself: Cosimo's "exemplary piety" was constantly commended by the papal nuncio, and it was universally applauded by his subjects, who almost never saw him except when he was accompanying a religious procession about the city on foot. Bishop Gherardi of Pistoia was almost as conspicuous: when he finally killed himself by preaching all through December of 1689 with a high fever in the ice-cold cathedral, huge crowds surged into his house to see how a saint passes into the next life. So was Federico Giannetti, rector of a parish at Sesto Fiorentino, canon of San Lorenzo, spiritual director of the convent of Santa Caterina in Via delle Ruote, and professor of moral theology at the university. When Giannetti died, his body had been so purified by the hair shirts and chains found in his room that—according to one witness—not a single fly dared to alight on it during the two and a half days before the burial.

The most famous of the heroes was none other than the Jesuit preacher Paolo Segneri, whose oratorical skill is still recognized in modern anthologies of Italian literature. From the moment God first spoke to him in 1663, Segneri constantly exercised his ingenuity in finding new ways of effecting his dedication to poverty, penance, and prayer. He "gave himself the discipline" three times a day, with little pins stuck in the whip to augment the flow of blood; and whenever he could find a collaborator, he had himself tied to a post and beaten (like Christ at the Scourging) until he fainted. In the winter, he recited psalms stark naked next to an open window. In summer, he threw himself into rose bushes, hung himself for hours by the hands, and slept on a table in a nail-studded gunnysack. And he still managed to walk some three hundred miles barefoot each year from one sensational preaching mission to the next.

Religious heroism knew no bounds of sex, age, or national origin. One of its models was a woman: Lavinia Felice Cenami Arnolfini, the wife of the ambassador from Lucca, who mortified her flesh by wearing a hair shirt and spiked stockings under her party dresses. One was an aristocratic man of letters: Luigi Strozzi, who strove to "purify all [his] actions" by examining his conscience four times a day, taking a two-week retreat once a year, and observing six hours of silence on each of a dozen saints' days. One was an art critic and historian: Filippo Baldinucci, who cured his headaches and resisted the temptations of the devil by abandoning himself completely to the will of God—even to the point of suppressing his love for his children. One was a foreigner: the naturalized Danish scientist Nicholas Steno. He had been so impressed by the sight of a Corpus Domini procession in 1666 that he went right to the Laurenziana Library to look up the relevant passages in the Greek New Testament. He then learned from Magalotti how to distinguish between the essence and the externals of Catholicism, and he learned from a nun named Maria Flavia Del Nero about the horrible fate of all Protestants in the next world. Soon after his conversion, in November 1667, he began the theological studies that were soon to qualify him for an appointment as instructor in religion, as well as in science, to the royal princes. In 1677 he was consecrated a bishop *in partibus* and sent off as a missionary to northern Germany. And from 1955 on, his sanctity, as well as his learning, have been abundantly commemorated by the republication of all his works, by the edition of several volumes of scholarly studies devoted to him, and by the foundation of a periodical bearing his name, the *Stenoniana Catholica*.

In the anticlerical nineteenth century, many of these practices would be denounced as an unnatural renunciation of human sentiments; and in the post-Freudian twentieth century they may look like manifestations of masochistic tendencies. But in the seventeenth century they were commended as worthy of universal emulation, even by the crusty old scientist, Borelli, who eventually placed a sacred image over his bed and began attending daily Mass. And they were commended by Magalotti, too. Magalotti was no novice in theology, after all. He had studied enough of the church fathers to help Dati pick out literary references in Tertullian. He was well enough versed in the Old Testament to assist Vincenzo Capponi in composing his scriptural commentaries. And he was familiar enough with the New Testament to write a preface to a translation of Cornelius Jansen's *Concordia Evangelica,* one of the best works of late sixteenth-century biblical scholarship. Magalotti was no novice in the practice of piety, either. He recited the clerical office every day. He regularly meditated upon the many spiritual manuals he had sent to him from Spain, particularly on those that were "written with gracious simplicity . . . and speak directly to the heart." It is thus not surprising that the failure of his most recent search for a vocation should have led him to religion—and to a reconsideration of certain problems that had first occurred to him during his second trip to England, over a decade before.

One of these problems had already been solved: the problem, that is, of how so upright and learned a man as Robert Boyle, to whom he had addressed an open letter in 1672, could still adhere to an imperfect creed. For by now Magalotti had read extensively in Luther and Calvin, and he recognized the basic Catholicism of most Protestant doctrine. He had also read Saint-Evremond, and he had come to appreciate at least some of the current efforts aimed at reunifying the churches. He had discovered that most of what Anglicans held against Catholics was the result of misinformation, and that most of what Catholics found inadmissible in Anglicanism could easily be removed by references to the Anglicans' own theological authorities. To be sure, it never occurred to him that his argument was vitiated from the start by his inability to regard non-Catholics as members of legitimate institutions. There was only one true church, he thought; and reconciliation was merely a matter of bringing individual stray sheep back to the fold. But neither could he have anticipated changes in Catholic ecumenical thought that were still two centuries away, nor could he have remained untouched by the current wave of optimism in Catholic Europe. Several very prominent "stray sheep" had recently been converted—a high official Steno had met in the Dutch government, the historiographer of the Académie Française, and, most prominent of all, the queen of Sweden. And the conversion of all England was ardently, if groundlessly, expected upon the accession of the Catholic king, James II. When, in the early 1680s, Magalotti found that both Protestants and Catholics were faced with the same frightening enemy—atheism—he was sure of being able to knock down the last barrier that separated them. All he had to do was convince Protestants that they, albeit unwittingly, had been largely responsible for engendering the enemy; they would then immediately rush for refuge to the sole bastion of what was, after all, their faith as well as his.

There were probably no real atheists, either secret or professed, in the whole of Italy at the time. But everyone thought there were. Or at least many Italians still worried about their country's reputation abroad as a seminary of incredulity; and some of them had heard enough about the scurrilous novels of certain Venetian aristocrats to be moderately frightened by an occasional pulpit tirade against them. One such tirade had dwelt so much on what it was supposed to condemn that it was put on the Index soon after its appearance in 1665. That was *The Atheist Convinced by Reason Alone* of a certain Filippo Maria Bonini, whom Magalotti may have run into during one of his trips to Rome. Another such tirade was just then in preparation: a point-by-point catechism aimed at an ill-defined *Inexcusable Unbeliever* ("L'incredulo senza scusa"), which Paolo Segneri dedicated to Prince Gian Gastone de' Medici in 1690. Still another, Benedetto Menzini's *Tenth Satire,* had won acclaim both for its literary qualities and for the vagueness with which it described its hypothetical hero:

> Who's been so hardened by his ill deeds
> that nothing's left but doubting creeds
> and laughing at Eternity.

Magalotti realized that Italian atheism was largely the invention of Italian anti-atheists, and he wisely refrained from even mentioning Giovanni Francesco Loredan, Ferrante Pallavicino, or any of the other standard villains of his generation. After all, even Segneri traced atheism not to Italians but to travelers returning from abroad, thus inaugurating a tradition of Italian theological xenophobia that was to last right down until the belated translation of the Dutch Catechism at the end of the 1960s. But Magalotti knew that atheism was indeed a real problem in northern Europe. He had encountered it himself in the conversations of courtiers, in the satires of that most profligate of all courtiers, John Wilmot, Second Earl of Rochester, in a book he had picked up in Augsburg, and in the works of the anti-atheists of France and Germany.

Atheism, Magalotti discovered, was not a philosophy or even a doctrine. It was rather an attitude and a way of life, one which under the cloak of a religious creed professed "complete indifference in all matters of religion." It was seldom expounded explicitly: "those closed-mouthed Brutuses and Cassiuses are the ones who trouble me," he confessed; "for they keep quiet in their misbelief; and instead of arguing, they just laugh." Atheism was spread about not from pulpits or lecture platforms but in "the academy of women and good food and in the mysterious meetings at the home of My Lady N.N." Its chief motivation was moral, or rather amoral: "you need account to no other tribunal than yourself," he noted; "you have no law other than the law of convenience." Finally, it accorded very well with the usual life-style of the European aristocracy of the day. "You are loved by your patron, esteemed by your generals . . . courted by the ladies, and (what is most important of all) . . . little troubled by your wife. You eat and drink merrily. You come home at two in the morning. And to bring on sleep you read a chapter of [Spinoza's] *Tractatus Theologico-Politicus* or [Hobbes's] *Leviathan*."

Yet the atheists occasionally sought to justify this attitude by appealing to theoretical arguments. Some of them went back to Aristotle; and after depriving the Unmoved Mover of the power to create or legislate, they pretended to be as scandalized by stories of his incarnation as the king of Sweden had been on hearing that "un si grand homme que monsieur le Cardinal [Richelieu] s'amuse parfois à dire la messe."* Some of them went back to Lucretius, and accordingly turned spirit into matter and the universe into a fortuitous concourse of atoms. Most of them professed one or another version of the age-old "imposter" thesis; they accordingly accused Moses and Numa, as well as Jesus and Paul, of fabricating their respective religions solely for the purpose of dominating other men. All of them delighted in picking out internal contradictions and scientific inaccuracies in the Old Testament as evidence of the absurdity of any belief that claimed to be based on it.

Magalotti did not find it hard to demolish these arguments, largely because he adopted an approach very different from that of most previous apologists. Instead of trying, like Segneri, to furnish the same old apologetic formulas with a new string of anathemas, instead of trying, like Bishop Burnet, to defend the literal accuracy of the Scriptures, instead of trying to prove the validity of religion by the traditional argument from universal consent, instead of trying to induce God from the visible order of nature, he simply showed that not believing in God required just as great an act of faith as believing in him. Going back to Aristotle, he asserted, meant accepting the word of "the richest, proudest, and most ambitious master that ever was on earth," one who let his pupils believe in gods he knew did not exist, and one who immobilized God in order to glorify the mobility of Alexander the Great. Going back to Lucretius meant accepting the whole of the *De Rerum Natura,* including its purely decorative gods. Professing

* "That so great a man as Cardinal Richelieu amuses himself occasionally by saying Mass." In French in the original.

the "impostor" thesis—and Magalotti checked on it in its earliest source, Origen's *Contra Celsum*—meant making civilized Romans inferior to Venezuelan cannibals, who proudly refused to be "deceived" by the viceroy's missionaries. Rejecting the Bible because of its scientific inaccuracies meant assuming it to be a textbook of natural science, which Augustine as well as Galileo had shown it most decidedly not to be. Scoffing at the Genesis account of creation meant ignoring the simplest rules of literary criticism, which carefully distinguished between theses and illustrations.

Thus atheism—or at least the kind of negative, nonconstructive, highbrow atheism that had been kept hidden in certain closets of European culture ever since the mid-sixteenth century—turned out to be a religion. By robbing it of reason, which was the only foundation it dared admit, Magalotti demolished it once and for all, at least on paper. Had he been more familiar with the works of one of his famous contemporaries, Spinoza, he might then have gone on to forestall the birth of this atheism's heir in the next century, philosophical deism. Had he been more familiar with the works of another contemporary, the biblical critic Richard Simon, he might have anticipated his successors by prescribing a return to the Bible, rather than a flight from it, as the most effective antidote to deism.

But in the meantime, Magalotti had inadvertently run into a category of religious writers that had usually been overlooked by the dogmatic and apologetic theologians. He had read Bernard of Clairvaux, John Tauler, Antonio Cordores, Armande de Rance of La Trappe, and, above all, John of the Cross and Teresa of Ávila. They, the mystics, had started him thinking about another problem, one that was far more important than atheism to his friends in Florence: the religious implications of Galilean science. From the mystics he learned finally that "faith can never be the daughter of human reason" because it begins only after reason has been extinguished. It was they who showed all metaphysical systems to be as irrelevant to religion as they were to science. It was they who demonstrated the purely relative validity of all scientific knowledge—of the latest remedy for stomach cramps as well as of Bartoli's descriptions of China. It was they who proved the arbitrary nature of the very foundation of scientific knowledge—Euclid's axioms as well as Descartes' *Cogito ergo sum*. And it was they who turned one of Galileo's insights into a truth. If "infinite slowness" ended up in the same place as infinite fastness, then indeed "this blessed thing called time—these days, years, and centuries—are simply names that we invent to suit our modes of understanding." Time, space, and the proposition that two parallel lines never meet were merely artificial constructions of a purely human logic, and were completely devoid of an objective reality of their own. The realm of the finite was one that started nowhere and ended nowhere—one in which all the recent achievements of Redian medicine left Florentines living and dying just as they always had, one in which 1 + 1, when compared to ∞, still added up to 0. Magalotti thus found himself in the same dilemma he claimed to have read about in Galileo, although he had actually read about it in Pascal. The infinite could be reached only by a blind leap, not by walking upwards from the finite.

Yet its very inability to approach the Truth enabled Galilean science to support religion much more effectively than any of its metaphysical predecessors. First, it denied the possibility of either rejecting God or imprisoning him, as Magalotti put it, on the mezzanine floor of the human brain. For it affirmed God to be no more invisible than atoms, and it held knowledge from the senses— or rather from formless blotches on the retina—to be no more reliable than knowledge from revelation. Second, it affirmed the possibility, as Pierre Daniel Huet's Pyrrhonism could not, of distinguishing among various grades of un-certainty. For it showed the testimony of a few impressionable nuns about Maria Maddalena de' Pazzi to be less reliable (or more unreliable) than the testimony of William of Clairvaux, "a monk of extraordinary prudence . . . for those times," about St. Bernard. And it showed both to be inferior to the testimony of Gregory the Great as validated by his scrupulous Protestant editor, William Cave. Third, it demanded the same assent to observable instances of incursions of the infinite into the finite as it did for observable acts within the finite alone. Whoever admitted that Redi's flies were born from eggs, said Magalotti, could not deny what had been seen by "a great number . . . of ladies and gentlemen of the highest nobility of Florence"—namely, that after six years of painful immobility, Lisabetta Capponi Orlandini had been suddenly cured of a broken leg, and that the cure could be traced to no other cause than the intercession of St. Peter Alcántara. Finally, by affirming the scientific validity of miracles that could be observed in the present, Galilean science could also affirm the relative validity of those that were reported to have occurred in the past. For it proved that the Catholic church was the normal, if not the sole institution in which these miracles were performed. It thus raised what the church remembered about the resurrection of Jesus, the rapture of Paul, and the ecstasies of John of the Cross to the same plane as what everyone could confirm for himself by dropping in any morning after Mass at the Ognissanti for an interview with Lisabetta. Thus, far from being a potential enemy of Catholicism, as the Holy Office bureaucrats vainly pretended in 1633, Galileo turned out to be its most effective ally. And Steno's conversion turned out to be not an exception but the consequence of a general rule—the rule that whoever became a Galilean had also to become a Catholic.

Along with its two subsequent appendices, containing the letter to Angelo Querini on infinity and the letter to Robert Nelson on miracles, Magalotti's *Lettere familiari contro l'ateismo* ("Familiar letters against atheism") might have been hailed as one of the most original and certainly the most readable theological work of his heavily theological age. It had been awaited anxiously by all the many friends who had contributed notes, suggestions, and additional information for one revision after another of the original version of 1681–83. It had been awaited even more anxiously by Magalotti's theological advisors in Rome, who were looking forward finally to shedding their scruples about the motion of the earth. Well before the last draft was finished, in August 1690, and well before copies of the manuscript began penetrating into the four corners of the peninsula, its author came to be referred to, in hushed sincerity, as "that saintly soul."

But Magalotti could not bring himself to publish his masterpiece, any more than he had been able to publish his minor works. For one thing, he had no intention of involving himself in the kind of endless word-juggling and tiresome proofreading that had been imposed upon him as author of the Cimento's *Essays*. For another, he doubted that the customary five hundred copies would be any more effective in converting atheists than all of Redi's treatises had been in converting pharmacists. His contemporaries agreed with him. Few of them published anything in their lifetimes except elegantly bound volumes of occasional verse that were meant to be given away, at their expense, rather than sold for profit or for the dissemination of their contents. Most of their writings that are available in print today are the results of the labors of eighteenth- and nineteenth-century literary historians.

Moreover, Magalotti eventually realized that theology was untenable as a human discipline, for it sought rational explanations for phenomena that were beyond the scope of reason. As one of his favorite poets had put it:

> To seek for reason
> in the wisdom of God
> is ridiculous temerity.
>
> For the numbered rays
> of man's mind are naught
> 'gainst the measure of infinity.
>
> And this mortal life
> is but fog beneath the sun:
> 'tis but a shade without solidity.
>
> Ah, sorry fate of man!
> What's here beneath the sky
> that's not but empty vanity?
> (Ciro da Pers, *La divina predestinazione*)

The one enterprise in which he had realized a good measure of success and the one field in which he could legitimately claim to have found a vocation turned out to be "empty vanity."

This discovery might have had no further consequences had Magalotti continued to regard his venture with the detachment of an impartial investigator. But as he began to lose faith in theology as a discipline, he began to be personally affected by the conclusions it forced him to draw. As the search for clarity led him inexorably into the "dark night" of John of the Cross, he noticed that the same old rash reappeared on his hands; and the rash was soon so painful that he had to wear gloves and refrain from striking his breast during the Confiteor.

There was only one way out. He would have to put aside his manuscript and enter the "dark night" himself. He would have to annihilate the finite and then wait patiently for the infinite to rescue him. That is just what he did at Lonchio for five long months. Then, after nothing happened, he decided that the infinite would feel more at home in a place it had already visited. Without telling anyone, not even the grand duke, and without closing his house or disposing of his affairs, he vanished—just as quietly and as suddenly as he had vanished from Vienna fourteen years before. Not until several weeks later was he at last discovered —in a cell in the monastery of the Oratorians at Rome.

6

How Magalotti stopped trying to
become anything at all

At first, Magalotti was sure that his plunge into a still darker night would succeed where all other quests for a vocation had failed. This step had been taken only after due reflection—after having "thought about it for many years and resolved upon it for at least two." It had been taken only after he had subjected himself to the best known means for discovering the divine will: the Spiritual Exercises of Ignatius Loyola, which were administered to him by one of the most skilled directors of consciences in all Italy. He had chosen a religious community, the Oratorio, that was Florentine in origin and that had recently built a church in Florence just a few steps from his ancestral property in Via de' Magalotti. And he could not have been more warmly received by the prior, who drove over to the Gesù in a carriage to pick him up.

But it did not take long for Magalotti to realize that this, the highest of all vocations, was not meant for him. The Oratorians turned out to be far different in his day from what they had been in the days of their founder, the jovial, bizarre mystic of Counter-Reformation Rome, Filippo Neri. None of them was his equal by birth, only one of them showed the slightest interest in scholarship, two were thieves, and the rest did little but sponsor concerts and manage elaborate picnic pilgrimages to the seven basilicas. The mystical "consolations" that he had looked forward to so eagerly failed to occur. Week followed week, but there were no levitations, no ecstasies, not even a simple vision. The fault, Magalotti knew, was solely his own, however much he ranted at his patient, puzzled hosts in moments of anguish. Mystical experiences were bestowed by God alone for his own inscrutable purposes. They were not earned or acquired by men. Any attempt to force the rain to fall on St. Teresa's garden amounted to a grave sin of pride. By Holy Thursday he had fallen into such a "state of great misery" that none other than the busy preacher Paolo Segneri had to be called over from the Gesù to comfort him. By mid-May he was so "beside himself" that he was "no longer capable of rational discourse." Finally, on July 18, after writing out a brief apology to the Oratorians, he fled from the monastery. And he did not rest until he had locked himself securely behind the doors of his villa at Lonchio.

From Magalotti's point of view, the best thing he could have done upon returning from Rome would have been to die. Death would have spared him the mortification of having his misfortunes reported all over Europe—even in the manuscript news-bulletins of northern Germany, which is where Leibniz read about them. Better still, it would have spared him the recurrence of his habitual financial woes. He sadly noted that his investments in land—estimated at the substantial sum of 47,200 *scudi*—brought him a clear annual profit of only 600 *scudi*; that was hardly enough to "widen my coat a bit for what little of life still remains." He observed that his investments in state bonds had fallen in proportion to the decline in their market value, from 116 to 80 *scudi* apiece. For awhile he thought of recouping his losses by the sale of one of his villas, particularly after a rather important lawsuit in Rome had gone against him. But every time he received an attractive offer, he raised the price; and soon even the most interested prospective buyers withdrew. He thus found himself once again in a state of annoyance every time a bill came due or every time the December tipping season came around. He applied the old proverb to himself: "Carnival without an appetite, Easter without devotion, and Christmas without a penny in your pocket."

Yet the God who had declined to visit him in the Oratorio now refused to come to his rescue in his villa at Lonchio, not even during the course of a serious illness in the spring of 1692. Magalotti found himself obliged to adjust to another two, four, six, and, as it turned out, twenty-one years in this world. His friends were willing to forgive him, in spite of their surprise at his having marred the religious annals of their age with the first instance of backsliding from a higher to a lower rung on the ladder of spirituality. Even the grand duke was willing to forgive him, in spite of his understandable disappointment in not being able to add still another saint to the Florentine calendar. He even gave him a couple of special commissions—one to study the feasibility of putting Tuscan wines in the place of French wines on the English market, and another to look into the establishment of a "community chest" and workhouse for the unemployed in Florence. And finally, in October 1693, he gave him back his former seat on the Council of State.

All that was left for Magalotti to do was to forget. Accordingly, he began to "moderate a bit the rigors of solitary life and come into the city more often." He stopped worrying about his reputation and learned to regard all persons—even nuns and peasant women, whom he particularly disliked—with the same charming polite detachment. Best of all, he discovered a vocation that had the great advantage of not being a vocation at all. It consisted in assembling trivial details about the most trivial of the items in contemporary curiosity collections and in making himself an authority on the least reliable of the unreliable five senses—the sense of smell. By the summer of 1695, when he began to display the fruits of his studies in a series of letters to the wife of his friend Leone Strozzi, he had succeeded completely in hiding his personal tragedy behind an impenetrable mask of witty, and apparently effortless, serenity.

Certainly no one was better qualified than Magalotti to write about *buccheri*, those earthenware vases from Peru, Chile, and Portugal that emitted a delicate odor when dampened and that were then the latest rage among more sensitive aristocrats all over Europe. As early as 1665 he had tried to measure a possible loss of weight in odorific substances. He had then made a collection of exotic recipes from all the countries he visited—recipes for "thrush legs browned over candle flame, split woodcock's heads on a grill, the horns of young deer, bears' feet, Cochin Chinese lark nests . . . and many other strange adaptations of the frivolity of modern meat-carvers." He had mastered the art of making sherbet (fruit juice packed in a silver jar under snow and salt). He had brewed a new kind of tea recently imported into Holland that provoked urination. He had designed a chocolate set that included a tiny Mexican fan for cooling the liquid after it was poured. He had searched Rome for new perfumes on behalf of Cardinal Francesco Maria. He had kept an eye (or a nose!) on all "those precious quintessences that are manufactured in the grand duke's foundry." He had manufactured some new ones of his own that were good enough to attract clients from as far away as London and Vienna. And he had developed his nasal sensitivities to the point where he could "discourse as a master" about any of "a thousand rare oriental odors."

Thus the *Letters on Buccheri* might have sought to investigate scientifically the phenomenon of sense perception, as did, for example a *Treatise on the Organs of Taste* that had been written some years earlier by one of Borelli's Florentine disciples. The *Letters* might also have satirized the contemporary craze for Chinese porcelains, Japanese teas, and Brazilian medicines, which are abundantly described in the opening pages. They might have illustrated the decline of classical scholarship into the pointless plundering of "Seneca, Pliny, Atheneus, and whatever poet happens to have let fall the words 'vase,' 'cup,' or 'pitcher.'" They might have exposed the fallacy of tracing etymologies through Castilian, Arabic, Finnish, Persian, Incan, and many other languages that had nothing in common but a few fortuitous homonyms. They might have denounced the amorality of current power politics, as they seem to do in the long account of a mock war between ambergris and the ladies of Paris. They might have provided a final proof in the absurdity of metaphysics, as they seem to do in the closing lines of Letter No. 5:

> Opinion, opinion of opinions, everything is mere opinion: everything, that is, except the Truth that I am the most obsequious of all the servants of the Marchesa Strozzi.

The *Letters* did none of these things. They were not meant to discredit baroque poetry, much as the Arcadians may have taken some passages for a parody of Marino. They were not meant to stimulate an interest in epistemology, much as the English philosopher David Hume may have found some passages relevant to his discussion of the objectivity of color. They were not meant as a manifesto of the kind of "modern European sensibility" so dear to the critics of the *Decadentismo* school of the 1920s and '30s. They were not meant as examples of "literary wastefulness," as at least one critic of the post-World War II era thought them to be. They were not meant to satirize anything, since they denied the very basis of satire—the existence of principles of judgment and the possibility of an alternative to what is satirized. They were not meant to do anything but provide Ottavia Strozzi with "a great royal platter of whipped cream," as lacking in substance as it was in durability—a platter into which she might dip for her amusement, but certainly not for nourishment or enlightenment. "Who builds on love builds on mud," Magalotti remembered "our Messer Niccolò" as having once pointed out. "Who build on odors," he added, unconcerned at having misquoted Machiavelli, "builds on wind." He himself found his construction so lacking even in "buccheresque science" that he expected it to be blown away as soon as one of the sensitive nuns in a well-scented Madrid convent read the first pages.

Yet for Magalotti, the *Letters* represented an important achievement. They reduced all the fields in which he had once searched for a vocation to the level of vanities. And when they made Teresa of Ávila into nothing but an initiate of the "ineffable mysteries of the Duchess of Alba's collection of *buccheri*," they reduced the highest of all vocations to the level of the vainest of vanities. For Magalotti's friends, too, the *Letters* represented an important achievement. At last they had a philosophic justification—one happily devoid of the least trace of philosophy—for not ever having sought a vocation in the first place. All of them applauded enthusiastically: scientists unable to discover a purpose for science, antiquarians oblivious to any relation between the past and the present, artists unmindful of any but the purely formal or decorative aspects of art, preachers caught up in the same worn-out themes of Counter-Reformation homiletics, diplomats accustomed to seeing all their plans dissolve before the whims of an irresponsible prince, poets despairing of finding a subject to write about. Nothing anyone did, they admitted, could make any discernible impression upon a world that was by its very nature static and unchangeable. Hence the Cimento's method of "testing and retesting" might just as well be applied to the purely apparent, if not purely subjective, effects of *buccheri*. The words in the Crusca's *Vocabolario* might just as well be ordered into epic poems about nothing, like the *Bucchereide* (the title parodies Virgil's *Aeneid*) of the anatomist-poet Lorenzo Bellini:

> Oh Count Magalotti,
> you who have taught me
> the tricks on which gluttons are dined;
> While mine's on the ground
> your genius has found
> a meal for to nourish my mind!
>
> (*Bucchereide*, p. 16)

"Vanity, vanity, all that is, is vanity": so went the song of Filippo Neri that Magalotti probably heard at the Oratorio. But since all that was showed no sign of ceasing to be for some time to come, Magalotti concluded that he might just as well put up with it, if not actually enjoy it. He accordingly returned to his collection of miscellaneous scientific information—information about the pugnacious character of British cocks, about the strange behavior of Norman earthworms, about the odd appearance of a new kind of bear called an *earaqulaq* recently acquired for the grand duke's zoo. He resumed his responsibilities as host to the English colony, so ably that the English resident minister wrote a Latin ode in his honor and a Latin panegyric of the city of Florence. He began corresponding with another Englishman of letters, John Sommers: and he kept up with what was going on in England through the copies of the *Tatler* that Sommers had sent to him. He started teasing the antiquarians again by claiming, for instance, to have "found [historical] monuments proving that the first birthday greeting had been given by Adam to Eve in the fiftieth year of the Julian Era." He started patronizing the poets again, and he carefully read and criticized the manuscripts they sent him. He reread the favorite ancient poet of his generation, Anacreon, finding him "most capable of banishing every unpleasant thought and of giving me all the relief I could hope for from my troubles." He went back to his favorite pastime of translating foreign books into Italian; and he found one of them to be interesting not only linguistically but also philosophically—Saint-Evremond's *Oeuvres meslées* ("Assorted essays"), which perfectly suited the state of his "present fortunes." He revived his interest in exotic travelogs—"such gallant, curious stuff, just the thing for really delicate tastes." He helped one of his friends translate Antonio de Solis's *History of the Conquest of Mexico*. And he would have added Aztec to his long list of languages if his most recent correspondent in Spain, Francisco Antonio Yriarte, had sent him the dictionaries he requested. More important still, he began once again to keep careful track of current politics and diplomacy; and he did it so conscientiously that he managed to save the grand duke from several near-disasters. Most important of all, he maintained his reputation as an expert on matters of religion and spirituality. He read the strange poems of the latest Spanish mystic. He listened to the vibrant declarations of Segneri's nephew and heir, Paolo, Jr. And he followed with amused curiosity the pietistic practices of his pampered godson, Lorenzo Maria Gianni, who earned beatification by keeping his eyes glued to the ground as he walked from his well-furnished palace to his stall in the cathedral every morning.

Yet Magalotti returned to all these former occupations in a completely different spirit from the one in which he had originally taken them up. He now became a scientist in the same way that Teresa of Ávila had become a founder of convents: all that he did, no matter how conscientiously and efficiently, meant no more to him than their external acts did to mystics in the state of union.

He could thus patronize a bright young botanist without ever having to commit himself to this or that new system of plant classification. He could instruct a bright young diplomat without ever feeling frustrated over the obvious short-comings of diplomacy. He could read St. Augustine—even those passages in Augustine that had once caused him such distress—and then bury them, without the slightest remorse, in a mass of ridiculous quotations from Pliny the Elder.

The world was one thing. Magalotti, the sharp-eyed observer of the world, was quite another. What was observed no longer had any power to affect the observer. Only once did he venture an explicit criticism, and that was simply because he feared that the multiplication of compendia, like the famous *Dictionary* of Pierre Bayle, would make learning available to an unprepared public—to a public, that is, which might take learning seriously. Only once did he venture to participate in a current dispute, and that was just because he feared that the ingenious thesis of a mathematics instructor at Pisa—Guido Grandi—might put a crack in the impenetrable wall between human knowledge and revealed religion. If zero multiplied by infinity really did yield a positive number, as Grandi proposed, and if his formula, $0 \cdot \infty = x$, were to replace Magalotti's formula, $1 + 1 = 0$, then Creation ex nihilo was not a mystery but a scientific fact, and mathematics, the one system of logic recognized by the Galileans, was not an instrument of science but a system of metaphysics.

Thus Magalotti finally found his vocation in the deliberate renunciation of a vocation. As his once-worried eyes took shelter beneath a wrinkled forehead, and as his once-handsome cheeks slid into flabby jowls, his pursed lips became fixed in an imperturbable smile. Having been thrown off the highest rung of Jacob's ladder, he had no intention of trying to grab onto a lower one. For he had now mastered the art of enjoying the fruits of mysticism without having to go through the troublesome, time-consuming stages prescribed in the handbooks of mysticism. He had found a way of remaining in the world instead of turning his back on it or rebelling against it.

But all Magalotti's friends and disciples mistook what was really an expression of inward serenity as a sign of unfathomable wisdom.

> Of all that moves, man's highest,
> for his head above them soars;
> and higher still's the wisdom
> that in his head he stores.
> Of all wise men the wisest
> is Count Magalotti, you know;
> above him on wisdom's ladder,
> 'tis vain to seek to go.
>
> (Bellini, *Bucchereide,* p. 54 of the 1779 edition)

His protestations of incompetence, they thought, were merely a way of "pretending not to know what he really possesses most marvelously." On the very morrow of his death, in 1712, they began searching frantically through all the great mass of manuscript letters, notes, poems, and treatises that he himself had not thought important enough even to destroy. Within five years, when the first samples of what he had written began coming out in print, they had elevated him to the rank of a sage. And within the next half-century they succeeded in transforming him into a proponent of "the prosperity of the people, commerce and manufacturing, the happiness of the state," and a number of other noble causes that were as congenial to the mind of the Enlightenment as they had been utterly foreign to the purposeless age in which he had lived.

BOOK V
FLORENCE
IN THE 1730s
How Giovanni Lami discovered the past
and tried to alter the present

PROLOGUE

The journalist

Friday, January 1. 1740. The library behind Palazzo Medici-Riccardi, on Via Ginori.
From the middle of an infinite heaven, which Luca Giordano had painted onto
the vaulted ceiling some eighty years earlier, Divine Wisdom looked down
through puffy clouds crawling with playful cupids, over the heads of two busty
nudes trying to tempt a stucco Hercules, past the gold leaf on the carved wooden
balconies along the upper tier of packed bookcases, and fixed her eyes on the
black skullcap of a man whose boyish cheeks, delicate mouth, and neck-length
locks suggested far fewer than the forty-two years he had just completed.

Giovanni Lami pulled his thick black cape more tightly over his narrow
shoulders: Marchese Vincenzo would never have permitted magnificence to be
sacrificed to comfort with one of the tile stoves that the Lorraine officials had
brought with them from France and Austria. He adjusted the small white collar
that placed him, along with so many other bachelors of his age, in a vague but
respectable middle ground between the laity and the clergy. He took a sip of hot
milk and coffee, a delicacy which at last enabled Florentines of sensitive digestions
to eat breakfast, but one which until recently had been beyond the means even of
a pampered courtier like Francesco Baldovini:

> Of godless Egypt the Hebrews broke
> in empty deserts the cruel yoke;
> but there they found a crueler dearth,
> till God-sent Manna restored their mirth.
>
> So I now wander through crooked ways,
> and weak and helpless consume my days.
> A rain of coffee, this do I implore;
> for nothing else can now my life restore.
> (D. M. Manni, *Veglie piacevoli*, VII, 125)

And he set to work correcting proofs on what was to be the most important venture of his adventurous career: the *Novelle letterarie,* the "Literary News," of which the first issue was announced for that day.

Periodical publications were no novelty to the Florentines of 1740. They had been reading weekly news-bulletins and market quotations since as early as 1596. Literary journals were not particularly new to them either. Many of them had at least heard of the more famous ones in northern Europe—the *Acta Eruditorum* of Leipzig, of which Magliabechi had been a correspondent, the *Journal des sçavans,* published under the auspices of the French crown since 1703, the *Mercure de France,* the weekly newspaper of Paris, and the French Jesuits' *Mémoires de Trévoux.* Some of them, for professional reasons, kept up with the acts of transalpine scientific societies, of which the *Philosophical Transactions* of London, the *Histoire et mémoires* of the French Académie des Sciences, and the *Mémoires* of the antiquarians' Académie des Inscriptions were the best known.

Few Florentines, it is true, still remembered the abortive attempts of the preceding century at transplanting literary journalism into Italy. The thinly disguised imitation of the *Journal des sçavans* founded at Rome in 1668 had gone out of business in 1679. Benedetto Bacchini's courageous and controversial *Giornale* of Modena had been forced out of business in 1696. The Venetian *Galleria di Minerva* had stopped publishing in 1717. Another *Giornale* in Forlì had lasted no more than four years. But most Florentine readers kept up with Angelo Calogerà's *Raccolta d'opuscoli* ("Collection of short literary and scientific works"), an eighteenth-century cross between *Scientific American* and the *Atlantic Monthly.* They still remembered the exhortation addressed to their fathers about the importance of journals by Bacchini's most eminent disciple, and now the dean of Italian scholarship, Lodovico Antonio Muratori of Modena. They had followed the most successful attempt to put Muratori's exhortation into practice, the *Giornale de' letterati d'Italia* ("Journal of Italian Men of Letters"), founded in Venice in 1710 and revived, after a five-year lapse, just three years before. And they had watched with interest two recent attempts to supplement the *Giornale*—the weekly *Novelle,* put out by some enterprising bookdealers in Venice, and the vivacious, pungent *Osservazioni letterarie,* written by the noisiest gadfly of the Italian Republic of Letters, Scipione Maffei of Verona.

Still, none of these journals was edited in Florence; none of them, consequently, could do much to remedy one of the greatest weaknesses of Florentine cultural life—namely, an anachronistic and badly organized book trade. Everyone complained about it. Buyers complained because they could not find what they wanted in the stores. Publishers complained because they could not sell their products outside of a very restricted market. Authors complained because "the world is so jammed with books these days that most men of letters get upset stomachs just on hearing of a new publication."

The fault lay partly with the government, which still imposed a 12 percent duty on books exported even to Siena—within the grand duchy. It lay partly in the absence of any but the most rudimentary forms of advertising—which may explain why so much of contemporary letter-writing was taken up with book news. But it lay mostly with the printers and with the guild system that they still looked upon as a panacea for declining profits. In 1707 they had persuaded the grand duke that books were too noble a commodity to be displayed on the stalls of "any old used-clothes dealer, junk peddler, or scrap-iron vendor." Thereafter they enjoyed a virtual monopoly of the sale as well as the printing of books, subject only to the nominal supervision of the consul of the Accademia Fiorentina.

Hence, none of the printers bothered to contact agents for handling their products in other cities. None of them would agree to stock the products of their competitors except on the basis of an exchange of merchandise. None of them thought of following the example of the Venetian bookdealer, Michele Hertz, whose ample profits came largely from the great variety of books he kept on hand from all the countries of Europe. None of them was willing to distribute the customary one-sheet publication announcements, to enlist prepublication sub-scribers, or to have books crated at Livorno for overseas delivery. Those administrative chores were left completely to the authors. Even those few printers, like Giuseppe Marmi and Giuseppe Moücke, who were "moved to contribute to the advancement of learning," could think of no better source for new manuscripts than the back shelves of the libraries of the city. It is not surprising, then, that of the thirty-one titles announced by Manni between 1718 and 1729, almost all were either reprints of Tuscan verse or else the dissertations, lectures, and "language texts" of modern Florentine academicians. Books in Florence were a strictly local product serving a strictly local market. Far from broadening the horizon of Florentine readers, they tended to increase their isolation from the rest of the world.

Lami realized, therefore, that his new journal had a very specific, and very important, service to render. It would have to be written in Italian—not in Latin, which he had been thinking of doing as late as the preceding November. It would have to include reviews of a great number of different kinds of books; and the reviews would have to be at once short enough to hold the attention of the nonspecialist and long enough "to say in a few words what the author says in many." It would also have to include longer informational articles about "those literary events which cannot be found in books and which can be learned about only with difficulty." It would have to be critical enough to help out those readers who had neither the time nor the money to read everything themselves. And yet it would have to be impartial enough to avoid the excesses of Maffei's

Osservazioni letterarie. It would have to devote at least half of each issue to news about Florence which could not be found in the other journals; and it would have to enlist foreign correspondents to contribute news from all over Europe. Finally, it would have to be reasonably priced. And 15 *paoli* for an annual subscription (or 21½ for elegantly bound volumes of back-issues) was not too expensive, considering that an ordinary book cost 4 *paoli* and that seats at the Cocomero Theater cost 2 *paoli* and up.

From Santa Croce to Florence

Lami's decision to found a journal came as the result of many years of experience in many different branches of knowledge. He had been born of modest but somewhat pretentious parents in the sleepy village of Santa Croce nestled along the river dikes of the lower Arno valley. He had been brought up by three doting bachelor uncles, one of whom had worked as a clerk in an English trading house at Livorno, and one of whom had read fairly extensively in the works of recent French economists. He had been educated at the Jesuits' Collegio Cicognini in Prato, an institution that performed for ambitious provincials the same function as a fashionable preparatory school that the Collegio San Giovanino performed for wellborn Florentines. After an adolescent spiritual crisis, and after further tutoring from his uncles, he had completed his education under three of the most prominent professors at Pisa: the pugnacious mathematician and philosopher Guido Grandi, who had once troubled Magalotti with his speculations about infinity; the canon lawyer Lazzaro Migliorucci, who was one of the first to interpret canon law in the context of ecclesiastical history; and the super-pious scientist-jurist Giuseppe Averani, who was largely responsible for the revival of humanist jurisprudence in the next generation.

Lami moved to Florence as soon as he graduated, in 1720, with the intention of applying the methods of his teachers in the practice of law. He arrived at a fortunate moment. Cosimo III had reached the last years of his overlong reign, and the heavy hand that once had "chopped down all the noble plants and left nothing but thistles and poisonous weeds" in the learned world of the capital was now rapidly withering. The government simply ignored an underground edition of Galileo's still-forbidden *Dialogue on the Two World Systems* that had been circulating since 1710. It openly sanctioned the first big, luxurious edition of his *Collected Works* (minus the *Dialogue*) sponsored by the Accademia della Crusca in

1718, even though the Holy Office moratorium had not yet been lifted. It closed its eyes to the disrespectful ditties that passed around the city at its expense:

> Fraud and ignorance today exult;
> liars and hypocrites now triumph.
> Greed and pull will get all you want,
> while the poor man sweats in vain.
> (quoted by M. Bencini in *Il vero G. B. Fagiuoli*, p. 9)

One last attempt to encourage "the scrupulous" turned into a minor disaster. Baccio Bandinelli's "Adam and Eve" was ordered removed from the cathedral—not because it was bad art, for no one had yet read Benvenuto Cellini's comments on it, but only because the figures were "nude." The public responded not with the usual acquiescence but with the only means of protest left to it under the grand ducal regime: a barrage of "bizarre and critical poems," which Lami still remembered twenty-five years later.

In 1723, Cosimo III finally died, and Florence was suddenly plunged into an atmosphere somewhat like that of the regency in France after the death of Louis XIV. Foreign tourists began coming to town, or at least enough of them to warrant republishing Raffaello Del Bruno's guidebook with a new map and an additional "promenade" of suburban villas. The works of Gassendi were published in 1726, with Lami acting as assistant to the chief editor, Niccolò Averani, a brother of Lami's former professor at Pisa; and no one said a word about the dangers of "atomism." Vincenzo Viviani's bequest for a monument to Galileo was at last executed. A huge piece of polychrome marble was set up in Santa Croce, and the bust that Giovan Battista Foggini had done from Sustermans' portrait was put on top of it. Orders for the indispensable symbolic sculptures were handed to the most skilled artists in town. And in 1734, just one year more than a century after the condemnation, Galileo's bones were carried in a solemn procession to the final resting place that had been prepared for them, right across the nave from the tomb of Michelangelo.

Unfortunately for Lami's career, no one was particularly interested either in what professors said about the law at the university or what their disciples said about it in the tribunals. And of all Florentines, the one who was the least interested in the law was the undisputed leader of the intellectual community—the jovial, loquacious, chubby preceptor of two generations, "the honor and joy of the present century and the wonder of all centuries to come," Anton Maria Salvini. Though already in his seventies, Salvini was still as busy, and still as fond of good food and wine, as ever. He made no distinctions among men: "everyone," he observed, be he peasant or artisan, scholar or aristocrat, "has something of value and a place in the world, and is worthy of respect." He was therefore perfectly willing to admit an unsophisticated, overeducated youth from the provinces into the circle of his many devoted disciples. He made no distinctions among subjects, either. "I keep my tastes universal," he pointed out, "for everything fascinates me, and I manage to find some good in every book I pick up." He was famous for being able to whip up a lecture on anything from Petrarch to John the Baptist and from wigs to earthquakes in as little time as it took to walk across the Piazza della Signoria.

> The proof we have in o'er a thousand sheets,
> that still record innumerable feats
> of his vast wisdom; and so a sparkling crown
> shines o'er the world to witness his renown.
> (G. B. Casaregi, sonnet of 1731)

Salvini claimed to be "just an ordinary, unrefined man," not a "genius." He belonged, as he put it, not among the "inventors," like Galileo and Amerigo Vespucci, but to the no less useful category of the "translators, commentators, and editors of works of others." The field that best seemed to suit this kind of talent was the study of languages. His first love was Greek, "in which," according to Lami, "his knowledge far exceeded that of all others of his age," and which provided him with his salary as public professor in the *Studio*. Between 1717 and 1725 he published Italian translations of Homer, Anacreon, Theocritus, and Plotinus. In 1728, the year before his death, he proved that he could translate in the opposite direction as well, with Greek versions of Catullus and Phaedrus. And it was to him that Lami owed his knowledge of Greek, a language that was to be of such importance in his theological studies of later years. Salvini's second love was the Tuscan language, which he constantly compared favorably with all others, ancient and modern. He spent much of his time annotating that treasure of Florentinisms, *La fiera* of Michelangelo Buonarroti, Jr., and correcting the non-Florentine expressions in the most authoritative current manual of literary criticism, the *Perfetta poesia* of Lodovico Antonio Muratori. His third love was, to the surprise of his compatriots, the English language. The English, he found, were a "free, frank, spirited, inventive, and thoughtful nation," and their literature was "less wordy and more substantial" than that of the French. When the English diplomatic agent in Florence gave him a copy of Addison's *Cato* during a hunting expedition in 1713, he set to work immediately on an Italian version, which was printed in 1725 with the translation and the original on facing pages.

The study of these languages, as well as of Spanish, Hebrew, and all the others that had earned Salvini the epithet "hundred-tongued" in Redi's *Bacco in Toscana,* served one purpose only: amusing himself and his friends. That also, as far as he was concerned, was the only purpose of the sciences and of mathematics, which he knew as well as any other of the former students of Viviani. It was the only purpose of the study of "antiquities," whatever Migliorucci and Averani may have thought to the contrary. It was certainly the only purpose of the study of law. He himself had put away his law books as soon as he could safely defy his father's orders, and thereafter he referred to them only when he wanted to show off his skill as a philologist. It is not surprising that Lami too, Salvini's most recent disciple, soon lost interest in the profession his uncles had chosen for him and that he turned to the less lucrative but more prestigious pursuit of letters.

As Salvini was the most important individual, so the most important cultural institution of the city was the Accademia della Crusca, of which he was the most prominent member. The Crusca was so important that it managed to have one of its recalcitrant members—the playwright Girolamo Gigli—thrown out of the grand duchy for no other crime than having proclaimed St. Caterina of Siena to be a better writer than Giovanni Boccaccio of Florence. The Crusca was not interested in the law, either. It was interested first of all in maintaining the authority of Florence, and therefore of itself, as the linguistic and literary arbiter of all Italy. It invited authors to have their books approved for linguistic orthodoxy before publication. It commissioned Salvini's younger brother, Salvino, to restudy the works of Leonardo Salviati and to prepare another biographical history of the Accademia Fiorentina. It appointed a special committee to bury its critics under another avalanche of quotations from still more "approved" authors. It commissioned Salvini to begin work on an appendix of technical terms. Between 1729 and 1734, after fifteen years of hard work, it published a much enlarged fourth edition of its dictionary, the *Vocabolario,* in five thick volumes.

The Crusca was also interested in reviving the Florentine literary heritage. Or at least it was interested in reviving that part of the heritage which offended no one's political or patriotic sensitivities. That excluded, for the moment at least, all the humanist writers of the fifteenth century and most of the political, historical, and satirical writers of the sixteenth. But it did not exclude Galileo and the last generation of Galileans—Magalotti, Redi, and Menzini. It included, surprisingly enough, that most uninhibited of all Florentine prose writers, Benvenuto Cellini, whose autobiography just happened to pop up during a search for unpublished "language texts." It included one long-forgotten predecessor, St. Francis of Assisi, as well as one addition to the short list of "uncorrupted" Renaissance writers, Leon Battista Alberti—largely because his *On the Family* was incorrectly attributed to the notoriously Latin-free traditionalist, Vespasiano da Bisticci. It included Machiavelli's *Discourse on Language,* which the secretary of the Crusca discovered in 1725 and which was first published, anonymously, in the appendix of Varchi's *Ercolano* five years later. It included the academic orators from Giovanni Della Casa to Salvini and the epistolographers from Bembo to Magliabechi; and Carlo Dati's plan for an anthology of *Prose fiorentine* ("Florentine Prose") was forthwith stretched out into a dozen pocket-size volumes. Above all, the Crusca's program of text-editing included a long list of long-forgotten minor writers of the "Golden Age"—Buonaccorso da Montemagno, Ricordano Malespini, Neri Capponi, Dino Compagni, et al. Many of the editions of these writers that were first published under its auspices in the eighteenth century are still the only ones available today.

Finally, the Crusca was interested in creating an even more vital Florentine literature for the future. It was not yet willing to take lessons from foreigners—as the Sienese comic playwright Girolamo Gigli did so successfully when he imitated Molière. Nor was it willing to condone the mere copying of the ancients—which is what the Neapolitan jurist Gian Vincenzo Gravina did so unsuccessfully with Euripides. Rather, it reasserted the program that it had passed on to all Italy through the many new branches, or "colonies," of the Accademia dell'Arcadia. It held up its approved language-texts as models of "that force, that brevity, that clarity, that beauty, that simple grace . . . which our language possessed at the time of Boccaccio and that it ought to acquire again today." It suggested still new forms of literary expression—blank verse, for instance, which was particularly suitable to "philosophical themes," and amorous verse, which, it insisted, even ecclesiastics could indulge in with impunity. It then told its members to write, write, write. And it awarded the compositions that managed to pass through the rigorous course of selection, censorship, debate, and approbation with the honor of transcription into a specially bound book called the *Tramoggia*.

The passion for versification was common to all Europe in the eighteenth century. In France, for instance, no less than 1,069 "poems" were composed by no fewer than 278 different "poets" in the small provincial town of Caen alone. But in Italy, the passion was particularly encouraged by a new form of public entertainment: extemporaneous recitals. The contestants would be given a theme. They would be allowed fifteen minutes to figure out their rhymes. And the packed audience would then wait breathlessly as they brought forth "precious relics, to be jealously preserved, and to be exposed for veneration in all ages to come." The passion was justified by a theoretical principle that the Roman Arcadia, still the arbiter of literary tastes all over Italy, regarded as axiomatic. Spontaneity alone, Arcadia insisted, could separate creative imitation from mere copying; and quantity, it added, was the best guarantee of quality. In other words, get enough people to sing as often as possible in the way everyone thought Petrarch had sung, and one of them was sure to come up eventually with something as good as the *Canzoniere*.

Salvini occasionally had doubts about some of the aspects of the Arcadian principle. Many of its faithful adherents, he noticed, seemed to suffer from a "want of real, solid things to write about." Most of them tended to overgeneralize concrete words and pad out lines with mere sounds. And all of them at times came up with lines such as these:

> Questa fu verginella intatta e pura.
> voi la martirizzate a dirittura.*

* Here is a rough English version:

> She was a young virgin, intact and pure,
> and you make a martyr of her for sure.

As if *a dirittura* was at all comparable in intensity to *e pura,* and as if a fashionable Florentine convent had anything whatever to do with lions in the Coliseum!

But no one in Florence had even heard of Vico, the misunderstood Neapolitan philosopher who proposed an aesthetic exactly the opposite of Arcadia's. No one had yet been exposed to the pious adaptations of the *Decameron* (or the *Ierodecameron,* the *Pentameron,* or the *Gierotricameron,* depending on how much time you were willing to waste on Hellenic pedantry) by Giovanni Bottari, Lami's ally of later years on theological questions. And no one had yet listened to Giovan Battista Casaregi as he exhausted all the hundred different ways of saying exactly the same thing whenever another noble lady took the veil.

Hence, not even Salvini could deny that the principle was basically sound. Nor could he deny that it was backed up by a mass of very convincing empirical evidence. The most prolific of the extemporaneous poets, a certain Bernardino Perfetti of Siena, was awarded Petrarch's laurel wreath on the Campidoglio in 1725. The most prolific libretto writer of the age, Pietro Metastasio, began his spectacular rise from poverty to the position of court poet at Vienna when the Neapolitan jurist and literary critic Gian Vincenzo Gravina discovered him composing verses on the streets of Rome. That indomitable Arcadian of Verona, Scipione Maffei, finally produced, in 1713, what Italians had sought in vain for centuries: the *Merope,* a tragedy worthy at least of Voltaire, though not perhaps of Euripides or Corneille; and Florentines expressed their gratitude by twice republishing it in the following decades and by having it translated into English. That overproductive Arcadian of Florence, Giovan Battista Fagiuoli, began the gradual revolution in the comic theater that was finally completed, two decades later, by the greatest Italian comedian of all times, Carlo Goldoni. Fagiuoli got rid of masks. He put a few credible human beings beside the stock characters of the *commedia dell'arte.* He forbade puns and extraneous jokes. He added descriptions of real contemporary situations to the usual ridiculous intrigues. And in the reconciliation scene at the end of his immensely popular *Marito alla moda* ("The Fashionable Husband"), he managed to introduce a touch of real sentiment. True, Fagiuoli could be exasperatingly tedious, particularly for anyone who tried to read through the five thick volumes of the first edition of his collected plays. But he received the most enthusiastic congratulations from Metastasio, from Maffei, and even from the dean of contemporary Italian comedians, Luigi Riccoboni. And what he lacked in talent he made up for in personal charm: "he was known by ordinary people, acclaimed by the rich, appreciated by the learned, loved by Florentines, esteemed by foreigners. He talked affably with everyone and gave pleasure to all [who met him]."

Thus the academicians of the Crusca went right on scribbling out the same old metaphors about the same flat heroes on the same standardized occasions— births, deaths, marriages, battles, sermons, monastic vows, and appointments to office. They continued to ignore individual peculiarities and to describe Prince

Eugene of Savoy, for instance, as if he were a carbon copy of Alexander the Great. They clung to abstract categories that made the War of the Spanish Succession sound like just another Trojan War. They failed to inquire whether Senator Vincenzo Riccardi, Lami's future employer, felt any differently toward his well-dowered bride than Petrarch had felt toward Laura. And it never occurred to them that the questions they debated—"Which is better, beauty or nobility?" "Which is more moving, a lady's smile or her frown?"—had nothing whatever to do with the real problems of eighteenth-century Florentines. The only would-be poet of the generation who tried to write about a subject of current interest was too far ahead of his times to succeed. Giovan Lorenzo Stecchi's "philosophic poem" *Delle meteore* turned out to be just a feeble adaptation of Marchetti's Lucretius—all content, no beauty, and massive footnotes to explain more fully the latest devices for measuring altitude and rainfall.

Both his birth and his age barred Lami from the exclusive circle of Florentine patricians and well-tried men of letters who ran the Crusca. But he was soon welcomed into its junior and less aristocratic counterpart, the Accademia degli Apatisti. The Apatisti talked about the same subjects—the passion of Our Lord, the panegyrics of Isocrates, the poems of Petrarch, anatomy, food, wine, and ball-playing. They had some of the same members—Salvini, for instance, his brother Salvino, and his successor as public professor of Greek, Angelo Maria Ricci; and they had many others who would, after proving themselves, be adimtted to the Crusca. But their chief efforts went into the "Game of the Sibyl": an unknown child brought in from the street would be presented with one of the usual academic "questions," for example, "Is virtue natural or is it acquired?" The contestants would then take turns piling up quotations and rhetorical flourishes to prove that whatever nonsensical grunt the child might make was the right answer.

Lami quickly mastered all these arts. He learned to spin out unpoetic rhyme well enough to use it effectively, and unpoetically, against his literary enemies of later years. He learned to dash off extemporaneous discourses with such ease that he soon thought himself dispensed from making second drafts, even when he wrote for publication. He learned to check words in the Crusca's *Vocabolario* and to defend his departures from the rules—an archaism here and a Latinism there—by reference to Trecento models. He learned that the chief obligation of writers was "not to transform the Tuscan language but to maintain it in its purity and marvelous elegance." And he learned that "eloquence and polish" and "ornament and beauty in discourse" were indispensable even in technical treatises.

But Lami owed much more to the Apatisti than just lessons in speaking and writing. He also owed to them his introduction into Florentine society—or at least into what was left of Florentine society after Grand Duke Gian Gastone locked himself up in his bedroom and after his sister, Anna Maria Luisa, secluded

herself in one convent after another. Most of society centered about private
dinner parties, which were numerous enough to keep the party-hopping playwright Fagiuoli busy every other evening. The Riccardi still occasionally put on a
gala reception at the Gualfonda gardens, as in the days of Galileo, with music,
dancing, and plenty to drink. Once a week Princess Violante Beatrice, the
grand-duke's sister-in-law, assembled the nearest thing Florence had to a court
at the Villa Lampeggio. It was there, at Lampeggio, that Lami first had a chance
to shine in public, with one of the "extemporaneous scholarly speeches" that
were an indispensable part of the entertainment.

   Society, in turn, meant sociability. And for a young man whose piety
bordered on the morose, whose unfailing egotism led him to lie even to himself,
whose sureness of his own talents drove him to seek out opponents simply "in
order to demonstrate his invincible resistance," and whose manners appeared
"abnormal and strange" even to his admirers—for a young boor like Lami,
sociability was no mean accomplishment. He discovered that "pleasant walks in
the country" were as recreative as pilgrimages to Impruneta, that good food and
wine were as necessary as fasts and vigils, that evenings in a tavern (*osteria*) were
as profitable as meetings of his many confraternities, and that conversation with
those "who are not men of letters [nor] skilled in sciences" provided an
indispensable complement to "concentration on serious matters." Best of all,
Lami discovered that humanity was composed of two sexes, even in Florence,
which had nothing resembling the French *salon*. Although he never became
seriously attached to any one woman, he at least learned to appreciate female
companionship. He also learned that "women are as disposed to the intellectual
disciplines as men," and he rejected the almost universal belief to the contrary
as "a strange popular opinion." Even in more advanced years he was willing to
interrupt pressing business in order to devote himself completely to a "charming
young lady" who just then happened to walk into his office.

2

From librarian to historian

After six years of being educated and civilized, however, what Lami really needed was a job; and he accepted the first one that his former teacher Guido Grandi managed to find for him, even though it involved moving about in the train of the wealthy diplomat who hired him as a librarian. Lami was disgusted with Genoa, his first stop, where people starved. He was amused by Vienna, his second, where people thought of nothing but "eating, drinking, sleeping, and having a good time." But he profited from both. He discovered the works of a number of recent, if somewhat shocking, transalpine authors whose names were scarcely mentioned in Florence: the "Socinian" Jean LeClerc, the "atheist" Spinoza, the "heretic" Bayle, and, worst of all, John Locke, who had written "a pestiferous and impious book entitled *The Reasonableness of Christianity*." Out of his reading came his own first treatise: an outdated defense of Catholic orthodoxy against the old charge of tritheism, entitled *De Recta Patrum Nicaeorum Fide* ("The True Faith of the Nicaean Fathers"), which was published at Venice in 1730.

Then, when his employer threatened to take him off to Malta, Lami decided "to wander about and see the world" all on his own. Accordingly, in April 1729 he left for Geneva, then Lyon, then Marseilles; and at the end of November he finally arrived in Paris, where he settled down, except for a brief vacation in the Netherlands, for two years of study and observation. This second trip turned out to be even more profitable than the first. Lami discovered that Calvinists were hospitable, that Lyonnais Catholics were gullible, that French hotels were much less expensive than Italian, and that even uneducated Parisians read "all the Sacred Scriptures and books of theology" usually reserved for the initiate in Italy. More important still, at least for his subsequent intellectual formation, he was exposed to the last blasts of the century-old Jansenist controversy, and he soon realized that many of the theological doctrines he once had thought fixed forever actually "changed with the climate." Most important of all, he was introduced to the well-stocked library of the Benedictines of Saint-Maur, the home of the most productive school of historical scholarship in all Europe. And out of his reading, which now extended from the Greek fathers to the English Deists, came his second treatise, the *De Recta,* or "True Opinion of Christians Concerning the Mystery of the Divine Trinity." The treatise sought to save the doctrine of the Trinity from the Deists' accusation of being a Platonic addition to an originally "reasonable" religion. It sought to do so by denying to John the Evangelist, and to all the other authors of the New Testament, any knowledge of Greek philosophy. And it succeeded well enough to get a three-page review in the Venetian journal *Novelle della repubblica letteraria*—and thereby to elevate its author to membership in the Italian Republic of Letters.

This second treatise also succeeded in getting the author what he needed most at the moment: a permanent job. Like most other aristocratic families, the Riccardi of Florence had long been avid collectors of miscellaneous bric-a-brac— pots, books, inscriptions, medals, statue fragments, exotic plants, and artifacts. As early as 1595 they had given their business agent at Rome carte blanche to buy anything of the sort he could find. More recently, Anton Maria Salvini had suggested that some articles in their collection might serve another purpose than that of mere decoration. They had accordingly hung many of their Greek and Roman inscriptions opposite Giovan Battista Foggini's new monumental staircase in the courtyard of their palace, the Palazzo Medici-Riccardi. Thus when Lami, who had just returned from an apprenticeship in one of the most famous libraries of Europe, suggested that they also put their books in order, they forthwith offered to pay him to do so. To add a bit of luster to a title that otherwise might have suggested the rank of a domestic servant, they persuaded the grand duke to give him an honorary professorship at the Studio as well.

Being a librarian was not exactly what Lami had in mind. What he really wanted was a chair at Pisa. And as the years went by without any sign of an invitation, he came to regard one after another of his friends as enemies solely on the suspicion of their having frustrated his ambition. Still, being a librarian was not without important advantages. That was the position Magliabechi had held when he aspired to the tyranny over the Italian Republic of Letters in the 1680s. That was the position Lodovico Antonio Muratori, the historian, essayist, and literary critic, had held when he was accorded the honorary presidency of the republic in the 1710s. And that was the position which was to give several of Lami's colleagues in the next two decades a degree of influence and authority equal to that of any university professor. Moreover, the position of librarian was no longer a sinecure. Libraries had by now become not simply ornaments of nobility but sources of information, and hence necessary tools for anyone, regardless of social status, who sought education or instruction. They rapidly grew in size and number: all the new literary and scientific academies established book-buying funds and lending privileges for members. Some libraries concentrated on particular fields, like botany, law, linguistics, and medicine. Most of them were now catalogued during the lifetime of the owner, so that they could be more easily consulted, rather than at his death, as had previously been the rule, so that they could be appraised for sale.

Thus librarians had to be cataloguers as well as scholars; and many of their catalogues, elegantly printed in folio volumes or carefully inscribed on vellum sheets, were so meticulously supplied with bibliographical information that they are still in use today. Lami himself was not satisfied with merely "a sterile list of names and titles." Whenever possible, he gave a history as well as a description of each codex. And he put off publishing his catalogue of the Riccardiana until he had checked every entry one more time. To be sure, the system of cataloguing generally adopted was rather cumbersome by Library of Congress standards. It was based not just on subjects (theology, patristics, natural philosophy), but also on language and on genre (poetry, oratory . . .). But at least it was superior to the *ordine di collocazione* ("order of acquisition") that is still the rule in some modern Italian libraries. It avoided the necklace-length call numbers that American libraries today must dream up for unforeseen categories. And it enabled the reader familiar with the traditional organization of learning to find what he was looking for with a minimum of effort.

Cataloguing had other advantages, too. It cut down on what was the inevitable consequence of disorganization: the loss of books. That turned out to have been the fate of some of Leonardo Salviati's manuscripts when a committee of the Accademia Fiorentina tried to find them in 1700, as it was almost to be the fate of Galileo's papers and of Giovan Battista Doni's "Catalogue of Florentine Writers" in the following decades. Cataloguing also put a stop to what was rapidly becoming a wholesale pillage of Florence's treasures by foreign book-buyers. The papers of the sixteenth-century philologist Pier Vettori had already started on the long pilgrimage that was to end eventually in Munich and London. The Corsini collection had been transferred to the new papal palace on the Tiber. Emperor Charles VI had been bidding successfully under a third name at Florentine auctions. Armed with their catalogues, the librarians assumed the responsibility of guarding Florence's literary heritage. And finally, on December 28, 1754, the government decided to support them. It prohibited the exportation of precious books and promised to buy all the major Florentine collections as they came onto the market.

At the same time, libraries were rapidly acquiring the status of public institutions. Francesco Marucelli had led the way in 1703, when he left his books not to one of his relatives but to his fellow citizens. Magliabechi had followed his lead in 1714, when he left instructions that his immense collection be made available "for the benefit of all, and especially of the poor priests and laymen who have not the means to buy books." Lack of money frustrated the executors of

21. Biblioteca Riccardiana, Reading Room

the two wills for many years. But when another great collector, Anton Francesco Marmi, threatened to withdraw his offer if it were not honored within ten years of his death, the grand duke himself intervened. Cataloguers were appointed, space was provided, and finally, in 1747, the Marucelliana and the Magliabechiana were opened to the public for stated hours on alternate days of the week. Lami and Angelo Maria Bandini then made similar provisions for the Riccardiana and the Laurenziana; and when the grand duke ordered the Medici-Palatina opened in 1765, Florence had five public libraries. What happened to the libraries also happened to other kinds of collections—to the fossils of Niccolò Gualtieri, to the plant specimens of Pier Antonio Micheli, and to the scientific instruments that soon were to form the core of what is today the Museum of the History of Science.

The libraries grew rapidly thereafter. They attracted other big donations from private collectors. They were generously endowed for further acquisitions. Because the nineteenth-century distinction between "domestic" and "foreign" books was still unknown, they rapidly became pan-European in content. More important still, they revolutionized Florentine reading habits. What had been the privilege of a few was now made available to all. What had been a way of withdrawing into the intimacy of a private study was turned into a way of associating with others in a common public reading-room. Reading, in other words, became a social rather than an individual activity; it became a stimulus rather than a deterrent to conversation.

Thus Lami had no reason to turn down the offer to be a librarian. Vincenzo, Gabriele, and Bernardino Riccardi may have been patrons rather than men of letters. They were certainly more interested in lavish living than in libraries. And they were usually too busy as managers of their widespread family investments, as magistrates, and as counsellors to the grand duke to have much time left over for books. But they were kind to everyone, regardless of social class; they once went out of their way to pay a surprise visit on Lami's mother while she was working in her cellar at Santa Croce. They were generous, too. In return for a "poetic applause" at Vincenzo's wedding in 1733 and the prospect of future book dedications, they promised Lami full freedom to say, do, and print whatever he pleased, as well as eventual support for his publishing ventures. They were unswervingly loyal. Never once, during the next thirty-seven years, did they ever go back on their promise, not even when they found themselves beset by grave financial problems, and not even when their librarian got involved in some rather embarrassing quarrels.

So Lami settled happily into the handsome halls on the Via Ginori, little suspecting that he would remain there for the rest of his life. At last he had the

financial security and professional status that he needed to begin building what
he really desired above all: a reputation. And since, for librarians, the best way
to build a reputation was to multiply pages in print, he began searching about for
something to publish. Having nothing of his own at hand, and realizing that his
recent translation of Fénelon's *Adventures of Telemachus* would probably not
appeal to an Italian reading public, he turned for advice to a Scolopian priest
named Alessandro Politi. Politi's careful editions of several little-known Byzantine
texts had just won him a chair at the university. His knowledge of "the abstruse
matter of ecstasies, revelations, and raptures" was soon to win him a place on the
papal commission charged with reforming the martyrology. His opinion thus
carried some weight. Lami listened attentively as Politi outlined the advantages
of preparing an *Opera Omnia* of the early seventeenth-century Dutch philologist,
Jan van Meurs, many of whose writings were available only in manuscript or in
rare first editions.

The project was sure to be well-received abroad, where scholars had long
been tapping Meurs's somewhat chaotic erudition for their own treatises. But it
would probably be well received in Florence, too. Few Florentines cared much
about ancient Attica or modern Leiden, which had been Meurs's two main areas
of research, but many of them, particularly Salvini's former students, professed to
be very interested in the Greek language. At least they were more interested in it
than the self-styled Hellenic specialist in Italy, Scipione Maffei, whose performance
seldom matched his pretensions. And they were more interested in it than their
colleagues in England, whose university chairs in Greek had by now become little
more than sinecures. Salvini himself had done a translation of the *Iliad*—one
which, whatever its defects, was more faithful to the original and less accommodating to the "polite" tastes of modern audiences than those of Mme Dacier and
Alexander Pope. Angelo Maria Ricci had dedicated parts of Plutarch, St. Basil,
and St. Gregory Nazianzen to Lami's patron, Gabriele Riccardi; and he was just
then delivering a long series of "Homeric dissertations" to his students. Lorenzo
Del Riccio had translated Demosthenes, and he was currently preparing a new
version of Theocritus for the Crusca. None of these energetic Hellenists was
aware of Vico's "Discovery of the real Homer." All of them continued to imagine
the ancient Greeks as models of eighteenth-century gentlemen, "the delight of
princes, the mainstay of the clergy, and the admiration of men of letters." They
could hope to be original only by padding their texts with explanatory and
philological footnotes. What Lami did was to bring to their attention some of the
immense accomplishment of the northern European and, in particular, German
philology of the preceding century. Thanks to him, they could now look up the
information they needed in Meurs rather than having to dig for it themselves in
the Laurenziana.

Lami went right to work. He wrote to Berlin, Leiden, Stockholm, and
Copenhagen for manuscripts. He procured several critical essays from Johann

Christoph Wolf in Hamburg and a specially written "Letter on Ancient Carts" from Politi. He drew a large map of Attica and located all the places mentioned in the texts. He searched through Florentine collections for additional illustrations. He hired Vincenzo Franceschini to make copper plates of the appropriate busts in the Medici gallery. He carefully saved all the laudatory letters he had received from his correspondents abroad. And when the first luxurious volume was finally published in 1742, with the letters ostentatiously displayed in the preface, the whole world could see that the editor was now known in the farthest corners of Europe as *eruditissimus Lamius,* "one of the chief ornaments of Italy."

Lami's next two projects were designed to win him the same recognition among his compatriots. The first one he entitled "Memorabilia of Outstanding Italian Scholars"—*Italorum Eruditione Praestantium.* The *Memorabilia* fit perfectly into a genre of literature that was as old as Vasari in Florence and that was to become ever more popular in the next decades—the biographical dictionary. It also had the advantage of requiring a minimum of effort from the editor. Some of the material, like Muratori's notes on Rinaldo d'Este, was already available and had only to be written up in final form. Much of it could be obtained from friends in other cities, even at the risk of having them write eulogies of themselves and then complain about typographical errors. Current standards of biography called for the delineation not of individuals but of types. It required not real men with their defects as well as their qualities, as one observer complained, but imaginary men "deprived of everything peculiarly human." All the biographer had to do was provide a family tree, a record of vital statistics, a note on physical features, a list of virtues, a bibliography, and an account of a pious death. In spite of several unforeseen delays, Lami's first articles were finished by the spring of 1742. They were then published periodically, at the rate of two sheets a month, until they finally filled three large, bound volumes.

The second project—a collection of rare texts from Florentine libraries—was well supported by the example of none other than the dean of Italian letters, Lodovico Antonio Muratori. Muratori had first won a name for himself by pulling long-forgotten manuscripts out of the Ambrosian Library in Milan. He had then consolidated his reputation by pulling manuscripts out of all the libraries of Italy. The immense documentary collections for which he is justly famous even today—the *Antiquitates Italiae Medii Aevi* ("Antiquities of Medieval Italy") and the *Rerum Italicarum Scriptores* ("Writers of Italian Affairs") were still coming out with inexorable regularity. The methods, too, had already been worked out. They could be found ready-made in Jean Mabillon's *Ars Diplomatica* or in Scipione Maffei's *Istoria diplomatica*—a guide to the technique of reading ancient diplomas.

By the mid-1730s, such subjects had already aroused enough interest in Florence to justify the creation of a special institution devoted to them. One evening in 1732 a certain Girolamo de' Pazzi, who had a whole villa full of manuscripts, inscriptions, and ancient coins—as well as microscopes, gems, and plant specimens—gave an intimate dinner party in the tower of his town house. The roast dove was so good, and the conversation was so "learned," that the guests decided to call the tower the *Colombaria* ("Dove Coop") and to dine there regularly. They were encouraged, a little later, by the elevation of Florence to the lofty status of an archaeological quarry: a Roman mosaic was found on Pazzi's own estate, and a number of ancient Christian tombs were discovered underneath the floor of the church of Santa Felicità. In 1735 they were encouraged still further by the visit of Karl Mencke, the son of the former editor of the *Acta Eruditorum* of Leipzig. That gave them a direct connection with the world of German scholarship. Then on May 1 of the same year, they were presented with a stone bearing the seal of the Accademia dei Lincei. That gave them a direct connection with the greatest of the Lincei academicians, their own Galileo. They forthwith elected a secretary to keep regular "Annals," adopted an emblem (two doves [*colombe*] kissing on a branch), and opened their sessions to "anyone of honest condition and wise bearing." The *Società Colombaria* was born. In 1742 it set up a museum in Pazzi's house. In 1745 it established permanent headquarters in Via dello Studio, the academic center of the city. In 1747 it issued the first of three volumes of the best dissertations read at its sessions. The Colombaria was so successful that, thanks to two subsequent "revivals," it still exists today, with an office and a small library on Via S. Egidio, near Santa Maria Nuova.

Lami's *Deliciae Eruditorum* ("Delights of Learned Men") were warmly applauded from the moment they started appearing, in 1736. There was enough material in the Riccardiana and in the other libraries of Tuscany to please all tastes: a chronicle of the emperors after Charlemagne, a ballad of Ser Durante of San Miniato, a Pisan chronicle of 1289, a charter of the hospital at Altopascio. . . . All Lami had to do was transcribe the documents, add appropriate footnotes, and write a preface. But he could also insert reflections of his own on almost any subject in the guise of a critical comment. Hence, the *Deliciae* became the favorite of his many undertakings, and he continued to work on them right up until the year before his death, when the eighteenth volume was completed. Yet Lami still remembered what Guido Grandi had taught him at Pisa, and he soon realized that the documents he was editing might serve purposes other than that of simply catering to the antiquaries and advancing his own reputation. For example, the Gospel of St. John had already proved to him the falsity of Socinianism. Similarly, the letters of an obscure Byzantine theologian, the first of which he had discovered just in time to put into the last pages of the *De Recta,* had proved to him that the doctrines of the Greek and the Latin churches were not so far apart as was usually assumed. He concluded, therefore, that manuscripts and inscriptions were more than just *anticaglia* (ancient objects). They were the means by which the past could be reconstructed, by which the present could be explained, and by which the future could be planned for.

This conclusion had several very important consequences. It did not reject the antiquarians. It did not deny that they had provided the only effective answer to the Cartesians, the Jesuit rhetoricians, and all the other Pyrrhonists of the preceding century, who had questioned the very possibility of historical knowledge. Nor did it deny that establishing the reality of at least certain remnants of the past was an indispensable first step to establishing the reality of the past as a whole. What it did do was transform antiquarianism into history. To the realm of the absolutely certain, which the antiquarians had staked out with the help of "diplomatics," it added a realm of the relatively certain. It made possible not only the formulation of true theses about a particular document but also more-or-less true hypotheses about the age from which the document descended. It not only admitted the statement that an emperor named Hadrian had rebuilt the Via Cassia from Chiusi to Florence. That fact was clearly recorded on a milestone now in the Opera del Duomo:

> ...HADRIANVS...
> VIAM CASSIAM VETVSTATE COLLAPSAM
> A CLVSIONORVM FINIBVS
> FLORENTIAM PERDVXIT

It also admitted the statement that Florence had probably been an important city long before Hadrian put the milestone in place.

More important still, Lami's conclusion suddenly knocked down the barrier that his forefathers had carefully erected at the time of Scipione Ammirato and that the antiquarians still thought was as impenetrable as ever: the barrier between the past and the present. It made both past and present subject to the inevitable corollary of time: change. The beliefs, practices, and institutions of the present were thus bereft of their quality of permanence and inalterability. They were reduced to the level of human inventions. As such, they could be altered as soon as they no longer seemed to be in accord with the intentions of their inventors. The best way of altering them, moreover, was first to consult whoever had had the most experience in similar affairs, no matter when he might have lived. In this way the words of the ancients acquired a new significance. No longer could they be used merely as ornaments in museums or rhetorical flourishes in academic dissertations. These words once again became what they had been in the Renaissance: a means of communication between men of different generations. No longer could a true "student of antiquities" be blind to "how much wisdom shines forth from the institutions, laws, and forms of government of ancient peoples." The student must seek to learn, not just to be amused. He had to be a historian, not just an antiquarian.

Lami did not have to reach this conclusion all by himself. It had already been fully presented in France by the Benedictines of Saint-Maur, who were just then training a whole generation of Catholic apologists to prefer the "solid truth" of their document collections to "the vain ornament of eloquence." It was rapidly being accepted by the nobility of the robe, which applauded the publication of La Curne de la Sainte-Palaye's *Manners and Usages of the Century of Theodosius the Great* in 1740. It was soon to be accepted by the Académie des Inscriptions, which finally recognized that Montfaucon had not written just for monks. It was about to be accepted even by the scientific *Journal des sçavans,* when it commended the *philosophe* Mably for going beyond "names and dates" to "the causes of events" and for making history a prerequisite for political philosophy. The same conclusion had been repeated over and over in Italy by Muratori, who had long since realized the futility of providing dossiers for lawyers. He had stopped trying to document the territorial claims of his patrons, the dukes of Modena, which the politicians of Europe paid no attention to anyway. He had turned instead to a much less immediate, and far more historical, work, the *Annali d'Italia.* And it was he who once again reminded Lami, in 1739, that facts alone were meaningless. They become significant, he insisted, only when they are made relevant to a question posed by the investigator.

All Lami had to do, then, was to promulgate in Florence what Muratori and the Benedictines had already done beyond the Alps and Apennines. And by the late 1730s, he had personal as well as intellectual reasons for doing so as quickly and forcefully as possible. Several theses in his *De Recta,* it seems, had stirred up a rather dangerous controversy. Calling St. John the Evangelist a "rustic" ran counter to one of the basic axioms of post-Tridentine Italian Catholicism, namely, that nobility and learning were prerequisites for sanctity. Suggesting that a few passages—and even a whole epistle—usually attributed to St. John might actually be later interpolations (as Erasmus had suggested two centuries earlier) looked like an attack on the authority of the Vulgate. Inviting Protestants to join forces against a common enemy seemed like a denial of the self-sufficiency of the Roman Church. And when at least two Protestants denounced the invitation as just one more Catholic plot against the Scriptures, it seemed like wasted effort as well.

Lami attempted to bolster his theses with new documents—and with another blast of uncharitable epithets—in a much larger volume, which he published under the title of *De Eruditione Apostolorum*—"On the Learning of the Apostles"—in 1738. But in vain. He found himself confronted not with individual prejudices or casual opinions, but with an entire system of philosophy, one, he wailed, that was as bitterly defended as it was "full of sophisms" and fraught with "erroneous and impious consequences." This philosophy, he claimed, had provoked the Protestant rebellion in the sixteenth century and stifled the rise of science in the seventeenth. Worse yet, it had perpetrated a kind of piety that had little in common with true Christianity except the name. The attention of the faithful was drawn not to Christ but to the "sweet nails that tore, ripped, cut . . . and lacerated . . . those most delicate members." The actions of the Apostles waned before the "singular virtues" of the most recent Florentine "mystic," a young nun named Maria Anna Piazzini, who beat herself with a chain until she hemorrhaged internally, who wrote letters in her own blood, and who sucked liquid out of a painting of St. Francis's stigmata—all in defiance of the rules of her convent. The majesty of God retreated before the prodigies of the Virgin of Impruneta and the miracles of the Crucifix at Porta Pinti. Good works were superseded by vows to die on behalf of the still-undefined doctrine of the Immaculate Conception —vows like those which certain Sicilian monks had been collecting by the thousands since 1720. This kind of piety, said Lami, was based on "the Holy Scriptures, Apostolic traditions, [decrees] of the Councils, constitutions of the supreme pontiffs, and the consent of the Universal Church"—all of which had an objective, unalterable existence of their own. They rested on myth. And myth could easily be manipulated for the financial benefit of the custodians of certain shrines and the members of certain religious orders.

Lami realized that this kind of piety could be checked only by introducing a very different kind. What he had to offer in its place was the piety of Augustine, of Basil, and of the fifteenth-century bishop of Florence, St. Antonino, whose *Summa Moralis* he helped edit in 1741. It was also the piety of the moderate Augustinians of the preceding generation and of "that learned personage," as he called Magalotti, "who ruled the hearts of princes and of all men of letters and culture." It promoted morality by imitation rather than by "cases of conscience" and "cold, sterile speculations." It looked forward to substantial changes in the structure and the practice of ecclesiastical institutions. Finally, it rested firmly on verifiable, documentary fact. Its chief weapon, the weapon Lami was certain would finally defeat his opponents, was history.

Yet introducing history into Florence turned out to be a very difficult task. Guido Grandi's attempt to do the same thing some thirty-five years earlier had long since been forgotten. Or rather it had been effectively squelched by a Florentine Oratorian named Giacomo Laderchi, whom Pope Clement XI made official historian of the Roman Church. None of Laderchi's arguments against history was particularly original. Most of them had been fully exhibited in 1695 by that archenemy of the Bollandists, Sébastien de Saint-Paul. But Laderchi felt obliged to repeat them for the good of his compatriots, especially since the campaign to wreck the Bollandists' great *Acta Sanctorum* had momentarily collapsed. The study of the past, Laderchi insisted, was a dangerous occupation. It tended to "put everything in doubt," to replace "it was" with "it seems to have been," to turn truth (*vero*) into apparent truth (*verosimile*), and to diminish "the veneration we owe to tradition, to antiquity, and to the church." Moreover, it was redundant.

The past had already been recorded once and for all by his illustrious predecessor, Cesare Baronio. And since Baronio was supported not so much by the validity of his sources as by the authority of the Papacy, any deviation from what he recorded was worthy of the Index. That, indeed, is just what Laderchi recommended for Tillemont's *History of the Roman Emperors,* which Lami hailed as one of the greatest monuments of modern scholarship when a third edition was launched in the late 1730s. Finally, the study of the past was a waste of time. What counted was the "perfection" of the church, not its origins. What best supported the church was not what men did for it with the help of God, but what God did all by himself in complete disregard for the natural capacities of men. To prove his point, Laderchi collected so many miracles done in the name of St. Peter Damian that three large volumes were not enough to record them all.

Laderchi's fellow ecclesiastical historians agreed with him. The only possible justification for history, they insisted, was to "glorify God," "console the clergy," and manifest their own "great veneration" for their religious orders. One of them decided to bring the century-old *History of the Servites* down to his own time. What he really did was to demonstrate once again the marvelous ability of his congregation to generate candidates for canonization. Another decided to separate the truth from the growing legends about Magalotti's pious young disciple, Lorenzo Maria Gianni. What he really did was to prove that St. Gaetano had kept Gianni's mother from suffering labor pains and that St. Maria Maddalena de' Pazzi had kept Gianni himself from breaking his arm in a fall downstairs. The most any of these authors would concede to the new historical scholarship was to forego "the slightest shade of exaggeration" and to add a number of purely decorative documents in their footnotes.

The efforts of Giuseppe Averani, Lami's former law professor at Pisa, fared no better than Grandi's, at least when he tried to venture beyond the walls of academic jurisprudence. That is just what the government commissioned him to do in 1720. In order to avoid having Tuscany swallowed up by the Hapsburg monarchy, he was asked to demonstrate that Florence had always been, and therefore still was, an independent republic, no matter what statements to the contrary might be deduced from the declarations of Charles V, Philip II, or Cosimo I. Unfortunately, the only documents Averani had time to consult were those that had been collected two centuries earlier by Vincenzo Borghini. Borghini was a historian, not a lawyer, and he had lived in an age when history as a discipline was still alive. He had therefore put his documents in a historical, not a juridical, context. They proved, that is, that certain juridical relationships had existed in the thirteenth or the sixteenth century. They did not prove that the same relationships did or ought to exist in all times. So the lawyers in Vienna quickly made hash of them. Moreover, Averani soon realized that his arguments were completely inapplicable to the current situation. Florence could not become a republic again, for its aristocracy had neither the will nor the ability to turn itself back into a responsible patriciate. The powers of Europe were not interested in reestablishing a former situation but in creating a new one. Hence, politics was a matter of might, not right—of armies and marriage contracts, not of historical precedents. And Averani resolved never to touch it again.

Then, in 1727, history was dealt one final blow. The trouble had been brewing ever since 1712, when the Dutch jurist Heinrich Brenckmann had first come to Florence in order to examine the famous text of Justinian's Pandects. Brenckmann soon recognized Averani's methods as his own—and as those of their common humanist predecessors. He therefore put Averani in contact with Dutch booksellers and arranged to have his *Interpretationes Juris* published at Leiden, then the capital of European jurisprudence. And that, more than any supposed historical inaccuracies, is probably what really annoyed Grandi. Never one to let prudence temper jealousy, Grandi wrote a blistering attack on Brenckmann's *History of the Pandects* and then published it with a dedication to Averani himself. The battle was on, with the rector of the university and the government in Florence on one side, armed mobs of enraged Pisan citizens on the other, and the students caught in between. The battle culminated in the resignation of one of Averani's most gifted disciples, Bernardo Tanucci, who immediately emigrated to Parma and became, a few years later, prime minister to the king of Naples. It dragged on until 1764, when the Pisan nobleman Borgo Dal Borgo published one last *Dissertation on the History of the Pisan Codices*.

Because of the triviality of the issues it was fought over, the "Battle of the Pandects" brought the whole historical approach into disrepute. History was being used not to sustain either the antiquity or the continuing validity of Roman law in Italy. On that question everyone agreed. Rather, it was being used solely to decide whether the manuscript in the Laurenziana had been stolen by the Pisans at Amalfi or whether it had been copied from an earlier version at Bologna. And it was being used to determine whether the manuscript should be called the "Pisan Pandects" after its supposed captors, or the "Florentine Pandects" after its present owners. As the Camaldolese monks needed saints, so the Pisan citizens needed heroes. And they were ready to ostracize or crack the skull of any historian who failed to serve them.

Both of the two premature heralds of history gave it up. Averani turned instead to concocting "scientific" explanations of New Testament miracles (the "darkness over the earth" at Jesus' death was caused by gigantic sunspots). As his disciples started talking about what a great jurist he "had been," he became increasingly morose, to the point of mental instability. He rewarded visitors at his sickbed with insults. He ended by accusing Lami of impiety for doing just what he had taught him to do many years before at the university—being a historian. Grandi, similarly, retreated from history to myth-making. He had already been guilty of doctoring up a few documents in his *Camaldolese History* of 1705. When some of his colleagues complained to him about a lacuna in their calendar, he obliged them by writing a "twelfth-century" biography of the largely legendary St. Bonomo. He then passed off his composition as a copy of a manuscript acquired from Queen Cristina of Sweden by none other than Muratori's mentor, the incorruptible Benedetto Bacchini. And he got away with it. Two decades later the Congregation of Rites sanctioned the cult of St. Bonomo. Not until 1916 did anyone uncover the fraud.

3

The end of the Medici

Yet Grandi's and Averani's contemporaries had good reasons of their own for refusing either "to investigate the past or to worry about what will happen in the future." "Enjoying the present" was about the only consolation they had left. "The decade of the 1730s," according to the most recent authority on the age,* "marked the lowest point of political disintegration, economic depression, and intellectual disillusionment in eighteenth-century Italy." This process of disintegration had begun in 1701, perhaps the most catastrophic year in Italian history since 1494. The ascent of a Bourbon to the throne of Spain moved the battlefield of Europe from the Rhine to Italy—and this time not just to Lombardy and Piedmont, which alone had borne the brunt of Hapsburg-Bourbon rivalries in the seventeenth century, but also to central and southern Italy, which had been almost entirely free of war since 1559. In 1707, the Austrian occupation of Milan and Naples transferred the hegemony of the peninsula from Madrid, where it had rested for over 150 years, to Vienna. Then, in 1714, the Peace of Radstatt cracked the very foundations of the whole Italian state system, the system that had been worked out so laboriously in the century between the Peace of Lodi and the Treaty of Cateau-Cambrésis. By giving one-third of the Duchy of Milan to the duke of Savoy, it simply whetted his appetite for the other two-thirds. By attaching Mantua to Austrian Lombardy, it threatened the independence of the other minor Po Valley states. By giving Malta and Majorca to England, and by detaching Sicily from Naples, it invited the active intervention of still another great foreign power. By robbing the Venetians of their hard-won conquests in Greece, it proved that no Italian state could hope to control its destiny. By excluding King Philip V of Spain altogether, it encouraged his Italian wife, Elisabetta Farnese, and her Italian advisor, Cardinal Giulio Alberoni, to play on the nostalgia of the Spanish in order to further her own family ambitions at home.

* Franco Venturi.

Meanwhile, the death of Louis XIV removed the only justification for concerted action among the powers. International politics became a free-for-all among contesting dynasties. Secret clauses belied the public texts of each new treaty. Alliances collapsed as soon as they were ratified. Not even the oldest frontier was any longer secure. Since Italy was by now completely excluded from active participation in the contest, no one could tell on one day who would rule any particular Italian state on the next, or indeed whether the state would even continue to exist. As three native ruling houses headed for extinction, and as the rulers of Spain, Savoy, and Austria traded Sicily, Sardinia, and the Tuscan fortresses back and forth among each other, even the wildest projects gained an aura of probability. One more shift of the balance of power might well have given the Este the succession to the lands of the Countess Matilda—and to those of the Medici—and it might well have permitted Elisabetta Farnese to carve out a kingdom for her son between Siena and Piacenza.

For Florentines, this state of uncertainty was particularly onerous, because it coincided with the gradual disappearance of the last remaining guarantor of the political order they had enjoyed for over two hundred years—the dynasty. Cosimo I had saved the Medici family from extinction in the sixteenth century, principally by begetting children at the rate of almost one a year during the lifetime of his wife. But all of Cosimo III's efforts to have his sons imitate their great ancestor came to naught, partly because the wives he chose for them were all as repugnant as his own. Gian Gastone, the last surviving male heir of Giovanni da Bisticci and the last Medici grand duke of Tuscany, had shown considerable promise in his youth. He was "a most learned prince," as Lami still remembered him many years later, "a follower of Leibniz in philosophy and not one to let priests and monks lead him around by the nose." But overindulgence had ruined his health; by 1724 when the sculptor Pianmontini reproduced him in bronze, his "Medici lip" had all but vanished beneath enormous jowls. A disastrous marriage to a Bohemian amazon and a winter spent trailing around after her from one hunting expedition to another had spoiled whatever taste he may have had for women; his lowborn boyfriends took over Palazzo Pitti as soon as he had cleared it of his father's friars. He had then taken to the bottle, and he regularly ruined dinner parties by insulting his hosts, telling dirty stories, and throwing up all over the table. All the desperate and costly diplomatic missions of the last decade, he realized, had accomplished nothing. They had achieved only one insignificant victory: the title to a small feudal domain near Ascoli Piceno; and he owed this victory largely to the ineptitude of the claimants' lawyer, Alfonso de' Liguori, who thereafter abandoned the law for theology. Gian Gastone therefore gave up international politics altogether. He made one last public appearance in 1729. And he spent the last eight years of his life in bed.

The fate of the grand duchy was thus left to the powers of Europe. And after innumerable changes of mind, they finally settled on Don Carlos of Bourbon, the elder son of Elisabetta Farnese. Don Carlos was young, handsome, energetic, and gay. Thanks to his half-Italian upbringing, and thanks to two months of careful coaching by Vincenzo Riccardi, he succeeded in ingratiating himself with senators and plebeians alike from the moment he set foot in his future capital, in March 1731. So well did he succeed, indeed, that no one complained about the six thousand soldiers he brought along with him. No one even bothered to reflect that the last of the Medici was being forced to sanction exactly what the first Medici grand duke had spent the first years of his reign getting rid of: a Spanish army of occupation.

Then, just as the Florentines were becoming accustomed to their prince-to-be, and just as Gian Gastone had eased the transition by "adopting" him as a ward, the War of Polish Succession broke out. Don Carlos marched off to Naples, where he threw out the Austrians and became the first resident king since the early sixteenth century. Tuscany fell back into the cauldron of European power politics, unable to defend itself even against food-stealing raids into the Maremma by the commander of Orbetello. As a result of the war, the elector of Saxony was given the Kingdom of Poland, the king of Poland was given the Duchy of Lorraine, and the duke of Lorraine, Francis Stephen, or Francesco Stefano as he was called in Italy, was given the succession to Tuscany. Accordingly, the Spanish troops moved out of Livorno and Portoferraio in the winter of 1736–37, and six thousand German troops moved in to take their place.

As far as Florentines were concerned, this was the worst of all possible solutions. Francesco Stefano happened also to be the promised consort of Maria Theresa, the only child of Emperor Charles VI and heir apparent to the dominions of the house of Hapsburg. Moreover, he was the Hapsburg candidate to succeed Charles VI as Holy Roman Emperor; and eight years later, after a long but futile attempt to break the traditional Hapsburg succession, the imperial crown was duly conferred upon him. Obviously, the new grand duke would not be able to reside in Florence even if he wanted to, which he did not. He would have to govern his new subjects, about whom he knew little and cared less, from a distance. Worse yet, his bride's title to her hereditary states hung on a flimsy agreement called the "Pragmatic Sanction"—an agreement by which each of the powers of Europe separately promised to recognize a female succession, but which bound none of them any more than all the other treaties signed, sealed, and then torn up during the preceding fifty years.

Florentines were about to lose what for centuries they had valued above all else. It was the threat to their independence that alone, in moments of crisis, had kept their ancestors of republican times from cutting each others' throats. It was the restoration of their independence that had reconciled their ancestors of the sixteenth century to the Medici principate. It was the preservation of their independence that had kept their country free from the ravages of the great wars of the seventeenth century. And it was their independence that they now were about to lose. Whatever the latest peace treaty said about a separate status, it looked as if Tuscany would be reduced to the rank of an Austrian province, much like Milan, and that it would then be bled dry to prevent the dismemberment of the Hapsburg monarchy, with which it had almost no interests in common. Florentines had good cause to weep, then, when Gian Gastone finally died in July 1737:

> Ah yes, 'tis true, I've heard the sad lament:
> great Cosmo's seed this day at last is spent;
> your end, Oh Florence, I know is now decreed.
> (Anon., *Crusca Tramoggia*, Cr. 14)

The new government did little to reconcile Florentines to their fate. Prince Marc de Craon, whom Francesco Stefano sent down as his plenipotentiary, tried to pass himself off as a representative of French culture, and he took credit, later on, for having Voltaire elected to the Crusca. But his unpolished speech betrayed him as a "Lorrainer," or, in Italian, as a *Lorenese,* a term that quickly acquired the additional connotation of "carpetbagger." Even the English ambassador found the *Lorensi* "vastly ignorant and insignificant," interested only in playing quadrille and piquet. The doors of Florentine high society remained as tightly closed to them as they were open to genuine Frenchmen—like the president Charles de Brosses, who was enthusiastically welcomed during his visit to the city in 1739.

Craon's colleague, the financial expert Emmanuel de Richecourt, was brighter and abler. Those who got along with him found him "clean-cut, gracious, eloquent, pleasant in private conversation, acute in his ability to know men and to understand the most minute details of government." But he was also vain, as Lady Margaret Walpole, the sister of the prime minister of Great Britain, discovered when he started paying court to her. Above all, he was rigid, self-righteous, and authoritarian. "He wanted to do everything by himself," admitted one of his admirers, and he relentlessly knocked down anyone who got in his way—from the wealthy, influential Florentine, Carlo Ginori, whom he sent off as governor to Livorno, to poor Craon, whom he eventually had recalled to Vienna. He thought of himself as "the absolute lord of Etruria," even to the point of single-handedly violating the immunities of the English merchants at Livorno. He disliked everything in Florence that differed from what he had known in Nancy. To celebrate the short, and only, visit of the new grand duke and duchess in 1739, he tore down an ancient column in the Piazza San Marco and hired a French architect (as if there were no architects in Florence!) to erect the hideous "French" triumphal arch that still mars the Piazza San Gallo (or Piazza della Libertà, as it is now called). He denounced the Tuscan administration as an illogical mixture of monarchy, aristocracy, and democracy, "a chaos almost impossible to disentangle." He began his administration by abruptly firing all of

Gian Gastone's court officials and taking away whatever power was still left to the urban magistracies.

Richecourt may, then, have been conscientious and concerned about the "common good." But his power was actually not as great as he pretended. The Supreme Council for Tuscan Affairs in Vienna frequently ordered him to do the opposite of what he recommended. And the grand duke was willing to receive secret petitions sent in over his regent's head. Hence, Richecourt was commonly blamed for everything that went wrong and given no credit for anything that went right. Even a well-meaning attempt to rule by consent backfired. When, in 1740, he accepted a recommendation from the head of the hospital to change the standards of accreditation for physicians, he brought down the wrath of the whole medical guild, which politely but firmly reprimanded him for not having first looked up the precedents in Tuscan law.

The minor Lorraine officials simply added to the unpopularity of their chiefs. They immediately abolished all the traditional holidays connected with the former dynasty: the birthday of Cosimo the Elder, the election of Cosimo I, and the elevation of Clement VII. They tore down the "six balls" from all public buildings and crowded anything symbolic of Florence into less than one-sixth of a new shield, which was covered with French lilies, bold horizontal stripes, an eagle, and a Lorraine cross. They tore up the "family compact" of 1731, which had guaranteed the possession of Medici family property to Gian Gastone's sister, Anna Maria Luisa. She responded by cultivating the nostalgia of Florentines for the extinct dynasty and by supervising the completion of the Medici mausoleum behind San Lorenzo. They took over all the more important posts in the bureaucracy and left the officials they replaced with little choice but to emigrate en masse to Naples. They disbanded the traditional militia, which they—with good reason—deemed to be expensive, inefficient, and unreliable. They filled the Fortezza with Lorraine troops and turned the cannons around so that they pointed toward the city, not away from it. Since they could not control their mercenaries, they let them wander about freely, and the citizens were soon compelled to respond with the same kind of "law and order" that was meted out to them. The first serious riot broke out in July 1738, when two soldiers were beaten up for having cut a rag collector's nose off. Another riot almost broke out on July 1, 1741: Craon was loudly booed when his chariot won the *palio* at Santa Maria Novella, and eight soldiers who had started softening up one of the booers just made it into a church before a furious mob could catch them.

Thus Florentines may well have been ready, as de Brosses reported, to give one-third of their possessions to have the Medici back and another third "pour n'avoir pas les Lorrains." But for the moment, however, they fully expected their new masters to vanish as suddenly as they had come. One more switch in alliances, they thought, and Francesco Stefano could well be replaced by the half-Italian brother of Don Carlos, Elisabetta Farnese's second son, Don Felipe.

The Spanish ambassador did his best to encourage these hopes. He personally paid for the restoration of Santa Maria Novella, where he had long resided. He trained crowds of paupers to shout *Viva la Spagna!* whenever he threw coins at them from a balcony. He constantly intrigued with all the disgruntled patricians, especially with Carlo Rinuccini, formerly chief counselor to Gian Gastone and now the manager of all of Anna Maria Luisa's business affairs.

Insecurity was perhaps the greatest defect of the Lorraine government. It was promoted by the attitude of the Lorrainers themselves, who wanted nothing more than to return to Lorraine. It was emphasized by the continuing presence of a Spanish garrison in the Maremma fortresses. And it was exacerbated by the outbreak of the War of Austrian Succession in the fall of 1740. If Frederick II of Prussia could so easily grab Silesia, which had been ruled by the Hapsburgs for over two hundred years, if Karl Albrecht of Bavaria could claim the crown of Bohemia and then that of the Holy Roman Empire, both of which had belonged to Hapsburgs for over three centuries, then why could not Don Felipe take possession of a state that had been Hapsburg—and then only by marriage—for only four years? Perhaps, on the other hand, Florentines might be rid of both Spaniards and Germans all at once: that, at any rate, was the suggestion the first minister of King Louis XV tantalized them with in January 1745. And just as the minister released his "Memorandum on a League to Establish Peace in Italy," one of his compatriots wrote a still more daring "Plan for Setting Up a Republic in Tuscany," which was soon published in a Florentine magazine, the *Giornale de' letterati*.

Even Maria Theresa's separate peace with Fredrick the Great in 1746, which permitted her at last to send an army into Italy, did not settle the matter. Nor did the death of Philip V, which withdrew the backing of Spain from Elisabetta Farnese's maternal ambitions. In December of the same year the people of Genoa, who were supposed to be as supinely accommodating to foreign armies as all other Italians, rose in rebellion and threw the Austrians out of the city. Thus not until the Treaty of Aachen was finally ratified in October 1748 did the status of Tuscany at last become clear. Francesco Stefano remained the grand duke, and he was freed of his only serious rival by the installation of Don Felipe as duke of Parma. But he was forbidden to unite his own domain with those of his wife. He was obliged to name his second or third son, not his first, as his personal successor. He was held to these conditions by the realization of all the great powers that a balance among themselves could best be preserved by moving Italy from the center back to the periphery of their fraternal squabbles—and by leaving it alone. Italy thus won, or was granted, a degree of autonomy far greater than any it had enjoyed since 1559. When the next, and the most famous reversal of European alliances made allies of the former contenders for hegemony in the peninsula, it was granted a half-century of peace as well.

Meanwhile, some forty years of political instability had undermined still further the precarious economic situation inherited from the seventeenth century. Tuscany did not suffer alone, to be sure. It was just one of the victims of a long-range economic recession that affected the whole of Europe during the same period, a recession that kept over 18 percent of the inhabitants of Bayeux in Normandy on relief rolls and most of the artisans of Genoa on weak minestrone. But the recession was compounded in Tuscany by forced levies: the bill for the Spanish troops alone in 1737 amounted to 1,120,827 *scudi,* or about 13 percent of the total revenues of the state. It was compounded still further by the anti-economic measures adopted by the government to meet the levies: more *monti* (bond issues), higher excise taxes, and, in 1720, a 4 percent across-the-board surcharge on all incomes. Tuscan currency faltered, or at least so thought Scipione Maffei, who could not find out whether the Florentine *scudo* was worth 8 *paoli* or 11.5 *paoli* in 1724. The secretary of finance (*depositario generale*) threatened to default on interest payments. And the state debt soared. It was still so high in 1737 (14 million *scudi*), even after Gian Gastone's economy measures, that the Lorraine government tried to get out of recognizing it.*

In spite of good intentions, neither Richecourt nor his Florentine collaborators did much to remedy these fiscal abuses. They forcibly reduced interest payments on the debt—which, of course, just robbed their creditors of that much of their capital. They reestablished a state lottery, which Gian Gastone had succeeded in abolishing and which Muratori had just shown to be ruinous as well as immoral. And they sold parts of the state domain, an important source of future income, just to meet current expenses. True, they knew in general what had to be done, and they even appointed a commission to look into a thorough overhaul of the entire tax structure. But their plans were wrecked by the grand duke himself. Without even consulting them, Francesco Stefano suddenly turned over all the revenues of the state to a "farm" (*appalto*), or a private tax-collecting corporation. The farm in turn expressly forbade any change in the existing structure, and it forthwith laid hands on everything it could, from the estate of Craon's daughter-in-law to the presents left by Anna Maria Luisa to her servants. Worse yet, all the partners under the first ten-year contract were foreigners, and they agreed to pay 2.8 out of their 4.2 million *lire* fee directly to the grand duke. Hence, much of the tax revenue was piped right out of the country. Even more was piped out in the form of subsidies to the bottomless Austrian war chest—over 12 million *scudi* by 1756—and in the form of bribes to the German troops "wintered" in Tuscany.

One former source of considerable "invisible imports" was lost forever,

---

* Warning: these and most of the following statistics are the result of my calculations from figures given by Parenti, Dal Pane, and Zobi, supplemented by occasional references in contemporary correspondence. Hence, they are highly tentative. The financial and economic history of this period still remains to be written.

when the grand duke sold off as his own the extensive Medici family possessions abroad. When monetary resources were exhausted, he turned to human ones. He ordered three thousand recruits to be sent to Germany in 1757, of whom only three hundred survived the first battle. When he demanded a thousand more in 1761, the Tuscan army deserted en masse, and the English fleet used the levy as an excuse for violating the neutrality of Tuscan ships in the Mediterranean. The final blow occurred in 1765, at the death of Francesco Stefano. Almost crushed with the enormous expenses of the Seven Years' War, his wife and son simply incorporated the "huge fortune" he had sucked out of Tuscany into the Austrian treasury. And not a *soldo* of it was ever returned.

Under these circumstances, any thought of lowering the state debt had to be abandoned: it was still almost as high in 1758 as it had been in 1737, even though taxes had gone up by some 20 percent. And Tuscan taxpayers could console themselves only by noticing that the debt of the Hapsburg monarchy as a whole had almost doubled in the same period. When the government was called upon to meet a sudden emergency, it found itself unable to move. For example, in 1742 it ordered the Magona ironworks to furnish building material, and it ordered the *Monte* to furnish capital for the relief of Livorno, which had been half-destroyed by a disastrous earthquake. "But lo! The Magona has no iron, nor the Pietà any money"; and the Livornesi were left to fend for themselves.

As taxes went up, taxable income went down. Frightened by an increasingly troubled economic situation and by a rapidly declining demand for fine Florentine silks in Germany, the big aristocratic families finally consummated the withdrawal from commercial and industrial activities that had begun two centuries earlier. In the 1720s, they still held 59 percent of the capital invested in Florentine business concerns, and some of them still took an active part in management, particularly in wool, silk, and banking. But by the 1750s, they held only 28 percent; since their holdings were not transferred to new investors at anything like their original value, the total invested capital declined by some 37 percent during the same period. Even Livorno was struck—partly by warfare on the Mediterranean, partly by competition from the free port at Genoa, and most of all, after 1737, by doubts concerning its neutral status. Consequently, the Livornesi were induced to take the much more risky and less promising business of handling money transactions and supervising smuggling activities for the benefit of the rebels in Corsica.

Some of the capital thus withdrawn went into land. Grain prices rose slowly but steadily, from 60 to 84.83 index points, between the 1720s and the 1740s. Florentine investors, untroubled by the erratic fluctuations of such markets as that of Turin, could look forward to a gradual improvement in the modest 3–4 percent return they were assured initially. Some of the capital vanished in a series of bank crashes. Senator Vincenzo Antinori declared bankruptcy for 33,000 *scudi* on Christmas Day, 1737, "an event which amazed the whole city."

according to a contemporary diarist. The big Franceschi firm in Via de'
Guicciardini collapsed in 1741, dragging with it the two sister firms of the
Franchini and the Gerini and forcing its president to take refuge from his creditors
in the Church of Santo Spirito.

Much of the capital was just thrown away in high living. Furnishings became
more elegant: of the 80,000 *scudi* that Cosimo Riccardi took out of his silk
companies between 1719 and 1739, 3,764 went into one order of crimson velvet
for chair covers, and 1,182 went into one order of elegant Bristol cloth. Parties
became more sober, since sherbet and lemonade replaced wine (which was much
cheaper) as the normal refreshment; but they also became more elaborate. A
single reception at the Feroni palace in Via de' Serragli on May 2, 1741, filled
some sixteen rooms, lit by "thousands of lights" and decorated with "prodigious
quantities of pictures, statues, bronzes, etc." Weekend jaunts into the country
became more extravagant: even Falco Rinuccini, the Florentine *antiquis moribus,*
whom Tanucci compared to the patriarchs of the Republic, spent much of his
enormous annual income of 50,000 *scudi* putting on plays and concerts at his
villas for a hundred-odd hangers-on. Coaches became more "superb and
sumptuous" than ever: they were adorned with "noble wood carvings, curious
paintings . . . exterior and interior gold leaf . . . rich drapes, and velvets of
various colors—so that they seem to be portable sitting rooms." Indeed, the
"insane display of human pride" outran the capacities of many pocketbooks. The
English ambassador, Horace Mann, whose garden parties were among the most
popular in the city, noticed that his guests often stuffed his glasses into their
pockets as they departed. One nobleman was forced to raise ready cash by
raffling off his paintings. Three others took advantage of their public offices to
steal from the public granaries—until they were arrested by order of the grand
duke in 1748.

In other ages, the Florentine aristocracy might have used its ingenuity to
recoup its lost fortunes. But in the mid-eighteenth century financial bankruptcy
was frequently accompanied by moral bankruptcy, and many members of the
aristocracy preferred to waste their time in a complicated game known as
cicisbeismo. This game was the most recent solution to the age-old and still
inflexible system of arranged marriages. It strictly limited the relationship between
husband and wife to the preservation of the family estate and the procreation of
heirs. Outside the home, neither spouse was permitted to be seen in the company
of the other. A lady could be accompanied to her theater box or detained for
intimate chit-chat behind one of Horace Mann's softly-lit orange trees only by
her *cicisbeo,* while his wife was off attending to someone else. Her husband, in
turn, was expected to dedicate himself exclusively to his *cicisbea,* pouring her
chocolate in the morning and seeing her to her carriage in the evening.

Cicisbeismo had notable advantages over the arrangement that had preceded
it in the seventeenth century—marriage with prostitution. For one thing, it

finally enabled women to enter society on the same footing as men. For another, it made possible a sentiment that contained at least some elements of love, or at least a bit of serious flirting. Even those who laughed at it could think of no viable alternative. Giovan Battista Fagiuoli's "Fashionable husband" (*Il marito alla moda*) ended up retracting his own objections to his wife's visitors and even rejecting the objections of his old-fashioned father. None of the ecclesiastical moralists ever ventured to denounce *cicisbeismo*. And when, many years later, the lay moralist Antonio Cocchi (who happened to be one of the few happily married men in the city) delivered a tongue-in-cheek tirade against matrimony, his outraged critics were left defenseless. For they had never thought of matrimony as anything but part of "the political and ecclesiastical system of the country." They could thus do no more than accuse him of trying "to ruin and corrupt men . . . with a bunch of revolting impieties already fried and re-fried by innumerable transalpine hacks." Or else, like Lami, who happened to be one of Cocchi's good friends, they could simply overlook his latest book by praising all his others.

In general, however, the disadvantages of *cicisbeismo* far outweighed the advantages. First of all, it made the life of a host miserable. He had to remember the family names not only of husbands and wives, but also of their current *cicisbei*; he had to make sure, for instance, that Giovanna Dini was seated next to Fernando Pandolfini, her "man," and not next to Luca Antonio degli Albizi, to whom her parents had married her. Second, it ruled out what even Antonio Cocchi, the author of the treatise against marriage, admitted to be a physical necessity—sex; and to judge from the absence of reported illegitimate births, it did so successfully. Hence, it probably exacerbated the constant bickering that made so many gatherings "cold [and] insipid" in the 1740s. Indeed, bickering became so general that it eventually affected even Lami's patrons, the Riccardi. From 1741 on, the aging Cosimo Riccardi constantly quarreled with his sons, to whom he had turned over the management of the family estate, over the size of the allowance they had agreed to accord him, and in 1746 he tried to increase the allowance without their consent by placing their jewels on the market in Lisbon and London. The result of this quarreling was near ruin, at least for the creditors of the family, who were left empty-handed when Cosimo's son and his grandson died within a few days of each other in 1752.

Thus in Florence, as in most of the other cities of northern Italy, the nobility gradually lost some of the prestige they had enjoyed for almost two centuries as the cultural and economic leaders of the community. They were denounced in Milan by the poet Giuseppe Parini for wasting "morning, noon, and night" (the titles of his trilogy) on meaningless ceremonies. And they were denounced in Florence by a Tuscan bureaucrat in 1738 for taking money out of agriculture and throwing it away on foreign luxuries and law suits.

Meanwhile, the steady decline of capital available for investment left the rest of the population ever less able to support itself. And unfortunately the rest of the population grew in numbers. True, Florence did not grow as fast as Bologna, which suffered all the same hardships except political insecurity. Nor did it grow as fast as a rather exceptional city like Strasbourg, which benefited from its recent incorporation into the French monarchy. But Florence finally recovered the losses it had endured after the plagues of 1631–33. The diocese as a whole passed from 182,427 residents in 1676 to 215,433 in 1738. Even the slight decline in the following two decades—from 213,427 in 1745 to 212,219 in 1751—was insufficient to offset the continued growth of the grand duchy as a whole—from 899,605 in 1738 to 924,625 in 1753. That meant so many more mouths to feed, just as the economy of the country became ever less able to feed them. Consequently, the severe famine of 1733–34 was only a warning that the worst was still to come. When it finally did come, in 1763–65, almost nothing could be done to allay it. Thus Giuseppe Zocchi was probably not too inaccurate when he drew a group of beggars with hands outstretched on the steps of San Firenze, or when he showed two men in rags sleeping on the rubble along the Lungarno Guicciardini, and when he pictured half-starved children playing on driftwood seesaws in front of Piazza Ognissanti. Even the tourists who bought his magnificent engravings could not have ignored the misery that surrounded the monuments they came to admire.

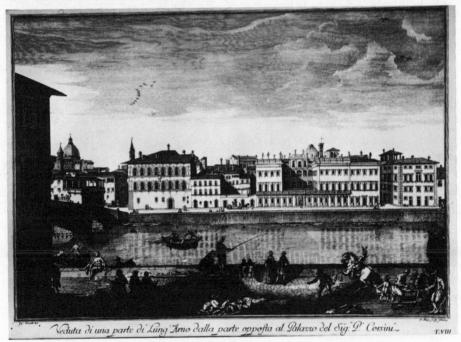

Veduta di una parte di Lung'Arno dalla parte opposta al Palazzo del Sig.r P.e Corsini.   T.VIII

22. Zocchi, Palazzo Corsini

4

Lawyers in office

Apparently, then, Lami could not have picked a less auspicious moment for trying to make his compatriots think in historical terms. Fortunately, he was unaware of how inauspicious it was. For he was still just as oblivious to politics and economics as every other Florentine man of letters had been since the sixteenth century. He considered "those people who like political reflections" to be simply curious time-wasters, and he declined to serve them with any more than two-line reviews in the *Novelle*. He considered such matters to be the exclusive domain of princes—or perhaps of God, since the new dynasty had obviously been chosen *divino consilio,* "by divine counsel." Yet if he had paid some attention to these matters, he would have noticed that the change in dynasties was somewhat less of a disaster than most Florentines thought it to be. The change left Tuscans in charge of many important areas of internal administration, and it also provided them with a much greater freedom of initiative than had been possible under the vigilant or somnolent gaze of the last two Medici. From 1739 on, all but extraordinary affairs were entrusted to a Council of Regency (hence the name *Reggenza*—"Regency"—usually applied to the whole period between 1737 and 1765). The Council included not only Craon and Richecourt, but also several of the most energetic Florentine ministers left over from the preceding reign.

The most energetic of these ministers was Giulio Rucellai. Rucellai was head of one of the oldest and wealthiest families of the city. But his professional competence and his sense of political responsibility kept him from being affected by the general decline of the class he was born into. Rucellai was something of a man of letters: he wrote one adaptation of Addison's *Drummer* and another of Molière's *Misanthrope*. Though his plays made "a woeful appearance" on the stage, their characters and situations were sufficiently Florentine to make Tanucci, the busy prime minister of Naples, read them with nostalgia and amusement. Rucellai was also "a valiant and good connoisseur," at least of things like

Horace Walpole's expensive snuffboxes. And he was an expert *cicisbeo,* so expert that he even managed to take Lady Margaret Walpole away from Richecourt.

But above all, Rucellai was a lawyer—one who, like the hero of his *Misantropo,* had "done his studies at Pisa" under Averani and had then taught there for three years after graduation. His studies had convinced him that law was the most effective instrument for improving the lot of those who were subject to it. Then, after 1733, when he became minister for ecclesiastical affairs, his practical experience convinced him that the greatest obstacle to the proper use of law lay in the existence of two separate, though overlapping, jurisdictions: the state and the church. This obstacle was made particularly formidable by the number of the clergy: 3.04 percent of the population in Tuscany, as compared to 0.7 percent in Alsace, 1.25 percent in Piedmont, and 2 percent in Naples. It was made still more formidable by the misery of most ordinary priests, many of whom had to beg for their bread, and by the extraordinary wealth of their superiors, who ate up most of the immense 14 million *scudi* a year of church income. And it was made almost insuperable by the "dead hand" (*manomorta*) clauses, which forbade the sale of ecclesiastical property and thus kept a sizeable portion of the arable land of Tuscany (as much as one-third in the Valdinievole) out of the hands of those most interested in increasing its productivity.

As a jurist of the humanist, or historical, school, Rucellai realized that this obstacle was a product of historical circumstances, not of natural or divine law. Armed with texts from Muratori, and conscious of the example of his sixteenth-century predecessor, Lelio Torelli, he determined to overcome it. Gian Gastone had already given him considerable freedom of action, at least with regard to protecting the Jews and planning for the suppression of decadent convents. The advent of the new dynasty gave him the opportunity he had been waiting for. It put the power of the Austrian monarchy, and eventually the prestige of the imperial crown as well, on his side of the bargaining table. And it promised "bold acts" if diplomatic negotiations should break down. When the test case came up, all Rucellai had to do was sit tight.

On April 28, 1738, Pope Clement XII issued a bull which threatened any Catholic who became a Freemason with no less than death and confiscation of goods. The bull might have passed unnoticed in Florence, even though, as a Corsini, Clement was a Florentine by birth. Its terms were far too harsh to be carried out, and its language alone was incapable of doing what an army of preachers was finally to accomplish in the following two centuries—making Freemasonry the scapegoat for all the ills of the world between the French Revolution and the return of Palmiro Togliatti from Russia. But it so happened that the grand duke himself was a Freemason and that an informal Masonic lodge had been founded in Via Maggio a few years earlier by some English residents, or so, at least, reported the ambassador from Lucca. Craon accordingly forbade the publication of the bull in Tuscany, dryly notifying the nuncio that the

Freemasons were not a religious organization and hence not subject to ecclesiastical laws.

But the Florentine inquisitor was apparently unaware that a century and a half had passed since the pontificate of Pius V, and he had evidently forgotten about the troubles his colleagues in Naples had provoked in a similar situation some forty-five years earlier. He dared not touch the English, first because they were not Catholics and second because they were protected by their king, who was the most powerful ally of the grand duke's father-in-law, the emperor. But he could pick on a few Florentines who, because of their knowledge of the English language, seem to have been admitted to the Florentine lodge. And on May 9, 1739, he had his henchman kidnap the most defenseless of them, an obscure poet by the name of Tommaso Crudeli, whom he had once heard recite some indiscreet verses about the rights of monarchs.

Third-degree interrogations and torture liberally applied while the victim was suffering from asthma, headaches, and abdominal hemorrhaging, failed to elicit any worthwhile information. The inquisitor could only conclude what an apologist claimed six years later—that the lodge was "the best behaved, the most pleasant, and the most useful society" in the city, and that it neither permitted sexual promiscuity nor imposed secrecy. But it was the government, not Crudeli, that the inquisitor was after. He was furious over the failure of a prank the nuncio had tried to play on Craon: slipping a memo on his desk which, if signed, would have turned over all episcopal appointments in Tuscany to the Roman Curia. So he searched about for other charges, no matter how trivial they might be. He had Crudeli accused of having made a joke about a Holy Office official in some coffee house, of having read a life of Paolo Sarpi, of having talked about Marchetti's translation of Lucretius, and of having once called scholastic theology "useless and superfluous." The government was helpless, particularly after some of its agents had been caught trying to arrange for Crudeli's escape from the prison of Santa Croce: and it dared not provoke any further hostility among the clergy before they granted the sizeable donation requested of them for the year 1741. What finally made possible a resolution of the affair was not the intervention of the state, but the conscience of one of the inquisitor's consultants, who spilled the whole story to the nuncio. Crudeli was accordingly transferred to the Fortezza da Basso, then confined in his house at Pioppi in the Casentino, and finally released, only to die a few months later from the ill-treatment he had received.

No one in Florence felt obliged to follow the example of the Neapolitan jurists of the 1690s in denouncing the Inquisition. The injustice and, above all, the inefficacy of its proceedings were now perfectly evident to the most unquestioning believers, and perhaps even to the pope. Hence it was simply allowed to lapse into relative inactivity until 1753, when its power was officially trimmed down, "on the Venetian model." It was finally abolished, almost without a murmur, in 1782.

Rucellai was thus left free to move from the juridical to the financial sphere. While one of his colleagues dug up the republican decrees of 1414 and 1427, which demonstrated to his satisfaction "the superiority of statutory over canon law" throughout Florentine history, he himself worked out a plan for undermining the economic as well as the juridical foundations of clerical immunities. On March 11, 1751, the Regency promulgated a law that even Tanucci, the most vigorously anticurial statesman in Italy, found too far ahead of the times. Monetary bequests to ecclesiastical organizations were limited to the small sum of 100 *zecchini*; bequests of real estate were prohibited altogether. The one-way flow of capital from the laity to the clergy, from negotiable investments to sterile investments, was suddenly halted. The state was well on its way to becoming the sole master of its own house.

What Rucellai did in the realm of ecclesiastical jurisdiction, his younger colleague, Pompeo Neri, sought to do in the realm of civil law. Like Rucellai, Neri had studied under Averani at Pisa—so successfully that he was given an instructorship as soon as he graduated. But he had also studied at Siena. And there he had come into contact with a group of Sienese patricians who were just then trying to put together what they read in the works of contemporary French economists with what they observed on their estates in the surrounding countryside. In 1739 they sent one of their members, Sallustio Bandini, who had already written several memoranda on economic problems, to Florence. Bandini handed the grand duke a bold new plan for the resuscitation of his country.

Since industry had vanished, Bandini pointed out, the prosperity of Siena depended wholly on the agricultural production of the Maremma—the broad, barren stretch of hills, plains, and swamps between Massa Marittima and the Papal border. The Maremma, he recalled, had once been, and might once again become, one of the most productive areas in Italy. It now had only 25,000 inhabitants, about one-seventh of what it had in the thirteenth century. Most of them lived in poverty and ill-health, and their annual harvests were barely enough, even in good years, to feed the mere 16,000 people left inside the walls of Siena. The fault, said Bandini, was not nature's, but man's; and the remedy lay not in physical improvements, which had been proven ineffective ever since the time of Cosimo I, but in legislation. Nature, Bandini insisted, was beneficent. Let nature alone; get rid of internal and external trade barriers, obligatory harvest censuses, fixed prices, and all the other restrictions aimed at forcing the country to produce for the cities. The self-interest of the proprietors would then automatically raise production in accordance with the demand on the world market.

Thanks to Neri, his Sienese friends obtained at least some concessions. The *annona* system, which controlled prices and distribution in Siena, was left standing, and customs duties were retained for the benefit of the tax farmers. But Maremma proprietors were granted permission to export two-thirds of their harvests for the next twelve years. Unfortunately, the grand duke came up at the same time with what he thought to be a still better plan. Flattered by petitions from some of his former subjects and misled by a somewhat racist notion that Northerners were more industrious than Mediterraneans, he brought in two thousand colonists from Lorraine and settled them on plots of abandoned land near Massa and Sorano. When it came to providing them with cattle, tools, capital, and accessible markets, however, he remembered that his wife had a war on her hands; and guns, in the unenlightened eighteenth century, took precedence over plows. In spite of the heroic but unbudgeted efforts of the Florentine superintendent, and in spite of the pleas of the local bishops, the colonists were left to die of starvation and malaria. By 1766 only ninety-four of them were still there.

Neri had nothing to do with the colonization scheme: he had already moved on to the study of much more basic reforms. In private life, it is true, he did not act like a reformer. He was better known as a lady-killer, one whom Tanucci described as a "sex-hunter" unable "to silence the urgings of nature" even at the age of fifty. But in public life, he was grave, reflective, tactful, taciturn, and a bit timid—a man with little taste for original ideas, but with an enormous penchant for bureaucratic efficiency. He was the son of a successful lawyer, auditor of the High Court (*Ruota*) of Florence, and justice counselor to Gian Gastone. Through his father's influence he had risen rapidly in the civil service, to become, in his early thirties, secretary to the Ministry of Finance. It was largely Neri's hard work that prepared for the most progressive legislative innovations of the Regency. All the special feudal jurisdictions that had accumulated since the time of Cosimo II were abolished, thus bringing the whole of Tuscany under a uniform court system. The right to establish inalienable inheritances (*fidecomissi*) was restricted to the nobility, thus putting still more property on the open market. And the legal distinctions between patricians (descendants of office-holding republican families), nobles (those given titles by the Republic or the Principate), and citizens (those with rights of election to minor offices) were formalized in such a way as to bring the civil nobility of birth more in line with what Neri defined as the "natural" nobility of talent.

Still, all these new laws were intended only as single elements in a much vaster plan of reform. In 1745 Neri was appointed head of a commission to collect all the various and often conflicting municipal laws of all the various political fragments of the grand duchy and melt them down into a single code. His appointment coincided with a general interest in codification in all the more advanced monarchies of Europe—in Prussia, Piedmont, Modena, Naples, and even Austria. It had the support of the Lorrainers, who had been brought up during the extensive reorganization executed by the grand duke's father in his war-ruined country after the Peace of Utrecht. Unfortunately Neri's project, after four years of hard work, was tabled. His insistence that Roman law be retained, indeed even extended, as the common law of Tuscany collided with Richecourt's insistence that it be replaced by statutory law—as it could more easily have been in a non-Roman law country like Lorraine. Rather than fight it out, Neri left Florence to accept a similar position in Milan. But when he returned a decade later, having successfully reformed the entire system of tax assessments in Austrian Lombardy, he was all but unopposed. He rewarded the Sienese by helping them renovate their university and reopen their Accademia dei Fisiocritici. And he set to work planning for the thorough overhaul of the administrative structure of the state that was to be carried out after the accession of a new grand duke in 1765.

Although he knew nothing of politics, then, and although he explicitly banned lawyers' manuals and judges' *decisiones* from the pages of the *Novelle,* even Lami could not remain wholly indifferent to what the regents were doing. Not since the time of Cosimo I had the government of Florence undertaken such far-reaching reforms. Moreover, these reforms had received the blessing of one authority whom Lami dared not overlook—Muratori. Muratori published his epoch-making *De' difetti della giurisprudenza* ("On the Defects of Jurisprudence") in 1742. When he was attacked the following year, in such virulent pamphlets as the *Jurisprudence without Defects* of a prominent Venetian lawyer, Lami felt obliged to defend him. He thus ended up accepting Muratori's three main theses. What is, is not necessarily right, Muratori held. "Public happiness" is the proper aim of legislation, not "reason of state." And laws are made by men and can therefore be altered by men.

Meanwhile, several Florentines whom Lami admired for other reasons were lending the support of Tuscan jurisprudence to Muratori's theses. Leopoldo Guadagni, with whom Lami corresponded on philological subjects, further developed Averani's methods in his voluminous *Institutions of Civil Law,* finally published in 1758. Antonio Niccolini, a polyglot, cultivated, wealthy nobleman, who paid for Averani's funeral monument, tested these methods in practice as an ecclesiastical lawyer in Rome before bringing them back to Florence. A young law instructor named Anton Francesco Pieri denounced the old jurisprudence as "a mass of futile and empty words" from his chair of Lombard law at Pisa. And two of Lami's favorite disciples were soon to publish eloquent manifestos of the new jurisprudence: Anton Maria Vannucchi in his *Method for Acquiring Critical Jurisprudence* of 1750 and Miglioretto Maccioni in his *Observations and Dissertations* of 1764.

More important still, one of the ablest of the Tuscan jurists was finally breaking down the barriers that so far had confined jurisprudence to the class-rooms of the university. Giuseppe Maria Buondelmonti was a descendant of one of the families whom Dante had accused of starting the Guelph and Ghibilline factions in the thirteenth century. Bad health had kept him from finishing his studies at Pisa, and, except for two years of administrative service in Rome, he had been forced thereafter to live in semiretirement on the income from his ample estates. He was a man of many tastes; he translated Pope's *Rape of the Lock* and wrote commentaries on Milton's *Paradise Lost* and the French *Encyclopédie*. It was probably his literary accomplishments, as well as his social rank, that led to his appointment as official orator at several state funerals: for Gian Gastone in 1737, for Charles VI in 1741, and for Princess Charlotte of Lorraine, the grand duke's mother, in 1745.

Still, Buondelmonti's chief interest was the law. He read the works of Alberigo Gentili, Grotius, Pufendorf, Barbeyrac, Locke, and all the other great transalpine jurists of the past century and a half. In his funeral orations, he turned what he had read into clear, easy-to-understand expositions for the benefit of his large and largely unprofessional audiences. Thanks to Buondelmonti, jurisprudence became a current subject of conversation in the cafés, in the dining rooms, and even in the Accademia della Crusca, where he gave still another lecture on it in 1755. The artist Giovan Domenico Ferretti paid tribute to the new fashion by baptizing the half-naked Roman athlete he painted on the wall of the Palazzo Curini-Quaratesi in Pisa " Justinian," and by having him burn one set of laws as he dictated a new one under the eyes of several cloudfuls of gods and goddesses.

Even Lami eventually picked up some knowledge of what so many Florentines were now talking about. He skimmed through the writings of Andrea Alciati, the greatest of the Italian humanist-jurists of the sixteenth century, or at least through enough of them to find some witty anecdotes. He corresponded with a friend in Livorno about the meaning and applicability of Lombard law. He applauded the appearance, in 1757, of Giovan Battista Almici's Italian (and "Catholic") version of Pufendorf. He joined in ridiculing the "old-style lawyers" for memorizing textbooks and "sitting on a file-case of citations" instead of "penetrating into the spirit of the laws." And he remembered that he too had a law degree and could therefore qualify as a "jurisconsult—and something else besides."

Still, Lami never succeeded in comprehending the most important innovation of the new jurisprudence: its insistence upon the unity of theory and practice and upon legislation as the only legitimate end of the study of law. What he found commendable in Catherine the Great was not the laws she gave to the Russians, but her subsidies to artists and writers. What he found praiseworthy in Sallustio Bandini was not his *Discourse on the Maremma,* but his big collection of scientific books.

Even less did Lami succeed in distinguishing between the two different and, to some extent, antithetical tendencies among the jurists of his day. The first of these tendencies was philosophical in approach and was supported by the concept of natural law that was fast becoming normative in all the more advanced states of Europe. It looked upon jurisprudence as a deductive science, as one that began not with the texts of the Romans or with any other positive law code, but with "a philosophical examination of man and his passions." It held, in Lami's words, that "the law is nothing but that rule of human action which reason discovers to have been commanded by the Supreme Legislator of the World." It assigned to the jurist the task of discovering the "principles of natural right." It left to the legislator simply the task of applying those principles in particular cases. The second of the two tendencies, on the other hand, was historical in approach and was backed up, in the 1740s and 1750s, by the republication of several important Renaissance law texts—for example, those of Jacques Cujas, of Antonio da Pratovecchio, and of François Hotman. This tendency looked upon jurisprudence as an empirical and to some extent even experimental science. It held, as Lami realized, that no law was ever "absolutely just and perfect in itself, but only . . . admissible with regard to the circumstances, persons, customs, and institutions of a particular people." It assigned to the jurist the task of discovering not what the law ought to be but what it had been—among the Etruscans and Goths as well as among Greeks, Romans, and medieval Florentines. It assigned to the legislator the task of applying the experience of the past in order to produce the effects he desired through new laws in the present. To Lami the two tendencies were merely complementary aspects of the same phenomenon. The law, he said in his review of Guadagni's *Institutions* in 1759, is a matter both of logic and of erudition. And since all the jurists he knew cited each other as if no real conflict actually existed, he was at least partly justified in saying so.

Lami could not shake off his distaste for the law in general. But there was one law he had to pay attention to, because it directly affected the success of his new enterprise: the press law of March 28, 1743. Actually, the law had been some time in preparation. Gian Gastone had let lapse the harsher provisions of the 1707 ordinance "on booksellers, printers, and stationers." He had appointed the leading Florentine men of letters as civil censors: men like Anton Maria Salvini and Filippo Buonarroti. He had closed his eyes to such tricks as the one played on the ecclesiastical censors by the editors of the *Prose Fiorentine* in 1732: they restored in the second edition the passages they had been forced to remove in the first, but they left the earlier date of publication on the title page and thus avoided having to apply for a new approbation.

What Gian Gastone had begun, the Regency completed. With the new law of 1743, the regents transferred all powers of censorship to the hands of state officials alone. They required consultations with a bishop only in the case of books which they, not he, decided were on theological subjects. They then sat tight and waited until the storm raised by the furious and offended Roman Inquisition—and by the anti-Lorraine faction among the Florentine cardinals— finally blew over. And a storm there was: the Papal frontier was immediately closed to all Florentine publications; printers who complied with the law were threatened with excommunication and imprisonment; Rucellai was subjected to another round of verbal attacks; and Florence was portrayed as a hotbed of heresy and licentious living. To all this the grand duke himself replied with clipped comments on "the ancient laws of my states" and the "novelties" and "abuses" perpetrated by the Holy Office. The purpose of the law, he explained, was to prevent any offense against "religion, good morals," and "the rights of His Royal Highness." After the Crudeli affair, the Inquisition knew exactly what he meant by that. But the purpose was also to "provide for the freedom of printing in our states and of introducing foreign books," and thus "to increase learning, spread knowledge, and give subsistence to a part of the population." The secretary of state accordingly instructed the new state censor—who happened to be one of Lami's collaborators on the *Novelle*—to avoid creating "any impediment to the printing business, which it is the intention of the Most Serene Grand Duke to favor and protect as much as possible."

The policy worked. The Holy Office prudently decided not to carry out its threats, particularly after even the future Pope Clement XIV began laughing at them. A case of books that Lami was sure would be sequestered on its way through Papal territory in late July arrived safely at Venice without even being opened.

At first Lami was more puzzled than pleased with the new law. He himself had opened a print shop and bookstore in 1741, which he called the Centaur Press; and he feared anything that might endanger his heavy investment in type and stock. Like most of his contemporaries, he defined freedom of speech to mean freedom for him and the Index for his enemies. He probably also expected to make some money from the clandestine "open letters" that were the inevitable consequence, in Florence as elsewhere, of official censorship. Like one of his friends who had been a state censor during the fight over the Pandects, he knew that two centuries of restricted freedom had trained his compatriots to manifest their frustrations in slander rather than in arguments; and he was as expert a slanderer as any of them. Like Muratori, whose volume of historical documents had been held up by the governor of Milan because of some anti-German expressions in the texts themselves, he knew that civil censors could be as intolerant as ecclesiastical censors. He knew, for instance, that the Pisan patrician Flaminio Dal Borgo had been jailed the year before because he "had not been able to hold his tongue" about the merits of the Spaniards and the defects of the Lorrainers.

Just how intolerant the civil censors could be, he found out only later. On August 30, 1745, they crossed out half of one of his tracts, even though, he whined, it was "full of moral precepts." Two weeks later, they banned an entire issue of the *Novelle,* and Lami had to have it hastily printed on inferior paper in Lucca and distributed "secretly, without saying anything to anyone." The next year they blocked a new edition of *Le Cene* by Anton Francesco Grazzini ("Il

Lasca"), apparently because they found it to be just so much more sixteenth-century pornography. They did so even though Lami had made a special arrangement with the chief censor, and even though he had protected the censor by putting "Stambul" instead of "Florence" on the title page. Then, when Lami tried to fool them by printing a tirade against the Jesuits ("harmful to society, useless to themselves, servants of vice and falsehood . . .") under the name of the young jurist Vannucchi, they made him replace all the specific references with dots—and even blot out by hand one of the references they had missed on the first reading. The biggest blow fell on June 9, 1747. Armed with an order from the regents, the police suddenly seized the Centaur and walked off with all the type and printed sheets they could find. Everything was returned a week later. But the firm never fully recovered. After deducting court costs, Lami managed to recover only 5 percent of his original investment when he finally sold it in 1751.

But in general the government of the Regency remained true to its word. It usually intervened only when the authors carried their name-calling contests well beyond even the ample limits of discretion recognized at the time. It did its best to avoid becoming a tool for private interests, as it did most notably in 1746, when it restored a pamphlet that the piqued bishop of Pistoia had managed to have burned publicly. The regents ridiculed the prohibition of Rucellai's *Tamburro* in Rome in 1750 as nothing but a bit of revenge upon the Tuscan minister for ecclesiastical affairs. And they rebuffed Tanucci's attempt to block some criticisms of the excavations at Herculaneum a few years later with the dry comment: "This Council cannot imagine how the opinion of a scholar might be offensive to the king [of Naples]."

One of the objectives of the press law was soon realized. "Looking at it from a commercial point of view," reported a government inspector after a survey in 1764, "the printing business . . . has never before flourished as it has in the present century." Besides one government printing house with fifteen employees, and one bookstore that specialized wholly in French books, there were eight private firms in Florence alone, not counting those in the provincial cities, which had doubled in number in the past two decades. And although none of these firms could rival the Bodoni of Parma in quality or the printers of Lucca in ingenuity—the inspector had the recent edition of the French *Encyclopédie* in mind—they managed to produce regularly "a great number of . . . respectable and voluminous books," which represented, he noted, an appreciable contribution to the Tuscan economy. The second objective was soon realized as well. Authors could now write and printers could publish much more freely than any of their predecessors since the Council of Trent and even more freely than many of their contemporaries in other parts of Europe. Lami himself eventually became convinced of the advantages of freedom. "How many sacrileges, scandals, and persecutions" might have been avoided in the last two hundred years, he reflected,

Veduta della Badia Fiorentina, e del Palazzo del Potestà presa dalla Piazza della Chiesa de PP. dell' Oratorio

23. Zocchi, Piazza San Firenze

if "a couple of words of explanation" had taken the place of anathemas. Differences of opinion were inevitable and even commendable, for they derived "from that liberty of thought given us by God and Nature." The old tactic of advancing one opinion by getting its opposite condemned, he decided, was worthy only of ignorant Dominicans.

For a man of letters, then, Florence was a very profitable city to work in. It was a pleasant city too, in spite of the economic depression. The streets were safe, and that, noted Horace Mann, was far more than could be said for London. "There are no assassinations, no robberies, and no great crimes," reported another visitor a few years later; and "nothing seems more useless [here] than the officers of justice." Also, the streets were still beautiful. "How enchanting," exclaimed that hard-core anti-Florentine, Giuseppe Baretti, after a one-day tour in 1766, "to walk about . . . among those splendid palaces, those churches, those marble and bronze [statues], across those bridges, and along that beautiful, arch-beautiful river Arno!" Better still, the streets were now provided with a new institution, the *caffè* (or coffeehouse), where news, books, gossip, and opinions were passed around with such alacrity that the government occasionally tried—in vain—to intervene. No one of any importance, Lami included, could let a day go by without stopping in for a cup of coffee, chocolate, or café-au-lait and an hour of vivacious conversation at Panoni's in Via Por Santa Maria or at the Svizzero ("the Swiss") near the cathedral. "Only two cities can rival Naples," confessed Tanucci, "Rome for its stones and Florence for its brains. . . . You have a beautiful countryside, beautiful gardens, beautiful habitations; you have a land that produces excellent fruit and a people that can provide with its industry for many pleasures. Enjoy it!"

Florence had recently become a mecca for foreign tourists, so many of them, particularly after the Peace of Aachen, that the English ambassador Mann was "absolutely ruined in feasting them." Montesquieu came in 1728, La Curne de la Sainte-Palaye and the President de Brosses in 1739, the son of the French minister of foreign affairs in 1746, Condamine (the apostle of smallpox vaccinations) and Jean-Jacques Barthélemy in 1755, Mme Dubocage in 1757. They came mainly to see "that arsenal of masterpieces." But, unlike their successors in later ages, they came also to meet their Florentine peers, with whom they often remained in correspondence thereafter. Many of them stayed on for years, particularly the English, who in Lami's generation founded the colony that was to become famous in the following century. According to one traveler, the hotels were better in Florence than anywhere else in Italy—which may be one reason why Goldoni set the scene of his *La locandiera* there. So, apparently, was the food, even though *pastasciutta* had not yet been introduced from Naples nor *lasagna* from Bologna. At least if innkeepers followed the instructions of Giovan Francesco Upezzinghi, a Pisan patrician who composed Anacreontic verses for the local Arcadian colony and who published a rhymed cookbook in 1719, they knew how to make creamed soups out of dried beans, peas, and onions, how to tenderize beef by soaking it in butter or oil, how to spruce up even the plainest boiled fish with wine sauce, how to decorate roasts with parsley, and how to prepare a succulent pear tart known as *sfogliata di pere*.

As foreigners became more numerous, foreign publications became ever more easily available. By the mid-1740s, the new French bookstore of Bouchard & fils was regularly receiving enough of them, on a vast variety of subjects of current interest, to fill thirty-one tightly printed pages in its annual sales catalogue. Florence's century-old self-sufficiency and isolation were rapidly breaking down. And as the world began coming to them, fewer and fewer Florentines found it necessary to follow Antonio Niccolini on the "grand tour." For nowhere, as Lami put it, could one be more effectively "stirred up by domestic examples and spurred on by foreign examples" than right there in "the most ample theater of letters and fine arts," the home of "Ficino, Vettori, Buonarroti, Salvini, Gori . . . ."

5

Bottoming out

At the same time, even the economic depression seemed to be bottoming out. The government adopted at least a few progressive measures. It negotiated a commerical treaty with the Turks, although the increasing poverty of the Levant hardly justified the enormous expenditure in presents to the sultan. It reduced grain duties between the two main "states" of the grand duchy. And it opened up new markets for Florentine silks in Hungary and Austria, with the result that at least one student was crowded off his barge in the late 1740s by bales of finished cloth that were being exported through Pisa. Still, most of the initiative came from private citizens. Several proprietors undertook extensive reclamation projects. By 1736 they had already added 41,128 *staia* of arable land to the Valdichiana alone. Several others decided to exploit the area around Signa for a completely new industry: straw hats. Soon,

> Of ten inhabitants you'll find but two
> without some straw beside them;
> white mats they make from green stalks new
> grown in the fields about them.
>
> (Marco Lastri. *Cappello di Paglia*)

And indeed, they continued to do so right down until the industrial revolution of the 1950s.

The most enterprising businessman of all was the indomitable Carlo Ginori, the archenemy of Richecourt on the Regency Council, the governor of Livorno, the first importer of *kin-yu* goldfish from China, and the first owner of Angola sheep from Africa. Ginori was a man whose "great variety of knowledge and tastes" were matched by a tireless "energy and zeal." While on a diplomatic mission in Vienna in 1737, he persuaded an Austrian porcelain artisan to bring back to Ginori's "spectacular" villa at Doccia the secret that Grand Duke

Francesco I had looked for in vain. There he started producing miniature copies of the statues in the Uffizi, oval serving plates with oriental scenes, and flowers *à la Sassonie* designed to cater to the extravagances of the European aristocracy. By the mid-1750s the firm was out of the red, and Ginori thought of sending off a boatload of his produce to America. By the late 1760s, when his son Lorenzo succeeded in anticipating the neoclassical tastes of the next generation, it began making good profits. Today, under the name of Richard Ginori and with a big modern factory at Doccia, it produces some of the handsomest wedding-present china in the whole Common Market.

Tuscany, then, may not yet have generated anything comparable to the new flax industries of Bohemia or the new paper and silk industries of the Venetian uplands. But it had at least accomplished the first step.

What Ginori did with porcelain, others did with paint and marble. Florence could not support its artists very well in the early eighteenth century, particularly after Gian Gastone decided to trim his father's overgenerous subsidies. Few new buildings went up, the Hospital of Bonifazio, the facade of San Firenze, Palazzo Capponi, and the Marucelliana Library being the most notable exceptions. And few proprietors felt sure enough of their revenues to risk remodeling the old ones. Hence Florence exported some of its best talent. Ferdinando Fuga went to Rome, where he experimented with concave-convex architraves on the Palazzo della Consulta and the Palazzo Corsini; he became one of the chief architects for that Neapolitan version of Versailles, the royal palace at Caserta. Sebastiano Galeotti spent most of his life traveling back and forth between Vicenza and Genoa. After covering the walls of the Castello di Rivoli in Piedmont with wiggling balconies and twisted pillars, he settled down, in the 1740s, as the director of the Academy of Arts at Turin. Alessandro Galilei, sometime superintendent of royal buildings for Cosimo III, worked mostly in Rome, where the simple flat pillars and high, nervous arches of his facade seemed designed to bury Borromini's interior of San Giovanni in Laterano. These Florentine émigrés, whose native tradition had never fully comprehended the architectural novelties of the preceding century, may well have been responsible for introducing the first elements of the subsequent neoclassical revolution into the three main centers of Italian high baroque.

Some of the talent, nevertheless, stayed at home. Most of the masters of Magalotti's generation—Gherardini, Foggini, Gabbiani, and Giovan Camillo Sagrestani—were still there when Lami first came up from the university. Most of their pupils stayed on after the masters died. Vincenzo Meucci, whose ceiling at Monticelli Lami called "truly a beautiful painting," covered the dome of San Lorenzo with serene celestial figures on a commission from Princess Anna Maria Luisa in the 1740s. Ferdinando Ruggieri rebuilt the church of Santa Felicità,

where the Colombaria's Christian tombstones were found, between 1736 and
1739. Girolamo Ticciati carved a bust of the Florentine pope Clement XII for the
Corsini chapel at Santo Spirito, a statue of St. John of Salerno for the cloister of
Santa Maria Novella, and a bas-relief allegory of the Medici family for the Palazzo
Corsini in Via del Prato. His chief assistant, Gasparo Brucchi, modeled the
terracotta portrait of Gian Gastone that Lami wrote an inscription for in 1737
and eventually went to work for the Ginori company. Ignazio Hugford, a
Florentinized Englishman who had come to study with Gabbiani in his youth,
decorated the monastery of Vallombrosa for his brother, the abbot Ferdinando
Enrico. Giovan Domenico Ferretti continued the work of Gabbiani in the Palazzo
Capponi in the 1720s. He did the frescoes in the Badìa in the 1730s. He painted a
"Death of St. Joseph" for the cathedral and a "Life of Christ" for the Annunziata
in the 1740s. And he finished several canvases for the Carmine in the 1750s,
before being buried there in 1768.

None of these artists ever produced anything comparable in quality to
Tiepolo's huge frescoes in the Veneto and at Würzburg, to Antonio Galli
Bibbiena's theaters in Bologna, Pistoia, and Siena, to Giuseppe Maria Crespi's
wild, eerie moonlight scenes, to Alessandro Magnesco's mysterious, spot-lighted
landscapes, or to the works of many other of their famous contemporaries
elsewhere in Italy. Some of them experimented in the kind of daily-life vignettes
that became such an important aspect of Italian painting in the age of Pietro
Longhi. Ferretti, for instance, did a whole series of *commedia dell'arte* figures for
Fagiuoli's theater group and a number of *scene giocose* with doll-like dwarfs dressed
up as judges, ladies, and peasants. Some of them tried mixing media. Thus the
tapestries designed by Meucci in the 1730s were indistinguishable from his
paintings, and Giovanni Baratta's marble bas-relief of Raphael and Tobias in
Santo Spirito looks as if it is made out of stucco. But most of them could think
of nothing better to do than to go on imitating Pietro da Cortona and Luca
Giordano, as their masters had done, and to modify their models only to the
extent of toning down the colors, making the draperies crisper, softening the
clouds, and adding or subtracting cupids from the diagonal whirlwinds.

What principally distinguished Florentine from other Italian artists in Lami's
generation was their conscious return to a particularly Florentine tradition. And
by the Florentine tradition was meant, at least according to the Accademia del
Disegno (Art Academy), which proclaimed itself the "depository" of standards,
the styles of the Florentine High and neo-Renaissance. The academy's program
was encouraged by the republication of the classics of sixteenth-century art
theory—Raffaello Borghini's *Il riposo* in 1730, Lodovico Dolce's *L'Aretino* in
1735, Ascanio Condivi's *Life of Michelangelo* in 1746, and Vasari's *Lives* in 1759.
It was strengthened by Ferdinando Ruggieri's *Studio d'architettura civile* in 1728,
which proposed to architects nothing more than designs copied from Buontalenti,
Vasari, and "the divine Michelangelo." But it was not supported by any theoretical

justification except, perhaps, the constant repetition of the same old formula about the priority of draftsmanship (*disegno*) and a few weak echoes of Maffei's tirades against "the corruption that began with Borromini." The nearest thing Florence had to an art critic, the superintendent of the academy, Francesco Maria Gabburri, was really just a connoisseur—one who could identify an artist by the way he painted hands but who could not judge the quality of the painting. It is perhaps not surprising, then, that what Florentine artists produced is better appreciated by historians today than by critics. Nor is it surprising that Ferretti's huge canvas for the cathedral at Pisa has been marked "untraceable"—like so much of the art of the age—in the storage room register ever since World War II. For no one has ever protested against the desecration of the quiet, dignified interior of San Giovannino by a string of electric candles and by a Disney-like plaster statue with a blazing crown of stars; and even the meticulous 1950 edition of the Touring Club guidebook did not see fit to mention the harmonious blend of gray-green marble facing, speckled gray colunms, and white capitals that Giovan Domenico Arnaldi commissioned in 1733.

Still, the Florentine tradition did have one big advantage: it saved the Tuscan countryside from Strawberry Hills and Chinese pagodas, which Mann, with his copy of the *Aedes Walpoliana* in hand, tried in vain to advertise in 1749. But it also had disadvantages. It blinded Florentines to the suggestions about the qualities of Greek sculpture put forward by Lami's scholarly friend Giovanni Bottari from the Corsiniana in Rome—suggestions that were soon to be developed into a complete aesthetic and then accepted by artists all over Europe. It closed their eyes to the proposals of a certain Carlo Stendardi that they take inspiration from the Newtonian cosmos, "the only model of true beauty," as he called it. It even deafened them to the complaints of some contemporary artists, particularly those whose letters Bottari collected for publication. No Florentine ever dreamed of reversing the patronage system, that is, of making patrons buy what the artists did on their own rather than letting them tell the artists what to do beforehand. And none of them ever questioned the superiority of *storie*—of representations of a scene from history or mythology—to all other forms of art. Gabbiani himself could do no more than ask Salvini for still another theme each time the preceding one turned out to be too complicated for a single ceiling.

Thus no one paid any attention when Lami proposed that modern artists look for inspiration to other moments in the past than just the sixteenth century. True, he had no previous experience with art and he certainly had no credentials for writing about it. Moreover, he ran up against the universal conviction that any art before Masaccio and Donatello was not even worth preserving. Ticciati covered an ancient altar in the Baptistry with stucco clouds and golden light-bursts—and no one complained. The masterpieces of Giotto and Cimabue in Santa Croce were left "so discolored, so covered with dirt, that you can hardly see the outline of the figures"—and no one bothered to clean them. Even such

distinguished travelers as Addison, Montesquieu, and De Brosses assured their
hosts that "Gothic" buildings were little more than curiosities, and Maffei called
them "ridiculous extravagances." Hence, when Lami discovered that, Vasari
notwithstanding, both Italians and Greeks had been producing good art for two
centuries before Cimabue, his compatriots refused to take him seriously, not even
those of them who may have read Bottari's recognition of "the great simplicity,
truth, and expression" of pre-Renaissance frescoes. And they left it to the theorists
of art in Rome to explore the artistic potentialities of what the antiquarians and
archaeologists were digging out of the distant past.

Actually, the Florentine artists had no need to follow any of these suggestions.
What they were asked to do was not to create but to copy—to produce exact
replicas of all the masterpieces of Tuscany and to put the whole contents of the
Uffizi on copper engravings. It so happened that just then the successful issue of
the Glorious Revolution and the wars of Louis XIV had launched the English
gentry and aristocracy into a feverish competition to cover their countryside
with Palladian villas. From 1710, when the Duke of Marlborough put in his
first big order for Blenheim, they descended upon Florence in search of pictures
and statues for their new country seats. Since what they wanted was not the art
of Ticciati or Foggini but the art of Raffaello and Cigoli, the Florentine artists
found that returning to their tradition paid much better than moving toward the
future. They also discovered that the English tourists who wandered into their
workshops wanted something like the modern postcard to take home with them;
Giuseppe Zocchi, among others, obliged them by publishing the magnificent
engraved reproductions of his scenes of Florence that are now known the world
over. Thus art in Florence became a business. As the English ambassador had to
spend more and more of his time negotiating contracts and arranging for
shipments out of Livorno, the art business provided the hard-pressed economy
with an appreciable, although undeterminable, amount of foreign credit.

6

The university and the church

Lami knew too little about either politics or economics to be sensitive to these encouraging signs. But he could not but be affected by recent changes in the two institutions he was most interested in. The first was the university, about which his friends in Pisa kept him fully informed in almost weekly letters after 1740. After years of neglect, a rector (*provveditore*) was finally appointed in 1733. He was Gaspare Cerati, an energetic, bright, well-read, and open-minded patrician-turned-Oratorian from Parma. Cerati knew enough about the current state of Italy to have been appointed advisor to Don Carlos the year before. He knew enough about the rest of Europe to qualify as Montesquieu's closest friend and most regular correspondent south of the Alps; and in 1741 he supplemented his knowledge of the contemporary world by extensive visits to Paris, London, Leiden, and Berlin. He was a moderate Augustinian and anti-Probabilist in theology—which made him completely sympathetic to Lami's program, even though he could never stomach Lami as a person. Above all, he was an administrator, so much of one that he was willing to trouble himself with such bureaucratic minutiae as the wearing of gowns in the classroom and the "inopportune, scandalous" behavior of professors at masked balls. Within a few months of his appointment, he drew up a complete program of reform and revitalization. He spent the rest of his thirty-five year term in office putting it into effect.

Cerati's job was not an easy one. Enrollment had dropped to less than two hundred, from more than six hundred a century earlier, and it had become almost wholly Tuscan in composition. Income from the "tenth" (*decima*), which Cosimo I had cornered Pope Paul III into according when the university was reopened in the 1540s, still provided most of the revenue; but with the decline in the economy, it now barely sufficed to pay salaries, leaving not a *soldo* for equipment and overhead. The archbishop stubbornly maintained his right to pass on degree candidates and had a crisis of conscience whenever a professor said something that did not square with his notions of orthodoxy. The university *auditore* in Florence kept sending down curt reminders that anyone might go over the rector's head in controversial questions. The regents, prodded by Richecourt, who had a grudge against Cerati, kept sending down memos about "abuses." And the students constantly complained about "intolerable restrictions," such as closing the gates of the colleges at 9 P.M. sharp, that interfered with their "honest recreation"—catcalling in the lecture halls, beating up citizens, bringing in dogs to bark at the singers in the theaters, and insulting the police, who were barred by law from touching them.

Cerati was undeterred by any of these obstacles. He increased the number of tuition and maintenance scholarships on which most students lived, and he established a university library well-stocked with the latest foreign books. He extended to all the professors the privilege conceded to one of them by Gian. Gastone in 1731: that of teaching whatever he judged to be "the best and the most true," and of discarding prescribed texts that were "not only useless, but ridiculous in a century as enlightened as ours." He loosened up the curriculum so that students might choose whatever courses most suited them, and he let those whose interests were not covered by courses—as happened with one of Lami's disciples—do reading on their own. He introduced instruction in subjects like chemistry, experimental physics, and navigation, which were just then rising to the dignity of academic acceptability. He got the government to come through on its long-delayed pledge to build an astronomical observatory. He encouraged the resident scientists to carry the experimental method into new fields—like artificial respiration, which did not work in one experiment of December 1749 because the victim was not treated until twenty hours after his body had been fished out of the Mediterranean.

Miraculous though it may seem, Cerati managed to get the professors to arrive at the beginning of the academic year, to stay until the end, and to give the required seventy rather than the customary thirty-odd lectures in between. He even reduced student rowdiness without resorting to billy clubs or expulsions, merely by reading stern admonitions: "Let no one dare to stir up noise or any kind of tumult . . . or have the temerity to interrupt any public function." Best of all, he completely redefined the role of the university in society. No longer, he insisted, should it serve merely as an instrument by which the Florentine and provincial nobility might monopolize the best positions in church, state, and the professions for its sons. Rather its task should be to spread knowledge to all the people of Tuscany, to enable them to "perform honorably in every kind of employment," to "preserve and promote the more noble disciplines in this province," and to encourage "sublime geniuses" to make "ever more progress and ever new discoveries for the advantage and pleasure of all mankind." Just how far he succeeded in implementing this redefinition was to become evident a generation later, when the beneficiaries of his reforms finally rose to positions of authority.

The other institution to which Lami was especially dedicated—and the only one of which he felt himself a responsible member—was the church. About the church, Lami had even more reason to be encouraged than he was about the university. To be sure, the reigning pope, Clement XII, was something of an anachronism. He thought of himself as a great Renaissance prince, a cross between Leo X and Paul V. He considered external pomp to be the most effective way of exalting his authority. He believed the spiritual power of the church to be directly proportional to its political power. And he was ready to use both to further the material interests of his family. But for Lami, what counted was that Clement XII tried to be a patron of letters—and, above all, that he had been born in Florence. During his pontificate the new Palazzo Corsini in Trastevere became one of the meeting places for a sizeable group of well-beneficed Florentine intellectuals, as well as for the usual army of Florentine businessmen, fortune-seekers, and hangers-on, who had swarmed to Rome the moment their compatriot was elected. The other meeting place was the "hermitage" of the worldly and world-wise Cardinal Domenico Passionei, an assiduous reader of Pascal, Arnauld, and Quesnel, an admiring correspondent of Montesquieu, Voltaire, and eventually Rousseau, and an insatiable collector of ancient and modern books—over 28,000 of them by the time of his death.

The most active member, first of one and then of the other, of these groups was one of Lami's most faithful friends, the tall, thin, unbending, and prematurely bald art critic and art historian, Giovanni Bottari. Bottari was a man of many trades. He had been a linguist and a literary expert, one of the principal authors of the fourth edition of the Crusca's *Vocabolario* of 1729. He had then become an ecclesiastical historian, a theologian, and a church administrator. His position on current issues was almost identical to Lami's: a rigorist in ethics, a relativist in philosophy, an Augustinian in theology, a biblicist in piety, and a staunch anti-Jesuit in questions of ecclesiastical polity. Since he constantly had the ear of the pope's two nephews, Prince Bartolomeo and Cardinal Neri Corsini, it looked as if these positions would soon become those most acceptable in the very capital of Catholic Christianity.

Within a few months of the first number of the *Novelle,* this prospect was suddenly realized, or so it seemed. One of the longest, stormiest, and most undignified conclaves in history finally ended, on August 17, 1740, with the election of Prospero Lambertini as Pope Benedict XIV. The new pope was already well known as an ecclesiastical reformer. As a theologian, he had sought to change hagiography into a search for models of Christian living—and to avoid the kind of morbid fascination for wonder-working that had been manifested as recently as 1729 in the canonization process of the sixteenth-century Florentine mystic, Caterina de' Ricci. As archbishop of Bologna, he had sought to revitalize the church at the diocesan and parochial level; and to do so he had gone back beyond the authoritarian, centralizing measures of the Counter-Reformation

Papacy to the ideals of the Council of Trent and the Catholic Reform. As a man of religion, he had sought to discourage such purely emotional and unscriptural "devotions" as the cult of the Sacred Heart. As pope, he promised to rid the Breviary of legends, to raise the religious quality of holy days by reducing their number, to encourage free discussion in the place of "subterfuges" under "false names," and to emphasize the religious rather than the temporal mission of the church.

Lami was elated by the election of "a pontiff of such learning and of so enlightened a mind." But there was no need for him to go to Rome himself. He was soon represented there by one of his favorite pupils, Pier Francesco Foggini, the son of the sculptor Giovan Battista and the author of several myth-smashing dissertations on Florentine saints. Through Foggini, as well as through his other friends in the Florentine colony, Lami could wield enough influence to get good jobs for his protégés. The pope was soon represented in Florence by an archbishop whose views were apparently identical to his own, Francesco Gaetano Incontri. Incontri defined the church not as a hierarchy but as "a vast body of faithful united in Jesus Christ." He looked for sanctity in "the firm resolution to do the will of God . . . in whatever role he has given you in this life," not in "ecstasies, miracles, [and] the gift of tears." He quoted Paul, Chrysostom, Filippo Neri, and François de Sales in his pastorals, rather than Bellarmine and Aquinas. He exalted the Mass, at the expense of "devotions," as the "most august and venerable mystery of the church," and he called upon the laity to participate actively in its celebration. After such expressions as these, Lami was sure he could count on the support of the new archbishop—as well as on the sympathy of the pope, of the most influential cardinals, and of the most active intellectual circles in Rome. The moment for action had at last arrived, political instability and economic depression notwithstanding. "Get to work," Muratori told him, "for the wind is blowing in our direction."

This optimism about the present was confirmed by Lami's study of the past. As antiquarianism turned into history, the past ceased to be, as it had been since the days of Ammirato, an undifferentiated chaos from which the present had happily been delivered. Arcadia had already imposed a new chronology in the 1690s, at least in the domain of literature; the chaos, it held, had twice before been overcome, first in the age of Theocritus and Virgil and then in the age of Petrarch and Boccaccio, and it was about to be overcome once and for all in the age of Redi and Crescimbeni. Muratori had inserted another literary great age: that of Bembo, Della Casa, and Sigonio, in the middle of the sixteenth century. Later, as he moved from poetry to politics, economics, manners, mores, and many other aspects of human life, he subtracted two ages from the list—the Arcadians' Rome and Maffei's and Vasari's Quattrocento. He added two others in their place: the age of the Goths and the Lombards, when Italy was united and peaceful, and the age of the communes, when it was independent. He thus prepared the way for the classic formulation of Saverio Bettinelli, whose *Il Risorgimento d'Italia dopo il Mille* ("The Rebirth of Italy after the Year 1000") was to provide the basic chronological concepts for Italian historiography until the end of the century.

These great ages were no more historical than were the four "great ages" of Muratori's more famous contemporary, Voltaire. Nor were they any less compromised by the assumption that civilization and creativity belonged exclusively to only a very small number of times and places. But by the 1740s, these ages were gradually being put into a sequential relationship with each other, and the gaps between them were being filled up. From exceptions, they were being turned into the products of history; they were shown to be the result not of chance but of the conscious decision of great men. "The provident Regulator of human affairs," according to an anonymous editor of the following decade, has from time to time "transfused a ray of His divine light into the minds of a few [men]." Since the great men of one great age built on the achievements of their predecessors, the long-range effect of their achievements added up to progress. Petrarch, for example, went beyond Dante, whom no one really appreciated until the advent of romanticism. The Principate went beyond the Republic, which a new edition of a sixteenth-century political tract still associated with "civil dissensions," its prosperity notwithstanding. Ammirato, whose *History* was reprinted in 1750, improved upon Bruni and Machiavelli, "in spite of his errors," just as Muratori surpassed the erudite historians of the sixteenth century, whose works he read and republished. Galileo, "the father of whole new mathematical sciences . . . and of true philosophy," paved the way for "the truly golden and happy times" of Magalotti, "when men of science were united by a sincere bond of friendship." Finally, the "so enlightened [eighteenth] century" surpassed all its predecessors, for it had a far greater number of "wise men of letters."

This concept of progress did not mean that Thucydides was wrong when he called history "a perpetually useful possession."* Nor did it rule out the utility of the knowledge of the past. It allowed for the discovery of "what wiser human eyes ought to be directed toward" as well as for the exposure of "what ought to be avoided." And it encouraged the restoration of what had wrongly been forgotten as well as the destruction of what had unfortunately been preserved. Indeed, the economic reformers of the next generation were to discover in history far more utility than even Lami suspected. Giovan Francesco Pagnini, for example, after reading Bolingbroke's *Letters on the Study of History* as well as Guicciardini's *History of Italy,* declared that history revealed "the secrets of the

---

* I translate literally from Domenico Maria Manni's "una perpetua utile possessione," except for turning one adjective into an adverb. The more common English translation from the end of book 1, chap 1, of *The Peloponnesian War* is: "as a possession for all time" (Crawley tr., Modern Library).

human heart" as well as the events that derived from them; he looked to history for the constant relation between cause and effect upon which all actions "profitable to the commonality of mankind" necessarily depended. Hence, the superiority of the eighteenth century consisted not in its actual but in its potential achievement. Never before had there been so promising a prospect for finding out the lessons of history and applying them successfully. And never before had there been so effective an instrument for making them known to others—the periodical journal.

7

The collaborators and the disciples

All Lami needed, to get started, was a few collaborators. He soon found them in three men whose special fields of competence complemented his own. The first was the timid, gentle, and aging cleric, Anton Francesco Gori—"the nicest man in the world," according to the abbé Barthélemy some years later, a man "without passion or jealousy . . . and universally respected by his compatriots and foreigners alike." Gori was usually penniless, even after Metastasio finally pulled the right string in Vienna and got him appointed provost of San Giovanni in 1746. Every extra penny went into down-payments on the luxurious, plate-filled tomes he turned out one after another: the *Description of . . . the Columbarium of . . . Livia Augusta* (1726), the *Florentine Museum Showing the More Significant Monuments of Antiquity* (12 vols., 1731–62), the *Etruscan Museum* (3 vols., 1737–43), the *Cortona Museum* (1750), the *Various Essays on Literary Symbols* (10 vols., 1748–53), the *Treasury of Ancient Gems* (1750), etc., etc. He was willing to risk controversy only on the question of the interpretation of ancient inscriptions, a question he scrupulously cut off from any reference to the contemporary world. He was even careful not to get "too much affection for the pagan philosophers" for fear of "straying from the right path" of Christian orthodoxy. In other words, Gori was Lami's exact opposite in character and ideology. But even Lami admitted that he was unexcelled as an antiquarian and that antiquarianism, outdated though it was with respect to history, still took up a sizeable portion of current books to be reviewed. He also knew that Gori was the "arbiter" of the Società Colombaria, as well as the correspondent of half the scholars of Italy. Hence, he could be expected to bring in some wealthy and influential subscribers for the *Novelle*. Finally, he knew that Gori was a tireless and meticulous worker, one who had traveled to every corner of Tuscany and who could make up for Lami's own haste in composition and distaste for proofreading.

The second collaborator was a poet, metallurgist, and physician from Livorno by the name of Giovanni Gentili. A young and relatively unknown

man, Gentili had as his only real accomplishments in the following years a few
academic quarrels at Pisa and a book on the earthquake of 1741. He eventually
left Florence to become a technical consultant to Maria Theresa's prime minister.
But he had one impeccable recommendation: his close friendship with the most
distinguished physician of the capital, Antonio Cocchi, a man whose "rare
qualities of mind," as Lami put it, and whose "vast and profound knowledge"
had earned him "the veneration of this city and the esteem of all the more
cultivated provinces of Europe." As a physician, Cocchi was a follower of
Francesco Redi and Lorenzo Bellini, whose works he published. Like them, he
was opposed to most current medicines. He insisted upon the priority of diagnosis
and description, and he emphasized preventative rather than curative medicine.
He was also a follower, and a popularizer, of the leading transalpine physicians
of the day, particularly Richard Mead, John Friend, and Hermann Boerhaave,
whom he had gotten to know during his stay in London and Holland in 1726–28.
He first applied their teachings as a practitioner, particularly among the members
of the English colony; many of his clients, like Horace Walpole, continued to
consult him by correspondence after their return home. He next applied his
mentors' teachings as professor of anatomy and surgery at the Studio Fiorentino,
as one of the directors of the Hospital of Santa Maria Nuova, and as head of
several governmental committees charged with drawing up medical and hygienic
regulations.

But Cocchi was much more than a physician. He was also a linguist, one who
spoke English and several other European languages without an accent and who
filled his voluminous diary with passages in Hebrew and Arabic—to the dismay
of historians of the period ever since. He was an accomplished antiquarian,
capable of deciphering and editing a ninth-century Byzantine manuscript of the
works of the ancient Greek surgeons. He was a philologist—the one, indeed, who
discovered and published the *Autobiography* of Benvenuto Cellini. And he was a
literary critic. His laudatory epistle on Voltaire's *Henriade* provoked an equally
laudatory response from the author and appeared in all the subsequent editions
of the eighteenth century. Cocchi was too timid and taciturn to get involved in
anyone's campaign on behalf of anything, in spite of the free-flowing hair and
messy, unbuttoned shirts that made him look like a Lord Byron before the
times. Still, through Gentili, Lami hoped to have Cocchi's assistance for
the *Novelle* in the field of medicine, about which he himself admittedly knew
nothing.

The third of the collaborators was Cocchi's twenty-eight-year-old assistant as
director of the Magliabechiana Library, Giovanni Targioni Tozzetti. Targioni
had begun his career as a botanist under the direction of Pier Antonio Micheli—
the poor, self-educated plant-lover who had adapted the new classification of
Joseph de Tournefort (1700) to the flora of Tuscany. On his return from the
university in 1734, Targioni had helped Micheli revive the *Società Botanica*

("Botanical Society"), a group of gentlemen dilettantes who had subsidized his endless jaunts around Tuscany since 1718. On Micheli's death in 1737 he had succeeded his teacher as director of the Botanical Garden, and he had acquired his immense collection of plant and mineral specimens. Targioni then became a historian of science. He studied the works of his sixteenth-century predecessor, Andrea Cesalpino. He published several volumes of the letters of Magliabechi's correspondents. And he recovered a great mass of manuscripts that once had belonged to the Accademia del Cimento. Finally, he became a naturalist. Inspired in part by Sir Robert Sibbald's *Scotia Illustrata* of 1684, and in part by Micheli's travel notes, he embarked upon an extensive survey of the flora, fauna, minerals, historical monuments, agricultural products, and human resources of Tuscany— a survey that filled six volumes in the first edition of 1751-54 and ten volumes in the second edition of 1768-77, and that was imitated or paralleled all over Europe during the following decades.

Lami had some reason for being a bit suspicious of the scientists. Some of them, like the author of a *History and Nature of Coffee* of 1731, were primarily interested in proving that coffee had grown in Tasso's Garden of Armida and that Turks never got stomachaches. Others of them, like Carlo Taglini, a professor of philosophy at Pisa and a corresponding member of both the Royal Society and the Académie des Sciences, sought to amuse rather than instruct. They sugarcoated expositions of Descartes with quotations from Petrarch and Boccaccio, and they mustered references from the *Philosophical Transactions* to show why the chirping of magpies was pleasant to the ear. Still others did for the eighteenth century what the Jesuit casuists had done for the seventeenth. They put out "medical histories" that actually amounted to so much pornography, even though Lami did his best to find something useful in them. That, at any rate, is what he tried to do with Giovanni Bianchi's *Brief History* of the autopsy of a lesbian. It was written, he said, "in a Boccaccio-like Tuscan style," and it treated "many anatomical questions, particularly regarding the sexual organs."

Still, Lami knew that the "mechanical medicine" of contemporary physicians was capable, as none of its predecessors had been, of "leading the intellect to an explanation [of maladies] and to the [correct] choice of remedies." He knew that Muratorian historiography rested on the same methods that had made possible all "the miraculous advances . . . in the philosophical disciplines." They rested, that is, on the methods first discovered by Galileo and most recently popularized in a translation of Voltaire's essay on Newton (*La Metafisica di Neuton* in Italian), which was dedicated to Lami's patron, Gabriele Riccardi, and published by his Centaur Press in 1742. Finally, Lami knew that both historians and scientists shared the same enemies: all those monks, seminarians, professors, and bureaucrats who still held Aristotle to be the last word in metaphysics, Suarez and Molina to be beyond criticism in theology, and the status quo in church, state, and literature to be normative throughout all ages.

Lami was no longer a lone individual. He was now the moderator of a coalition. Galilean science and Muratorian historiography, neo-Augustinian theology and neo-Cultist jurisprudence, Newtonian physics and Arcadian poetics —all had joined forces in a common cause. And the *Novelle letterarie* became their organ of debate and propaganda.

The first ten years of the new journal proved Lami's prognosis to have been correct. In spite of military campaigns, which frequently interrupted postal service to the north, in spite of the inefficiency of the business manager, who often got behind in mailings, and in spite of the negligence of the agent in Rome, "the slowest man in the whole world about keeping his promises," the journal flourished. Sales continued to rise—from at least 250 in 1745 to about twice that number in 1750; the first ten volumes had to be reprinted to keep up with the demand for back issues. Readers multiplied, since many subscriptions were institutional rather than individual, like the ones for the Collegio Ferdinando in Pisa and for the *Spedaletto* near Cremona. By 1750 the *Novelle* were hailed in Rome, where most of the cardinals had become subscribers, as an indispensable "alarm clock [to] keep us Italians from falling asleep in the letters and sciences."

24. Tito Lessi, *Lami with His Friends in the Riccardiana*

With editorial success came fame for the editor. Lami was delighted to learn, in 1745, that "he was very well known and much talked about" in Milan, where someone even composed a Latin ode to him. He was even more delighted, four years later, to hear that he was "favored by the first literary men of Germany" and well spoken of in all the proper circles of Vienna. He was elated to receive, shortly afterwards, a printed *Hymn in Honor of Doctor Giovanni Lami* from a certain "Ferindo Vatiliano, Pastor d'Arcadia." He was even eventually honored by the government. The regents commissioned him to do an inscription for Francesco Stefano in 1751. Richecourt had him write a position paper in 1753. And the emperor-grand duke gave him the title of state theologian in 1761.

Lami's cause also gained the support of a number of members of important institutions. Faithful to their Galilean heritage, most of the Scolopians adhered to it. In 1741 they brought out a new textbook that included references to "the learned, zealous [that is, anti-Jesuit] bishops and priests of France" and "some exercises in sacred history"—as well as a pile of miracle stories and anti-Lutheran tirades that Lami apparently did not bother to read. In 1745 they even set up a special Academy of Practical Moral Theology for the purpose of weaning priests from what Lami called "the theology of accommodation." Some of the Dominicans adhered as well, or at least so did the best of their current historians, the Florentine Giuseppe Agostino Orsi, who became secretary of the Index in 1740. Doctrine, said Orsi, could be formulated only on the basis of verifiable historical documents; he accordingly modified his radical position on papal infallibility when the documents happened not to back him up. Similarly, several bishops came to recognize "the close relationship" that Lami insisted upon "between sacred and profane scholarship"; they accepted his challenge to "free their people from vain fables" by writing critical histories of their dioceses. One bishop went so far in replacing "the muddy swamp of laxist casuistry" with "councils, holy fathers, and the purest [historical] sources" that he turned his see into "a seed-bed of saints." At least one convent was transformed into a bluestocking reading society dedicated to "perpetual discussions . . . of history," thanks largely to a mother superior, who was also known as Eurilla Aracneia, *pastorella d'Arcadia*. The seminaries of Florence, San Miniato, and Volterra revised their curricula in accordance with Lami's recommendations. The Accademia della Crusca finally admitted him to membership in 1737, along with a good number of other less wellborn scholars and teachers whom it hoped would rescue the organization from five years of relative inactivity. It thereafter sanctioned the books of piety he recommended and permitted him to introduce historical dissertations into his proceedings. Even the confraternities eventually began sponsoring sermons in which the usual "cases" gave way to long quotations from Erasmus and Pascal. Or at least they did so in the sermons of Andrea Pietro Giulianelli, sometime schoolmaster at Pescia, professor of eloquence at the Florentine seminary, assistant director of the Laurenziana Library, and occasional contributor to the *Novelle,* before he killed himself with too much work in 1767.

Lami soon succeeded in building up a group of loyal admirers and disciples. A few of them were his contemporaries, like Domenico Maria Manni, the brother of the Crusca's text publisher, Giuseppe. After his death at the age of ninety-eight, in 1788, Manni was known more for his longevity than for his accomplishments, and during his lifetime he was known more for his industry than for his brilliance. But no one could deny that he was a tireless worker: as an editor of the Crusca's *Vocabolario,* as an official in a whole string of city magistracies, as a contributing member of all the academies of Tuscany, and as the father of no less than eighteen children. Nor could anyone deny that his unending stream of treatises, essays, and annotated texts were faithful to Lami's rules about the importance of archival documents. For in 1755 he explained how to use them in what soon became a standard manual, his *Method for the Easy and Profitable Reading of the Histories of Florence.* Much of what Manni wrote may indeed have amounted to "pages and pages of senseless facts drawn out of so many old and insignificant codices." But at least the facts were well established. If Manni could demonstrate the truth about the origins of the Befana (the fairy who brings presents on Epiphany), about the invention of eyeglasses, about the artist Ghirlandaio, and about the traveller Francesco Carletti, then he could also provide exact information about the shrines of Rome—so much of it that Christians could benefit fully from the Holy Year by staying at home and reading his book. And that is exactly what Lami applauded Manni for doing.

Still, most of the disciples belonged to the younger generation. After all, it was not to professors but to students that Lami turned for information about current academic quarrels and for aid against his enemies at the university. And it was not the Crusca that provided him with a forum for his ideas: indeed, the consul reprimanded him for inviting his young charges to lectures. It was rather the Accademia degli Apatisti, the teen-age word-game club which he had belonged to in his youth and which he reorganized for the benefit of vacationing university students in 1748.

Many of these disciples produced works of lasting value. For example, a Torinese Jesuit named Giuseppe Richa, who had been sent to teach philosophy at San Giovannino, turned to history as a relief from his academic obligations. With Lami's help he soon finished a ten-volume catalogue of all the artworks, relics, and traditions of every church in the city, a catalogue which is still an indispensable reference book for historians. A Tuscan priest named Ferdinando Paoletti sought to respond to Lami's call for a learned clergy by inviting specialists to lecture at the seminary of San Miniato, of which he was rector. Paoletti eventually set an example himself by becoming an exemplary country curate and a political economist at the same time—in fact, one of the most influential political economists of the next reign. Alfonso Niccolai prepared a running commentary on the Old Testament, with citations to Maupertius and Galileo as well as to Augustine, for the benefit "of all classes and all ages." Antonio Martini, the future archbishop of Florence, took advantage of the papal bull of June 13, 1757, to begin work on the Bible; he eventually produced what is still today the classic Italian translation of both Testaments.

Lami's favorite, and certainly his most docile disciple, Angelo Maria Bandini, was only "in his salad days" when Lami first met him in 1740. But he soon made such "admirable progress . . . in the path of noble studies" that he "achieved in little time what others take many years to do." He followed his master's footsteps to Pisa, where he wrote articles for the Meurs edition between classes, and then to Vienna. When he went off on a benefice-hunting expedition to Rome, he obeyed Lami's orders to put away his pen and open his eyes and ears. When he returned to Florence to become director of the Laurenziana, he carried on Lami's work in Byzantine patristics, and he extended Lami's researches into early Christian and medieval Florence down into the Renaissance. Imitating the methods Lami had applied to the books in the Riccardiana, he eventually produced one of the greatest of all the eighteenth-century library catalogues: a detailed description of all the Greek and Latin manuscripts in the Laurenziana. It was through Bandini's publications, and through the scholars all over Europe who came to him for advice, that Lami's labors became known abroad. And it was through Bandini that the results of these labors were finally immortalized, even after the great work of the German philologists of the nineteenth century, by being included in Migne's still-standard collection of the Greek church fathers.

8

The battles

Thanks to the support of these friends and disciples, and thanks to the diffusion of the *Novelle,* Lami was able to embark on four different pen-and-ink battles at the same time. The first one had been prepared by Bandini's predecessor at the Laurenziana, Anton Maria Biscioni. Biscioni spent some of his extra time entertaining his friends, including the playwright Fagiuoli, at musical dinner parties. He spent the rest of it copying every reference to every Florentine writer of every century onto thousands of little slips of paper, amassing them (alas!) in alphabetical order by first names, and then depositing them in the fifteen enormous folders that have collected dust in the Magliabechiana ever since. But he also managed, in 1736, to produce an edition of the letters of Florentine saints, an edition that provided real, living models of Christian virtue and at the same time recorded many "pure, plain, and clear [Tuscan] words" for the use of the lexicographers. The battle was then launched by Foggini, just before his departure for Rome. In some five hundred note-filled pages, Foggini proved that St. Peter had never set foot in Florence, that St. Zanobi, the legendary first bishop of Fiesole, could not have lived before the fourth century A.D., that the *Acts* attributed to him could not have been written before the eleventh century, and that all pious beliefs to the contrary were false and therefore prejudicial to true piety. Manni, Buondelmonti, and Gori joined the fray, with Lami at their head. St. Luke the Evangelist, they proposed, had never been an artist. A man, not an angel, had painted the face of the Annunziata. The Crucifix at Porta Pinti had not even been credited with miracles before 1720. St. Peter had not sent a portrait of the Virgin to the people of Fiesole, none of whom were Christians at the time. Pontius Pilate had not been born in Arezzo. And the powers attributed to the Virgin of Impruneta rested solely on "false, incoherent accounts."

Such propositions derived directly from the theses Lami took from Augustine: that incredulity is less damaging than superstition, and that the truth is more precious than any scandal its publication might provoke. They were fully confirmed by the classic manifesto of the new piety in 1747: Muratori's *Della regolata devozione* ("On the Well-Ordered Piety of Christians"). But such propositions were to the liking neither of the monks of Camaldoli, nor of the Jesuits of San Giovannino, nor of a political economist of the Papal State, who bitterly resented any opinion derogatory to the prestige of his government. "The filthy Mr. Lami of Santa Croce" was accused of heresy, of Jansenism, and of being "a sponge for wine, a habitué of taverns, more drunk in the morning than at night." His collaborators were called respectively "a miserable, dirty little priest," "a mule-shit medic," and "neither fish nor meat, since he is inedible either raw or cooked" (sic). St. Romulus was declared to be a martyr: first because no pope had ever disapproved of his cult, second because the records of his martyrdom were obviously divinely inspired, and third because a sheep belonging to no less than Cosimo the Elder had been found covered with blood after a fall into the well where the saint had died. St. John the Evangelist was a scholar because he was referred to as such by "Saint" Dionysius the Areopagite, who was still identified as the disciple of Paul and bishop of Athens three centuries after he had been proved to have been no such thing. St. Peter's visit to Florence was verified by his well-known passion for traveling and by the impossibility of his having missed a city of such importance. And so on.

To all this Lami responded in kind. "This book is meant for pleasure," he said of one of them, "for it is full of amusing stories." "This one," he said of another, "is based on the testimony of much later writers" and is therefore "not worthy of mention in these pages." "Spinning out these devout stories," he said of still another, "is to pour ridicule on Catholicism" and to reduce it to an amusement of "half-witted old women."

Lami might have let the matter drop at that point. After all, his arguments were irrefutable on his own terms. Anyone who admitted the relevance of the documents he cited had no choice but to accept or to despair—which is what one of his opponents did when he complained about "transforming an important chapter of . . . ecclesiastical history into a . . . confused mixture of many true and false Saint Romuluses, and many [more] dreamed-up martyrs, confessors, bishops, and laymen." But to Lami superstitions were more than just products of popular imagination. They were deliberate falsifications. They were created to make money for the keepers of various churches, shrines, and altars ("offerings" for a single procession could run as high as 500 *scudi*). They were also created to support the doctrine of Probabilism, a doctrine which, according to Lami, took moral choice off the shoulders of individual Christians and put it into the hands of clever, retrograde, power-hungry "specialists."

If ever you've heard a Jesuit talk,
at fallacious speeches you'll certainly balk.

Molina, it seems, is all that he reads,
and in physics on none but Ptolemy he feeds.

(*I pifferi della montagna*)

Since these same specialists controlled much of secondary education, Lami felt morally obliged to expose them to their hapless pupils:

There in his corner, where he's worth not a pr———,
he shits on himself, and on the muses does stick
all his satirical stench;
then out comes a verse, so obscene and so blunt,
that it makes us desire to match pr——— to cu——
e'en with a pox-covered wench.*

(Ibid.)

All the pent-up spleen left over from his school days at Prato was now poured out onto the one ecclesiastical body he held to be responsible for the corruption of religion in Italy: the Society of Jesus. He even accused the society of betraying its own heritage: of forgetting Ignatius, of ignoring the Bollandists, of mistreating those few of its members who still remained faithful to the heritage, and of downgrading the benefits of the *Spiritual Exercises,* which he still recommended to Foggini in 1745. His efforts against the society—together with those of the anti-Jesuits in Rome, Spain, France, and elsewhere—were eventually successful. In 1744 a project to publish an Italian translation of the French Jesuits' *Journal de Trévoux* wilted before an outburst of patriotic indignation. In 1758 the general himself ordered the editor of the society's counterpart to the *Novelle* to go easy in his constant barbs at Lami. Meanwhile, the reputation of the Jesuits in Florence had fallen so far that tourist guides habitually pointed to first the Palazzo Medici-Riccardi and then to San Giovannino next door, with the explanation: "There is the cradle of literature, and there is its tomb." Finally, in 1759, the prime minister of Portugal initiated the process by which the society was suppressed in one state after another—in a manner that often shocked even Lami—until it was formally disbanded throughout the church by Pope Clement XIV.

Lami's second battle had actually begun some twenty years before he became involved in it. Back in the 1710s, when Salvino Salvini was preparing his *Fasti* of the Accademia Fiorentina, he had come across a long-forgotten manuscript by Thomas Dempster, the Scots refugee who had taught at Pisa in the days of Galileo. Salvino was not particularly interested in the treatise. All it did was to attribute the invention of everything from city walls to boxing not to the Romans, as had long been customary, but to the little-known predecessors of the Romans on the Italian peninsula, the Etruscans. No one else had ever been much interested in

* The blank letters in the translation correspond exactly to those in the original.

the treatise either, even though, as Lami soon discovered, a few isolated Florentines had been at least curious about the Etruscans ever since the time of Leonardo Bruni. But when Salvino's brother, Anton Maria Salvini, gave the treatise to a visiting English nobleman, Thomas Coke (later Earl of Leicester), and when the expert antiquarian Filippo Buonarroti then published it, with a subsidy from Coke and a great quantity of notes and engraved illustrations, "the whole world applauded."

The cultural revival of the provincial cities of Tuscany had suddenly endowed Dempster's theses with an apparent utility. If it could prove that the Etruscans were the teachers of the Romans, then it could also prove that Cortona, Arezzo, Siena, and Volterra, which the Etruscans had founded, were superior to Florence, which had never claimed to have been founded by anyone but Romans. Etruscology, the systematic study of the Etruscans, was born. The new Academy of the *Occulti* at Cortona immediately changed its name to the Etruscan Academy (*Accademia Etrusca*), with a *lucumone* (the Etruscan word for *prince*) as president. The old Academy of the *Sepolti* of Volterra endowed its sixteenth-century name ("buried from the world") with an archaeological connotation ("digging up buried treasures") and began collecting for the famous museum that still bears the name of its chief patron, Cardinal Mario Guarnacci. Scipione Maffei rushed back to Verona to insert a whole section of cribbings from Buonarroti's notes in his *Istoria diplomatica*. Archaeologists, with Gori at their head, set out on a methodical hunt for new tombs and inscriptions all over Tuscany. Monks started digging around their monasteries. Landlords started expelling peasants from fields that promised a harvest of ancient coins and pottery. The sale of miscellaneous artifacts (and pseudo-artifacts) became a profitable business, or at least it became so for a certain Sig. Caglieri, whose shop in Florence was soon well enough known to merit a diploma from the greatest of all the patrons of "antiquities," Cardinal Alessandro Albani.

By 1742, when Lami's "Letters from Gualfonda" (the Riccardi garden) began appearing in the pages of the *Novelle,* the phase of discovery had given way to the phase of interpretation, judgment, and wild speculation. The Etruscan alphabet had already been worked out, at least well enough so that, with a few minor exceptions, Gori's version of 1737 is still basically the one accepted today. But just what the letters of that alphabet meant when they were put together, and where the people who wrote them came from, were questions that had as many hotly-defended answers as there were scholars with reputations to advance. One of them insisted that the Etruscan language was the parent of Latin. Another held that it derived from Greek, or from a common ancestor like Pelasgian or Tyrrhenian. Another said that it was the "language of Noah," and therefore related to Hebrew. Still another—the secretary of the French Académie des Inscriptions—claimed that it was Gallic in origin.

On the condition that Illyrians or Indo-Europeans be substituted for the passengers on the Ark, all these answers are still maintained today by one or another specialist in the field. But in the 1740s they were seriously compromised by several current misconceptions. They were all based on the assumption that what was oldest was by definition best, that the quality of any group or community depended upon its past rather than upon its present achievements, and that language was a gift of God rather than an invention of men—Vico notwithstanding. Hence, the proper sequence of archaic and classical was reversed, The "naturalistic" statues that today are attributed to later Greek and Roman influence were put first on chronological lists. And texts that are now considered largely unintelligible were "translated" by picking homonyms from any other language— whether Phoenician, Phrygian, or "Rhaetian"—whenever the root language failed to provide one to the liking of the translator.

Thus Lami was to some extent justified in coming out with still another answer to the questions, even though his arguments for the affiliation of Etruscan with Latin are far less convincing than those presented by Raymond Bloch in 1952. Nor was he completely unjustified in denouncing the whole of Etruscology as the flag-waving of local patriots. For one thing, it was not really history at all, but exasperated antiquarianism. It supposed that "one rare metal medallion" bearing the inscription HRCVL "provided absolutely certain testimony that the Campania had been inhabited by Etruscans." It built vast empires out of a pile of funeral stones that said little more than variants of "here lies so-and-so." Rather than encouraging men to right what was wrong in their own times, it distracted them with the wonders of a largely imaginary and utterly unattainable Golden Age in the past.

Still, Lami's denunciation had some unfortunate consequences. It misled at least one scholar into a sterile search for Latin homonyms. It discouraged another —Giovan Battista Passeri—from developing further the one method of deciphering the language that later was to prove the most fruitful, the method, that is, of examining the same word in different contexts without regard to similarities in other languages. It branded even the serious work of the Cortonese academicians as a revival of fifteenth-century document-forging (they eventually gave it up). Worse yet, it blinded most Florentines to the importance of the two other great archaeological discoveries of the century, Herculaneum and Pompeii, even though one Florentine—Gori—and one Tuscan—Marcello Venuti—were the first to smuggle descriptions of them past the jealous eyes of the Neapolitan censors. These discoveries, Lami proclaimed, amounted to just another "magic lantern," "full of so many visions, incoherencies, errors, contradictions, [and] imaginary interpretations" as to be practically worthless. It is thanks largely to his attitude that Florence never produced anything comparable to the fantastic landscapes of one of the first illustrators of the discoveries, Giovan Battista Piranesi.

The third battle was similar to the second, in that it was fought over the question of the relevance of scholarship. It began in November 1740, when a shy, twenty-five-year-old bookworm named Lorenzo Mehus proposed to the Centaur Press an edition of the letters of Coluccio Salutati and Leonardo Bruni, the founders of Florentine humanism in the early Renaissance. The project looked at first like a continuation of the Crusca language-text editions. It also looked—particularly since the letters were in Latin rather than Italian—like an addition to Muratori's historical documents, which were just then being complemented by a four-volume collection of the Florentine historians of the fifteenth and sixteenth centuries. But it soon became apparent that Mehus had something else in mind. He was interested in applying the criteria not of Muratori but of the Dutch and German philologists, who had started printing humanist texts some thirty years before anyone in Italy even heard of them. That meant following the manuscripts word for word, just as they came out of the archives, with no notes other than lists of variants. It also meant backtracking even with respect to Salvino Salvini, who had discovered in Alberti's *On the Family* not only words for the *Vocabolario* but "absolutely noble and very important subject matter . . . regarding the affairs . . . of civic life" and "truly golden precepts . . . worthy . . . to be impressed on the minds of everyone."*

To Lami, the project was useless, and he turned upon Mehus with the fury of a rejected counselor. Books unread were a waste of time, he said; and no one could be expected to read the Latin of "those barbarous times" unless the spelling were modernized, unless the references were identified, and unless the significance of the contents for the eighteenth century were fully pointed out. Actually, the two positions were not irreconcilable. Indeed, they exist side by side today—one in the Walpole, Jefferson, and Madison "factories" of American universities, and the other in the "source books" of undergraduate humanities courses. Even Lami admitted, moreover, that an "explained" text ought to be based on a "correct" one. But unfortunately he was too accustomed to dealing with diplomas, charters, inscriptions, and other nonliterary documents to appreciate the problems of alternate readings. And he was too apolitical to understand any better than Mehus the significance of these particular texts. After one try at putting out a rival edition of Salutati, he turned instead to violent denunciations. Mehus stumbled on against increasing obstacles until he at last finished his edition of the works of Ambrogio Traversari in 1759. Then he gave up altogether. The rediscovery of Renaissance civic humanism had to wait for the more favorable and more politically charged atmosphere of the 1770s and '80s.

* Most of the adjectives of the original are in the superlative and cannot be properly translated.

The fourth of Lami's battles was the most bitter of all, for it struck at the very basis of the distinction between theology and the sciences that he had inherited from Galileo and Magalotti. It began suddenly and unexpectedly when, in the late fall of 1745, Lami received a small booklet for review entitled *Of the Existence and the Attributes of God . . . According to Philosophy Alone: Metaphysical Essays of Signor****. He had no grudge against the author, a university professor by the name of Giovan Gualberto De Soria. In fact, he rather admired him for having introduced Newton into the classroom at Pisa and for applying Newton in an easy-to-read, and strongly antischolastic textbook of 1741. De Soria was a great talker, one "who knew how to take a few general principles from his potpourri of philosophy, sprinkle it with a couple of metaphors, and throw it into a sea of words." He was also an amateur poet, one who could explain air pressure in rhymed verse for the amusement of the Pisan Arcadians. He was a bit proud of having risen into academia from humble origins: his father was a poor postal clerk from Elba who had exhausted his pocketbook sending his son to the college at Prato. De Soria was otherwise inoffensive. His only real reason for printing his *Essays*—with wide margins on small pages—was his fear of being caught by Cerati's new publish-or-perish regime at the university; at thirty-eight years of age, he still had only one publication to his name.

But Lami was horrified. To pretend that human reason without the aid of faith could comprehend the fundamental doctrines of Christianity was to deny the point he had made about St. John the Evangelist: that the doctrines depended on revelation alone. It also meant yielding completely to the Jesuits, to the Aristotelians, and, for that matter, to the Socinians. It meant opening the door for theologians to meddle in history and for scientists to meddle in theology. He covered his own copy of De Soria's book with invective. He wrote to Rome to press for a condemnation—which De Soria barely averted by quickly putting out an amended edition. He got Bandini to stir up trouble at Pisa. He ran a series of long and violent articles in the *Novelle,* which were then collected in a separate volume the following year. He finally relented only after his poor victim had been denied a raise in salary, ruined in a lawsuit, insulted and threatened by his students, and finally forced to turn to lighter, less compromising subjects like the amusing *Dialogue between a French Gentleman and an Italian Concerning the Qualities of Their Two Nations,* which first appeared in 1766.

9

The retreat

Thus the battles were won. But somehow, the fruits of victory never quite matured. To some extent, the fault was Lami's. So convinced was he that he could do no wrong and that whoever disagreed with him could do no right, that he ended up alienating even those who most admired him. "There's not an honest man around who has not broken with him," said one of them in 1750. "I cannot but respect him, for he's very learned; but I won't bother trying to be his friend, because the laws of friendship are unknown to him." Even by 1742, the "immense horde of [his] enemies" had grown to the point where some of them launched a sort of anti-*Novelle*, for which they borrowed the prestigious title of the recently deceased *Giornale de' letterati*—the "Journal of Learned Men"—of Venice. The *Giornale* failed to match the *Novelle* in style, in polemical verve, or in regularity of appearance. Its articles were too long, too "learned," and more intent on telling Florentines what went on abroad than in letting them speak for themselves. Still, it served for many years as the organ for a heterogeneous coalition of university professors and Jesuit sympathizers, and for the members of the Colombaria and the hangers-on of that irreverent homosexual aesthete from Austria, Philip von Stosch.

What held the coalition together was a common distrust of Lami. And what continually nourished it with new adherents was Lami's inability to get along with his own collaborators. Even Gori soon tired of being publically reprimanded, particularly when his sin consisted only in minor bibliographical oversights and typographical errors that in fact were listed in the *corrigenda* at the end of his books. His relations with Lami finally degenerated into a ridiculous fight over the value of a bronze tablet bought by the Riccardi in 1745, a fight that was finally extinguished by a peremptory order from Vienna. The intellectual community of Florence thus split into warring fragments. "One Florentine is still worth ten Venetians," admitted Muratori. But "a hundred Florentines, each one with his brain on fire and passionately attached to his own opinion . . . [is still] worth less than one Venetian."

At the same time, Lami's dedication to his cause occasionally led him to confuse marginal issues with essential ones. It also led him to back himself into embarrassing corners. In 1744, for instance, he became interested in a certain Father Norbert of Bar-le-duc in Lorraine—a hotheaded Capuchin who was subsequently thrown out of Rome for his violent tirades and who then had the nerve to ask Richecourt for a bishopric. Lami promptly made himself an expert on the old question of the Chinese and Malabar rites, a question that had been brought up one last time by the Propaganda Fidei in 1737 and by Veyssière La Croze's book on Ethiopia in 1739. He did so not by reading any of the huge mass of literature then available on the Far East. He did so by editing the diary of an Italian monk who had gone to Macao in 1720 for the sole purpose of building a case against the Jesuits. He did so also by reading Norbert's inflammatory *Historical Memoirs Concerning the Missions in the East Indies,* which was promptly placed on the Index, and by taking seriously everything he read about the book in the hysterical pages of the *Nouvelles ecclésiastiques,* the underground newspaper of the Jansenist extremists in France.

It never occurred to Lami that the Jesuits were doing for the Chinese and the Indians simply what Paul had done for the Greeks and what he himself was trying to do for post-Galileo Catholics (Vatican II was to sanction such efforts two centuries later): putting Christianity in terms that their audiences could understand. Nor did it occur to him that Benedict XIV's decree against the rites would have the effect of limiting Christianity to an insignificant minority of the population in all non-European countries that could not be conquered by a Catholic power. It did not even occur to him that Norbert, who practically boarded at the Riccardiana for several months, was more an apostle of the Capuchins than of Christian orthodoxy, and more a victim of his own frustrations than an apostle of anything. Lami might have been discredited by the whole affair if Norbert had not been packed off to northern Europe and finally dropped from his order.

Even more serious was Lami's involvement in a controversy of the early 1750s that had no relevance to any contemporary issue whatsoever—the controversy over the morality of the theater. Lami had already learned that rigorism could be carried to absurd extremes. For instance, he had not hesitated to back up Maffei's explanation of the difference between interest on capital and usury, for he knew by heart all the passages in the Scriptures and in the works of the church fathers regarding usury, which the Lombard economist Gian Rinaldo Carli had republished in 1747. In the theater controversy, he ought to have known, historian that he was, that in some cases Augustine was talking in the very specific context of his own times, and that the degenerate spectacles of the fourth century A.D. had very little to do with the dramas of Metastasio, Fagiuoli, or even Voltaire. But when the Dominican Daniele Concina came out with two huge volumes, both of them as packed with quotations from the fathers as they were devoid of references to modern playwrights, Lami began to waver. When Foggini republished what Filippo Neri, François de Sales, and Carlo Borromeo had said about the theaters of the sixteenth century, he began to feel himself bound by ties of friendship. When he then remembered that plays formed an important part of Jesuit school curricula, and when he found out that one of the staunchest contemporary defenders of the theater was having an affair with an actress forty years his junior, he made up his mind. The controversy ended in breaking off whatever relations he still maintained with Maffei, the proud author of the *Merope*. And it turned out to be completely ineffective. "We have thirty-two theaters open here," he moaned in 1761. "Just look what good the Florentines have made of all those books against [them]!"

To some extent, however, these setbacks were not so much the fault of Lami as of those in whom he had put his confidence. The archbishop was partly to blame. In spite of his promises, Incontri refused to press for a reduction of holy days in 1741; he went right ahead and exposed the relics of St. Zanobi in 1743; and he showed a notable want of courage "in uprooting Molinism" when he discouraged the publication of anti-Molinist treatises in 1757. The government was partly to blame, too. From 1754 on, it regularly told Lami what not to print and forced him to remove whole sentences from what he had already set up in type. Then, in 1758, Richecourt was replaced by the "incompetent and wicked" general from Pavia, Antonio Botta Adorno, who was well remembered for having provoked the popular uprising of Genoa in 1746. Botta let the ecclesiastical censor interfere once again, to the point where Lami often had to choose between being boringly evasive or being silenced, in spite of his position as imperial theologian.

But above all, the fault was the pope's. Benedict XIV turned out not to be the hero Lami—and Muratori—thought him to be. According to Mann, he was "an old Bolognese doctor" and "a beat and a *coglione* . . . [who] amuses himself with making saints" while the administration of his states crumbles. He was not interested in keeping the church out of politics: in 1750 he got into a jurisdictional quarrel with the Venetians that proved to be even more degrading than the one of his unfortunate predecessor, Paul V. He was not really interested in rewriting the Breviary; and he even congratulated one of Lami's fiercest enemies for his valorous defense of the legendary St. Romulus, who thus continued to inspire pious priests for another two centuries. He was not interested in reforming the habits of the Curia, where "imposture [was still] worth more than learning" in procuring promotions. He was not even interested in following the precepts of justice that his personal friend Muratori had proposed to him in 1742. He was so annoyed at having been taken in once by a noisy Lorrainer, whom the grand duke had made bishop of Volterra, that he had him thrown into the Castel

Sant'Angelo; and there the poor man stayed for the remaining thirty-two years of his life, forgotten by all. "Thus Rome declares itself continually less faithful to Augustinian doctrine," Lami moaned. Under Benedict's successor, it abandoned the doctrine altogether. For Clement XIII may have been a model pastor when he became archbishop of Padua in 1747. But one of the first things he did when he became pope was to condemn the new catechism of Mésenguy, even though it had already been adopted at Naples. And that shattered any hope of ever getting the catechism of Bellarmino out of the schools.

At the same time, Lami had to admit that one of the most important elements of his program had backfired. Opening Italy to transalpine literature had indeed proved to be an effective stimulant to Italian culture and a powerful support for what he held to be true Catholicism. It had been so, that is, as long as what northern Europe had to offer was the *Mémoires* of the Académie des Inscriptions, the *Histoire et mémoires* of the Académie des Sciences, the poems of Alexander Pope ("who had the glory of not having abandoned the Roman Catholic religion"), and the plays of Crébillon *père*. But in the late 1740s and early 1750s, it started producing very different kinds of books. Some of them Lami endorsed without reserve. The botanical works of Charles Linnaeus, for instance, seemed to offer a system of classification considerably more accurate than that of Tournefort and Micheli, and they were duly translated into Italian by the Florentine botanist Saverio Manetti in 1757. Similarly, the *Mémoire* on inoculation by Charles Marie de la Condamine seemed to offer a remedy to the age-old curse of smallpox; Lami's former colleague Targioni showed how it could be applied successfully to a large number of people in the fall of 1756.

But some of these books left Lami considerably perplexed. John Locke's metaphysical treatises were still as unacceptable as ever, and he could not understand why Angelo Tavanti and Giovan Francesco Pagnini wore out their eyes translating the difficult prose of Locke's treatises on money. Montesquieu's *Spirit of the Laws,* which was to become a textbook for the next generation of Florentine jurists, was exhaustingly prolix, particularly when compared (and the comparison was Lami's) to *The Prince* of a certain "celebrated author." The *Encyclopédie* of Diderot and d'Alembert was clearly aimed at "introducing everywhere a universal skepticism." Rousseau's *Emile* was "a detestable work," and his *Social Contract* "a marvelous mixture of correct and false conclusions." As the French *philosophes* moved more and more toward an open rejection of Christianity, and as the Holy Office began condemning their works almost automatically as they appeared in print, Lami's basic assumption became ever less tenable. This was the assumption that all contributions to the letters and sciences, whatever their source, could be only beneficial to the Catholic cause. As philosophy and the church moved rapidly toward open conflict, Lami found the neutral ground between them giving way, and he reluctantly moved off toward one of the two extremes. One last attempt at reconciliation proved to be a failure—the attempt to counter De la Mettrie's *Man-Machine* with Magalotti's theory about the souls of animals.

No one cared any longer. A return to geographical isolation was impossible, for Florence had now, thanks largely to Lami's efforts, been permanently annexed to the European cultural community. All he could do was to acknowledge grudgingly that the French Jansenists had been "filled with the spirit of schism." All he could do was to applaud sadly the full-scale attack launched against the Enlightenment by the Parlement of Paris in 1759 as "wise," "useful," and necessary.

At the same time, Lami had to admit that the problems and passions of his generation were losing their appeal. Gori's antiquarian volumes became increasingly difficult to sell—and to subsidize. The Crusca was denounced as an anachronism, its dictionary was proclaimed inferior to Dr. Johnson's, and its authorities were ridiculed as "bastardized wiseacres"—*imbastarditi saccenti*. The Colombaria stopped studying gems and inscriptions and "passed the evening in pleasant conversation." The guidebooks of Arcadian criticism were written off as "boring nonsense." Even Lami's disciples failed him. They wrote pages and pages of well-documented facts; but they then refused to draw practical lessons from them, even about such a potentially relevant personage as Filippo Neri. To the last representatives of the old generation in the late 1750s, it seemed as if "literature was gradually becoming extinct in this country" and that "we will [soon] relapse into the barbarism of the seventeenth century." The age of the scholars and historians was giving way to the age of the agronomes and the political economists; and all Lami could do was wring his hands.

What interested the new generation was not descriptive science but applied science, not diagnoses but effective remedies for grain diseases, not botany but scientific agriculture, not piety but politics, not accounts of medieval festivals but concrete information about "the various sectors of public revenue and administration—information that may be less elevated and less difficult, but closer to us and therefore more important." The change was one of degree rather than of kind, and Lami tried to keep abreast of it. In 1753 he joined the new Accademia dei Georgofili, the first of the many agricultural societies that were soon to spread over the whole of Italy. He even "showed off his good taste concerning the cultivation of vines" in one of the first sessions. More often, he was content merely to repeat what he had been saying for the past thirty years. He republished the *De Eruditione* in 1769, not for the purpose of updating it but merely to "take revenge on his censors and accusers." He added footnote to footnote until his texts were crowded off the page. Although his scholarship remained sound enough to be quoted authoritatively as late as 1968, it became increasingly difficult to read.

Similarly, when Lami himself tried his hand at writing manuals of piety, he produced something much closer to what he had condemned than to what he had called for in his programmatic appeals. His manuals, particularly the one he wrote for his mother, may have been historically accurate, but they were still hagiographical, still as far as ever from the Bible and the fathers. They really proved only that he could not write for a popular audience. Thus when Alfonso de' Liguori's charming stories of the adventures of a Neapolitan mother-mistress-goddess named The Virgin started pouring off the presses, Lami did not bother to respond, even though the stories were specifically designed to save the church from Muratori. He was completely unaware of the enormous advantages that his opponents stood to gain from the kind of emotional, nonliturgical, nonscriptural piety offered by Liguori. It very effectively kept the noses of the laity out of the administrative and doctrinal affairs of the church and made them subjects of the hierarchy rather than responsible members of a *Respublica Christiana.* Nor, needless to say, was Lami at all aware of the potential benefit to his own cause of the execrated doctrine of Probabilism. He never dreamed that it might one day be used to defend the consciences of individuals against the arbitrary orders of the Curia, as it was very effectively in 1967 by a professor at an institution with the ominous name of The Bellarmine School of Theology, in Illinois. Consequently, it was Paul of the Cross, not Paul of Tarsus, who became the model for Catholic missionaries in the next two centuries. And it was Liguori's *Theologia Moralis,* not Augustine, Pascal, or Muratori's *Well-Regulated Devotion* that filled seminary bookshelves right down until the 1960s, when all of the innumerable editions of Liguori's work were suddenly dumped onto the secondhand book market.

So Lami gradually retired. He reviewed books without reading them. He amused himself, and various visiting dignitaries, by playing the game of the Sybil and debating for hours on such questions as "Who is the greater, Aristotle or Alexander?" He took trips around Tuscany, jotting down notes on archives and inscriptions—and ignoring everything else, even the beauty of the landscape. He spent more and more of his evenings in the taverns—at the *Svizzero* and at the *Porco* ("The Pig")—"discussing at length a line from some poet, an epithet, a word," or just exchanging wisecracks "as if he didn't know how to do anything but joke." He kept up his youthful appearance. Even at sixty-four he had hardly a wrinkle on his face; and his slightly wavy, shoulder-length hair still showed no signs of thinning. But he was getting old nonetheless. He increasingly turned over the direction of the *Novelle* to Bandini and another bright young disciple named Marco Lastri. As he denounced once more the "wolves" and the "esprits-forts" of the age, his successors called, practically to his face, for the immediate trans-lation into Italian of "the celebrated French Encyclopedia . . . the one work in all the world that merits to be translated into all languages." When he finally died, in February 1770, one of the leading spokesmen of the new generation irreverently remarked: "One less dog to bark at men of merit."

BOOK VI
FLORENCE
IN THE 1780s

*How Francesco Maria Gianni spent
twenty-five years building a model state only
to see it torn down in a single morning*

I

Peasants, plebeians, and proprietors

Tuesday, June 9, 1790. Piazza dell'Olio—the slightly widened alley behind the archiepiscopal palace in Florence. About six o'clock in the morning.

The peasants had been there since daybreak, unloading barrels, setting up stands, and putting out measuring cups. They had done tolerably well on previous market days. One of them still had 10 *paoli* in his pocket from last week's sales— enough to feed a whole family for five or six days. They had no reason to believe that they would do any less well today. The last restrictions on the movement of foodstuffs within Tuscany had been removed some fifteen years before, by the law of August 24, 1775, and the peasants who brought their produce into Florence had by now become accustomed to selling it at prices established by the law of supply and demand, rather than at prices dictated by the urban magistracy ironically called the *Abbondanza* ("Abundance").

Similarly, the last restrictions on the importation and exportation of food-stuffs across the Tuscan border had been removed in 1781. Now, in years of plenty, the big proprietors could ship their surpluses to Marseilles, where profits often ran as high as 20 percent; and the peasants, or at least those of them within carting distance of the city, were no longer faced with glutted markets at home. Grain prices in Tuscany followed the upward trend of those everywhere else in Europe at the time: from 12 *lire* a sack before 1763 to 18.19 in 1771, to 20 in 1783, and finally, with a few temporary regressions, to 23 in 1790. So did oil prices: even in so felicitous a year as 1786 they dropped only 4 *lire* after the harvest, from 83 to 79. The rising prices were no longer simply the consequence of dearth. Oil production increased considerably in the late 1780s, thanks in part to a tree-planting contest launched by the Accademia dei Georgofili. Wine production had risen so much by 1785 that some of the grape harvest was turned into spirits, which the grand duke obligingly freed from the control of a state monopoly. Grain production, at least according to one well-informed observer, increased by 24 percent between 1765 and 1792, from 8,356,942 to 13,033,031 sacks a year. Population rose by only 11 percent during the same period—a rate (.047 percent per annum) which would give some satisfaction to contemporary populationists, but which was considerably lower than the .57 percent registered for the years 1961–67. The age-old spector of famine had all but disappeared. At the same time, the demand for Tuscan agricultural products abroad rose even faster than domestic production. And while a rise in grain exports from zero to 624,845 sacks a year in the first ten years of the reign did not convert Tuscany into the creditor it was to become in the late 1960s, when 29 *lire* went out of the area for every 56 *lire* that came in, it at least got rid of the prospect, as frightening as that of a famine, of having a year's work wiped out by an overabundant harvest.

Certainly the peasants were not well-off. Almost none of them had received anything like an equal share of the benefits of rising prices, since they were usually obliged to pay rent not in cash but in kind. But many of them were at least better housed. The grand duke alone had spent over a million *lire* in repairs and new construction; that may be one of the reasons why so many of the farmhouses—with huge stone ovens, enormous fireplaces, and terracotta pipes—that are now being bought up as weekend retreats by Florentine businessmen date from the late eighteenth century. Some peasants benefited from a notable increase in their landlords' capital investments: 600 *scudi* had been plowed back into Orlando Del Benino's estates at Villamagna each year since 1775, for instance. A few of them had even managed to climb all the way up to the dignified level of the eighteen-member family that dined Giuseppe Pelli in style on September 25, 1787. "They live in perfect patriarchal harmony," reported Pelli, who was a bit ashamed of continuing to live in Florence rather than on his own estate in the upper Valdarno. "They bring prosperity to their landlords and to themselves, [and] they cultivate the land so skillfully that even the wisest *agronome* could hardly do better."

Just how much of this modest flicker of rural prosperity passed on to the inhabitants of the city depended largely on how each person made his living. Those whose income derived largely from the land they owned in the country were the most direct beneficiaries; they kept their cellars stocked with their own produce, in accordance with the rules of domestic economy codified centuries before by Leon Battista Alberti. Those much further down on the social scale, whose income derived from services to the landowning classes, seem at least to have "earned enough to live decently." That, at any rate, is what a tall, hollow-cheeked, forty-year-old tailor's assistant named Giovan Battista Giambaccini told the police when he was brought in on a pickpocketing charge in the spring of 1790. Giambaccini was paid by the piece in the shop of the master-tailor Jacopo Mastagni at the Badìa. But Giambaccini also accepted orders of his own on the side, and, on the morning of his arrest, he had just been paid 32 *paoli* by a Mugello landowner for making him a suit. At the same time, Giambaccini's wife, Teresa, earned enough by winding silk thread and cutting ribbons to clothe herself and their three children. Out of what he estimated as an average daily income of 3½ *paoli* Giambaccini could not afford to buy sea fish, which before the invention of refrigerator cars were fairly expensive. But he could spend 7 *crazie* (0.7 *paoli*) on bread, anywhere from 4 *crazie* (on weekdays) to 10 (on holidays) on veal, Arno eel, and other *companatico* ("things to eat with bread"), and 11 *quattrini* for half a *fiasco* of wine. He thus enjoyed a standard of living comfortably above even late twentieth-century poverty levels. And he had enough left over to dress with some style: a yellow leather hairband, a three-cornered black felt hat, a dark brown suit with a green *giubba,* a red-and-white striped *panciotto,* white linen stockings, and black leather shoes with silver-plated buckles.

Government employees, on the other hand, of whom there had been 1,335 in 1765, were rather less fortunate. Most of them still lived on the same fixed salaries that even an outspoken defender of government policy admitted to be increasingly inadequate. Many of them had recently been deprived of the traditional means of rounding out their salaries through tips and semilegal bribes: that, at any rate, is what happened to the customs officials when the Tariff Law of 1781 freed most goods from any duty at all and made weight, which was constant, rather than estimated value, which was subject to wrangling, the sole basis for taxing those goods still left on the list. And all of these workers were in constant danger of having their jobs wiped off the roster in the wake of the next administrative reform.

By far the greatest number of Florentine workers, however, were employed in the various branches of the cloth industry—25,570 of them in 1765, of whom over a third were employed in the silk industry. The prices of manufactured goods in general had remained fairly constant during the twenty years of rising food prices. But the price of silk had actually fallen. Worse yet, after a rather encouraging rise from 121,038 bales in 1778 to 159,377 in 1786, exportation of silk had recently dropped sharply. An anonymous petitioner of 1788 was probably exaggerating when he asked the grand duke, in terms as vague as those of most anonymous petitioners, "to go into the houses and see [for yourself] how many people sleep without sheets on the floor, how many children go naked, crying with hunger." But even the French ambassador had to admit, between one eulogy of the government and another, that "salaries are not sufficient to buy bread at 3 *sols*; and the consequence is poverty."

It never seems to have occurred to the Florentine silk-workers that their troubles were caused by low wages rather than by high prices. None of them seems to have realized that gradual inflation might stimulate production, that the difference between real and artificial prices always had to be paid back in taxes, and that freedom to withhold grain from the market at one moment was the best way to assure its presence at the next moment. Needless to say, none of them ever dreamed of organizing for self-improvement, particularly in the light of the

government's phobia concerning anything that looked like a "corporation."
Indeed, none of them could even conceive of the possibility of progress in the
future. Improvement meant simply returning to a largely imaginary status quo
ante. And any alteration of that status quo was immediately blamed not on price
curves, devaluations, or economic *conjonctures,* but on that traditional strawman of
all preindustrial societies, the "monopolist." Thus one of the great pastimes of
Florentine workers in the spring of 1790 was hunting for flesh-and-blood versions
of the strawman. In May, the San Giovanni police station was bombarded with
so many reports of collusion among neighborhood shopkeepers that even the
rather bewildered, and not terribly efficient, district captain began to believe them.
A few weeks later the Santo Spirito district captain had to go in person to the
store "Dalla Buca" in Via San Giovanni in order to save the innocent proprietor
from being plundered.

To be sure, hard times were nothing new for the working classes of the
capital. At least there is no reason to believe that the times were any harder in
the 1780s than they had been during the long economic depression of the mid-
seventeenth century or during the political turmoil of the early eighteenth. There
is good reason to believe that the overall cost of living was actually lower in 1790
than it had been in 1770–74. But previously economic discontent had usually
been siphoned off into religious emotion. And, at least since the late sixteenth
century, religious emotion usually ended by strengthening the established
political and social order, or by leaving it unscathed after a display of harmless
fireworks. However, by 1790 this safety valve had been severely damaged. Just
five years before, on March 21, 1785, the government had ordered the dissolution
of the only institutions over which ordinary lay Florentines still maintained a
certain amount of control: the confraternities. It dissolved so many of them that
merely listing them all in the various cities of Tuscany takes up eleven closely
written folio pages of the inventory in the Florentine State Archives. When it
then confiscated the endowments as well, it put an end not only to the processions
and vigils that for so long had distracted the poor from their misery, but also to the
small handouts in money and bread that, however inefficiently, had frequently
kept them short of starvation.

On May 9, 1789, the government took one further step. It ordered the
removal of the "cloaks of massive silver" that had always hidden the "portrait"
of the Virgin at the Annunziata on all but very special occasions. The following
November the Servites finally got around to carrying out the order in a three-day
ceremony featuring the archbishop, the grand duke "with his usual deep devotion,"
carloads of indulgences, and an "extraordinary concourse of every class of
people." But not everyone present was convinced of the government's perfectly
valid theological reasons for the unveiling. Most of them were sure that unveiling
did to images what haircuts had done to Samson: it robbed them of their potency.
Having despaired of the earthly assistance of the confraternities, the poor now

found themselves bereft of supernatural assistance as well. One well-qualified but "indifferent" observer warned that raising such a basically "superfluous" question might end by "disturbing the public peace." He was proved right in the last weeks of May 1790, when handmade posters began appearing with alarming frequency in the Mercato Nuovo demanding the restoration of the veils and the reestablishment of the confraternities.

In themselves, the posters would have been no more dangerous than the wall-scribblings of later generations. But at the time they represented the sentiments not only of many Florentine plebeians, but of a large part of the regular clergy as well. In 1775, the government had restricted their right to admit new members. In 1779, it had forbidden them to send money abroad. In January 1782 it had expelled all of their associates who were not born or naturalized Tuscan subjects. In July of the same year it had abolished all their exemptions from local episcopal control. In 1786 it had forbidden all but the mendicants from soliciting private donations. In the meantime it had begun closing down all those religious houses that it alone chose to define as "superfluous" or "underpopulated." In other words, the regular clergy were faced with extinction. Most of them did not have the will to resist. The only arguments they could muster on behalf of monasticism at the end of the antimonastic eighteenth century were obviously a hundred years out of date. Few of them dared to resist, particularly after appeals to their superiors in Rome had been forbidden by the edict of October 2, 1788. The mere suspicion of involvement in an uprising at Pistoia in 1787 had led to the immediate reclassification of the local Zoccolanti and the Capuchins as "superfluous." But there was one exception: the Dominicans of San Marco. They still remembered their fights against Cosimo I in the 1540s and against Jesuits, Augustinians, and Jansenists ever since. And they had no intention of suffering passively the fate already meted out to eleven of their sister communities in other parts of the country. Ten years before they had not hesitated to rush to the defense of their former leader, Giuseppe Agostino Orsi (a sometime ally of Giovanni Lami), when someone published a new edition of a pamphlet written fifty years earlier against Orsi's defense of Aquinas's and Melchior Cano's theses about something called "the material use of the word *No.*" Their success in smaller things spurred them on to succeed in bigger things. They first won over the archbishop of Florence, thus undercutting any justification for government intervention on behalf of episcopal authority. They then unleashed one of their most fiery fellows in the pulpit, who denounced the whole current ecclesiastical policy in one blistering sermon after another all through the spring of 1790.

Thus the alliance between throne and altar that had lasted for two centuries began to fall apart. Ever since the days of Giovanni Botero and Roberto Bellarmino, the clergy had proclaimed itself the surest guarantor of civil government; and the civil government had returned the gesture by freely using religion as an *instrumentum regis*—an instrument of political power. Now, suddenly, at

least a part of the clergy broke with the government and went over to the side
of the very element of the population that had the least to gain from the preservation of the established order. The new alliance had already gone into action in
other parts of the country. On April 24 a large mob of peasants and plebeians,
with the tacit consent of some of the nobility, had taken over the city of Pistoia,
driven the bishop out of town, ripped his coat of arms off the episcopal palace,
set back up the altars he had taken out of the churches, and then paraded up and
down the streets for three days. On May 31 a mob of dock-workers in the "Little
Venice" section of Livorno had reopened all the suppressed chapels, ripped up
the marble steps that had been bought by the synagogue from a closed church,
put the miracle-working Madonna di Montenegro (Livorno's equivalent of the
Virgin of the Annunziata) back in place, sent the ecclesiastical provost and two
of his secretaries running off to Florence, and forced the governor, with a
coccarde pinned awkwardly on his hat, to promise to give the monasteries back to
their former owners. During the next two or three days similar disturbances
occurred at Colle Valdelsa, at Chiusi, and at Montevarchi, all apparently with
similar results.

Strangely enough, the upper classes of the capital paid very little attention to
these disorders. According to one observer, the affair at Pistoia amounted to
nothing but a display of "popular tempers" concerning "certain totally unimportant practices . . . that had nothing to do with the essentials of religion"—
an affair which could easily have been blocked by a timely muster of the troops
camped just outside the city walls. The only disorders that attracted any interest
among most Florentine newspaper readers were the ones that had been taking
place in France during the preceding year. And they, it seems, had so far produced
much more good than evil. They had gotten rid of one or two undeserving
individuals like the Cardinal de Brienne, whose haughty manners had made such a
bad impression during his tour of the Uffizi in May 1789. They had enabled
"twenty-four million others to start a new life." And they had avenged "the
sins of all his predecessors since Francis I" by taking power away from an
incompetent despot and giving it to men very much like the doctors, lawyers,
and landlords of Florence.

A few Florentines, it is true, were a bit worried that what they immediately
identified as a revolution in France might spread to their own country. During
the summer of 1790 the police were occasionally warned about secret agents: a
French-speaking monk whom they escorted out of the Porta San Frediano on
July 9, in spite of his pleas of innocence; a French citizen whose "imprudent
and seditious speech" had made him persona non grata in Naples a few months
before; a heavyset man "with a red, ardent, enflamed face" named Tagliatesta

("off-with-their-heads"), who was credited with killing hundreds of people in Avignon and Nîmes and who was rumored to be on his way to Tuscany on July 14. But even those who worried were quickly comforted by their long-time friend, the French ambassador. The National Assembly, insisted the ambassador, was doing nothing other than promulgating in France the very same principles that their own government had been observing for over two decades. Tuscany, they knew, was "free of politics, plots, and military spirit." It was too far away to be affected by "the great tempests that blow across the broad fields of northern Europe." Its population was "probably the quietest and most submissive" in the world. Its capital city was "certainly the happiest in all Italy." And it enjoyed "a degree of public safety such that anyone can walk about at any hour of the day or night without receiving so much as a slight insult." Even if certain elements of the population were discontent, they "lacked the qualities necessary to create a tumult worthy of attention." Nothing like the storming of the Bastille could ever take place in Tuscany—first because there was no Bastille, and second because there was no one to storm it.

This state of optimism was in part the result of misinformation. For political as well as for cultural reasons, Florentine newspapers tended to be as sparse in information about the Hapsburg monarchy as they were abundant in news about France, England, and America. Their readers had no way of knowing that revolutions could be regressive as well as progressive. They never thought to put the events of Pistoia and Livorno into the context, not of Paris and Philadelphia, but of Belgium and Hungary. They never realized that the defense of "liberties," privileges, and tradition could spark a revolt just as easily as the demand for "liberty," justice, and reason.

Optimism was also encouraged all during the winter and spring of 1789–90 by one of the gayest social seasons in memory. "Never before," reported the weekly *Gazzetta toscana,* "have the parties been more brilliant and more crowded." For nine months the architects Giulio Mannaioni and Giuseppe Baccani had been at work transforming the Pergola from a baroque into a neoclassical theater. On December 26 over a thousand guests danced all night to celebrate its reopening. In January, the blind playwright Cosimo Giotti introduced at the Cocomero the most startling of his anticlassical evocations of the Middle Ages—the prose tragedy *Ippolita e Rinaldo,* or "The Guelphs and the Ghibellines," which "so enchanted the numerous spectators that they shouted for a repeat performance and made the author accompany the actors to the stage." Two weeks later, the choreographer-composer Paolino Franchi presented a ballet version of the recent capture of Belgrade, which the Andolfati company then rewrote as a musical play, with real soldiers lent for the occasion by the grand duke. Luckily for those of festive spirits, the inevitable royal deaths coincided that year with the beginning of Lent. Official mourning for the grand duke's daughter-in-law did not begin until February 24, and the news of the death of his brother, Emperor

Joseph II, simply let loose a bustle of activity that culminated in the elaborate funeral directed by the architect Ignazio dell'Agata and the painter Luigi Molinelli at Santa Felicità one month later. At the end of March the Accademia degli Armonici sponsored a concert by the celebrated singers Francesco Porri and Carolina Perini, which was crowned, as usual, with a sonata by the ubiquitous and tireless violinist Pietro Nardini. Then on April 19 the theaters reopened with Cimarosa's popular *Giannina e Bernardone,* sung by the same combination of a male and a female soprano that Italian audiences still held to be a perfectly justifiable suspension of natural law. Foreigners poured into the city, so many of them that the Aquila Nera Hotel overflowed and the grand duchess had to offer a thirty-eight-plate dinner just for the more distinguished of them. All Florentines who could afford to follow this constant round of entertainment were up too late each night to pay much attention to what went on during the day.

Thus optimism combined with distraction to blind Florentine newspaper readers to the appearance of a completely new element in the disorders at Livorno: the demand for the abolition of free trade. They were deaf to the shouts of *Viva l'Abbondanza*—"Long live the Price Control Office"—that arose from mobs of women in the streets of San Frediano during the first week of June. And they failed to notice the rapid transformation of what had been a religious issue into an economic one. Even the police seemed to be undisturbed. They themselves had torn down a violent pro-*Abbondanza* poster in the Mercato Nuovo on June 7. They knew that two "bad, fanatic priests, capable of dangerous acts against the government," were busy making even more violent posters concerning long-discarded rites. They knew that carriages were regularly being stopped and the passengers warned that their days were numbered. They knew that one of the regents had been receiving so many anonymous threats that he had decided to move to the country. They knew that "seditious discussions" were going on every night in certain taverns around Santa Croce and in Giovan Antonio Betti's bookstore at Santa Trinita. But they did nothing.

The police seem not even to have paid much attention to the increasingly alarming reports about the existence of a plot to channel discontent into an open revolt. Just who was actually involved in the plot will never be known, since the subsequent investigating committee was too unsure of its authority to step on any but the most defenseless toes. But at least the committee managed to identify someone who could pass as a leader: an intelligent but "visionary and fanatic" baker of San Frediano named Antonio Mazzanti. Mazzanti, it seems, had read in the newspapers "about the revolts in several other nations," although his definition of a republic as "something like what they have in Genoa" suggests that he missed some of the context. When he read about the revolts at Pistoia and Livorno, he got together with a certain secondhand clothes dealer named Vincenzo Santini. The two of them, supposedly all alone, drew up a program that included not only the restoration of the images, the confraternities, and the *Abbondanza,* but also the dismissal of several ministers, the deportation of the bishop of Pistoia, and the reestablishment of a professional army and navy—articles, that is, which no baker or secondhand clothes dealer would ever have thought of, but which the investigating committee chose not to trace back to the real instigators. Mazzanti next called a series of meetings in Via della Carraia and on the Costa San Giorgio, meetings attended by as many as fifty persons each. And there he presented his plan of action: march from San Frediano to the ghetto and to several patrician palaces in order to collect a war chest. Distribute some of the money so collected in order to attract recruits. March to the Annunziata and win the support of the whole population by replacing the Veil. March back up to the Fortezza Belvedere, which Mazzanti and Santini had already inspected to determine its vulnerability to mob attack. Turn the cannons on the city. And keep them there until the Council of Regency appointed a delegation of noblemen to carry their program to the grand duke in Vienna.

To the President of the *Buon Governo* (Minister of Police), this plan probably seemed too fantastic to warrant any special measures. But he should have realized that, fantastic or not, it could very easily have been carried out. Florence was practically defenseless. Ten years earlier the grand duke had all but disbanded the regular mercenary army and had replaced the garrison of the capital with a volunteer citizen militia. Then in February 1790 he had disbanded the militia as well. The few vagabonds, delinquents, and miscellaneous down-and-outs who had since been recruited under the new plan for assuring a minimum of public safety were still too green to inspire much confidence. Indeed, the dozen or so of them stationed at the Belvedere had been ordered not to move from their posts for fear of being cut off from behind. The colonel of the cavalry was a man "with a head so small and confused that it's of no use whatever." And the captains of the infantry were respectively "mediocre" and "invalid."

Florence was also practically without a government. For twenty-five years Florentines had been trying to keep up with Grand Duke Pietro Leopoldo's constant round of orders, counterorders, edicts, and decrees. For twenty-five years they had learned to expect to find him peering over their shoulders from one minute to the next. It thus came as somewhat of a surprise to them to remember that he was also the younger brother and heir apparent of Emperor Joseph II. He did his best to keep his subjects calm after the arrival of the news of Joseph's death on February 25: he waited for four days and then crept as quietly as possible out of his residence at Pisa and over the pass at Abetone toward Modena and Vienna. But early in May they became fully conscious of the consequences of his departure. On May 3, at four P.M., his second oldest son, the future grand duke Ferdinando III, rode out of the Pitti, followed at five o'clock by four of his other sons and three days later by his wife, the grand duchess Maria Luisa, with the rest of their fourteen children. A few days later Florentines watched dumbfounded as cart after cart rolled through the Porta San Gallo bearing what they thought to be the entire furnishings of the Palazzo Pitti. On May 26 they read in the newspapers that all the horses, mules, and equipment at the royal stables in Piazza San Marco—formerly the Medici zoo and later to become the seat of the University of Florence's Faculty of Letters—had been put up for auction. Suddenly they found themselves without a prince and faced with a situation that made them "fear the worst, or at least lose all hope of future happiness."

Pietro Leopoldo had not abandoned his subjects altogether. Just before leaving he had appointed a Regency Council with a full authority to govern in his name. But at the same time he had undercut the Council's effective power by refusing to settle the question of his son Ferdinando's succession, by demanding to be informed of everything the council did, and, above all, by appointing as members not men of strength and initiative, but bureaucrats accustomed by years of routine "to hiding their real sentiments and suffocating their talents." As president of the council he appointed a man who incarnated both its virtues and its shortcomings: Senator Antonio Serristori, a man whom the grand duke himself described as, "honest, moderate, prudent, sufficiently talented, and well versed in practical affairs," but also "very old and desirous only of peace and quiet." When difficulties began to arise, the council acted as expected. Instead of sending soldiers into Pistoia, it asked the nobility to set an example by moving out; and it then rewarded the rioters with a general amnesty. Instead of sending soldiers into Livorno, it sent the archbishop of Pisa down to tell the rioters they would get everything they wanted. Even as late as June 7 it refused to consider the recommendation of one of its members that measures be taken to forestall the spread of violence to the capital. And it let the reports of the district police captains sit on the desk of another member, the president of the *Buon Governo,* Giuseppe Giusti, a man who seems to have been more interested in controlling "the promotion of judges and court employees" than in using any of his "power to do good and evil."

Giusti's policy served him well. For he managed to hang onto his job through all the various changes of government that were soon to follow. But the lesson was not lost on the impoverished silk-workers, unemployed porters, disgruntled government clerks, and dispossessed friars, as the investigating committee admitted in its recommendation for leniency:

> With the example of the recent disturbances in other parts of the grand duchy in mind, sure of encountering no more opposition and resistance than had been encountered elsewhere, and certain of receiving the same pardon accorded to the others. . . .

If ever they were going to take action, this was the moment. They had every-thing to gain. And they ran the risk of losing very little in the process of trying to gain it.

2

The riot

Suddenly, about six o'clock on the morning of June 9, a mob of some hundred ragged men, with *coccarde* on their caps, and torches, clubs, and hatchets in their hands, rushed into the busy Piazza dell'Olio shouting "*Abbondanza! Abbondanza!* Down with the prices!" The peasant vendors were too accustomed to being browbeaten, humiliated, and cheated by city dwellers of all classes to think of resisting. At least one of them was immediately relieved of every *soldo* in his pocket. Another was dragged around the corner and released only after promising to deliver all the oil in his possession to a local merchant whose identity the investigating committee seems not to have bothered trying to establish. Many of the others who happened to be on the streets during the rest of the day were robbed and beaten. When even Archbishop Antonio Martini—the only man of authority in all Florence still able to command the respect of all classes and groups—failed to calm the mob and at last vanished behind the window of his palace with a futile blessing, there was no choice left but surrender. The price of oil was accordingly lowered from 76 to 50 *lire*. Within an hour the market was completely sold out. The sellers had lost not only their expected profits, but much of their investment in time and labor as well.

The mob then moved down the Via Cerretani, around Giambologna's statue of Hercules and the Centaur (now in the Loggia dei Lanzi) and down to the house of the Ambra family in what is now the Via dei Rondinelli. It pushed through the main door, broke the marble tables, splattered oil all over the yellow damask wall-coverings, and emptied the storerooms of their contents. It then proceeded to the house of Ugolino Vernaccia, an eighty-six-year-old landowner who, like the Ambra, had no connection with the government, but who had taken advantage of the government's free trade policy to amass a considerable fortune. Vernaccia tried to placate the rioters by throwing some 120 *scudi* worth of coins from an upstairs window. But within minutes one group of them was

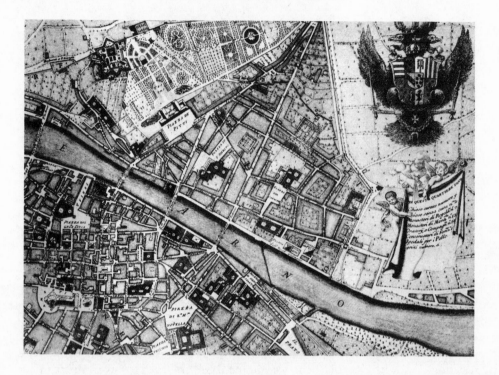

25. Ferdinando Ruggieri, Map of Florence, 1755 edition, with coat of arms of
the House of Lorraine

holding him on the sill and threatening to push him over unless he sent a written
order to his estate manager for immediate delivery of all his stocks. Another
group set up armed sentinels in the cellar and rationed out supplies to whoever
wished to come in. The rest wandered freely about the house, breaking everything
that looked like a box or chest, pocketing some 500 *scudi* in cash, and making off
with all the jewelry in the apartment of Vernaccia's young wife, Caterina Antinori.

By this time some of the original members of the mob had wandered off—
one man, for instance, who had a whole mule-load of plunder, and one boy, who
had an armful of shoes and silver buckles. But some four hundred others had
taken their places. And whoever by now had assumed Mazzanti's position as
leader, or at least whoever had drawn up the itinerary of plunder later found on
Vernaccia's floor, decided that the mob had grown large enough to be divided
into two parts. One part was accordingly directed down to the Mercato del
Grano, or the Grain Market, which was then located in what has since become
the lobby of the Capitol movie theater behind the Palazzo Vecchio. And it there
applied the same treatment that had been meted out to the peasants in the Piazza
dell'Olio. While the handsome axes stolen from Palazzo Vernaccia waved in the

air, and while the peasant vendors stood by helplessly, the sacks were sold off one by one at the ridiculous price of 4 *lire* a *staio* until none was left.

The success with which the initial demands for lower prices had been put into effect now encouraged the rioters to advance to the second stage of their plan: from plunder to politics. They crossed the Ponte alle Grazie and headed for the magnificent sixteenth-century palace of the president of the Regency Council, Antonio Serristori. Luckily, one of Mazzanti's agents arrived just in time to keep them from breaking down the main door. The delay permitted Serristori himself to appear—first to pledge his cooperation in getting their political demands accepted, and second to suggest that their wrath be redirected toward the one of his fellow regents least likely to cooperate. The rioters were persuaded. They marched around the back of Palazzo Serristori and up the Borgo San Niccolò to the house of Senator Francesco Maria Gianni, even though Gianni's name did not appear on the original itinerary. And after appropriating 20 *scudi* worth of grain and trampling down a few plants in the garden, they settled down to drinking the contents of the wine cellar on the spot.

Apparently, many of the participants were becoming either satiated or drunk; and at least a few of them had become so satisfied with the mere act of plundering that they began returning what they had taken. They were thus ready to accept a face-saving way out of their adventure when the parish priest of San Niccolò and several unidentified noblemen arrived with a proposal. Instead of damaging Gianni's house, they suggested, why not put their case before one of his neighbors, Marco Del Rosso? That Del Rosso was a man of no political influence whatsoever seems not to have bothered anyone, and Del Rosso, probably informed in advance of what was expected of him, played his part perfectly. The rioters stood respectfully out on the street while a twelve-man delegation went inside. The delegates in turn received Del Rosso's assurances of assistance in negotiations with the government, accepted a 10 *paoli* "donation" (less than one-third of what the tailor Giambaccini charged for making a suit!), and then, as if to emphasize the difference between a riot and a revolution, "kissed his hands twice in gratitude" and went home.

Meanwhile the other half of the mob left behind at Palazzo Vernaccia had re-formed in the Piazza dell'Olio and was preparing for an attack on the ghetto. The plan required some courage. Cosimo I had erected the three-block area between what is today the middle of the Piazza della Repubblica, Via Roma, and the colonnade on Via Brunelleschi more for the protection than for the segregation of the residents. Access to the three small piazze onto which the tall houses opened was provided only by two small entrances at the north and the south end. But the myth that the Jews were wealthy proved stronger than fear. Archbishop Martini's proclamation that Christian feet would enter the ghetto only over his dead body was greeted by shouts of "Money! Money! *Io vuo' de' quattrini!*" Similarly, the Jews' attempt to give the mob some of what it asked for just whetted its appetite. The four delegates elected to distribute 25 *zecchini* apiece ran off with the bags—all, that is, but one of them, who threw his sack into the air to avoid being torn apart. A servant sent out with another bag of 200 *scudi* managed to escape only after his clothes had been ripped off. And by the time another bribe of 300 *scudi* was announced, the doors of the first houses had been broken down and the safe in the chancery office had been broken open.

The attack on the ghetto turned out to be the beginning of the end of the riot. The rioters apparently forgot that Florentine Jews had managed to preserve what Florentine Christians had sacrificed for security with the foundation of the principate: a sense of community. The ghetto had always been self-governing, and, eight years before, the grand duke had turned over the ownership of its property and buildings to a corporation composed of the more prominent residents. The rioters also forgot that the Jews of Tuscany had gained, after two centuries of vigilant government protection, what the Jews of Lessing's Germany had not yet dared to dream of: a determination not to be pushed around. In 1753 they had successfully appealed to the stringent protective law of June 22, 1735 (galleys for the least molestation) in a suit against the composers of a carnival song with anti-semitic overtones. In 1757 they had obtained an order closing an academy in Livorno until its discriminating rules were abrogated. In 1789 they had forced the owners of a theater to guarantee them a block of boxes each year and to prohibit the slightest unflattering reference on the stage. At the same time they secured admission to municipal offices on exactly the same conditions as other citizens, except that they were not required to attend the usual religious services. Thus when state protection suddenly vanished, the Jews decided to meet force not with tears, resignation, or more bribes, but with force. The community leaders sent out an appeal for help to the Mercato Vecchio, where the merchants were easily persuaded that they would be treated no differently if the ghetto fell. As the chancery clerks began throwing successive groups of invaders "heads over heels downstairs with their fists," the better-armed merchants filed in through the south entrance with reinforcements.

As the riot became increasingly violent, two private citizens, neither of whom had any connection with the government, decided that the moment for action had come. The government, they realized, had abdicated its role as the prime mover of society, for the first time in 253 years. And if the city were to be saved from a general sack, it would have to save itself. One of these citizens was the handsome, dashing, athletic young nobleman Alamanno de' Pazzi. The other was the former militia officer Orso D'Elci. Pazzi put on his most elegant clothes and mounted his most expensive horse. He made such an impression, by his voice and his bearing, when he rode into the ghetto, that he persuaded the rioters to follow him home—to the same palace in Via del Proconsolo where the poet Berni had once entertained the pleasure-bent guests of Cardinal Cibo in the days of Duke Alessandro de' Medici. At the same time D'Elci quietly contacted a number of his more trustworthy friends. He then provided them with red and white armbands according to rank, divided them into "flying squads"—*corpi volanti*—for patrolling the streets, and induced the terrified regents to give them the official title of "Defenders of the Country," or national guardsmen.

By late afternoon the riot was all but over—thanks not to the Regents, or to the City Council, or to the police, or to any other representatives of legitimate civic authority, but to the Jews, the merchants of the Mercato Vecchio, Marco Del Rosso, Alamanno de' Pazzi, and Orso D'Elci. It might have ended in a total defeat of the rioters had not the regents, or at least the four of them still left in the city, made a last-minute attempt to regain the authority that they had progressively frittered away since the riot in Pistoia. They did so by issuing two decrees.* The first sanctioned "the restoration of certain exterior forms of worship"—veils, processions, confraternities. And it empowered the three archbishops, in consultation with their suffragans, to make all future decisions in questions of liturgy. It thus extended to the rest of the country what had been conceded under constraint at Pistoia and Livorno. And it abandoned to the ecclesiastical hierarchy one of the principal areas over which the state had sought to establish its primary jurisdiction during the preceding fifteen years. The other decree prohibited the shipment of foodstuffs out of the capital or out of the country. It also imposed upon the city council the ungrateful task of fixing prices on the urban markets. In this way it legalized what had been imposed by violence that morning in the Piazza dell'Olio and in the Grain Market. And it sacrificed to the violent what for years had been considered one of the most fundamental elements of Tuscan economic legislation.

But the rioters were not therefore the victors. Neither of the two decrees said anything about most of the planks in Mazzanti's program: firing ministers, hiring porters, expanding the army, or even lengthening the business hours of the taverns. They said nothing about who was going to pay for the restoration of the old confraternities now that the former endowments had long since vanished. As late as June the next year the financial condition of those confraternities that had been restored by voluntary subscription was still so precarious that they could not even participate in the Corpus Domini procession. The decrees said nothing about the level at which prices were to be fixed. And three days later the City Council single-handedly raised the price of coarse bread, the mainstay of the plebeian diet, by 75 percent—from 4 to 7 *quattrini* a pound.

More important still, the prospects of concerted action to maintain what had been won became dimmer by the hour. The recruiting stand set up by the National Guard at the Palazzo Vecchio the next morning was swamped with

---

* Some historians accept the date of June 8 that appears on the printed version of the decrees. After studying the material in ASF Carte Gianni 12, 242, in the context of the events of June 9, I conclude that the regents deliberately falsified the date in order to give the appearance of not having acted under constraint.

applications. The commander of the Fortezza da Basso was overburdened with volunteers, at least one of whom brought along a hundred armed retainers and offered to serve "in any part of the grand duchy where there is danger of another tumult." Moreover, the formation of the Guard encouraged the regular law enforcement agencies to come out of hiding. On the very night of June 9 a detachment of soldiers from the Belvedere slipped down into San Frediano and waited near a crowd of women for the return of the wives' plunder-laden husbands. At the same time a detachment of police crept into Palazzo Pazzi and wrote down all the names it could hear mentioned among those who had followed Alamanno home from the ghetto. Thus when some of the rioters turned up in Piazza della Signoria the next morning for the purpose of infiltrating the Guard, they were immediately identified and escorted straight to the Bargello. Soon 108 men as well as several dozen women and children were behind bars.

Strangely enough, at least by twentieth-century standards of how to handle rioters, none of the arrested was starved, beaten, humiliated, put into a "hole," or forced to make a confession. The provisions of the 1786 criminal code were observed to the letter. The police stuck scrupulously to their assigned tasks of collecting depositions, booking the prisoners under clearly stated charges of "public violence and repeated theft," and providing comfortable quarters, ample rations, and clean beds. The Supreme Tribunal of Justice, which alone had the legal authority to pass judgment, made every effort to distinguish among various degrees of culpability, to rule out partial or unreliable evidence, and even to provide living allowances for the dependents of the detained. But it did not hesitate to impose the maximum penalties on those it finally found guilty. The leaders were given life in the galleys and forthwith shipped off to Messina. The others were given long prison terms in Tuscany or lifetime banishment in the Maremma or Volterra. Meanwhile, the police systematically applied the current laws against idleness and filial disobedience in order to enroll as recruits for the Austrian army all able-bodied men who seemed "not to want to work," who "hung around the taverns and got drunk instead of attending to [their] business," or who, like a certain Pietro Castagnali of the Santo Spirito district, "refused to heed the orders of his father and abandoned himself to dissipation." Even though most of the condemned eventually obtained mitigation of their sentences (Mazzanti was unchained from his Neapolitan oar after only eighteen months), the possibility of their once again disturbing the peace of Florence was very notably diminished.

The rioters thus gained very little from the riot. But the government gained even less. For one thing, the regents were kept so nervous by the obvious signs of continuing unrest that they dared not revoke the decrees of June 9. Insults, rocks, and occasionally whole buckets of gravel were regularly hurled at passing patrols, without the police ever being able, or willing, to track down the culprits. Menacing handbills continued to appear on the walls of the city—like the one entitled

THE FLORENTINE PLEBEIANS SERRVE NOTISSE*

found near Serristori's garden on the morning of July 9. Seditious sonnets continued to be circulated for the benefit of those who could memorize more easily than they could read. The authors were not only semiliterate visionaries like Mazzanti, but also men of some means—like "a certain fat gentleman with a wig and a rather barbarous physionomy" who "lived on revenues" and spent most of his time holding forth from a bench in Borgo Santi Apostoli. The peace of the capital was constantly menaced by the turbulence of Pistoia, which, two and a half centuries after Cosimo I had stamped out the last sparks of its age-old civil discord, once again assumed its role as the witches' cauldron of Tuscany. After seven months of vainly trying to get his orders carried out, the governor asked for a transfer. "The animosity of the people," he explained, made it impossible to remain in the city "without constant hardship and danger."

The regents found themselves hamstrung by orders and counterorders from Vienna. Pietro Leopoldo suffered the most violent outburst of temper of his whole temperamental career when he heard of the events of June 9. The economic and ecclesiastical system "which I have established after so many years of hard work and with such . . . benefit for the public," he howled, had been overturned by "a troop of the very lowest order of people" in a single day! But he was now too busy trying to keep a vast empire from dissolving into its component parts to give more than momentary attention to the minor miseries of a peripheral province. The letters he hurled at the heads of his ministers every ten days or so for the rest of the summer are remarkable above all for their inconsistencies. At one moment he seemed bent on arrogating all their authority to himself. At the next he seemed equally bent on letting them stew in their own juice. At one moment he told them not to yield another inch. At the next he sarcastically pointed out that price controls would now oblige them "to force people to bring their produce to the market and to lay hands violently and unjustly on their property." At one moment he told them to call in all the regular troops from the frontiers. At the next he told them to arm the Jews. And at still another he told them to get ready two palaces for a German regiment that he, not they, would command. At times the regents quietly ignored his orders, as they did when he told them to reinstate the death penalty which he for years had boasted about being the first monarch in Europe to abolish. But most of the time they were kept obedient and attentive by the one danger they feared more than another riot: annexation to Austria. And Pietro Leopoldo took care not to let them see his act of renunciation in favor of Ferdinando until February 1791, a full seven months after he had signed it.

---

* Similar misspellings in the original: FASSI NOTIZZIA DALLA PLEBE FIORENTINA. . . . The bottom part of the handbill is torn off.

Meanwhile, the regents, with full approval from the grand duke, gradually scuttled the only instrument by which a clear victory might have been secured: the National Guard. They moved cautiously at first, partly because the Guard alone was capable of keeping the peace, and partly because it provided a very convenient scapegoat for the inevitable rise of food prices back toward open-market levels. But as more and more troops arrived from Lombardy, they began suggesting to D'Elci that he keep his volunteers at home. Then, one Sunday morning in September, they invited all the officers to a formal reception in the Pazzi Chapel. There, instead of distributing medals and honors, they treated their guests to "a languid expression of thanks" and a curt announcement of the termination of their commissions.

Thus the riot of June 9 turned out to be much more than just a momentary mishap. It put an end to twenty-five years of intensive reform legislation. It turned the contents of ministerial memoranda and grand ducal decrees into subjects for public debate. It laid bare one of the chief contradictions inherent in the experiment of "enlightened despotism," both in Tuscany and in the rest of Europe, the contradiction, that is, between government for the people and government by the people. It endowed the urban plebeians with an active role in politics, a role they had not assumed since February 1537, when they had saved Cosimo I from his uncles. And it laid the groundwork for the coalition between plebeians, peasants, and dissident clergy that was actually to take over the country nine years later, during the popular uprising of 1799.

At the same time, the riot drove out of politics once and for all the two people who had been most closely associated with Pietro Leopoldo during the last years of his residence in Florence. The first was probably the most disagreeable, the most intransigent, and certainly the most disliked man in Tuscany, Bishop Scipione de' Ricci of Pistoia and Prato. Ricci had inherited the accumulated pride of two ancient patrician families (his mother was a Rucellai). The presence on his genealogical charts of one of the most spectacular saints in Florentine history, the sixteenth-century mystic Caterina de' Ricci, made him sure of his infallibility in all matters of religion. No one could contradict him—neither the archbishop of Florence, whom he despised as a weakling, nor his fellow Tuscan bishops, whom he accused of betraying him at the National Synod of 1787, nor even the pope, whose authority outside the diocese of Rome he considered to be purely nominal. The only person he had any respect for whatsoever was the grand duke. But even Pietro Leopoldo noticed that Ricci became "riled at the least opposition" and was "a persecutor of whoever does not share his opinions," and he learned to keep a certain distance from him. For almost two months Ricci had been trying in vain to get a response out of the vicar he had left behind when he fled from Pistoia in April. Not willing to resign outright, and thus to leave the clergy still loyal to him completely defenseless, he talked his doctor into prescribing a rest cure on the banks of Lake Como. He had just started out of Florence when the news of the riot reached him. Petrified at the thought of being assailed by one more angry mob, and terrified by the realization that the grand duke was now too far away to rescue him, he dismounted, walked for a half-day under a blazing sun, and disappeared into the Chianti. There he remained for the next several months, in such carefully guarded hiding that even his vicars had to communicate with him through secret messengers. Two years later most of what he had done as bishop was formally condemned in Rome. He was forced to give way to a more conciliatory successor. He never again set foot in the diocese he had ruled with an iron hand for almost ten years.

The other major victim of the riot was the second most disliked man in Tuscany, one whose sole saving virtue, according to his enemies, was that Ricci hated him more than anyone else. This man was Francesco Maria Gianni, senator, councilor of state, member of the Regency Council without portfolio, and principal adviser to the grand duke on financial and economic problems. Gianni also descended from an old Florentine family, one that went back at least to the early thirteenth century. Most of his family's wealth had come from the success of his great-grandfather, Ridolfo, in buying up land in the Mugello in the early seventeenth century. The wealth had been preserved largely by the success of his father, Niccolò, in putting all of his three surviving daughters in convents and enrolling the eldest of his three sons in the Knights of Malta. The nearest the family could come to a saint was that saccharine, dainty-fingered "venerable," Lorenzo Maria Gianni, whom Magalotti had thought worthy of inclusion in his list of religious curiosities during the last years of his life. All of the family's former patrician spirit had been thoroughly diluted by the appointment of many of its members to minor positions at court. This spirit was at last converted into a bureaucratic one by the appointment of Niccolò as one of the permanent trustees (*protettori*) of the Monte Comune in 1723.

Unfortunately, Gianni suffered from one major character defect: a complete lack of sensitivity to other human beings and, consequently, a total inability to get along even with those who agreed with him. The attitude of his collaborators varied from stiff-lipped tolerance to violent hostility. To some he was "a miserable, vile, insolent creature . . . a poisonous animal without a trace of wit or judgment." To others he was "a very dangerous man—so much the more so because he is smart." To Pietro Leopoldo he was an unrivaled expert on the political and economic conditions of the country, one who had to be consulted "on all matters, particularly on the more important ones." But he was also, the grand duke admitted, so anxious "always to be in the right" that he would at times sustain with equal acrimony exactly the opposite of what he had previously sustained—just to avoid admitting that he had erred. He tried constantly to dominate those who were dependent on him and to "discredit [anyone] who does not blindly support all his views." And he showed "such animosity and disdain" for everyone else that it was "impossible to run a meeting in his presence."

For Gianni, the riot provided an easy way out of an increasingly uncomfortable situation. Actually, he had no reason to run away on the morning of June 9. The wrath of the rioters was directed against the rich proprietors and the Jews, not against him; when they finally did think of raiding his house, they proved to be "more reticent than bold," as he himself admitted. They took their political grievances to Serristori, the president of the Regency Council, not to him, the least of the regents, whom they knew to be wholly without influence on his colleagues. The accusation that one rioter had offered himself as Gianni's assassin was dismissed by the court as a bit of personal slander. Nevertheless, Gianni was so obsessed by his usual persecution complex, and he was so convinced "that all the other ministers are shown signs of respect while I alone am attacked," that he fled anyway. He was so sure of being followed that he turned off the main highway at Scarperia and took a side road over the Futa pass. And he did not rest until he was firmly locked inside the house of the Tuscan consul at Bologna that evening.

For the regents, on the other hand, the riot provided the opportunity they had long awaited for getting rid of Gianni once and for all. They might have seized the opportunity even more vigorously had they seen what he wrote about them in his secret letters to the grand duke. But all they had to do was to answer his plaintive queries with the warning that conditions were still too unsettled, even two weeks after the riot, to assure his physical safety within the borders of the grand duchy. When he did finally return, toward the end of the summer, he took care to come no nearer the capital than Pisa.

At first Gianni was bitter. He launched one virulent attack after another on "ministerial irresponsibility" and on thousands of unnamed "ambitious, intriguing, jealous souls, who hide their iniquity behind a mask of zeal and tenderness." But gradually he came to realize that his thirty years of uninterrupted service to the state had come to an end. He therefore took trips around northern Italy. He settled down for a while on an estate in Liguria. He put together the immense number of memoranda and legislative drafts that today form one of the largest collections of private papers in the Florentine State Archives. He wrote a number of general treatises on political economy that were published in two volumes after his death. Except for a brief return to power during the French occupation of 1799, he spent the last thirty years of his life in retirement.

3

How Gianni became a professional bureaucrat

Gianni could have foreseen neither his spectacular rise nor his precipitous fall when, in May 1750, he secured "a very minor position" with "a very small salary" in the finance office of the district of Florence. A university degree was still all but prerequisite to advancement in government service, and "the barely average talent" with which he seemed to have been endowed did not warrant, in his father's opinion, the expense of maintaining him for four years at Pisa. Indeed, he took the position not because he wanted it, but because he needed it. His older brother had just signed over to him the rights of primogeniture, and therefore the obligation of begetting heirs. Since his relations with his pinch-penny father were anything but cordial, he knew he would have to procure at least some revenue outside the family patrimony for some years to come.

Still, it was not long before Gianni became fascinated with even the "low, material affairs" that crossed his desk. In fact, he became so fascinated with them that he lost all taste for "the pleasures and pastimes of most young men of my age." He married rather young, for the times, in September 1752, and rather well—to the daughter of Senator Pietro Paolo de' Medici. But family life always remained for him a function of his professional life. He was careful to see that his wife was invited to the right ladies' parties, just as he made sure that he himself was seated next to the right persons at *calcio* (soccer) games. The few letters that he wrote to his two sons and his daughter are really nothing but personal apologies or political tracts, meant to be read by the public at large and devoid of the least trace of paternal affection.

Undistracted by the arts and letters, about which he claimed to know nothing, and undisturbed by the historical, religious, and juridical questions discussed in the Riccardiana Library, where he never set foot, Gianni had nothing better to do in his spare time than to "gather information . . . concerning the finances and commerce of Tuscany." He soon learned the art of summarizing the results of his inquiries in the form of written reports—reports in which orderly expositions of detail were carefully interspersed with rhetorical pleas on behalf of his recommendations for action. By 1758 his first report was ready for presentation: a "Historical Essay on the Tariffs and Taxes of Pisa." He also learned to pull strings on behalf of friends and relatives. He learned how to go over the heads of reluctant superiors. And he learned to combine reminders of his irreproachable honesty and untiring industry with hints about his availability for still more responsible charges.

These efforts soon brought rewards: a promotion in the office of the General Inspectors (*Soprassindaci*) in the fall of 1750, an appointment as director of the customs office at Pisa in 1754, a recall to Florence as Supervisor (*Provveditore*) of the Silk Guild in 1759, and, finally, on November 17, 1760, an elevation to the now purely honorary, but still much coveted, rank of senator. By the age of thirty he had arrived at a position that could correctly be called "comfortable"; he could now begin "to aspire to the sort of fame" which only from the vantage point of the years after 1790 would seem to be "really misery" in disguise.

Yet Gianni would probably have remained nothing but an efficient secretary had he not had the good fortune to encounter three of the most distinguished representatives of Tuscan culture in the generation of Giovanni Lami. One was Gaspare Cerati, the rector of the university, who gave him books on economics to read and who helped him meet several members of the faculty. Another was Pompeo Neri, who expressed "a very high opinion of [his] actions" during an interview in 1758 and who sent him on a very educative investigating mission to Siena in 1759. The third was his second cousin, the well-traveled, worldly-wise, and wealthy patrician, Antonio Niccolini, who became a kind of tutor to him during his first years at Pisa, and who became his chief protector and his sole personal correspondent for some two decades thereafter.

Thanks to these three men and their willingness to judge him by his brains rather than by his personality, Gianni began to reflect upon his day-to-day experience in the light of what they taught him about Tuscany in the past and about Europe in the present. He gradually came to think of his work as something more than just a way of satisfying his "avarice and ambition." He increasingly became aware of a moral as well as a professional obligation that went well beyond simply carrying out uncritically the instructions handed down by his superiors. He finally decided that the purpose of public administration was not to serve the interests of the administrators or even those of the monarch. It was rather to serve the interests of all the citizens, and to do so as effectively and as inexpensively as possible.

Gianni himself admitted that there was nothing original in this conclusion. He could easily have found it in the works of "Monsignor Melon, Monsieur de Montesqui, Monsieur D'Hume, l'Ami des hommes," and the other "masters of new theories in our century," whom he had by now at least heard about, even if he could not yet spell their names correctly. He could even have found it in some of the memoranda presented to Francesco Stefano's Regency Council some fifteen or twenty years earlier. Where he actually did find it, however, and where he found it much more practically and less philosophically stated, was in some of the papers tucked away in the back files of his office at Pisa—that is, in the commerical decrees of the Florentine Republic in the early sixteenth century. If the principles of good government were no longer observed in practice, he decided, it was because they had been strangled in bureaucratic red tape. No one knew better than Gianni, after he took the trouble to find out exactly what each commune in the province of Pisa owed in butchers' taxes each year, how strong the tape was. Just issuing new regulations would do no good, for harassed bureaucrats were simply too tired to plow through still more pages of fine print. What was needed was a thorough reform of the entire structure, one that would replace the miscellaneous accumulation of ad hoc measures issued in response to thousands of different and long-since forgotten problems with a rational and intelligible system.

For the moment, Gianni saw little hope for realizing any such sweeping reform. Most public servants were utterly devoid of civic spirit and intent only on making more money. Government authority was divided between Florence, Vienna, and the Tax Farm Corporation, each of which usually acted independently, and often in contradiction, of the other. The wealth of the country was constantly being drained off in the form of special contributions and donations to be spent abroad. Any suggestion for change was sure to be blocked by such unimaginative conservatives as Antonio Serristori, the same Serristori who was to put an end to Gianni's public career in 1790 and who, as one of the chief stockholders in the Tax Farm Corporation, did his best to thwart Gianni's attack on it in the 1750s. In such circumstances even closing down one of the many uneconomical toll stations in the Apennines required nothing short of moving a mountain. And, indeed, not until a providential landslide wiped out the station in December 1761 did Gianni finally manage to cross it off his crowded ledger.

Then, suddenly, everything changed. On August 31, 1765, the Emperor-Grand Duke Francesco Stefano died. In accordance with the latest dynastic reshuffling, the title to his personal domain passed not to his first son, who was to succeed him as Emperor Joseph II, but to his second son. Thus on August 31 the new grand duke Peter Leopold, or Pietro Leopoldo, as he was to be known thereafter south of the Alps, headed over the Brenner Pass, accompanied by his Austrian advisers, several Florentine ladies-in-waiting, and his bride, the Spanish princess Maria Luisa, whose marriage to him on the eve of his father's death had forged one more link between the rival houses of Hapsburg and Bourbon. Two weeks later, early enough in the morning to forestall an official reception, the royal couple rode into the Palazzo Pitti.

Few Florentines knew much about their new ruler. They might have reflected that, at barely eighteen, he was about the same age as Cosimo I had been at the moment of his election, although no one could have guessed how much the restorer of the grand duchy was to resemble its founder. They might have seen a copy of the rather ridiculous rococo engraving published in Vienna to celebrate his birth—although they could not have foreseen how tenaciously he was to cling to the keys as well as to the sword that hung over the engraving's inappropriate biblical inscription: *Claves tibi Petre dabo* ("To you, Peter, I will give the keys"). Some of them may have been comforted by the thought that he had been brought up by an admirer of Muratori, that he had been stuffed with the favorite law texts of the modern Tuscan jurists, and that he disapproved of his mother's expensive chateau parties. They might also have been disturbed by the thought that his heavy educational curriculum included not a single line about the past or the present of the country he was called upon to rule. All he knew about either, in fact, was what he had just read in a last-minute memo jotted down by his father, whose own information was second-hand at best.

Few Florentines were particularly concerned about such details. Two crop failures since 1762 had produced one of the longest and severest famines since the early fourteenth century. The cold damp summer of 1765—when "not even in the dog-days was it ever hot enough to make one sweat"—seemed to promise little relief in the future. The government was incapable of doing much to mitigate the tragedy, which was common to the whole Mediterranean basin and which was the result not of a temporary mishap, but of a long-term decline in agricultural productivity.

Nonetheless, most Florentines were still sure that the only possible way out of their plight lay in having a grand duke resident in Florence. When one suddenly appeared, they accorded him their complete confidence, regardless of his particular qualifications. The Collegio dei Nobili commissioned a cantata appropriately named "The Landing of Aeneas in Latium." The Hebrew Nation constructed a gigantic triumphal arch opposite Palazzo Pitti on the equally significant theme of "Lycurgus bringing the Laws to Sparta," and kept it floodlighted all night with a myriad of wax and oil torches. Other celebrations became so numerous in the last weeks of 1765 that the first issue of the new weekly newspaper, the *Gazzetta Toscana,* on January 1, 1766, was devoted wholly to listing them. Nature itself seemed to join in the gaiety. On the very day of Pietro Leopoldo's arrival, the sun finally came out. And it stayed out all through an unusually warm and pleasant fall. Even the hordes of half-starved refugees from the stricken countryside had at least a momentary respite from their miseries when Pietro Leopoldo distributed 1,000 *scudi* in honor of his deceased father from the steps of the cathedral.

Actually, the new government was not all that different from the preceding one. Pietro Leopoldo felt obliged to turn to his father's appointees for practical information about what for him was still a strange and unknown country. He dared place his confidence in no one but his sole friend, Franz Thurn. And he soon discovered that his mother's exclamation, "Hélas, vous êtes souverain," had been intended more as a metaphor than as a statement of fact. She constantly reminded him that as "a German prince" he should make even the Florentines at his court learn German. She complained bitterly whenever a courier arrived without a letter. Through a number of informal spies she checked up on what he himself told her—the most faithful of the spies being none other than Thurn's wife.

Just how closely Florence was still tied to Vienna became clear within a few months of Pietro Leopoldo's arrival. Joseph needed every penny he could lay hands on to relieve the Austrian treasury of the expenses of the Seven Years' War. After a desperate search, he finally succeeded in uncovering a will his father had made in 1751, one which, in defiance of subsequent agreements, named his first son as his universal heir. Pietro Leopoldo was forthwith notified that "the cash in the Tuscan treasury belongs to me." He tried to delay. He fell into fits of melancholy. He forgot to answer letters. But eventually he had to yield—to send off the immense sum of almost 4 million *lire* in coin and to apply to a Genoese bank for a loan to cover the costs of one more natural disaster: two months of subfreezing weather during the winter of 1765–66.

Yet Gianni's exclamation was not wholly unwarranted: "Finally, through the mercy of God, we are no longer a province" (that is, the dependency of a foreign power). And the "universal jubilation . . . of all the people" during the coronation ceremonies the following June were not wholly without foundation. The young grand duke flattered his Tuscan ministers from the start by taking copious notes on everything they told him. He soon got rid of his mother's chief agent in Tuscany, Botta Adorno, and sent him off with an honorary title to his native Pavia. He gradually shifted his confidence to the three leading exponents of reform left over from the previous government: Angelo Tavanti, Giulio Rucellai, and, above all, Pompeo Neri. After Thurn's sudden death in February, he took as his chief German advisor the brilliant and attractive, if rather spendthrift, diplomat from Styria, Franz von Rosenberg Orsini—or Rosemberg, as the Florentines usually called him. Rosemberg immediately won the affection of the grand duke's subjects without—incredible as it seemed at the time—losing that of Maria Theresa and Joseph. He soon discovered that his own empirical observations in the Austrian foreign service at London, Copenhagen, and Madrid led ineluctibly to the same program of political reform as the one proposed by his Florentine colleagues. Within a few months he had won his master over to the program as well.

Thus when, in late May, Pietro Leopoldo embarked on the first of the many trips around the country that were soon to make him as familiar to his subjects as Cosimo I had once been, it became clear that he would no longer spend his days brooding in a chemistry laboratory. When he began preferring what had always been his second language to his first—when he spoke and wrote almost exclusively in Italian and when he had his third son baptized Giovanni (for Florence's patron saint, John the Baptist) rather than Johann—it became clear that he was now grand duke of Tuscany first and representative of the House of Hapsburg second. When, in November 1766, he appointed a commission with full powers to conduct a thorough inquiry into the economic conditions of the country, it became clear that he intended to rule in his own name. The four foreign states accredited at the Tuscan court accordingly promoted their chargés-d'affaires to the rank of plenipotentiary ministers.

For Gianni, the restoration of independence marked the beginning of a rapid rise in his chosen profession. The first appointment came in November 1766, as a member of the seven-man economic investigating commission, a post that enabled him to perfect the art of drawing up questionnaires and sorting out the answers. The next appointment came in April 1768, as supervisor of the department of *Revisioni e Sindacati,* a post that put before him the account books of the entire bureaucracy. In 1769 he was made "chief steward" (*maggiordomo*) of the royal household, a post that kept him busy ordering butter and cream for the grand ducal table, but one that also put him into constant contact with the grand duke.

As long as the older generation of statesmen lived on, Gianni could go no further. Pompeo Neri was clearly the most worthy candidate for the presidency of the new Council of State in 1780. Moreover, by the time the older generation began to die off, Pietro Leopoldo had become too sure of himself to want any more strong personalities in high places. After Tavanti's death, he gave the finance ministry not to Gianni, who might have aspired to it, but to Serristorri, who could be counted on to keep his younger rival in check. Actually, Gianni did not need a ministry. He quietly built up a faithful following of carefully placed dependents. He obtained an unending series of ad-hoc assignments—to review the administration of the Order of Santo Stefano (1770), to audit the books of the Magona iron works (1771), to investigate the management of communal lands (1776), to look into the possible reduction of the public debt (1779), and so on. Because he insisted upon "going around in person" and accepting as true "only what I see with my own eyes," he soon acquired a fund of precise, concrete information about every corner of the grand duchy, information that made him an indispensable consultant on every project of legislation. Occasionally he exceeded the limits of his commission, as when he got it into his head to talk as authoritatively about Transylvania and Bohemia as he usually did about Pisa and Siena. But as long as he stuck to the subjects assigned to him, his master paid attention. And as an informal, nonofficial adviser during the last ten years of the reign, he succeeded in exerting more influence upon the conduct of public affairs than any other civil servant, including those whose titles were more elevated than his own.

Still, ever since he became conscious of his vocation, Gianni had looked upon his personal success only as a means, not as an end. And most of his energies in the first years of the new reign went into realizing the project he had been working on since the early 1760s—the streamlining of the bureaucracy. The first target was his former employer, the tax farm. Once Tavanti had demonstrated that the original justification for its creation had disappeared, and once Gianni himself had described it as an impediment to even the most modest financial reform, its negative effect on the economy became "perfectly clear in the eyes of whoever knows anything about this country." Accordingly, on August 16, 1768, it was abolished and the collection of taxes was once again made the exclusive responsibility of officials hired directly by the state. The second target was the customs office or, rather, the myriad of posts authorized to collect a myriad of tolls on an interminable list of products at costs that often surpassed the amounts collected. Most of the posts on the frontiers—especially on the craggy, unguardable frontiers to the south and the east—were withdrawn. By 1785 the eighteen posts still left in the province of Siena succeeded in raising more net revenue than forty-three of them had raised twenty years before—in spite of drastic reductions in tariffs. The third target was the principal state offices. Gianni was charged in November 1771 with drawing up a list of those positions in the Finance Ministry that could safely be eliminated; legislation based upon his recommendations was immediately put into effect. The last target was the whole gamut of republican magistracies: those which Cosimo I had left standing while depriving them of all but nominal authority, and those like the Senate and the Council of the Two Hundred, which the Constitution of 1532 had erected as a sop to the nostalgic republicans. According to Neri, the magistracies no longer did anything but stick their noses into many "minute matters that can be better dealt with on the spot" and "trample upon the rules of decency and economy." One by one they were shifted about, then renamed, then amalgamated with other magistracies, and finally dissolved altogether. By 1784, when a new roster of state employees was drawn up, none was left. All the old elective and rotating offices had been replaced by appointive offices. The number of higher-level officials on the government payroll, which had risen from 325 to 585 between 1551 and 1736, had fallen to 525. Thus two and a half centuries after it had been abolished in substance, the Republic was abolished in form as well. The Principate, which had been erected on the foundations of the Republic, now completed its transformation into an absolute monarchy.

Gianni's proposals for the reform of the bureaucracy were based on two complementary assumptions: that bureaucracies had a natural tendency to expand in size and in functions, and that their efficiency was inversely proportional to their size. Reform consisted largely in trimming down, in avoiding the accumulation of too many charges in one office, and in "getting rid of useless occupations . . . that [often] take the place of real business." Even if they were dangerous, however, bureaucracies were necessary; the grand duke could not attend to every little detail himself. Whenever the volume of business warranted an increase in personnel, Gianni was always willing to recommend it. And whenever specialized services were required, he always insisted upon adequate compensation. Finally, bureaucracies were composed of men, each with his own tastes and talents. Hence "the selection of persons" had to be considered, as well as the prescription of their functions. And no person, particularly if he had proven "absolutely faithful in spirit and in will [through] many years of service," ought to be deprived of his means of support, even if the office he held was slated for abolition.

Fortunately, the grand duke agreed with Gianni on almost every point. "The simplification and clarification of the administration," he told his brother, "is the most useful and necessary work . . . you can undertake." Indeed, he became so infatuated with "exact rules, method, and order" that he tried to extend them even into the realm of culture. He noticed that botany was no longer a discipline in its own right, as it had been in the days of Pier Antonio Micheli. He therefore abolished the Accademia Botanica and turned its property over to the Accademia dei Georgofili. He then noticed that agriculture had recently become associated with political economy. He therefore reorganized the Georgofili as the Royal Academy of Sciences and instructed it to study not only "agriculture in the broadest sense of the term" but also all questions pertaining to "public and private economy." At the same time he decided that poetry, philology, and lexicography were logically interrelated. He therefore declared the Accademia Fiorentina, the Crusca, and the Apatisti to be obsolete, even though they were still conducting their sessions as regularly as ever. He gave the members one year to sign up in the new Accademia Fiorentina, which was formally inaugurated in the spring of 1784. Finally, he came to the conclusion that "draftsmanship"—*disegno*—was only the foundation of the arts, not their essence. He therefore transformed the Accademia del Disegno into the Accademia delle Belle Arti ("of Fine Arts"). He assigned it a triple function as a school for apprentices, a union of professionals, and a meeting place for art lovers. He increased its state subsidy. And he moved it into the former convent in Piazza San Marco where it still is today—and where the unmistakable neoclassical decor of its gallery still recalls the tastes of the time in which it was restored.

Yet Tuscany did not therefore turn into a completely modern bureaucratic state, even after the centralization of all administration under a single Council of State on August 6, 1789. For one thing, Pietro Leopoldo contradicted his own standard of promotion through talent alone by excluding Florentines from most subordinate positions. For another thing, he occasionally reverted to Hapsburg tradition in preferring foreigners to nationals—that is, in dipping into what was left of the international pool of administrative talent, where loyalty to employer was immune from loyalties to family or country. Finally, he was careful "to move employees frequently around from one department to another," not for the purpose of training them but for the purpose of preventing "their becoming too attached to [any particular] superior."

Gianni was in complete agreement with this policy, for he was firmly convinced that public office invariably corrupted the most virtuous officeholder. The policy did have one notable advantage. It made the bureaucracy more efficient, less costly, and thoroughly "capable of carrying out and enforcing the [laws] that Your Royal Highness may be pleased to introduce," as Rosemberg put it on the eve of his departure. But it also had some notable disadvantages. It encouraged the advancement of mediocrities, like the "poor, proud gentleman of little talent and application" who "went happily ahead . . . with full honors" by doing no more than he was told to do. It left bureaucrats with no other means of self-expression than spontaneous slow-downs, about which both Gianni and Pietro Leopoldo constantly complained. Worst of all, it robbed them of any trace of esprit de corps and of any sense of collective responsibility toward the community as a whole. Thus when a crisis of political authority suddenly occurred in the spring of 1790, the bureaucracy was incapable of acting on its own. As soon as the ever-vigilant eyes of the grand duke were removed, it simply stopped working.

4

How Gianni tried to replace a controlled economic system with a free one

The Technicians.

No one at the time ever really expected the bureaucracy to govern. No one ever dreamed that it would one day be expected to carry on all the ordinary functions of a parliamentary democracy between the fall of one ministry and the investiture of another. The principle laid down by Cosimo I in the mid-sixteenth century was still accepted as axiomatic: government was a function inseparable from the person of a prince, and a bureaucracy existed only to carry out his orders. If the prince had nothing but the usual routine orders to impart, he could leave the bureaucracy much as he found it. That is what all the Medici grand dukes, from Ferdinando I to Cosimo III, had done, since for them governing meant simply enjoying what had already been won. But by the middle of the eighteenth century most of the monarchs of Europe had been forced to define new goals. The king of Prussia was trying to make a poor state pay for a large army. The king of Sardinia was trying to keep the French out of Turin. The empress of Austria was trying to keep her hybrid empire from falling apart. The duke of Modena was trying to avoid having to sell off the rest of his paintings as the price of independence. And most of their royal cousins were trying to increase the flow of money from private pockets into the public, or at least the military, treasury.

Pietro Leopoldo's goals were rather different. He did not have to worry about his personal authority at home, since his predecessors had managed to avoid even the suggestion of dissent for some two hundred years before him. He did not have to worry about the security of his frontiers, since neither he, nor any of his neighbors, nor any of the great continental powers, had any interest in changing them. What he had to do, on the other hand, was to keep his subjects from starving. That was the conclusion reached by a Sienese magistrate after an independent survey of the Maremma just the year before. It was also the conclusion that emerged from the report of the Investigating Commission of 1766. And much the same conclusion was proposed thereafter by all the many other investigating commissions that were soon to turn Tuscany into one of the best documented, most minutely described, and most carefully mapped countries of the age.

All this new documentation was anything but comforting. Half the population of Grosseto, it showed, spent at least part of the year in an understaffed, ill-equipped public hospital. None of the sharecroppers in the rest of the province made more than 20 *scudi* a year—which was two-thirds of what the Georgofili set as the rock-bottom minimum and one-sixth of what they paid their secretary for travel expenses alone. Of the 500 inhabitants of one commune on Mount Amiata, 220 were listed as *miserabili*—unable to support themselves at all. Few of the peasants on the Niccolini estates at Ponsacco ever ate anything but rye and millet. Most of those in the rich Arezzo plain had to live on less than the equivalent of one-half kilogram of bread a day, according to calculations made by the bishop himself. Three thousand of them died of hunger alone in 1765, and many others were found lying about "half alive, with grass in their mouths" before the new harvest of 1773. Thus underproduction produced undernourishment which then depressed production still further. By 1766 some areas of Tuscany were producing as much as 50 percent less than they had a century earlier.

What could be done to halt this downward spiral? The first answer the grand duke's advisers came up with was one that had the full backing of the Galilean tradition. That tradition was just then undergoing another of its periodical revivals, a revival stimulated by the discovery of the long-lost records of the Accademia del Cimento, by the foundation of a natural history museum (now the Museum of the History of Science in Piazza dei Giudici), and by the publication of a new eulogy of Galileo under the name of the most acclaimed scientist at the University of Pisa, Paolo Frisi. The answer, said the advisers, lay in science. Science had already unveiled the secrets of the universe. Therefore it should now be able to solve the problems of the economy as well.

Much of Tuscan science in the late eighteenth century was still occupied with the kind of tasks that Francesco Redi had set for it in the late seventeenth century: picking holes in what the Redians called the latest incarnation of Aristotelian system-building, Buffon's *Natural History*; finding out whether certain kinds of frogs were as poisonous as Redi's reptiles; observing the effects of castration on pigs; and calculating the dilation of a cat's iris in a dark room. Public demonstrations were still as popular as ever. One professor from Pisa gave "a complete course in mechanics" while home on vacation in 1784. A visiting professor from France created such a stir by a private exhibition at the Pitti in 1786 that he had to repeat it on two successive nights before packed audiences at the Theater of the Intrepidi. Sometimes the interest in physics became so intense that it erupted into violent quarrels. In 1785 two scientists succeeded independently in verifying the thesis of Lavoisier about the transformation of boiling water into "breathable air." Their claims to priority, motivated to some extent by the considerable sums each of them had invested in the necessary equipment, were spread about the city on printed posters and in polemical pamphlets. Finally the chief of police himself—the same Giuseppe Giusti, by the way, who was still to be chief of police during the riot of 1790—had to step in to halt what he called "a distasteful affair" and what was turning into a very expensive lawsuit.

Tuscan scientists were still interested in medicine, too. Or at least they were interested in the kind of "experimental" medicine that Redi had taught in the 1680s and that Antonio Cocchi had practiced in the 1740s. One of the chief propositions of Redian medicine had been spectacularly confirmed in the mid-1760s: the proposition that most maladies were physical or physiological in nature. The method of smallpox inoculations worked out at Santa Maria Nuova proved so successful that one of Cocchi's pupils took it to France; there he applied it to the family of none other than the French *philosophe* Helvétius. The proposition was confirmed once again in 1772, when the Collegio Medico developed a way of reviving the victims of drowning solely by the application of physical pressure; it was so pleased with the results that it asked the government to put its manual on artificial respiration into the hands of every citizen. By 1781 the proposition seemed to be so certain that one of the best-known physicians in the city declared influenza to be noncontagious. It was caused, he said, by a succession of hot days and cold nights and by a resultant excess of bile in the blood. The explanation was eventually to vanish with the discovery of bacteria. But the typically Redian prescription—sober living and moderate diet—was effective enough, at least as a deterrent, to be repeated almost verbatim during another epidemic forty-six years later.

The second proposition of Redian medicine was that the least medication usually works the best cure. As Angelo Nannoni, the leading surgeon of Florence in the 1780s, put it: "Nature should [always] be followed, and it need only occasionally be aided." Nannoni had seen far too many "abuses of medicaments" during two years of postdoctoral study at Rouen and Paris in 1747 and 1748. He had found ample support for what he had learned earlier in Florence in the works of the English physician, John Ray, to whom Cocchi probably introduced him. He therefore prescribed operations only as a last resort. And he sought to heal wounds with fresh air rather than with the oils, balsams, and resins that commonly took the place of disinfectants before the discovery of iodine.

What Nannoni began, his brilliant son Lorenzo carried on. Lorenzo had been thoroughly exposed to the sight of blood and knives since he was old enough to stand beside his father's operating table. He had published his first medical treatise and received his first professional appointment at the age of nineteen. He had presented a paper to the Surgical Academy of Paris at the age of twenty-nine. He had worked out new ways of treating cataracts, syphilis, hernias, and babies born without an anus. After his return from England and France in 1779, he never left the hospital before one or two in the morning, to the annoyance, perhaps, of his wife, but to the delight of his adoring students, one of whom eventually married his daughter. Nannoni did all he could to make his patients less uncomfortable: soaking them in warm baths, swabbing their gums with opium before filling their teeth, and letting them get up and walk as soon after an operation as possible. He occasionally made some strange miscalculations, like placing the moment of greatest fertility in females immediately after menstruation (for the perfectly orthodox Redian reason that the irritability of the sexual organs was then greater). But he always remained faithful to the doctrine that science was meant to serve people, not people science. He declared artificial insemination in human beings to be ridiculous, no matter what the great Lazzaro Spallanzani said to the contrary. Who is she, he asked, "who would prefer an annoying little squirt to a sweet, pleasant, virile instrument and then abstain from the use of the latter for nine whole months, just to test the thesis of a philosopher?"

The third proposition of Redian medicine was that no kind of human ailment was exempt from medical treatment. The law of January 23, 1774, had already recognized insanity as an illness and not, as the laws of most other European states supposed, an incurable derangement or a sign of diabolical possession. Its causes, according to a bright young physician named Vincenzo Chiarugi a few years after his graduation from Pisa in 1780, were no different in nature from those of other illnesses. Sometimes it was the result of brain damage. But sometimes it was the result of a disorder of the passions. Since the passions became manifest in facial expressions, they could be observed and classified. Since "strength, courage, ferocity, animosity" and the like were determined either by sense perceptions or, as one of his colleagues put it, by "nutrition, air, and situation," they could be controlled. So Chiarugi set out to find a cure. He began by turning the Hospital of Bonifazio, of which he became director in 1785, into a well-furnished, comfortable rest home—just the opposite of the prison which London's "Bedlam" was to remain for many years to come. He had detailed case histories compiled for all the patients, forbade their being subjected to any greater physical constraint than padded straitjackets, and insisted that they always be treated as persons. He sought to gain their confidence through kindness and gradually to "instill reason" into them through long, confidential conversations. Thus Florence had a psychiatric clinic long before any other city in Europe. And if its founder has since been forgotten, the fault lies partly with the French painter C. T. Theury, who put not him but his chief rival in the famous portrait of the chain-breaker of 1879.

To these three propositions, the physicians of the late eighteenth century added, or reaffirmed, two others. Hygiene, they insisted, was the best preventative for disease; and medical treatment was the right of all citizens regardless of class or income, not just the privilege of those who could pay. True, not everyone could afford to take advantage of the sober neoclassical pavilion that Pietro Leopoldo had erected at Montecatini in 1773. And almost no one could afford one of the special services offered there: medical advice and exercise at the same time, while riding horseback through the country in the company of a physician. But anyone who could get to Montecatini could drink the water, which at least had a mild laxative effect even if it did not actually cure everything from hemorrhages to hypocondria, as advertised. And anyone could breathe the wind-swept air, which was held to be as essential to good health in the unpolluted eighteenth century as it is in the asphyxiated twentieth. The chief promoter of the project, Alessandro Bicchierai, was no one to cater solely to the rich. He was as proud of his humble origins as he was of having, in good Redian fashion, "banished so many useless and harmless remedies from his clinic." And he took care to show how the construction of the baths benefited the pocketbooks, as well as the health, of all the residents of Montecatini.

The residents of Florence benefited even more than those of Montecatini. In 1780 the loggia outside the Porta al Prato was converted into a public bath, fully equipped with lockers, dressing rooms, and separate facilities for men and women; it was open to the public free of charge. The new establishment had one great drawback. It enabled the grand duke to put the Arno off-limits—ostensibly because of the danger of drowning, but more probably because no one had thought of protecting his prudish eyes by inventing swimming trunks. But the prohibition was soon forgotten. Twenty years later the chief of police was still complaining about "the abuse of bathing in the Arno in defiance of current laws, at any time of the day and without regard [for propriety]."* And the public bath must have had a salutary effect on the noses as well as on the bodies of the citizenry in an age when domestic bathrooms were all but unheard of.

The main hospital of the city, Santa Maria Nuova, was reorganized and enlarged according to the recommendations of a special commission appointed by the grand duke soon after his accession. The endowment, which had been badly depleted during the famine years of the 1760s, was considerably expanded. An aqueduct was built all the way to Montereggi in order to assure a perennial supply of fresh water. A centralized kitchen and heating plant were installed at considerable savings in fuel. A new "anatomical theater" and several new laboratories were constructed, and the pharmacy (which is still in operation today) was doubled in size. Many new wards were added—in the ex-convent of the *Oblate* between Via dell'Oriuolo and Via S. Egidio, as well as in the central building behind Buontalenti's magnificent archways. The former hospital of Sant' Eusebio outside the walls was transformed into a clinic for skin diseases.

* A copy of the decree of June 3, 1801, now hangs appropriately over the president's desk at the Rari Nantes swimming club on Lungarno Francesco Ferrucci.

The teaching staff was increased by the incorporation of the Collegio Medico (the "Florentine Medical Association," which controlled the licensing of physicians) and by regular salary raises, while courses in new specializations, like obstetrics, were added to the curriculum.

At the same time, the treatment of patients at the hospital was notably improved. Every corner was swept daily and mopped twice a week. Bigger windows were put in to improve ventilation, and perfume was regularly sprayed in the wards to banish bad odors. Anyone brought into the reception room was immediately admitted, washed, given a hair- and nail-cut and a shave, put in a hospital nightshirt (*camicia, gabbanella, e berretto*), and assured of 8 ounces of bread, $10\frac{1}{2}$ ounces of wine, and 3 ounces of meat twice a day—which is more than most of them ever ate at home. Whoever could not pay was assured of free treatment, free medication, and even free house-calls after discharge, without the slightest discrimination. Whoever could pay was charged strictly in proportion to his income. A staff of medical students and fifty "paid servants" (not a bad proportion for 1,034 beds) was constantly on duty "to answer all calls from said patients even for the most menial service." And in 1783 a new set of regulations was issued, regulations which completed the redefinition of medicine as public health rather than private treatment and made Florentine medicine fully worthy "of the enlightenment that is the honor of our century."

Actually, the reform of the hospitals may have been a bit too successful. Santa Maria Nuova became so attractive that the rich stopped having themselves cared for at home and the poor feigned illness just to be admitted. As one amazed foreign tourist put it, "In Tuscany, the hospitals are apparently the grand duke's palaces." But the public health officials were too proud of their accomplishment— and still too loyal to Counter-Reformation definitions of the obligations of the rich toward the poor—to be disturbed by such abuses. An investigating commission of 1816 even boasted that Florence still cared for three patients for every one in Paris and three and a half for every one in Vienna, while the government supported some thirty-five other hospitals spread about the rest of the country. The commission could think of no other remedy for the disorders left after twenty years of French occupation than to restore "the grandious creation of the incomparable genius of the IMMORTAL LEOPOLDO"—or, to be more accurate, of Marco Covoni, director of the hospital since 1782, who had actually done most of the work.

A similar transformation took place in another branch of science that had long enjoyed considerable prestige in Florence: technology. In the days of the Cimento, technology had served largely to assist a few wise men to satisfy their curiosity about the structure and content of nature. Now it acquired a much loftier purpose: that of promoting the physical and economic well-being of all the citizens. Now it had to be judged, in the words of one scientist, according to the new criterion of "true utility and nothing but utility."

At times, the utility of certain technological innovations was not immediately evident. For instance, the "aerostatic balloon" that one Francesco Hendrion set off on January 20, 1784 (after producing hydrogen, or "inflammable air," with iron filings and sulphuric acid) did little but amuse the huge crowd that watched it soar three miles straight up from the Ponte alla Carraia. The most that could be said for it was what the playwright Vittorio Alfieri had said about a similar experiment the year before in Paris: it was "a majestic and noble spectacle, more fit for poetry than for history." But for Hendrion, a minor employee in the *Decime* tax office,* the balloons were at least profitable. He sold them for 30 *zecchini* apiece, and by December 1786 he had apparently made enough money to warrant putting a new, improved model on the market. For the Accademia Fiorentina, the balloons marked the beginning of a new age, an age in which man would finally free himself from the bonds of gravity and conquer space. Indeed, the only really skeptical observer was the grand duke. When Pagani and Company published a translation of the Academy of Lyon's balloon-making manual, and when everyone from the Benedictines of the Badìa to the archaeologists of Cortona began following the instructions, the grand duke decided that some of the experiments were being conducted "more for entertainment than for research." He therefore ordered the experimenters to secure licenses from the government and to accept financial liability for eventual damages. When, on February 2, 1788, a balloon that had been successfully suspended in mid-air over the Piazza della Signoria suddenly went crashing into the tower of the Palazzo Vecchio, many Florentines became skeptical as well:

> Behold the mob there, gazing at the sky,
> pushing, shoving, all for . . . know you why?
> Well, someone's made a ball of paper fly!
> (Lorenzo Pignotti, "I palloni volanti")

They finally concluded that the age of air travel was not nearly as imminent as the Accademia Fiorentina thought it to be.

An occasional failure, however, by no means dampened the almost unlimited faith in the potentialities of scientific technology that Florentines shared with their British and French contemporaries. The same poet who mocked the balloons was something of an inventor himself. After repeating Joseph Priestley's experiments on the separation of oxygen and nitrogen, he was sure that rainfall was caused by exhalations of "heavy air" from deep within the earth, and that it could therefore be regulated. When none other than the director of the Natural History Museum repeated the same experiment (by putting an electric charge through a closed tube), he was sure he had found a way of extracting good air,

---

* That is where the newspaper report of the event said he worked. Actually, he worked in the office of the *Camera delle Communità,* where R. Burr Litchfield has found his name listed. The *Decime* office had been abolished eight years before.

that panacea for so many ailments, from bad air. If he failed in the long run to persuade Florentines to sleep with their windows open, he at least gave the hospital directors a scientific argument on behalf of ventilation.

Several of the more famous foreign inventions of the age were immediately adopted in Tuscany. Lightning rods were put up on the Torre del Mangia in Siena as early as 1777, and Franklin stoves were installed at the Doccia porcelain factory in 1774. Still other inventions were the work of Tuscans themselves. One of them perfected a device for transporting oil presses up and down hills. Another developed a grain mill that moved without air or water power. One figured out how to exploit the peat bogs in the lower Arno for "a new combustible substance that costs nothing"—at least compared to the exorbitant price of wood. Another constructed a "machine run by fire that lifts water out of the sea . . . and onto the salt flats" at Castiglione alla Pescaia. Still another made a water-driven "machine for amalgamating the ashes" at the mint, thereby recovering whatever gold and mercury may have fallen into them. And the secretary of the Georgofili was specially commissioned to put chemistry and engineering together for "a quicker and less expensive way of crystallizing salt" from the mines at Volterra. Perhaps the most intriguing invention of the age was a small desk-size piano "that yields to none in sweetness of harmony" and that cost as little as 35 *zecchini*—only a little more than Hendrion's balloons, that is, and much less than those currently imported from England. Apparently the invention was a financial success; it was further developed three years later to include four registers and a removable case.

Having long been accustomed to collaboration between technicians and philosophers for the advancement of science, Florentines had no difficulty now in accepting the collaboration of technicians and businessmen for the purpose of reducing costs and increasing production. They began by trying to improve the three traditional staples of Tuscan agriculture. They encouraged seed selection and less wasteful planting methods. They compensated for the fragility of wheat by introducing more resistant grains, like "Siberian oats" and *gran nero*. They sought to make Tuscan wine "travel," and thereby to save some of "the thousands of *zecchini* . . . sent out of the country each year" for bottled luxuries from Champagne and Cyprus. At least twice, they thought they had discovered the proper formula for durable wine. And at least once they were happy enough with the results of their experiments to have explanations of them translated into German. Unfortunately, even Montepulciano continued to spoil before it reached England—to the annoyance of the prospective customers, who had often picked up a taste for it during their "grand tour." The efforts of the experimenters failed to bear fruit for another half century. The nearest they came to a commercial success was merely a by-product, one which the inventor claimed to be as good for the stomach as it was good to the taste, and which he patented under the name of *vermut*.

The next step was crop diversification, if for no other reason than to mitigate the consequences of a failure in any one crop. Not all the various kinds of flora that the Georgofili read about in their foreign periodicals or had shipped in from abroad were adapted to the particular geographical and meteorological conditions of Tuscany. The handsome tree that one Filippo degli Albizi brought back from the Levant and appropriately baptized *albizia* turned out to serve no other purpose than that of enhancing "the delight of our gardens." The director of the botanical garden was therefore charged with separating the practical from the merely exotic, and with converting botany from a branch of medicine into a branch of agriculture. Every spring he presented the academy with a plan of research for the coming year. And every summer he gave public lectures in the garden on how to apply general principles in practice.

What passed the first test was then tried out on the estates of the members. Monetary prizes were regularly advertised for specific innovations. Managers and peasants as well as landowners were encouraged to report the results of their own independent experiments. An ordinary gardener was elected to membership by acclamation in 1780 for having successfully grafted orange and lemon trees and for having produced double carnation blossoms. The academy then undertook to publish whatever was turned over to it in one of the two current agricultural magazines, the *Magazzino toscano* or the *Giornale fiorentino di agricoltura, arti e commercio*. It also invited everyone to visit its "model farm"—a small estate attached to the parish church of Villamagna, just two miles up the road from the present suburb of Badìa a Ripoli. The pastor-proprietor happened to be the same Ferdinando Paoletti who had collaborated with Lami as rector of the seminary at San Miniato. And Paoletti was one of the city's leading economists as well as a practical agriculturalist. The Georgofili's most famous honorary member, the traveling ambassador of the English "agricultural revolution," Arthur Young, did not particularly like the farm when he visited it in 1789. But that was largely because he disliked everything to the degree in which it differed from what he knew in England. All he noticed after a day-long exposure to a chilling *tramontana* wind was the truth of the principle that Italy is a land of sunshine only when the sun shines. But all the other visitors were enthusiastic; and many of them were inspired to go and do likewise.

The third task facing the Florentine agronomes was how to bring more land under cultivation, particularly in the most deserted part of Tuscany, the Maremma. According to the enthusiastic, energetic Jesuit engineer Leonardo Ximenes (who is still remembered today as the founder of the state weather station in Florence, the Osservatorio Ximeniano), the answer lay in drainage canals, dikes, and aqueducts. This answer was basically no different from the ones that had been put forth from time to time ever since the days of Cosimo I. But Ximenes was more than just an engineer. He was a mathematician, one who had been hired as a tutor by none other than Lami's patron, Vincenzo Riccardi. He was an astronomer, one who had corrected current calculations of the distance between the earth and the moon with the help of a "meridian line" drawn on the floor of the cathedral, and one whose refinements on Nicholas-Louis de La Caille's instruments for measuring parallaxes were duly reported all over Europe. He was also something of a historian. After reading Orlando Malavolti's seventeenth-century *History of Siena,* he came to the conclusion that the once-prosperous Maremma had been ruined by the wars between the thirteenth and the sixteenth century and that it had been kept in ruins thereafter by "the physical constitution of the air and the water." Finally, Ximenes was an organizer and a promoter. He managed to secure assurances of full financial backing from the grand duke in the very first days of the new reign. By 1768 he had completed a new road down from Siena, new dikes along the Ombrone, a network of drainage ditches in the Grosseto plain, and a "Royal Canal" meant eventually to wipe out the Lake of Castiglione.

Certain of having at last found a solution to an age-old problem, the government forthwith advertised for colonists, and Ximenes organized guided tours for the gaping visitors who descended upon him from Florence. Even Gianni was convinced of the efficacy of these triumphs of technology when he saw them imitated by Pope Pius VI in 1780—little realizing that the Pontine Marshes project was soon to become more famous for the money it drained out of the papal treasury than for the water it drained off the plains. Indeed, some results were immediately visible. Most of the marshes actually did dry up within a few years, and by 1774 grainfields stretched for at least nine miles out of Grosseto. Still, the province that Ximenes tried so hard to revive was destined to remain *Maremma amara* ("Bitter Maremma"), as the folk song has it, for another century. But that was not his fault. He had no way of knowing that malaria was spread not by "bad air" (*mal aria*) but by mosquitoes. And he had no way of foreseeing the hundreds of tile-roof farm houses that the land reform program of the late 1940s was eventually to sprinkle over the once empty plains.

Thus the Tuscan countryside underwent its first major change since the late Middle Ages. Much of what had long remained barren or seasonally covered with water was now planted. What had once been dedicated exclusively to wheat was now interspersed with vines and olive trees, with potato fields, fruit orchards, cattle pastures, meadows planted in *erba medica* and alfalfa, and rows of mulberry trees. One old crop was on the verge of producing bigger profits, namely, canapa, which a new process promised to refine into cloth almost as smooth as silk. One new crop—tobacco—turned out to be profitable almost immediately, especially after the grand duke removed all legal restrictions on its sale and after the Georgofili issued a free pamphlet on its cultivation. Tobacco was used to make insecticides and snuff as well as the tough, twisted cigars that are still the consolation of strong-stomached Tuscans. It was prescribed as a medically sound remedy for "humid heads" and running noses. It continued to thrive right down until the late nineteenth century, when a new national monopoly gradually suffocated it with controls and inspection teams.

As Tuscan agriculture became more diversified, so did Florentine diets.

No longer did anyone have to be content with the same sauces on the same cuts of meat and fish prescribed by the rhymed cookbook of 1719. In 1788 a new cookbook, written in simple, clear prose, offered a choice among hundreds of recipes. It prescribed vegetables in abundance—a great relief from the traditional excess of protein and starch; and one of its vegetable dishes seems to have used the "extraordinarily large artichoke" developed by the Georgofili in 1786. It added *gnocchi alla tedesca* (German dumplings), *ravioli di ricotta,* and stuffed Neapolitan macaroni to the more traditional forms of *pastasciutta,* even though it elevated none of them to the rank of today's indispensable *primo piatto.* It still allowed for game; but it suggested that birds and hare be varied by wrapping them in pie crust or covering them with biscuit dough.

The authors of the *Oniatologia* apparently expected one person in each household to spend sixteen hours a day over a big wood stove that never went out. But at least they sought to make the cook's life easier by deriving many different plates from a few standard recipes. For instance, the same kind of *pasta frolla* ("pâte feuilleté") could be used to make any number of succulent desserts out of fresh or dried fruit. Similarly, a basic *brodo bianco* ("white broth") was made by boiling 1 whole chicken, 2 lbs. of beef, 4 lbs. of lean veal, a handful of herbs, a sliced onion, a pinch of cinnamon, and $\frac{1}{2}$ ounce of salt. It could then be blended with another chicken, 12 almonds, and 4 hard-boiled eggs, chopped up in a double boiler, and then poured, as a puree, on toasted bread slices. Or it could be strained with dried peas and bits of ham to make something like traditional American split-pea soup. At the same time the authors addressed themselves specifically to Florentine readers. Their Lenten recipes emphasized eels and eggs (devilled in a half-dozen different ways) rather than sea fish; and they could turn almost any kind of leftover into the *crostini* that have always been an essential garnish on Tuscan tables. Like the experimental agronomes in the Georgofili, they welcomed whatever could be conveniently imported from abroad. They specifically recommended deep-fried egg batter with powdered sugar, *budino di riso all'inglese* (English rice pudding), *pasta brise* (sic.), and cod fish *alla provenzale,* all of which have since become standard items in Florentine foodstores. At the same time, they rejected what could not easily be adapted. They did not even mention *polenta* (corn meal), which could not be grown easily in Tuscany even though it was the staff of life in the nearby Po Valley.

Thus the plebeians of June 1790 may have been upset about the price of bread. But for whoever had property in the country, or could afford to take advantage of the markets of the city, the table was becoming an enjoyable pastime, one that was now based on quality and variety rather than just on quantity.

The foreigners.

Yet even Ximenes realized that technology alone was not enough. No one would plant more olive trees, he admitted, unless oil could be sold at a profit. And no one would ever take advantage of his new canals and highways unless "better agrarian and political laws" made them commercially attractive. Gianni had come to much the same conclusion in 1764, when the Sienese magistrates complained to him about the legal restrictions on the use of their land in the Maremma. Giovan Francesco Pagnini, the translator of John Locke's treatises on money, repeated the conclusion in 1765, after he had concluded a detailed study of the history of Florentine and English economic legislation. It was good laws, insisted Pagnini, not nature, that had brought prosperity to Florence before 1492 and to England after 1688. It was the current bad laws, insisted Gianni, that in the mid-eighteenth century "depleted food supplies in good years and provided little more than imaginary relief in bad years." The ancient wool industry had been permanently ruined by the shift of trade routes to the Atlantic, they argued. But, they noted, "the country is still the same, and the men who live in it are the same." There was therefore no reason why modern Florentines could not do with agriculture what their ancestors had done with manufacturing.

Neither Gianni nor Pagnini thought that laws could engender or even preserve wealth. Indeed, the experience of the preceding decades, particularly of the years since the promulgation of the stringent laws of 1747, seemed to prove just the opposite—that the quantity of law was directly proportional to the degree of poverty. What they were asking for was a completely new kind of economic legislation—legislation that would abolish laws, not make them, and that would leave the economy alone ("laisser faire"), not cajole, guide, or force it. Observation had convinced them that their request was fully justified. All they now needed was some good theoretical arguments to back it up. They could think of no better way to find such arguments than to follow the example set by Lami in the fields of theology and historiography: to read the latest books written on similar subjects by authors in other countries.

Fortunately, this task was much easier for them in the second half of the eighteenth century than it had been for Lami in the first. Florence had now become more closely united to the rest of Europe than it ever had been before— and than it ever was to be again until after the Second World War. A few Florentines went abroad permanently. One of them—Scipione Piattoli—worked so hard to save Poland from one last partition that he was confined for eight years in an Austrian prison; he finally became an important official in the Russian foreign office. Another—Filippo Mazzei—wandered all the way from the Balkans to Virginia; after an unsuccessful attempt to pass himself off as a Florentine Jefferson during a brief visit home in the late 1770s, he settled down as Piattoli's correspondent, and the king of Poland's representative, in Paris. Many more Florentines went abroad and then came back to tell their compatriots about their experiences. Vincenzo Martelli, for instance, finally accepted a pension from Pietro Leopoldo after teaching Italian for some thirty years in London; he forthwith furnished Florentines with detailed background information on the most spectacular events of the day by publishing his *History of England and Her Colonies* in the fateful year of 1776. Giorgio Santi of Pienza returned to Florence when the grand duke outbid the Margrave of Baden's offer of a diplomatic post at the French court; he then wrote a series of *Voyages through Tuscany* on the model of those he had already written about Paris and Montpellier. Angelo Fabroni, later rector of the University of Pisa, got to know Condorcet, Condillac, and even those "bandmasters of impiety," Diderot and Rousseau, while on a scholarship in Paris; he then went all the way to Berlin to meet the Piedmontese historian Carlo Denina at the court of Frederick the Great. Giovanni Fabbroni, one of the brightest of the younger Florentine political economists, became a member of the Loge des IX soeurs, the chief salon of the post-*Encyclopédie* philosophes in Paris; after a long residence in London, he acted as intermediary between Thomas Jefferson and Benjamin Franklin and their English correspondents.

At the same time, far more foreigners began coming to Florence. A few of them—the English penologist John Howard, for instance—came to collect specific information on Tuscan institutions. Some of them came

> To meditate in sad and sacred silence
> o'er the relics of the ruined Forum.
> (L. Pignotti, *Poesie* (1798), I, xx)

Like their prototype, Edward Gibbon, who had spent the summer of 1764 in Florence, they stopped on the way to "observe the rarities of Tuscany"—the Uffizi, the Pitti, and the cathedral, which Charles Dupaty described ecstatically in his letters of 1785. At least one of them "very quickly became . . . a patriotic citizen of the province he was destined to inhabit" for over twenty years: Louis Durfort, who succeeded Horace Mann in 1786 as the most popular diplomatic representative in the city. His contributions to Tuscan cultural life eventually led to his election as honorary president of the Accademia Etrusca of Cortona. But most foreigners came just to have a good time in a pleasant, and relatively inexpensive, environment. They packed the Pergola for the opening performance in 1786, and most of them stayed on for the rest of the fall theater season.

Some of these visitors left almost as soon as they arrived. The German playwright Lessing, for instance, found the heat so unbearable in July of 1775 that he forgot all about the resolution he had made just two months before "to live and die in Italy." Pierre-Jacques Bergeret was so afraid of catching cold on December 1, 1773, that he left for Rome on the next day—after having himself driven around to look at all the facades and all the churches. Mozart stopped off only long enough to give one concert in April of 1770 before being rushed off to more enthusiastic receptions at Rome and Naples. Others, however, were less pressed. Henry Frederick, Duke of Cumberland, the brother of King George III, had to stay at least long enough to attend the parties given in his honor by the grand duke, Mann, Durfort, the nuncio, and just about everyone else who discovered in time who the "Count and Countess of Dublin" really were. On one day the entertainment began at 12:30 P.M. with a state reception at the Pitti. An intimate twenty-nine-plate dinner was then followed by an opera at the Intrepidi Theater. A masked ball at the Pergola, with flowers in every box and with special scenery designed at a moment's notice by the manager, Andrea Campigli, finally broke up about six o'clock the next morning.

Many visitors actually became permanent residents. George Nassau Clavering, Third Earl Cowper, arrived in 1760, and not even the loss of his seat in Parliament was enough to get him back to England before 1789. He bought a large palace in Via Ghibellina with the rents his English tenants paid through the bank of Francesco Veraci. He played a prominent role in Florentine cultural life thereafter, as informal music adviser to Pietro Leopoldo, as president of the Coreofili theater company, as a member of the Crusca, and as sometime *lucumone* of the Accademia Etrusca. One of Cowper's compatriots, whom Florentines called "Milord Tilney" (all Englishmen were *Milordi*!) shared his responsibilities for entertaining the constant stream of wellborn sons on the Grand Tour. He had a large enough establishment to provide all-night dancing and food for the entire Florentine nobility, some of whom learned what to expect on such occasions by reading Chesterfield's *Letters to His Son*. Luisa Stolberg, better known as the Countess of Albany from her unfortunate marriage to the last of the Stuart pretenders, settled in Florence for over a decade after 1775. She returned in 1793 as mistress to the poet Vittorio Alfieri and as leader of a brilliant literary salon on the Lungarno near Ponte Santa Trinita. The English poet Robert Merry became a close friend of the Florentine poet Michelangelo Giannetti after losing all his money on gambling in 1782; the two of them, together with Lorenzo Pignotti, with another English expatriate, Allan Ramsey, and with the English wife of an Italian singer, published a joint anthology of Italian and English poems entitled *The Florentine Miscellany*. The English colony was by far the largest. It soon grew to the point where it included not only respectable noblemen, but also a good number of rather bohemian art students. One of them, Thomas Linley, studied violin with Nardini for over a decade. Another, Francis Harwood, spent every *soldo* he owned on plaster casts and shocked his Florentine visitors by drinking himself to sleep on wine every evening.

Tourism thus became an important business in Florence. Florentine businessmen were quick to realize the financial advantages of making their new customers' sojourns as attractive and comfortable as possible. They imported foreign delicacies like *gelati* (ice cream), which the firm of Francesco Grossi and Costantino Tommasi adapted from a Neapolitan recipe and began selling at Florence's first *gelateria* near the Cocomero Theater in 1790. They published new guidebooks with bilingual texts, lists of prices and post-horse stations, and suggested itineraries for easy sightseeing. They brushed up on foreign languages, particularly on French, which "all the best members of the nobility" learned according to an "original and simple method" from one M. Depois of Paris at a studio on the Canto dei Calderai (Via de' Pucci). They expanded and improved their hotel accommodations. The Aquila Nera was doubled in size by the purchase of a former seminary building on the Via Ognissanti in 1786, and all the rooms were redecorated *alla francese*. The Locanda dello Scudo di Francia moved from Via Maggio into a large palace opposite the Badìa in 1780, "with quarters all fitted out in the most modern style." Two new hotels, the Albergo della Gran Bretagna at the end of Lungarno Guicciardini and the Locanda di Giacomo Megit in Santo Spirito, were designed specially to cater to guests from England. Another, the Locanda Della Rossa, was built big enough to accord "splendid hospitality" to a whole train of heavy-spending Neapolitan nobles in 1781. All the hotels seem to have lived up to the high standards of personal attention and prompt room service that were set forth in an operatic version of Goldoni's *La Locandiera* at the Pergola in 1781.

Yet Florentines did not really have to talk to foreigners in order to find out what was going on abroad. Their magazines and newspapers kept them very well informed, not only about recent books, as they had in Lami's day, but also about current political events. By mid-July of 1776, for instance, they were fully aware that "the colonies of Great Britain know their rights; . . . sooner or later English America will be free." By mid-August they read a full report on the Declaration of Independence in a long article sent in by the London correspondent of the *Gazzetta universale,* Peter Timothy. By September they had the text of the Declaration in Italian translation, "signed on July 4 by the oft-mentioned Sig. Giovanni Hancock." Thereafter they kept close enough track of the progress of the war to be coolly critical of abbé Raynal's *Philosophical and Political History of the European Settlements in the Two Indies,* which Bindi in Siena began publishing in a serial translation in November. Whatever books the magazines reviewed could now be bought directly at local bookshops, some of which managed to cut shipping costs by using the Tuscan consuls in Paris and Genoa as agents. Anyone who could not afford to buy a book could read it—along with a selection of some two dozen foreign journals—by paying a mere 10 *paoli* annual fee (or 18 with borrowing privileges) at Filippo Stecchi's lending library in Via dei Tavolini near Orsanmichele.

Much of what Florentine readers liked best soon became available in Italian translation: Gibbon's *Decline and Fall,* William Robertson's *History of America* and *History of Charles V,* and the unending stream of technical, medical, economic, and religious works that came off Tuscan presses a few weeks after they had first been published abroad. Similarly, some of what they preferred to read in French but could not easily obtain from abroad they could read in Italian reprints. Thus Montesquieu's *Letters to His Italian Friends* appeared in Florence in 1767, and a voluminous *Collection of Tragedies, Comedies, and Dramas Selected from the Most*

Celebrated Modern Authors began appearing in Livorno in 1774. The most famous venture of this kind was the Livorno edition of the *Encyclopédie,* which was begun in 1769 by the same firm that had made a "scoop" with the first edition of Cesare Beccaria's *Of Crimes and Punishments* five years before. To Pietro Leopoldo— and to Rosemberg, who advised him to approve the application for a subsidy —the venture had two notable advantages. It gave the government a chance to sneer at the ecclesiastical censors, who had been largely responsible for the "Christianized" version of the *Encyclopédie* put out at Lucca a few years earlier. And it assured the Tuscan economy of a bit of much-needed foreign credit, since the edition could be sold all over Europe. He therefore not only accepted the dedication but also put up some 23,000 *lire* of the capital. By the time the first volume was ready in 1771, more than 1,200 subscribers had been signed up from as far away as Holland. All the other volumes were soon on the shelves of almost every library in Tuscany.

Florence thus became an integral part of a single European cultural community. No one ever suggested that this community be extended into the realm of politics. For the chief consequence of political disunity, international wars, seemed to have been banished to the extremities of the earth, at least after the Treaty of Paris in 1783. Nor did anyone ever suggest that Florence be incorporated into a political unit—like a single Italian state—halfway between Tuscany and Europe. For even Gianni still used the terms "patriotic" and "national" to refer solely to relationships among Pisans, Sienese, and Aretines; and in many ways Amsterdam and Montpellier seemed closer to him than Rome or Venice. National distinctions were severely condemned. "It is high time," admonished the *Novelle letterarie* in 1787, "that men of letters stop fomenting national prejudices . . . and take advantage of every opportunity to show how enlightenment brings the various nations together and teaches them to respect one another." The faith in the superiority of the Florentine language vanished with the dissolution of the Crusca; except for a few old-fashioned cranks, even Florentines began writing according to the rules of the chief anti-Cruscans of the age, Pietro Verri and Melchiorre Cesarotti. The faith in the superiority of Italian culture, which Muratori had done so much to propagate just a half-century before, vanished as well. In fact, it vanished to the point where the most popular Florentine poet of the time, Lorenzo Pignotti, put Alexander Pope in the niche hitherto reserved for Petrarch:

> To me he turned,
> humbly, reverently prostrate on the ground:
> his eyes were flushed with flaming, noble ire;
> And thus he spake: Who art thou to dare,
> with Tuscan lyre on banks of Thames to sing?
>
> (Pignotti, *L'ombra di Pope*)

He advised his colleagues to read through Hume's *History of England* in search of new heroes, and he proposed William Penn as a worthy replacement for Gian Gastone and Eugene of Savoy:

> From rum'rous Europe didst thou bring
> O gentle citizen, the arts of peace;
> And happy, golden mean didst thou then set
> to flourish in another world.
>
> (Pignotti, *Robert Manners*)

As Europeans first, and as Tuscans or Italians second, Florentines no longer hesitated to appropriate for themselves whatever appealed to them in the cultural heritages of their neighbors. Hairdressers copied the latest coiffures from France. Tailors adapted the new dress patterns sent down at the beginning of each season from Paris. Florentine readers discovered that many of the authors they previously had shunned were really very interesting after all. Voltaire, for example, turned out to be not an atheist but a deist, as one of his former Italian secretaries, Cosimo Collini, insisted when he returned home in 1775 with inspiring stories about the charity continually showered upon the poor people of Ferney. Similarly, Helvétius turned out to be not really a materialist but a philosophic poet almost as good as Tuscany's own "immortal Marchetti." Even Montaigne turned out to be anything but "vacillating in the principles of religion"—particularly after he had been proven perfectly orthodox by a scholarly Benedictine of Bordeaux in 1773. Even though he had lived "in a century very different from our own" and in a time "when the light of true philosophy had not yet begun to shine," he was still able "to illuminate every class of men" by teaching them to know themselves. In fact, he had only one serious defect: "an unstitched and badly connected tyle." And Giulio Perini provoked some harsh criticism from his friend Marco Lastri when he tried to reproduce Montaigne's style in eighteenth-century Italian.

Becoming citizens of Europe, however, did not mean that Florentines stopped being citizens of Tuscany. Nor did it mean that they had to accept whatever was offered to them. For example, the English had many good qualities. But their taste in interior decorating was dubious at the best, particularly when they painted the floors of their Florentine houses to look like marble and covered their walls with colored paper. Their food and drink were utterly incompatible with Florentine stomachs, as poor Angelo Fabroni found out after four months of indigestion in London. Their sexual relations were a combination of strait-laced duty and outright frigidity, as Lorenzo Cantini pointed out in his dramatic exposition of "the character of the British nation":

Salm: Ah, you are therefore a rigid observer of a too austere virtue!
Elson: Yes, but it is a virtue worthy of an Englishman!

(*Salm ed Orami,* 1789, Act I, sc. viii)

Their ostentatious spending was offensive, particularly to those Italians who thought the credit of the English came largely from the sale of *baccalà* (salt cod) in Italian ports. And their much-vaunted civil liberty was merely the result of juggling among corrupt interest-groups, groups which proved all too willing to embrace "despotism" the moment true liberty was proclaimed on the other side. of the Channel.

The French had many good qualities, too. But their government was in the hands of incompetents, as the firing of Necker in 1781 clearly demonstrated to "all intelligent people." Some of their writers were just armchair literati who "think they can throw light on agriculture, politics, and commerce without ever having had any practical experience." Others were little more than shallow scandalmongers, whose "works walk in darkness." In fact, the minute any French writer began talking about religion, and the moment any of them began constructing still another "system of nature" on the basis of "fantastic and imaginary" rather than real men, Tuscan readers started yawning. And they finished by putting aside "the all-too-celebrated" constructions of Holbach, the "absurd principles" of Helvétius, and the *Discourse on Inequality* of Rousseau.

Florentines bothered to counterattack only when their honor was at stake. They did so, that is, only when the English meteorologist Richard Kirwan based his rainfall calculations solely on reports from Padua—as if those from Pisa and Florence had never been published. They did so only when an Italian translation threatened to contaminate even Italy with the numerous errors in William Roscoe's life of Lorenzo the Magnificent. And they did so once again when the French astronomer and traveler Jérôme de La Lande filled his *Voyages* (1769 and 1786) with "fabulous stories, false or misconstrued information, precipitous judgments, and a thousand bits of ridiculous and vain frivolity." What Lalande said about *l'amour* in Florence obviously came from the scurrilous jokes of some doorman, they decided. But they failed completely to understand how a personal friend of Ximenes could say that a fire had destroyed the Pergola in 1755, that Florentine ecclesiastics moonlighted as theater managers and fencing teachers, or that Baccio Bandinelli had invented the art of engraving. The editors of the *Novelle letterarie* soundly blasted the book for fear that it might mislead thousands of innocent French tourists for years to come.

The Economists.

Florentines of the late eighteenth century carefully avoided the practice of some of their ancestors in the fifteenth century (and of some of their descendants in the mid-twentieth century, for that matter) of positing a "model state" either in the past or somewhere else in the present and then criticizing their own country to the extent that it fell short of the model. Just because England and France prohibited the exportation of certain commodities, warned Giovanni Fabbroni in 1789, was no reason why Tuscany should do the same. "I keep arguments from authority a thousand miles away from my mind," he said, in good Galilean fashion, "and I accept only arguments based on reason. Admittedly those nations do many good things; but they do many bad things as well." Since Florentines were proud of contributing to others as much as they borrowed from them, they never suffered from inferiority complexes. "I was born," wrote Fabbroni to Jefferson ten years earlier, "in a part of Italy where servitude was much less grave than it was elsewhere. I now live under the most humane prince in the universe, one who . . . has abolished every trace of despotism . . . and who has assured a more than sufficient freedom of conscience to every individual. It is these circumstances," he concluded, and not any desire to escape into some sort of terrestrial paradise, "that make me so want . . . to come visit your happy republic."

The general rule that Florentines applied in this task of selective borrowing was the same one that they had inherited from their forefathers in the Accademia del Cimento, as the Neapolitan political economist Antonio Genovesi observed as early as 1764. The rule was to adopt only what experience showed to be useful in solving the particular problems of Tuscany. Florentines had to be especially rigorous in applying this rule, largely because none of them could afford to follow the example of those of their contemporaries abroad who engaged solely in theoretical speculation. As responsible members of the government, as prominent investors in the domestic economy, or as conscientious associates of the Accademia dei Georgofili, they were not free to let their or anyone's theories run through to logical conclusions. They knew that a mistaken idea, no matter how solid its theoretical justification might be, could spell disaster both for them and for the mass of citizens under their jurisdiction. Hence none of them ever managed to become any more than a third-rate theorist—not even Aldobrando Paolini, whose *Legitimate Freedom of Commerce* provided at least a rudimentary explanation of the economic reforms during Pietro Leopoldo's reign; and not even Gianni, who tried hard to rework some of his memoranda into systemic treatises after Pietro Leopoldo's departure. The editor of the "Classics of Italian Political Economy" series had no end of trouble when, in the first decade of the next century, he started looking for theoretical texts worthy of Tuscany's well-known practical accomplishments.

This, then, was the rule they adopted whenever they turned to that body of contemporary foreign literature which seemed most relevant to their current problems. They had already begun, in the late 1750s and early 1760s, to read John Carey, David Hume, Bernardo de Ulloa, Geronimo de Ustariz, and needless to say, the Neapolitan friend of the founder of the Georgofili, Antonio Genovesi, who had read all the others. At least one of them, Stefano Bertolini, the polyglot bureaucrat from Siena, set to work distilling whatever economic doctrine he could from the most prestigious foreign author of his generation, Montesquieu. Several others got their hands on the two most recent, and novel, tracts of the moment: the Marquis de Mirabeau's *Ami des hommes* and François Quesnay's articles in the *Encyclopédie*. There they found all the extra arguments they needed to support Gianni's and Neri's campaign against government warehouses, obligatory harvest declarations, and privileged markets. The result was the law of September 18, 1767, which swept away most of the restrictions on the movement of grain from one part of Tuscany to another. This first law was quickly followed by many others—laws which, one by one, abolished internal tariff barriers, controls on the baking and sale of bread, and most of the hundreds of miniscule excise taxes which, as Gianni pointed out from ample documentation, usually discouraged commerce while barely covering the costs of administration. Even pastry-makers were freed, on January 1, 1780, from what the grand duke discovered to be intolerable "vexations and law suits." They were given permission thereafter "to keep, cook, and sell any and all kinds of meat, fowl, game, etc."

Meanwhile, a number of the more prominent French economists had joined together into a kind of school, a school which was certain of having at last found the absolute laws upon which all economic affairs depended. According to the Physiocrats, as the members of this school soon came to be called, all new wealth ultimately comes from agriculture. Commerce and industry do nothing but transform what has already been created. Thus an increase in wealth can be obtained only by increasing the amount of money regularly invested in the land. And the only really productive class in society is the one composed of those capable of making such investments: the proprietor-managers, or *fermiers*.

When the Physiocrats heard about the law of 1767, they were elated. At last they could look forward to supplying their doctrine with what it still lacked: an empirical base. Florentines were elated too, when the most recent, and most prominent, convert to Physiocracy, the Marquis de Mirabeau, dedicated a detailed statement of the school's creed to none other than Pietro Leopoldo. Soon the names of Le Mercier de la Rivière, Nicholas Baudeau, Guillaume Le Trosne, and Du Pont de Nemours (which Americans have good reason to remember even today) became as frequently mentioned in the debates of the Georgofili as the names of plant diseases and sowing techniques had been before.

The most convinced Physiocrat in Florence was none other than the Georgofili's model farmer, the curate of Villamagna, Ferdinando Paoletti. Since none of the improvements so far introduced had succeeded in raising his share-croppers' incomes much above mere subsistence, Paoletti became convinced that more radical measures were necessary. Relations among men, he discovered, are governed by a moral law that is just as immutable and beneficent as the physical laws that govern the inanimate universe. Positive (or political) law consists of nothing but "the exposition of the rights and duties that men have naturally and necessarily among themselves." Therefore, he concluded, the government has but four main duties. It should educate the citizens to the point where they can perceive natural law all by themselves. It should get rid of every remnant of any restriction that might falsify the "just price" set by the free play of supply and demand. It should reject even the modest ceiling on wheat prices and the tariff protection for domestic wines that he himself had called for three years before. And it should then *lasciar fare*—"lassier faire."

Paoletti's Tuscanized Physiocratic doctrine provided a theoretical framework for the new legislation that the grand duke and his ministers were just then working on. The law of August 24, 1775, guaranteed complete freedom of trade, both internal and international. The law of August 30, 1781, the masterwork of the finance minister, Angelo Tavanti, then abolished all differences of tax rates inside the grand duchy, moved most of the customs houses to the frontier, and freed imports as well as exports from any but minor revenue duties. Tuscany thus became a single economic unit; at the same time it opened itself to the outside world. What the French had struggled in vain to achieve ever since the time of Colbert, Florentines boasted, had been accomplished by "this magnanimous and energetic prince" in less than fifteen years. Mirabeau accordingly honored him with the epithet "worthy Son of Heaven."

Meanwhile, the process of transforming property-holding into property ownership, a process which had begun with the first struggles of the mercantile communes against feudal law in the early Middle Ages, was at last brought to completion. The absolute right of owners to fishing, hunting, and grazing privileges was extended even to the subsoil, Roman-law precedent notwithstanding. The transfer of property from less to more enterprising owners was encouraged by reducing contract taxes and abolishing all the remaining permanent trust holdings (*fidecommissi*—laws of March 14, 1782, and February 23, 1789). The disposal of the fruits of private enterprise on domestic markets was facilitated by the establishment of uniform weights and measures eleven years (July 11, 1782) before the National Convention established them in France. The disposal of these products on foreign markets was facilitated by a number of bilateral commercial treaties with other states.

The government took seriously the Physiocrats' admonition to "encourage investment in agriculture, the sole source of true wealth." It decided to reverse the century-old flow of capital from business into state bonds and to "put back into circulation the conspicuous quantity of money" that had already been immobilized. On August 25, 1778, it set down guidelines for what was to be one of the most audacious financial operations of the age. On December 16, 1780, it recalled a big block of bonds (*luoghi di monte*) and gave the holders less than two years to redeem them. In 1784, shortly after the death of Tavanti removed one of the chief opponents of the plan, Gianni was charged with working out a way of recalling the rest of the bonds. On March 7, 1788, his recommendations were put in the form of a legislative decree. And by the time of his flight to Bologna—just a year after the ancien régime had collapsed under the burden of the state debt in France—two-thirds of the state debt in Tuscany had been liquidated.

Finally, the government took seriously the Physiocrats' admonition to get rid of the privileged position that all its predecessors, republican as well as grand ducal, had accorded to industry. Just as agriculture should not be exploited for the sake of industry, the government argued, so industrialists and merchants should be free to "transform" the products of agriculture in any way they saw fit. One by one the private monopolies, or *privative,* were torn down; one by one the state monopolies, particularly those on iron and tobacco, were turned over to private managers. All prohibitions against manufacturing outside Florence were withdrawn, and the inhabitants of the *dominio,* the district, and the subject cities were accorded—for the first time since their submission—the same economic rights as those enjoyed by the inhabitants of the capital. Then, six years before a much more moderate version of the same measures ended in one more ministerial crisis in France, the very cornerstone of the whole medieval corporate structure of the economy was removed, namely, the guilds (February 1, 1770). Ten years later all the laws were withdrawn which since 1585 had sought to brake the decline of the silk industry by maintaining the quality of its products. And on May 29, 1781, the Chamber of Commerce (*Camera di Commercio*), which had been entrusted with liquidating the remaining business of the former guilds, was closed up. Tight controls had been replaced by complete freedom. The making, buying, or selling of any product in all parts of the grand duchy was turned over completely to the initiative of private citizens.

Even its warmest adherents, however, soon became aware that Physiocratic doctrine contained several serious shortcomings. For one thing, it was highly abstract. Although "economic axioms from which all questions can be deduced with certainty" might appeal to Gianni's cousin, the "educated farmer," Matteo Biffi Tolomei, they were often annoying to a busy administrator like Gianni himself. He frequently indulged in anti-intellectual outbursts against "the good, the bad, and the inept productions of few true authors, of many copiers, and of many sellers of their pens." Second, most Florentine "economists" had read too much Muratori to be able to view economics solely from a scientific point of view. Talking only about "interest" and never about "justice," in accordance with Mirabeau's advice, might be persuasive in France; but it convinced no one in Tuscany. Even Paoletti, who was a parish priest with the cure of souls as well as an economist, padded his dissertations with quotations from St. Antonino, St. Clement of Alexandria, St. Paul, and "many other fathers of the church." Any traces of bad conscience he might have had about mixing moral and economic principles were swept aside in 1776, when Pompeo Neri finally made available in print the highly moralistic passages in Sallustio Bandini's *Discourse on the Sienese Maremma.*

Florentines were too well read in contemporary pamphlet literature not to realize that the Physiocrats constituted only one of several current schools of political economy. Indeed, the precipitous fall of the French finance minister, Turgot, in May of 1776 made them wonder if that school were not perhaps the one least likely to win out. One of the few books that Gianni ever admitted reading was none other than Voltaire's scathing satire of the Physiocrats, the *Homme aux quarante écus*. Among the books his colleagues read were those of the contemporary Spanish economists, who convinced them that "Spain was becoming daily more enlightened" in spite of its intellectual isolation from France. They also read the book that was soon to replace those of the Physiocrats as the leading economics textbook of the day: Adam Smith's *Wealth of Nations*. And they soon became aware that the example of Holland as well as of England disproved one of the Physiocrats' main theses, since the Dutch managed to get all the wealth they wanted while importing much of their food from abroad. Even Pietro Leopoldo, "the doctor," who had a standing order for all new books from the Desaint firm in Paris, was kept informed of the grave differences of opinion abroad by his diffident ambassador, Raimondo Niccoli. He knew that one of the most vigorous attacks on the Physiocrats had been written by an Italian, Ferdinando Galiani. And he could not but notice that many of Galiani's arguments were as applicable to Tuscany as they were to Naples. Hence Gianni was not completely alone when he concluded: "I have found among the authors so many various ideas ... that I have not been able to adopt any one of them without serious reservations."

Most important of all, Florentines were too well read in their own history to believe that manufacturing was really unproductive. They did not object, therefore, when the government openly contradicted Physiocratic teaching by exempting straw-hat makers from taxation, by renewing the special privileges of the Ginori porcelain company, and by turning over the Fortezza da Basso to a manufacturer of wool cloth "in the French and English fashion." Nor did they forget Pagnini's lesson of 1765: that what made taxes "just" was not the nature of the objects taxed but the consent of the taxpayers. Hence Gianni's conclusion: the Physiocrats' much-advertised single tax on land might make sense in France. But in Tuscany it would be unjust, difficult to exact, and disturbing "to the comfort and the tranquility of the subjects," particularly to the peasants, who would probably end up paying most of it. He therefore dismissed the project as "so much hot air."

At times Pietro Leopoldo was willing to contradict even his own principles of free trade. For instance, he sanctioned the opening of a government rope factory at Pratolino that ended in bankruptcy after having severely damaged its private competitors in Borgo San Lorenzo and Prato. In 1787 he yielded to the constant whining of the silk manufacturers and granted them a premium for exportation. By the time he realized his mistake, the beneficiaries had realized a tidy profit from smuggling back into Tuscany what they had already exported to purely imaginary foreign customers. Even Gianni was occasionally hesitant about accepting the full consequences of the principles. After all, until its dissolution, he had been president of the silk guild. He thus found it hard not to sympathize with the manufacturers, who were ill-prepared after centuries of comfortable protection to face the full impact of foreign competition, even in domestic markets. The snob value of buying French rather than Florentine silks was actually encouraged by Pietro Leopoldo, in spite of all his moralistic sermons about unnecessary foreign luxuries, when he had his daughters' expensive trousseaux made not in Florence but in Lyon. Gianni could only regret the shortsighted way in which the manufacturers chose to take advantage of abolition of controls—that is, by spreading deprecating rumors about each other abroad and then cheating their customers with hidden cuts in quality. As a politician rather than a businessman, he could not even dream of advising them to do what their successors in the twentieth century normally do when faced with foreign competition, namely, make an imitation that is better than the original and then ship it abroad for sale right under the competitor's nose. Instead, Gianni persuaded the grand duke to contradict himself once again. Accordingly, some of the old privileges and exemptions were restored, and raw materials were pushed down to artificially low prices by forbidding their exportation.

Yet neither those of the grand duke's advisors who might be called moderate Physiocrats, nor those who might be called, however inaccurately, moderate protectionists, were ever committed to any particular economic doctrine. Giovanni Fabbroni, for example, attributed the origin of all his ideas to "an inborn taste for agriculture" and to a careful testing in "experience" of the hypotheses spontaneously born of his observations. As late as 1796 the Georgofili refused to accept a paper sent in from France because "in applying . . . his general principles . . . to the particular circumstances of our country, [the author] shows a lack of that specific knowledge which is indispensable for success." Florentines were not surprised, then, to discover that some of their projects turned out to have effects very different from the ones they expected. For example, absolute property rights quickly led to a general slaughter of game animals; and the grand duke was obliged to restrict the hunting season to the months between September 20 and the beginning of Lent. Even worse, absolute property rights soon threatened to wipe out one of Tuscany's most precious natural resources: the forests. The Georgofili did not need to wait for Giulio Perini's translation of Henri-Louis Duhamel de Monceau's *De l'exploitation des bois* to remember that deforestation inevitably produced floods. They therefore applauded the government's prohibition of woodcutting within a certain distance of the crest of the Apennines. And they appealed to their members for suggestions on how to remedy the damage that three years of complete liberty had already wrought.

The grand duke's ministers, however, were rather distressed when their appeals to private initiative got the willing entrepreneurs in trouble. That is just what happened in 1782, when a cloth manufacturing firm in Arezzo went bankrupt

—apparently from overexpansion. But they were even more distressed when no one chose to respond to their appeals at all. Many projects for new industries got no farther than papers presented to the Georgofili, like Giovanni Fabbroni's proposal for making paper out of mulberry bark. Not even Pietro Leopoldo's offer of a 500-*zecchini* prize and a guarantee of high prices managed to elicit a single operating anthracite mine, in spite of help from a technical manual published in 1791. Thus Gianni could not but conclude that at times private initiative was incapable of undertaking programs of immediate importance to society as a whole. In such cases, he admitted, the government was perfectly justified in interrupting the course of nature until a qualified private bidder turned up. Prospective entrepreneurs could be led to flowing water, in other words, but they could not be made to build mills on it.

Even agriculture did not respond as much as it might have to the new laws, as Gianni discovered after a trip through the province of Siena in 1786. However much his hosts boasted about "certain small improvements" and an occasional "extension of land under cultivation," the reforms had not yet succeeded in engendering anything like "a fountain of riches." The results elsewhere in Tuscany were more encouraging, but even there the twofold rise in land prices had cut the return on new investments to not much more than Biffi Tolomei's rigged figure of $3\frac{1}{2}$ percent—which was about the same as it had been in Naples in 1764 and not enough to warrant the expenditure of still more capital.

In general, however, most of the reformers agreed with Gianni's overall judgment, much as they might disagree with him in particulars. "Anyone who thinks that a society founded on the free play of particular interests is without defects fools himself," he admitted. "But anyone who thinks that [these defects can be cured] by replacing private with governmental administration fools himself even more." He need only read "the deplorable history" of government regulation in the past to become aware of its inevitably "unhappy results" in the present. For one thing, Tuscan currency succeeded in maintaining its official value in gold, partly because the ministers were still too loyal to the famous florin of 1252 and too frightened by the recent fate of the American continental dollar to be dragged along by the French government's policy of periodic devaluations. For another thing, the major Tuscan export industry, silk, managed to increase the value of its exports, in spite of the debacle of 1786–87, from 746,966 *lire* in 1760 to 1,035,816 *lire* in 1793. Some small rural industries continued to thrive: shoes at Montalcino and San Quirico, cloth-dyeing at Sarteano, paper-making in Valdorcia. A hat factory was founded in Livorno by a certain Vincenzo Mazzini, who had invented the machinery and trained the personnel to operate it; by 1793 he was able to fill an order for 30,000 red fezzes from a single Algerian merchant. A pencil factory was established in no less appropriate quarters than the Camaldolese monastery at Volterra; Pietro Leopoldo was so excited at not having to import pencils any longer that he naturalized the monk who established it and exempted his lay colleague from all future taxes. In Florence an optics laboratory opened shop in Via Por Santa Maria, specializing in portable telescopes and eyeglasses *all'uso moderno*. A print shop was set up by the state printer, Cambiagi, with equipment so modern that it could be operated by children—who seem to have been the principal victims of all these enterprises. And two factories for making various products of starch were opened within four years: one by a certain G. B. Cappugi and the other by Antonio Bambi and Giorgio Guadagni, with outlets, respectively, next to the Badìa and on the corner of Via de' Calzaiuoli and Via Porta Rossa.

In industry, then, the results may have been rather modest, particularly in comparison to what was happening in Birmingham and Manchester. But at least they provided a first step toward the somewhat more intensive industrial growth that was to take place in the first years of the Restoration. And the audience that listened to Antonio Targioni Tozzetti's glowing report of October 1, 1817, was duly shocked to learn of the existence of a few people in Florence still so short-sighted as to regret the demise of guilds, inspections, and fixed prices. In agriculture, the results were somewhat more encouraging. In 1772 inclement weather suddenly caused a harvest failure almost as bad as those of the mid-1760s. "Nevertheless," reported the finance minister Tavanti, who apparently looked more closely at the markets of the capital than at the starving peasants of the Valdichiana, "the people have not once been without bread of good quality. For assured of complete liberty in their transactions, the merchants of Florence and Livorno have had the courage to bring in grain from abroad—all of which clearly proves that the system of liberty is the only one capable of contributing to the happiness of nations." Tavanti's proof was not invalidated in the spring of 1773, when a minor disturbance broke out in response to a sharp jump in prices. Florence experienced nothing like the full-scale bread riots that broke out at the same time in Paris, Albi, and Aix-en-Provence. Tavanti's proof seemed to be fully confirmed during the next two years, when harvests rose far above pre-1772 levels.* Solemn *Te Deums* were duly celebrated throughout the country in thanksgiving for the new laws.

Thus neither the grand duke, nor his ministers, nor the journalists, nor the members of the Georgofili were wildly jubilant. They all looked to the future rather than to the past or the present for a definitive confirmation of what they were the first to qualify as an experiment. But at least they were moderately pleased with what they had accomplished so far. Above all, they were sure that they were heading in the right direction.

---

* His proof may still be somewhat valid even today, at least with regard to a country like the Republic of Mali where economic conditions are somewhat similar to those of eighteenth-century Tuscany. At least his argument is very similar to the one made about the effects of removing Mali agricultural controls in an article published by the Paris daily *Le Monde* on May 20, 1970.

5

How Gianni tried to turn an absolute monarchy into a constitutional monarchy

The Written Constitution.

It soon became obvious, at least to Gianni, that the new economic system would succeed only to the extent that the beneficiaries could be induced to take advantage of the opportunities it offered them. Yet two centuries of omnipotent government had carefully inculcated in most of them a habit of avoiding even the appearance of spontaneity. Therefore, some way had to be found of turning passivity into a sense of responsibility and obedience into a spirit of collaboration. Some way had to be found, that is, of "encouraging civic activity, stirring up patriotic zeal, and raising subjects once again to the rank of men."

One such way had already been suggested as early as 1767, namely, making the subjects assume some of the tasks hitherto monopolized by the government. In that year the city councilors of Castel Fiorentino decided at last to try solving their own water-control problems, instead of waiting, as usual, for the grand duke to come do it for them. Their example soon received the support of historical precedent, when Muratori's successor at Modena risked his job to proclaim republican city-states as the only form of government suitable to Italians. When some of the dependents of the Finance Ministry threatened to step into one of the areas the prince had vacated in deference to the principle of laisser-faire, Gianni realized that local self-government afforded the only effective protection against what he feared most: government by irresponsible bureaucrats.

Accordingly, all the old Florentine magistracies originally designed to suffocate the autonomy of the subject cities were abolished; and all the local magistracies which had made the subject cities ungovernable even before their submission were abolished as well. In 1772 two "pilot" communes were erected, one in Arezzo and one in Volterra. Their elected officers were given the titles of *gonfaloniere* and *priore,* which were reminiscent of ancient republican traditions, rather than "governor" or "intendant," which might have been reminiscent of the centralizing policies of the absolute monarchies. In 1773 the experiment was extended to the towns of the upper Valdarno, in 1774 to those of the district of Florence, in 1777 to Pisa and Pistoia, in 1778 to Siena. By 1781 the experiment seemed to have worked well enough elsewhere to warrant its extension to the capital.

Thus on November 20, 1781, the names on the electoral list prepared by a grand ducal chancellor the previous July were distributed in four different ballot boxes, or *borse*: one for patricians, another for citizens (as defined by the law of 1750), a third for taxpayers above 2 *fiorini* a year, and a fourth for all of the above plus the owners of any kind and any amount of fixed property. On January 1, 1782, the first name was drawn from the first box, and Giuseppe Maria Panzanini became mayor, or *gonfaloniere*. Three more names were drawn from the first box and four each from the next two boxes to form the Board of Priors, or *Magistrato Supremo*. Twenty were then drawn from the fourth box. All the males over thirty so designated accepted nomination as members of the city council (any women or institutions picked had alternates named for them)—if for no other reason, at least for that of avoiding a 100 *lire* fine for refusing to serve. On March 1, the newly elected magistrates and council-men assembled in the new city hall, the Palazzo di Parte Guelfa. They were formally invested with the exclusive right to impose real estate taxes up to 10 percent of value. And they were given complete control over waterways, streets, bridges, sewers, charitable institutions, and markets.

Thus Florence once again had an autonomous city government, one which, in spite of very specific limitations, enjoyed at least as much authority as do the communes under the constitution of the Italian Republic today. It once again had a chief executive, the first one since the abolition of the office in 1532; and the *Gazzetta toscana* could not resist the temptation of calling Panzanini, however inaccurately, the heir of Pier Soderini. It once again had a city council, one far more representative of all the people than any of its predecessors since the fall of the Ciompi. And it once again had a flag. In fact, the first thing the priors did— after voting themselves salaries, needless to say, and after sending a research delegation to the Magliabechiana library—was to adopt the red lily on a white field that has represented the city ever since.

The new city government soon provided Florence with several notable improvements. In 1786 it put up street signs on every corner; at last strangers could find their way about simply by following the new map of 1782 or Placido Landino's street index of 1779, which was conveniently republished just as the signs were completed. In 1788 it installed several new sewers and repaved many of the streets in accordance with an instruction booklet the merits of which, said the editors of the *Gazzetta toscana,* far exceeded "the highest eulogy that could be bestowed upon it." In 1789 it moved the coal and straw market away from the front of the Baptistry. Later the same year it ordered the construction of a large restaurant and snack bar (for *merende*) at the end of the Cascine. Consequently, the famous park became more pleasant and popular than ever:

> Neath oak and pine, broad elm and bay
> delightful smiles and jovial laughter stay;
> While gaiety innocent and loving pleasures play
> and breathe the air of Paradise.
>> (Michelangiolo Giannetti, *Ottave* . . .
>> *per le magnifiche feste* . . . *1791*)

As a pedagogical device, the new communes seem to have worked fairly well. At times, indeed, they seem to have worked even too well. When the grand duke "suggested" that the Florentine commune put up street lights, the priors politely reminded him that they, according to his own theory, were supposed to know more about such matters than he; and the mayor for 1783, Francesco Guazzesi, firmly refused to burden the taxpayers with an annual bill of 13,659 *scudi* just for oil, when corner shrines and private doorway lamps—at least in his opinion—provided plenty of light already.

But as effective organs of local government, the communes, or at least the commune of Florence, left much to be desired. The council never managed to figure out just what it was supposed to do, in spite of several queries to the royal auditor. It therefore left practically all business to the priors; and since the priors were by law selected from the bigger property owners, their main preoccupation was keeping property taxes as low as possible. Similarly, the annual rotation of both priors and councilmen might have had the salutary effect of giving many people some experience in self-government. But since incumbents could not be reinstated for a year after the termination of their first term, the system prevented the accumulation of experience from one year to the next. The aims of pedagogy, in other words, came into conflict with the aims of efficiency. "Even though taxes haven't gone up," observed one attentive citizen after examining the balance sheet for 1786, "the zeal and intelligence of the magistrates has certainly gone down, and the general upkeep [*polizia*] of the city has gotten noticeably worse."

Election by lot might have had good historical precedent; but even Savonarola had known that it produced mediocrity rather than quality. It left city officials unprepared to face the constant harassment of job seekers and contract wranglers, as in the case of the marble manufacturer who lobbied so hard against painted street signs. It left them even more exposed to interference by state bureaucrats, who, as Gianni complained bitterly in his memoranda on local government, took every opportunity to arrogate to themselves the tasks specifically assigned to the communes. Above all, it left them utterly helpless before the impetuous about-faces of the grand duke himself. For Pietro Leopoldo was sure of being able to do everything better than anyone else. And he was perfectly capable of forgetting all about the limitations he had imposed on himself whenever something went wrong, which is just what he did when negotiations over the street lighting question finally broke down.

To be sure, many of these weaknesses might have been overcome by the institution of a "Tribunal of Interpretation," as one legal expert suggested in 1788—a sort of supreme court charged with keeping all parts of the government, the grand duke included, within their respective jurisdictions. But Gianni refused even to consider such a "mutilation of sovereignty." None of his colleagues seems to have remembered the balance of powers theory they had read about in Montesquieu several decades before. Yet none of them had forgotten Muratori's— and Beccaria's—invective against the rule of judges.* Consequently, the priors busied themselves not with important questions of policy, but with minuscule questions of administrative routine: a petition from a priest to spend 13 *scudi* on house repairs, a request from the chaplain of the Salviati to take 28 *scudi* out of his endowment, an order to sell off abandoned goods at the customs house, a plea from the wife of a convict to get her wristwatch back. They got so bogged down in such questions in June 1790 that they barely noticed the trouble taking place on the streets. And they had no time at all to work out any remedies.

Even well-functioning local governments, however, would not have been able to fulfill one other condition for the success of the new economic system: longevity. As the experience with occasional concessions to free trade before 1765 had shown, the very suggestion of a possible time limit was enough to discourage long-term investment in favor of quick profit-taking. Hence, all the laws promulgated after 1765 were specifically defined as irrevocable. But as long as all law—customary, communal, or Roman—continued to be subject to the will of the prince, any particular law could be considered irrevocable only as long as the prince chose not to revoke it. Pietro Leopoldo himself was hardly a model of consistency. He showed the utmost disrespect for the very law that his Medici predecessors had permitted to acquire at least the aura of permanence: the constitution of 1532. In any case, there was little he could do to assure that his eventual successor would comply with any single decree of his will.

Somehow, then, a rule had to be found by which those laws that could be changed might be distinguished from those that could not. Fortunately just such a rule had already been worked out in the early 1770s: the law of nature. This

---

* Muratori's judgment was still current as late as 1927, when the American jurist Morris R. Cohen said, in the midst of the debate over Realism in jurisprudence, "To be ruled by a judge is, to the extent that he is not bound by law, tyranny or despotism." Quoted by Edward A. Purcell in "American Jurisprudence between the Wars," *American Historical Review* LXXV (1969): 435.

rule appealed especially to Pietro Leopoldo, who had been stuffed with natural law theories by the time he was twelve. The rule had been saved from the taint of relativism by none other than the leading Tuscan authority on Montesquieu, Stefano Bertolini, who showed Grotius's theses to be eternally valid by finding them in Thucydides.

But the main architect of the law of nature in Tuscany was the pugnacious, gregarious, garrulous forty-year-old jurist from Rovezzano, Giuseppe Maria Lampredi, whose improvised verses were the life of literary parties in Florence, and whose lectures were the delight of the law students at Pisa. Lampredi had begun his career as an amateur Etruscologist, and he was delighted when an appointment at the university at last gave him an opportunity to avenge the Roman conquest of the Etruscans, who, he claimed, had anticipated all the scientific, political, and economic novelties of the eighteenth century. He achieved his revenge by completing the process begun a generation earlier by Giuseppe Averani. He subjected the code of Roman law to the light of "universal justice." He then relegated it once and for all to the historians. And he transferred the basis of modern jurisprudence to "reason alone," amid a barrage of citations from Bacon, Locke, Bodin, Spinoza, Mably, et al.

Lampredi thus swept aside the labors of those of his colleagues, like Leopoldo Guadagni and Anton Maria Vannucchi, who were still trying to find out what the law had been. At the same time he scoffed at Rousseau, who, he maintained, wasted his time dreaming up purely imaginary Gardens of Eden. He then drew two general principles out of what he claimed were perfectly obvious, and therefore undeniable, aspects of human nature. First, "Each man should pursue his own happiness without infringing on that of others." Second, "Each man should pursue the happiness of all mankind without harming himself either in spirit or in person." From these two principles he deduced a whole string of absolutely certain corollaries: that government rested on the consent of the governed; that the state's first duty was to promote "manufacturing, agriculture, and external and internal commerce"; that "laws regulating food distribution, granting monopolies, and fixing the working conditions in shops" were contrary "to public happiness"; that proprietors had the right to do whatever they pleased with their property; and that belligerents could not rightly touch anything belonging to neutrals (for example, at Livorno). He drew out a number of other corollaries, too, in the intimacy of his classroom, but no one suspected what they were until his most famous student, Filippo Buonarroti, tried applying them in the "Revolt of the Equals" against the French Directory in 1797. Meanwhile those corollaries that seemed more relevant at the moment he gathered into three volumes and published under the title of *Universal Public Law* in 1775.

Some readers scoffed at first: this is "nothing but a formless, undigested mass of quotations from Grotius mixed up with abstruse terms taken out of Pufendorf," remarked one of them. But Pietro Leopoldo was delighted. All his economic laws were really carbon copies of the law of nature, he now realized. Since he had discovered them, not made them, they could be altered only at the risk of defying nature itself. Better yet, Lampredi's book was written in "a simple, terse, concise style" that could easily be understood by the young. It became, in the second revised edition of the next year, a required textbook for all Tuscan law students. It remained authoritative for decades thereafter, partly because many of its theses were confirmed five years later by the most famous of all Italian law texts of the age, Gaetano Filangieri's *Science of Legislation*.

What Lampredi did for the lawyers and judges, an obscure clerk in the Secretariat of State was about to do for all those Florentines who had been brought up by Lami to think of history as the key to progress. Riguccio Galluzzi had had no particular training as a historian. His mother had dumped him on his paternal grandfather when she remarried shortly after his father's premature death; and the dwindling fortunes of his old Volterran family had been barely sufficient to get him through the local seminary. He had studied law and theology, not history, at Pisa. He had taught moral philosophy at the Accademia dei Nobili at Florence. In 1767, with Neri's help, he had started the slow climb up through the bureaucracy that was to make him state book censor in 1769 and state counselor in 1784.

Galluzzi soon showed a particular talent for one bureaucratic task to which Pietro Leopoldo, with his mania for putting everything in the right place, attached particular importance—the organization of archives. Volumes and volumes of documents were just then being moved into the capital from monastic and communal libraries all over the country, and the grand duke himself was buying up every private collection that threatened to come onto the market— as the famous Strozzi library did when the heirs died off in 1784. All items of cultural or literary value were sent respectively to the Laurenziana and the Magliabechiana, and all the cataloguers trained or left over from the last generation —from Angelo Maria Bandini to Ferdinando Fossi—were put to work sorting them out. All items regarding charitable institutions were sent to Santa Maria Nuova, where the director, Marco Covoni, spent four years rearranging them. All items of a political and administrative nature were deposited in what was soon to become one of the world's greatest centers of historical research—the State Archive, or *Archivio di Stato,* which was founded by the decree of December 24, 1778. Since documents alone were found to be "completely useless either to scholarship . . . or to public and private law," Galluzzi was hired to compile an index for one of the major categories. That is just what he was busy doing when, within months of the appearance of Lampredi's textbook, Pietro Leopoldo asked him to supplement the juridical justification of the achievements of his reign with a historical one.

At the outset, Galluzzi apparently rejected several possible courses. He may have thought at first of following Lampredi's example and of creating a golden age in distant Etruria to match the new golden age in modern Tuscany. After all, his father had dug up enough Etruscan artifacts to warrant their being sold to the grand duke in 1773. His compatriot Mario Guarnacci, the guiding light of the Accademia dei Sepolti, of which he was a member, was just then working on one last flicker of midcentury Etruscological mythmaking, the *Origini italiche*. Even the sober geographer Targioni Tozzetti was tempted, as late as 1770, to inspire his fellow members in the Georgofili with the thought that "a people as rich and peaceful as the Etruscans" must have known how to make wine that traveled. But the academicians of Cortona were the most adamant of all. Almost twenty years later they were still willing to misread hundreds of undecipherable inscriptions for precedents of "the florid state of commerce that in the golden reign of Pietro Leopoldo forms a great part of our happiness." They were thus fully prepared to bring history around through a full cycle, even at the risk of having to resurrect Lars Porsena in a powdered wig and silk breeches beneath the pastel cupids of the neoclassical ballroom of Palazzo Pitti.

Galluzzi may also have thought of following Lami's example and of looking for precursors of the present in the archival remnants of the Middle Ages. Lami's example was still very much alive. It was officially remembered every year, when the *Magistrato Supremo* presented two hundred poor girls with the dowries he had provided for in his will. It was also remembered every time his disciples started fighting over his spiritual heritage—which is what happened most notably in 1787, when the author of the most recent eulogy forgot to mention another eulogy that had been published fifteen years before. Lami's defects were soon forgotten. He was now applauded as "a great man, a great writer, and a great theologian." One week after the riot of June 1790, the curate of Santa Felicità could think of nothing better to say in a panegyric on his predecessor than to quote Lami's favorable judgment of him. The kind of scholarly historiography that Lami had promoted continued to inspire works of value: another continuation of Muratori's *Rerum Italicarum Scriptores,* which included a number of now-famous Quattrocento texts; a series of medieval documents published under the Lamian title of *The Delights of Tuscan Scholars* (*Delizie degli eruditi toscani*) by Ildefonso di San Luigi; a monumental historical guide to all the monuments of the city, Marco Lastri's *Osservatore fiorentino*; and a succession of biographical dictionaries that are still indispensable references for historians of the Medicean period of Florentine history.

Still, Etruscology soon lost those supporters who had managed to survive Lami's barbs. Guarnacci's chronology of the colonists from Babel provoked nothing but laughter when it appeared in 1771, particularly after he tried to get Pietro Leopoldo to fire one of his critics from a chair at Pisa. By 1791 the only explanation left for the continued study of Etruscan inscriptions was that "nobody understands them and [therefore] everyone reads them as he pleases." Scholarly historiography also lost its powers of persuasion, in spite of Vincenzo Fineschi's

Thucydidean introductions to local church histories, in spite of Angelo Maria Bandini's well-paid commissions to do research for British scholars, and in spite of the Accademia Fiorentina's proclamation that "the study of antiquity" could be easily "combined with the philosophic spirit of the present century." Turning scholarship into propaganda convinced no one. Probably very few people ever bothered to read Adami's tract against *manimorte* laws, Mehus's pamphlet against confraternities, or an anonymous demonstration of "the disorders caused in church and state by the mendicant friars." Abusing scholarship for the purpose of "applauding our past achievements," as a *Dissertation on the Excellence and Greatness of the Florentine Nation* did in 1780, brought nothing but sarcastic admonitions "to work [instead] on some new achievement and thus earn the praise of future generations." And one attempt to mold history into a patriotic hero-gallery—the Accademia Etrusca's offer of a prize for the best biography of Amerigo Vespucci—turned into such a mud-throwing contest that all the essays were rejected, even though one of them came to the flattering conclusion that the new United States constitution was merely a copy of "the economic and administrative laws presently in vigor under the philosophical reign of Pietro Leopoldo."

Galluzzi therefore chose to write what ever since the time of Pietro Giannone had been called "civil history." The method of research he took from Muratori, whose *Annals of Italy* remained constantly open on his desk; that is, he took all his specific information from the documents in the collection now known as *Mediceo del Principato*. Even his most persistent detractors have never managed to catch him in errors of fact. His form, on the other hand, he took from Guicciardini, from Carlo Denina, and perhaps even from Voltaire and Robertson. The range of his subject matter he took from the principal concerns of his own generation. Letters, arts, science, religion, and court scandals, all of which previously had been treated separately, were now consolidated about one central theme: the state. Economic affairs, backed up with statistics that are still today quoted as authoritative, were accorded the same importance in the sixteenth as was normally given them in the eighteenth century. The result was one of the best historical works of the age, a work that might receive the recognition it deserves from historians of historiography today were its subject Sweden or Louis XIV instead of *The History of the Grand Duchy of Tuscany under the House of the Medici*.

Some of Galluzzi's readers were furious. To those for whom papal infallibility extended to every gesture of the pope and to every act of every religious order, he was guilty of impiety. To those who judged the quality of scholarship by the length of the footnotes, he had written "a pack of lies." But Pietro Leopoldo, as well as the critics of the literary journals, was well pleased. The elegant 20 *paoli*-a-volume edition was quickly followed both by a 3½ *paoli*-a-volume pocket edition and by a French translation. Although the *History* did not succeed in exalting the present regime by denigrating its predecessors, as both Gianni and Pietro Leopoldo apparently hoped it would, it did something much better. It showed that much of the new legislation had been anticipated two centuries earlier. It attributed the subsequent decline of the grand duchy to the failure of the later grand dukes to follow the lead of the first one. And it suggested that what Pietro Leopoldo was doing in the 1780s was really the fulfillment of what Cosimo I, the unmistakable hero of the *History,* had done, under less favorable circumstances, in the 1540s. Galluzzi confirmed what Lastri had pointed out seven years before: "that, whatever many people think, the population of Tuscany was much lower in the last century of the Republic than in the first century of the Principate" and that "the peace and prosperity of the sixteenth century" was largely the work of one "who without fear of flattery can be compared to Augustus." As the Georgofili then rediscovered the works of the sixteenth-century agronomers, Giovan Battista Tealdi and Bernardo Davanzati, the reigns of Cosimo I and Ferdinando I emerged as two of the great ages in Florentine history. The reforms of the 1780s turned out to be not only manifestations of an external natural law but also the culmination of a long historical process.

What law proved and history corroborated could still be brushed aside by a less well-read or an incorrectly educated successor to the throne. The prospect of having the system die with its creator became all too evident in 1778, when Pietro Leopoldo arrived in Vienna for an extended visit. He discovered that his brother Joseph was intent upon governing with methods very different from his own. He also discovered that Joseph would stop at nothing in order to impose those same methods on Tuscany, either by annexing it outright or by bringing the infant archdukes to Austria for indoctrination. He therefore began looking for some means to save his country, not from his subjects, but from his brother or his sons. He spent his spare time reading the new constitutions of Virginia and Pennsylvania. He took side trips to study the political institutions of the various parts of the Austrian Empire, those very institutions that Joseph was determined to wipe out. By the time he got back to Florence in March 1779, he thought he had found a solution. What Tuscany needed, he decided, was a written constitution. He forthwith summoned Gianni, handed him some scattered notes, and told him to get to work on a first draft.

Gianni was dumbfounded. An absolute monarchy limited by nothing but whatever "light [might be] infused into the spirit of the monarch . . . by Eternal Providence" was the only kind of government he had ever thought of. Those of his colleagues whom he consulted on the project agreed with him: a monarch reduced to the role of "a first citizen or a first magistrate" was "a dream." But as successive drafts passed back and forth between his and his monarch's desks, he gradually became converted. A representative assembly, he realized, would form a fitting complement to the new communal councils. It would funnel into the central government all the new energy that the autonomous communes were supposed to generate at the level of local government. It would prevent an enlightened monarchy from ever degenerating into a tyranny—and he took time off to scribble out a "Memorandum on Despotism" so frightening and so full of bombastic imprecations that he hid it even from his children. A constitution would guarantee to all citizens "honest social liberty in the exercise of their intellectual and personal faculties." And it would change taxes, which subjects felt justified in trying to avoid, into contributions, which citizens voluntarily imposed on themselves.

Gianni set to work on a plan to make sure that "the right of making laws resides nowhere but in the General Will." The eligible voters in the communes should elect a college in each of twenty-seven districts. Each college should then send two deputies to an annual meeting of a National Assembly. The Assembly should be empowered to discuss any matter in perfect freedom, and all of its resolutions receiving royal assent should have the force of law. Then, just to make sure that neither assembly nor monarch would ever be tempted into contradicting their own best interests, Gianni wrote all the reform legislation of the preceding fifteen years right into the first thirty-nine articles. He thus solved the problem of the longevity of this legislation by subtracting it completely from the realm of statutory law and elevating it to the rank of constitutional law.

On September 8, 1782, the final version was ready. It was the first European constitution of modern times to be written by practitioners rather than theorists of government. It was the first one to reject the traditional separation of "estates" and to recognize no other difference between "active" and "passive" citizens than the possession of property. Had it been adopted, it would certainly have received the assent of the literate classes of Florence. These classes were just then provided by one of their own ancestors, Machiavelli, with a theoretical justification for the kind of government that Pietro Leopoldo's constitution envisaged. The fabrication of a letter supposedly recounting Machiavelli's pious death freed their consciences from the warnings of the ecclesiastical censors. A long preface assured them that *The Prince* had been intended merely as a trap for despots. A bit of timely trimming from the letters of 1514 and 1515 shielded eighteenth-century Florentines from all evidence contrary to the picture of the author as a virtuous republican. And the republication of the *Discourses* more than two centuries after the promulgation of the Tridentine Index suddenly exposed them to a theory of popular participation in a "mixed" government. Florentines discovered in Machiavelli a "science of politics" capable of generating in their own country the same public spirit they had come to admire so much in contemporary America. Accordingly, on January 28, 1787, Mayor Alberto Rimbotti repaired to Santa Croce for a carefully prepared public ceremony. When he lifted the veil from Vincenzo Spinazzi's neoclassical bust and Antonio Vacca's "simple but noble" inscription, Machiavelli was finally transformed from a misunderstood skeleton in the closet into "the honor of Etruria . . . one of the greatest men Italy has ever produced."

But instead of adopting the constitution, Pietro Leopoldo tabled it. His program of fundamental reforms was still far from finished, and he knew that promulgating decrees took much less time than listening to the debates of the inexperienced voices of a still inarticulate General Will. Also, his habit of commanding was so ingrained after seventeen years of absolute rule that he shrank before the prospect of having to yield to the opinions of his former subjects. Above all, he was afraid of his brother, whose limitless ambitions had been freed of their last restraint by the death of Maria Theresa two years before. According to Joseph, the Russians had to be beaten in the game of dismembering the Ottoman Empire. The Hungarians and the Flemings had to be taught to speak German. The Venetians and the Bavarians had to be forced into helping round out the crooked frontiers of the Austrian Empire. And the Tuscans had to be made to foot some of the bill.

The first set of demands was presented the following December, when the emperor himself stopped off at Cosimo I's old hunting lodge in the Mugello. The second set was presented in the spring of 1784, when he came to inspect the grand duke's court at Pisa and Livorno. The third set was presented in June of the same year, when Joseph summoned his younger brother all the way to Vienna. Pietro Leopoldo had too many children in need of respectable positions to offer any but the feeblest opposition. He dared not even mention the constitution, which would have given away his real intention never to carry out what he had been forced to promise. He dared do nothing more than write notebooks full of pungent barbs in a code that remained unintelligible until Adam Wandruszka finally broke it in the 1960s. So Gianni locked up the constitution in a drawer. No one heard of it again for another fifteen years.

The Piecemeal Constitution.

Abandoning the constitution as a whole, however, did not prevent the constitution-makers from implementing bits and pieces of it under the disguise of ordinary legislation. The grand duke continued to solicit advice and suggestions from all interested citizens, even though they were not formally gathered in a national assembly. He turned the Accademia dei Georgofili into a semiofficial senate for economic affairs very much like the "patriotic" academy proposed by Gianni in 1793. He gradually disbanded the standing army which Gianni never stopped denouncing as a waste of money in a country where the interests of government and people were identical. And he replaced the soldiers with four "civic companies" drawn from the lists of what the constitution defined as "active citizens." After inflicting one or two spectacular defeats on the Berber pirates, and after letting neutral Tuscan ships make a good profit on the war-torn

Bristol-Livorno route, he then disbanded the navy, too, that "giant, useless, expensive machine," as Gianni called it, which served no other purpose than that of furthering the careers of the officers. He entrusted the frontiers instead to the traditional Medici policy of strict neutrality. With legal help from Lampredi, he snuffed out the two current "causes" that might possibly have enticed his subjects into dangerous adventures. He refused to establish relations with the revolutionaries in America, since to do so would surely have gotten him into trouble with his best customer, England. And, like Cosimo I before him, he avoided even the suggestion of aiding the rebels in Corsica, who were optimistically relegated to the care of "the excellent government of France" in a rather prosaic comedy put on in the fall of 1781.

At the same time, Gianni was put to work separating what the Medici had deliberately mixed up ever since the days of Lorenzo the Magnificent—the possessions of the crown and the personal possessions of the grand ducal family. He tried to save the former from the kind of spoliation that Joseph II had tried to perpetrate soon after the death of Francesco Stefano. Lampredi was put to work procuring for Tuscany what Muratori had long ago procured for Modena and what Frederick the Great had long ago promised to procure for Prussia: an organic, rational code of all civil law. Meanwhile, the various parts of the standing criminal laws that Cesare Beccaria had denounced as barbarous and use-less back in 1764 were gradually withdrawn. Finally, on December 9, 1786, a completely new criminal code was published—one which abolished torture, mutilation, confiscation, and even the death penalty; one which removed from the books all those crimes "improperly called *lèse-majesté,* invented with refined cruelty in a perverse age"; one that instituted careful legal safeguards for accused persons and witnesses as well as for convicts; and one that fully conformed to the Beccarian principle of punishment for correction rather than for vengeance.

The Tuscan jurists were well pleased, one of them because the code vindicated his attacks on Beccaria's ecclesiastical censors, another because it incorporated his arguments about the uselessness of imprisonment for debt, and still another because it at last admitted a difference in gravity between parricide and cattle-thievery. The bishop of Fiesole was delighted, and he immediately commissioned a Scolopian poet to write a pastoral poem in honor of the code. The academic orators were enthusiastic: "While foreigners admire dumbfounded a work so worthy of a philosopher-prince," one of them announced, "it is up to us to celebrate." The Accademia Fiorentina accordingly staged a formal public assembly for all the men of letters in the city. Ordinary Florentine citizens were jubilant: within three days they had oversubscribed a spontaneous appeal for an equestrian statue of Pietro Leopoldo to be erected in Piazza San Marco. "Oh times, oh customs, oh religion!" they cried (in good Florentine, needless to say, not in Ciceronian Latin). "Let us thank Providence for being born in this age and for having the masters we have." The grand duke himself was pleased, since—according to the Supreme Tribunal of Justice as well as to the far from impartial French ambassador—the crime rate dropped just as he predicted it would.

The courts began carrying out the prescriptions of the code even before the texts were published. When a certain Giuseppe Gori was acquitted of theft charges in August 1786, he was freed without bond or surety. Instead of being asked to pay the charges for his maintenance in prison, as had always been customary everywhere in Europe, he was reimbursed from the state treasury for the inconvenience his detention had caused him.

Even more important than specific legislative measures were the government's efforts to put into practice one of the basic principles of the constitution: freedom of speech. It got rid of the last remnants of ecclesiastical censorship. As early as 1769, in fact, one state official congratulated an editor for having incurred the hostility of the Holy Office. After all, he noted, "prohibited books are the ones that are most sought after and that sell for the highest prices." The government continued to maintain an office of civil censor in accordance with the law of 1743, but it turned the office over to none other than the historian Galluzzi. Although Galluzzi occasionally raised questions of taste or tact—and although he once suggested to the author of a play about Bianca Cappello that he get rid of what looked like direct references to Pietro Leopoldo's mistress—he almost never made an outright prohibition. Thus Tuscany soon came to enjoy in fact a degree of free speech far greater than that promulgated in theory by the much-heralded Austrian press law of 1781. And the edict of January 4, 1792, which finally codified the practice of the preceding decades, saved Tuscany thereafter from the repressive measures adopted by most other European states as an antidote to revolutionary propaganda.

A few Florentines were shocked by "the current liberty to write any kind of error and to spread it about with impunity." One of them blamed freedom of the press for "an infinity of troubles to state, manners, and religion"; this was the bigoted bibliophile Domenico Moreni, who saved his soul by compiling a still indispensable bibliography of local history and by donating his large library to the Riccardiana. Most Florentines fully supported the government's policy. They were now prepared to accept the responsibilities of freedom. They realized —as Lami never had—that freedom "must be exercised with prudence, not passion." They banished "exaggerated panegyrics," "ironic adulation," and "invective" to the realm of bad taste. Even Lampredi insisted that his critics be able to write whatever they pleased against his books. They discovered that freedom was both pleasant and useful. For, insisted one of them—perhaps with the famous thesis of Tacitus and Leonardo Bruni in mind—freedom alone could prevent the talent the state so badly needed from being perverted into timorous mediocrity. "To feel myself free," he said, "to be sure of being free, and to think freely, is a great good."

Best of all, Florentines discovered that freedom was profitable. It was so partly because publishers soon learned to cater to, as well as form, the tastes of their public. "You know the country well," said one successful publisher to his colleague, "and you therefore know what will be sure to sell." Magazines introduced light poems and humorous asides when their readers complained that the contents were too heavy. Big hard-cover editions were often followed by cheaper pocket-size paperbacks, like Pagani's *Youth Instructed in Practical Arithmetic* of 1780, which included a table of the weights, measures, and moneys used in all the commercial centers of Europe. The best of serious literature frequently gave way to subjects that no one would have dreamed of committing to print a generation earlier—subjects like that of the *Ladies' Encyclopedia: Work Dedicated to their Instruction and Delight,* which included "handsome colored designs" of the latest fashions and directions for using hair curlers.

Publishing houses multiplied. While Cambiagi remained the official printer to the grand duke, Antonio Benucci bought out the old Allegrini-Pisoni Company in Piazza Santa Maria in Campo in 1780. Several new firms were founded: Francesco Pagani, Francesco Bartolini in Piazza San Firenze, Rinaldo Bonini in Piazza del Duomo, Della Rovere at Santa Maria Maggiore, Giuseppe Tofani in Piazza Pitti, the Stampa della Rosa in Piazza San Giovanni, Filippo Stecchi in Via dei Tavolini. Book sellers multiplied, too, many of them doubling, as they often do still today, as paper merchants. The number of books available for purchase increased proportionately. First editions rose from an average of 500 to 1,000 copies each—which, by the way, is exactly the same number that a particularly courageous publisher in London, breaking precedent, assigned to Gibbon's *Decline and Fall* at about the same time.

Periodicals flourished even more than books. "Say what you will," insisted one editor, "periodical publications are generally useful." They reached a wholly new reading public, one composed of "those many people who do not want to build up a library of their own . . . but who would like to have access to the more practical and workable aspects of the latest discoveries." The nature of periodicals had changed considerably since the foundation of the first of them back in 1740. Some, like Angelo Faboni's *Giornale de' letterati* of Pisa and Marco Lastri's *Novelle letterarie,* continued to concentrate on critical book reviews. Others, particularly the *Gazzetta toscana* and its international counterpart, the *Gazzetta universale* (which offered joint subscriptions for the two at a considerable reduction), were much like modern newspapers. A good number of them were dedicated to special fields of interest—the *Giornale fiorentino di agricoltura, arti e commercio,* for instance, which served eighteenth-century Tuscany in much the same way that *Ventiquattr'ore* serves twentieth-century Italy. Still others were frankly almanacs, which were written "for every class of persons, including Jews" (one of them included Jewish feast days on the calendar), and which claimed to "get knowledge into the heads even of those who make a point of never reading anything." A few, finally, amounted to what today would be called popular magazines: a *Biblioteca galante,* which ran serialized stories like "A History of Ugong, Emperor of Persia," and a monthly *Giornale delle dame,* "a collection of novelettes, anecdotes, reflections, and news," which claimed that "the conversations of a lady's dressing room these days are more serious and instructive than the meetings of an academy." Occasionally these periodicals were accused of printing little but "insipid nonsense." Some of them lasted for only a few years or a few issues. But thanks to the invention of advertising and want-ads, most of them managed to make money with prices not too much higher than those of their twentieth-century counterparts, and with as few as 250 subscribers.* No one read them more avidly than Pietro Leopoldo himself, who used them as one of his chief sources of information.

At the same time the piecemeal constitution had numerous drawbacks. One of its articles, the one that banished the use of armed force, could be effective only so long as the powers of Europe found it advantageous to observe the peace of Italy. Without a navy, there was nothing the grand duke could do to prevent the War of the American Revolution from infringing upon the neutrality of Livorno; and there was not much he could do to keep the French from capturing the merchantman *Pietro Leopoldo* on the high seas. Another article, the one guaranteeing national independence, depended on the determination of Pietro Leopoldo not to drag Tuscany along with him when he succeeded his brother as emperor; as Joseph II slowly slipped into the grave, Florentines became so apprehensive that they could do nothing but build "castles in the air," one more gloomy than the other. Still other articles, those that turned legislation and defense over to at least a large minority of the citizens, depended on Pietro Leopoldo's willingness to respect the integrity of their elected or appointed leaders. And that was the one rule the grand duke could never bring himself to observe. When he was still only twenty years old, he had had the effrontery to tell wise old Pompeo Neri to his face that one of his proposals "meant nothing, amounted to nothing, and was worth nothing." By the time he was thirty-seven, he had become so skilled in the art of frightening his subordinates with unannounced inspections that none

* My calculation for prices: The *Novelle letterarie* cost 15 *paoli* a year for 52 numbers. A joint subscription to the *Gazzetta toscana* and the *Gazzetta universale* cost 18. One volume of Hugford's beautifully illustrated *Elogi de' pittori* cost 10½ *paoli*—a book of the kind that would sell at about $12 in 1970. That makes a weekly magazine come to about $16 a year and a newspaper to $9 a year, prices which, considering the relative size of circulation, are not too expensive.

of them felt secure. On May 7, 1786, for instance, he descended on the managers of the royal estates near Chiusi. On May 8 he popped in on the bishop of Cortona. After rearranging the furniture in the cathedral, interrupting classes in the seminary, and doing a tour of the hospitals, he rushed on to see what was happening at Castiglion Fiorentino. Some of his subordinates eventually learned simply to "wait until the screaming died down," as Gianni put it, realizing that his outbursts of temper never lasted very long. But most of them were so intimidated—or so frightened of what some volunteer spy might tell the grand duke as he strolled around the lobby of the Pergola listening for gossip—that they preferred to protect themselves by doing as little as possible. Thus in February 1790, when the civic companies were abolished without a word of warning or explanation, not even those officers who had dedicated ten years to the bold new experiment dared whisper a complaint.

Pietro Leopoldo seemed at times to be incapable of abiding even by his own rules. He constantly portrayed himself as a rigorous moralist, one who prescribed black dress at court, outlawed prostitution, and prohibited dice and card playing. Indeed, he set an example of civic behavior by walking to public events at the Uffizi instead of adding to the already chaotic carriage traffic. But every time he made a tour of the country, he left behind a string of violated peasant beds. While in Florence he spent most of his free nights not with his rather homely consort, who was almost always pregnant, but with Lord Cowper's wife, Lady Anne, or, after 1786, with a charming young dancer named Livia Raimondi. And Livia gladly repaid the favor by diligently doing the reading he assigned her in Thomas à Kempis, Fénelon, and a whole shelfful of Jansenist moral theologians.

Pietro Leopoldo occasionally tried to cultivate popularity by providing great crowds of all classes with endless quantities of food, wine, and dance music at all-night parties in the Boboli. He also opened the Pitti to whoever wanted to come and talk about anything, a practice one German tourist found *eben so nachahmungswerth als lobenswerth*—"as worthy of imitation as of praise." And a sign on the door warned visitors that offering a tip was as offensive as receiving one. At the same time he closed down several theaters, put an end to the age-old "Game of the Bridge" at Pisa, and made the "Baptist" in the traditional San Giovanni parade put on clothes. He constantly lectured about justice and the rule of law. He also kept a box for the deposit of anonymous accusations in Piazza Pitti, and he promised to split the fines with anyone whose accusation led to a conviction. Even free speech was gravely compromised at times. When the innocent editor of the *Giornale fiorentino* stirred the wrath of vested interests in Livorno with an unfavorable review of a Metastasio opera, he was clapped into the dungeon of Volterra without trial; his more fortunate colleague escaped the same fate only by getting across the Apennines just a few hours before the police arrived at the frontier. Almost all the theological pamphlets published in Rome in 1787 were banned under heavy penalties, as if mature Tuscan readers could not themselves identify the kind of "fanaticism, calumny, and injurious phrases" typical of the press in despotic regimes. The Tuscan author of a pamphlet critical of the bishop of Pistoia in 1788 was thrown out of the country. And the authors of the *Florentine Miscellany* found it advisable to have their unflattering references to the grand duke printed separately and pasted only into the copies sent to London. Even the mails were not always safe, or at least Lampredi did not think they were when he told his Rome correspondents to send letters only through the Genoese, never the Tuscan, post office.

Actually these infringements on civil liberty were wholly unnecessary. All

26. Casa di Livia, Piazza San Marco

the government really had to do was recognize the well-established patterns by which society itself punished its individual members for the slightest deviation —as a poor little rich girl named Giulia Tramontani found out to her sorrow in 1789. Giulia had always been kept shut up at home in preparation for her future marriage to a certain Pietro Chierici. She was therefore utterly defenseless before the first smile of one of her father's frequent houseguests, a handsome but not yet "settled" young man, named Luigi Cheluzzi. When, on March 10, Luigi dropped in to announce his immediate departure for Milan, she did not hesitate for a moment. By nightfall the couple had made it over the same road that exiles had taken for centuries, and that Gianni was to take just fourteen months later. At the Hotel San Marco in Bologna, according to the police report, Luigi "lay with the said lady in the same bed, and after many embraces and caresses finally managed to deflower, abuse, and know her carnally; and he kept her with him for the space of five hours, or, more precisely, until the time of their arrest in the said hotel on the morning of March 11." Neither Giulia's father nor the Supreme Tribunal of Justice were the least bit moved by Giulia's ardent declarations of coresponsibility: women, according to contemporary notions of sexual psychology, were supposed to be completely passive in such matters. They refused even to accept quietly what looked like the inevitable. Instead, they shut her up in a detention home and subjected her to intensive brainwashing. By mid-April she had been brought around to denouncing the marriage to Luigi she had once hoped for as "a thing cursed by heaven." And by October she had learned to write nice little notes to her arranged bridegroom, notes that were probably as sincere as they were shallow. Thus Florentine society triumphed over love. Giulia could look forward to a lifetime of respectable tedium. Pietro could look forward to a lifetime of idle opulence; for he had been bought off with the promise of a sinecure, a fully furnished apartment, a steady allowance, and all the educational expenses of any eventual offspring. And Luigi could look forward to rotting in prison, deliberately forgotten by everyone, including Pietro Leopoldo's impeccable justice officials.

The Illustrated Constitution.

The piecemeal constitution thus ran the risk of being severely compromised by its very authors, unless they could find some way of drawing attention away from its defects and on to its merits. Luckily, Florentine tradition provided excellent lessons in how to do just that. Benozzo Gozzoli had raised the family of Cosimo the Elder to the rank of Magi kings. Giorgio Vasari had eternalized the victories of Cosimo I on the walls of the Sala dei Cinquecento. And Pietro Tacca had hidden the expensive colonial ventures of Ferdinando I in the shadow of the huge equestrian statue in Piazza Santissima Annunziata. All Pietro Leopoldo needed to do, then, was to call in the artists and the poets, and the economic system would soon have been immortalized in stone, song, and color.

The moment could not have been more propitious. The beginning of the new reign had coincided with the promulgation of what everyone for the next half century took to be the absolute principles of aesthetics—principles, that is, which were held to be just as binding in the arts as the law of supply and demand was in economics. These principles had first been proposed by an Italianized Saxon named Johann Joachim Winckelmann, who was known in Florence as the cataloguer of the Baron von Stosch's gem collection as well as the author of the epoch-making *History of Art in Antiquity,* translated into Italian in 1779. The principles were then applied in practice by Winckelmann's equally Italianized compatriot, Anton Raphael Mengs. And they were then worked out in detail by the Italian art critic, Francesco Milizia.

According to the neoclassicists, as the followers of Winckelmann, Mengs, and Milizia eventually came to be called, art begins with philosophy. Nature can give only the elements of beauty, whereas the duty of an artist is to portray beauty itself by the use of true, or faithful (*verosimili*), representations. Anything that is purely ornamental or purely delightful, or anything that suggests violence, confusion, or rapid motion, must be banished. All the various styles which the neoclassicists lumped together under the pejorative title "baroque" had to give way to the new ideal of *Stille Grösse*—"Quiet Grandeur," which could be achieved only by "doing the most with the least." The artist had to begin by studying those monuments of the past in which the *Stille Grösse* had been most closely approximated: namely, the statues of the Hellenistic sculptors (which Winckelmann thought to be Hellenic) and the paintings of Raffaello (hence Meng's middle name). The artist could then set out to surpass his models. And since he could appeal, in the enlightened eighteenth century, to a kind of philosophy far superior either to the Platonism of the fourth century B.C. or the NeoPlatonism of the early sixteenth century A.D., he could be sure of following in the footsteps of Mengs, whom most critics held to have already surpassed his famous namesake.

Neoclassicism was peculiarly Roman in origin. Rome was not just one of many cities; it was still the undisputed art capital of Europe. Since this latest of Rome's stylistic innovations claimed to be more universal, more eternal, and more infallible than all its predecessors, it spread rapidly over the whole world, from the palaces of St. Petersburg to the county courthouses of Ohio. The Florentines, who had produced nothing in the way of art theory since the time of Raffaello Borghini, succumbed as rapidly as all their neighbors. By 1781 two of the four professors at the Accademia del Disegno were Romans, and a third was a Saxon—which was almost the same as being a Roman. Pietro Leopoldo had his first major portrait done in Rome by the highest paid neoclassic portrait painter of the age, Pompeo Batoni. And the Rinuccini opened their palace in September 1781 so that all their fellow citizens could come and admire the "superb drawing of the Deposition in chalk and black pencil" they had just purchased from Mengs.

Not since Cigoli went to Rome and Pietro da Cortona came back from Rome had Florence been in such danger of losing its artistic autonomy. All that Florentines could do to defend themselves, however, was to insist upon a few concessions to their national heritage and to draw attention to whatever they could find of non-neoclassic theory elsewhere in Europe. They reprinted the *Lives* of Vasari and Baldinucci. They translated the treatises of Joshua Reynolds— whose one attempt to contact Batoni in Rome was well known to have ended up in a *dialogue de sourds*. They discovered the *Treatise on Painting* by the Tuscan counter-hero to Raffaello, Leonardo da Vinci. They rescued Michelangelo from the charge of having lived too long and of thus corrupting Italian art at its height with the "mannerism" of his later works. They attributed whatever they could not but admit as defects in their heritage to the influence of "foreigners" like Luca Giordano and Salvator Rosa. Those of Mengs's unfavorable comments that could not be ignored they attributed to the author's having been sick when he wrote the last chapters of his book.

Fortunately, this campaign of self-defense was not necessarily in conflict with neoclassical theory. While exalting the works of Raffaello and the Carracci as the closest realization of their ideal, the neoclassicists never forgot their debt to archaeology. And they never failed to credit even such "corrupt" artists as Bernini and Borromini with at least technical accomplishments of lasting value. Hence the very theory that occasionally jarred Tuscans' patriotic sensitivities also encouraged them to embark on what soon turned out to be their most valuable contribution to art: the systematic restoration of their artistic heritage. They ransacked dissolved monasteries for forgotten canvases, some of which were discovered to be in a shocking state of disrepair. They denounced as a sacrilege the customary practice of touching up paintings and whitewashing over frescoes that were no longer fashionable, a practice that had most recently ruined the works of Giotto in Santa Croce and those of Pontormo in San Lorenzo. Adamo Fabbroni took time off from his experiments in wine preservation to work out a new way of cleaning oil paintings. Vincenzo Fineschi made an exact description of the lunettes in Santa Maria Novella in order to prevent their ever being altered by some future restorer. Carlo Lasinio did copper engravings of some sixty painted facades, in order at least to preserve the memory of what time was rapidly deteriorating and what the neoclassicists denounced as a ridiculous extravagance. Antonio Lumachi wrote a description of the Baptistry to commemorate its complete restoration in 1782. And when Tommaso Puccini, the head of the Royal Gallery in 1793, heard that a curate in San Casciano was about to demolish a cupola by that least Hellenic of all Florentine painters, Giovanni da San Giovanni, he curtly reminded him that "in the reign of Ferdinando III" works of art of whatever epoch "are not to be destroyed but jealously preserved." Indeed, only one historical monument was lost in the quarter-century after 1765. And it was lost only because the monks of San Pier Maggiore had so long neglected the upkeep of their church that the walls collapsed practically on the heads of the masons who were trying to repair them.

Thus the custodians of art—the museum directors and the art historians—finally managed to end their age-old servitude to the producers of art. Giuseppe Pelli Bencivenni, who succeeded Antonio Cocchi's son Raimondo as director of the Uffizi in 1775, dedicated himself completely to reorganizing the gallery according to genre and chronology. In March, 1784, with huge new glass windows along the corridors to assure adequate lighting, the gallery was opened to the public free of charge—and with a specific prohibition against tipping the guards. At the same time Pelli's colleague in the Uffizi (and Ximenes' sometime colleague in the Society of Jesus), Luigi Lanzi, dedicated himself to reorganizing the history of painting. After successfully righting the customary inversion of archaic and classical Etruscan statues, and after then visiting almost every church and gallery north of Naples (where ex-Jesuits dared not set foot), he finally came up with a new classification based on stylistic similarities. Thanks to the rapid diffusion of his *Storia pittorica d'Italia* in Italy and of William Roscoe's English translation abroad, Lanzi's classification became standard in museums and textbooks all over the world for the next century and a half.

Having been granted their independence, the museum directors were all too happy to accept the neoclassicists' aesthetic principles, which they were sure would soon engender a second Florentine Renaissance. So was Pietro Leopoldo. He filled the classrooms of the Accademia delle Belle Arti with plaster casts shipped up by sea from Civitavecchia, as can be seen in the charming little scenes that serve as *cul-de-lampes* in Lastri's book *Etruria pittrice*. He gave annual prizes to those students who best reproduced the casts in paint, managing thereby to multiply the square footage of colored canvas in Florence even faster than Vasari's academic festivals had done two centuries earlier. He commissioned his chief architect, Gaspare Paoletti, to redecorate the interior of Poggio Imperiale and to construct a new ballroom (the "Sala degli Stucchi") in the Pitti. He added a whole new wing in the Boboli, little caring, apparently, about the obvious disharmony between its delicate lines and Buontalenti's heavy masonry nearby. He had the living room of Livia's house in Piazza San Marco painted in sky blue and white trompe l'oeil, with no more than three cupids, those devils of the neoclassicists, permitted to play among the translucent clouds. More important, he had one of the most celebrated monuments of Hellenistic sculpture, the Niobe, brought up from the Villa Medici in Rome and installed under Paoletti's impeccably neoclassical ceiling in the Uffizi. But his real chance came on the night of January 28–29, 1771, when the Church of the Carmine—all of it, that is, except the Corsini and the Brancacci chapels, which are all most tourists look at today—was completely destroyed by fire. When, after twelve years of hard work by the royal architect, Zanobi Del Rosso, and after enormous expenditures by

27. Sala di Niobe, Uffizi Gallery

the grand duke and the Corsini family, the simple, motionless, monochrome interior was at last exposed to the admiration of the public, even the official orator could do nothing more than quote from Psalm 117: *A Domino factum est illud. Et est mirabile in oculis nostris.**

The victory of neoclassicism was complete, although it may have done little to alter the external appearance of the city. The heritage of the past two centuries simply could not admit such a radical departure. Hence, the basilica of San Marco was given a watered-down baroque facade, and the Carmine was left without any

* The Confraternity version may be more accurate, but it is much less moving: "By the Lord this has been done; it is wonderful in our eyes."

28. Church of the Carmine, interior

facade at all. But neoclassicism did much to alter Florentine interiors: at the Oratorians' church of San Firenze, for instance, where Zanobi Del Rosso's off-white chapel was opened in 1776, and at Palazzo Pazzi, which was completely redone in the 1780s. It did even more to alter the figures of Florentine women.

Indeed, it created a whole new ideal of feminine beauty: "long, blond hair falling over shoulders of ivory; a serene forehead unshadowed by the least trace of a cloud; placid blue eyes that come marvelously alive when she speaks . . . arms, hands, breasts, and flanks as perfectly befit a gentle matron." Teresa Pelli Fabbroni, wife of the economist Giovanni, adopted daughter of the museum director Pelli Bencivenni, close friend of the tragedian Cosimo Giotti, the poetess Corilla Olimpica, and the jurist Lampredi, was the first woman in Florentine history to organize anything like a French intellectual salon. She also inspired the first attempts since the sixteenth century to reconsider the role of women in society:

> Who is he who once condemned
> the fairer sex to servitude?
> Who gave them needle, thread, and yarn,
> who called them weak and soft of heart,
> who cast them out of higher realms
> of virtue and brave deeds?
> (Pignotti, dedication to Teresa of the 1798
> edition of his *Poesie,* p. xxi)

She was the incarnation of the new ideal. As early as 1783, when Pietro Leopoldo stood as godfather to her first child, she looked like a Thermidorian before her time. And anyone who wanted to look like her had only to call for an appointment with Giuseppe Nobili, the Roman hairdresser who opened a beauty shop in 1786 and who knew how to transform the softest Florentine head into an ancient marble bust.

Poetry was somewhat less promising than the plastic arts. It was just as "philosophic," to be sure. Or at least Carlo Gastone della Torre di Rezzonico, the leading Italian critic of the age, said it was. The editors of the *Giornale de' letterati* repeated the same opinion again and again for the benefit of their readers in Tuscany. But unlike the artists, the poets had no models. Arcadia had worn Petrarch to shreds. And the orators of the Accademia Fiorentina never managed to work up any but a historical interest in Boccaccio and Francesco Redi. When Florentine poets looked abroad for models, they found not only Pope but also Ossian, Edward Young, Thomas Gray, and other such cloudy Britons, whose works could simply not be fitted into neoclassical categories even with the help of Melchiorre Cesarotti's translations.

Only one Florentine poet succeeded in making a fortunate choice. That was Lorenzo Pignotti, the son of a ruined shoemaker in Figline Valdarno, who supported himself teaching physics and medicine while climbing up to social prominence on the shoulders of his students' parents at the Accademia dei Nobili. Pignotti took the advice of Tommaso Crudeli, his most worthy predecessor of the last generation. He put the theoreticians aside: "One of Mengs's paintings," he said, "is far more valuable than all his treatises put together." Instead, he read Aesop and La Fontaine—in between the interminable cups of coffee that endangered his health and the frequent rounds of ball playing, riding, and fencing that restored it again. He then set out to combine "the most pleasant and varied productions of the inventive fantasy" with "the most instructive and philosophical products of Reason." What actually emerged from this combination was a bookful of rhymed fables that may have instructed no one, but that delighted Teresa Fabbroni and some of her friends enough to warrant its being expanded and reprinted a half-dozen times before the end of the century.

All of Pignotti's contemporaries, however, got caught in one of three dead ends. Some of them tried to write the kind of "scientific" poetry that certain critics were constantly praising for its utility rather than for its beauty. Others of them got involved in long projects, like Raimondo Cocchi's epic poem *Luni,* that an unpoetic age was incapable of sustaining. Many of them went on pursuing the same old chimera of extemporaneous versification, particularly when one of them, Signora Maria Maddalena Morelli Fernandez of Pistoia, better known as Corilla Olimpica, received Petrarch's (and Bernardino Perfetti's) laurel crown on the Campidoglio in Rome and a formal apotheosis in the Accademia Fiorentina. Most Florentines forgot about their poets. They turned instead to 10-*soldi*-an-issue comedies and farces—to "The Second Day of Marriage," "The English Shoemaker in Rome," "The Wife of Her Husband," "A Strategem of Love," and scores of other such titles which, alas! none of the stuffy book collectors of the time ever thought worth saving for posterity.

Music, on the other hand, was much more promising. For music, according to the traveling British critic, Charles Burney, was the one field in which Italians could still "boast of a superiority over the rest of Europe." In spite of some complaints about unphilosophic poets, even the more old-fashioned music authorities agreed that "beauty in music . . . , as in painting and sculpture consists in the most difficult facility [*facile difficilissimo*] by which the simplicity of nature is imitated." Such standards were no novelty in Florence, as even the leading authority, Stefano Arteaga, admitted by paying tribute to Vincenzo Galilei. But the standards were now modified to make music, vocal as well as instrumental, independent of its setting—just what late sixteenth-century Florentines refused to permit. Thus no one blamed contemporary audiences for ignoring the lyrics that were sung on the stages, not even those critics who lamented the destruction of the dramatic and scenic elements of recent opera. No one reproached one nervous conductor who, in 1786, when Michele Neri Bondi became too sick to finish *La Locandiera,* simply lifted what he needed for the work's first performance from another score. The hero of the 1779 comedy *Discord in the Theater* stated the current position clearly: "Who cares if I clip out the recitatives and leave only the arias?" he asked. "No one has bothered to read the words for over thirty years. And if one scene no longer fits with the next, the discreet listener can easily supply whatever connection he wishes."

Since music no longer had to be justified in terms of poetry, it could now be related directly to philosophy. Hence Florentine music critics had no difficulty in adopting neoclassical terminology. They were sure that "the most severe and philosophic study" would produce in music the same "kind of beauty which is not subject to changes in time and taste" that it did in the other arts. In fact, they were sure that philosophic music had already been created. Mengs himself assured them that Arcangelo Corelli deserved the same respect as a model for musicians that Raffaello held as a model for painters. Moreover, they were happy to note that Corelli had bequeathed his music to them through his friend Giuseppe Tartini's favorite pupil, "the violinist of love," Pietro Nardini. And the soft, melodic sonatas that Nardini composed and played—as well as his carefully cultivated stage presence—continued to reduce Florentine audiences to tears at every concert for some three decades after his return to the city in 1767.

The most convincing proof of the validity of neoclassical musical theory lay in the quantity of music that was composed in its name. Florence in the late eighteenth century abounded in concerts, performers, and composers. Two opera seasons began in five different theaters every September and Epiphany. Hardly an evening passed even in Lent without at least one recital and an oratorio. And no parish pastor or major religious order dared let an important religious holiday go by without presenting a new High Mass—in spite of one bishop's vain attempt to start a premature back-to-Gregorian movement.

Music in late eighteenth-century Florence, as in all of Italy, for that matter, was a popular and commercial rather than a "court" activity. It was a business in the hands of professional musicians and managers who toured the peninsula as regularly as they crossed the Alps and who enabled Florentines to enjoy the current international favorites, Cimarosa and Paisello, almost as often as Neapolitans. But the importation of music did not dampen domestic productivity. Florentines could always count on the voice of the male soprano Giovanni Manzuoli, surnamed (rather inappropriately) *Succianoccioli*; on the violin of Nardini's favorite pupil, Luigi Campannelli; and on Eugenio Sodi's harpsichord, which could be heard clearly over a full orchestra at the Pergola. They could count on Giuseppe Moneta to write scores for operas and intermezzi, on Disma Ugolini to sell her sonatas for 6 *paoli* each at her father's chinaware store in Via Ginori, and on Vincenzo Panetai to compose instrumental works which "for their exactness and expressiveness always make music lovers desire only that he go on composing."

Florence produced one composer who eventually became one of the most acclaimed opera writers of all Europe: Luigi Cherubini, whose name is still

29. *Rustic Concert*, panel in Villa Poggio Imperiale

preserved in the title of the Florentine state conservatory. A scholarship from
Pietro Leopoldo, who much admired the Solemn Mass Cherubini had written at
the age of eighteen, enabled him to continue his formal studies in Milan. The
operas he launched at the Pergola in 1782 and 1784—*Armida e Massenzio* and
Quinto Fabio—made him famous overnight. Unfortunately for Florence, they
also brought him invitations from the most powerful monarchs of the age. In
1785 he accepted one of these invitations and never again returned to his native
city. He became head of the Italian theater and then director of the national
conservatory in Paris. By the beginning of the next century, he was the all but
absolute master of music in the whole Napoleonic empire—so absolute, indeed,
that he dared talk back even to the emperor.

Yet the most promising of all the arts was the theater. And it was so in part because neither the playwrights nor the public would put up with the rules that Milizia, Napoli Signorelli, or any of the other authorities tried to impose upon them. People were bored with Metastasio. They were tired of "Furies, Mercuries, and Plutos" and with themes that were completely irrelevant "to the manners and the thoughts of [modern] spectators." They were fed up with characters that served merely as sounding boards for monologues: "It's high time that confidants be thrown off the stage," said one of them; such devices "are just copied from the Greeks, whose way of life has nothing whatever to do with our own." They were increasingly impatient with the "unities." And they wanted the actors to stop talking in the stilted, antiquated language which was to continue to make opera librettos ridiculous for another century. Even the most conservative Tuscan critics admitted that "genius needs complete liberty in order to show its vigor," at least on the stage. Pignotti flatly declared that "if a poet has to break the rules in order to move or delight his listeners, then blame the rules, not the poet."

Most Florentine dramatists proceeded cautiously in putting into practice the freedom they claimed to have won. Pietro Bicchierai, for instance, proudly demanded the right to do anything Shakespeare had done. But he was very careful to keep the action of his *Virginia e Cloe* of 1767 within the confines of a single Roman piazza and to have the presence of a crowd only indicated by the gestures and references of the main characters. A few dramatists, however, went so far as to throw aside the orthodox unities in the name of historical accuracy. One of them annoyed his audience by using sixteenth-century speech in a sixteenth-century plot. Another—that interminable scribbler, Modesto Rastrelli—ruined an excellent subject by trying to pack all his miscellaneous scholarship into *The Death of Duke Alessandro*. Still another, Giulio Perini, proved that scholarship and art were not necessarily related when he had to try polite blackmail to get the Cocomero Company even to consider his comedy *The Women*.

But there was one Florentine dramatist who succeeded beyond all expectations: Cosimo Giotti. Blindness may have stimulated Giotti's imagination, for the rich descriptive passages in his dialogues read as if he were unsure of having any help from one of the most flourishing ancillary arts of the age, stage design. His *Massacre of the Innocents* terrified theatergoers in 1782: they were completely unprepared even for the carefully-rationed amount of violence he put before them. His *Agide, King of Sparta* kept them spellbound for nine packed performances in 1786, even though he carefully toned down the murder scene at the end; they howled so long when the curtain went down that the actors had to lift him bodily onto the stage. The audience suddenly forgot its century-old habit of chattering right through the performance—a sacrifice that one satirist thought possible only in Utopia. In *Gusman d'Almeida,* at the beginning of the next season, they were kept in a constant state of shock, as one character stabbed herself right in front of their eyes, as a Muslim proved himself to be more human and more virtuous than his Christian antagonist, and as the hero abandoned the woman he loved for the woman to whom he was bound by law and political expediency. "No one has ever before dared put [such a] terrible situation on the stage," noted the critics. They scratched their heads in wonder as the printed copies sold out immediately and a Florentine company took the production on a tour of northern Italy. After they had been held in suspense right through the last horrible scene in *The Guelphs and the Ghibellines* of 1790, it is not surprising that Florentines failed to warm to the only Italian tragedian of the age whom modern literary historians have thought worth studying: Vittorio Alfieri. For Giotti kept them electrified with at least one new breach of the neoclassic rules, and one new dip into what textbooks now call "romanticism," every other year until the turn of the century.

Florentine culture could thus offer the government all it needed to reinforce the piecemeal constitution with lasting illustrations. But the government declined the offer. Gianni, for one, was color-blind, tone-deaf, and scornful of anything not directly connected with his work. He probably agreed with one of the Georgofili's favorite economists: "Artisans leave a permanent trace of their industry. But [artists], that numerous mob of useless, frivolous, sterile consumers, live totally at the expense of society, like parasitical plants . . . on a tree." Pietro Leopoldo patronized the arts because he was expected to, because he liked to be "entertained" occasionally, and because concerts and plays gave him a chance to spy on the audience. But unlike many other heads of state, both past and future, he was utterly indifferent to the political potentialities of the arts. In 1808, after the incorporation of Tuscany into the French Empire, the Accademia delle Belle Arti was set to work doing mosaics of the emperor-king. But under Pietro Leopoldo, it was asked to paint "Tancredi Mourning Clorinda" and "Lucretia Extracting her Sword" rather than, say, "The Return of Ceres" or "The Rebirth of Commerce." The academy's magnificent, impeccably neoclassical interior (which now houses the original *David*) was permitted no other reference to the munificence of the founder than a set of grand ducal arms on the pastel ceiling.

The dramatists were treated the same way. Instead of being encouraged, they were harassed, even though some of Giotti's heroism might well have been channeled into support for one reform law or another. So were the engravers. Giovan Battista Cecchi was left to copy Giuseppe Fabrini's portraits of the grand ducal family rather than to make new ones from real life; and his copper plates ended in a purely commercial venture. Pignotti's fable "The Tiber and the Arno" showed clearly what poetry could do to serve the state:

> How joyfully I gazed, and oh, how often
> did I behold sweet Flora at my shore;

there industry did dwell, and craftsmen labored,
with mighty trade and commerce at their door. . . .

Now at last I see my joy returning;
all my wounds are healed, my wealth's recaptured.
There is he for whom Etruria's long been yearning,
there is he who Flora rules, enraptured;
Behold him: Leopold!
(Lorenzo Pignotti, *Il Tevere e l' Arno*)

And his long ode on *The Happiness of Austria and Tuscany* fulfilled the promise. But Pignotti was ignored. A year later he dropped poetry for history. By the time of his death, he had brought his five-volume *History of Tuscany* down to within three years of the time when Galluzzi's had begun. Similarly, Giuseppe Pelli's citizens' committee was all set to show that Innocenzo Spinazzi and Giovan Battista Capezzoli could do for the grand duke in stone what the master of their profession, Antonio Canova, had done for the pope. Instead of welcoming their spontaneous offer to create a statue of him, Pietro Leopoldo declared that statues were nonproductive investments. When they then submitted the "useful alternative" of a public fountain, he brusquely, and with utter disregard for the most elementary rules of public relations, ordered them to give the money they had collected back to the subscribers. Thus the one serious attempt to put the arts to work for the state ended in a wave of perfectly understandable bad feelings. Because the organizers could not bring themselves to believe a grand duke capable of such indiscreet behavior, they put the blame on one of his ministers who was rapidly becoming the scapegoat for all the defects of the regime: Gianni.

6

How Gianni tried to turn a hierarchical society into an egalitarian society

Actually, Pietro Leopoldo and Gianni may not have been entirely wrong in relegating the arts to the realm of decoration. Had they succeeded in carrying out all their other projects for consolidating the new regime, whatever embellishment the artists added would indeed have been superfluous.

The first project consisted of winning the support of public opinion abroad. That is just what Benjamin Franklin had done in 1778, to no little advantage of the nation he represented. And that is just what certain disgruntled Tuscans had tried to do in 1775, when they caused consternation at home and bewilderment elsewhere with the misleading articles they had published in French journals. The grand duke therefore made a point of receiving all the distinguished or influential foreigners who came through town, and of regaling them with lectures about the wonders of the reign. Some of his guests may have found the lectures a bit trying. But few of them failed to include the main theses in the travelogs they published when they got home. Only one of them ever scoffed openly, the grand duke's brother-in-law, King Ferdinando of Naples, who responded with a soon-famous joke about how many Tuscans preferred living in his own unenlightened domains. But Pietro Leopoldo knew very well that, except for a few worthy men like Luigi Targioni, who went there on serious business, most of his subjects resident in that paradise of patronage seekers were just the kind of unproductive hangers-on that he was happy to have off his payroll.

Fortunately, Pietro Leopoldo did not have to pursue this advertising campaign all by himself. Several of his bishops regularly sent copies of his ecclesiastical legislation to correspondents abroad. Giulio Perini wrote the article *Toscane* for the first major imitation of the *Encyclopédie* in 1783, one which finally made up for the appalling paucity of information about Tuscany in its more illustrious predecessor. The French ambassador in Florence filled his weekly dispatches with so many enthusiastic descriptions, and with such thick appendices that his superiors sometimes wondered which government he was representing. What the grand duke's voluntary collaborators may have missed was carefully filled in by Gianni in a *compte-rendu* that he published anonymously in 1787. By the time the final version of *The Government of Tuscany during the Reign of His Majesty Leopold II* came out in 1791, Florence had acquired a new international reputation. It was no longer the mother of fine arts, the guardian of good language, or even a museum of past glories. It was now the capital of a model state and the seat of a philosopher-king. Its new role would probably have been much more widely noticed had not the outbreak of the French Revolution suddenly focused the attention of all Europe exclusively on Paris.

The second project was much more audacious. It consisted of establishing a system of public education that would, to use Gianni's words, "change the manners of the entire nation in a few years." Unfortunately, none of Pietro Leopoldo's ministers or advisers had any clear idea of what to teach or how to teach it. Bishop Giuseppe Ippoliti of Cortona could find no better guides for his new seminary than Quintillian and Muratori. Paoletti's chapter on "The Necessity of Instructing the People" was too full of contradictions. Pietro Leopoldo's own "Ideas about the Organization of Schools in Tuscany" was too sketchy to be of much use. Gianni did not get around to composing his vague and verbose "Plan of National Education" until 1796. Some Florentine officials may have heard of the many pedagogical schemes that were favorite pastimes of the age of Rousseau, of Pestalozzi, of Filangieri, and—closer to home—of the Lombard economist Gian Rinaldo Carli, whose essay *On Public Schools* appeared in 1774. All of them were at least sure that elementary education was a more pressing concern than secondary or higher education, that the practical should take precedence over the theoretical, that modern languages were more useful than ancient languages, that morality and piety could be taught without recourse to theology, and that learning to sew, sow, and keep account books was far more important than learning to wage verbal battles over "abstract questions" and "the dreams of delirious philosophers."

Fortunately, one group of teachers in Florence was already prepared to meet at least some articles of this program: the Scolopians. The rector of the Scolopian school was an accomplished anatomist and a fair composer of music, as well as a Latinist. The superior of the Tuscan province was a Muratorian historian and a close friend of Lami's sometime Scolopian associate, Alessandro Politi. One of the leading professors had translated Fontenelle's *Plurality of the Worlds* as well as a whole list of French economic tracts; he had written treatises on Etruscan antiquities, practical hydraulics, and weights and measures; and he had published a long series of *Small Works of Interest to the Public and Private Good of the Agricultural Population*. Another taught French and Italian literature by using eighteenth-century rather than fourteenth- or sixteenth-century texts—a real departure from set practice; and he wrote biographies of Alberti, Magalotti, Lorenzo the Magnificent, and his own less famous contemporaries. Still another might have been "the greatest dramatist in Italy" had teaching not taken so much of his time. Two others were expert mathematicians who did not let their professional commitments prevent them from writing elementary textbooks.

In other words, the Scolopians were still as open-minded, versatile, receptive to novelty, and dedicated to teaching as their forefathers had been in the early seventeenth century. They were still as interested in looking for more effective methods; one of them, Stanislao Canovai, published some well-pondered *Reflections on Public Schools* in 1775. They still remembered that their founder had suffered as much as Galileo himself on behalf of Galilean philosophy. Then, suddenly, after 150 years of hard work and humiliation, their oldest enemies were delivered into their hands. On August 3, 1773, a grand ducal commission knocked on the door of the College of San Giovannino carrying a copy of Clement XIV's bull against the Society of Jesus and a corresponding royal decree nationalizing all its property. Every volume, every chair, every inkwell, was carefully registered. The twenty-five doddering remnants of past glories were then informed that they would have to move out by the end of the day. Several months later the Scolopians were invited to take their place.

The victors were wise enough to avoid being vindictive. As Pietro Leopoldo, almost alone among Catholic monarchs, gave the ex-Jesuits pensions, freedom, and even an occasional job, so the Scolopians reinstalled the most able of them, the canal-builder Ximenes, in his former apartment. They could afford to be charitable. With 596 out of a total of 935 Florentine students registered in their schools, they were now in a position to dominate secondary education in Florence. Through the public recitals, orations, and oratorios that they put on with even more pomp than the Jesuits had in the days of Giovan Battista Fagiuoli, they were also in a position to influence, or at least to provide political, moral, and economic precepts for, a much wider public.

What the Scolopians could not do was to carry out the functions their founders had assigned to them. As heirs of the Jesuits, they had also fallen heir to the Jesuits' class preferences. Once they had moved into the pleasant realm of tuition-paying students, they decided to concentrate their resources exclusively on turning the sons of doctors and landlords into other doctors and landlords. Yet the health of the state now required that silkworkers and peasants be educated as well, whatever some Physiocrats might have said about the economic advantages of illiterate farmhands. At least these farmhands had to be turned into "honest and useful citizens," fortified against the temptations of idleness and delinquency, made receptive to technical improvements in their respective occupations, and given a sense of the moral as well as the economic value of their work. Several organizations spontaneously offered their services. The Third Order Franciscans of Figline opened a free "school for domestic education" in 1778 with funds from an unexpected inheritance and with a timely donation from

Antonio Serristori, the future president of the Regency Council. The Georgofili invited proposals on how best to establish an "agrarian school for country children" as well as a center for the training of veterinarians. Ferdinando Paoletti put into practice at Villamagna the ideas he had borrowed from that Lycurgus of contemporary pedagogy, Antonio Genovesi. Many of his fellow parish priests conscientiously followed Paoletti's example.

Still, the main burden fell on the state, in accordance with Giovanni Fabbroni's formula: "It is in society's own best interest to assume the responsibility for educating those whose parents alone cannot bring them up as useful and operative citizens." The state therefore founded "Schools of San Leopoldo" in each of the four quarters of Florence and in all the major cities of the grand duchy. By 1782 several hundred poor children were duly attending classes in Corso de' Tintori, in the former hospital of San Paolo, and in the former convent of San Salvatore. They were being regularly instructed in writing, *abbaco,* knitting, spinning, and the catechism.

But the state could not afford to maintain all the schools, even though teachers cost as little as 27 *scudi* a year (less than a third of the ordinary starting salary at the university), and even though it specifically earmarked for education the properties confiscated from some of the dissolved monasteries and confraternities. It therefore resorted to various expedients, like turning convents into teaching "conservatories" and making the communes foot the bill for lay schools. No one ever asked whether monks and nuns were necessarily good teachers; and the fact that two-thirds of the convents elected to adopt strict closure indicates, instead, that some of them had doubts about the vocation the state suggested to them. No one ever figured out how actually to turn seminaries into normal schools. And no one, not even in that statistics-conscious age, ever bothered to collect figures on just how many future citizens actually benefited from the bold schemes designed for them.

The third project was the most audacious of all. It consisted of rescrambling the traditional social classes and of creating another class more directly tied to the regime. Tuscany had never known anything like the tripartite division of nobility, clergy, and third estate that prevailed in much of northern Europe, or anything like the feudal, curial, and forensic classes of southern Italy. The Medici grand dukes had carefully prevented either of the two groups that provided its chief support—the Florentine patriciate and the bureaucracy—from ever developing a sense of corporate identity. Neither these groups, nor the three classes defined as privileged by the law of 1750 (patricians, nobles, and citizens), ever enjoyed what constituted the most meaningful privilege of the nobility in other countries: tax exemption. And the "notwithstanding" clauses introduced into all the fiscal laws of the late eighteenth century made sure they would never enjoy it in the future.

Pietro Leopoldo was convinced that even the shadow of a nobility was antisocial and uneconomic. Most of his more vocal subjects agreed with him. While
insisting that economic equality was a "chimera," they found any infringement
upon "the greatest possible equality" in the way each individual was treated to be
wholly incompatible with the spirit of "this philosophic century." They accordingly banished from biographies and academic eulogies the genealogical
introductions that had been considered indispensable since the days of Scipione
Ammirato. If they referred at all to the "smoke-stained images" in someone's
family gallery, it was only to show what obstacles he had had to overcome in
order to develop fully as an individual.

Pompeo Neri had long before insisted that talent, not birth, was the sole
characteristic of a "natural" nobility. Gianni added one more: work; that is,
making a positive contribution to the material or cultural prosperity of the country.
Thus Pietro Leopoldo had little trouble getting rid of the external signs of the
legal or traditional nobility. Elegant and ostentatious clothing was barred from
all public offices. Genuflecting and hand kissing were prohibited in court
ceremonials. Shopkeepers were forbidden to advance any more than short-term
credit to expectant heirs. Household heads were held strictly accountable if they
browbeat or underpaid their dependents. With the dissolution of the republican
magistracies, the abolition of perpetual trusts, and the requirement of a doctorate
for nomination to all higher ecclesiastical offices, the Florentine patriciate was
left with just two "privileges": a separate ballot box in municipal elections and
the right to send children to the Accademia dei Nobili. Hence the purely honorary
title of *senatore,* which Gianni earned in 1761, came to be more highly regarded,
even after the dissolution of the Senate, than the mock-feudal title of *marchese,*
which Gianni's former superior Serristori had acquired only by the accident of
birth. Patricians were left with a choice between falling into the category of the
"idle," along with beggars and the unemployed, and redefining themselves as
agriculturalists. By the 1780s the real class structure of Tuscany had come to
resemble fairly closely the one described by Gianni on the basis of occupation:
landowners, farm workers, merchants and manufacturers, and industrial or
commercial employees.

This initial rescrambling had no sooner gotten under way, however, than it
began to show signs of instability. Only the first of the four occupational classes
was in a position to take full advantage of the free-trade laws. It alone, therefore,
could accumulate the capital necessary to take advantage of the transfer of
property from the public or semipublic to the private domain. It thus threatened
to gobble up the other three classes; and those whom the removal of all restrictions
on property ownership had already made the absolute masters of half the land in
Tuscany threatened to become masters of all of it.

According to some members of the Georgofili and to several of the grand
duke's closest advisers, that was exactly what ought to have happened. Agricultural

productivity was proportionate to capital investment, as all good Physiocrats knew. Hence as much land as possible should be owned by those capable of making the necessary investments. *Latifundia* would be the salvation of Tuscany, whatever some crabby Romans had said about it sixteen unenlightened centuries before. Unfortunately, this argument ran head-on into another economic principle that had come to enjoy the status of an axiom: productivity was proportionate to the proximity of ownership and operation. Self-interest, said the anti-Physiocrats, impels the owner of a house to make repairs that a tenant neglects. And, they pointed out, large landownership generally encouraged absentee ownership, which had already been as much the ruin of modern Tuscany as it had of ancient Italy. The Physiocratic argument also ran head-on into the pastoral preoccupations of certain Muratori-reading ecclesiastics, most notably Bishop Ippoliti. Old Testament in hand, Ippoliti issued a severe warning. Either the present sharecropping contracts would be modified, he proclaimed, or God would send the Assyrians to avenge the wrongs inflicted on the starving, humiliated peasants who were bound by them.

Something, then, had to be done to improve the relative position of those whom Fabbroni called "the most valuable and most praiseworthy part of society." The only solution Ippoliti could think of was an appeal to the moral conscience of the landowner. But the landowners had a good answer for him: property comes before piety. And they actually managed to push a bill across the grand duke's desk decreasing by nine months the waiting period required after a cancellation of contract. A somewhat more practical, even though very limited, solution was to get rid of the extra obligations, in kind or labor, that were still imposed on tenants after the laws of 1578 and 1580. By 1786, when road repair was turned over to the communes, the last of them finally vanished.

Gianni had a still better solution: turn the sharecroppers into landowners. They would then work harder, since their industry would benefit their heirs, not some unknown successor on their temporary plot of land. They would become eligible for election to the municipal councils and would thus be able to prevent the kind of legal violence that occurred when the proprietors in the commune of Bientina, now fully in control, grabbed all the rights enjoyed by the nonproprietors before the implementation of the local government reform. Above all, peasant-owners would provide a solid, numerous, and eternally grateful power base to which the grand duke could turn for support whenever he got into a quarrel with one of the other classes.

Gianni knew very well that none of the peasants of Tuscany would ever be able to buy land or even to obtain a guarantor for future payment. But he also knew that neither the state nor any of the communal or charitable institutions under its control could afford to give the land to them outright. He therefore proposed refurbishing a kind of half-tenancy, half-ownership contract that had been used off and on since the Middle Ages, particularly in lands newly brought under cultivation: the *livello*. The recipient would make an initial payment equal to one year's estimated income and agree to pay a fixed annual rent thereafter. In return, he would receive complete freedom to cultivate the land as he pleased and to sell it or pass it on to his heirs in perpetuity.

This proposal found some favorable response from the beginning. Sallustio Bandini and Giulio Rucellai, among others, had already suggested extending *livello* contracts to all ecclesiastical properties. The Austrian reformer Joseph von Sonnenfels was just then suggesting the use of a similar contract as a way of alleviating the particularly depressed conditions of the peasants in Bohemia. As early as 1767 Gianni had noticed that the *livello* farms in the Pisan plain looked more prosperous than the sharecropper farms. In 1769 he was given an opportunity to put *livello* contracts more widely into operation on the lands belonging to the Hospital of San Bonifazio. Within two years he had persuaded the grand duke to make them obligatory on many of the royal estates as well. "Land in the hands of those who work it," he insisted, "is usually the best cultivated." It is the duty of the government, added one of his sympathizers, "to sustain the weakest classes of society, in which are to be found the persons most useful to [the state]."

Unfortunately, Gianni's plan soon ran into serious obstacles. Well-to-do landlords found that they could easily outbid peasants at the auctions, even when bidding instructions specifically favored the current sharecroppers. And they found that residency requirements for bidding could easily be circumvented either by bribery or by being a relative of the auctioneer. Whenever they could get a whole estate, rather than single farms, put up in block, they needed to worry only about a possible repetition of what happened when the Bardi family obtained the *livello* for all the forest land around Montemurlo: the enraged residents marched into the forest and tore it down. And if none of these subterfuges worked, the present landlords could always keep peasants away from the auctions by threats of physical violence.

At the same time, opposition to *livello* contracts continued to mount. The charitable organizations were apprehensive about being stuck forever with artificially low rents. Communal officials were unhappy about not being able to get rid of unproductive tenants. Treasury officials insisted that sale alone could provide the income they needed to liquidate the state debt. And the Physiocrats in the Georgofili, most notably the monetary expert Pagnini and the future regent Serristori, were horrified by what was obviously a bastardization of the concept of private property. Even Gianni had eventually to admit that his goals were more social than economic, that increasing productivity and maintaining hospitals was less important than "freeing cultivators from every kind of slavery." And the kind of slavery he was talking about, the kind that kept sharecroppers' incomes low enough to maintain a constant pool of cheap day-labor, was just what the big landlords needed to operate their rationalized, moneymaking agricultural enterprises.

More unfortunately still, the peasants themselves failed to live up to Gianni's image of them. Except in a few cases where groups of them took the initiative in demanding *livelli,* and except in a few other cases where a number of them had already managed to achieve a certain level of prosperity, most peasants were unprepared to take what was offered them and even less prepared to keep what they had taken. By 1779, only 30 percent of the Bonifazio *livelli* were still in the hands of peasants; by 1794 the percentage had sunk to 22. Cut off from the direction of a large landowner capable of coordinating production with demand, and unassisted by anything like the cooperatives and farm banks that have made peasant proprietorship profitable in modern Japan and Mexico, the new peasant half-proprietors were soon caught again in what had always been the heaviest chain around their necks: debt. They thus sold their *livelli* to whoever could bail them out—in the Bonifazio case, 38.52 percent of the *livelli* were sold to local merchants and professionals and 14.8 percent to "nobles." And the peasants sank back into the category of sharecroppers.

The fault was partially that of Gianni and his partisans. With all the statistical surveys they conducted year in and year out, none of them ever bothered to ask the peasants themselves what they wanted. But the fault was mostly that of all their ancestors for the preceding six centuries, who had systematically cultivated a prejudice against those it suited them to exploit. Even Paoletti, that Tuscan *ami des hommes,* confessed that his loving peasants were hopelessly ignorant, slothful, and stubborn; and he could see no other way of promoting their own best interests than keeping them under the vigilant eye of a gentleman supervisor. Even Marco Lastri, the one man of letters who thought seriously about how to make scientific information available to the illiterate, wrote his periodical "Peasants' Almanach" (*Lunario per i contadini della Toscana*) in such a condescending style that no peasant could have had it read to him without being offended— particularly if he were a Tuscan. Finally, even Gianni, for all his convictions about the eventual political and economic role of peasants, shrank back from any measure that might have made him associate with them as equals. The peasantry was glorious. But peasants were pretty grubby. Having been consistently treated as such for so long, they themselves had come to share the judgment.

To some extent, then, the bishop of Cortona was right. A moral and spiritual regeneration would have to precede an economic and political regeneration. Since neither the landlords, nor the bureaucrats, nor the technicians in the Georgofili were able to initiate such a regeneration, there was no choice but to enlist the assistance of the only category of educated persons whom the peasants would listen to with respect, or at least with deference: the clergy.

7

How Gianni tried to keep a civil society from turning into a theocracy

In the first years of Pietro Leopoldo's reign, the possibility that the clergy might collaborate in the regeneration of the peasantry seemed fairly bright. Lami's exhortations and Muratori's tracts had succeeded in producing a number of conscientious curates, men like Giovan Battista Landeschi, the "rustic Socrates" of San Miniato, whose learning might have won him a life of scholarly ease, but who chose instead to "live solely for the care of his people." One of these new curates invented a farm house that provided twice the comfort at a third of the price. Another figured out how to build roads in the Casentino less expensively with paid than with conscript labor. One translated St. Bernard's sermons "as food for the piety of the faithful." Another defied all current language authorities by writing a version of *The Imitation of Christ* in the spoken idiom of his un-schooled parishioners. Still another persuaded the citizens of San Marcello Pistoiese to pool their traditional doles in a "community chest," thus providing a more effective and less humiliating form of relief for the poor. And both the provost of San Lorenzo in Florence and his assistant, later the rector of the university, spent up to half of each day visiting the sick and counselling the healthy among the thirteen thousand souls assigned to their care.

Thus the parish, after centuries of eclipse, seemed to be on the verge of revival as the center of Florentine religious life. This revival was facilitated by several recent manuals of popular piety—for instance, Geremia da Vernazza's *Pastor's Diary,* with sermon suggestions for each day of the year, and Pierre Étienne Gourlin's *Catechism,* which avoided the failings while emphasizing the merits of its controversial predecessor, the catechism of François-Philippe Mésenguy. This revival was also supported by the government, or at least by Giulio Rucellai, who stayed on as minister for ecclesiastical affairs during the first decade of Pietro Leopoldo's reign. Many of Rucellai's measures, to be sure, were of little pastoral significance, except insofar as they got rid of embarrassing abuses and protected the pastors from outside annoyances. The right of asylum was at last abolished, and the royal *exequatur*—a sort of civil censorship on all decrees emanating from Rome—was reestablished. The monastic prisons were closed. Exempted institutions were once again placed under episcopal jurisdiction. Ordination examinations were made stiffer. The Florentine Holy Office, or what was left of it after the Crudeli affair, was formally abolished in 1782. The office of the nuncio was reduced, with all possible deference to the person of the very respected nuncio, to the rank of an ordinary embassy.

But other measures were of immediate importance to the parish pastors. Both the new "companies of charity," which replaced the old confraternities, and the new "conservatories," into which many of the former convents had been transformed, were made directly dependent upon the parishes in which they were located. Even the units of the civic guard were not permitted to elect a chaplain without the consent of the local pastor. Hermits, those age-old profiteers of rural ignorance and superstition, were outlawed. Preaching missions, those hysterical interruptions in normal community routine, were subjected to strict controls. The bishops were requested to remind their clergy of "the obligation to instruct the people in Christian doctrine" and to avoid rhetorical displays that no one but specialists could understand. And "all those things which are meant more for exhibition and pomp than for edification" were strongly discouraged, especially if they siphoned off money from more productive investments.

In other words, the liturgical, scriptural, community-centered piety so fiercely fought for a generation earlier had now received official backing. That it was backed by Palazzo Pitti rather than by the Vatican seemed to disturb no one. In its religious and ecclesiastical aspects, it amounted to little more than a belated application of the reform decrees of the Council of Trent—so much so, indeed, that the Vatican itself had difficulty finding valid theological objections to measures it opposed for nontheological reasons. In its jurisdictional aspects, it was no different from what had already been put into practice in Naples and Venice, and it was considerably milder than what was soon to be put into practice in the Austrian Empire.

Moreover, no one any longer had illusions about the ability or desire of the Church of Rome to do anything but hamstring the efforts of local churches to reform themselves. It had too long been bogged down in civil wars between Jansenists and Jesuits, Augustinians and Molinists, Constitutionalists and Appelants. It had gotten still further bogged down of late in a hopeless and not very convincing struggle against what it defined as modern philosophy. After the dissolution of the Society of Jesus, after the wholly gratuitous persecution of the last Jesuit general, and after the humiliating pilgrimage of Pope Pius VI to Vienna, the Papacy had lost much of its remaining prestige. With a spendthrift antiquarian as pope, with well-paid agents of the great powers as cardinals, and with once-proud religious orders rapidly sinking into quarrelsome immobility, the Church of Rome could offer nothing comparable to the well-published image of a prudish, puritanical grand duke washing the feet of twelve poor men in the presence of the entire court. "The services of our holy religion being above all else in the heart of our most pious sovereign . . . ."

Although they were often strained, then, relations between Rome and Florence did not break. Pope Clement XIV was considered something of a hero by the Tuscan reformers. Pope Pius VI was praised as "a wise prince" even by ardent anticurialists. Both popes were often more willing to cooperate than to veto; this is what happened, for example, in the case of the double benefices brought to their attention by "our most beloved son in Christ . . ." in 1775. In return, Pietro Leopoldo was often willing to yield, at least in matters of practice. In 1776 he agreed to close down the rather strident monthly magazine, the *Gazzetta ecclesiastica*. In 1780 he listed so many tiny questions that might still be forwarded to Rome for decision that the bigger questions, including his right to have made such a list in the first place, were momentarily overlooked.

Finally, in 1781, Pietro Leopoldo nominated an archbishop whom the new pastors considered a perfect incarnation of all their models, and one whom the pope had already found worthy of another episcopal see in northern Italy. Antonio Martini was as ugly in appearance as he was serious and sympathetic in tempera- ment: a gigantic nose, staring eyes, a long pointed chin, and a blanket of short frizzy hair. A former disciple of Lami and a good friend of Lami's friends in Rome, he had spent the previous fifteen years of his life on a benefice from the king of Sardinia, working on the first official Italian translation of the Bible. He did not intend his work as a delight to scholars, even though he enlisted the help of many of them on difficult passages in Hebrew and Greek. He intended it rather as a way of "spreading among all [the people] . . . the principles of true piety," of protecting them against "the arrogant impiety of so many current books that alter and shake their faith," and of wiping out the remnants of what Lami had identified as the root of all religious error: the thesis that doctrine can be derived as well from "natural reason" as from revelation.

Martini knew how to steer clear of extremes. He placated his opponents by printing the Latin text opposite the Italian in the first edition; it was Marco Lastri of the *Novelle letterarie,* who, without Martini's consent and against his wishes, took the Latin out of the second edition printed in Florence. He padded his pages with well-accepted Patristic interpretations, which Lastri melted down for fear that boredom would overcome the readers before they got beyond Genesis. And he appealed, successfully, to the bull of Benedict XIV of 1757 and to Pope Pius VI himself whenever Holy Office bureaucrats tried to delay the appearance of each successive volume.

But he was firm when it came to scholarship. He had Michelangelo Buonarroti's dictionary-play *La fiera* to back him up on questions of Italian vocabulary. He kept a copy of the appropriate Tridentine decree ready to show to whoever might object to his deviations from the Vulgate. He gave full backing to the state-directed reform of the Tuscan church in weekly sermons carefully patterned on those of St. Augustine. "Concentrate all your efforts and your works of charity in your parish church," he exhorted his listeners, while reserving to himself the right to absolve any of them who ventured to attend Masses in other churches for more than three Sundays in a row. Remember that all the Jews, he added, and not just a few prophets, were specially chosen by God; anyone who molests them interferes with God's plan to have them regenerate the church sometime in the future. All Christians, he insisted, not just monks and canonized saints, are "the sons and heirs of Grace . . . and brothers and coworkers in the service of souls." The way to sanctity lies not in spectacles but in the command of Paul: "imitate me as I imitate Christ."

Yet even as Martini was speaking, the ecclesiastical reform program was running into trouble. The new pastors themselves were never quite able to accept the thesis that Paul IV, Pius V, Roberto Bellarmino, and their own St. Augustine had vehemently rejected: that a civil society could also be a just society. Even Martini, for all his praise of "the new regulations of our august sovereign," gave one of the pastors a stern reprimand for reporting a criminal to the police instead of smoothing over his crime in the secret of the confessional. Also, the kind of unliturgical, unscriptural, and purely individualistic piety that they thought had been buried kept coming back to life. Someone in Siena let it be known that he had figured out a mathematically infallible formula for calculating the relation between numbers of days in Purgatory and numbers of Ave Marias on earth. Someone in Florence "opened up Purgatory" altogether "to the piety of the living." Someone else put up posters about a stairway that rewarded whoever crawled up it with countless indulgences. Still others put on "pious functions" in their own houses or even in front of street-corner shrines "in order to attract a crowd."

The most successful counterattack on neo-Tridentine piety came from abroad. The cult of the Sacred Heart had been launched almost a century earlier by an English convert to Catholicism and by a French mystic. It had then spread across northern Europe as far as Poland. Finally, in the 1770s, it had begun to penetrate Italy, in spite of the stern disapproval of Pope Clement XIV. Even the opponents of ecclesiastical reform in Tuscany declared it to be "more worthy of the fanatical and superstitious centuries than of our own." But when certain Dominicans and Servites realized that it might be effective in winning back some of the moral and financial support that Pietro Leopoldo and Martini were channeling into the parishes, nothing could prevail against the cult, neither the threat of fines nor constant declamations against "a spirit of vanity totally opposed to the true maxims of religion."

Even one of Lami's most faithful cultural heirs, a bookish monk with the curious religious name of Ildefonso di San Luigi, fell victim to what his archival research should have revealed to him as an anachronism. The result was a miracle-studded life of the latest candidate for canonization which, except for the date on the title page, could have been written much more easily in 1673 than in 1773. A girl named Teresa Margherita Redi, it seems, born in 1747, had thrown out her dolls before she was six years old and had closed herself in her room with toy altars and homemade icons. She dispensed with a mattress as soon as her parents got her into the blue-blood convent of the Florentine Carmelites. There she began showing an immense "love for the poor," not by associating with any of them—God forbid!—but by talking constantly with her guardian angel and by "exciting her pious and generous father" to spend in alms what was left after paying her dowry. She then started showing an immense love for her fellow nuns, all of whom still bore just as aristocratic surnames as their predecessors had in the days of Maria Maddalena de' Pazzi. And she did so not by talking to them, for she "always walked about with her head modestly bowed," but by getting the Blessed Virgin to cure their sore feet and headaches. Best of all, she died at the age of twenty-three. Her crucifix, pieces of her habit, and dead flowers from her grave worked some forty-one documented miracles in less than three years. "The news of these incredible feats deeply moved the whole people of Florence and Tuscany," noted her biographer. It also contributed effectively to building up the hysteria that was to burst forth in the image-veil riots of 1787 and 1790.

All these spectacular reversals made it possible for Pietro Leopoldo's enemies in Rome to step up their pressure in Tuscany. Much as Pius VI tried to steer an even course, the Curia could not long overlook a decree that banned the payment of ecclesiastical taxes outside the country. It condemned the new catechism in 1781, and it secured the appointment of a new master of the sacred palace who was all the more intransigent for having once been one of Lami's followers. At the same time Pietro Leopoldo began reading books on theology as well as books on political economy. One of the books he picked up—a manual for pious princes written by a French Jansenist in the 1720s—convinced him that his obligation for his subjects' eternal salvation was even more important than his obligation for their material well-being. He thus came to think of himself as an "external bishop." With a vigor equal to that of the Holy Office of yore, he prescribed textbooks for the clergy, banned what he considered to be unorthodox titles from seminary and convent libraries, seized all the patronage rights of the communes and parishes, and paid the Companies of Charity to carry out the projects he himself assigned to them. He thus proclaimed that citizen participation was as undesirable in ecclesiastical affairs as it was desirable in civil affairs. For unlike the general will, which was common to all, theological verities were communicated to one man alone.

Thus jurisdictionalism—the policy by which the state was separated from the church—gave way to a kind of Caesaropapism—a policy by which the church was absorbed into the head of the state. That was a policy that Martini, tolerant and tactful though he was, found difficult to accept. Hence, Pietro Leopoldo had to look around for another clerical collaborator. He soon found one in the person of the new bishop of Pistoia and Prato, Scipione de' Ricci. Ricci had also been a disciple of Lami in his youth, and had been brought up under the guidance of Bottari and Foggini in Rome. He had been slow to take sides on current theological issues, partly because he happened to be the nephew of the last general of the Society of Jesus and was charged, in the months after the dissolution, with trying to get his unfortunate uncle out of jail. Even as an assistant to Martini's aging predecessor in the late 1770s he had kept fairly quiet. He ably avoided what might have been the first storm of his career by getting the archbishop himself to read the works of Machiavelli that some of his friends were editing, prohibitions notwithstanding. But all along Ricci was gazing with fascination at the last flickers of French and Dutch Jansenism. As soon as he discovered how far reality in his new diocese differed from the ideal described in his theology books— in spite of the noble efforts of his predecessors—he let the possible become hopelessly mixed up with the desirable. He resurrected for Pistoia Florence's long-forgotten role as the New Jerusalem of Italy. He also resurrected the original prophet of the New Jerusalem: "a man of pure and inviolate faith, of innocent zeal, of lively intelligence and the purest morals, a man capable of prescribing extreme remedies for extreme ills," namely, Girolamo Savonarola. Two centuries after Archbishop Alessandro de' Medici had erased him, Savonarola, the patron saint of Ricci's saintly ancestor, Caterina, was restored to his place on the calendar, thanks in part to an eloquent *Apologia* published in Florence in 1782.

Many of Ricci's measures left their victims defenseless, particularly those who all too obviously had nothing to defend but their own "interests and comfort." The Dominican confessors were indeed misbehaving in the convents of Santa Lucia and Santa Caterina, and not even a rather poorly engineered miracle could save them from expulsion. The veneration of images and the devotion of the *Via Crucis* really were full of superstition, however sound they may have been in theory. And the Roman Breviary really did contain numerous historical errors, as Muratori had pointed out four decades before.

Translating parts of the Mass into Italian was only a continuation of the policy of Ricci's predecessor, who had authorized vernacular versions of the Psalms, the Ave, and the Pater, although having laymen read the Passion was perhaps an unwarranted anticipation of the late twentieth century. Even what Ricci envisaged as the main instrument of reform, the diocesan synod, was so impeccably Tridentine that the pope himself could raise no more valid objection than its "inopportuneness."

But Ricci insisted upon backing up his measures with a flood of translations from authors either condemned or suspect at Rome. He insisted upon throwing out *all* the regular clergy, not just the offensive ones. He insisted upon banning all the devotions, even those which centuries of practice had proved to be innocent at the best and harmless at the worst. He took Gregory VII, Pius V, and all the other authors he did not like out of the Breviary and put in others who had never been recognized by any constituted authority. He closed chapels, demolished altars, transferred parishes, confiscated endowments, and moved clergy from one job to another without even informing the persons involved beforehand. He forbade "uniting Christ with Belial" during the only time of the year when most of his flock could interrupt their dreary routines: he told them "to work even harder ... during these noisy days [of Carnival] and thus offer their bodily fatigue as reparation for their sins." He did all this without consulting his metropolitan, his fellow bishops, or the Roman Curia. In fact the only people he consulted on anything were a few faithful correspondents abroad. Even his priests, whom he constantly exalted as the foundation of the church, were told to be quiet and listen when he brought in theologians from Pavia to tell them what to talk about. Thus when his famous diocesan synod finally met in 1786, it made the still more famous synods of Carlo Borromeo in Counter-Reformation Milan seem like democratic free-for-alls in comparison.

Meanwhile the polemics became more and more acrimonious. Ricci's organ, the *Annali ecclesiastici,* blasted away at dissent at home and at opposition abroad. It turned Rome into Babylon, the Roman Curia into "the soul of intrigue [against] the most precious truths of religion," and Ricci himself into a "lamp in the sanctuary" and an "ornament of the Church of God." The anti-Ricci *Giornale ecclesiastico,* founded in Rome in 1785, answered in kind, with a lead article marked "Pistoia" at the beginning of almost every issue. As hostility mounted, the Riccians became increasingly convinced that the center of Christianity had become hopelessly corrupt. To protect themselves, they dipped freely into recent episcopalian and presbyterian doctrine to prove that each diocese, or at least each national group of dioceses, was completely self-sufficient; that all the bishops, and not just the *primus inter pares,* were equally vicars of Christ; and that the reform of the universal church should proceed from diocesan to national synods and to an elected ecumenical council much like the one Savonarola had called for in the days of Alexander VI. Since Rome refused to cooperate in such a venture, the Riccians were forced to turn for protection to their prince. And since Pietro Leopoldo seemed disposed to reassume the Emperor Constantine's office as convenor of the clergy, they started pushing the Tuscan Church down the path already trod by Ricci's friends in the schismatic Church of Utrecht.

That was the point where Gianni began to back out. First of all, it was perfectly clear that the Riccians were not at all interested in political economy, constitutional monarchy, peace, or prosperity. In fact, they were violently opposed to anything that distracted the minds of the faithful from the pursuit of salvation. Horace, they said, was "dishonest." Bayle's *Dictionary* was "a monstrous collection of obscenities." Lessing wrote nothing but "impudence that nauseates even the least delicate stomachs." Anyone who read any of the "novels, stories, and fables, overgrown with dreams, scandals, and impiety" that poured across the Alps from France was sure to lose his soul.

Second, the Riccians threatened to hit at the very core of the regime by preempting all the revenues from the suppressed ecclesiastical institutions in the dioceses they controlled. In theory they may have been right. But in fact such property had always fallen within the jurisdiction of the state. And Gianni had not the slightest intention of letting it go. "Until now we have heard nothing but the purity of religion, the correctness of doctrine, and the restoration of discipline," he remarked ironically. "Now all we hear about is temporal interests, material goods, money, and authority." By taking sides in a quarrel of clerics, he insisted, the government had made those it favored seem incapable of defending themselves. It was now threatening to let the entire system of political and economic legislation he had worked so hard to construct be torn apart in a civil war over issues that were trivial and irrelevant. Pistoia had poisoned Florence in the days of Dante with its factions of Blacks and Whites. It was now on the verge of destroying it altogether with an army of ravenous Jesuits and a horde of barbarous Jansenists.

Meanwhile, Pietro Leopoldo had come to a similar conclusion. Instead of going along with Ricci's plan for other diocesan synods, he convoked all the bishops of Tuscany to a meeting at the capital on April 24, 1787. He then sauntered out of town and let Lampredi, lawyer turned theologian for the occasion, smash down the Riccians with his forensic oratory until they were reduced to a minority of three. Official state policy thus reverted from Caesaropapism to jurisdictionalism. And Pietro Leopoldo stopped up his ears to Ricci's incessant and idolatrous petitions. So did many of his subjects, who, unable "to laugh over our wounds," tried to draw "a thick veil over an event that will always be shameful to the human spirit . . . and to Tuscany." After all, wrote Paoletti to a friend, veterinary science "is much more useful and interesting than Jansenism. *Addio!*"

But the damage had been done. The bishop of Montepulciano had been pitted against the archbishop of Florence, who was suspected of Jesuitism for having gone along with the pope's permission to eat eggs and cheese in Lent. Martini had consequently become distrustful of any further ecclesiastical reform. Ministers were pitted against ministers, bureaucrats against bureaucrats, the librarian of the Riccardiana against the librarian of the Magliabechiana. Galluzzi was called a Jansenist, Lastri a "mundane theologian," Francesco Fontani "an

astute B . . . ,* a Jesuit at heart," and Lampredi a sellout to the Court of Rome—
which, by the way, his secret correspondence shows him most certainly to have
been. Everyone put the blame on Gianni, who was incorrectly credited with
being able to govern the grand duke, and hence with having provoked the
whole crisis in the first place.

Just at a time, then, when it might have served the cause of social progress,
the clergy were too busy fighting among themselves to serve anyone. Hence, the
livello program was quietly scrapped, leaving behind a few fortunate worker-
tenants who had managed to survive the first years, and adding hundreds and
hundreds of hectares to the big estates, which were to dominate most of Tuscany
for another century and a half. Gianni's plan of bringing the peasantry into the
body politic was forgotten; it remained a dead letter until the civil war of 1943–45,
when the Italian Communist Party did for clearly stated reasons of its own what
Gianni only dreamed of doing for reasons that were never too clear to anyone.
The economic weaknesses of sharecropping were passed onto the next generation,
which had to go over the same sorry statistics and encounter the same sharp
differences of opinion. Sharecropping lasted as the predominate form of agricultural organization right down to the 1950s, when the Italian parliament decreed
its demise and when the peasants finally walked off their farms and into the
factories of the Economic Miracle.

Consequently, the urban workers went on thinking of inflation as an
unmitigated evil. The agricultural workers went on looking to divine intervention
rather than to organization for an escape from their plight. Both came to believe
that veiled images had something to do with free trade. A gulf had been dug
between educated and illiterate, between rich and poor, between curialists and
anticurialists. To many of those on one side, violence seemed to be the only way
of getting to the other side. Gianni, who had admitted the legitimacy of violence
as an expression of a frustrated general will, could only accuse them of a tactical
error when they decided to resort to it.

* The word left blank in the original is probably *bischero,* a common Florentine term of
denigration.

8

The invasion

March 25, 1799. At the Porta San Gallo.

The few Florentines who showed up to watch the troops of the French Republic file through Francesco Stefano's arch that morning were neither enthusiastic nor bitter. They knew that their government had done everything possible during the past five years to postpone this moment. It had scrupulously adhered to the traditional Tuscan policy of unarmed neutrality, even to the point of prohibiting insults against either side in the war and of backing French bills of exchange on Florentine banks. It had permitted complete freedom in current discussions about the relative merits of the Revolution and had adamantly refused to adopt the restrictive measures by which all other Italian states sought to immunize themselves against change. In 1794 it had tried to persuade the French National Convention—through a personal letter of the abbot of the Badìa to Lampredi's former pupil, the archrevolutionary Filippo Buonarroti—that the objectives of the Grand Duchy were exactly the same as those of the Republic. In 1796 it had tried to persuade the Directory, through its personal representative to General Bonaparte in Bologna, that a French invasion would add nothing to what Tuscans had already accomplished by themselves.

Yet most Florentines also realized that even the best informed Frenchmen were incapable of imagining a revolution in any but Gallic terms. Indeed, what most impressed the new French ambassador was not how far Tuscans had gone in realizing a revolution of their own, but how successful they had been in approximating the institutions and rhetoric of revolutionary France. He therefore took the very arguments advanced in support of the independence of Tuscany to support a policy of immediate occupation. Since Tuscans were "the best people in Italy," he insisted, they could be won over almost without firing a cannon. Since Florence was the Athens of Italy, all the other Italian cities would automatically follow its lead. As revolutionary fervor waned in Paris, and as tricoloring the map began to take precedence over the spreading of new ideas, this argument became ever more persuasive. By the end of 1798 Tuscany was surrounded by a sea of French-style republics: the Ligurian on the northwest, the Cispadine on the north, and the Roman and the Parthenopean on the south. The French commander was just waiting for a legitimate pretext in order to complete his government's policy of gallicizing the whole peninsula.

To some Florentines, the arrival of French troops seemed like the final solution to a decade of debate. The decrees of June 9, 1790, had been quietly annulled the following November. In January, 1792, the Georgofili had launched a full counterattack on the opponents of free trade with a public competition on the loaded theme, "Is it more advantageous . . . to favor manufacturing by controlling commerce in raw materials, or should the latter be left in total freedom?" In July and August of the same year a royal commission had come up with still more statistics designed to prove the folly of protectionism. Even Gianni soon realized that the exceptions he had requested on behalf of the silk industry were logically and practically inconsistent. When another attempt to impose price controls failed even more disastrously than the first, when grain production dropped as European grain prices soared, and when riots and miracles again broke out all over the country, the grand duke decided to restore his father's economic laws in full. He appointed as his chief minister the most vociferous exponent of those laws at the moment, Vittorio Fossombroni, whose political career was to continue well into the next century. Thus free trade became an indelible part of the Florentine heritage. As late as 1848, one Florentine statesman, in discussing proposals for a new constitution, declared that "it [free trade] could not be taken away from us without producing a complete social revolution." And the French military commander made good his promise to respect it in 1799 by giving the Finance Ministry to none other than Gianni, who was both pleased with the prospect of returning to power and fearful that his refusal might lead to the appointment of a Frenchman in his place.

Thus many Florentines were disposed to believe that the French government would amount in essence to a return to the regime of Pietro Leopoldo. Ever since his death in 1792, the former grand duke had gradually been freed of the memory of his defects and elevated to the rank of a hero-lawgiver, the greatest, suggested the editors of the *Novelle letterarie,* since the time of David. The last major attack on his reputation—a kind of "secret history" published in 1796 by a bankrupt would-be Procopius who had never stopped resenting the appointment of Galluzzi as state historiographer—was quickly obliterated when Giovanni Fabbroni published a corresponding apotheosis. Indeed, Fabbroni's judgments soon rose to the level of self-evident axioms. In 1808 the "immortal" Pietro Leopoldo was credited with having "realized the philanthropic speculations of all the philosophers." In 1813, at a time when such eulogies were generally reserved for Napoleon, he was hailed as "the philosopher sovereign," "the wonder of Europe," whose "great name cannot be heard without evoking a sense of veneration and gratitude." After 1823 "his name was constantly on the lips" of the members of the Georgofili, according to the historian Gino Capponi, who was busy composing the first full history of his reign. And in 1846, just as all Italy was about to plunge into a revolution of its own, the statesman Giovanni Baldasseroni could think of no better way to save the state than to restore "the honest freedom of the press, the autonomy of local administration, the compilation of good law codes, and the publication of the acts of the government" that Pietro Leopoldo had instituted over a half century before.

Unfortunately, it soon became apparent in the spring of 1799 that the French commander was primarily interested in maintaining an army of occupation for the sole benefit of, and at no cost to, his own government in France. Florentines did not particularly mind hanging a portrait of "Liberty" in the Loggia dei Lanzi, erecting a "Liberty Tree" in front of the Palazzo Vecchio, changing the name of Piazza del Granduca (now della Signoria) to Piazza Nazionale, turning academies into "patriotic societies," and rebaptizing provinces as "departments." After all, they had invented philology three centuries before. They had learned to live with many other kinds of images eight years before. And they were not now about to start confusing signs with substance—or exchanging fireflies for lanterns.

Florentines did begin to have serious doubts when, two days after the invasion, Grand Duke Ferdinando III was forced to flee, even after they had assured the French that he was nothing but "the first gentleman [*galantuomo*] of the state, the first subject of its laws," and therefore a figure perfectly consonant with the most advanced constitution. Some of them soon came to the conclusion that their legitimate sovereign—the son of the sovereign whose farsighted constitution Gianni had just brought out for their inspiration—was far more democratic than the military despot who was currently hiding behind a curtain of democratic rhetoric in the Palazzo Vecchio. Others came to the conclusion that French order meant plunder, particularly when the museum directors were kept awake all night trying to prevent the wholesale robbery of Florence's art treasures. Still others came to the conclusion that French justice meant blood, particularly after the decree of 3 *pratile* VII (May 22) ordered the total destruction of the cities of Arezzo and Cortona. Most of the "patriots" who thought they could best serve their country by collaborating with the occupier soon became disillusioned. Gianni resigned his office after a month. He refused to come in from the country even in July, when the senators were suddenly transformed into a senate and authorized to govern in the grand duke's name after the retreat of the French.

Thus the invasion of 1799 turned out to be the beginning of an end—the end, that is, of Tuscany as an independent state. What Cosimo I had spent a lifetime creating, what Ferdinando I had so methodically strengthened, what Cosimo III had tried so desperately to avoid losing, and what Pietro Leopoldo had so skillfully saved from the grasp of his avaricious brother—all this had been swallowed up in the vortex of a continent-wide revolutionary war over which Tuscans had no control whatsoever. The mobs of Aretine peasants brought the Grand Duchy back in July, to be sure, though more for the sake of processions and free bread than out of loyalty to the grand duke. The French renamed it the Kingdom of Etruria soon after their return the following year, even though they used it mostly as a storage place for a stray Bourbon prince whom they could not find room for elsewhere. Napoleon continued to recognize it at least on paper when he incorporated it into the French Empire in 1808. But even after the Austrians restored it in full at the Congress of Vienna, and even after they sent back the old ruler who had so irritated them during his exile by refusing to speak anything but Italian, the Grand Duchy had become provisory at the best. The movement of Italian unification increasingly condemned all the various states of the peninsula as intolerable anachronisms. When Tuscans voted for annexation to Piedmont-Sardinia in 1859, they recognized that no exceptions could be made even for the one of the states that worked fairly well, that had solid historical foundations, and that still enjoyed the affection of the vast majority of its citizens.

A POSTSCRIPT

30. Luca Giordano, *Apotheosis of the Medici*
Palazzo Medici-Riccardi

July 28, 1970. Palazzo Medici-Riccardi: the Hall of Luca Giordano.
The fifty members of the Tuscan Regional Council were presented with a full agenda when, at about 10:30 A.M., they were finally called together in their second formal·session. They first had to appoint an interparty committee to look into the validity of their mandates, thus blocking the efforts of at least one councilor to discredit the regional government from the start by questioning the eligibility of its members. They next had to adopt a rule limiting the number of executive officers (*assessori*) to the minimum of eight, rather than to the maximum of sixteen permitted by law. They thus accepted a principle very similar to the one enunciated by Francesco Maria Gianni two centuries before: small bureaucracies are easier to control than large ones. At the same time they comforted those many citizens who had feared the creation of one more bureaucracy in a country already overburdened with bureaucrats. They then had to listen attentively while a

spokesman for the majority outlined the serious political, economic, and ecological problems they would soon be called upon to solve. They had to listen patiently while he embroidered his outline with the usual rhetorical flourishes about "the class consciousness of the workers" and the "imperialistic power politics" of current international "military blocs."

The program itself was generally acceptable. But the question of who should be charged with carrying it out provoked a long and acrimonious debate. The Socialists defended their decision to collaborate with the Communists in Florence while maintaining their alliance with the other three Left-Center parties in Rome: practical politics, they insisted, had at times to take precedence over unrealizable ideals. The Christian Democrats chastised the Socialists for embarking on a dangerous political adventure. The Social Democrats condemned the Christian Democrats for not insisting that the Socialists abide by the thesis of either a minority Left-Center government, or no government at all. The one Republican councilor upbraided all his colleagues for talking about generalities and not getting down to particular issues.

Actually, the answer to the question had already been determined by the results of the election of June 7. No government could be formed without the participation of the Communists, who had won a sizeable plurality of seats on the Council; and the Communists could not organize a majority without the help of the Socialists as well as of their minor allies to the left, the Social Proletarians (PSIUP). By early July, the details of the future coalition had been worked out. With the express consent of their own party headquarters in Rome, and with the tacit consent of a good number of Christian Democrats, the Socialists accepted the almost irresistible concessions offered them in exchange for their support. No one was surprised when the votes were counted: twenty-six in favor, twenty-four abstentions. No one was particularly disappointed, either, for the majority's candidate had exceptional qualifications for his new office. Lelio Lagorio was a veteran of the Resistance movement of the 1940s. He was a distinguished intellectual, having taught constitutional law at the university. He was an experienced administrator, having served as mayor of Florence. He was an able politician, having long been active in the Florentine branch of the Italian Socialist Party. He had acquired an exceptional knowledge of all Tuscany as chairman of the unofficial Regional Planning Commission. Last but not least, he was by far the handsomest political leader in all Italy. Everyone applauded when, later that afternoon, he was proclaimed first president of the Region of Tuscany.

Thus some 112 years after it had been reduced to the status of a geographical expression, Tuscany once again became an autonomous political entity. All that remained to be done was to provide for Florence, which, now that it had been raised to the dignity of a regional capital, could no longer be abandoned, as it had so often in the past, to the care of a commissioner sent out by the Ministry of the Interior in Rome. In Florence, unfortunately, the elections of June 7 had produced a city council in which a majority could be put together only by reestablishing the Left-Center coalition—by returning, that is, to the very formula that had just been repudiated at the regional level. Consequently it took another six weeks of wrangling before the four parties that had parted ways on July 28 could be brought back together. Not until September 15, amid shouts of "Resign! Resign!" and "Prague! Prague!" from the gallery, but with the backing of the Socialists, the Social Democrats, and the Republicans, as well as his own Christian Democrats, was Luciano Bausi finally elected mayor.

Surely none of the councilors present at the session of July 28 was unaware of the historical significance of what was being done. But probably few of them were aware of the equally significant events that had once occurred within a few meters of where they were sitting. They had come in through the main entrance to the great baroque hall without noticing the house next door, where Lorenzaccio had murdered Duke Alessandro in 1537, thus precipitating the transformation of the Florentine republic into a monarchy. They had perhaps looked up, in moments of distraction, at the fresco on the ceiling without realizing that it had marked, in the 1680s, the surrender of a four-hundred-year Florentine artistic tradition to an international style brought in from the outside. They may have noticed the small door on the right without remembering that it led into the library where, in 1740, Giovanni Lami had launched Florence's first periodical journal.

But then, the councilors had little reason to recall the accomplishment of their ancestors during the two and a half centuries between the election of Cosimo I and flight of Ferdinando III. Much of it had since been destroyed, defaced, or flooded out. Much of it had been studiously ignored, both by recent historians of the city, whose interests lay almost exclusively in the periods before 1527 and after 1870, and by the school teachers, whose prescribed programs of study emphasized national history at the expense of local or world history. Much of it still suffered from the negative value judgments passed upon all of post-Renaissance and pre-Risorgimento Italy by such authoritative critics as Francesco De Sanctis and Benedetto Croce. Thus when one informed contributor to the letter-column debate in the daily *La nazione* suggested that the Six Balls of the family that had created Tuscany would be more appropriate on the new regional banner than an obscure Etruscan lion, he was denounced as an apologist for tyrants and poisoners.

Moreover, by 1970 Florence had become a very different city from what it had been before 1799. The population had risen from less than 100,000 to more than 450,000, not counting another 400,000 in the surrounding metropolitan area. The four ancient quarters had been combined, at least on the tables of the urban planners, into a single *centro storico* ("historic center"), and their place as major subdivisions of the city had been taken by Rifredi and Gavinana, Novoli and Coverciano. The Mercato Vecchio had been demolished to make way for the Umbertian arcades of Piazza della Repubblica, and the descendants of the food vendors of 1790 were now clerks in the new neighborhood supermarkets. The public baths at Porta al Prato had been replaced by the municipal swimming pools in the Cascine and at Bellariva, and the walls north of the river had given way to car-packed boulevards. The color of the Arno had changed from light blue to dark brown, and the prevailing odor in the streets had changed from that of horse manure to automobile exhaust. The focus of religious fervor had moved from San Marco to Isolotto. The focus of athletic fervor had moved from Piazza Santa Croce (which was now a parking lot) to Campo di Marte. And the cry *Evviva Fiorenza!* had been drowned out by the cry *Forza Viola!* *

Yet the age of the Principate had not yet wholly vanished from the memories of the citizens. It was still present in the names of many streets: Via Benedetto Varchi and Via Scipione Ammirato, both of which are much longer than the tiny Via Leonardo Bruni; Viale Francesco Redi, which leads from the railway station to the Fiat service garage; and Piazza Pietro Leopoldo, which opens on to the *vie* of the chief agronomes and state officials of the late eighteenth century. It was still present in its chief architectural monuments: the Palazzo degli Uffizi, where Cosimo I lodged the city magistrates and where Pietro Leopoldo put the state archives; the Boboli Gardens, which Buontalenti built for Grand Duke Francesco and which the children of modern Florence now enjoy; San Firenze, which still houses the Fathers of the Oratory (as well as the State Tribunal); and the Teatro della Pergola, which still hosts most of what is left of the theater in Florence. Above all, it was still remembered in what turned out to be its most lasting achievement: the cultural, economic, sentimental, and now the political unity of the former Grand Duchy. When, early in 1970, the national government finally recognized the folly of imposing Napoleonic centralization on a country as diverse as Italy, no one had any doubts about where to draw the boundaries of the Tuscan region. No one had any doubts where to put the capital, either; and instead of tearing down their own cities, like the citizens of Reggio Calabria and Aquila, in a fit of anachronistic local flag-waving, the representatives of Livorno, Siena, and Arezzo quietly assembled in Florence, just where their ancestors would have assembled in the 1780s had Pietro Leopoldo succeeded in promulgating his constitution.

La nazione was not just coining a humorous anachronism when it bestowed the title of "the optimistic grand duke" on the man the regional councilors chose as their president on July 28. Had any of them looked upward at that moment, he might have noticed a smile of contentment on the faces of Lagorio's Medici predecessors as they looked downward from Luca Giordano's tumultuous heaven painted on the ceiling.

* The cry of the Florentine professional soccer team.

Bibliographical Note

Most of what is said in this volume comes from the published and unpublished works and letters of the various personages mentioned in the text. I cite specific titles only when a more general indication might be confusing or when a modern critical edition is available. In accordance with the aims stated in the Preface, I give only the principal archival or manuscript sources rather than specific page or folio references. And once I have cited a title in the bibliography for one Book, I generally do not repeat it even when the subject matter regards succeeding Books as well. I use the following abbreviations throughout.

Libraries and archives

ASF	Archivio di Stato, Florence
AVat	Archivio Vaticano
BNF	Biblioteca Nazionale Centrale, Florence
BUP	Biblioteca Universitaria, Pisa
Laur	Biblioteca Laurenziana
MAEPar	Ministère des Affaires Etrangères, Paris
Mag	Magliabechiana collection of the BNF
Mar	Biblioteca Marucelliana
Ricc	Biblioteca Riccardiana
VG	Private archive of the Venturi Ginori Lisci family, Florence

Periodicals and general reference books

AMCol	Atti e memorie dell'Accademia Toscana di Scienze e Lettere "La Colombaria"
ASI	Archivio storico italiano
BHR	Bibliothèque d'humanisme et renaissance
BSE	Bollettino storico empolese
BSL	Bollettino storico livornese
BSMar	Bollettino storico maremmano
BSPis	Bollettino storico pisano

BSPist	Bollettino storico pistoiese
BSPrat	Bollettino storico pratese
BSSP	Bollettino senese di storia patria
CS	Critica storica
ES	Economia e storia
DBI	Dizionario biografico degli Italiani
GCFI	Giornale critico della filosofia italiana
GSAT	Giornale storico degli archivi toscani
GSLI	Giornale storico della letteratura italiana
IS	Italian Studies
MKHIF	Mitteilungen des Kunsthistorischen Instituts, Florenz
RBA	Rivista delle biblioteche e degli archivi
RdA	Rivista d'arte
REI	Revue d'études italiennes
RLI	Rassegna della letteratura italiana
RMI	Rivista musicale italiana
RSAT	Rivista storica degli archivi toscani
RSCI	Rivista di storia della Chiesa in Italia
RSI	Rivista storica italiana
RSRis	Rassegna storica del Risorgimento
RST	Rassegna storica toscana
SFI	Studi di filologia italiana
SSt	Studi storici

The place of publication of all books is Florence, unless otherwise indicated.

Prologue

The fullest account of the siege is that of Benedetto Varchi in his *Storia fiorentina,* which can now be read in a recent reprint (Salani, 1963), but which I read in the edition of his *Opere* (Trieste: Lloyd Adriatico, 1858); Giovanni Batista Busini's letters, "Sugli avvenimenti dell'Assedio di Firenze," from which Varchi took much of his information are included in appendix to vol. I, pp. 445–517. Other contemporary accounts are helpful, both for their description of the events and for their point of view, for example, Bernardo Segni's *Storie fiorentine,* which I read, along with his biography of Niccolò Capponi, in the edition of 1728 (Palermo: Rapetti); Jacopo Nardi's *Istorie della città di Firenze* (LeMonnier, 1888); Baccio Carnesecchi's brief memoranda published by Umberto Dorini in *RSAT,* III (1931), 100–112; and Francesco Guicciardini's classic *La storia d'Italia,* available in numerous editions and now also in English translation.

Of the modern accounts of the siege, the best is still that of Cecil Roth, *The Last Florentine Republic* (London: Methuen, 1925), which will probably be read with pleasure as well as with confidence for a long time to come, as Roberto Ridolfi pointed out in *ASI,* XII (1929), 273–91; but much relevant material can still be found in the older *Assedio di Firenze* by Pio Carlo Falletti Fossati (Palermo: Giannone e Lamantia, 1885), much of it taken from the reports of the Venetian ambassadors, which I consulted in the original published by Eugenio Albèri in *L'Italia nel secolo decimosesto, ossia Le relazioni degli ambasciatori veneti* (Società Editrice Fiorentina, 1858). I have also consulted

Baccio Valori's "Rendiconto delle spese fatte nell'Assedio," ed. Luigi Passerini, in *GSAT,* I (1857), 106–62; "Cartelli di querela . . . tra Lodovico Martelli e Giovanni Bandini," ed. Carlo Milanesi, *ASI,* n.s. IV² (1857), 3 ff. (a good example of the mentality of the besieged); the reports of the imperial generals in Alessandro Bardi, "Carlo V e l'Assedio di Firenze," *ASI,* ser. V, vol. XI (1893), 1–85; and the first letters of Francesco Guicciardini to Bartolomeo Lanfredini published by André Oţetea in *Dalla fine dell'Assedio di Firenze al secondo convegno di Clemente VII e Carlo V* (Aquila: Vecchioni, 1927), which are put into historical perspective by Agostino Rossi in *F. G. e il governo fiorentino dal 1527 al 1540* (Bologna: Zanichelli, 1896–99), and by Roberto Ridolfi in *The Life of F. G.,* trans. Cecil Grayson (New York: Knopf, 1968). On Francesco Ferrucci there is a considerable bibliography, much of it hagiographic. I generally follow the *Vita* by Filippo Sassetti, ed. C. Monzani, *ASI,* IV² (1853), 425 ff., but also available separately in G. Daelli's "Biblioteca rara" series (Milan, 1863).

Two of the militia speeches are published by Manlio Fancelli in *Orazioni politiche del Cinquecento* (Bologna: Zanichelli, 1941). Their spirit is recalled by Donato Giannotti in his *Della Repubblica Fiorentina,* of which I have the edition of Venice (Hertz), 1722. Some subsequent commentary is published in the appendix to Rudolf von Albertini's fundamental work, which I use extensively in Book I, *Das florentinische Staatsbewusstsein im Uebergang von der Republik zum Prinzipat* (Bern: Francke, 1955). I have found examples of republican legislation against recalcitrant citizens in the Newberry Library collection. Successive constitutional debate is described by Felix Gilbert in "Alcuni discorsi di uomini politici fiorentini e la politica di Clemente VII . . . per la restaurazione medicea," *ASI,* XCIII² (1935), 3–24, and in Gilbert's "The Venetian Constitution in Florentine Political Thought," *Florentine Studies,* ed. Nicolai Rubinstein (Evanston: Northwestern University Press, 1968), pp. 463–500 (Marvin B. Becker's "The Florentine Territorial State and Civic Humanism" in the same volume, pp. 109–39, describes the background for what I say about the Republic's policy toward the subject cities); the reaction of certain nonpartisan Florentines to the disaster is documented by the short *Lamento di Fiorenza* (Bologna: Commissione per i testi di lingua, 1968), which includes the text of the truce of August 12.

The location of the Imperial army outside the walls can be seen from the chart drawn by L. Zumkeller, now in the Museo di Firenze Com'Era, and from Giorgio Vasari's famous mural in the Sala dei Cinquecento in the Palazzo Vecchio.

The two most recent histories of Renaissance Florence follow the example of their predecessors in stopping short of the siege: Alberto Tenenti, *Firenze dal comune a Lorenzo il Magnifico,* trans. from the French original (Paris: Flammarion, 1968) published by Mursia in Milan (1970), and Gene A. Brucker, *Renaissance Florence* (New York and London: John Wiley, 1969). Ferdinand Schevill's well-known *History of Florence from the Foundation of the City through the Renaissance* (New York: Harcourt Brace, 1936) mentions the siege simply as the last act of a great tragedy. But all are helpful, as is the rest of the vast amount of scholarly research recently devoted to Florentine politics and culture before 1527, in providing an explanation of why the siege took place.

Of the modern histories of Florence that cover the rest of the period treated in this volume, Romolo Caggese, *Firenze dalla decadenza di Roma al Risorgimento d'Italia* (Seeber & Lumachi, 1912–13), gives the fullest account of political events, although Antonio

Panella, *Storia di Firenze* (Sansoni, 1949), is helpful in spite of its brevity. Both of them supercede their immediate predecessors, Alfred von Reumont, *Geschichte Toskanas* (Gotha, 1876), and George Frederick Young, *The Medici* (1919, but most readily available in the Modern Library edition); but none of these books contains anything like the wealth of information about political and economic affairs, especially for the sixteenth century, that is to be found in Riguccio Galluzzi's still indispensable *Istoria del Granducato di Toscana sotto il governo della casa Medici* (Cambiagi, 1781, but I usually use the edition of Livorno: Vignozzi, 1820–21, in 7 vols.), which I discuss in Book VI.

Besides Galluzzi, I use several general reference books throughout this volume, and I mention them here once and for all. For buildings and places in Florence, Walter and Elisabeth Paatz, *Die Kirchen von Florenz* (Frankfurt-a-M.: Klostermann, 1955); Giuseppe Richa, *Notizie istoriche delle chiese fiorentine,* 10 vols. (Viviani, 1754–62); Demetrio Guccerelli, *Stradario storico biografico della città di Firenze* (Rome: Multigrafica, 1967, a reprint of the 1st ed. of 1929); Giuseppe Boffito, *Piante e vedute di Firenze* (Giuntina, 1926); Marco Lastri, *Osservatore fiorentino* (1821–); and Ugo Losacco, *Notizie e considerazioni sulle inondazioni dell'Arno* (Istituto Geografico Militare, 1967). I use the following biographical collections: Angelo Fabroni, *Historia Academiae Pisanae,* 3 vols. (Pisa, 1791–96); Jacopo Rilli, *Notizie dell'Accademia Fiorentina* (Matini, 1700); Salvino Salvini, *Fasti consolari dell'Accademia Fiorentina* (Tartini, 1717) and *Catalogo cronologico dei canonici della chiesa metropolitana fiorentina* (1751–); *Elogi degli uomini illustri toscani* (Lucca, 1771–74); and, especially for the artists, Giorgio Vasari, *Vite de' più eccellenti pittori, scultori e architetti,* which I usually read in the edition of Guglielmo Della Valle (Siena: Carli, 1791), and Luigi Lanzi, *Storia pittorica della Italia* (Bassano, 1795–96), also in English translation by William Roscoe (London, 1852–68). For members of the ruling family, I refer to Gaetano Pieraccini, *La stirpe de' Medici di Cafaggiolo,* 3 vols. (Vallecchi, 1924–25, 1947) (for the facts, not for the theses), and Umberto Dorini, *I Medici e i loro tempi* (Nerbini, n.d.) (particularly for the handy genealogical tables). On demographic and economic questions, I use Giuseppe Parenti, *Prime ricerche sulla rivoluzione dei prezzi in Firenze* (Cya, 1929); Karl Julius Beloch, *Bevölkerungsgeschichte Italiens* (Leipzig, 1927); and Marco Lastri, *Ricerche sull'antica e moderna popolazione della città di Firenze* (Cambiagi, 1775). The texts of many laws and edicts I have found in Lorenzo Cantini, *Legislazione toscana* (Albizzini, 1800–1808), and in the two miscellaneous collections in the New York Public Library and in the Newberry Library. And the texts of many of the treatises, orations, and letters I refer to are published in *Prose fiorentine,* begun by Carlo Roberto Dati in 1661 (as I explain in Book IV), and completed, in several editions (I generally use, for Parts I–III, the edition of Venice: Remondini, 1751) in the eighteenth century.

The map of north-central Italy is based partly on those of Giovanni Antonio Magini (1608) and Matteo Greuter (1630), which I found in the Novacco collection of the Newberry Library.

Book I

Almost all the purely political events mentioned in this book are recounted much more fully by two of the principal historians of the age, Varchi (through the summer of 1538) and Giovambattista Adriani, in *Istoria de' suoi tempi* (I use not the first edition,

1583, but the most recent, of Prato, 1822–23), which goes down to the death of Cosimo. Their reliability is assured by what Giovanni Miccoli says about Adriani in *DBI,* what Roberto Ridolfi says about Varchi in *ASI,* CXVI (1958), and what Richard Samuels says about Varchi in a current Ph.D. dissertation at the University of Chicago, as well as what is said about both of them by Michele Lupo Gentile in "Studi sulla storiografia alla corte di Cosimo I," *Annali della Scuola Normale di Pisa,* XIX² (1905), 1–64, and "Sulle fonti inedite della 'Storia fiorentina'...," reprinted from *Studi storici* (1906), and, to a lesser extent, by Benedetto Croce in *Poeti e scrittori del pieno e del tardo Rinascimento* (Bari: Laterza, 1932), pp. 129 ff. Bernardo Segni's *Istorie fiorentine,* cited above, is much less trustworthy, as Giuseppe Sanesi, in *ASI,* ser. V, vol. XXIII (1899), 260–88, and Roberto Ridolfi in *Belfagor,* XV (1960), 663–76, have shown, but it is valuable for Segni's firsthand observations. Paolo Giovio's reputation as a historian has at last been rescued from the unjust attacks of Varchi and Michele Bruto (*Florentinae Historiae Libri VIII* [Venice, 1562]) by none other than Federico Chabod, in "P.G.," *Periodico della Società Storica Comense,* XXXVIII (1954), 9–30, now reprinted in his *Scritti sul Rinascimento* (Turin: Einaudi, 1967). For general biographical notes on Giovio, I use Ettore Rota in *La letteratura italiana: I minori* (Milan: Marzorati, 1961), vol. II, pp. 927–48, particularly for what Giovio got from Cosimo himself. Unfortunately, the editors of the recent *Opera Omnia* (Rome: Istituto Poligrafico dello Stato, 1956–) have seen fit to limit the circulation of his *Historiarum Sui Temporis* by pricing it out of the market. Subsequent historians fill in some gaps and add some details, not so much Scipione Ammirato, for the reasons given in Book II, and certainly not Lorenzo Cantini (*Vita di Cosimo* ..., 1805), for whom Cosimo was merely a welcome antithesis to Napoleon (but there is a good selection of documents in the appendix), but above all Riguccio Galluzzi, cited above, for the reasons given in Book VI.

In addition to the historians, I have read extensively in some of the chroniclers and diarists of the time: in the rather superficial Giuliano Ughi (ed. Francesco Frediani in *ASI,* appendix vol. VII [1849]); in the rather provincial Bindaccio Guizzelmi (ed. Renato Piattoli, *RSAT,* V [1933], 222–38); in the cranky "Old Oligarch" usually called "Marucelli" (although Roberto Cantagalli, after a long search, has been unable to identify him more precisely), of which the clearest of several copies in the BNF is MSS Gino Capponi 105; in the anonymous author of the chronicle published by Roberto Ridolfi in *ASI,* CXVI (1958), 548–70; in the diligent William Thomas, whose *History of Italy* (1549) has recently been republished by George B. Parke (Cornell University Press, 1963); in the chatty and rather superficial Leandro Alberti (1479–1552), whose *Descrittione di tutta Italia* was published in 1550; and in the timorous, if unscrupulous, Sienese ambassadors, whose reports are edited in *ASI,* ser. V, vol. XI (1893), 278–338. I have not used the reports of the two Venetian ambassadors in the 1560s, because I found them grossly misinformed. A considerable number of relevant political documents are printed in Cesare Guasti's catalogue to the Strozzi papers in the ASF, which I have used extensively (along with the manuscript catalogue) while tracking down others that have not been published.

A very large quantity of contemporary correspondence has survived. The letters of Cosimo himself, for instance, would take years to plow through, even for someone patient enough to master his horrible handwriting, and no distinction can be made between his personal and his official letters. Of the "Carteggio universale" in the ASF, I have gone over the first five volumes of both series (Medici del Principato, 1 ff. and 330 ff.) and a random selection of other volumes for the later years, all with the help of Sergio Camerani's *Bibliografia medicea* (Olschki, 1964) and his printed index of the *Medici del Principato* series. But on the whole I have relied on the judgment of those scholars who for one reason or another have published a good number of the letters, all of whom are listed by the most recent of them, Giorgio Spini, in his edition of the *Lettere* (Vallecchi, 1940) and in his still indispensable *Cosimo I . . . e la independenza del Principato mediceo* (Vallecchi, 1945).

Particularly valuable for political and diplomatic affairs are the letters of Averardo Serristori (ed. Giuseppe Canestrini: Le Monnier, 1853), of Francesco Guicciardini (in vol. X of Canestrini's edition of *Opere inedite* [1867], since the current edition has not yet arrived at the later years), and of Francesco Vettori, Filippo Strozzi, et al., published in the huge appendix to G. B. Niccolini's drama, *Filippo Strozzi* (1847). What they say can sometimes be further documented by the two printed collections of French diplomatic papers dealing with Tuscany: G. Canestrini and A. Desjardins, eds., *Négotiations diplomatiques de la France avec la Toscane, 1311–1610* (Paris, 1865), and E. Palandri, *Les négotiations politiques et religieuses entre la Toscane et la France à l'époque di Cosme I et de Cathérine des Médicis* (Paris, 1908), though I have found still others in MAEPar, Toscane I, fols. 468 ff. I have also read the far greater selection scattered through the first sixty-odd volumes of the *ASI,* which are all listed in the indices (and therefore not here). But I leave to my successor the task of going through the archives at Simancas, which are probably one of the richest sources for the history of a state so closely tied to the Spanish Empire.

The published letters of contemporary men of letters are even more voluminous, given the appreciation among the humanists of letter-writing as an art. Those of Annibal Caro are available in sixteenth-century editions, but I recommend the most recent one, by Aulo Greco (LeMonnier, 1957), because the footnotes constitute a veritable index of the cultural life of the age. Those of Andrea Alciati I read in the edition of Gian Luigi Barni (LeMonnier, 1953) and in the partial selection of Roberto Abbondanza in *Annali di storia del diritto,* II (1958), 361–403 (which is also one of my main sources of information on the University of Pisa). Those of Pietro Aretino are published by Fausto Nicolini (Bari: Laterza, 1913–16); those to Aretino by Teodorico Landoni (Bologna: Romagnoli, 1873); those of Pietro Bembo (few of which are relevant here) in *Delle lettere . . .* (Verona, 1743); those of Anton Francesco Doni in *Tre libri . . .* (Venice, 1552) and *Lettere scelte,* ed. Giuseppe Petraglione (Livorno: Giusti, 1902); those of Donato Giannotti by Milanesi in *ASI,* n.s. vol. VII (1863), 155 ff., by Roberto Ridolfi in *RSAT,* I–III (1929–31), and by Randolph Starn in *Rinascimento,* XV (1964), 101–21, and now in *D. G. and His 'Epistolae'* (Geneva: Droz, 1968). Those of Paolo Giovio are published in the first two volumes of his *Opera Omnia* (1956—see G. G. Ferrero, the editor, in *GSLI,* CXIII [1939], 225–55); those of Cosimo's son Giovanni by G. B. Catena (Rome: Rossi, 1752); those of Michelangelo by Milanesi (LeMonnier, 1875); those of Isabella Guicciardini by I. Del Lungo (LeMonnier, 1883); those of Vincenzo Martelli by his Florentine friends in *Rime e lettere* (Giunti, 1563 and 1602); those of Vasari by Karl Frey in *Der literarische Nachlass G. V.'s* (Munich, 1923); and those of Pier Vettori—a brief selection of those extant—in *Epistolarum Libri X* (Giunti, 1586), by Gino Ghinassi (Bologna: Romagnoli, 1870), and by Pierre de Nolhac (*P. V. et Carlo Sigonio: Correspondance avec Fulvio Orsini* [Vatican, 1889]).

Some collected epistolaries are valuable, too, particularly the *Lettere d'uomini illustri conservati in Parma* (Parma, 1853) (for correspondents of the Farnese), *Lettere di XIII huomini illustri* (Venice, 1564), *Lettere di cortigiane del secolo XVI*, ed. L. A. Ferrai (the author of a well-documented biography of Cosimo published by the Libreria Dante in 1884), etc. But the most valuable of all are Johann Wilhelm Gaye's immense *Carteggio inedito* for the artists (Italian edition, Florence, 1839–40), and part IV of the *Prose fiorentine* (which I describe in Book V). I have not been able to go through the immense collection of letters addressed to Pier Vettori now in the British Museum (see Cecil Roth in *RSAT*, I [1929], 154–85), and I know only of those that have been published— by Angelo Maria Bandini in 1758 and by Ridolfi in 1929 (see above, under Giannotti). Nor have I had time to search out all the scattered letters of Varchi; and I have had to use the published sonnets as a sort of guide to Varchi's correspondents.

Of other works of men of letters of the age, I read Cellini's *Vita,* usually in the Einaudi paperback (1953), and Cavalcanti, Nardi, and Lorenzaccio in Manlio Fancelli's *Orazioni politiche,* cited above, in spite of numerous errors in transcription and in spite of the editor's apparent attempt to take a slap at the dull-witted directors of the Istituto Nazionale di Cultura Fascista, who paid for the publication. I read Varchi's *Della maggioranza* in Paola Barocchi's *Trattati d'arte del Cinquecento* (Bari: Laterza, 1960), and Luigi Giucciardini's *Del Savonarola* in Bono Simonetta's edition of 1959 (Olschki). Varchi's Latin verse is now available in a modern edition: *Liber Carminum,* ed. Aulo Greco (Rome: Abete, 1969).

At the same time, I have been considerably aided by a good number of critical and biographical studies. The best one on Cosimo himself is by Giorgio Spini, in *Unione Fiorentina: Secoli vari* (Sansoni, 1958), pp. 163–87 (together with Spini's remarks in *RSI,* LVIII [1949], 76–93). I accept Spini's judgment of his predecessors, particularly of those who have written in English, like Cecily Booth, *Cosimo I, Duke of Florence* (Cambridge University Press, 1921). The numerous contemporary eulogies and funeral orations are better documents of Cosimo's *image* than they are of Cosimo himself, although some, like those of Adriani and Domenico Mellini (written for Cristina of Lorraine), are remarkably unbiased (note G. E. Saltini in *ASI,* n.s., VI [1862], 52–60). For the compliments paid to Cosimo by Marc Antoine Muret, I am indebted to Kenneth Schellhase. On other personages, I have consulted Henri Hauvette's book on Luigi Alamanni (Paris: Hachette, 1903); Giuliano Innamorati's monographic studies of Pietro Aretino (Messina-Florence: D'Anna, 1957), which, though far from comprehensive, are more pertinent here than those of Alessandro Del Vita (1954) or of Giorgio Petrocchi (1948). I have consulted Detlef Heikamp on Baccio Bandinelli, in *Paragone,* no. 175—which I have in off-print—and no. 191 (1966), 51–62; Girolamo Mancini on Cosimo Bartoli in *ASI,* LXXVI² (1918), 84–135; Giorgio Spini on Antonio Brucioli (La Nuova Italia, 1940) (not W. T. Elwert in *Arte pensiero e cultura a Mantova* [Sansoni, 1965], which does not even mention Spini); Francesco Dini on Francesco Campana in *ASI,* ser. V, vol. XXIII (1899), 289–323; N. Jonard on Berni in *REI,* IX (1962–63), 100–25; Andrea Emiliani on Bronzino (Busto Arsizio: Bramante, 1960), whose *Saltarelli* are published by the Commissione per i Testi di Lingua (Bologna, 1968); Oddone Ortolani (though with reservations) on Pietro Carnesecchi (LeMonnier, 1963); Aulo Greco on Annibal Caro (Rome: Edizioni di Storia e Letteratura, 1950); Giuseppe Campori on Cavalcanti in *Atti e memorie ... provincie modenesi e parmensi*, IV (1864), 137–70; Carlo Cordil on Cellini in his introduction to the Ricciardi edition of the *Vita*; Abd-el-Kader Salza on Lodovico Domenichi in *Rassegna bibliografica della letteratura italiana*, VII (1899), 204–9; Giuseppe Fatini in the UTET edition of Firenzuola, whose *Ragionamento d'amore e altri scritti* are also available in the edition of Bartolomeo Rossetti (Rome: Avanzini e Torraca, 1961), as well as Adriano Seroni's *Bibliografia essenziale ...* (Sansoni, 1957) and Luigi Russo in *Belfagor*, XVI (1961), 535–54; Luigi Staffetti, Umberto Dorini, and R. Feliciangeli on the various members of the Cibo family; Cecilia Ricottini Marsili Libelli (Sansoni, 1960) and Michele Messina in *La letteratura italiana: I minori*, vol. II, pp. 1293–314, on Doni—rather than Mario Santoro in *Fortuna, ragione e prudenza nella civiltà letteraria del Cinquecento* (Naples: Liguori, 1967), who just strings together random quotations, and rather than Paul Grendler in *Journal of the History of Ideas*, XXVI (1965), 479–94, and now in *Critics of the Italian World, 1530–1560* (University of Wisconsin Press, 1969), for reasons I make clear in my review in *Catholic Historical Review*, LVII (1971), 72–74. For a full bibliography on Doni, I have consulted Ricottini Marsili Libelli, *A.F.D.* (Sansoni Antiquariato, 1960), and, for one incident in his life, Carlo Cordié, "Un 'racconto' di A.F.D. e la censura," *RLI*, LXXIV (1970), 134–38.

   I have hesitated to rely too much on Ireneo Sanesi's introduction to the UTET edition of Gelli after reading Raffaello Spongano's review in *GSLI*, CXXXI (1954), 108–16, or on Robert M. Adams in his translation of Gelli (Cornell University Press, 1963) after reading J. M. Whitfield's review in *IS*, XIX (1964), 114–16, although I am not competent to judge on the disputed points. I rely instead on three studies by Armando L. De Gaetano in *Italica*, XXXII (1965), 226–41, XLIV (1967), 263–81, and *GSLI*, CXXXIV (1957), 198–313. On Giambullari, I follow Pietro Fiorelli in *SFI*, XIV (1956), 177–210. On Il Lasca—who, strangely enough, is not even mentioned in Douglas Radcliff-Umstead's *The Birth of Modern Comedy in Renaissance Italy* (University of Chicago Press, 1969), even though he is well represented in Charles S. Singleton's edition of the *Canti carnascialeschi* (Bari: Laterza, 1936)—I follow Giovanni Grazzini, *NA*, CDXXIX (1960), 185–208, Luigi Russo, "A.F.G. detto 'Il Lasca'," in *Studi di varia umanità in onore di Francesco Flora* (Milan: Mondadori, 1963), pp. 379–91, Michel Plaisance, "Evolution du théâtre de la 'beffa' dans le théâtre de Lasca," *RET*, XI (1965), 491–504, and—for a review of Lasca's works rather than for the dubious statements about his "times"—Robert J. Rodini, *A.F.G.: Poet, Dramatist, and Novelliere, 1503–1584* (University of Wisconsin Press, 1970). On Jacopo Nardi, I follow Alfredo Pieralli in *La vita e le opere* (1901) and Luigi Falcucci in *Alcune osservazioni ...* (Sassari: Gallizzi, 1899). On Pontormo, whose *Diario* has been published by Emilio Cecchi (LeMonnier, 1956), I follow Janet Cox Rearick in *The Drawings of P.* (Harvard University Press, 1964), Doris Wild in *RdA*, XXXVI (1961–62), 53–64, Kent W. Forster, *P.* (Munich: Bruckmann, 1966), and Luciano Berti, *P.* (Edizioni d'Arte, 1966) (the most elegant of all), as well as the catalogues of the showing of 1956. On Pier Vettori, I follow Antonio Benivieni (1583), Angelo Maria Bandini (1756) (though with some reservations), and

Francesco Niccolai (Seeber, 1912). And on Francesco Vettori, I follow Louis Passy, *Un ami de Machiavel* (Paris, 1912).

Besides Rilli and Salvini, my main sources for the Accademia Fiorentina are the documents in Mar B. III. 52–54 (Annali), Mag IX. 91, and BNF II.IV. 1, though I am very much indebted to Armando L. De Gaetano's "The Florentine Academy and the Advancement of Learning through the Vernacular . . . ," *BHP*, XXX (1968), 19–52. On the Accademia del Disegno (and I am shocked to find in James S. Ackerman's recent book on *Palladio* [Penguin Books] the assertion that the "court" atmosphere of Florence barred artists from the "aristocratic" academies and forced them to organize an academy of their own), some of my information comes from Mary Ann Ward, who kindly let me look at the first draft of her Ph.D. dissertation at the University of Chicago; other information comes from Leonardo Olschki's article in *N. Ant.*, CCL (1926), 470–79. On the university, besides Fabroni, who is more reliable for the late seventeenth and eighteenth centuries than for the sixteenth, I have turned to one of his sources: the apparently well-informed article of S. M. Fabrucci in Calogerà's *Nuova raccolta d'opuscoli*, VI (1760).

For some personages, the bibliography is so immense that I have had to choose carefully. For Vasari (and for Michelangelo), there is Paola Barocchi, in several monographs and in her mammoth edition of the *Vita di Michelangelo* (Milan: Ricciardi, 1962), along with the articles published in *Studi vasariani* (Sansoni, 1952), where critical judgments often differ from those of Alessandro Bonsanti in *Unione Fiorentina: Il Cinquecento* (Sansoni, 1955), pp. 41–58. One aspect of Vasari's work is considered by Ugo Procacci in "Il V. e la conservazione degli affreschi della Cappella Brancacci . . . ," in *Scritti in onore di Lionello Venturi* (Rome: De Luca, 1956), vol. I, pp. 211–22; the defects of his scholarship are noted by Creighton Gilbert in *Studies in the Renaissance,* XIV (1968), 20. For Varchi I refer to Guido Manacorda's monograph (Pisa, 1903) in general and to Umberto Pirotti's articles in particular: *Convivium,* XXIX (1960), XXXI (1963), the latter translated and edited by me in my *The Late Italian Renaissance* (London: Macmillan; New York: Harper & Row, 1970). On Cardinal Ippolito de' Medici, I refer to the biographical sketch by Giuseppe Moretti in *ASI,* XCVIII[1] (1940), 139–78; on Lorenzaccio, whose *Aridosia* and *Apologia* were published first in Daelli's "Biblioteca Rara," vol. II (Milan, 1862), and then by Federico Ravallo (Turin: UTET, 1917), to Ridolfo Mazzucconi's monograph (Milan: Mondadori, 1927). For Guicciardini I have consulted Roberto Ridolfi, whose "F. G. e Cosimo I," *ASI,* CXXII (1964), 567–606, adds to his biography, *Vita di F. G.* (Rome: Belardetti, 1960), of which Grayson's translation has already been cited, and to Agostino Rossi's ample *F. G. e il governo fiorentino dal 1527 al 1540* (Bologna: Zanichelli, 1896), which is still valuable. For critical judgments of Guicciardini's work, however, I rely on Vittorio de Caprariis' *Dalla politica alla storia* (Bari: Laterza, 1950) and on the last chapter of Felix Gilbert's *Machiavelli and Guicciardini* (Princeton University Press, 1965).

Certain aspects of the subjects included in this Book are treated in greater detail in various monographic studies. The best account of Cosimo's election is by Antonio Rossi in *Atti dell'Istituto Veneto di S. L. e A.,* ser. VII, vol. I (1889–90), 369–435, though I have at last untangled (I hope) the chronological confusion of the events of January 5–9, 1537, first perpetrated by Varchi and then by all his successors, with the help of

A. Cappelli's *Cronologia e calendario perpetuo* (Milan: Hoepli, 1906), an invaluable manual. Vitelli's letters to Cardinal Cibo I found in ASF Med. 330, f. 10. Some of the imperial agents are mentioned in Hayward Keniston's *Francisco de los Cobos* (University of Pittsburgh Press, 1960), others in Federico Chabod's studies of Milan and in M. van Durme's recent book on Granvelle. The several genealogical compendia, from those of Scipione Ammirato described in Book II to those of Curzio Ugurgieri della Berardenga on the Acciaiuoli, Piero Ginori Conti on the Cambi, and Luigi Passerini on scores of other families (I have not felt obliged to read through all his immense collection of notes in the BNF), are helpful for straightening out family trees.

For the other cities of Tuscany I have taken what little I needed from such books as Michelangelo Salvi's *Delle historie di Pistoia* (Venice, 1672) and, on Arezzo, Giovanni Rondinelli's contemporary *Relazione,* first published in Arezzo in 1755, although my population statistics come from the latest authority, David Herlihy, in *Medieval and Renaissance Pistoia* (Yale University Press, 1967), pp. 76-77. For Piombino, I have consulted an article by Carlo Odoardo Tosi in *Arte e storia,* no. 5 (1906), and, for Empoli, one by Giuliano Lastaioli in *BSE,* II (1960-61). But for Lucca I have been able to rely on one of the best products of recent Italian historiography: Marino Berengo's *Nobili e mercanti* . . . (Turin: Einaudi, 1965), although I have also read the printed documents regarding the Burlamacchi affair. On Siena I have followed Arnaldo d'Addario's *Il problema senese* (LeMonnier, 1958) for the period before the outbreak of the war, and Roberto Cantagalli's *La Guerra di Siena* (Siena: Intronati, 1962) for the period thereafter, with assurances about its reliability from Berengo in his reviews: *RSI,* LXXIV (1962), 169-75, LXXVI (1964), 233-35.

The most thorough study of the matters considered in chapters 3 and 4 is still that of Antonio Anzilotti, *La constituzione interna dello Stato fiorentino sotto il duca Cosimo I de' Medici* (Lumachi, 1910), even though some of the theses are no longer wholly acceptable. The most recent contribution has been made by Arnaldo d'Addario in an edition of the census reports of 1551 and 1561: "Burocrazia, economia e finanze dello Stato fiorentino alla metà del Cinquecento," in *ASI,* CXXI (1963), 362-456. I have taken some details from Giovanni Antonelli in "Gli Otto di Guardia . . . ," *ASI,* CXII (1954), and from Renzo Ristori in "L'idea del principato civile," *Rinascimento,* VII (1956), 75-91. Danilo Marrara's *Studi giuridici sulla Toscana medicea* (Milan: Giuffrè, 1965) treats Florence only as an introduction to his main interest, Siena. For the army, there is a very thorough study by Jolanda Ferretti in *RSAT,* I–II (1929-30), and a somewhat more general book by Niccolò Giorgetti, *Le armi toscane e le occupazioni straniere in Toscana (1537-1860)* (Città di Castello, 1916), of which vol. I is applicable to the first five Books of this volume. Francesco Lottini's *Avvertimenti civili* may have been more important in the evolution of European political thought than I suspect: the French translations are discussed by Corrado Vivanti in *Lotta politica e pace religiosa in Francia fra Cinque e Seicento* (Turin: Einaudi, 1963), p. 194. For the Order of Santo Stefano I have consulted the original constitution, published by Torrentino in 1562, as well as the revised constitution published in 1745; and for one aspect of Cosimo's military policy, I have studied Piero Machiavelli's *Progetto . . . per cacciare di Toscana Francesi e Spagnoli e per istituire un'armata toscana* (1560), published by Jarro in 1863 and, in a very limited edition, by Dotti in 1907. John Hale is the expert on fortresses. His specific study of the Fortezza da Basso is published in Rubinstein, ed., *Florentine Studies*, pp. 501-33; it can be supplemented for the rest of the city by Bruno Zevi's "Le fortificazioni fiorentine," in Zevi and Paolo Portoghesi, eds., *Michelangiolo architetto* (Einaudi, 1964), pp. 377-424 (which also includes an important article by Portoghesi on "La Biblioteca Laurenziana," lavishly illustrated).

For the church and ecclesiastical policies, the bibliography is somewhat denser: Hubert Jedin on the first session of Trent in *RSI*, LXII (1950), 345-74 and 477-96 (as well as numerous references in his *History of the Council of Trent* [English trans., St. Louis: Herder and Herder, 1957-]). now complemented for the later sessions by the official correspondence published by Niccolò Rodolico in *ASI*, CXXII (1964), 5-9. Other matters are discussed by Aldo Stella in *BHR*, XXVII (1965), 133-82, by Antonietta Amati (on San Marco) in *ASI*, LXXXI (1928), 225-77 (and I have read the letter of Cosimo to the cardinals in BNF, II. III. 89, fols. 181-85), by Giuseppe Alberigo (on one of Cosimo's informants at Trent) in *RSCI*, XII (1958), 173-201, as well as the several relevant chapters in his *I vescovi italiani al Concilio di Trento* (Sansoni, 1959), and by A. Panella (on Cosimo and the Index of Paul IV) in *RSAT*, I (1929), 11-25. For the period of the 1550s and '60s, I have been guided by Ruth Prelowski Liebowitz, who has read all the papers regarding the Sienese Inquisition. I have taken some details on the Jesuits, though with caution, from Mario Scaduto's continuation of Pietro Tacchi Venturi's *Storia della Compagnia di Gesù in Italia* (Rome: La Civiltà Cattolica, 1964). At least one aspect of contemporary religious life is considered in great detail, with all the relevant documentation carefully edited, in Guglielmo de Agresti's several volumes on Caterina de' Ricci (Olschki, 1963). Delio Cantimori is my principal guide on the problem of heresy: there are numerous references to matters treated in this and in the next Book in his *Eretici italiani del Cinquecento* (Sansoni paperback, 1961) and his *Prospettive di storia ereticale italiana del Cinquecento* (Bari: Laterza, 1961). Cosimo's policy of toleration is illustrated in several pages of Valerio Marchetti, "Il gruppo ereticale dei Sozzini a Siena, 1557-1560," *RSI*, LXXXI (1969), 151 ff.

On economics and demography, Florence has been the object of several exemplary studies. Besides Giuseppe Parenti's *Prime ricerche* cited above, there is Pietro Battara's "Botteghe e pigioni ...," *ASI*, XCV² (1937), 3-37, and *La popolazione di Firenze alla metà del '500* (Rinascimento del Libro: 1935). Gian Francesco Pagnini's *Della decima* of 1765 (discussed in Book V) is still unsurpassed on matters of taxation and money; and a thesis by Lorenzo Pecchioli presented at the University of Florence has guided me through economic legislation. But research has only just begun in this area. A specific case of what Florentines thought about what they and Cosimo were doing is given by Spini in "Politicità di Michelangelo," *RSI*, LXXVI (1964), 557-600; the structure and interests of several prominent families of the age are described by Richard A. Goldthwaite in *Private Wealth in Renaissance Florence* (Princeton University Press, 1968).

Of the considerable literature on the "precedence" question, I have taken most of my details from the cases considered by Giuseppe Mondaini in *La questione di precedenza* (1898) and by Panella in *Pegaso*, I (1929). Some information on international business relations are in Giuseppe Canestrini's article on Portugal in *ASI*, Appendix III (1846), 93-110, S. Goldenberg's article on Transylvania in *ASI*, CXXI (1963), 255-88, and Ramón Carande Thobar's *Carlos V y sus banqueros*, vol I (Madrid: Revista de

Occidente, 1943), which mentions a few Florentine bankers in Spain, as well as Emile Picot's "Les italiens en France au XVIe siècle," *Bulletin italien,* I (1901), 124 ff., and II (1902), 108 ff. I have taken account of Vincenzo Piano Mortari's and Biagio Brugi's work on sixteenth-century jurisprudence, although neither of them touches directly upon Florence. My discussion of the "Academy of the Plain" is based on the documents in Mag IX 126; and for printing I have relied on Salo Bongi's book on Giolito, Angelo Maria Bandini's histories of the Giunti and the Torrentini, and two recent articles by G. J. Hoogewerff. Certain aspects of cultural life are treated by Detlef Heikamp in *Il Vasari,* XV (1957), 139–50, and by Marcello Vannucci in *Dante nella Firenze del '500* ("Leonardo da Vinci," 1965). For the visual arts, I have read through a good bit of the immense literature devoted to the question of Mannerism, from the classic work of Walter Friedlaender, *Mannerism and Anti-Mannerism in Italian Painting* (Columbia University Press, 1957), and the *Acts of the XX International Congress of the History of Art* (Princeton University Press, 1963), to John Shearman, *Mannerism* (Penguin, 1967), always being cautious of what many art historians say when they get off "art" and onto "the times," and taking advantage of Catherine Dumont's review article, "L'état de la question," in *BHR,* XXVIII (1966), 439–57. The wide differences of opinion among the authorities have usually forced me to make up my own mind about disputed points.

Particular aspects of the "remodelling" of the city are considered by Ida Maria Botto in *Proporzioni,* IV (1963), 25–45, by Anna Forlani in *Il Vasari,* LXVI (1963), 41–44, by Guido Pampaloni in the very elegantly printed *Palazzo Strozzi* (Rome: Istituto Nazionale delle Assicurazioni, 1963), by Cosimo Conti in *La prima regia di Cosimo I* (Pellas, 1893), by Umberto Dorini in "Come sorse la fabbrica degli Uffizi," *RSAT,* V (1933), 1–40, by Francesca Morandini in a brief sketch of the history of the Pitti in *Commentari,* XVI (1965), 35–46 (to which I refer again in subsequent Books), and by Gunther and Christal Theim in the magnificent and painstaking *Toskanische Fassaden-Dekoration* (Munich: Bruckmann, 1964). I have checked my remarks on Francesco's *Studiolo* with Mario Bucci's splendid volume in the Sansoni "Forma e Colore" series, and with Luciano Berti, *Il principe dello Studiolo* (Edam, 1967); and my description of Giovanni's wedding reception with Piero Ginori Conti's *L'apparato per le nozze* . . . (Olschki, 1936), recently illustrated by the exhibit of Vasari's designs in the Uffizi (1965–66), of which a longer description, including the scores for the music, has been provided by Andrew C. Minor and Bonner Mitchell in *A Renaissance Entertainment: Festivities for the Marriage of Cosimo I* . . . (University of Missouri Press, 1968). The current popularity of this subject is shown by the publication of Jacopo Giunta's account of Michelangelo's funeral, translated into English and annotated by Rudolf and Margot Wittkower (London: Phaidon, 1964), and of Alois Nagler's *Theater Festivals of the Medici* (Yale, 1964), which adds little but illustrations to the published sixteenth-century accounts of the events. Cellini's bust of Cosimo, now in the M. H. de Young Museum in San Francisco, is described by Walter Heil in *The Burlington Magazine,* CIX (1967), 4–12.

Book II

Considerably less personal correspondence has survived for the second than for the first half of the sixteenth century; and the tendency of letter-writers to cover up their real sentiments with unfelt compliments renders it far less useful as a historical source. Of that part of it which has been published, I have consulted the letters of Bernardo Davanzati in the edition of Giuseppe Manuzzi of Florence, 1852; those of Archbishop Alessandro de' Medici to Pietro Vasari in Alessandro del Vita's edition in *RBA,* n.s., vol. II (1924), 220–36, and those concerning his missions to France in the translation by Raymond Ritter, *Lettres du Cardinal de Florence sur Henri IV* ... (Paris: Gassel, 1965); those of Vincenzo Borghini in the edition of A. Lorenzoni (Seeber, 1912); those of Andrea Cesalpino in the editions of Ugo Viviani (in spite of its errors), *Vita e opere di A. C.* (Arezzo: Viviani, 1922), and of Carlo Minetti (LeMonnier, 1874); those of Francesco Pucci in the edition of Luigi Firpo and Renato Piattoli (Olschki, 1955); and those of Filippo Sassetti in the edition of Ettore Marcucci (LeMonnier, 1855) rather than that of Arrigo Benedetti, *Lettere indiane* (Turin: Einaudi, 1961), which has an excellent introduction, but which contains only those letters that regard India. I have tried to clarify what Florentines said to each other by what their contemporaries elsewhere said to or about them; and I have checked through the published letters of Battista Guarini, Joseph Scaliger, Sperone Speroni, Paolo Manuzio, Girolamo Muzio, and, above all, Torquato Tasso. The complete published letters of King Henry III of France contain nothing pertinent to Florence except for a letter of condolence to the "dowager grand duchess," whose name, Bianca Cappello, the king seems not to have known, and on whom Roberto Cantagalli's article in *NRS,* XLIX (1965), 636–52, is the most recent authority.

Of the works of Ammirato himself, I have preferred the 1848–49 edition of his *Istorie di Firenze* either to the first or to the third (and last) of Turin, 1853, because the text is easier to read, and I have read the Brescia, 1599, rather than the first (Florence, 1594) edition of his *Discorsi sopra Cornelio Tacito* because I happen to own it. But the choice of editions is unimportant, since none of them appears to contain textual variants. Many of his notes and the manuscripts of many of his writings are in Ricc 2302, 2424, and 2708—all of them carefully identified by the leading modern authority on the subject, Rodolfo De Mattei, e.g., in "Codici Di S. A.," *Accademie e biblioteche d'Italia,* XXX (1962), 25 ff. A good number of Ammirato's more important minor works and most of his surviving literary correspondence are included in the three volumes of his *Opuscoli,* published posthumously by Scipione Ammirato, Jr., between 1637 and 1642, although some of the pieces had already appeared either separately or in another volume also called *Gli opuscoli* (Marescotti, 1583). De Mattei has published a bibliography of Ammirato's known (as of 1959) writings in *Studi salentini,* IV (1959), 381 ff., and has published what few texts have since come to light—e.g. a lost chapter of the *Discorsi* in *GCFI,* XLIII (1964), 115 ff., and another discourse of doubtful authorship in *ASI,* CXXVI (1968), 407–19. The *novelle* are available in two private printings of the late nineteenth century (Bologna, 1856, and Livorno, 1881). What biographical information I have not taken from Ammirato's works and correspondence comes from the first biography, that of Domenico de' Angelis (1675–1718) in *Le vite de' letterati salentini* (Florence, 1710), from the short sketch in the *Elogi degli uomini illustri toscani,* vol. III, from the much more complete *La vita e le opere* of Umberto Congedo (Trani, 1904) (now very rare, and for some reason "missing" from all the libraries of Florence), and from the many articles of Aldo Vallone, some of which have been collected in his

Studi e ricerche di letteratura salentina (Lecce: Centro di Studi Salentini, 1959). The context of one of Ammirato's projects is given by Oscar Halecki in "Le projet d'une ligue anti-ottomane...," *Académie des Inscriptions et Belles-Lettres: Comptes-rendus des séances de l'année 1960* (1961), pp. 190–200, and Peter Barth, "'Marciare verso Constantinopoli': Zur Türkenpolitik Klemens VIII," *Saeculum*, XX (1969), 44–56. The context of his political philosophy is given by Gennaro Maria Monti in "Un avversario cinquecentesco dell'unità d'Italia...," *Studi in onore di Niccolò Rodolico* (Florence: Università, 1944), pp. 263–74, by Samuel Berner in "Florentine Political Thought in the Late Cinquecento," *Il pensiero politico*, III (1970), 177–99, and by De Mattei in an article on "Ragion di Stato" in *Rivista internazionale di filosofia del diritto*, XXXVII (1960), and in a study of another anti-Machiavellian in *ASI*, CXXV (1967), as well as in numerous other studies. De Mattei will eventually publish a full historical biography based on his exhaustive researches all over Italy and Spain. Meanwhile, his sketch in the *DBI* and the articles collected in his *Il pensiero politico di S.A.* (Milan: Giuffrè, 1963), are indispensable guides.

For the other *dramatis personae* of this Book, I have used Ferdinando Vegas's article on Bernardo Davanzati in *La letteratura italiana: I minori*, vol. II, pp. 1327–37, which supplements A. Silvio Barbi's *Una lettera di B. D. e il suo volgarizzamento di Tacito* (1897). Davanzati's treatise on money (1588) can most easily be read in the French translation of Jean Yves LeBranchu, in *Écrits notables sur la monnaie* (Paris: Alcan, 1934). On Giovan Battista Strozzi, Jr., I have used Barbi's *Un accademico mecenate e poeta* (1900) along with Strozzi's substantial, but sketchy and often illegible correspondence in Mag VIII. 1899. On Raffaello Borghini, whose *Il riposo* has recently been republished (Milan: Labor, 1967), I have referred to Elena Avanzini's brief notes published in 1960 (Milan: Gastaldi); and I have read Riccardo Scrivano's study of Raffaello's distant cousin, Vincenzo, in *RLI*, VII (1958), 22–37, which takes into consideration the text included in *Studi sulla Divina Commedia*, ed. Ottavio Gigli (LeMonnier, 1855), and the notes of Benedetto Croce in *Poeti e scrittori del pieno e del tardo Rinascimento*, vol. II, pp. 134–54. For Maria Maddalena de' Pazzi, I have supplemented M. M. Vaussard's biographical sketch, 2nd ed. (Paris, 1925) with Vaussard's translation of selections from the *Extases et lettres* (Paris, 1945), the many letters published long ago in Anton Maria Biscioni's *Lettere di santi e beati fiorentini* (1736), and the unpublished doctoral dissertation of Giuliano de' Agresti, "La dottrina dell'amore in S. M. M." (Gregorian University, 1959), kindly lent me by the author, who has published one of a projected series of volumes of Maria Maddalena's complete works. These documents and studies should suffice to steer unwary readers away from such pious, but wholly unhistorical rhapsodies as the *S.M.M. de' P.*, published anonymously by Presbyterium in Rome (1960). For Filippo Sassetti, I have taken account of a new letter published by Vanni Bramanti in *GSLI*, LXXXIII (1966), 390–406, of the remarks of Robert L. Montgomery, Jr., in "Allegory and the Incredible Fable," *PMLA*, LXXXI (1966), 45–55, of the studies by Leonardo Olschki in *La bibliofilia*, XL (1938), 289–316, and by Francis M. Rogers in Congresso Internacional de Historia dos Descobrimentos, *Resumo das communicaçós* (Lisbon, 1960), pp. 280–83; but Mario Rossi's *Un letterato e mercante fiorentino* of 1899 is still indispensable. For Giovan Vittorio Soderini, I have found nothing more recent that the biographical introduction to the "Classici italiani" edition of his *Della con-*

servazione delle vite (1806), and for Ciriaco Strozzi (and the world of scholarship he represented), nothing but an anonymous "Vita Kyriaci Strozae" of 1604 in ASF Strozziana, ser. 3, f. 40. For Francesco Pucci, I have consulted G. Radetti's sketch in *GCFI*, XII (1931), 109–31, even though Firpo's researches have made much of it obsolete.

The best known, or at least the most studied Florentine of Ammirato's generation is Leonardo Salviati, even though he may remain "uno dei grandi 'maltrattati' della storia letteraria," as Severina Parodi claims in an introduction to one of his unpublished letters in *SFI*, XXVII (1969), 147–74. Particular aspects of his career have been studied by Deanna Battaglin, in "L. S. e le 'Osservazioni al Pastor Fido' del Guarino," *Atti e memorie dell'Accademia Patavina di Scienze, Lettere ed Arti*, LXXVII (1964–65), pt. III, pp. 249–84, by Silvio Pasquazi in a collection of essays on the *Rinascimento ferrarese* (Caltanissetta: Sciascia, 1957), by Carlo Pincin in "Un quaderno di L. S.," *Atti dell'Accademia delle Scienze di Torino*, Classe Scienze Morali, vol. XCVII (1962–63), 57–67, and above all by Peter M. Brown—in *GSLI*, CXXXIII (1956), 544–72, CXXXIV (1957), 314–32, and CXLVI (1969), 530–49, in "L'edizione del 1873 delle *Prose inedite*," *Rinascimento*, VIII (1957), 111–30, and in "Il *Discorso sopra la ginnastica*...," *Annali della Scuola Normale Superiore di Pisa*, Classe Lettere Storia Filosofia, ser. II, vol. XXVI (1957), 98–111. What is still lacking, however, is a modern critical edition of his works. Nothing has yet replaced the "Classici italiani" edition of 1809 or the privately printed edition (Rimini, 1875) of his *Lettere edite e inedite* by Pietro Ferrato.

The first chapter of this Book relies on the portrait of Ammirato reproduced in the frontispiece of DeAngelis' biography, on the plans of La Petraia in the Museo di Firenze Com'Era, on the many illustrations in Giulio Cesare Lensi Orlandi Cardini's (alas! sparsely explained) *Le ville di Firenze* (Vallecchi, 1954–55), on Bertha Harris Wiles, *The Fountains of Florence* (Harvard University Press, 1933), which I use elsewhere, at least for the illustrations, even though the fountains are arranged by type, rather than by place or historical connection, and on Maria Luisa Gothein, *A History of Garden Art*, Eng. trans. ed. Walter P. Wright (London and Toronto: Dent; New York: Dutton, 1928). I am sorry not to have been able to use Bastiano Arditi's *Diario di Firenze*, ed. Roberto Cantagalli (Istituto Nazionale Studi sul Rinascimento, 1970), which I read about in *RLI*, LXXIV (1970), 482, as this volume was on its way to the publisher.

For the countryside, I have consulted Emilio Sereni's *Storia del paesaggio agrario italiano* (Bari: Laterza, 1961), as well as the much more reliable reports of the Venetian ambassadors for this period (1576, 1588, and 1589). For Livorno, I have consulted the monographs of Giorgio Mori, C. A. Vianello, and Giuseppe Gino Guarnieri, and above all the *Navires et marchandises à l'entrée du port de Livourne* of Fernand Braudel and Ruggiero Romano (Paris: Colin, 1951). For economic conditions and activity, I have followed Braudel's now-classic *La Méditerranée et le monde méditerranéen à l'époque de Philippe II*, 2d ed., revised and enlarged (Paris: Colin, 1966), as well as on Amintore Fanfani's *Storia del lavoro in Italia* (Milan: Giuffrè, 1943), which draws heavily upon Cantini's collection of laws, upon Parenti's study of price curves, and upon Galluzzi. Considerable light has recently been shed on Florentine commercial activities of the time by José Gentil da Silva in an article in *Revue du Nord*, XL (1959), 133, and in "Capitaux et marchandises, échanges et finances entre le XVIe et XVIIIe siècle," *Annales*, XII (1957), 287–300, by Henri Lapeyre in *Simon Ruiz et les 'asientos' de Philippe*

II (Paris: Colin, 1953), by Maurice Carmona in "Aspects du capitalisme toscan au XVIe et XVIIe siècles," *Revue d'histoire moderne et contemporaine,* XI (1964), 81–108, and "Sull'economia toscana del Cinquecento e del Seicento," *ASI,* CXX (1962), 32–46, by Giulio Mandich, *Le pacte de ricorsa et le marché italien des changes au XVIIe siècle* (Paris: Colin, 1953), and by Ruggiero Romano in the works cited in the bibliography for Book III. I have taken pertinent details from Guido Pampaloni's study of the Monte di Pietà in *Archivi storici delle aziende di credito,* I (1956), from Giuliano de' Ricci's diary in BNF Nuovi acquisti 985, reviewed by Giuliana Sapori in *Studi in onore di Armando Sapori* (Milan: Istituto Editoriale Cisalpino, 1957), vol. II, pp. 1063 ff., and an optimistic *relazione* of 1598 in Mag XXIV. 4, keeping in mind the questions posed by Amintore Fanfani in "Effemera la ripresa economica di Firenze sul finire del secolo XVI?" *ES,* XII (1965), 344–51, and Carlo Cipola, "The Decline of Italy: The Case of a Fully Matured Economy," *Economic History Review,* n.s., vol. V (1952–53), 178–87. The optimism of Florentines was shared by a resident English merchant at Pisa: see Raymond de Roover, "Thomas Mun in Italy," *Bulletin of the Institute of Historical Research,* XXX (1957), 80–85. The gambling regulations are contained in the collection of laws at the Newberry Library, mentioned above; and the Bolognese seeding machines are described by Carlo Poni in *RSI,* LXXVI (1964), 455–69.

The activities of Florentines abroad are mentioned briefly in the large volume of Hyppolyte de Charpin Feugergolles and Louis Fournier about Lyon, although Natalie Davis assures me that much more information could still be dug out of the Lyon archives. What I say about the foreign relations of the grand dukes comes in part from MAEPar, Toscane II (although the reports are rather sparse for this period), from *Agents ambassadeurs toscans auprès des Suisses sous le regne du grand-duc Ferdinand,* ed. Ernest Giddey (Zürich: Leeman, 1953), from Philip Argenti, *The Expedition of the Florentines to Chios* (London: J. Lane, 1934), from G. Uzielli, *Cenni storici sulle imprese . . . di Ferdinando I* (G. Spinelli, 1901), and from Sergio Camerani's study of Francesco's negotiations with the sultan in *ASI,* XCVII² (1939), 83–101, to be read keeping in mind what Dorothy Vaughan, among other recent authorities, says in *Europe and the Turk: A Pattern of Alliance, 1350–1700* (Liverpool: University Press, 1955). The many documents in the ASF regarding the exploits of the Knights of Santo Stefano have been studied by Alberto Tenenti in preparation for his exciting *Venezia e i corsari, 1580–1615* (Bari: Laterza, 1961), now in English translation as *Piracy and the Decline of Venice,* trans. Janet and Brian Pullan (London: Longmans, 1967).

For the physical aspect of the city, I have relied on Lastri's *Osservatore fiorentino,* on certain passages from Borghini's *Il riposo* (which I usually read in the "Classici italiani" edition of 1807), on the detailed map of 1584 printed in—among other places—Boffito's *Piante e vedute,* and above all on Francesco Bocchi's guidebook, *Le bellezze della città di Firenze,* first published in 1591 and frequently revised and republished thereafter. One of the best sources for the daily life of the times is Agostino Lapini's *Diario fiorentino,* first published in 1900. What I say about the members of the ruling house comes largely from Ammirato, e.g., his remarkably frank oration about Francesco, as well as from the reports of the Venetian ambassadors, Galluzzi, contemporary portraits, and the detailed *Istoria* (1880) of Ferdinando's administrative chief, Piero Usimbardi, later bishop of Arezzo. The only study of the bureaucracy I have been able to find is Guido Sommi Picenardi's article on Luigi Dovara in *ASI,* ser. V, vol. XLVII (1911), 49–129. What Fabrizio Winspeare says about court life in *Isabella Orsini e la corte medicea del suo tempo* (Olschki, 1961) should be read in the light of Giovanni Carrara's review article in *NA,* XCVI (1961), 517–24. A few other details may be gathered from Graziella Silla's anecdotal *Una corte alla fine del secolo '500* (Alinari, 1927), Leo Schrade's description of Bianca Cappello's marriage in *Les fêtes de la Renaissance* (Paris: Editions du Centre National de la Recherche Scientifique, 1961), and Gina Fasoli's article "Sulle ripercussioni italiani della crisi dinastica francesce...," *Memorie dell'Accademia delle Scienze dell'Istituto di Bologna,* Classe Scienze Morali, ser. IV, vol. IX (1949), 1–64. Much more information on political and social conditions in the years covered in this and in the next Book can be found in Samuel Berner's two articles: "Florentine Political Thought in the Late Cinquecento," *Il pensiero politico,* II (1970), 177–99, and "Florentine Society in the Late Sixteenth and Early Seventeenth Centuries," *Studies in the Renaissance,* XVIII (1971), 203–46, although I do not necessarily agree with all the theses.

Except for those portions regarding questions of literary criticism, which Bernard Weinberg published in *GSLI,* CXXXI (1954), 175–94, and described in *Italica,* XXXI (1954), 106–14, I have taken most of my information about the Accademia degli Alterati from Weinberg's microfilm of the manuscript diary in Laur Ashburnham 558 and from the statutes and lists in Mag IX. 134, with help from Domenico Maria Manni's *Memorie della fiorentina famosa accademia degli Alterati* (Stecchi, 1748) and Weinberg's encyclopedic *History of Literary Criticism in the Italian Renaissance* (University of Chicago Press, 1961), which contains a synopsis of all the pertinent treatises of the age and full bibliographies for each author. The most recent study of the Crusca's position on literary matters is a paper by Mario Sansone, published in the transactions of the conference of Ferrara, 1954, under the title *Torquato Tasso* (Milan: Marzorati, 1957). The Accademia della Crusca I describe on the basis of the manuscript diary preserved in the present seat of the academy, a diary kept by successive secretaries, with only occasional lacunae, right up until the dissolution of the academy in 1783, upon which are based the brief comments in Cartesio Marconcini, *L'Accademia della Crusca dalle origini alla prima edizione del 'Vocabolario'* (Pisa: Valenti, 1910), and [Giovanni Grazzini], *L'A. della C.,* published privately by the academy in 1965, as well as, for the later period, my own *Tradition and Enlightenment in the Tuscan Academies, 1690–1800* (University of Chicago Press; Rome: Edizioni di Storia e Letteratura, 1961), which I cite here once and for all. Most of the other academies of the period are listed in Michel Maylender's immense *Storia delle accademie d'Italia* (Bologna: Cappelli, 1926–30). On Tacitus and on Tacitism in historiography and prose style I have consulted Jose Ruysshaert's book on Justus Lipsius and the well-known biography by Jason Lewis Saunders, as well as an article by Morris W. Cross published in the *Revue du seizième siècle* in 1914. On historiography in particular I am indebted to Giorgio Spini's study of *ars historica* (1948), now translated and somewhat revised in my *The Late Italian Renaissance.* One of my chief sources is Vincenzo Borghini's *Discorsi,* in the 1755 edition, as well as the correspondence of his friends. William J. Bouwsma's somewhat negative view of Ammirato as a historian is expressed in his "Three Types of Historiography in Post-Renaissance Italy," *History and Theory,* IV (1965), 303–14.

What I say about religious life in Florence comes in part from the printed records of the diocesan synods, from the canonization papers of several of the saints—e.g., *Compendium Vitae, Virtutum et Miraculorum B. Catharinae de Ricciis* (Rome, 1746)—from Cesare Guasti's edition of the letters of Caterina de' Ricci, and above all from Guasti's heavily documented *Officio proprio per fra Girolamo Savonarola,* 2d ed. (Prato, 1863). But I have also used selections of contemporary hagiography, like Pandolfo Ricasoli Baroni's *Osservazioni celeste . . . contenute nella vita di . . . Angelo Maria Montusi* (1632), and the anonymous "Vita Leonis XI," in Biblioteca Casanatense, Rome, MS 4201, as well as such modern studies as Antonio Cistellini, "San Filippo Neri e la sua patria," *RSCI,* XXIII (1969), 54-119 (which I also use in Book IV), Valerio Marchetti, "Notizie sulla giovinezza di Fausto Sozzini da una copialettera di Girolamo Bargagli," *BHR,* XXXI (1969), 67–91, D. Alaleona, "Le laudi spirituali nei secoli XVI e XVII," *RMI,* XVI (1909), 1–54, F. Sarri, *Il venerabile fra Bartolomeo Cambi da Salutio* (Bemporad, 1925), and—particularly on the mystics and holy men—Arnaldo d'Addario, "Note di storia della religiosità e della carità fiorentina nel secolo XVI," *ASI,* CXXXVI (1968), 61-147. On censorship, I have taken note of A. De Rubertis, "La censura delle opere di fra Girolamo Savonarola," *La bibliofilia,* LX (1953), 54–58, and I have found one example of a censored text, Francesco Bocchi's history of the Flemish wars, in ASF Strozziana, ser. I, 275. What I say about the bishop of Fiesole comes in large part from Ammirato's portrait in *Familie nobili fiorentine*; what I say about Lorenzo da Brindisi from the chaotic chronicles of P. Arturo da Carmignano, which began being published in 1960; and what I say about Ferdinando's press from G. E. Saltini's thorough article in *GSAT,* IV (1860). Ferdinando's religious policy at Livorno has been fully recognized by only one recent historian of sixteenth-century toleration movements: Erich Hassinger, in *Religiöse Toleranz im 16. Jahrhundert* (Basel-Stuttgart: Helbing and Lichtenhan, 1965).

My remarks about philosophy have been guided by the references provided by Eugenio Garin and Paul Oskar Kristeller to Francesco de' Vieri, the old, but still standard, biography of Jacopo Mazzoni published by Giuseppe Rossi in *Rendiconti dell'Accademia dei Lincei,* ser. V, vol. XL (1893), pp. 163–83, and by Tullio Gregory's and Luigi Firpo's studies of Patrizi, one of the latter now available in English in my *The Late Italian Renaissance* (first published in *Rivista di filosofia,* LXI [1950], et seq.). My passages on utopianism are inspired by Firpo's *Lo Stato ideale della Controriforma* (Bari: Laterza, 1957); my passages on *imprese* take note of Mario Praz's *Studies in Seventeenth Century Imagery* (London: Warburg Institute, 1939), now also available in a revised Italian edition of 1964. My account of the trimming of the *Decameron* comes partly from the articles of Peter M. Brown cited above, partly from Pio Paschini in *Cinquecento romano e riforma cattolica* (Rome: Lateran, 1958), partly from the *Annotazioni* of Borgini's committee (I happen to use the 4th edition of 1857, with the notes of Angelo Maria Salvini), and partly from the somewhat justified tirades against Salviati by Il Lasca and by Traiano Boccailni (in *Pietra del paragone politico,* 1615).

On the arts, besides the more general sources already mentioned, I have consulted Eduard Vodoz's *Studien zum architektonischen Werk des Bartolomeo Amannati* (sic.) (Ph.D. diss., Zürich, 1942), which is very thorough, as well as Pietro Pirri's "L'architetto Bartolomeo Ammannati e i gesuiti," *Archivum Historicum Societatis Iesu,* XII (1943), 5–57, Andrea Bruscoli's diary, edited by Detlef Heikamp in *Proporzioni,* IV (1963),

David Summers's "The Sculptural Program of the Cappella di San Luca . . . ," *MKHIF,* XV (1969), and Eve Borsook, "Art and Politics at the Medici Court . . . ," ibid., XI (1965), XIII (1967). I have taken note of the theses of Mina Bacci in "Jacopo Ligozzi e la sua posizione nella pittura fiorentina," *Proporzioni,* IV (1963), of Ida Maria Botto in "Alcuni aspetti dell'architettura fiorentina della seconda metà del Cinquecento" in the same volume, of Federico Zeri, *Pittura e Controriforma: L'arte senza tempo di Scipione da Gaeta* (Turin: Einaudi, 1957), and of Eugenio Battisti, "La critica a Michelangelo dopo il Vasari," *Rinascimento,* VII (1956), 135–57. And I have taken a few details from Sabine Jacob, "Florentinische Elemente in der spanischen Malerei des frühen 17. Jahrhunderts," *MKHIF,* XIII (1967), 115–65, and from Jesús Hernández Perera, *Escultores florentinos en España* (Madrid: Instituto Velázquez, 1957). My brief reference to the Uffizi statue collection is taken from M. Müntz, "Les collections d'antiquités formées par les Médicis au XVIe siècle," *Mémoires de l'Accadémie des Inscriptions et Belles-Lettres,* XXXV² (1896), 105 ff., and from Antonio Zobi's *Notizie storiche sull'origine e progressi dei lavori di commesso in pietre dure* (1841) (2nd. ed.; 1853).

For music, I have relied on the 1934 offset copy of Vincenzo Galilei's *Dialogo della musica antica e moderna* and on his *Contrapunti a due voce,* ed. Louise Rood (Smith College, 1945), on Giovanni de' Bardi's "Discorso" translated in Oliver Strunk's *Source Readings in Music History* (Norton paperback), vol. II, and on Claude Palisca's edition of Girolamo Mei's *Letters on Ancient and Modern Music* (American Institute of Musicology, 1960) and his "Vincenzo Galilei's Counterpoint Treatise . . . ," *Journal of the American Musicological Society,* IX (1956), 81–96. For the background of the work of the Camerata, I have referred to Robert Weaver, "Sixteenth Century Instrumentation," *The Musical Quarterly* XLVII (1961), 363–78, and to Liliana Pannella, "Le composizioni profane di une raccolta fiorentina del Cinquecento," *Rivista italiana di musicologia,* III (1968), 3–47, as well as, concerning the connection between music and the theater, to Giulio Ferroni's "Le commedie di Raffaello Borghini," *RLI,* LXXIII (1969), 37–63. I have taken into consideration the well-known works of Federico Ghisi, Massimo Milo, Fabio Fano, D. P. Walker, and Nino Pirrotta, all of them mentioned by my chief guides through the technical complexities of the subject, namely, Howard Mayer Brown, whose "Psyche's Lament" will soon appear in a Festschrift for A. Tillman Merrit (Harvard University Press), and whose "How Opera Began: An Introduction to Jacopo Peri's *Euridice* (1600)" is published in my *The Late Italian Renaissance,* and by Edward E. Lowinsky, whose "Music in the Culture of the Renaissance," *Journal of the History of Ideas,* XV (1954), 509–53, is a good example of how such complexities can be made intelligible even to the layman. Further information on Galilei is to be found in Antonio Favaro's bibliographical article in *ASI,* ser. V, vol. XLVII (1911), 376 ff.

For science, I have relied on Alexandre Koyré to guide me through the work of Giovan Battista Benedetti and Francesco Buonamici, and on Ettore Bortolotti's *Studi e ricerche sulla storia della matematica* (Bologna: Zanichelli, 1928) to introduce me to contemporary mathematical problems.

I give further bibliographical references in my two essays: "The End of the Renaissance in Florence," *BHR,* XXVI (1965), 1–30, now with slight revisions in my *The Late Italian Renaissance,* and "The Florentine Background of Galileo's Work," in Ernan McMullin, ed., *Galileo: Man of Science* (New York: Basic Books, 1967). How much my theses differ from those frequently presented can be noted by comparing them with the concluding remarks of Andreas Grote in *Florenze*: *Gestalt und Geschichte eines Gemeinwesens* (Munich: Prester, 1965), especially p. 271.

Book III

The most important source for this Book is the "Edizione nazionale" of Galileo's *Opere,* 2d ed. (Barbèra, 1929–39). Volumes X to XVIII contain the complete correspondence to, from, and about Galileo. Volume XX has an index and a very helpful biographical dictionary of all persons mentioned in the texts. When possible, I have read individual works in the latest critical editions: *Il saggiatore,* ed. Libero Sosio, with an excellent introduction (Feltrinelli); *Dialogo sui massimi sistemi,* ed. Ferdinando Flora (Universale Rizzoli, 1959) and ed. Franz Brunetti (Laterza, 1963); *Discorsi . . . intorno a due nuove scienze,* ed. Adriano Carugo and Lodovico Geymonat (Turin: Boringhieri, 1958), with a magnificent commentary; and the somewhat older, but still standard, *Scritti letterari,* ed. Alberto Chiari (LeMonnier, 1943), The *Sidereus Nuncius* I read in the offset of the original edition published by the Domus Galilaeana in Pisa in 1964 (though I recommend the French edition of Emile Namer [Paris: Gauthier Villars, 1964], which provoked the comments on the difference between Galileo and Descartes by Jean-François Revel in *L'Express,* 30 Jan.–5 Feb. 1967). Carlo Maccagni's *Antologia galileiana* (Barbèra, 1964) is well planned, but it would be more valuable with notes and comments. I have usually done my own translations, though I have found the many now made available by Stillman Drake and I. E. Drabkin very useful because of their extensive notes. The tendency of some modern "historians of ideas" to slight Galileo in favor of Bacon and Descartes can be explained partly by the 330-year delay in translating one of his principal works into French—and by the decision of the publishers to price the new *Discours concernant deux sciences nouvelles* (Paris: Colin, 1970) out of the market at F 70.

The bibliography on Galileo has increased considerably as a result of the recent centennial celebrations, as may be seen in the long list prepared by Ernan McMullin and published, along with a number of pertinent studies by some of the best scholars in the field, in *Galileo: Man of Science,* cited above. I particularly recommend the many papers presented at the *Convegno internazionale di ricognizione delle fonti per la storia della scienza italiana dei secoli XIV–XVI* at Pisa and Florence, soon to be published *in toto.* The essays presented at U.C.L.A. and published as *Galileo Reappraised* (University of California Press, 1966) are often very original. So are some of those published by the Accademia dei Lincei as *G G: Celebrazioni del IV centenario della nascita* (Rome, 1965), by the Massachusetts Institute of Technology as *Homage to G.,* ed. Morton F. Kaplan (Cambridge, 1966), and by Laterza as *Fortuna di G.* (Bari, 1964)—although I avoid getting involved in the quarrel over Bertolt Brecht. Unfortunately, the demands of conference organizers have outrun the supply of talent. Thus the *Achievement of G.,* ed. James Brophy and Henry Paolucci (New York: Twayne, 1962), is something less than valuable. The enormous *Simposio* on *G. nella storia e nella filosofia della scienza* (which the editor, Maria Luisa Righini, kindly let me examine in proof before its publication in 1967) has rather more padding than substance. I feel fortunate, therefore, to have finished this chapter before having had to read the twelve projected volumes of *Saggi su G. G.,* soon to be published by the national committee in charge of the fourth centenary celebrations in Rome.

Of monographs on various aspects of Galileo's achievement, many of those of Antonio Favaro are still indispensable, even though they often consist of little more than running commentaries on the correspondence. The offprints of his articles are all assembled in the Favaro collection of the BNF, which is where I read them. His biographical sketches of Galileo's friends and foes have since been supplemented by Giorgio Abetti's *Amici e nemici di G.* (Bompiani, 1945) and by G. Gabrieli's "De-gl'interlocutori . . . ," in Accademia dei Lincei: Classe di Scienze Morali, *Rendiconti*, ser. VI, vol. VIII (1932), pp. 95–129. His exhaustive *G. G. e lo Studio di Padova* and *G. G. a Padova* have recently been reprinted (Padua: Antenore, 1966 and 1968). His biography was reprinted in paperback by Barbèra in 1957. I have found the following particularly helpful: Franz Brunetti's article on method in *Belfagor*, XI (1956); Bruno Busolini's study of motion in *Physics*, VI (1964); Ernst Cassirer's provocative thesis on Galileo's Platonism in *Studies . . . in Honor of George Sarton* (New York: Henry Schuman, 1947); Raffaello Colapietra's ' Il pensiero estetico galileiano," *Belfagor*, XI (1956), which complements Erwin Panofsky's well-known *G. as a Critic of the Arts* (The Hague: Nijhoff, 1954); I. E. Drabkin and Stillman Drake in their introduction to Galileo's *On Motion and On Mechanics* (University of Wisconsin Press, 1960); and, on a single aspect, Olaf Pedersen's "Sagredo's Optical Researches," *Centaurus*, XIII (1969), 139–50. Needless to say, I am much indebted to the many works of Marie Boas Hall and Thomas Kuhn for general direction in the history of science. Unfortunately, the standard reference work on the history of mathematics by Eric Bell skips the Galileans.

On the literary aspects of Galileo's work, I have followed Enrico Falqui in an article in *La Letteratura italiana*: *I minori*, vol. II; Nereo Vianello in *SFI*, XIV (1956) and in "Preoccupazioni stilistiche di G. lettore del Petrarca," *La critica stilistica e il barocco letterario* (LeMonnier, 1958); Raffaello Spongano in *La prose di G. e altri scritti* (Messina-Florence: D'Anna, 1949); and Dante Della Terza's essay in the volume *G. Reappraised* (U.C.L.A.) cited above. Galileo's relations with Sarpi and Campanella are documented by Firpo in "Appunti campanelliani, XXV . . . ," *GCFI*, XXXV (1956), 546, and are mentioned by Louise George Clubb in *Giambattista Della Porta, Dramatist* (Princeton University Press, 1965), pp. 32–35. I have taken the context largely from such authorities on baroque literature as Ezio Raimondi, e.g., in his *Letteratura barocca* (Olschki 1961), Franco Croce, particularly in his most recent *Tre momenti del barocco letterario italiano* (Sansoni, 1966), Uberto Limentani in *La satira nel Seicento* (Milan-Naples: Ricciardi, 1961) and in "L'antisecentismo nella prima metà del Seicento," *La critica stilistica e il barocco letterario.*

On the trial, I follow Firpo in *BHR*, XXVII (1965), as well as in his many studies of late Renaissance philosophy; and I have taken note of Gerhard Hennemann's article in *Zeitschrift für Religions- und Geistesgeschichte*, XX (1968), 61–69. Giorgio de Santillana's now classic *The Crime of G.* (Phoenix, 1955) is indispensable for this and all other aspects of Galileo's life and works. On Galileo's early writings, Raffaello Giacomelli's *G. G. e il suo 'De Motu'* (Pisa: Domus Galilaeana, 1949) is a helpful guide through a difficult subject. It should be read along with Alexandre Koyré on Galileo's debts to his colleagues at Pisa recently republished in his *Etudes galiléennes* ("Histoire de la pensée," vol. XV [Paris: Hermann, 1966]) and with Leonardo Olschki's still very valuable *G. und seine Zeit* (Halle: Niemeyer, 1927). On the medieval background, Anneliese Maier's *Die Vorläufer G's im 14. Jahrhundert* (Rome: Edizioni di Storia e

Letteratura, 1949) is still the last word, although Ernest Moody has modified the theses somewhat in *G. Reappraised* (U.C.L.A., 1966). On the Padua period, I follow, besides authorities already cited, Giovanni Polvani, "Il momento veneto nella vita . . . ," as well as the other articles in *La civiltà veneziana nell'età barocca* (Sansoni, 1959), and Luigi Bulferetti in *G. G. nella società del suo tempo* (Manduria: Lacaita, 1964), though I have relied heavily on the well-known books and articles of Gaetano Cozzi and take several bits from Paolo Sarpi's *Lettere ai protestanti,* ed. Manlio Builio Busnelli (Laterza, 1931).

On technical and philosophical questions, Guido Morpurgo Tagliabue's two studies, *I processi di G. e l'epistemologia* (Milan: Edizioni di Comunità, 1963) and "G., uomo d'oggi," in *Cusano e G.,* ed. E. Castelli (Padua: CEDAM, 1964), are essential, as are Vasco Ronchi's numerous restatements of the important thesis he propounded in *Il cannocchiale di G.,* 2d ed. (Turin: Einaudi, 1958), e.g., *Storia del cannocchiale* (Pontificia Accademia delle Scienze, 1964). I am very much indebted to two brilliant essays by Adriano Carugo, one published in *Nuove questioni di storia moderna,* ed. Luigi Bulferetti (Milan: Marzorati, 1964), the other in *SSt,* I (1959–60), as well as to the recent works of such well-known authorities on Renaissance philosophy and science as Antonio Corsani, in "G. e le macchine," *GCFI,* XLV (1966); Paolo Rossi, in *I filosofi e le macchine (1400–1600)* (Feltrinelli paperback, 1962); and Eugenio Garin in *Scienza e vita civile nel Rinascimento italiano* (Universale Laterza). Giovan Battista Della Porta's *De telescopio,* which Ronchi cites at length, is now available in a modern edition (Olschki, 1962); it is put into its Neapolitan context by Nicola Badaloni in an article in *SSt,* I (1959–60). What I say about Galileo's influence on his own and on the next generation come in part from Spini and from a monograph by Pasquale D'Elia, S. J., *G. in Cina* (= Analecta Gregoriana, XXXVII) (Rome: Gregoriana, 1947).

The seventeenth-century biographies of Galileo by Niccolò Gherardini and Vincenzo Viviani, the latter now republished along with the trial documents by Ferdinando Flora in a Rizzoli paperback, are still interesting and valuable to read. Of current biographies, the one by Pio Paschini (Vatican City, 1964) is very bulky and rather old-fashioned (it was actually written in 1943), and the one by Giovanni Paoli (Turin: Società Editrice Internazionale, 1943), is popular and superficial. The best biography for lay readers, and certainly the best written one, is Lodovico Geymonat's *G. G.* (Turin: Einaudi, 1957), now available in English translation by Stillman Drake (New York: McGraw Hill, 1965). Very valuable for my purposes is Maria Luisa Righini Bonelli's description of Galileo's residences, in *Universo,* XXXVII–XXXVIII (1957–58), as well as her articles on the Ptolemaic cosmos, on the revival of ancient science, and on the telescope, published respectively in *Cultura e scuola,* XXVII (1968), *Organon,* IV (1967), and *Ithaca* (1962).

While scholarly literature thus abounds for Galileo himself, it is very sparse for the environment in which he lived. Considerable anecdotal material for the years after 1640 has been gathered together in Gaetano Imbert's *Seicento fiorentino* (1906; 2d ed., Milan: Athena, 1930). Several of the episodes in Galluzzi were expanded into books at the turn of the present century, namely, Gino Bandini, *Un episodio mediceo della Guerra dei Trent'Anni* (Seeber, 1901); G. G. Guarnieri, *L'ultima impresa coloniale di Ferdinando I* (= *Annali dei RR. Istituti Tecnico e Nautico di Livorno,* ser. IV, vol. IX [1908–9]); *Origine e sviluppo del porto di Livorno durante il governo di Ferdinando I* (Livorno: Meucci, 1911), *Lo sviluppo . . . di*

Livorno . . . *Cosimo II* (Livorno: Formichini, 1912), and, more recently, a huge miscellany entitled *Il Principato mediceo nella scienza del mare* (Pisa: Giardini, 1963). These have since been supplemented by J. D. Mackie, ed., *Negotiations between James VI* . . . *and Ferdinand I,* with a selection of documents (London, 1927), by Achille De Rubertis, *Ferdinandi I* . . . *e la contesa fra Paolo V e la Repubblica veneta* (Venice: R. Deputazione Editrice, 1933). I have taken additional information from the reports of the Tuscan resident in London, Ottavio Lotti, to Andrea Cioli in Florence in ASF Mediceo 4188, from the report on internal administration of September 28, 1627, ASF Mediceo 6410, from the edicts on the university of January 25, 1611, in Mag IX. 49, 13. Tuscan territorial acquisitions are listed by Pompeo Neri in a Relazione in ASF Gabinetto 122. For Livorno, besides these and the works already cited, I have looked at the contemporary *Discorso cronologico* written for Ferdinando II by Nicola Magri and published at Naples in 1647, as well as the reports of the Genoese consul summarized by Giulio Giacchero in *Storia economica del Settecento genovese* (Genoa: Apuania, 1951), especially pp. 23–24. On the queen of France, I follow Salvo Mastellone in *La reggenza di Maria dei Medici* (Messina–Florence: D'Anna, 1962).

Only a few modern studies bear even indirectly upon the economic affairs of Florence, namely, the articles by Guido Pampaloni and Romolo Camaiti in *Archivi storici delle Aziende di Credito,* vol. I, Torban Damsholt's resumé of the findings of Parenti and Fanfani in *Scandinavian Economic History Review,* XII (1964), and the two small masterpieces of Ruggiero Romano published respectively in *Annales,* VII (1952), and in *RSI, LXXIV* (1962). I have therefore tried to interpret the documents I use with the help of the studies of European economy in general by François Crouzet (e.g., in *Annales,* XXI [1966]) and by Roland Mousnier, particularly in the relevant sections of *Les XVI et XVII siècles* (Presses Universitaires de France, 1954). I have added the documents on population in ASF Strozziana ser. I. 24, to what has already been published in Pardi, Belloch, and Galluzzi, even though their inconsistencies and contradictions render them suspect—all of them, that is, except for the annual baptismal figure on fols. 143 ff. For the plague, I have relied mostly on the contemporary accounts mentioned in the text, that is, those of Mario Guiducci and Francesco Rondinelli, as well as on an article by Achille De Rubertis in *Memorie domenicane,* LXIV (1947). My survey of Tuscany under Ferdinando I is based largely on "Una relazione inedita dello Stato del granduca di Toscana nel 1607," ed. Agostino Zanelli, BSSP, XXXIII–XXXIV (1926–27). My statements about Tuscany in the 1640s are based in part upon the "Descrizione di tutto lo Stato vechio" (sic.) in ASF Strozziana, ser. I, 24. My survey of the quarter of Santo Stefano in 1631 comes from ASF Strozziana, ser. I, 19. My calculations of admissions to citizenship are taken from the "Nota de' cittadini fatti in Firenze nel tempo del Principato fino al 1646," in the same collection, ser. II, 74.

The art of the period has been more thoroughly studied, although the judgments of the students are often at variance with one another and difficult to fit into an interpretation of the period as a whole. Baldinucci is still basic. But so now are a few catalogues: the *Mostra del Cigoli* (published by the Cassa di Risparmio of San Miniato, 1959), the *Casa Buonarroti* (published by the Cassa di Risparmio of Florence, 1966). Felice Stamfele and Jacob Bean, *Drawings from New York Collections* (New York: Metropolitan Museum, 1967), vol. II, and above all *Settanta pitture e sculture del 600' e*

'*700 fiorentino,* ed. Mina Gregori (the authority on the subject) (Vallecchi, 1965). For individual artists, I have used the study of Lorenzo Lippi by Fiorella Sricchia (*Proporzioni,* IV [1963]), of Giovanni da San Giovanni by Edoardo H. Giglioli (Florence: S.T.E.T., 1949), of the Casino by Anna Rosa Masetti (*Critica d'arte,* nos. 49–54 [1962]), of Carlo Dolci by Carlo del Bravo (*Paragone,* no. 163 [1963]), of Volterrano, in his Petraia period, by Matthias Winner (*MKHIF,* X [1963]), of Cecco Bravo by Anna Rosa Masetti (Venice: Neri Pozza, 1963). By far the most complete study of Pietro da Cortona is the one by Giuliano Briganti (Sansoni, 1962), who, however, is prejudiced against all things Florentine. His book must, therefore, be read along with the catalogues of the showings at Cortona in 1956 (Rome: De Luca) and of the drawings at Florence (Olschki, 1965), along with the invaluable article by Malcolm Campbell, editor of the second catalogue, published in *Art Bulletin,* XVIII (1966), in anticipation of Campbell's book on Cortona, along with W. Vitzthum's *P. da C. a Palazzo Pitti* (Milan: Fabbri, 1965), and along with the documents published by Anna Maria Crinò in *RdA,* XXXI (1959). My judgments of Cigoli are shaped by Walter Friedlaender's long article in *Festschrift für Ludwig Heinrich Heydenreich* (Munich: Prestel, 1964). My references to Agucchi are from Denis Mahon's *Studies in Seicento Art and Theory* (London; Warburg Institute, 1947); my details on decorative arts come from Antonio Morassi's lavishly illustrated *Il tesoro dei Medici* (Milan: Sylvana, 1963), now available in English (New York Graphic Society, 1964). And many of my observations on the whole of contemporary art come from the long, scholarly, but well written *Patrons and Painters* by Francis Haskell (London: Chatto & Windus, 1963).

The principal studies of music in this period are Angelo Solerti, *Musica, ballo . . . alla corte medicea dal 1600 al 1637* (Bemporad, 1905), the more recent *Alle fonti della monodia* of Federico Ghisi (Milan: Bocca, 1940), and "La nascita del melodrama" of Massimo Mila, *RMI,* LVI (1954), and those by Brown cited under Book II. I have therefore done my own unprofessional dipping into the works of Giovan Battista Doni, particularly his *Lyra Barberina,* ed. A. F. Gori (Florence, 1762), his *Compendio del Trattato de' generi e de' modi* (1635), his correspondence, edited by Gori as *Commercium letterarium* and published with A. M. Bandini's *De Vita et Scriptis* in 1754 and 1755, and his letters included in Mersenne's *Correspondence,* which is still in process of publication (Paris: Beau Chesne). But wherever possible I have followed the suggestions of D. P. Walker and Claude Palisca, the latter in "Scientific Empiricism in Musical Thought," *Seventeenth Century Science and the Arts* (Princeton University Press, 1961).

The publishing business declined in the early seventeenth century. Most of what came from the presses in these years consists of orations and miscellaneous verse. And even that is usually more easily accessible in later editions, e.g., for orations, the *Prose fiorentine.* Poetry, however, often contains a mine of information about the life and times of Galileo's contemporaries. Except for *La Firenze, poema* (Ferrara: Rinaldi, 1777), I read the poems of Gabriello Chiabrera in my copy of the *Opere* (Venice: Baglioni, 1805) and his *Lettere* in the second edition of Genoa, 1829, with help from the somewhat anodyne *Vita* by his nephew, published in San Miniato in 1913, and from the authoritative articles by Giovanni Getto, in *Lettere italiane,* VI (1954), and in Getto's *Barocco in prosa e in poesia* (Rizzoli, 1969). The *Rime* of Stefano Vai have been reprinted by the Commissione per i Testi di Lingua (Bologna, 1968). I have read the poems of

Giambattista Marino in the original editions and his *Lettere* in the well-annotated and indexed edition of Marziano Guglielminetti (Turin: Einaudi, 1966). The *novelle* of Andrea Cavalcanti are listed in Giovanni Papanti, *Catalogo dei novellieri italiani* (Livorno, 1871). Although literary historians have generally ignored them, the works of Jacopo Soldani, Francesco Ruspoli, Lorenzo Lippi, Antonio Malatesti, and the other *beaux esprits* of the time are still very amusing to read today. So, particularly, are those of Michelangelo Buonarroti, Jr., who has finally received the attention of two critics (particularly Giorgio Petrocchi) in *Atti del Convegno sul tema*: "*La poesia rusticana nel Rinascimento*" (Accademia Nazionale dei Lincei, 1969). So, finally, are those of the Neapolitan poet and artist Salvator Rosa, who lived in Florence in the 1640s: see U. Limentani's edition of his *Poesie e lettere inedite* (Olschki, 1950).

None of the extant collections of personal letters and memoirs can even approach Galileo's in quality and quantity. The letters of Carlo Strozzi in ASF Strozziana, ser. III, 45, for instance, are as dull to read as the plodding author must have been to listen to. But they can be supplemented by the memoirs and business records that I have found in the same collection, ser. III, 40, 137, 182, and 203. Those of Giovanni Ciampoli (I have consulted an anonymous biography of him in Mag IX. 100, as well as the one by Favaro and, more recently, Mario Costanzo's *Critica e poesia del primo Seicento,* vol. I: *Inediti di Giovanni Ciampoli* [Rome: Bulzoni, 1969]) are highly "auto-censored" in the printed version (Rome: Hertz, 1661), and carefully omit mention of some of the views that the author hid in his still-unpublished letters to an equally tedious letter-writer, Jacopo Gaddi (Mag VIII, 1279–81), whose Selva politica, Mag XXX, 158 and 179, as well as his numerous printed works I also refer to. Somewhat more frank is Girolamo da Sommaia in his "Zibaldone" (Mag VIII, 75 and 28). The memoirs of Cardinal Guido Bentivoglio, published in Venice in 1648, are concerned almost exclusively with curial ladder-climbing at the beginning of the seventeenth century, and reflect the author's rather narrow range of interests. Those of Cesare Tinghi (BNF Gino Capponi 261, until 1618, and thereafter in the ASF), which are well known to art historians, suffer from the limitations noted in the text. The Memorie diverse... of Andrea Cavalcanti (ASF Strozziana, ser. I, 11) are much more interesting, but they begin only in 1640. The Relazione of Francesco Carletti (on whom: Gemma Sgrilli, *F. C.* [Rocca San Casciano, 1905]), of which parts can be read in *Le più belle pagine,* ed. L. Barzini (Milan: Treves, 1926), and the whole in Lorenzo Magalotti's edition discussed in Book IV, deals more with the Indies than with Florence. It is now available also in English (New York, 1964). And the voluminous *Epistolario* of José de Calasanz (Giuseppe Calasanzio, in Italian), still in the process of publication by the Edizioni di Storia e Letteratura in Rome under the editorship of Leodegario Picanyol, is fascinating to read. The part of it which refers to Florence has been examined by Pasquale Vannucci in *NA,* CDLXVIII (1956). The Settimani diary is, of course, the product of a later age. But it is full of details about this period that are not available elsewhere.

Several collections of scientific and diplomatic documents of the period are available in print, e.g., Michele Cioni, *I documenti galileiana del S. Ufficio di Firenze* (Libreria Editrice Fiorentina, 1908), and Giuseppe Gabrielli, "Il carteggio scientifico ed accademico fra i primi Lincei (1603–1630)," Accademia Nazionale dei Lincei, Classe scienze morali . . . , *Memorie,* ser. VI, vols. I–II (1923). The largest collection of those that have not been printed, the Galileo papers in the BNF, has been described by Angiolo Procissi, author of, among other things, *Le traduzioni italiane delle opere di Archimede* (Bologna, 1953), in his *La collezione galileiana* . . . (Rome: Istituto Poligrafico dello Stato, 1959), although the manuscript catalogues still must be consulted for details. Some material in this chapter comes from the volume Toscane II in MAEPar. The material regarding the academies comes from Edoardo Benvenuti's *Agostino Coltellini e l'Accademia degli Apatisti* . . . (Pistoia: Tipografia Cooperativa, 1910), from the works of Benedetto Buonmattei (particularly from G. B. Casotti's biographical preface to *Della lingua toscana* in the second edition of 1760), from the biographical introduction to Benedetto Fioretti's *Osservazioni di creanze* (1675), and from the MS Diario Terzo of the Accademia della Crusca (from 1640), in the academy's archives, as well as from the standard reference books already cited.

For religion and the church, I have used the printed decrees of the various synods in Florence and Pisa, Giovan Battista Neri's *De Iudice S. Inquisitionis, Opusculum* (Matini, 1685), the "Relazione" on Cardinal Carlo de' Medici in BNF Gino Capponi 161 (and other details in 125 and 261), the *Monumenta Ordinis Servorum Sanctae Mariae a Quibus Eiusdem Ordinis Presbyteris Edita* (Rome, 1920), *Florentina Beatificationis Ven. Servae Dei Eleonarae Ramirez Montalvo Viduae Laudi* (Congregation of Rites, S. Hist. Nr. 130; Vatican, 1965), an account of the "pious objects" donated to the Accademia dei Lincei in 1612 (which shows that the scientists had no quarrel with "baroque" piety) published by Giuseppe Gabrieli in *GCFI*, VIII (1927), 386, the published works of the principal preachers and pastors, from Domenico Gori to Pandolfo Ricasoli Baroni, and, finally, the fascinating *La Semplicità ingannata* of that seventeenth-century precursor of Women's Lib, Arcangela Tarabotti (Venice, 1644), which I found in the Newberry Library while tracing down a reference of Giorgio Spini in his indispensable *Ricerca dei libertini* (Rome: Universale di Roma, 1950) (which I use extensively in Book IV as well). Many of the letters of Maria Celeste Galilei from her convent were translated by Mary Allan-Olney and published in 1870 (London: Macmillan). All of them have been studied by Enrica Viviani Della Robbia in *Nei monasteri fiorentini* (Sansoni, 1946). The reference to Maria Felice Orsini comes from an article by Ferdinand Boyer in *ASI,* CXXI (1963). And the story about Giovan Battista Cavalcanti is condensed from the long report in BNF Gino Capponi 305. My judgments of the histories of the religious orders have since been confirmed by Sergio Bertelli, who kindly let me read his forthcoming *Ribelli, libertini e ortodossi nella storiografia dell'eta barocca* in manuscript.

The published travelogs of foreign observers—from Franciscus Schottus, *L'itinerario* (Padua, 1628–29), and Pierre Du Val, *Le voyage et la description d'Italie* (1644, published in Paris, 1656), to John Evelyn, *The Diary* . . . , ed. E. S. de Beer (Oxford: Clarendon, 1955), Balthasar de Monconys, *Voyages* (*enrichie* edition of Paris: P. Delaulne, 1695), are sparse and usually superficial in this period. Milton's stay in Florence is described in an article by Piero Rebora in *Il Sei-Settecento,* in the Unione Fiorentina series (Sansoni, 1949). Except for the short notes by Cecil Roth in *AMCol* (1934–35), the available biographies of the romantic adventurer, Robert Dudley, who compiled the enormous portolan-gazetteer *Arcano del mare* (1646–47), are disappointingly old-fashioned. The *Toscane françoise* of Jean-Baptiste L'Hermite de Souliers, *dit* Tristan (Paris: Mesnier, 1658) amounts to no more than what is said of it in my text, and it can be used only as a supplement to the manual of behavior in BNF Gino Capponi 124 209 ff.

Biographical material is available for some of the personages mentioned. Of those not cited above, the best known is certainly Evangelista Torricelli, whose *Opere* and *Carteggio* began coming out in Faenza (Montanari) in 1919, and whose *De infinitis spiralibus,* with a comment by Ettore Carruccio, was published by the Domus Galilaeana in 1955. For a few years a periodical was devoted to studies about him. Commemorative celebrations were put on in Florence (University) in 1951 and in Faenza in 1958. The biographical studies of Marina Berardi Ragazzini in *Studi Romagnoli,* VIII (1957), and of Angiolo Procissi (Florence: University, 1951) are fairly complete, while the many articles of Luigi Tenca describe thoroughly his accomplishments as a mathematician. For Niccolò Aggiunti, I have used (besides Favaro), the *Orazione* of Marcantonio Pieralli (Pisa: Francesco delle Dote, 1638); for Alessandro Adimari the article by Arnaldo d'Addario in the *DBI;* for Cosimo de' Bardi, the *Orazione* by Francesco Maria Gualterotti (Florence, 1632); for Paganino Gaudenzio, Felice Menghini's *P. G.; Letterato grigionese del '600* (Milan: Giuffrè, 1941); for Curzio da' Marignolle (whom I have mentioned only once), the introduction to the *Rime varie* by C. Arlía (Bologna, 1885); for Antonio Malatesti, the notes in Pietro Fanfani's edition of his works (Milan, 1865); for Giovan Battista Rinuccini, the preface of G. Aiazzi to his *Nunziatura in Irlanda* (a fascinating document) (Florence: Piatti, 1844); for Pope Urban VIII as a poet, the note by Mario Costanzo in *GSLI,* CXLIV (1967), 329–39; for Carlo di Tommaso Strozzi, A. M. Bandini's article in *Novelle letterarie* (1786), cols. 34 ff., 49 ff., and 65 ff.; for Filippo Salviati, Niccolò Arrighetti's *Delle lodi* (Giunti, 1614); for Jacopo Soldani, the notes of Giuseppe Bianchini in the 1751 (Albizzini) edition of his *Satire.* Besides the other biographical dictionaries already cited, I use for this Book the *Pinacoteca* of Gian Vittorio Rossi ("Jano Nicio Eritreo") (Köln, 1643–48), which is not very thorough.

Book IV

Some of Magalotti's personal letters, like those of his contemporaries, were probably lost in the mails, as Francesco Redi complains in his *Opere,* cited below, vol. VI, p. 3. But an enormous number of them has survived. Stefano Fermi listed 1,108, not including the diplomatic letters, in his *Biobibliografia magalottiana* (Piacenza: Favari, 1904): Fermi's list is far from complete, as he admitted in his "Per un'edizione completa delle lettere . . . ," *Miscellanea di studi critici pubblicati in onore di Guido Mazzoni* (Galileiana, 1907), vol. II, pp. 261–75. Many of them are in print: *Lettere scientifiche ed erudite* (Tartini, 1721; Venice: Occhi, 1742; Venice: Pasquali, 1772); *Delle lettere familiari di L. M. e di altri insigni uomini a lui scritti,* ed., with a biographical introduction, by Angelo Fabroni, 2 vols. (Cambiagi, 1769) (one of the fullest collections); *Scritti di corte e di mondo,* ed., with a critical introduction, by Enrico Falqui and arranged by subject rather than by chronological order (Rome: Colombo, 1945); *Lettere inedite di L. M., Francesco Redi . . . ,* ed. Iarro (Seeber, 1889); "Due lettere . . . ," ed. D. E. Rhodes, *Studi secenteschi,* VII (1966); and *Lettere inedite di uomini illustri,* ed. Angelo Fabroni (1773–75). Those to Ascanio Piccolomini are published by Laura Corso in *BSSP,* VIII (1937), from among the many still in manuscript in Biblioteca Comunale, Siena, D.V.7; seven of those to Alessandro Segni by Ferdinando Massai in *RBA,* XXVIII (1917) and XXIX (1918); and others by

Sergio Camerani in *ASI,* XLVII (1939). Selections from the diplomatic correspondence are published by Cesare Guasti in *GSAT,* VI (1861) and V (1862) (also in offprint); extracts from those about England by Anna Maria Crinò in *Fatti e figure* (cited below); and a few of those on art by Alfredo Agostini in *I Melani a Firenze* (Pisa: Nistri, 1878).

Much of the correspondence still remains in manuscript, however. The richest collection is that in the private archive of the Venturi Ginori Lisci family in Florence, which includes also the original drafts of almost all his formal and informal writings and his official commissions at court (VG 251 E). The letters to and from Redi are mostly in Laur Redi 206 (with a few others in Redi 86), only some of which are included in Redi's published epistolaries. Those to Viviani are in Ricc 2487, those to Guido Grandi (which I consider briefly at the end of chapter 6) in BUP MSS Grandi 93. Mamy others are in BNF Palat. Cassetta Magalotti and MSS Galileo-Cimento III (mostly on his scientific activities). The diplomatic correspondence is preserved partially in ASF Strozziana ser. I (for example, 363 contains his letters from Sweden), and partly in ASF Mediceo 4412, 4491, 4510, 4518, and 4519. Those to him by Regnier Desmarais are in Bibliothèque Nationale, Paris, Fonds Italiens 517—in copy: the originals (some of which do not appear in the Paris copies) are in VG. Other earlier editions of one or more letters are listed by Fermi and need not be repeated here.

Magalotti's other writings exist in numerous versions. Lorenzo Montano published an anthology, *Le più belle pagine di L. M.,* in 1924 (Milan: Treves). The *Saggi di naturali esperienze,* of which a second edition appeared in 1691, has most recently been republished by Enrico Falqui (Rome: Colombo, 1947) (which is the edition I use, because I own a copy of it). The reports on various of his travels through Europe are published in part by Walter Moretti, *Relazioni di viaggio in Inghilterra, Francia e Svezia,* "Scrittori d'Italia," no. 241 (Bari: Laterza, 1968), though with a number of mistaken readings that have been corrected by Anna Maria Crinò in a review soon to appear in *SFI.* I began reading the autograph copy of Magalotti's diary of Cosimo's trip in BNF Conventi Soppressi SS. Annunziata G.9.1863; but as soon as possible I switched from Magalotti's own atrocious handwriting to Crinò's carefully transcribed and carefully annotated version, *Un principe di Toscana in Inghilterra e in Irlanda nel 1669* (Rome: Edizioni di Storia e Letteratura, 1968), which now replaces its only predecessor, the rather inaccurate anonymous translation published by Mawman in London, 1821. For Spain I have consulted the edition of Angel Sanchez Rivero, *Viaje de Cosme de Medicis por España y Portugal* (Madrid: Rivadeneyra, 1933). The illustrations, by the way, have once again been reproduced, in vol. III of *Historia social y económica de España* by Juan Regla and Guillermo Léspedes del Castillo, ed. Jaime Vicens Vives (Barcelona, 1957). For other countries I followed the easier-to-read copies in BNF II, III.430 and in Laur Med. Palat. 123, along with the supplementary diary of Jacopo Ciuti (Crinò has established the authorship) in ASF Misc. Med. 835 and as much as my eyes could take of the diary of Giovan Battista Gornia in ASF Misc. Med. 836. Magalotti's other travel literature I have read either in manuscript—the reports on China and Guinea in BNF Galileo-Cimento 292—or in the printed editions of 1697, 1825, and 1845, of which some passages have been reprinted in such anthologies as *Il genio vagante* (Parma, 1691–92), *Relazioni varie* (Manni, 1693), *Varie operette* (Venice: Pizzolatto, 1779), and *Varie operette del conte L. M.* (Milan: Silvestri, 1825).

Of Magalotti's literary works, I read several of the poems, e.g., "Sopra l'acque del Reno," in Laur Redi 206, fols. 11–14, "La Madreselva" and "Canzoni" in Ricc. 2304, 3407, and 3490; and still others in his *Canzonette anacreontiche* (Tartini & Franchi, 1723), *La donna immaginaria* (Bonducci, 1762), with a good introduction, and *Poesie scelte di vario genere ... stampate da un socio colombario* (Viviani, 1754). One of the novels is published by Gaetano Domenico Poggiali in his *Novelle di alcuni autori fiorentini* (Milan: Silvestri, 1815); one of his lectures is published by Costantino Arlìa in *Il propugnatore,* XV (1882), from a manuscript in the Biblioteca Angelica in Rome. The *Commento sui primi cinque canti dell'Inferno di Dante* was published in Milan in 1819 (Imp. Regia Stamperia). Of the *Lettere familiari contro l'ateismo,* I have consulted the manuscript copies in Laur Ashb. 1003, in Biblioteca Casanatense, Rome, 1392, and BNF Gino Capponi 137—but not the ones in Bibliothèque Nationale, Paris, Fonds Italien 515 and 113; and I read through the most recent edition (although several sections appear in Mario Praz's edition of the *Buccheri*) published by Nobili in Bologna in 1821, with notes by Domenico Maria Manni and Luigi Muzzi. A modern critical edition of Magalotti's most important work is long overdue. I read the "Concordia della religione e del principato" in Laur Ashb. 1207 and have transcribed parts of it in the appendix to my article, "The Failure of Political Philosophy in Seventeenth-Century Florence," *Renaissance Studies in Honor of Hans Baron,* ed. Anthony Molho and John A. Tedeschi (Sansoni and The Newberry Library, Chicago, 1970), pp. 559–76. I looked at Magalotti's translation of *Le regole della Trappa* first in the original in VG and then in Cesare Guasti's edition (Bologna: Romagnoli, 1883) ("Scelta di curiosità letterarie inedite o rare," no. 196). I read the *Lettere sopra i buccheri* in Praz's edition of 1945, while referring to that of Enrico Falqui (*Lettere odorose* [Bompiani, 1943]) because it contains the relevant correspondence with Leone Strozzi; and I read Magalotti's letters to Saint-Evremond in the preface to his translations of the essays in *Opere slegate,* ed. Luigi de Nardis (Rome: Ed. dell'Ateneo, 1964). Several of Magalotti's academic discourses are printed in the *Prose fiorentine* along with those of several of his contemporaries.

Fortunately, I have not had to read through all this material without some guidance. I have consulted the eighteenth-century biographies by Gaetano Cambiagi (in his edition of *La donna immaginaria,* cited above), by Angelo Fabroni, and by Pompilio Pozzetti (*L. M. Elogium,* 1787), the comprehensive biography (indeed the most comprehensive to date) by Fermi, *L. M. letterato e scienziato* (Piacenza, 1903) (as well as the manuscript "Cronologia" in VG 263, 6/1, that was probably composed by Fermi), the somewhat less comprehensive biographies by Giuseppe Raimondi (Milan: Alpes, 1929), by Enrico Falqui in *La letteratura italiana: I minori,* vol. III, pp. 1793–1826, and by E. Cecchi, "Carrattere del M.," *Paragone,* no. 42 (June, 1953). Most of the biographies suffer from a lack of patience on the part of the biographers, who draw their conclusions from only part of Magalotti's writings and from almost none of the writings of his contemporaries. This defect is even more pronounced in the more specialized studies of particular aspects of his work: e.g., Sebastiano Timpanaro, "L. M. e la scienza," in his *Scritti di storia e critica della scienza* (Sansoni, 1952); Walter Moretti, "L. M. e il suo secolo," *AMCol,* XXI (1956), 213–307 (to be read in light of the reviews by Franco Croce in *RLI,* LXI [1957], 568–70, and by Giorgio Bárberi in *GSLI,* CXXXV [1958], 143–45, and of Moretti's edition of the *Relazioni,* cited above, by Giovanni da Pozzo in

Belfagor, XXIV [1969], 237–44); Georges Güntert, *Un poeta scienziato del Seicento*: L.M. (Olschki, 1966) (which deals solely with Magalotti's literary work: see Leonard R. Mills in *BHR,* XXIX [1967], 722–25); Attilio Momigliano, "Le Lettere sopra i buccheri," in his *Ultimi studi* (La Nuova Italia, 1954); and the prefaces to almost all the partial editions of Magalotti's works cited above.

Magalotti's adventures in England have been the subject of several studies: R. W. Waller, "L. M. in England, 1668–69," *IS,* I (1937); Piero Rebora, "M. e gli inglesi," in his *Interpretazioni anglo-italiane* (Bari: Adriatica, 1961); Adolfo Faggi, "Hume e M.," *Atti dell'Accademia delle Scienze di Torino,* LIX (1923–24), 348–52; F. Viglione, "L. M. primo traduttore di Milton," *Studi di letteratura moderna,* I (1913); as well as in the several studies by Crinò cited above. Michele Ziino reviewed most Magalottiana before the date of publication of his "Rassegna di scritti magalottiani," *Leonardo,* III (1932), 441–43. Another such review would be helpful today; it might steer future scholars away from the pitfall of chopping up Magalotti or any of his associates into such artificial categories as "baroque," "antibaroque," and "pre-Arcadia."

The "context" I have sought to reconstruct in part from the reports of the work of Florentines in contemporary periodicals, e.g., the *Journal des sçavans* (which tried to be international in spite of its annoying Gallophilia), of the *Acta Eruditorum* (which succeeded in being international because Germans were not yet infected by nationalism), of the *Philosophical Transactions* of the Royal Society of London, of the courageous but shortlived *Giornale de' letterati* of Parma (see Book V), and of another, more successful journal with the same title published in Rome. I have also reconstructed the context from contemporary diaries and guidebooks, particularly Ferdinando Del Migliore's *Firenze illustrata* (1684), Giovanni Cinelli's updated edition of Bocchi's *Le bellezze della città di Firenze* (1677), Galeazzo Gualdo Priorato's *Relazione della città di Fiorenza e del Granducato di Toscana* ("Colonia": Pietro de la Place, 1668), an anonymous series of "Varie notizie prese alla giornata ... 1637 fino all'anno 1698" in Ricc 3175, and, above all, the fascinating and packed "Bidosso, o vero Diario" of Francesco Bonazini, BNF Mag XXV.42 (which I have on microfilm).

But I have reconstructed the context mostly from the works and correspondence of, and from the studies about, Magalotti's friends and associates. Several good biographies are published in Giovan Maria Crescimbeni's *Le vite degli Arcadi illustri* (Rome, 1708–14) and *L'istoria della volgar poesia* (1698; 3d. ed., Venice: Basegio, 1730–31), largely because some of Magalotti's fellow Florentines became Arcadian heroes. My main authorities on Pope Alexander VII are the *Vita* by Sforza Pallavicino (Prato, 1839), Giovanni Incisa Della Rochetta's "Appunti autobiografici," in *Mélanges Eugène Tisserant* (Vatican, 1964), vol. VI[1], pp. 439–57; Alfonse Dupront in *Forschungen und Studien zur Geschichte des Westfälischen Friedens* (Münster- i-W.: Aschendorff, 1965), as well as what his Florentine contemporaries say about him in their letters. On Filippo Baldinucci, besides his published works (the *Notizie de' professori del disegno* and the *Raccolta di alcuni opuscoli,* which I read in the edition of 1765), all with biographical notes, which are my principal guide through the art of the age, I have consulted his *Vita* of Bernini edited by Sergio Samek Ludovici (Milan: Edizioni del Milione, 1948), his son Francesco Saverio's edition of his *Vita* of Pietro da Cortona, published by Samek Ludovici in *Archivi,* ser. II, vol. XVII (1950), 77–91; his immense bundle of notes in BNF II.II.110, and, particularly for chapter 5, his spiritual diary in Ricc Moreni 18. His work as a collector is partly documented by Roseline Bacou and Jacob Bean in *Dessins florentins de la collection de Filippo Baldinucci* (Paris: Editions des Musées Nationaux, 1954) (and an Italian version published at the Farnesiana in Rome in 1959).

On Giovanni Borelli, I have followed the biography by Tullio Derenzi in the *Celebrazione della Accademia del Cimento,* cited below; it is partially documented by Derenzi's edition of several of Borelli's letters to Marchetti in *Physis,* I (1959), 224–43. On Maria Selvaggia Borghini (with whom Magalotti corresponded in the 1690s and 1700s), I have read the *Saggio delle poesie di S. B.,* ed. Domenico Moreni (Magheri, 1827). And on Cosimo III, as well as on Gian Gastone in Book V, I have consulted Harold Acton's *The Last Medici* (London: Faber and Faber, 1932) (Ital. trans. Turin: Einaudi, 1962).

On Carlo Roberto Dati there is a considerable bibliography: the *Elogio* by Francesco Fontani (1794), the introductions to his *Lettere* (Magheri, 1825), to his *Prose,* ed. Ettore Allodoli (Lanciano: Carabba, 1913) (all sources extensively used in this Book), and to the *Scelta di prose,* ed. B. Gamba ("Alvisopoli," 1826), as well as Carlo Andreini's "C. D. e l'Accademia della Crusca," in *Miscellanea di studi critici . . . in onore di Guido Mazzoni,* vol. II, pp. 81–101, and *La vita e l'opera di C. R. D.* (Rome: Dante Alighieri, 1936), to which I add two earlier "Lives"—one by Antonio Magliabechi in Mag IX, 50, and one by Angelo Fabroni in his *Vitae Italorum,* vol. XVI. The most recent monograph is Antonio Minto, '*Le vite dei pittori antichi' di C. R. D. e gli studi erudito-antiquari nel Seicento* (Olschki, 1953), from which also comes much of my information about antiquarian studies in general. I have read as much as my eyes could stand of Ottavio Falconieri's letters to Magliabechi in Mag VIII. 649, along with Anton Maria Salvini's biography of Ottavio's brother Paolo in *Le vite degli Arcadi morti* and Paolo's abjuration of Peripatetic philosophy in Jacopo Soldani's *Satire* of 1751, pp. 74–76. My judgment of Anatasius Kircher is indebted not only to my own reading of his works, but also to Paolo Rossi in *Clavis universalis* (Milan: Ricciardi, 1960), p. 195, to Arnaldo Momigliano in *RSI,* LXXVII (1965), 780, and to P. Friedländer in Pontificia Accademia Romana di Archeologia, *Rendiconti,* XIII (1937), 229–47.

Only a small part of the extensive surviving correspondence of Prince, later Cardinal, Leopoldo de' Medici is in print, e.g., in Sergio Camerani's "Amicizie e studi di Leopoldo . . . ," *ASI,* LCVII¹ (1939), 27–40, in Huygens' *Oeuvres* cited below, and in later editions of the letters of his contemporaries. The same is true for the still more extensive correspondence of Antonio Magliabechi, most of which is still in manuscript in the collection of his personal papers in the BNF. I have read only a small part of it, most notably Magalotti's letters to him in Mag VIII 1176 and 733, and the excerpts transcribed by one of the first curators of his collection, Antonio Cocchi, in the 1740s: Mag VIII. 1343. More often I have consulted the letters written to Magliabechi published as *Epistolae Clarorum Belgarum . . . ad A. M.* (1745) and *Venetorum* (1745–46), and letters by him to certain Neapolitans, reviewed by Biagio De Giovanni in *Saggi e ricerche su Settecento* (Naples: Istituto Italiano per gli Studi Storici, 1968), p. 10. Those to and from the Bollandists and Maurists have been studied by Andrea Dal Pino, OSM, in *Studi storici dell'Ordine dei Servi,* VII (1955–56), 75–126. A description of Magliabechi by Muratori is published by Tommaso Sorbelli in *Miscellanea muratoriana* (1950), pp.

174–76, and one by Ugo Foscolo is in Foscolo's *Opere* (LeMonnier, 1850), vol. IV. There is a bust of him in the entrance of the BNF.

Some of the Cimento's activities are documented in the various studies of Marcello Malpighi, e.g., that by G. Gherardoni in *Studi e memorie dell'Università di Bologna,* N.S., vol. I (1956), and that by Arturo Castiglioni in *Rassegna clinico-scientifica,* VI (1928). On Alessandro Marchetti, the current authority is Mario Saccenti, first in an article published in *Convivium* (1953), and then in his *Lucrezio in Toscana* (Olschki, 1966), which mentions all the previous bibliography. Some of Marchetti's literary battles are described by Luigi Tenca in "I contrasti fra A. M. e Vincenzo Viviani," *Rendiconti dell'Istituto Lombardo delle Scienze e Lettere,* LXXXV3 (1953), 293–313, and by Niccola Carranza in "Antonio Magliabechi e A. M.," *BSPis,* XXVIII–XXIX (1959–60), 393–446. Several letters to or about Magalotti appear in the published works of the English resident, Henry Newton, *Epistolae, Orationes & Carmina Latina* (Lucca, 1710). Much of Enrico Norris's correspondence with Magliabechi is published in *Epistolae ... Venetorum ad A. M.;* and biographies of him previously written are listed in the preface, including the one I have generally used, Francesco Bianchini in *Vite degli Arcadi illustri.* Unfortunately I have not been able to consult the two more recent studies of his work by Léon Pélissier. Several letters of Gian Paolo Oliva, general of the Society of Jesus, are pertinent to matters discussed in this Book and are published in his *Lettere,* 2 vols. (Rome, 1681). One of my principal sources has been Lorenzo Panciatichi, *Scritti vari,* ed. Cesare Guasti (LeMonnier, 1856).

Francesco Redi is perhaps the best-known member of this generation. Many of his works have been republished in recent editions—from the "Classici italiani" edition of the early nineteenth century, in nine volumes, to such partial collections as Pietro Fanfani's *Lettere precettive di eccellenti autori* (Barbèra, 1855), Piero Giacosa's *Le più belle pagine* (Milan, 1925) (the main purpose of which is to exalt the Italic genius), Vittorio Osimo's *Lettere e consulti* and *Naturali osservazioni* (Milan: Signorelli, 1927), and A. Ferrini-Baldini's *Quattro lettere inedite* (Arezzo, 1959). But I most often use the edition of the *Opere* in the second Neapolitan edition of 1778. The *Bacco in Toscana,* recited by Arnaldo Foà, is now available on a record published by La Nuova Italia; the *Experiments on the Generation of Insects* are available in the English translation of Max Bigelow (Chicago: Open Court, 1909; reprinted 1969). I have consulted several biographies, from those of A. M. Salvini and Angelo Fabroni in the eighteenth century to Gaetano Imbert, *F. R., uomo di corte e uomo privato* (offprint from *NA,* October 15, 1895); Ugo Viviani, *Vita ed opere inedite* (Arezzo, 1924) and *Vita, opere, iconografia ... Vocabolario inedito delle voci aretine ... e dei 'Ricordi'* (Arezzo, 1924–28), which, together with Viviani's edition of *La vacchetta* (Arezzo, 1931), are usually better for the specific information and documentation they contain than for their historical judgments. More comprehensive is Ranieri Schippisi, "F. R.," in *La Letteratura italiana: I minori,* vol. III, pp. 1765–92. Somewhat more useful are the studies of specific aspects of Redi's work, e.g., Luigi Belloni, "F. R. als Vertreter der italienischen Biologie des XVII. Jahrhunderts," *Münchener medizinische Wochenschrift,* CI (1959), 1617–24; Alfonso Bertoldi, "Tra Daniello Bartoli e F. R.," *Rivista d'Italia,* X2 (1907), 895–99; Ferdinando Massai, *Lo 'Stravizzo' della Crusca ...* (Rocca San Casciano, 1916); and Guglielmo Volpi, "Le falsificazioni di F. R. nel Vocabolario ... ," which I read in offprint from the *Atti dell'Accademia della Crusca* (1915–16).

There are several editions of Orazio Ricasoli Rucellai's *Dialoghi*; but I usually use the one edited by Giuseppe Turrini (LeMonnier, 1868), with guidance from the abundantly documented *Della vita e degli scritti* of Augusto Alfani (Barbèra, 1872). Paolo Segneri's works are available in numerous editions, the most recent being P. S. and Daniello Bartoli, *Prose scelte*, ed. Mario Scotti (Turin: U.T.E.T., 1967). The *Lettere inedite,* ed. Giuseppe Boero, S.J. (Milan: Silvestri, 1851), contains the *Quaresimale* as well; and the *Lettere inedite ... al granduca* (LeMonnier, 1857), upon which part of chapter 6 of this book is based, contains the eulogy by Giovanni Pietro Pinamonti, Magalotti's spiritual director during the Exercises of March, 1691; I supplement them with "Lettere inedite di P. S., di Cosimo III e di Giuseppe Agnelli ...," ed. Pietro Tacchi Venturi (who also wrote the biographical article in *Enciclopedia italiana*), *ASI*, XXXI (1903), 125–65; and with such works of and about his successors as Pinamonti, *Opere* (Parma, 1718); Francesco Maria Galluzzi, *Vita del P. Paolo Segneri juniore* (Rome, 1716; Lucca, 1719); and Pietro Pirri, S. J., "Ludovico Antonio Muratori e Paolo Segneri juniore, un'amicizia santa," *RSCI*, IV (1950). All these pieces should be read with guidance from Emilio Santini, *L'eloquenza italiana dal Concilio Tridentino ai nostri giorni* (Milan: Sandron, 1923), G. Marzot, *Un classico della Contriforma*: P. S. (Palermo: Palumbo, 1950), Giovanni da Locarno, *Saggio sullo stile dell'oratoria sacra nel Seicento* (Rome: Istituto Storico O.F.M. Capp., 1954) (on which, see Cesare Segré in *GSLI*, CXXXII [1955], 463–66, and Benedetto Croce on pp. 438 ff. of the 1929 edition of his *Storia dell'età barocca* [Laterza]). All the works of Nicholas Steno (Niels Stensen) are now being republished, largely through the efforts of the late Gustav Scherz, who wrote several biographical studies as well: *N. S. Forscher und Denker im Barock* (Stuttgart: Wissenschaftliche Verlagsgesellschaft, 1964); *Pionier der Wissenschaft*: *N. S.* (Copenhagen: Munksgaard, 1963), and the English preface to Steno's *Lecture on the Anatomy of the Brain* (Copenhagen: Nyt Nordisk Forlag, 1965), as well as notes to the *Disputatio Physica de Thermis,* in photostat from the original 1660 edition published at Montecatini in 1966, all of which are amply documented by Scherz' edition of the *Epistolae et Epistolae ad Eum Datae,* 2 vols. (Copenhagen: Nyt Nordisk Forlag, and Freiburg-im-Br.: Herder, 1953). The most helpful introductions to particular aspects of Steno's life and work are Max Bierbaum, *N. S.*: *Von der Anatomie zur Theologie* (Münster-i-W., 1958), and Maria Luisa Righini Bonelli, "The Accademia del Cimento and N. S.," *Analecta Medico-Historica,* III (1968), 253–60, as well as Francesco Rodolico's two articles published respectively in *Atti della Società Toscana di Scienze Naturali*, LX (1953), and *Rivista storica delle scienze naturali,* I (1955). The most recent additions to Steno's known correspondence are several more letters of Magalotti published by Scherz in *Centaurus*, XII (1968), 167–81. The biography by Raffaello Cioni (LeMonnier, 1953) is hagiographic in tone and intent, which may account for its having been translated into English (New York: Kenedy, 1962). Domenico Maria Manni's *Vita* (Vasi, 1775) is antiquarian in tone, but still useful. Vincenzo Viviani's vast correspondence in the Galileo-Cimento collection of the BNF is reviewed by Antonio Favaro in "Documenti inediti per la storia dei manoscritti galileiani nella Biblioteca Nazionale di Firenze," *Bullettino di bibliografia e di storia delle scienze matematiche e fisiche*, XVIII (1886), 80–92; and Viviani's *Vita* of Galileo is studied critically by Favaro in *ASI*, LXXIV² (1916), 127–50.

On the Roman Oratorio, where Magalotti's search for a vocation ended, I have consulted Carlo Gasbarri's *L'Oratorio romano dal Cinquecento al Novecento* (Rome-Bologna:

Cappelli, 1963); and for its spiritual ties with Florence, the many contemporary eulogies and biographies, e.g., that of Carlo Roberto Dati in Mag XXXV. 51 and the poems of Giovan Maria Casini and Bernardo Adimari in their *Canzonette spirituali* (Brigonci, 1703).

Chapter 1 relies to some extent on the very informative histories of science written in the eighteenth century, principally Giovan Battista Clemente Nelli, *Saggio di storia letteraria fiorentina* (Lucca: Giuntini, 1759) and Giovanni Targioni Tozzetti, *Notizie degli aggrandimenti delle scienze fisiche* (Bouchard, 1780), as well as on a number of articles published in the *Celebrazione dell'Accademia del Cimento nel tricentenario della fondazione* (Pisa: Domus Galilaeana, 1958), on Favaro's "Per la storia dell'A. del C.," *Atti dell'Istituto Veneto di S. L. ed A.*, LXXI² (1912), and on the description of the scientific instruments given by Maria Luisa Righini Bonelli in *Cimelli galileiani* (Olschki, 1962), *Il Museo di Storia della Scienza* (Olschki, 1960), and "Strumenti scientifici antichi" in *Enciclopedia Mondadori delle scienze* (1968), with magnificent color illustrations. But the history of the Cimento still remains to be written: even the first chapter of Martha Ornstein's *The Role of Scientific Academies in the Seventeenth Century* (University of Chicago Press, 1928), takes account of only a small portion of the available documentation. My main source for the earlier years of the academy has been the immense correspondence of Christiaan Huygens, published in his *Oeuvres complètes* (The Hague: Nijhoff, 1888–1950). On Huygens, I read Arthur Ernest Bell, *Huygens and the Development of Science in the Seventeenth Century* (London: Arnold, 1947), and Dora Shapley, "Pre-Huygenian Observations of Saturn's Rings," *Isis*, XL (1949), 12–17. Another important source is the published *Works* of Robert Boyle (London: Rivington, 1772), which includes an account of Boyle's trip to Italy (vol. I), but not, alas, the autograph diary that Anna Maria Crinò has consulted in the British Museum. On Boyle, I follow Robert Kargon, "Walter Charleton, R. B., and the Acceptance of Atomism in England," *Isis*, LV (1964), 184–92, and Marie Boas Hall, *R. B. and Seventeenth-Century Chemistry* (Cambridge University Press, 1958). For the Cimento's relations with non-Florentine scientists, I have consulted Léon Auger, *Gilles Personne de Roberval, 1602–1675* (Paris: Blanchard, 1962); Harcourt Brown, *Scientific Organizations in Seventeenth-Century France* (Baltimore: Williams and Wilkins, 1934); Richard S. Westfall, *Science and Religion in Seventeenth-Century England* (Yale University Press, 1958); Theodore Raab, "Puritanism and the Rise of Experimental Science in England," *Journal of World History*, VII (1962), 46–67 (which gets rid of the old myth about the dependence of modern science on Protestantism); as well as the standard histories of science for the period. My details about the "Gelli pill" come from Andrea Cavalcanti's Memorie diverse, ASF Strozziana, ser. I, 11, fol. 10 (November 27, 1653), Gello Gelli's *Trattato de' tumori* (1667), and the letters of Ricasoli Rucellai to Redi.

For the theoretical and philosophical implications of the Cimento's work, I have read Eugenio Garin, "Contributi alla storia del pensiero italiano del secolo XVII," *AMCol*, XXIV (1969), 297–327; Alberto Tenenti, "La polemica sulla religione di Epicuro nella prima metà del Seicento," *SSt*, I (1959–60), 227–43; Tullio Gregori, *Scetticismo ed empiricismo: Studi su Gassendi* (Bari: Laterza, 1961); the studies of Mario Saccenti cited above; Nicola Badaloni, "Intorno alla filosofia di Alessandro Marchetti," *Belfagor*, XXIII (1968), 282–316, and *Introduzione a G. B. Vico* (Milan: Feltrinelli, 1961);

Salvo Mastellone, *Pensiero politico e vita culturale a Napoli nella seconda metà del Seicento* (Florence-Messina: D'Anna, 1965), "Note sulla cultura napoletana al tempo di Francesco d'Andrea," *CS,* I (1962), 596–625, and now *Francesco d'Andrea: politico e giurista* (Olschki, 1968); Pietro Omodeo, "La biologia nei secoli XVII e XVIII," *Nuove questioni di storia moderna* [ed. Luigi Bulferetti] (Milan: Marzorati, 1964), vol. II, pp. 897–935, and "La disputa sulla generazione spontanea da Redi fino a Lamarck," *Società,* XIII (1957); Enrico Falqui, ed., *Antologia della prosa scientifica italiana del Seicento* (Vallecchi, 1943); Silvestro Baglioni's introduction to Giacinto Cestoni, *Epistolario ad Antonio Vallisnieri* (Rome: Accademia d'Italia, 1940); Pietro Franceschini, "Il secolo di Galileo e il problema della generazione," in *Physis,* VI (1964), 141–204 (which I, unlike at least one critic, found very helpful), and "La trasfusione del sangue nei primi documenti," which I read in an offprint kindly sent to me by the author, from *Atti del Simposio internazionale di storia delle scienze* (Florence-Vinci, 1960); Carlo Alberto Madrignani, "Il metodo scientifico di Francesco Redi," *RLI,* LXV (1961), 476–500; Jean Rostand in *Esquise d'une histoire de la biologie* (6th ed., Paris: Gallimard, 1945)—and for Pasteur's tribute to Redi: James Bryant Conant, *Pasteur's and Tyndall's Study of Spontaneous Generation* (Harvard University Press, 1952). Lorenzo Bellini's *Discorsi di anatomia,* referred to at the end of chapter 2, were published by Moücke in 1741–47, with a prefatory biography. Daniello Bartoli's scientific vocation is considered by Ezio Raimondi in "D. B. e la 'ricreazione del savio'," in his *Letteratura barocca: Studi sul Seicento italiano* (Olschki, 1961), and in a Ph.D. dissertation by John Renaldo at the University of Chicago. One of the young botanists referred to is Michelangiolo Tilli, whose papers are in BNF Galileo-Cimento 285. The subsequent fate of Lucretius is discussed by Frank Manuel in *The Eighteenth Century Confronts the Gods* (Harvard University Press, 1959), pp. 146 ff. And Cosimo III's abortive decree on the teaching of Aristotle at Pisa (which arrived conveniently *after* all the professors had left on vacation and which provoked from the rector only a promise to try to get it into their hands) is in ASF Misc. Med. 87, fol. 14.

Of travel literature referred to in chapter 3—besides that of Magalotti cited above— I have consulted Filippo Corsini's Viaggi d'Allemagna . . . fatti dal Ser.mo Principe Cosimo, ASF Strozziana 57; Filippo Pizzichi's *Viaggio per l'Alta Italia del . . . Cosimo,* ed. Domenico Moreni (Magheri, 1828); Susan Heller Anderson, ed., Cosimo Brunetti, *Three Relations of the West Indies in 1659–1660* (Transactions of the American Philosophical Association, vol. LIX, part 6 [Philadelphia, 1969]); Alessandro Segni's reports of the trips he and Francesco Riccardi took around northern Europe in Ricc Moreniana (no call number); Jacob Spon's *Voyage d'Italie* . . . (Lyon, 1678); Pietro Amat, *Bibliografia dei viaggiatori italiani* (Rome, 1874); Percy G. Adams, *Travellers and Travel Liars, 1600–1800* (Berkeley: University of California Press, 1962); Gaetano Branca, *Storia dei viaggiatori italiani* (Rome: Paravia, 1873); Frédéric Lachèvre, *Les successeurs de Cyrano de Bergerac* (Paris: Champion, 1922); Jules-Antoine Dumesnil, *Voyageurs français en Italie* (Paris: Renouard, 1865); and Roberto Wis, "Francesco Negri, voyageur italien," in his *Terra Boreale* (Helsinki, 1969), a book kindly brought to my attention by Anna Maria Crinò.

On Florentines in England, much material has been gathered by Crinò e.g., *I letterati della Restaurazione nella Relazione magalottiana del 1668* (Sansoni, 1956), *Il 'Popish*

Plot' (Rome: Edizioni di Storia e Letteratura, 1954), and *Fatti e figure del Seicento anglo-toscano* (Olschki, 1957). On the expectations of an imminent conversion of England, see Gustavo Costa, "Documenti per una storia dei rapporti anglo-romani nel Settecento," *Saggi e ricerche sul Settecento*; on Poland, several reports of Francesco Buonvisi in *Nunziatura a Varsavia,* ed. Furio Diaz and Niccola Carranza (Rome: Istituto Storico Italiano, 1965); and on Russia, Crinò in Università di Padova, Facoltà di Lingue in Verona, *Annali,* ser. II, vol. I (1966–67). On Florentines in France, there is some information in an article by Francesco Picco in *Miscellanea . . . in onore di Guido Mazzoni,* vol. II, pp. 111–78. I have not found very useful André Mabille de Poncerville's biography of the Italophile Valentin Conrart (Paris: Mercure de France, 1935). Gustave Cohen's articles in *Revue de littérature comparée,* V (1925) and succeeding volumes, confirm Magalotti's statement of having met Saint-Evremond in Holland. Leibniz's letters to Prince Ferdinando were published by Silvestro Centofani in *ASI,* n.s., vol. IV² (1857). The immense amount of information contained in the letters and reports of Florentine visitors and diplomats has been almost totally ignored by historians of the countries they visited, even by Hugo Hantsch and Pieter Geyl, whose *Geschichte Oesterreichs* (4th ed., Graz: Steierische Verlagsanstalt, 1962) and *The Netherlands in the Seventeenth Century* (New York: Barnes & Noble, 1964) could have benefited from it. What Magalotti says about the imperial court provides a valuable supplement to the reports of the Venetian ambassadors, which I read in vol. XXVII of *Fontes Rerum Austriacarum* (1867).

Some general background on the work of the antiquarians is given by Bruno Neveu, *Un historien à l'école de Port-Royal: Sébastien Le Nain de Tillemont* (The Hague: Nijhoff, 1969), and his essay in *Religion, érudition et critique à la fin du XVIIe siècle et au début du XVIIIe* (Presses Universitaires de France, 1968), pp. 21–32; Henri LeClerq, *Mabillon* (Paris: Letouzey & Ané, 1953–57); David Knowles, *Great Historical Enterprises* (London: Nelson, 1962); Sergio Bertelli, "Erudizione e crisi religiosa . . . ," *Atti e memorie della Società Storia Patria Modena,* ser. IX, vol. II, pp. 151–81, and "La crisi dello scetticismo . . . ," *Società,* XI (1955), 435–56; and Mario Battistini, "I padri Bollandisti Henschenio e Paperbrochio in Toscana nel 1661," *RSAT,* II (1930). The discovery of Petronius is explained by Martin von Schanz in *Geschichte der römischen Literatur* (Munich: Beck, 1890–1967), vol. II, pp. 509–20. Valerio Chimentelli's research notes are in Laur Ashb 1219.

The internal affairs of Tuscany, as well as the structure of the Tuscan diplomatic service, are documented not only in Galluzzi, but also in Niccolò Arrichi's Teatro di grazia e giustizia, ASF Misc. Med. 696; the *Istruzione per li capitani . . . dello Stato di Siena* of 1671 and 1692 (which I found in the New York Public Library); Marcantonio Savelli's *Pratica universale* (3d ed., 1696); Biagio Brugi, "Un lettore di erudizione legale a Pisa nel 1691," in his *Per la storia della giurisprudenza e delle università italiane* (1921), pp. 165 ff.; Carlo Strozzi's Cirimoniale, trattamenti di principi . . . , ASF Strozziana, ser. I, 363. Demographic statistics are given by R. Burr Litchfield in *Journal of Economic History,* XXIX (1969). Several anecdotes come from the lengthy diplomatic reports of the papal nuncio (in the Vatican Archives) and of the French ambassador (MAFPar), as well as from BNF Gino Capponi 124. fols. 127 ff.

On literature, I have consulted Mario Saccenti, "Firenze, il Seicento e i 'Panbaroc-chisti,'" *Convivium,* XXVIII (1960); Uberto Limentani, "Sulle satire di Benedetto

Menzini," *Studi secenteschi,* I (1960), 15–37; Walter Binni, "La formazione della poetica arcadica e la letterature fiorentina di fine Seicento" in his *L'Arcadia e Metastasio* (La Nuova Italia, 1963), pp. 3–46; Carlo Alberto Madrignani, "La poetica di Francesco Redi," *Belfagor,* XV (1960), 402–14, Maria Luisa Altieri Biagi. "Lingua e cultura di Francesco Redi, medico," *AMCol,* XXXIII (1968), 191–304, and, for one of Magalotti's favorite authors, Pier Vincenzo De Vito, *Ciro da Pers tra classicismo e barocco* (Udine: Accademia delle S.L.A., 1964). On Dante criticism, I have consulted Umberto Cosmo, *Con Dante attraverso il Seicento* (Bari: Laterza, 1946), and Limentani, "La fortuna di Dante nel Seicento," *Studi secenteschi,* V (1964), 3–49, and *The Fortune of Dante in Seventeenth Century Italy* (Cambridge University Press, 1964). Limentani's "L'anti-secentismo nella letteratura della prima metà del Seicento," cited in the bibliography for Book III, is also relevant here. On style, I have consulted Raffaele Colapietra, "Stile e scienza nei discepoli di Galileo," *Convivium,* XXIII (1955), 533–56; on Carlo de' Dottori, the monograph on him by Franco Croce (La Nuova Italia, 1957). Notes on the theater can be found in Alessandro Ademollo, *I primi fasti del teatro di via della Pergola in Firenze* (Milan: Ricordi, n.d.); an engraved illustration of the interior is in Ugo Morini, *La R. Accademia degli Immobili ed il suo teatro* (Pisa, 1926). The *Vocabolario* is discussed by Ferdinando Massai in "Le 'Origini italiane' del Menagio . . . ," *RBA,* XXVIII (1917), 1–22.

For music, my main sources are Leto Puliti, *Cenni storici della vita del . . . Ferdinando dei Medici,* in offprint from the *Atti dell'Accademia del R. Istituto Musicale di Firenze* (1874); and Mario Fabbri, *Alessandro Scarlatti e il principe Ferdinando de' Medici* (Olschki, 1961). On art they are Oreste Ferrari and Giuseppe Scavizzi, *Luca Giordano,* 3 vols. (Naples: Edizioni Scientifiche Italiane, 1966); Matthias Winner, "Volterranos Fresken in der Villa della Petraia," *MKHIF,* X (1963), 319–52; M. Muraro, "Studiosi, collezionisti e opere d'arte," and Lucia and Ugo Procacci, "Carteggio di Marco Boschini con il cardinale Leopoldo . . . ," both in *Saggi e memorie di storia dell'arte,* IV (1965); Giuseppe Bianchi, *Ragguaglio delle antichità e rarità . . . nella Galleria Mediceo-Imperiale* (Stampa Imperiale, 1759); Aldo Bartarelli, "Domenico Gabbiani," *RdA,* XXVII (1953), 107–30; Ignazio Hugford, *Vita di A. D. G., pittor fiorentino* (Moücke, 1762); and, above all, Klaus Lankheit, *Florentinische Barockplastik: Die Kunst am Hofe der letzten Medici, 1670–1743* (Munich: Bruckmann, 1962), with splendid illustrations and ample documentation in the appendix. Maria Margherita Pieraccini thinks Gherardini somewhat more original than I do in her "La difficile poesia di un ribelle all'Accademia: A. G.," *Commentari,* IV (1953), 299–305, since she bases her theses exclusively on the works of art. The most complete account of his work is Francesco Saverio Baldinucci's *Vita,* published along with a lengthy commentary by Gerhard Ewald as "Il pittore fiorentino Alessandro Gherardini," in *Acropoli,* III (1963), no. 2, pp. 81–132, a xerox copy of which was kindly lent me by Edward A. Maser. One resident foreign artist is mentioned by Kirsten Aschengreen Piacenti in *MKHIF,* X (1963), 273 ff. For general background, I refer to Jean Alazard, *L'art italien de l'ère baroque au XIXe siècle* (Paris: Laurens, 1960); and for Ferdinando Maria as a patron to Francis Haskell, *Patrons and Painters,* cited above.

Much of what I say about contemporary religion in chapters 5 and 6 is based on such documents as the "Obblighi de' fratelli della Congregazione della Buona Morte" and Luigi Strozzi's "Massime di pietà," in ASF Strozziana, ser. III, 33; the *Regole per le sorelle della Compagnia del Sacramento di San Marco* (Guiducci & Franchi, 1714); *Breve*

relazione delle feste fatte per la canonizatione di Santa Maria Maddalena de' Pazzi (Rome, 1670);
Giuseppe Maria Rossi, *Della vita del servo di Dio Lorenzo Maria Gianni* (Albizzini, 1735);
Luigi Strozzi, *Vita di Suor Maria Minima Strozzi* (Brigonci, 1701); Giovan Battista Neri,
De Judiciis S. Inquisitionis Opusculum (Matini, 1685); the Calendario di pietà in Mag
XXXVII. 199, as well as the printed and manuscript works listed above by author.
Throughout I have kept in mind the very convincing theses of Alberto Vecchi, *Correnti
religiose nel Sei-Settecento veneto* (Venice-Rome: Istituto per la Collaborazione Culturale,
1962), which may well serve as a model for future historians of religion.

For the general context of Magalotti's theological writings, I am particularly
indebted to Giorgio Spini's *Ricerca dei libertini,* cited in the bibliography for Book III,
which here should be read in the light of Paul Oskar Kristeller's observations in "The
Myth of Renaissance Atheism and the French Tradition of Free Thought," *Journal of
the History of Philosophy,* VI (1968). Strangely enough, one of the most important modern
studies of atheism does not even mention Magalotti: Fritz Mauthner, *Der Atheismus
und seine Geschichte im Abenland* (Stuttgart-Berlin: Deutsche-Verlags Anstalt, 1922),
perhaps because of the author's rather Nordic definition of *Abendland.* More helpful,
although equally oblivious to what took place in Italy, are the well-known studies of
"Libertinism": René Pintard, *Le libertinage érudit dans la première moitié du XVIIe siècle*
(Paris: Boivin, 1943); P. Vernière, *Spinoza et la pensée française avant la Révolution* (Presses
Universitaires de France, 1954); J. S. Spink, *French Free Thought from Gassendi to Voltaire*
(London: Athlone Press, 1960); A. Adam, *Les libertins au XVIIe siècle* (Paris: Buchet-
Chastel, 1964); Philip A. Wadsworth, "La Bruyère against the Libertines," *Romanic
Review,* XXXVIII (1947), 226–33; Walter Rex, *Essays on Pierre Bayle and Religious
Controversy* (The Hague: Nijhoff, 1965); and Richard Popkin, "Pierre Bayle's Place in
Seventeenth-Century Scepticism," in *Pierre Bayle, Le philosophe de Rotterdam,* ed. Paul
Dibon (Amsterdam and New York: Elsevier, 1959), as well as Popkin's "Scepticism,
Theology, and the Scientific Revolution in the Seventeenth Century," in *Problems in
the Philosophy of Science* (Amsterdam: North Holland Publishing Co., 1968), vol. II;
and, on biblical criticism, Jean Steinmann, *Richard Simon et les origines de l'exégèse biblique*
(Paris: Desclée de Brouwer, 1960).

Book V
Lami seems never to have thrown away a single scrap of paper; since he was a historian
as well as a librarian, he took care to have himself well documented for the benefit of his
colleagues in later generations. The letters he received, together with the great numbers
of his drafts, notes, and all his publications, are preserved in the Biblioteca Riccardiana
(Ricc), of which he was the director, except for those few letters that are now in the
Biblioteca Nazionale (BNF). For the purposes of this Book, I have paid particular
attention to the autobiographical parts of the "Lettera d'Ippofilo fiorentino" (Ricc
3286), of his *Charitonis et Hippophili Hodoeporici* (= vols. X and XI of *Deliciae Eruditorum*),
and of his "Diario storico" (Ricc 3808), although almost everything he wrote has
autobiographical references, and although none of it is free of deliberate falsification or
self-deceit. Only a few of his letters have been published, mainly those from Vienna and
France, edited by Maurice Vaussard in *REI,* n.s., vol. I (1954) and II (1955). I have
concentrated largely on his correspondence with Foggini and Bottari in Biblioteca
Corsiniana, Rome, 1588 and 1598, with Bandini in Ricc 37, and with Gori in Ricc 3723.

Whoever eventually reads through *all* the letters both to and from Lami, including those to Angelo Calogerà now in Leningrad, which I was not able to consult but about which I read in Cesare De Michaelis, "L'epistolario di A. C.," *Studi veneziani,* X (1968), 621–704, as well as the many others scattered about in other libraries (Lami did not usually have a secretary to keep copies for him), will certainly have occasion to correct much of what I say about him.

The modern authority on Lami and on Florentine scholarship in this period is Mario Rosa, whose "Atteggiamenti culturali e religiosi di G. L. nelle 'Novelle letterarie,'" *Annali della Scuola Normale Superiore di Pisa,* ser. II, Vol. XXV (1956), I follow throughout. One aspect of the *Novelle* has been reviewed by Carlo Pellegrini in *GSLI,* CXVI (1940), 1–17. Emile Appolis, *Le 'Tiers Parti' catholique au XVIIIe siècle* (Paris: Picard, 1960) discusses Lami at length; Aldo Andreoli refers to one of Lami's *Vitae* in *Atti e memorie Dep. Stor. Patria Prov. Modenesi,* ser. IX, vol. II (1961), 139–40; and I have written a short biography, "G.L. e la storia ecclesiastica ai tempi di Benedetto XIV," *ASI,* CXIII (1965), 48–73, where I give other pertinent bibliography.

Biography (in the limited sense defined in this chapter) was one of the favorite literary genres of the mid-eighteenth century, and *vite* or *elogi* are available for almost all of Lami's friends, enemies, mentors, and disciples. I have made considerable use of Giuseppe Allegrini's *Serie di ritratti* (Florence, 1766–73), esp. vol. IV, which has copperplate engravings for each "life"; of Angelo Fabroni's *Vita Italorum ... Qui Saeculis XVII et XVIII Floruerunt* (Pisa, 1778–), of Lami's own *Memorabilia Italorum ...* (Centauro, 1742–); of the prefatory *vite* in all posthumous publications of contemporary authors; and of the abundant information in the journals. All surnames that begin with the first 1½ letters of the alphabet, of course, can be found in the *DBI,* namely, the three Averanis (Niccola Carranza), Sallustio Bandini (Mario Mirri), and Angelo Maria Bandini and Benedict XIV (Mario Rosa). The last has been expanded into a long essay and published together with a number of other studies on "the Age of Muratori" in the author's *Riformatori e ribelli nel '700 religioso italiano* (Bari: Dedalo, 1969). I have written short biographies of Buondelmonti, Cocchi, and Lami, which may some day appear, along with selections from their writings, in another volume of Franco Venturi's *Illuministi italiani* (Ricciardi).

Some of the *dramatis personae* have received more recent attention. For Guido Grandi (whose portrait is engraved opposite the title page of his *De Infinitis Infinitorum* [1710]), Niccola Carranza's "Prospero Lambertini e G.G.," *BSPis,* XXIV–XXV (1955–56) (as well as his other studies mentioned in the last Book) is the most complete. Luigi Tenca has discussed his mathematical works in many different articles; Gerhard Schwartz in *Neues Archiv der Gesellschaft für ältere deutsche Geschichtskunde,* XV (1916), 185–241, and Giovanni Tabacco in *La vita di S. Bonomo ... e l'abate G.G.* (Turin: Facoltà di Lettere e Filosofia, 1954) have exposed his *Fälschungen,* and Nicola Badaloni adds a detail in his "Una polemica scientifica ai primi del '700 ...," *Società,* XIV (1958), 1142–60. Here as elsewhere, however, contemporary accounts are still indispensable, e.g., the *elogio* in the *Giornale de' letterati* of Florence, I (1742), 210 ff., and Lami's *Vita* (Massa [but probably the Centauro], 1742), which is not always very objective.

Mario Benvenuti discusses one part of Giuseppe Averani's career in his "L'erudizione al servizio della politica," *NRS,* XLII (1958), 484–506; anyone who wants to study him thoroughly will have to begin with the *elogi* of Gori and Antonio Niccolini, and with the big mass of notes collected by Gori in Mar XXIX 15. On Anton Maria Salvini, I have consulted Carmelo Cardaro's *A.M.S.* (Piacenza: Favari, 1906); on Gaspare Cerati, Carranza's "Monsignor G. C., Provveditore dell'Università di Pisa," *BSPis,* XXX (1961), 103–290; on Gian Gastone, Harold Acton, Galluzzi, and, on his law suit in Naples, an article by Oreste Gregorio in *Archivio storico per le provincie napoletane,* n.s. XXXIV (1955). 181–95; on Pompeo Neri, the somewhat dated "notizie" of Gaetano Rocchi and Ida Masetti Bencini as well as the introductions to his writings by Franco Venturi in *Illuministi italiani,* vol. III (Ricciardi) and the necrology in *Novelle letterarie,* VII (1776), col. 689 ff.; on Sallustio Bandini, Venturi's introduction in the same volume as well as the earlier biography by Glauco Tozzi (Accademia dei Lincei, *Memorie,* ser. VI, vol. V [1933]) and a long manuscript kindly lent to me by the author, George Baker, who has published two pertinent articles in *BSSP,* XXIV (1965); on Cocchi, the still-standard biography by Andrea Corsini (Milan: Agnelli, 1928), the notes by Salvatore Rotta in *RLI,* LXII (1958), 348–49, and, above all, the considerable documentation preserved in the private archive of Count Enrico Baldasseroni, who generously permitted me to work for several days in his house in Florence. Rotta discusses De Soria, and gives all pertinent bibliography, in "Idea di riforma nella Genova settecentesca ... ," in *Movimento sociale,* XVII (1961). I have read the relevant unpublished material in the Biblioteca Labronica of Livorno.

On Giovanni Bottari (whose principal works I cite below), I have consulted Romana Palozzi's article in *Annali della Scuola Normale Superiore di Pisa,* ser. II, vol. X, pp. 70–90, as well as a whole chapter in Enrico Dammig, S.J., *Il movimento giansenista a Roma* ... (Vatican, 1945); on Giovanni Targioni Tozzetti, the two articles in the *Rivista geografica italiana,* one by O. Marielli, XI (1904), and the other by R. Concari, CLI (1934)—though nothing has yet replaced the *elogio* in the *Novelle letterarie,* ser. II, vol. XIV (1784), 97 ff., republished in *Atti dell' Accademia dei' Georgofili,* II (1795), 22–29. Micheli's importance in the discovery of fungi spores has been recognized by Arthur Buller in Royal Society of Canada, *Transactions,* ser. III, vol. IX, sect. 4, pp. 1–15, though Targioni's *Notizie della vita e delle opere* ... , ed. Adolfo Targioni Tozzetti (LeMonnier, 1858) is still unsurpassed. Lami's *papalino* foe, Leone Pascoli, has been studied by Luigi Dal Pane in an article now republished in his *Lo Stato Pontificio e il movimento riformatore del Settecento* (Milan: Giuffrè, 1959), pp. 207–37, and Lorenzo Mehus by Mario Rosa, in "Per la storia dell'erudizione toscana del '700 ... ," *Annali della Scuola Speciale per Archivisti e Bibliotecari,* II (1962), 41–96, upon which I rely heavily throughout.

Half way through this Book, my faithful companion through all the preceding ones, Galluzzi, gives out; his place is taken by his competent nineteenth-century successor, Antonio Zobi, whose *Storia civile della Toscana,* 5 vols. (L. Molini, 1850–53) goes from 1737 to 1848. Zobi also wrote a more technical *Manuale storico degli ordinamenti economici vigenti in Toscana* (Baracchi, 1858). On the countryside, Targioni Tozzetti's immense *Relazioni d'alcuni viaggi,* discussed in the text, is invaluable, particularly when supplemented by Manuele Repetti's *Dizionario storico fisico della Toscana* (1843), and, particularly for Livorno and Pisa, by the recently discovered diary of a little-known German traveler, Georg Christoph Martini, translated into Italian by Oscar Trumpy and published as *Viaggio in Toscana* (Massa and Modena: Aedes Muratoriana, 1969). Much of the cultural and intellectual life of the age is described in my *Tradition and Enlightenment,* to which I refer for more ample bibliographical notes. On politics, I make considerable use of the several works by Niccolò Rodolico, from *La Reggenza lorenese in Toscana* (Prato: Vestri and Spighi, 1908) and *Stato e Chiesa in Toscana* . . . (LeMonnier, 1910) to "Emanuele di Richecourt . . . ," in his *Saggi di storia medievale e moderna* (LeMonnier, 1963), all replete with documents. Antonio Anzilotti's classic "Le riforme in Toscana . . ." is still valuable for suggestive hypotheses, and is now reprinted in his *Movimenti e contrasti per l'unità italiana*, 2d ed. (Milan: Giuffrè, 1965). Luigi Dal Pane is the current authority on economic affairs, with his *La finanza toscana dagli inizi del sec. XVIII alla caduta del Granducato* (Milan: Banca Commerciale, 1965), although work in this field has so far been limited to the examination of government orders and reports and has still come up with very little about the actual conditions of the economy. R. Burr Litchfield knows more about contemporary social structure than anyone, thanks largely to his efficient use of IBM cards. I am very indebted to him for permission to read his "The Business Investments of the Florentine Patricians in the Eighteenth Century" in manuscript. The article is now available in French translation in *Annales*, XXIV (1969), 685–721. Population statistics come from Beloch, from Giovan Francesco Pagnini, and especially from Giuseppe Parenti, *La popolazione della Toscana sotto la Reggenza lorenese* (Rinascimento del Libro, 1937), which I compare at one point with the statistics given by Atho Bellettini in *La popolazione di Bologna dal sec. XV all'unificazione italiana* (Bologna: Zanichelli, 1961). The affair of the Freemasons is described by Ferdinando Sbigoli in *Tommaso Crudelli e i primi framassoni in Firenze* (Milan, 1884), and recently by Ernesto Baldi, *L'Alba: La prima loggia massonica a Firenze* (Coppini, 1959). The fiasco in the Maremma is described by Alberto Mortara in "Un tentativo di colonizzazione . . . ," *NRI*, XXII (1938), 40–63, 338–94, and again with new documents by Candeloro Giorgini in *La Maremma toscana nel Settecento* (Ed. ECO, 1968), from which I have taken other information about the state of the clergy. The later development of the English colony is fully, and amusingly, described by Giuliana Artom Treves in *Anglo-fiorentini di cento anni fa* (Sansoni, 1953). A brief sketch of the period as a whole is given by Giuseppe Panzini in a paper presented at a meeting in 1966 and published as *La Lorraine dans l'Europe des Lumières* (Nancy: University, 1968).

I have found some very enlightening (but not always too reliable) observations in the letters and reports of visitors from abroad, most notably those of Carlo Goldoni (*Mémoires,* in many editions), Montesquieu, Charles de Brosses, Pierre Jean de Grosley, the Abbé Barthélemy, and particularly, Gian Rinaldo Carli, whose "Saggio" can be found in the 1784 edition of his *Opere*.

Much of my information comes from contemporary periodicals, both Tuscan and non-Tuscan. Much of it comes from the works of contemporary authors—all those mentioned in the texts and many more besides. Two diaries (besides those of Lami) are well supplied with scenes of daily life: that of Giovan Battista Fagiuoli (Ricc 3457) and that of an anonymous (and apparently rather simpleminded) author in Ricc Moreniana, Acquisti diversi, 64. VII. For Florentine "high society," however, nothing can compare to Horace Mann's correspondence with Horace Walpole, published in several volumes by the Yale University Press. The diaries of the three principal academies here discussed—the Crusca, the Colombaria, and the Etrusca—are preserved in the present headquarters of the academies. I have made extensive use of the published correspondence of Muratori, ed. Matteo Càmpori (Società Tipografica Modenese, 1922), of Maffei, ed. Celestino Garbotto (Milan: Giuffrè, 1955), of Bernardo Tanucci, ed. Enrica Viviani Della Robbia (Sansoni, 1932), of Giovanni Bianchi, ed. Maria D. Collina (Olschki, 1957), of Giuseppe Baretti, ed. Luigi Piccioni (Bari: Laterza, 1924), and of Benedict XIV, ed. Emilia Morelli (Rome: Edizioni di Storia e Letteratura), and of that of Anton Maria Salvini (*Prose fiorentine*), Bottari's artist-friends, and Pope Clement XIV, published in the eighteenth century. Of the still unpublished correspondence, I have made considerable use of Gori's (in the Marucelliana), and of Bottari's and Foggini's (in the Corsiniana).

Most matters concerning the government—and the Lorraine government followed its predecessors in sticking its nose into just about everything—are recorded in a whole section of the Archivio di Stato called the *Reggenza* (Regg). I have used principally Rucellai's reports in Regg 780. 48, and Regg 35 (along with a curious plan for suppressing convents of 1734 in VG 225.19), Richecourt's memo of July 13, 1737, in Regg 194, the regulations regarding the Holy Office in Regg 339, the Memo of May 1749 on canon law (and on the law system in general) in Regg 29 bis., the "Rapports du Conseil" in 186, and Francesco Pecci's report on the book industry in Regg 778. Cocchi's memo on physicians' qualifications is in BNF II. V. 172.

Niccola Carranza is the leading authority on the history of the university, and I follow faithfully his "L'Università di Pisa e la formazione culturale del ceto dirigente toscano . . . ," *BSPis*, XXXIII–XXXV (1964–66), 469–537, as well as his biography of Cerati. Unfortunately Fabroni's *Historia* stops with those professors appointed before 1737. I have also looked at length through the files on university affairs in the ASF, namely, Regg 634–637. Cerati's reform program I read in ASF Misc. Med. 87.

On the porcelain industry, I have consulted Arthur Lane, *La porcellana italiana*, Ital. trans. by Dino Pavolini (Sansoni, 1963), and Giuseppe Liverani, *Catalogo delle porcellane dei Medici* (Faenza: Lega, 1936) and *Il Museo delle porcellane di Doccia* (Sesto Fiorentino: Richard-Ginori, 1967). Baldinucci's place as my main guide to the artists is taken, for this period, by Francesco Milizia in *Vite dei più celebri architetti* (Rome, 1768); [Luigi Lanzi], *Serie di uomini più illustri nella pittura, scultura e architettura* (1774) and *Storia pittorica d'Italia*, cited in bibliography for the Prologue, *L'Etruria pittrice, ovvero, Storia della pittura toscana*, 2 vols. (Pagni & Pardi, 1791–95); Giovanni Gori Gandellini, *Notizie istoriche degl'intagliatori* (Siena: Pazzini, 1771); and Pelegrino Antonio Orlandi, *Abecedario pittorico,* in the updated edition of Pietro Guarienti (Venice: Pasquali, 1753). Elements of contemporary art theory I have gathered from Giovanni Bottari, *Raccolta di lettere sulla pittura, scultura ed architettura* (Rome: Pagliarini, 1752–53) and *Dialoghi sopra le tre arti del disegno,* "corretti e accresciuti" (Lucca, 1754; Florence, 1770; and Naples, 1772). I have also taken them from the introduction to the 1730 edition of Raffaello Borghini's *Il riposo,* from Carlo Stendardi's "Inno della natura" in his *Ines de Castro ed altri componimenti poetici* (Bonducci, 1761), Ferdinando Ruggieri's *Studio d'architettura civile* (1722–28), republished by Bouchard in 1755, and *Descrizione dell'arco inalzato dalla nazione brittanica . . . Livorno* (Tartini & Franchi, 1732), Ferdinando Bibbiena, *Direzioni della prospettiva teorica* (1732), of which I use the Venetian edition of 1796, Francesco Algarotti's *Saggio sopra la pittura* (Livorno: Coltellini, 1763—from the Venetian edition of 1755), and Anton Maria Salvini's translation of Roland Fréart,

Idea della perfezione della pittura, ed. Domenico Moreni (Carli, 1809). Lami's *Dissertazione relativa ai pittori e scultori italiani che fiorirono dal 1000 al 1200* is published by Fantoni in Leonardo da Vinci, *Trattato della pittura* (Pagani & Grazioli, 1792). Contemporary engraving is well illustrated in Andrea Gerini's text for Giuseppe Zocchi's now-famous *Scelta di XXIV vedute delle principali contrade di Firenze,* dedicated to Maria Theresa (Allegrini, 1744).

I have been aided in this reading by several recent monographs: Roberto Pane, *Ferdinando Fuga* (Naples: Edizioni Scientifiche Italiane, 1957); Nino Carboneri, *Sebastiano Galeotti* (Venice: Neri Pozza, 1955); Antonio Muñoz, "Classicismo artistico nel '600 e nel '700," *Rassegna italiana,* V–VI (1920), 560–68; Arnaldo Venditti, *Architettura neoclassica a Napoli* (Naples: Edizioni Scientifiche Italiane, 1961); Eugenio Battisti, "La critica a Michelangelo dopo il Vasari," *Rinascimento,* VII (1956), 135–57 (a subject that still needs further study); Massimo Petrocchi, *Razionalismo architettonico e razionalismo storiografico* (Rome: De Luca, 1947); and, above all, Edward A. Maser's study of Giovan Domenico Ferretti, Ital. trans. (Marchi & Bertelli, 1968), and Klaus Lankheit, *Florentinische Barockplastik: Die Kunst am Hofe der letzten Medici, 1670–1743* (Munich: Bruckmann, 1962), with magnificent illustrations and several important documents in the appendix, which I use for Book IV as well.

The standard guide to periodical literature is Luigi Piccioni's *Il giornalismo letterario in Italia* (Turin: Loescher, 1894) and his more recent anthology, *Giornalismo letterario del Settecento* (Turin: UTET, 1949), though there is nothing for Tuscany as thorough as Marino Berengo's magnificent *Giornali veneziani del Settecento* (Milan: Feltrinelli, 1962). M. A. Timpano Morelli has studied earlier Florentine newssheets in *CS,* VII (1968), 288–323. On the printing industry in general, see Maria Augusta Timpano Morelli, "Legge sulla stampa e attività editoriale...," *Rassegna degli archivi di Stato,* XXIX (1969), 613–98. The book catalogues I refer to are: Giuseppe Manni's advertisement in the appendix to his edition of Redi's *Opere,* vol. VII; the "cataloghi" of the books of A. M. Salvini in Mar A.248.8, of Marmi in BNF II.I.274–76; of Gaddi and Strozzi in Mar A.192.4 and 18 bis,; and of Gori in Colombaria, Annali 28. The flier of the Bouchard company is in BNF M.799.4.

On libraries and archives, I have consulted the monographs of Giuliana Giannelli, Domenico Fava, Carlo Angeleri, and Olga Pinto (on the Corsiniana: Olschki, 1956), as well as the material in the *elogi* of contemporary librarians and in ASF Regg 778. The recipes come from Upezzinghi's *Il cuoco in villa* (Urbino, 1719). Selections from the naturalists have been published by Francesco Rodolico in *La Toscana descritta dai naturalisti del Settecento* (LeMonnier, 1945), and by Leonello Vincenti, *Viaggiatori del Settecento* (Turin: UTET). The best histories of Etruscology are still those by Gori, Passeri, Maffei, and Lami (see my *Tradition and Enlightenment,* pp. 165 ff.), though one theory is discussed by M. Renard in *Latomus,* III (1939), and Coke is described by Valdo Vinay in *Studi di letteratura, storia e filosofia in onore di Bruno Ravel* (Olschki, 1965), pp. 597–615. On modern Etruscology, I refer to the well-known works of Pericle Ducati, Massimo Pallottino, et al., and to the "état de la question" article by Raymond Bloch in *Annales,* VII (1952), 319–28. On jurisprudence, I use Paola Berselli Ambri's *L'opera di Montesquieu nel Settecento italiano* (Olschki, 1960), conditioned by the observations of Mario Rosa in *RSCI,* XIV (1960), 410–28, and the very thorough study of Vincenzo

Piano Mortari, "Tentativi di condificazione in Toscana nel sec. XVIII," *Rivista italiana per le scienze giuridiche,* LXXXIX (1951–53), 285–387. Such works on contemporary piety as Raimundo Tellería's *San Alfonso Maria de Ligorio* (Madrid: El Perpetuo Socorso, 1950), and P. Julien Strucher, C.SS.R, *Le voeu du sang en faveur de l'Immaculée Conception* (Rome: Academia Mariana, 1959), are exhaustive, but not yet wholly integrated into other aspects of the life of the times. The modern theologians I refer to at the end are Denis Meade, O.S.B., and Richard A. McCormick, S.J.

Putting Florence into the context of Italy as a whole is much easier today than it was fifteen years ago, thanks to the recent growth of interest in the eighteenth century among Italian historians. In the field of literary history I follow such well-known authors as Mario Fubini and Walter Binni; the latter's "Il teatro comico di Girolamo Gigli," *RLI,* LXIII (1959), 417 ff., is immediately pertinent to my analysis of Fagiuoli. In politics and diplomatic relations, I refer constantly to the works of Guido Quazza, particularly to his *Il problema italiano e l'equilibrio europeo, 1730–1738* (Turin: Deputazione Subalpina di Storia Patria, 1965), and his "L'Italia e l'Europa durante le Guerre di Successione," in Nino Valeri, ed., *Storia d'Italia* (Turin: UTET, 1965), vol. II, and to those of Franco Valsecchi, especially in his most recent *L'Italia del Settecento, 1714–1788* (= vol. VII of the Mondadori *Storia d'Italia*). On economic and social problems, the bibliography is very long. I have taken a few specific details from Giulio Giaccero's *Storia economica del Settecento genovese* (Genoa: Apuania, 1951), from Bruno Caizzi, *Industria e commercio della Repubblica Veneta nel XVIII secolo* (Milan: Banca Commerciale Italiana, 1965), from Raffaele Ciasca's edition of the reports of the Genoese ambassadors (Istituto Storico Italiano per l'Età Moderna e Contemporanea, 1967). On scholarship and historiography, I rely largely on Sergio Bertelli's long monograph on Muratori and his subsequent discussion of "erudizione e crisi religiosa" in *Atti e memorie Dep. Stor. Patria Pröv. Modensi,* ser. IX, vol. II (1962), together with Giuseppe Giarrizzo's study of Muratori, Vico, and Giannone in *RSI,* LXXIX (1967), and, more recently, Mario Fubini's article on Muratori in Vittorio Branca, ed., *Sensibilità e razion alità nel Settecento* (Sansoni, 1967). I have summarized other recent works in my own "Muratori: The Vocation of a Historian," *Catholic Historical Review,* LI (1965), 153–72, as well as in "The Settecento Medievalists," *Journal of the History of Ideas,* XIX (1958), 35–61, which may be of help to those who do not read Italian. Giuseppe Silvestri has written a good general biography of Scipione Maffei (Treviso: Canova, 1954), though for Maffei's place in the history of scholarship, Arnaldo Momigliano is the best guide: "Ancient History and the Antiquarian," now in [*Primo*] *Contributo alla storia degli studi classici* (Rome: Edizioni di Storia e Letteratura, 1955). A couple of details on Bettinelli I have borrowed from an article by Bartolomeo Genero, "Ricerche bettinelliane," *GSLI,* CXXXVIII (1961), 365–401. For Rome in Lami's day, I have used L.-P. Raybaud, *Papauté et pouvoir sous les pontificats de Clément XII et Benôit XIV, 1730–1758* (Paris: Vrin, 1963), Giuseppe Vella, *Il Passionei e la politica di Clemente XI* (Rome: Dante Alighieri, 1953), and Alberto Caracciolo, *Domenico Passionei tra Roma e la Repubblica delle lettere* (Rome: Edizioni di Storia e Letteratura, 1968) (which doesn't go much beyond 1720), as well as the book by Dammig cited above. Benedict's fight with the Venetians is recounted by Federico Seneca in *La fine del Patriarco aquilese, 1748–51* (Venice: Deputazione Storica, 1954). For all aspects of the age I am particularly indebted to the various works of Franco Venturi, especially to his recent *Settecento riformatore*: *Da Muratori a Beccaria* (Turin: Einaudi, 1969), of which the first chapter appeared as "Gli anni '30 del Settecento," in *Miscellanea Walter Maturi* (Turin: Giappichelli, 1966).

Putting Florence into the context of Europe as a whole, on the other hand, is made difficult by the immensity of the bibliography. I will mention only those works from which I have borrowed specific references: Furio Diaz, *Filosofia e politica nel Settecento francese* (Milan: Feltrinelli, 1962); Franklin Ford, *Strasbourg in Transition* (Harvard University Press, 1958), Jean-Claude Perrot, "Villes et Société au XVIIIe siècle," *Annales*, XXIII (1968); Françoise LeMoal, "Les dimensions du Socinianisme," *Revue d'histoire moderne et contemporaine* XV (1968); Robert A. Kann, *A Study in Austrian Intellectual History* (New York: Praeger, 1960); Giuseppe Ricuperati, "Spinoza, Toland, e il 'Triregno'," *RSI*, LXXIX (1967); Emmanuel de Broglie, *Bernard de Montfaucon et les Bernardins* (Paris: Plon 1891); Lionel Gossman, *Medievalism and the Ideologies of the Enlightenment: The World and Work of La Curne de Sainte-Palaye* (Johns Hopkins University Press, 1968); Hippolyte Delehaye, S.J., *The Work of the Bollandists* (Eng. trans., Princeton University Press 1922); Bruno Neveu, *Un historien de l'école de Port-Royal; Sébastien Le Nain de Tillemont, 1637–1698* (The Hague: Nijhoff, 1966); Emile Egger, *L'Hellénisme en France* (Paris: Didier, 1869); M. L. Clark, *Classical Education in Britain, 1500–1900* (Cambridge University Press, 1959); René Lanson, *Le Goût du Moyen-Age en France au XVIII siècle* (Brussels: Van Oest, 1926); Olwin H. Hufton, *Bayeux in the Late Eighteenth Century* (Oxford: Clarendon, 1967); Gustav Otruba, *Wirtschaftsgechichte Maria Theresas* (Vienna: Bergland, 1969); François Bontinck, *La Lutte autour de la liturgie chinoise aux XVIIe et XVIIIe siècles* (Louvain: Nauwelaerts, 1962); Leonora Cohen Rosenfield, *From Beast Machine to Man Machine* (New York: Oxford, 1940) (alas, not a word about Magalotti or any other Italian!).

Book VI

None of the contemporary accounts of the riot of June 9 is free of bias, and no two of them agree even on the general course of events. Jacopo Tolomei Pucci was a disgruntled aristocrat for whom the machinations of the Jansenists explained everything. But his Diario dell'insurrezione (Mar Palagi 65, ins. 1) has the advantage of immediacy and is full of specific information not available elsewhere. The report of the police (ASF Buon Governo, Negozi Polizia [1790] 514) is impaired by the efforts of the authors to cover up their inability or unwillingness to intervene; but all the other cases in the same immense file contain many interesting details about social conditions at the time that are of considerable help in understanding both the background and the aftermath of the riot. The report of the investigating committee, prepared under the auspices of the Supremo Tribunale di Giustizia (ASF S.T.G. Giornale, 1790, vol. 14, fols. 177 ff.) for submission to the grand duke, is the most comprehensive; it also is warped by the attempt of the committee to find impotent scapegoats. The account of the papal nuncio, Tommaso Ruffo Scilla (AVat Nunziatura Firenze 88, fols. 188 ff.: Giornale dell'accaduto in Firenze dal lunedi 7 giugno 1790 a tutto il sabato 12) is both thorough and objective, since the author had no axe to grind. The same cannot be said of the comments of the French ambassador, Louis Durfort, as I have shown in my article on him in *RSRis*, XLV (1958), 199–218. His "explanations" are often as ridiculous as the specific references are correct, and I have taken many of the latter from his correspondence in MAEPar Toscane 143B and 144. Gianni's account, published in the form of a letter to his son Ridolfo as "Memoria sul tumulto" in his *Scritti di pubblica economia* (Niccolai, 1848) (2 volumes containing many of his treatises, which I have used extensively elsewhere) is several months posterior to the events, of which Gianni was not a witness; and it is as full of vague name-calling as almost everything else he wrote. His immediate reaction to the two decrees is in ASF Carte Gianni 12 ins. 242 (fols. 1124–1212) and 248 (fols. 1262–1276). His letters to Serristori are published by Zobi in *Storia del Granducato di Toscana,* vol. II, pp. 529 ff., along with Pietro Leopoldo's correspondence with the regents. Much of Zobi's own reconstruction of events is colored by his efforts to exalt both Pietro Leopoldo and Gianni, but it is apparently based in part on the report of the investigating committee. Gianni's differences with Ricci are evident from his "Memoria . . . sulla rappresentanza del vescovo Ricci" (*Scritti di pubblica economia*) of 1788. Ricci's own letters after the riot are in ASF Carte Ricci 53. The troubles of his followers at the end of 1790 are well recorded in the abundant diary of his secretary, Carlo Mengoni (ASF Carte Ricci 119); and conditions in Prato and Pistoia are amply documented in a report of April by Cesare Marchetti, ed. Guido Feri in *BSPist,* LXIX (1967), 129–35, and in Ricci's letters to his vicar in Prato during the summer, ed. Aldo Preti in *BSPrat,* XXXIII (1957) and XXXIV (1958). The bitter attacks on both Gianni and Ricci by Giuseppe Maria Lampredi are published by Mario Battistini in *RSAT,* I (1929), 45–66.

I have plotted the course of the riot as well as I could (given the contradictions in the sources) with the help of the splendid *Pianta della città di Firenze* of 1783 (a copy in the Museo di Firenze Com'Era) and of *Studi storici sul centro di Firenze* published by the Commissione Storico Archeologica Comunale in 1889 (when the center of town was gutted and rebuilt in its present form). Views of the Mercato Vecchio as it appeared before the nineteenth-century "urban renewal" projects—and as it probably appeared in 1790 as well (there is no illustrator comparable to Zocchi in the last decades of the century)—are published by Corrado Ricci in *Cento vedute di Firenze antica* (Alinari, 1906). The best modern account of the riot, and of all the riots that followed until the end of the century, is by Gabriele Turi in "*Viva Maria*": *La reazione alle riforme leopoldine (1790–1799)* (Olschki, 1969), extensively reviewed by Furio Diaz in *RSI,* LXXXII (1970), 387–99. It largely replaces its predecessor by Renato Mori in *ASI,* C² (1942), 53–94.

Much of the rest of this chapter is based on a chronologically selective reading in the many contemporary journals and newspapers, which I discuss in the text, as well as on many of the books and pamphlets that I first found mentioned in their reviews. Many of the periodicals are briefly mentioned in the general histories of journalism cited in the bibliography for Book V; only one has been the subject of a monograph: Carlo Capra, *Giovanni Ristori, da illuminista a funzionario, 1755–1830* (La Nuova Italia, 1968), which I have used extensively in other contexts as well. Excerpts from the *Giornale fiorentino istorico-politico-letterario* regarding the American Revolution have been translated by Howard R. Marraro in *Forum Italicum,* V (1971), 67–81. This Book is also based on two important diaries: that of Marco Lastri in Ricc Moreni Frullani 32 and that of

Giuseppe Pelli Bencivenni in BNF, uncatalogued MS: Efemeride, in many volumes. Other memoranda and collections of correspondence are used in specific circumstances: Durfort's reports to Paris, cited above; the letters of Angelo Tavanti to Raimondo Niccoli in *Rivista di studi napoletani,* VII (1968); Giorgio Santi's diary in *BSSP,* XXXIII (1926); and Ximenes's letters in BNF Galileiana 288. I had hoped to use the Mann-Walpole correspondence more extensively. But the letters get duller and more trivial as the authors approached the grave. The Yale edition, cited above, is still without an index. Texts of contemporary legislative decrees are usually cited in the series of *Bandi e ordini da osservarsi nel granducato di Toscana* begun in 1737 and kept up throughout this period, although the more important ones are quoted in Cantini and in the newspapers, and all those with bearings on economic and administrative matters are fully described by Abele Morena in "Le riforme e le dottrine economiche in Toscana," published in eight parts in successive numbers of *Rassegna nazionale* from XXVII (1886) on, as well as in other monographic literature. The state archives are so bulging with official reports, drafts, and memoranda for this period that it would take several lifetimes to go through them all; I have consulted only those files to which I have been led either by a reference from a competent scholar or by curiosity—e.g., ASF Gabinetto 107 and 117; Reggenza 1050; and Acquisti e Doni 94. Since some of the legislation was prepared with technical assistance from the Accademia dei Georgofili, I have used the academy's records as cited in my *Tradition and Enlightenment.*

For Gianni himself, the chief source is the immense collection of his personal papers and other documents pertaining to his various government jobs in the Carte Gianni of the ASF, described, none too impartially, by Francesco Dini, in *ASI,* ser. V, vol. XI (1893), 348–75. I read many of them in the original before the future editor kindly permitted me to read those he had typed up in preparation for an edition of Gianni's *Opera Omnia* (which will include also his letters in the private archive of the Niccolini family), and before I found selections from several unpublished works well annotated and introduced by Franco Venturi in volume III of *Illuministi italiani* (Ricciardi) (which includes selections from three other Tuscan economists as well). The Gianni family tree I found where it might be expected, in BNF Passerini, Gianni 188. My guide to all the material on Gianni has been Furio Diaz, who has indeed read through all the papers and who is currently the leading authority on the period as a whole. His several preliminary studies are now brought together in his thorough account of the development of Gianni's thought, *Francesco Maria Gianni* (Milan-Naples: Ricciardi, 1966). Some of Pietro Leopoldo's personal correspondence was published long ago by Alfred von Arneth, e.g., *Joseph II und Leopold von Toskana: Ihr Briefwechsel,* 2 vols. (Vienna: Braumüller, 1872). His personal memorandum to his son is now being edited by Arnaldo Silvestrini as *Relazione sul governo della Toscana,* of which one volume was published by Olschki in 1969. And it forms an indispensable supplement to the official apologia of the regime entitled *Il governo della Toscana sotto il regno di sua maestà Leopoldo II* (2d ed. [duplicate of 1st ed. of 1790]: Bonducci, 1791) (translated into German as *Die Staatsverwaltung von Toscana . . .* [Gotha, 1795]). My guide to this literature, as well as the source of much of my information, has been Adam Wandruszka, author of several brief character sketches of the grand duke, e.g., in *Historische Zeitschrift,* CXCII (1961), 295–317, and *RST,* XI (1965), 179–91, who had edited at least one contemporary character sketch, by a friend, in *ASI,* CXVIII (1960), 289–91, and who has incorporated all his other many monographic studies of the period in a two-volume biography, *Leopold II* (Vienna and Munich: Herold, 1963–65).

On economic and social conditions at the time I have used—besides such contemporary sources as the material in ASF Biffi Tolomei 189–191 and the writings of the economists themselves—a number of recent monographs: two studies on the demographic characteristics and the business affairs of the Florentine patriciate by R. Burr Litchfield, published respectively in *Journal of Economic History,* XXIX (1969), and in *Studies in Honor of Hans Baron,* cited above; two articles by Giulio Prunai, one on the Sienese customs offices and another on the Maremma, published respectively in *ASI,* CXXXI (1968) and *BSMar,* no. 7 (June, 1963); Ildebrando Imberciatori, *Campagna toscana del '700* (Accademia dei Georgofili, 1953); Luigi Dal Pane, "I lavori preparativi per la grande inchiesta del 1766," in *Studi storici in onore di Gioacchino Volpe* (Sansoni, 1958); and two articles by Giorgio Mori on the exploitation of Tuscan mineral deposits published in *ASI,* CXVI (1958), and in *Rivista delle società,* III (1958); and, for modern comparisons, Giannino Parravicini, *L'economia della Toscana* . . . (Vallecchi, 1969), Robert Forster, "Obstacles to Agricultural Growth . . . ," *American Historical Review,* LXXV (1970), 1600–15, and Michel Morineau, "Y a-t-il une révolution agricole en France au XVIIIe siècle?" *Revue historique,* CCXXXIX (1968), 299 ff. Population statistics come either from Marco Lastri's *Ricerche sull'antica e moderna popolazione,* or from G. Pardi, "Disegno storico della demografia di Firenze," *ASI,* (1916), 3–84, 185–245, and "Disegno della storia demografica di Livorno," *ASI,* LXXVI (1918), 1–96, or, for later parallels, from Pierfrancesco Bandettini, *L'evoluzione demografica della Toscana dal 1810 al 1889* (Torino: ILTE, 1969), and *La popolazione della Toscana dal 1810 al 1959* (Camera di Commercio, 1961).

Various aspects of the political and social reforms have recently been studied—after a hiatus of some thirty years since the appearance of the pioneering articles of Antonio Anzilotti—by Lorenzo Tocchini in "Usi civici e beni beni communali . . . ," *SSt,* II (1961), 223–66; by Giorgio Giorgetti, "Per una storia delle allivellazioni leopoldine," *SSt,* VII (1966), 245–90 and 51–84; and by Mario Mirri in "Proprietari e contadini nelle riforme leopoldine," *Movimento operaio,* VII (1955), 173–229. These three studies have done what none of their predecessors ever attempted: they have gone beyond the texts of the laws to find out just how the laws were carried out in practice within certain areas. The only studies of the local government reform are by Lea Bernardini in an unpublished thesis (kindly lent to me by the author) entitled "La formazione della comunità di Firenze" (Università di Firenze, Facoltà di Magistero) and by Pietro Paolini, "Cenni storici sulla comunità civica di Pistoia," *BSPist,* LX (1958), 67–79. The thought, as contrasted with the action, of the reformers (although it is questionable that the two can be separated) is considered by Renato Mori in *Le riforme leopoldine nel pensiero degli economisti del '700* (Sansoni, 1951), with a complete bibliography of their printed works in the footnotes, and in an older article by Luigi Dal Pane, "Influenze francesi . . . ," *RSRis,* XXIII (1936); interesting parallels are offered by André J. Bourde in a huge study of *Agronomie et agronomes en France au XVIII siècle,* 3 vols. (Paris: SEVPEN, 1967), and by Lucio Villari, *Il pensiero economico di Antonio Genovesi* (LeMonnier, 1958) (which should be read together with Venturi's introduction to vol. V of *Illuministi italiani*). The background of the law code projects is given in part by M. Roberti in *Rivista di storia del diritto italiano,* IX (1936), by B. Donati in his introduction to L. A. Muratori, *Scritti giuridici* (Modena, Soc. Tip. Modenese, 1942); land by M. C. Nannini in *Atti e memorie . . . provincie modenesi,* ser. 9, vol. II (1962), as well as by Mario Rosa in a biography of Lampredi's colleague, Cosimo Amidei, in *DBI.* Background for another hotly-debated question at the time is given by N. Jonard in "Le Luxe en Italie au XVIIIe siècle," *REI,* XV (1969), 295–321.

Church affairs and ecclesiastic reform have been the subject of numerous studies, beginning with Francesco Scaduto's *Stato e chiesa sotto Leopoldo I* (Ademollo, 1885), if not with the publication of Ricci's controversial *Memorie,* which I read in the edition of Agenore Galli (2 vols.; LeMonnier, 1863) (not to mention the far more controversial version of the *Mémoires* originally published in French by Louis de Potter [1828]). Some important information is still to be found in the studies of Niccolò Rodolico published in the 1910s. The degree to which the whole issue can still be polemical is well illustrated in a long article by Ciro Cannarozzi in *RST,* XII (1966), in several of the articles published in the *Nuove ricerche storiche sul giansenismo* (Rome: Gregoriana, 1954), in an article by P. Savio in *Italia francescana,* XXXII (1957)—or, from a very different point of view, in two of the major works of Ernesto Codignola, *Il giansenismo toscano nel carteggio di Fabio de Vecchi* (Vallecchi, 1944) and *Carteggi dei giansenisti liguri,* three huge volumes (LeMonnier, 1941–42), both full of documents that are indispensable for the study of the period.

One of the two principal authorities today is Ettore Passerin d'Entrèves, whose "Il fallimento dell'offensiva riformista . . . ," *RSCI,* IX (1955), 99–134, another in *RST,* I (1955), 6–27, and a general reconsideration (with Francesco Traniello), "Ricerche sul tardo gianesenismo italiano," *Rivista di storia e letteratura religiosa,* III (1967), 279–313, are especially valuable. The other principal authority is Mario Rosa, two of whose chapters in *Riformatori e ribelli del settecento religioso* (cited in the bibliography for Book V) are immediately pertinent. For the specific aspects indicated in the title, I follow Carmelo Caristia, *Riflessi politici del Giansenismo italiano* (Naples: Morano, 1966). My information on Martini and the Bible comes in part from two funeral orations by Giuseppe Casini and Antonio Longo (1810), from the documents of Foggini in ASF Carte Ricci 217, and especially from Cesare Guasti, "Storia aneddotica del volgarizzamento dei due Testamenti," *Rassegna nazionale,* XXV (1885)—a long-forgotten article that was pointed out to me by a fellow student of Florentine antiquities, Count Bernardo Rucellai. My details about Teresa Margherita Redi come from Ildefonso di San Luigi as well as from the article on him by Gabriele di S. Maria Maddalena, C.C.D., in *Ephemerides carmeliticae,* IV (1950), 519–623, though the author finds the whole matter somewhat more inspiring than I do. I reconstruct the expulsion of the Jesuits from the official record in ASF Magistrato Supremo 3491. Both the civil and the religious aspects of the reforms were thoroughly reconsidered at the meeting of the Società Storica Toscana in 1964, and the *Atti,* published in *RST,* XI (1965), along with, more recently, Bernard Plongeron, "Questions pour l'Aufklärung catholique en Italie," *Il pensiero politico,* III (1970), 30–58, provide currently the best introduction to the whole period.

A few studies have been made of specific aspects of contemporary science: Andrea Corsini, "La medicina alla corte di Pietro Leopoldo," *Rivista Ciba,* no. 46 (April 1954);

George Mora (who seems to be the only person who has ever heard of this subject) in
two articles on Vincenzo Chiarugi in *Journal of the History of Medicine and Allied Sciences,*
XIV (1959), 434–33, and in *American Journal of Psychiatry,* CXVI (1959), 267–73 (and I
would not have heard of it either had not the author kindly sent me the offprints); and
several important pages of Anthony Pace's *Benjamin Franklin and Italy* (Philadelphia:
The American Philosophical Society, 1958). Otherwise I have turned to the works of
the scientists themselves, as well as to some of the many contemporary eulogies of them,
like that of Alessandro Bicchierai by Giovan Gualberto Uccelli (Pagani, 1798). My
information about the hospitals comes in part from Michelangiolo Giannetti's *Orazione
per l'apertura* . . . (Della Rovere, 1783), in part from the regulations themselves, and in
part from *Rapporto sopra lo stato degli spedali* . . . (Marenigh, 1818).

On Florentine literature, scholarship, and theater in the later eighteenth century,
almost nothing has been written. There are several pages on Pignotti in the introduction
to Ugo Frittelli's *Favolisti toscani* (Vallecchi, 1930), but they do not supplant the much
longer contemporary biography printed in the 1821 edition of his *Storia della Toscana.*
The title of Ettore Levi Malvano's "Pietro Leopoldo e la cultura in Toscana," *Il Sei-
Settecento* (Unione Fiorentina), is misleading: the article just repeats in different words
what the same author said over thirty years earlier about the Tuscan editions of the
Encyclopédie in *Revue de littérature comparée,* III (1923), 213–56; and what he said then will
soon be superseded by Mario Rosa's forthcoming book on the subject. Alessandro
Ademollo's old *Corilla Olimpica* (C. Ademollo, 1887) is important largely for its witty
scenes of contemporary high-life. Therefore my own critical judgments are authoritative,
however undisciplined and philosophically unsound they may be; and they will remain
authoritative until someone with proper preparation and training finally deigns to study
the authors I have cited (and the many others I refer to without mentioning by name).
In the meantime, the general works on literature and poetics of the time by Mario
Fubini, Walter Binni, and Bruno Migliorini are very helpful as guides to the main
literary trends elsewhere in Italy. What I say about the schools comes largely from the
writings of Stanislao Canovai and Pompilio Pozzetti (including an unmarked pamphlet
in BNF Misc. Pal. 4.E.4) along with one or two details from Ildebrando Imberciadori's
brief article on agrarian instruction in *ES,* VIII (1961). And what I say about the revival
of Machiavelli follows in part the theses of Giuliano Procacci, in *Studi sulla fortuna del
Machiavelli* (Rome: Istituto Storico Italiano, 1965), and in part those of Mario Rosa, in
Dispotismo e libertà nel Settecento: Interpretazioni "repubblicane" di Machiavelli (Bari:
Dedalo, 1964). Some details on scholarships are to be found in Luigi Gasparetti's
Le "Origini italiche" di Mario Guarnacci e l'utopia della "sapientia antiquissima" (Genoa:
Penella, 1926); a sidelight on the book collectors is to be found in Cesare Guasti's
Le carte strozziane . . . (Galileiana, 1884).

Even though Neoclassicism in general has been the subject of considerable debate
in recent years, Tuscan neoclassicists have been studied only marginally. Francesca
Morandini has described the changes in the Palazzo Pitti briefly in *Commentari,* XVI
(1965) (cited in bibliography for Book I), following C. Conti's *Il Palazzo Pitti* of 1887.
Ugo Procacci has assembled the documents regarding the reconstruction of the Carmine
in *RdA,* XIV (1932). Antonio Cristellini has chronicled the construction of the Cappella
della Madonna in a privately printed monograph of the same name (1961). And

Fernand Boyer, in *RST,* I (1955), and *REI,* n.s., vol. III (1956), and Paul Marmottan in *Les arts en Toscane sous Napoléon* (Paris: Champion, 1901), have talked briefly about what happened in the following decades. But none of them seems to have paid attention even to the printed orations of Tommaso Puccini and the other spokesmen for the academy. Nardini is barely mentioned in the typically England- and Germany-centered *History of Violin Playing* by David Boyden (Oxford University Press, 1965), and even Cherubini is only briefly noted in Adelmo Damerini's *Il R. Conservatorio di Musica* . . . (LeMonnier, 1941) and in his and Franco Schlitzer's *Musici toscani* (Siena, 1955).

Travel literature is fairly abundant for the late eighteenth century, and I have used it subject to the qualifications given in the text. Of special importance have been the letters of Lessing, *Mozart in Italia,* ed. G. Barblau and Andrea Della Corte (Milano: Ricordi, 1956), C. Burney's *The Present State of Music in France and Italy* (London: T. Becket, 1771), Young's *Voyages* (which I read by chance in a French translation of 1860), Dupaty's *Lettres sur l'Italie en 1785* (Lausanne: Mourer, 1789), Karl Philipp Moritz, *Reisen eines Deutschen in Italien in den Jahren 1786 bis 1788* (Berlin: Maurer, 1792), M. A. Tornézy, ed., *Bergeret et Fragonard: Journal inédit d'un voyage en Italie, 1773–1774* (Paris: Librairies et Impriméries Réunies, 1885). Gibbon's voyage is recorded by Salvatore Rotta, together with all the pertinent information on the translations of his works, in "Il viaggio in Italia di Gibbon," *RSI,* LXXIV (1962), 324–55. Martelli has a good number of pages in Ettore Bonora's edition of *Letterati memorialisti viaggiatori del Settecento* (Milan-Naples: Ricciardi, 1941). Piattoli has been studied by Giampietro Bozzalato in *Polonia e Russia alla fine del XVIII secolo: S.P.* (Padua: Marsilio, 1964), a work reviewed by Emanuele Rostworowski in *RSI,* LXXVIII (1966), 921–31. Filippo Mazzei's letters to Poland were published by Raffaele Ciampini in 1937 (Bologna: Zanichelli). His *Memoirs* were translated into English by Howard Marraro in 1942 (Columbia University Press). And his life has most recently been studied by Sara Tognetti Burigana, *Tra riformismo illuminato e dispotismo napoleonico* . . . (Rome: Edizioni di Storia e Letterature, 1965). The authority on the English colony in Florence is Brian Maloney, who has written an article on the Florentine Miscellany in *The Modern Language Review,* LX (1965), 48–57, and on Cowper in *IS,* XVI (1961), 1–33. On the Countess of Albany, I follow Carlo Pellegrini's book of the same name (Naples: Edizioni Scientifiche Italiane, 1951).

Biographical material is more abundant and far better (for reasons given in the text) for this than for any preceding period since the death of Benvenuto Cellini. Most contemporary biographical dictionaries have been used throughout this book, particularly those by the rector of the university, Angelo Fabroni; what he left undone was picked up by his successor in the early nineteenth century, Emilio de Tipaldo. Unfortunately Tipaldo's dictionary is *not* in alphabetical order; but someone has appended a manuscript index in the last volume of the set at the BNF. Some modern biographies are also available. Mario Mirri expanded his biography of Stefano Bertolini for the *DBI* into a long article in *BSPis,* XXXIII–XXXV (1964–66), replacing that by G. Giorgetti in *ASI,* CIX (1951), 84–120. He has published a study of the Tuscan ambassador to Paris in the *Annali* of the Istituto Giangiacomo Feltrinelli, II (1949), 55–120. He has also written a biography of Ferdinando Paoletti, and kindly permitted me to read an advance copy of it (La Nuova Italia, 1969). Anna Maria Becciarelli has written about Aldobrando

Paolini in *BSPist,* n.s., vol. V (1963), 35–83; Gianfranco Miglio about Lampredi in *La controversia sui limiti del commercio neutrale* (Milan, 1942) (but the introduction to Defendente Sacchi's translation of *Iuris Civilis Universalis* is still indispensable); Ines Carmen Madelle about Galluzzi in *R.G. e la sua opera storica* (Faenza, 1923) (but Nicla Capitini Maccabruni has dug up enough further information in the ASF to do it all over again); Giusta Nicco Fasola about Lanzi in *Miscellanea di storia ligure in onore di Giorgio Falco* (Milan: Feltrinelli, 1962); M. R. Caroselli about Ippoliti in *Critica alla mezzadria di un vescovo del '700* (Milan: Giuffrè, 1963) (though doing little more than paraphrasing letters and treatises that make better reading in the original); Leo Neppi Modona about Giulio Perini in *Il cristallo* of Bolzano, V (1963), 23–50 and 70–82, and in *REI,* X (1964), 81–91. Filippo Buonarroti has by far the biggest bibliography of all, given his subsequent notoriety and given the historiographical importance to Delio Cantimori's book about the Italian Jacobins. The latest are the studies of G. Saitta and Maria Augusta Morelli (who is the first to find out much about Buonarroti's life in Tuscany) published in *CS* from III (1964) to V (1966).

In chapter 8 I refer to the diary of Ferdinando Fossi published with an introduction by Leo Neppi Modona in *ASI,* CXXVI (1968), to Vittorio Fossombroni's *Memorie* published by LeMonnier in 1851, to the letters of the French ambassadors published by Baldo Peroni in *Fonti per la storia d'Italia dal 1789 al 1815 nell'Archivio Nazionale di Parigi* (Rome: Accademia d'Italia, 1936), to Gianfranco Torcellan's article on Francesco Becattini in *DBI,* to Ernesto Sestan on "Gino Capponi storico" and "Don Abbondio in Soglio" in his *Europa settecentesca ed altri scritti* (Milan-Naples: Ricciardi, 1951), to Giovanni Baldasseroni's *Memorie* edited by Renato Mori (LeMonnier, 1949), to Franco Catalano in *Illuministi e giacobini del '700 italiano* (Milan: Cisalpino, 1959), to Imberciadori's study of nineteenth-century sharecropping in *ES,* VIII (1961), 179–85, to Ettore Passerin d'Entrèves, "L'anticapitalismo del Sismondi . . . ," *Belfagor,* IV (1949), 283–99 and 402–409, and "La società toscana intorno al 1799, con un inedito di Francesco Maria Gianni," *Quaderni di cultura e storia sociale,* I (1952), 1–8, and to several of the contemporary accounts and later studies of the insurrection of Arezzo, all of which (together with an exhaustive bibliography) are discussed by Turi in "*Ave Maria.*" Unfortunately I did not discover many of the scattered articles by Mario Battistini on several aspects of Tuscan cultural life until my manuscript was in press. They are all listed in *De Gulden Passer,* XXXII (1954), 14 ff.

Since the Postcript concerns what were, when I wrote it, current events, it is based almost wholly on the modern heirs of the *Novelle letterarie* and the *Gazzetta toscana,* namely, on the only remaining Florentine daily, *La nazione,* and on the "local news" section of the national *L'unità,* supplemented occasionally by bits from other Italian dailies such as the *Corriere della sera* of Milan, which recently ran a series on the regions of Italy. On the opening sessions of the Tuscan Regional Council, I also read an interesting and informed review by Enzo Enriques Agnoletti in *Il ponte,* XXVI (July 31, 1970), pp. 789–92.

Index

NOTE. The index includes all persons and places mentioned in the text, but not those mentioned in the Bibliographical Note alone. It includes only those subjects that are relatively circumscribed in scope—e.g., "Medicine," but not "Science." It omits such headings as "Florence," "Tuscany," "Rome," "Italy," "Latin," and "Italian Language" that appear frequently throughout the volume. It gives the numbers even of those pages (outside the Bibliographical Note) where a person, place, or subject is referred to without being specifically named. Whenever a particular person who is mentioned elsewhere in the text by name is indicated only by his title or office, the corresponding number is given under his name in the Index—e.g., "Francis I" instead of "King of France." In accordance with Italian custom, Italian rulers of Italian or foreign states are listed under their family names, and Italian women are usually listed under their maiden, rather than their married, names. Foreign or foreign-born rulers of Italian as well as of non-Italian states are listed under their given names—e.g., "Carlo di Borbone (King of Naples)," but "Medici, Maria de' (Queen of France)." First names not given in the text are given in parentheses in the Index. Local place names in cities other than Florence are given under the cities in which they are located—e.g., "Louvre" is under "Paris." A number followed by "q" refers to a page where the person mentioned is quoted—e.g., 127q. Numbers in italics refer to pages where the person or subject is discussed in some detail. A Roman numeral, either alone or followed by an Arabic numeral and placed between parentheses—e.g., (V) or (V, 2)—refers to a whole book or to a chapter in a book where the person mentioned is discussed throughout.

Pius II (Pope), 152
Pius IV (Pope), 88
Pius V (Pope), 92, 101, 110, 122, 124, 127, 132, 135, 249, 356, 495, 498
Pius VI (Pope), 437, 483, 493–97
Plague of 1348, 196
  of 1529, 5, 54
  of 1631–33, 225–26, 353, 531
Plato, 57, 143, 145–46, 159, 204, 242–43, 277
Platonic Academy (Accademia Platonica), 67, 69, 133, 145, 242
Platonists, Platonism, 83, 156, 190, 242–43, 245, 280, 290, 330, 472, 529. *See also* Neoplatonists
Plautus, 146
Plebeians, 124, 149, 172, 205, 209, 345, (VI, 1–2), 438
Pléiade, 84
Pliny (the Elder), 155, 249, 312
Pliny (the Younger), 276, 309
Plotinus, 323
Plutarch, 32, 48, 131, 237, 338
Po (river and valley), 438
Pocetti, Bernardino, 153
Poland, Poles, 56, 99, 111, 127, 173, 271, 345, 439, 495, 544
  ambassadors, 101
  king of, 439
Pole, Reginald (Cardinal), 124
Police, Police Office (Otto di Guardia), 149, 194, 363, 400, 402, 404, 406–8, 414, 469, 495, 553
Politi, Alessandro, *334*, 485
Politi, Ambrogio Caterino, 124
Political Philosophy, 57–58, (II, 3), 193–94, 270–73, 297, 338, 354, 518, 522. *See also* Jurisprudence; Law
Poliziano, Angelo, 81, 140, 144, 151, 286
Polverini, Jacopo, 59
Polybius, 38, 57
Pompeii, 388
Pompey, 117
Ponsacco, 429
Pontine Marshes, 437
Pontormo, Jacopo, 23, 36, 71, *75*, 80, 153, 516
  San Lorenzo frescoes, 76, 473
Pontremoli, 48, 193
Pontus de Tyard, 157
Pope, Alexander, 334, 359, 394, 443, 477

Popoleschi, Giovanni Antonio, 98
Population, demography, 54, 58, 65, 112, 196, 198, 278, 353, 355, 429, 462, 507, 531, 544, 549, 556
Porcelain, 129, 366–67. *See also* Doccia
Porco (Il, tavern), 149, 396
Porphyry, 81, 144
Porri, Francesco, 406
Portoferraio, 47, 65, 100, 345
Portofino, 261
Portugal, Portuguese, 111, 261, 264, 309, 386, 519
  language, 262, 286
  physicians, 196
Porzio, Simone, 82
Possevino, Antonio, 124
Poussin, 283
Pozzo, Carlo da, 117
Pozzuolo, 238
Prague, 169, 174, 179
Prato, 23, 34, 59, 65, 95, 225, 275, 296, 450, 554
  Collegio Cicognini, 321, 386, 390
  San Vincenzo, 134
  Santa Caterina, 497
  Santa Lucia, 497
Press, printers, publishing, 69, 318–20, *361–63*, 443, 453, 461, *467*, 520, 532, 550–51
  booksellers, 380, 406, 442, 467
  see also Bartolini; Betti; Bindi; Bodoni; Bouchard; Cambiagi; Della Rosa; Della Rovere; Gioliti; Giunti; Grypho; Manni; Moücke; Pagani; Stecchi; Torrentino
Prices, 55, 401–2, 406, 409–11, 413, 453, 502, 519
  books, 320
  food, 296, 357, 399
  grain, 113, 195, 350, 399
  journals, 468
  land, 452
  money, 452
  paintings, 154, 280
  teachers, 487
  theory of, 448
  wool, 116
  see also Interest
Priestley, Joseph, 434
Priscianesi, Francesco, 69
Prostitution, 150, 272, 278, 296, 351, 469

ERIC COCHRANE is professor of history at the University of Chicago. He has written *Tradition and Enlightenment in the Tuscan Academies* and has edited *The Late Italian Renaissance*. He has also published numerous articles in scholarly journals.

[1973]